FORENSIC PSYCHOLOGY

FIRST CANADIAN EDITION

LAWRENCE S. WRIGHTSMAN
University of Kansas

STEPHEN PORTER
Dalhousie University

THOMSON

NELSON

Australia   Canada   Mexico   Singapore   Spain   United Kingdom   United States

Forensic Psychology, First Canadian Edition
by Lawrence S. Wrightsman and Stephen Porter

Associate Vice-President, Editorial Director:
Evelyn Veitch

Publisher:
Joanna Cotton

Senior Executive Marketing Manager:
Don Thompson

Developmental Editor:
Alwynn Pinard

Permissions Coordinator:
Indu Ghuman

Production Editor:
Julie van Veen

Copy Editor and Proofreader:
Valerie Adams

Indexer:
Jin Tan

Senior Production Coordinator:
Hedy Sellers

Creative Director:
Angela Cluer

Cover Design:
Brian Cartwright, Rocket Design

Cover Image:
www.firstlight.ca

Compositor:
Alicja Jamorski

Printer:
Transcontinental

Library and Archives Canada Cataloguing in Publication

Wrightsman, Lawrence S.

    Forensic psychology / Lawrence S. Wrightsman, Stephen Porter. — 1st Canadian ed.

Includes bibliographical references and index.
ISBN 0-17-641442-8

    1. Forensic psychology—Textbooks. I. Porter, Stephen, 1970– II. Title.

RA1148.W74 2005   614'.15
C2004-906513-0

Contents

Preface

In the first decade of the 21st century, the term *forensic psychology* has become increasingly salient in our society, and more and more students are seeking information about university courses relevant to this fascinating area. But what *is* forensic psychology? Certainly the term has been around for decades, but experts in the field often disagree as to the breadth of its coverage. Some reject (and even deride) portrayals of forensic psychologists (typically criminal profilers) in the media; others embrace the label "forensic psychologist," despite its controversial meaning. In recent years, more and more psychologists have applied their empirical and clinical knowledge to courtroom issues and have testified as expert witnesses or assisted lawyers as consultants. With such an expanding field, there are numerous temptations for the expert; these include making stronger claims than the data support, promising too much, using invalid procedures, and violating ethical guidelines. A recurring theme of this book is that the legal system offers a host of opportunities for the application of our knowledge, but that psychologists must remain vigilant and aware that their first responsibility is to their profession.

This book has two major foundations. First, it developed from the original text authored by Lawrence Wrightsman. His text is among the most well-respected, scholarly, and popular books in the area. Dr. Wrightsman based his text on a course he was teaching in the early 1990s in response to students' great desire for knowledge about the activities of forensic psychologists and the opportunities for training in the field. While I have endeavoured to maintain and build upon the high quality of the original text, I believed it was necessary to better meet the needs of students and professors in Canada. Since I began teaching the first forensic psychology course at Dalhousie University in 1998, I chose to use a collection of readings rather than an existing textbook heavy on American legal content. As such, this edition is very different from the original U.S. edition. The second major basis for writing this new edition lies in the great differences that exist between Canada and the United States in terms of our legal systems, the practices by forensic psychologists in the two countries, and our cultural landscapes in general. This new edition emphasizes the uniquely Canadian perspective, while discussing our field in its full international context.

In my course, as in this book, the content reflects several key beliefs:

1. *Forensic psychology, as a field, is still in a state of formulation and development.* For some, forensic activities evolve from the applied or clinical roles of the psychologist; for others, an experimental, applied cognitive, or social psychological background leads to involvement in forensic work research when they testify as expert witnesses in court. Thus, the coverage of a book entitled *Forensic Psychology* should be broad and inclusive. In this book, the reader will find coverage of everything from

deception detection to criminal responsibility, from competency assessments to criminal interrogations, from testifying about family violence to eyewitness testimony, from psychopathy to post-traumatic stress disorder.

2. *Forensic psychology is a profession.* This book is oriented around the variety of roles for the forensic psychologist and is directed toward the reader who is curious about just what forensic psychologists do. Specific chapters, focusing on activities such as police selection or child abuse allegations, describe how the psychologist can be useful to the legal system and, specifically, to the body of knowledge, techniques, and instruments available to the psychologist. The ethical considerations in applying this material to the legal system's questions are emphasized throughout the book.

3. *The practice of forensic psychology should be firmly based in empirical research.* As Leonardo da Vinci—arguably the first "scientist/ practitioner"—stated, "Science is the captain, Practice the soldier." When psychologists venture into the legal system, their claims and conclusions must be based on sound research, and not simply their own personal opinions (as often happened in the past). Throughout this text, there is an emphasis on the relevant research findings that can best inform the practices of psychologists in the legal arena.

4. *The forensic psychologist is a participant in the legal system and as such must be aware of the legal system's "rules of the game."* When psychologists move from their clinical examining rooms or academic offices to practise as forensic psychologists, they are on a different turf, with different rules and expectations. Judges, police officers, trial lawyers, and others have expectations for the forensic psychologist that may conflict with what the psychologist can ethically or realistically provide. A book on forensic psychology should consistently note the temptations and responsibilities when psychologists venture into the legal system.

5. *Sources of information about forensic psychology are rich, varied, and extensive.* A book about forensic psychology should include empirical evaluations about the effectiveness of various procedures, from the application of the polygraph to the assessment of trauma in sexual assault victims, but it also should include descriptions of real cases that provide provocative illustrations of the procedures and phenomena to be evaluated. Such a book should try to capture the vitality of a field that constantly confronts new inquiries and issues. Thus, each chapter includes examples and legal cases relevant to the topic under study, as well as suggested readings selected to reflect the richness of the field. The References section at the end of the book, with roughly 1500 entries, includes texts from psychological journals and law reviews, but also from court cases and popular periodicals. Further, a list of relevant Web sites is included on the Companion Website. Most cases described here are Canadian court cases, from an animal cruelty case in a provincial court in Corner Brook, Newfoundland (Chapter 7), to numerous cases in the Supreme Court of Canada, which has the final "say" on a legal issue.

6. *A book about a popular topic such as forensic psychology should be as user friendly as possible.* In addition to the extensive list of references and the suggested readings, each chapter of the book contains an introductory outline, a closing summary of its contents, and a list of key terms. Each of these terms is printed in boldface when introduced in the text. Boxes in each chapter provide further exploration of specific topics, case examples, and summaries of research findings.

We hope that for each reader this book realizes the goals we set in creating it. The curiosity generated by students inspired the book, and we constantly feel gratitude for the presence of students and for the opportunity to hear about their views and observations. Hortense Callisher has written: "The habit of the lectern instills the habit of knowing. The habit of writing instills the habit of finding out." It gives us joy to have become habituated to both.

ANCILLARY MATERIAL

Instructor's Manual/Test Bank to Accompany *Forensic Psychology*, First Canadian Edition

Each chapter of the Instructor's Manual with Test Bank includes questions for class discussion and/or essay examinations; suggested activities; and multiple-choice questions with the correct response noted, as well as a page reference. (ISBN: 0-17-641443-6)

Companion Website

The book-specific site is available at **http:// www.forensicpsych.nelson.com**

It features links to Canadian and international resources that are relevant to forensic psychology, including online discussion groups. This site also includes study resources and information on degrees and careers in psychology.

ACKNOWLEDGMENTS

If this book were solely the product of the authors, it would be very different from the book you are reading. I am greatly indebted to a number of people who contributed to the final version of this work.

Many thanks to Lawrence Wrightsman, whose original text provided an excellent foundation for this book. The writing of this adaptation was facilitated by the support and assistance of numerous individuals at Thomson Nelson. First and foremost, I am greatly indebted to

Joanna Cotton for proposing that I write the Canadian text in the first place, and for her support and patience during the almost three years from start to finish. Also, I would like to thank Alwynn Pinard. Her feedback and encouragement were much appreciated. Alwynn arranged for chapter reviews from the following experts in the field (among others who wish to remain anonymous):

> Deborah C. Connolly, Simon Fraser University
> Laura Melnyk, King's College at the University of Western Ontario
> J. Don Read, Simon Fraser University
> Joti Samra, University of British Columbia
> Marilyn Smith, University of Toronto
> Steven M. Smith, Saint Mary's University
> Oliver R. Stoetzer, Fanshawe College
> Margo C. Watt, St. Francis Xavier University
> J. S. Wormith, University of Saskatchewan
> Dan Yarmey, University of Guelph

The suggestions of these reviewers were much appreciated and contributed greatly to the quality of the text. I also thank my production editor, Julie van Veen, and my copyeditor and proofreader, Valerie Adams. They were an inspirational team with which to work.

I would also like to thank my excellent research assistant, Naomi Doucette, who conducted literature reviews, reviewed and formatted all chapters before they were passed on to Alwynn, and compiled the updated references. Appreciation is extended to all my superb graduate students who provided feedback during the chapter writing, in particular Michael Woodworth (now a professor at Okanagan University College in Kelowna) and Kristine Peace.

Finally, appreciation is extended to Sasha Porter, who contributed much time and energy in proofreading and editing my work, and who provided a vast amount of moral support as always.

Stephen Porter

About the Authors

Photo: Jack W. Brehm

LAWRENCE WRIGHTSMAN

Lawrence S. Wrightsman (Ph.D., University of Minnesota, 1959) is professor of psychology at the University of Kansas, Lawrence. Wrightsman is an author or editor of ten other books relevant to the legal system, including *Psychology and the Legal System* (4th edition, co-authored with Michael T. Nietzel and William H. Fortune), *The American Jury on Trial* (co-authored with Saul M. Kassin), and *Judicial Decision Making: Is Psychology Relevant?* He was invited to contribute the entry on the law and psychology for the recently published *Encyclopedia of Psychology,* sponsored by the American Psychological Association and published by Oxford University Press. His research topics include jury selection procedures, reactions to police interrogations, and the impact of judicial instructions. He has also served as a trial consultant and testified as an expert witness. Wrightsman is a former president of both the Society for the Psychological Study of Social Issues and the Society of Personality and Social Psychology. In 1998 he was the recipient of a Distinguished Career Award from the American Psychology-Law Society. This award has been made on only six occasions in the 30-year history of the organization; the preceding awardee was U.S. Supreme Court Justice Harry Blackmun.

STEPHEN PORTER

Photo: Sasha Porter

Stephen Porter (B.Sc. [Hons.], Acadia University, 1992; Ph.D., University of British Columbia, 1998) is an associate professor and director of the forensic psychology program in the Department of Psychology at Dalhousie University. As a psychologist in training, Porter worked at Mountain Institution (a federal prison), the Forensic Psychiatric Institute (B.C.), the B.C. Board of Parole, and a victim services organization in Vancouver. Porter now works in the area of psychology and law as an educator, researcher, and practitioner/consultant. At Dalhousie, he teaches courses in abnormal psychology, forensic psychology, and psychological assessment, and supervises a large number of graduate and undergraduate students. He has published numerous research and review articles on diverse forensic issues including deception detection, forensic aspects of memory (e.g., recovered/false memory), the criminal psychopath, and psychological trauma. As a practising forensic psychologist, Porter has conducted more than 180 psychological assessments on criminal offenders or accused persons, and has been consulted in numerous other cases, often concerning complainant and suspect evidence. Porter has been qualified as an expert witness in several legal cases in Canada. In addition, he has lectured widely and provided training to psychologists and other correctional staff with the Correctional Service of Canada and judges across the country as part of the National Judicial Institute training program. In July 2000, Porter was presented with the President's New Investigator Award from the Canadian Psychological Association. His recent major awards include an operating grant (2004–2007) from the Social Sciences and Humanities Research Council (SSHRC) and a discovery grant (2004–2009) from the Natural Sciences and Engineering Research Council of Canada (NSERC).

1

The Challenge of Forensic Psychology

The longstanding recognition that psychiatric or psychological testimony also falls within the realm of expert evidence is predicated on the realization that in some circumstances the average person may not have sufficient knowledge of or experience with human behaviour to draw an appropriate inference from the facts before him or her.
—Chief Justice of Canada Beverley McLachlin (*R. v. D.D.*, 2000)

WHAT *IS* FORENSIC PSYCHOLOGY?

The term **forensic psychology** has become increasingly salient at the start of the 21st century. But what is forensic psychology? As a beginning definition, this book proposes that forensic psychology is any application of psychological knowledge or methods to a task faced by the legal system. Bartol and Bartol (1999) offer a more detailed—but equally broad—definition:

> It is both (a) the research endeavor that examines aspects of human behavior directly related to the legal process (e.g., eyewitness memory and testimony, jury decision making, or criminal behavior), and (b) the professional practice of psychology within or in consultation with a legal system that encompasses both criminal and civil law and the numerous areas where they interact. Therefore, forensic psychology refers broadly to the *production* and *application* of psychological knowledge to the civil and criminal justice systems. (1999, p. 3, italics in original)

Thus, forensic psychology encompasses activities as wide ranging as child custody decisions, alleviating police burnout, carrying out competency evaluations, conducting risk assessments, serving as an expert witness, and more.

Consider the following six real-life examples:

- John Yuille is a well-known professor and forensic psychologist in private practice in British Columbia. In addition to conducting research on various forensic issues, he regularly acts as a consultant to the courts and to police in their investigations, sometimes providing expert testimony concerning children's testimony.
- Jeff Earle is a forensic psychologist working full time as the director of psychological services in a medium-security prison in Nova Scotia. He oversees the work of numerous psychologists who engage in a

variety of activities, including writing risk assessments and providing counselling to inmates. Further, he conducts research in the area of psychopathy and risk in collaboration with academic researchers.

- Hugues Hervé was trained as a clinical forensic psychologist. He has worked at a Regional Reception and Assessment Centre for the Correctional Service of Canada, conducting assessments on violent offenders and serving as a member of the Regional Research Committee. He currently works at the Forensic Psychiatric Institute in Port Coquitlam, British Columbia, providing treatment, conducting assessments, and doing research with persons who have been found not competent to stand trial or not criminally responsible for their actions. He remains active in the research community by engaging in collaborative research.
- David Fairweather received his Ph.D. in counselling psychology from the University of Ottawa; he now is a psychologist employed by our federal prison system (Correctional Service of Canada). In this capacity, he conducts and supervises risk assessments to aid decision-makers (e.g., the National Parole Board, case management personnel) in decisions surrounding parole and community release, assesses offenders' capabilities and personality characteristics, and makes recommendations for treatment. In a minimum-security prison, he provides individual counselling to offenders. At the community level, he provides individual and family counselling to offenders who are on conditional release. In his private practice, he conducts psychological assessments for a provincial child protection body (Ministry of Children and Family Development), focusing mainly on areas of parenting capacity and custody/access.
- Superintendent Glenn Woods is the director of the Behavioural Sciences Branch for the Royal Canadian Mounted Police (RCMP).

Trained as a police officer, he is only one of a few investigators in Canada to have received specialized training in psychological profiling. He now contributes to criminal investigations as a criminal profiler. He provides criminal profiles to investigators involved in the investigation of crimes of interpersonal violence, particularly homicide and sexual assault. This is done through a behavioural analysis of crime scenes to determine characteristics and traits of the unknown offender. Post-offence behaviour analyses and investigative suggestions also are provided to investigators.

■ Steven Smith received his Ph.D. in social psychology from Queen's University in 2000, and now works as an assistant professor at Saint Mary's University in Halifax. He is a young but already well-known researcher in the area of eyewitness testimony, and has investigated factors leading to mistaken identifications from police lineups. His work offers an important demonstration of the potential problems associated with relying too heavily on eyewitnesses in the legal system.

THE PROMISE AND THE PROBLEMS OF FORENSIC PSYCHOLOGY

The foregoing examples reflect the variety of activities that may fall under the label "forensic psychology." These examples were chosen for several reasons. First, note that the training and past experiences of these professionals who work in the field of forensic psychology differ greatly, depending on their role. A forensic psychologist who does court-ordered child custody evaluations (such as David Fairweather) comes from a background in clinical psychology and is likely to have had a diversified practice as a psychotherapist

before he or she came to concentrate on child custody. A forensic psychologist who works full-time in a prison may also have been trained in clinical or forensic psychology, but with more concentration on psychopathology and in the use of tests and other assessment devices to measure competency and malingering (faking a serious mental disorder, often to avoid punishment). Other forensic psychologists, such as expert witnesses on child eyewitnesses, may have been trained as experimental psychologists or social psychologists. Some psychologists such as Steven Smith spend most of their time devising experiments to test scientific theories and generate findings of relevance in the legal system. Subsequent chapters will detail the activities of many roles, including criminal profiling, police selection, the use of hypnosis in criminal investigation, and evaluating criminal responsibility and competency as well as the activities illustrated above.

But even though the day-to-day activities of forensic psychologists may differ from one another, they share common challenges and temptations. Because it is an applied field resting on a sometimes-uncertain science, forensic psychology runs the risk of sacrificing reliability for relevance. Some of these common temptations are described in Chapter 2.

To propose that forensic psychology is *any* application of psychology to the legal system, as is done here, does not acknowledge the controversy within the field as to just who is a forensic psychologist and how one should be trained to become a forensic psychologist. The development of doctoral training programs with *forensic psychology* (such as the University of British Columbia) or *psychology and law* (such as Simon Fraser University) in their title has accelerated in the last 15 years and is still evolving. Not all observers would agree that each of the six examples above reflects their definition of forensic psychology. Students, judges, and even the past president of the Canadian Psychological Association (CPA), James Ogloff, have observed the problems in trying to define this field. Ogloff

(2004, p. 84) noted that "While some attention has been paid to defining our field—variously known as 'forensic psychology,' 'psychology and law,' 'law and psychology,' and 'legal psychology'—there is still little agreement on appropriate definitions."

This book has opted for a broad definition because the field is relatively new and because controversies exist. In examining the definitions of forensic psychology offered in the professional literature, one can separate them into broad and narrow types (Brigham, 1999). The definition which began this chapter is, of course, a broad one; narrow definitions (as are often used in Great Britain, for example) limit the focus of forensic psychology to clinical and professional practice issues, such as assessing criminal responsibility or competency to stand trial, conducting child custody evaluations, and other activities that rely upon professional training as a clinical psychologist. This type of definition would exclude the evaluation-research function, as well as many specific activities, including those performed by the research psychologist who testifies as an expert witness on the effects of pre-trial publicity. Psychologists trained in experimental, social, or developmental psychology, but who lack clinical training, would not be eligible. Thus, it must be recognized that for many psychologists, forensic psychology is a specialization of clinical psychology (a position with which we disagree). As an illustration, forensic workshops offered at the annual conference of the CPA typically are focused on clinical psychology topics. For example, at the 2004 convention in St. John's, the two forensically oriented workshops focused on risk assessment and addictions.

Thus, much disagreement exists over how encompassing the definition should be. Right now, many psychologists are left in, to use John Brigham's (1999) term, a "definitional limbo." Consider Brigham's own situation: A social psychologist and a professor, he has not had training in clinical psychology. He carries out research on eyewitnesses' memory and sometimes provides expert testimony in criminal trials. If asked in court, "Are you a forensic psychologist?" he has said:

My most accurate current response would seem to be, "Well, it depends...." And, in my experience, judges *hate* responses of that sort, which they see as unnecessarily vague or evasive. (Brigham, 1999, p. 280, italics in original)

As more and more graduate students seek training in forensic psychology, the lack of an agreed-upon definition increases the magnitude of the problem. One manifestation of the issue is to question whether the CPA should certify a "specialty" or "proficiency" in forensic psychology as the American Psychological Association (APA) has done. Although it is true that the purpose of a **specialty designation** is to evaluate specific graduate-school training programs and not to credential individuals, a concern exists that such labels in the future may be applied to individual psychologists. So should a training program that seeks a specialty designation as forensic psychology include only clinical training or should it be broader? Or should such a specialty designation even be sought? Arguments have been offered for each perspective (see Brigham, 1999, and the responses generated by Heilbrun, 1998).

Throughout the above discussion, the issue has been presented as an either-or question—that is, should training for forensic psychology be limited to clinical psychology or should it include more? Some forensic psychologists have suggested a richer, less adversarial, conception of what training in forensic psychology should be. Kirk Heilbrun (described in Brigham, 1999) has offered a model, presented in Table 1.1, that reflects three training areas and two approaches.

Heilbrun's model is comprehensive, and the boundaries of forensic psychology used in this book are in keeping with his conceptualization. Note that among the training topics in his model are consultation in jury selection and in litigation strategy, policy and legislative consultation, and expert testimony on the state of the science, as well as traditional topics such as forensic assessment (all topics covered in various chapters throughout this text).

Table 1.1	Heilbrun's Conceptualization of Training in Forensic Psychology		
	Law and Psychology Interest Areas (with associated training)		
	Clinical (clinical, counselling, school psychology)	*Experimental* (social, developmental, cognitive, human experimental psychology)	*Legal* (law, some training in behavioural science)
Research/ Scholarship	1. Assessment tools 2. Intervention effectiveness 3. Epidemiology of relevant behaviour (e.g., violence, sexual offending) and disorders	1. Memory 2. Perception 3. Child development 4. Group decision making	1. Mental health law 2. Other law relevant to health and science 3. Legal movements
Applied	1. Forensic assessment 2. Treatment in legal context 3. Integration of science into practice	1. Consultation re jury selection 2. Consultation re litigation strategy 3. Consultation re "state of science" 4. Expert testimony re "state of science"	1. Policy and legislative consultation 2. Model law development

(From "What Is Forensic Psychology, Anyway?" by J. C. Brigham, 1999, *Law and Human Behavior,* 23, p. 282, Table 3.) Reprinted by permission of Springer, the language of science, and by permission of the author.

FORENSIC PSYCHOLOGY IN CANADA

In whatever manner we choose to define forensic psychology, many Canadians are recognized as leaders in the field on an international level. In the forward of a 1997 text by two Canadians (Chris Webster and Margaret Jackson), John Monahan at the University of Virginia, a towering figure in the field, commented on "the remarkably strong international presence of Canada in forensic psychology and psychiatry, a presence out of proportion to relative population size, not to mention relative crime rate" (Monahan, 1997, pp. x–xi). Ogloff (2004), now based at Monash University in Australia, noted that:

There are prominent research groups or individuals at the University of Victoria, the University of British Columbia, Simon Fraser University, the University of Saskatchewan, the University of Regina, Queen's University, the University of Toronto, Ryerson University, University of Guelph, Université de Montréal, Dalhousie University, and the University of New Brunswick…. In addition to prominence as researchers and clinicians, Canadians have distinguished themselves as editors of key journals in the field. (p. 84)

Once widely viewed as a subfield of psychology in which one might "end up working," forensic psychology is now one of the most highly respected areas of psychology. As one of us noted in a recent special issue of the CPA journal *Canadian Journal of Behavioural Science* devoted to forensic psychology, much of the ground-breaking research in major areas of forensic psychology, including eyewitness testimony, risk assessment, deception detection, victimology, psychopathy, and criminal behaviour, was and is conducted in Canada (Porter, 2004). In addition, Canadian researchers are having a major impact in society. For example, both the National Judicial Institute (NJI) and the Correctional Service of Canada (CSC) rely heavily on training provided by psychologists for their staff. Researchers such as Rod Lindsay at Queen's University contracted by the NJI have been given the opportunity to educate the judiciary in several areas, including eyewitness testimony and assessing credibility. These types of applications in Canada provide an excellent example of bridging the gap between our basic science and applied practice in the field.

THE CONFLICT BETWEEN PSYCHOLOGY AND THE LAW

Disagreement within the field of psychology as to the limits of forensic psychology is not the only problem we face. When psychology seeks to apply its findings to the legal system, it faces the task of working with another discipline, that of the law. Lawyers—including judges, trial lawyers, and university professors—are trained to look at human behaviour in a way that is quite different from the perspective of psychologists. It is the goal of this chapter to examine the nature of these conflicts between the law and psychology (and other social sciences). Only after that exploration may we move to a more extensive description of the various roles of forensic psychologists, in Chapter 2.

Laws and Values

Laws are human creations that evolve out of the need to resolve disagreements. In that sense, laws reflect values, and values are basic psychological concepts. **Values** may be defined as standards for decision making, and thus laws are created, amended, or discarded because society has established standards for what is acceptable and unacceptable behaviour (Wrightsman, Nietzel, & Fortune, 1998). Society's values can change, leading to new laws and new interpretations of existing laws. For example, 100 years ago society

looked the other way when a married man forced his wife to have sexual relations against her will, but society has become increasingly aware of and concerned about spousal sexual assault, and now Canada and other countries have laws that prohibit such actions.

Each discipline approaches the generation of knowledge and the standards for decision making in a different way. A lawyer and a social scientist will see the same event through different perspectives, because of their specialized training. Judges may use procedures and concepts different from those of psychology in forming their opinions. It is not that one approach is correct and that the other is wrong; rather, they have different goals.

Some lawyers consult with psychologists in evaluating and planning their case evidence, and Canadian courts now accept psychologists as expert witnesses on a variety of topics. But obstacles stand in the way of full application, and many of these obstacles are at the most basic level—the level of values and goals. Conflicts between the values of psychology and the values of the legal system serve as a focus for this chapter, because they play a role in evaluating the topics covered in subsequent chapters, especially in the degree to which psychology is successful in influencing the decisions of the legal system.

Many ways exist to distinguish these contrasting goals and values; John Carroll put it as follows:

> The goals of the law and the goals of social science are different and partially in conflict. The law deals in morality, social values, social control, and justifying the application of abstract principles to specific cases. In day-to-day operation, the system values efficiency and expediency…. In contrast, social science deals in knowledge, truth, and derives abstract principles from specific instances. These are thought to be value free. In operation, the scientific method values reproducible phenomena and underlying concepts and causes rather than the specifics or form in which these appear. (Carroll, 1980, p. 363)

The response of the CPA to "repressed" memories following several legal cases is an example of the expression of psychology's values. Since the 1980s, some allegations of crime have been based on memories "recovered" in psychotherapy or highly leading police interviews (see Porter, Campbell, Birt, & Woodworth, 2003). For example, Donna Cole (pseudonym) recovered memories of being sexually abused by her father at the age of 18 months. Her outlandish claims included that her father placed both her and her brother in a roasting pan in the oven, dismembered and buried a female hitchhiker, and raped the family dog after mutilating the animal. Her testimony led directly to her father's conviction. Such cases led the CPA to produce a 1996 position paper (spear-headed by James Ogloff) questioning the accuracy of recovered memory evidence in legal cases, based on increasing empirical evidence for the existence of false memories. For example, in 1994 Canadian researchers Stephen Lindsay and Don Read published a widely cited paper that examined memories of childhood sexual abuse as "recovered" in therapy and concluded that many were likely to be mistaken. Ultimately, in 1998, the CPA recommended to Anne McLellan, then the federal Minister of Justice, that a full judicial inquiry be conducted into all Canadian convictions stemming from such evidence. McLellan rejected the recommendation and many people remain in prison as a result of such evidence. Perhaps her reaction to the CPA was not surprising given the politics involved. However, some have argued for an **empirical approach** in applying psychology in the legal system "in which both existing standards and proposals for change would be carefully examined for their scientific merit" (Rogers, 1987, p. 841).

The Legal System's Reliance on Intuition over Empiricism

Psychologists are trained that the best way to answer a question about human behaviour is to collect data. A conclusion about behaviour is not accepted by psychologists until the observations are objectively measurable, they show **reliability** (they are consistent over time), and they possess **replicability** (different investigators can produce similar results). In contrast, lawyers are more willing to rely on their own experience, their own views of life, and their intuition or "gut feelings." J. Alexander Tanford (1990), a professor of law, proposed that courts tend "to approve legal rules based on intuitive assumptions about human behaviour that research by psychologists has shown to be erroneous" (p. 138).

For example, judges have long believed that they have special insight into whether a witness is lying or telling the truth based on "demeanour evidence." However, there is growing evidence that judges may not be well equipped to identify liars on the stand. Ekman and O'Sullivan (1991) found that judges and other groups performed at around chance in judging the honesty of videotaped speakers. A major problem in evaluating the credibility of witnesses is a widespread reliance on cues to lying that lack validity. Porter, Birt, and Woodworth (2000) found that many faulty credibility judgments are based on misleading strategies, such as relying on a single dominant cue or one's "gut instinct." Whereas judges may associate lying with speech disturbances, longer pauses, gaze aversion (the liar will not look you in the eye), body movements, and shifting positions, liars seem to show the opposite pattern (e.g., Vrij, 2000). There is evidence that Canadian judges may use the wrong approach to identifying liars (from case transcripts). For example, in the Canadian case *R. v. Jabarianha* (2001), the judge stated: "Mr. Corkum and Mr. Jabarianha were less than believable. Each exhibited classic signs of discomfort when challenged.... Each was evasive at times or his eyes shifted around. Thus in certain points of the story displayed signs of untruthfulness" (para. 29). Unfortunately, such remarks contradict the findings by researchers of deceptive behaviour. One might argue that it is our responsibility as students of forensic psychology to attempt to counteract the legal system's reliance on intuition over research evidence. As such, the NJI's approach of inviting researchers to lead some of their training sessions with Canadian judges is a step in the right direction.

Illustrations from the Courtroom

Two illustrations from the courtroom decisively reflect the conflict in values between the legal profession and scientific psychology. The first, a Canadian example, demonstrates the debate over whether psychologists should give expert testimony in the courtroom. In the other, an American example, the court's opinion was consistent with the position of the psychologist who testified as an expert witness, but the effect of the psychologist's testimony in influencing the outcome was unclear. These two examples reflect the difference of opinion both between disciplines and within each discipline.

A Canadian Example

In Canada, there has been much debate over when expert testimony should be admitted as evidence, and what defines an "expert." Do psychologists possess knowledge that would qualify as expert evidence?

In the 1994 case *R. v. Mohan*, detailed principles for assessing the admissibility of expert opinion were offered by the late Justice Sopinka. He established four criteria for admitting expert evidence: (1) relevance, (2) necessity, (3) absence of any exclusionary rule, and (4) qualification of the expert. Concerning relevance, the trial judge must assess the expert's relevance to the issue at hand, as well as the value of the expert's information versus the possible prejudicial (biasing) effect it may have on legal decision making. The court made it clear that the expert evidence must be more than simply "helpful." The higher standard requires that expert evidence be necessary and provide information "that is likely to be outside the experience and knowledge of a judge or jury" (summary para. 4), but not likely to distort the fact-finding process.

Does psychological testimony ever meet these criteria? Despite disagreement from some

legal professionals, in *R. v. Lavallee* (1990) (a battered spouse case detailed in Chapter 10), it was determined that expert testimony by both psychiatrists and psychologists "falls within the realm of expert evidence." The next question concerns what types of expert psychological testimony are acceptable to courts in Canada. The Canadian law makes it clear that expert evidence must go beyond "common sense" and can never replace the function of judges and juries (neither of whom are compelled to accept an expert's opinion). However, it is clear that the application of this principle can be problematic. For example, courts somewhat arbitrarily have decided that certain types of psychological evidence are "common sense" and others are not. Supreme Court of Canada judgments have decided in favour of expert evidence concerning the behaviours of sexually abused persons (*R. v. Burns*, 1994), and concerning battered women's behaviour (*R. v. Lavallee*, 1990). In *Lavallee*, expert evidence on the psychological effects of battering and the behaviour of affected spouses was viewed as both relevant and necessary because of the average person's negative reaction to a spouse who stays in an abusive relationship and because of the need to dispel inaccurate assumptions.

On the other hand, Canadian courts have resisted allowing expert testimony on eyewitness testimony or other aspects of witness credibility, with the apparent assumption that the evaluation of eyewitness testimony is a matter of "common sense." The difficulty with relying on the common sense of the trier of fact in judicial decision making was demonstrated by University of Guelph researcher Dan Yarmey (1986) in his test of the standards outlined by the courts for the assessment of eyewitness accuracy. Despite some of the court's commonsense notions for determining the accuracy of a given witness, he found that the accuracy of the witness's prior description of the accused and the witness's level of confidence at the time of the incident were not good predictors of accuracy. Many of the difficulties that arise during eyewitness testimony contradict the commonsense beliefs held by judges and laypersons about eyewitness memory (Yarmey, 2001).

The complexities here are certainly highlighted in the type of abuse cases mentioned above in which someone reports that he or she "recovered" a memory for a crime after repressing it for decades. To date, Canadian courts have no consistent approach to deciding whether such evidence is valid or determining the value of relevant expert evidence. In the case of *R. v. François* (1994), François was convicted of repeatedly raping a 13-year-old girl. The only evidence at trial was the complainant's testimony that she had "blocked out" the sexual assaults until her memory returned in a flashback years later. When François appealed his conviction to the Supreme Court of Ontario, it was upheld. The judge rationalized that:

> It was ... for the jury to determine, on the basis of *common sense* and *experience* [italics added], whether they believed the complainant's story of repressed and recovered memory, and whether the recollection she experienced in 1990 was the truth. The jury's acceptance of the complainant's evidence concerning what happened to her cannot, on the basis of the record, be characterized as unreasonable. In sum, the verdict was not illogical or speculative or inconsistent with the main body of evidence. (summary para. 4)

On appeal, François's conviction was set aside.

Although the judge's comments convey a belief that jurors can readily determine the credibility of recovered memory evidence based on common sense, in reality, the jury had been asked to act as experts on a very complex psychological issue. Most psychologists would agree that the judge contradicted the principle asserted in *R. v. Mohan* (1994)—that psychological testimony can and should be admitted as evidence in situations where the issue at hand is beyond the experience and knowledge of judges and juries.

What are we to make of this conflict between the perspectives of psychological science and the judiciary? First, we need to note that the goals of researchers and judges are different. Psychologists derive the truth from empirical proof. For example, as the CPA asserted to Anne McLellan, it has been shown in numerous studies that many recovered memories are actually false memories (e.g., Porter, Yuille, & Lehman, 1999), and that their assessment goes beyond the knowledge of most laypersons. Judges, on the other hand, wish to establish the truth through an evaluation of the evidence in a particular case and with certain assumptions about human decision making based on their own observations.

Both positions can be defended. As psychologists we have been trained to believe that empirical results define the truth, that data have power. In contrast, judges believe that each case is unique and that accumulated data may not be relevant in a single case.

An American Civil Case: *Price Waterhouse v. Hopkins* (1989)

The previous discussion concerned court decisions as to whether psychological testimony was relevant to types of cases and to the extent that it should be admitted. But what about the impact of such testimony once it does enter the courtroom? In the American case *Price Waterhouse v. Hopkins* (1989), the U.S. Supreme Court acknowledged the presence of sex discrimination in a civil suit, after reviewing the testimony of a psychologist about the nature of stereotyping. But how much difference did the testimony of the psychologist make?

Ann Hopkins, in 1982, was in her fourth year as a very successful salesperson at Price Waterhouse, a leading accounting firm. She had brought in business worth US$25 million; her clients raved about her, and she had more billable hours than any other person proposed for partner that year (Fiske, Bersoff, Borgida, Deaux, & Heilman, 1991). But she was not made a partner—not that year and not the next year. Price Waterhouse apparently rejected her because of her heavy-handed managerial style and her "interpersonal skills problems." She was described as "macho," lacking "social grace," and needing "a course at charm school." A colleague didn't like her use of profanity; another reportedly advised her that she would improve her chances if she would "walk more femininely, talk more femininely, dress more femininely, wear make-up, have her hair styled, and wear jewellery" (p. 1117). She was caught in a double bind; women were censured for being aggressive even though aggressiveness was, in reality, one of the job qualifications (Chamallas, 1990).

So Hopkins took the firm to court, claiming sex discrimination and a violation of the 1964 U.S. Civil Rights Act. The above information, though disturbing, was not enough; she had to demonstrate that the stereotypic remarks, quoted above, were evidence of discrimination in the decision to reject her as a partner. Thus social psychologist Susan Fiske was asked to testify as an expert witness, and she agreed, because she felt the case fit with the scientific literature on sex stereotyping in organizations to a striking degree.

An account by Fiske and her colleagues describes the nature of her testimony in the case:

> [The testimony] drew on both laboratory and field research to describe antecedent conditions that encourage stereotyping, indicators that reveal stereotyping, consequences of stereotyping for out-groups, and feasible remedies to prevent the intrusion of stereotyping into decision making. Specifically, she testified first that stereotyping is most likely to intrude when the target is an isolated, one- or few-of-a-kind individual in an otherwise homogeneous environment. The person's solo or near-solo status makes the unusual category more likely to be a salient factor in decision making. (Fiske et al., 1991, p. 1050)

Of 88 candidates proposed for partner status in 1982, Hopkins was the only woman; of 662 partners at Price Waterhouse, only seven were women.

Among many relevant matters, Professor Fiske also testified that subjective judgments of interpersonal skills—apparently essential in the partnership decision—are quite vulnerable to stereotypic biases, and decision makers should be alert to the possibility of stereotyping when they employ subjective criteria. She concluded that sexual stereotyping played a major role in the firm's decision to deny Hopkins a partnership.

In the Price Waterhouse decisions on partners, the opinions of persons with limited hearsay information were given the same weight as the opinions of those who had more extensive and relevant contact with Hopkins (Fiske et al., 1991, 1993), and Price Waterhouse had no policy prohibiting sex discrimination. As Fiske and her colleagues observed, "consistent with this failure to establish organizational norms emphasizing fairness, overt expressions of prejudice were not discouraged" (Fiske et al., 1991, p. 1051). Professor Fiske, in her testimony, noted that many of Price Waterhouse's practices could be remedied if the firm applied psychological concepts and findings.

At the original trial, the judge expressed some frustration over the psychologist's testimony. He seemed to have great difficulty understanding what the psychologist was saying, and "at times he undermined her position by changing the meaning of her statements and then challenging her to explain herself more clearly" (Chamallas, 1990, p. 110). But after considering all the evidence, the judge ruled in favour of Hopkins's claim, writing that an "employer that treats [a] woman with [an] assertive personality in a different manner than if she had been a man is guilty of sex discrimination" (p. 1119). Price Waterhouse—not surprisingly—appealed the decision, and in doing so, argued that the social psychologist's testimony was "sheer speculation" of "no evidentiary value" (p. 467). After the decision was upheld by the U.S. Circuit Court of Appeals for the District of Columbia, Price Waterhouse asked the U.S. Supreme Court to review the case, and because various appellate court decisions in *Hopkins* and other similar cases had been in conflict, the Court accepted the case for review. On May 1, 1989, the U.S. Supreme Court handed down its decision to uphold a significant portion of the decision.

Thus, it would appear that the testimony of a research psychologist had a significant impact on the judge's decision in a landmark case. But some of the justices were hostile to Professor Fiske's message; in his dissenting opinion, Justice Anthony Kennedy questioned her ability to be fair, implying that Fiske would have reached the same conclusion *whenever* a woman was denied a promotion. Even the majority opinion by Justice William Brennan downplayed the impact of the expert witness's testimony; the majority opinion stated:

> Indeed, we are tempted to say that Dr. Fiske's expert testimony was merely icing on Hopkins' cake. It takes no special training to discern sex stereotyping in a description of an aggressive female employee as requiring "a course at charm school." Nor ... does it require expertise in psychology to know that, if an employee's flawed "interpersonal skills" can be corrected by a soft-hued suit or a new shade of lipstick, perhaps it is the employee's sex and not her interpersonal skills that has drawn criticism. (*Price Waterhouse v. Hopkins*, 1989, p. 1793).

Fiske and her colleagues had the following reaction to this comment:

> One can interpret this comment in various ways; as dismissive, saying that the social science testimony was all common sense; as merely taking the social psychological expertise for granted; or as suggesting that one does not necessarily require expert witnesses to identify stereotyping when the evidence is egregious. (Fiske et al., 1991, p. 1054)

While any of these is a possibility, none is congruent with a claim that the social science evidence really made a difference in the U.S. Supreme Court's opinion.

Further, not all psychologists have endorsed the application of Fiske's conclusions (Barrett & Morris, 1993). Not only do judges disagree with each other, but so too is there less than unanimity among psychologists. In fact, the lack of agreement within the field creates problems for the establishment of agreed-upon procedures for forensic psychologists. For example, is there sufficient scientific evidence to justify a psychologist's testifying that a murder defendant's behaviour reflected the battered woman syndrome?

THE HISTORY OF THE RELATIONSHIP BETWEEN PSYCHOLOGY AND THE LAW

We have seen the diversity of activities by contemporary forensic psychologists and have begun to identify the complex interaction between modern-day psychology and the law. How did we get where we are today? What was the relationship of the two fields when they began to interrelate? How have matters changed?

The division between contemporary psychologists who conduct research (mostly in laboratories) in search of scientific laws and those who work toward the alleviation of detrimental behaviours in individuals can be traced back to the beginnings of the 20th century, and the distinction is certainly of relevance to the origin of forensic psychology. On the one hand, the courts have faced the challenge of dealing with people, who, because of mental disturbance or a criminal tendency, cannot conform their behaviour to legal requirements. On the other hand, psychologists in laboratories have studied various phenomena (such as accuracy of observers or how people behave when they are lying). Origins of the first approach can be traced to Césare Lombroso (1836–1909), an Italian considered to be the father of modern criminology, because he sought to understand the causes of crime. The development of separate juvenile courts in the United States—first done by Illinois in 1899— led William Healy, a physician, to initiate a program of study of the causes of juvenile delinquency. In doing so, he sought the advice of prominent academic psychologists such as Edward G. Thorndike, William James, and James

R. Angell. His founding of the Juvenile Psychopathic Institute in 1909, with a staff that included psychologist Grace M. Fernald, led to increased emphasis on the foundations of criminal behaviour. Dr. Fernald was one of the first psychologists to specialize in the diagnosis and treatment of juvenile delinquency (Bartol & Bartol, 1999).

Also, during the late 1800s and early 1900s Sigmund Freud was developing his theory of personality, and his writings about psychopathology influenced thinking about the causes of criminal behaviour. In a speech in 1906 to a group of judges, Freud proposed that psychology could be of practical use to their field (Horowitz & Willging, 1984).

The Role of Hugo Münsterberg

The other thread can be traced to academic psychology. Consider the following quotation from a prominent psychology-and-law researcher regarding his building facilities: "…visiting friends [would find], with surprise, twenty-seven rooms overspun with electric wires and filled with (equipment), and a mechanic busy at work" (Münsterberg, 1908, p. 3). Five pages later, this psychologist wrote: "Experimental psychology has reached a stage at which it seems natural and sound to give attention to its possible service for the practical needs of life" (p. 8).

A contemporary statement? No, that was from *On the Witness Stand* (1908), written by Hugo Münsterberg almost a century ago. Three months before the founding of the American Psychological Association, in September of 1892, Münsterberg, after receiving a Ph.D. from Leipzig University and studying with world-renowned Wilhem Wundt, came from Germany to the United States, to establish—at William James's invitation—the psychological laboratory at Harvard University. At the APA's first annual meeting in December 1892, a dozen papers were presented, of which Münsterberg's was the last. In it he criticized his colleagues' work as "rich in decimals but poor in ideas" (Cattell, 1894).

Despite the fact that interests in psycho-legal issues captured only a small portion of his professional time, Münsterberg's impact on the field was so prodigious that it is appropriate to call him the founder of forensic psychology. His choices of what to do are still somewhat reflected in current research activities of psychologists interested in the legal system. For example, the chapter topics of Münsterberg's 1908 book—memory distortions, eyewitness accuracy, confessions, suggestibility, hypnosis, crime detection, and the prevention of crime—in varying degrees define what some psychologists think of as topics for contemporary forensic psychology.

Münsterberg was by no means the sole instigator of a movement. In some ways, he was a less-than-ideal symbol; he was arrogant and pugnacious and he often engaged in self-important posturing. Even William James later described him as "vain and loquacious" (Lukas, 1997, p. 586). More importantly, there were other pioneers, too. Even before Münsterberg's book, Hermann Ebbinghaus (1885), using himself as a subject, had demonstrated the rapid rate of early memory loss. In France, Alfred Binet, as early as 1900, was seeking to understand children's competence as eyewitnesses (Yarmey, 1984). In Germany, Louis William Stern began publishing eyewitness research as early as 1902; during the next year he was admitted to German courts of law to testify as an expert witness on eyewitness identification. Stern (1903) established a periodical dealing with the psychology of testimony. Although it is true that much of the early work published there was classificatory (e.g., six types of questions that might be asked of an eyewitness), other contributions were empirical; for example, he compared the memory abilities of children and adults. Wells and Loftus (1984) observed: "Not surprisingly, the early empirical work was not of the quality and precision that exists in psychology today" (1984, p. 5). Yet the foundation was set.

Guy Montrose Whipple (1909, 1910, 1911, 1912), in a series of *Psychological Bulletin* articles, brought the *Aussage* (or eyewitness testimony) tradition into English terminology, introducing

American audiences to classic experiments relating testimony and evidence to perception and memory. Even prior to World War I, "law was acknowledged as a fit concern for psychology and vice versa" (Tapp, 1976, pp. 360–361).

But Münsterberg was the psychologist "who pushed his reluctant American colleagues into the practical legal arena" (Bartol & Bartol, 1999, p. 7), and thus he had the greatest impact—for good or bad. Some of the topics that first received their illumination by Münsterberg and his contemporaries continue to remain in the limelight. Especially with regard to the accuracy of eyewitness identification, the immense interest in recent times can be directly traced back to Münsterberg's work.

Münsterberg's Goals for Psychology and the Law

Münsterberg's mission has been described as raising the position of the psychological profession to one of importance in public life (Kargon, 1986), and the legal system was one vehicle for doing so. Loftus (1979) has commented: "At the beginning of the century, Münsterberg was arguing for more interaction between the two fields, perhaps at times in a way that was insulting to the legal profession" (p. 194). "Insulting" is a strong description but it is true that Münsterberg wrote things like this: "it seems astonishing that the work of justice is carried out in the courts without ever consulting the psychologist and asking him for all the aid which the modern study of suggestion can offer" (1908, p. 194). At the beginning of the 20th century, chemists and physicists were routinely called as expert witnesses (Kargon, 1986). Why not psychologists? Münsterberg saw no difference between the physical sciences and his own.

Münsterberg's Values

A description of Münsterberg's specific views toward the court system will help us understand the actions he took. More importantly, an examination of his views will cause us to ask: How different are our values and beliefs from his?

The jury system rests on a positive assumption about human nature, that a collection of reasonable people are able to judge the world about them reasonably accurately. As Kalven and Zeisel (1966) put it, the justice system:

> recruits a group of twelve lay [people], chosen at random from the widest population; it convenes them for the purpose of a particular trial; it entrusts them with great official powers of decision; it permits them to carry out deliberations in secret and report out their final judgment without giving reasons for it; and, after their momentary service to the state has been completed, it orders them to disband and return to private life. (1966, p. 3)

Further, our society values the rights of the accused; it protects suspects against self-incrimination and places the burden of proof on the state to show guilt beyond a reasonable doubt. As his biographer, Matthew Hale, Jr., saw it, Münsterberg took a very different view of society and the role of the psychologist as expert: "The central premise of his legal psychology ... was that the individual could not accurately judge the real world that existed outside him, or for that matter the nature and processes of his own mind" (Hale, 1980, p. 121). Thus police investigations and courtroom procedures required the assistance of a psychologist (who, in Münsterberg's view, could be more objective than other persons).

Three Types of Activities

Münsterberg reflected his desire to bring psychology into the courtroom by carrying out three tasks:

1. Demonstrating the fallibility of memory, including time overestimation, omission of significant information, and other errors.
2. Publishing *On the Witness Stand*, which was actually a compilation of highly successful magazine articles. As a result of these articles, he was, after William James, North America's best-known psychologist (Lukas, 1997). His

goal in these *McClure's Magazine* pieces was to show an audience of laypersons that "experimental psychology has reached a stage at which it seems natural and sound to give attention also to its possible service for the practical needs of life" (1908, p. 8).

3. Offering his testimony as expert witness in highly publicized trials. Perhaps most controversial was his intrusion in the Idaho trial, in 1907, of the labour leader "Big Bill" Haywood (Hale, 1980; Holbrook, 1957). The IWW (Industrial Workers of the World) leader was charged with conspiracy to murder Frank Steunenberg, a former governor of Idaho and a well-known opponent to organized labour. On December 30, 1905, in Caldwell, Idaho, Steunenberg had opened the gate to his modest home and was blown apart by a waiting bomb. The murder trial transformed Haywood into an international symbol of labour protest; Clarence Darrow offered his services as defence lawyer, and people like Eugene V. Debs and Maksim Gorky rallied support (Hale, 1980).

The case against Haywood rested on the testimony of the mysterious Harry Orchard, a one-time IWW organizer who—after a four-day interrogation—confessed to committing the bombing (as well as many other crimes) at the behest of an "inner circle" of radicals, including Haywood. Münsterberg firmly believed that one of psychology's strongest contributions was in distinguishing false memory from true. Thus he examined Orchard in his cell, during the trial, and conducted numerous tests on him over a period of seven hours, including some precursors of the polygraph. In Münsterberg's mind, the most important of these was the word association test. Upon returning to Cambridge, Münsterberg permitted an interview with the Boston *Herald* (July 3, 1907), which quoted him as saying, "Orchard's confession is, every word of it, true" (Lukas, 1997, p. 599). This disclosure, coming before a verdict had been delivered, threatened the impartiality of the trial, and Münsterberg was

rebuked by newspapers nationwide. Still, the jury found Haywood not guilty, as the state did not produce any significant evidence corroborating Orchard's confession, as Idaho law required. Two weeks later, Münsterberg amended his position by introducing the concept of "subjective truthfulness." His free association tests, he now concluded, revealed that Orchard genuinely believed he was telling the truth, but they couldn't discern the actual facts of the matter.

Despite the adverse publicity, Münsterberg maintained his inflated claims for his science. In a letter to the editor he wrote: "To deny that the experimental psychologist has indeed possibilities of determining the 'truth-telling' process is just as absurd as to deny that the chemical expert can find out whether there is arsenic in a stomach or whether blood spots are of human or of animal origin" (quoted by Hale, 1980, p. 118). His claims were couched in exaggerated metaphors; he could "pierce the mind" and bring to light its deepest secrets.

In fairness, it should be noted that Münsterberg did not limit his advocacy to one side in criminal trials. In one case he felt the defendant's confession was the result of a hypnotic induction and hence false, so Münsterberg offered to testify for the defence. In the Idaho case his conclusions (which, if not derived from his political ideologies, were certainly in keeping with his antipathy to anarchy and union protest) supported the prosecution.

Münsterberg, like most true believers committed to their innovative theories, may have exaggerated claims in order to get attention and convince himself of their merits. His biographer Matthew Hale (1980) has made a strong case that Münsterberg "deceived himself with alarming frequency, and his distortions in certain cases bordered on outright falsification" (1980, p. 119).

Reaction of the Legal Community

Not surprisingly, Münsterberg's advocacy generated withering abuse from the legal community. One attack, titled "Yellow Psychology" and written by Charles Moore, concluded that the laboratory had little to lend to the courtroom and expressed skepticism that Münsterberg had discovered a "Northwest Passage to the truth" (quoted in Hale, 1980, p. 115).

The article by John Henry Wigmore (1909), a law professor and a leading expert on evidence (cast in the form of a trial against Münsterberg during which lawyers cross-examined him for damaging assertions), was in the words of Wallace Loh, "mercilessly satiric" (1981, p. 316); it suggested that experimental psychology, at the time, lacked enough knowledge to be practical (Davis, 1989). Further, Wigmore argued that the jury system distrusted those outside interferences, such as Münsterberg's, that intruded upon their common sense judgments. But Wigmore made a telling point in this article. As Loftus (1979) has reminded us, in Wigmore's courtroom drama, "Before the jurors left the courtroom to go home, the judge took a few moments to express his personal view. He said essentially this: In no other country in the civilized world had the legal profession taken so little interest in finding out what psychology and other sciences had to offer that might contribute to the nation's judicial system" (p. 203).

A Period of Inactivity

Perhaps for these reasons—exaggeration by Münsterberg and avoidance by legal authorities—research by scientific psychology applicable to the courts languished from the First World War until the latter half of the 1970s. There were contributions in the 1930s, 1940s, 1950s, and 1960s, but they were infrequent. Historical treatments of the development of the field (e.g., Bartol & Bartol, 1999; Davis, 1989; Foley, 1993; Kolasa, 1972; Yuille, Daylen, Porter, & Marxsen, 1996) note that a few works examined the legal system from the psychological perspective; those included books such as Burtt's *Legal Psychology* in 1931 and Robinson's *Law and the Lawyers* in 1935 and some speculative reviews in law journals (Hutchins & Slesinger, 1928a, 1928b, 1928c; Louisell, 1955, 1957). But until the 1960s, more

work on the legal field was done by anthropologists, sociologists, and psychiatrists (Tapp, 1977).

The relationship between eyewitness confidence and accuracy is an example of the gap in research activity. Münsterberg did perhaps the first empirical test of this relationship (Wells & Murray, 1984). He had children examine pictures for 15 seconds and then write a report of everything they could remember. Subsequently they were required to underline those parts of their report of which they were absolutely certain. Münsterberg reported that there were almost as many mistakes in the underlined sentences as in the rest. Other studies in the first years of the 20th century, by Stern and by Borst, were reported by Whipple (1909). Paradoxically, no further empirical interest surfaced until almost 65 years later (Wells & Murray, 1984).

Explanations for the dead period came from Sporer (1981, cited by Wells & Loftus, 1984): "zealous overgeneralizations drawn from experimental studies that did not meet adequately the demands of complex courtroom reality" (quoted by Wells & Loftus, 1984, p. 6). Wells and Loftus offer another reason: that "psychological research during that time was oriented primarily toward theoretical issues with little focus on practical problems" (1984, p. 6).

Resurgence in the 1970s

Resurgence in interest by experimental psychologists and social psychologists did not occur until the 1970s. With regard to one example, eyewitness identification, Wells and Loftus (1984) estimated that more than 85 percent of the entire published literature surfaced between 1978 and the publication of their book in 1984.

Two Canadian researchers who began to tackle the accuracy of eyewitness identification at this time were John Yuille at the University of British Columbia (e.g., Yuille, 1980) and Dan Yarmey at the University of Guelph. In 1979, Yarmey published one of the first important modern texts on eyewitnesses, *The Psychology of Eyewitness Testimony*, which inspired numerous other researchers to start their own work in the area. Yarmey completed his book while on sabbatical at the University of Tennessee and then the University of Toronto. Early in his sabbatical, he was contacted by a lawyer from Michigan who had read his articles on facial recognition and wanted advice in a case. Yarmey decided to visit the law library to see what lawyers knew about eyewitness identification and concluded that they knew very little. He then decided to write his book, which went on to have a great impact in forensic psychology.

Why the rise of forensic psychology in the 1970s? A renewed emphasis on the necessity to make observations in natural contexts in order to understand social behaviour and memory was a reason, according to Wells and Loftus (1984). More generally, social psychology in the 1970s responded to a crisis about its relevance by extending its concepts to real-world topics, including health and the law (Davis, 1989). Nagel (1983) went so far as to claim: "The contemporary law and psychology movement has been the direct outgrowth of social psychologists' self-reflection on the failure of their discipline to advance social policy: it was an explicit rejection of the academically effete nature of much social psychological curiosity and an attempt to become more 'action-oriented'" (1983, p. 17).

James H. Davis (1989) took a different approach:

> It is tempting to draw a general parallel between the temporal sequence of the past: Münsterberg's proposals; reaction and critique of other scholars, disenchantment among social psychologists; and finally, abandonment of efforts at application of psychology to law. But something different happened "the next time around." The general disenchantment that was characteristic of the latter "crisis" period was not followed by an "abandonment phase." Rather, we have seen a continuous evolution and strengthening of some new developments during the succeeding years— a period in which *applied research in social psychology came to be recognized in its own right.* (1989, p. 201, italics in original)

The Present

Where do we stand now? Psychologists do research on a number of topics relevant to the real world of the legal system. Beyond the extensive work on jury decision making, psychologists have studied such diverse phenomena as sentencing decisions, deception detection, children's abilities as eyewitnesses, and the impact of the battered woman defence. Much of this work has been done in laboratories, with limitations to its applications to real-world decisions.

At the same time, judges, trial lawyers, police, and other representatives of the legal system are making real-world decisions—about the competency of a defendant, about which jurors to dismiss, about how to interrogate a suspect. Applied psychologists sometimes have an influence on such decisions as well as the thousands of others made daily in the legal system.

The credo behind this book is that it is time for psychologists to move beyond their laboratories and seriously ask how their perspective can improve the decisions made in law offices and courtrooms. In doing so, we need to face the obstacles discussed earlier in this chapter. Each profession and each discipline has its own way of doing things, its own way of seeing the world and defining the experiences in it. Police operate out of shared assumptions about the nature of the world; the experience of going through law school socializes lawyers to emphasize certain qualities; judges learn certain values and emphasize them in their decisions. Forensic psychologists must recognize these values (as well as their own) as they attempt to have an impact.

THE PERSPECTIVES OF PSYCHOLOGY AND THE LAW

If forensic psychology can succeed in any systematic way, it must first confront the conflicts between the goals and values of the legal profession and those of psychology. The following paragraphs examine some of these conflicts in depth (see also Box 1.1).

What Determines Truth?

The most fundamental conflict between psychology and law arises from the attempt to define what is true—in itself perhaps the most elusive and challenging quest. Suppose we ask a psychologist, a police officer, a trial lawyer, and a judge the same question: How do you know that something is true? Each might say, "Look at the evidence," but for each the evidence is defined differently. As noted earlier, psychologists base their answers on empirical observations. They are trained that speculation and armchair reasoning are not enough; such approaches may convince others but not the research psychologist. Even psychological theories, influential as they may be in directing the choice of research topics and procedures, are not accepted until they are validated by replicated research findings. "Being empirical" is the *sine qua non* of scientific psychology.

For the police officer, personal observation is a strong determinant of the truth. Police take pride in their ability to detect deception and their interrogative skills as ways of separating truth telling from falsification. Gisli Gudjonsson (1992), a psychologist and a former police officer, noted that many police interrogators have blind faith in the use of nonverbal signs of deception. Certainly they also rely on physical measures, too; speeding is determined by the reading on the radar gun; alcohol level by the blood–alcohol test. However, crime investigation may reflect either inductive or deductive methods of reasoning; see examples of this distinction, developed by Frey (1994), in Box 1.2.

As the police example above suggests, a belief in the validity of intuition is a part of a police officer's evidence evaluation. Hays (1992), a 20-year veteran of the Los Angeles Police Department, wrote: "Most cops develop an instinct for distinguishing the legitimate child abuse complaints from the phony ones" (p. 30). Police are willing to use a broader number of methods to determine truth than are psychologists. For example, a

---

BOX 1.1
Tensions between Law and Psychology

The tensions between law and psychology may be expressed as dichotomies (Haney, 1980). Nagel (1983, p. 3) and Haney (1980) list the following as the most frequently cited dichotomies:

1. Psychology's emphasis on innovation and counterintuitive thinking versus law's *stare decisis* model (that is, that courts must adhere to prior law and **precedent** where appropriate and when applicable, Laufer & Walt, 1992) and conservative stance, which resists innovation.
2. Psychology's empirical versus law's authoritarian epistemology, based on a hierarchy.
3. Psychology's experimental methodology versus law's adversarial process.
4. Psychology's descriptive versus law's prescriptive discourse.
5. Psychology's focus on the results of a number of studies versus law's focus on a single case.

6. Psychology's probabilistic and tentative conclusions versus law's emphasis on certainty, or at least the assumption that legal conclusions are irrevocable.
7. Psychology's academic and abstract orientation versus law's pragmatic and applied orientation.
8. Psychology's proactive orientation versus law's reactive orientation.

It should be noted that, though fundamental differences are agreed upon, some psychologists (cf. Laufer & Walt, 1992) argue that some of these differences may be more apparent than real. In particular, they believe that the influence of precedent on explanation in psychology has been underemphasized. For example, "normal science" imposes existing paradigms on interpretations and explanations of facts, and these paradigms direct new research endavours.

substantial number of police departments are willing to use psychics to help them solve crimes, whereas most psychologists would be appalled if someone argued that psychics could offer any valid avenues toward knowledge.

In a 1994 murder case in British Columbia, eight-year-old Mindy Tran was abducted while riding her bicycle outside her Kelowna home. She was found by 68-year-old Rex Fitzgerald of Nova Scotia. Fitzgerald, who had been contacted by the RCMP (because of his experience in similar cases), was able to solve a mystery that had confounded more than 400 searchers. He was quickly able to find Mindy's remains in a shallow grave with the use of a "divining rod" (usually used to find water) and a strand of her hair. He later said that he is not a psychic, but "It's just that I have the ability to work a divining rod. I don't know why. I feel it's an energy of some sort" (*Calgary Herald News*, August 11, 1999).

A lucky coincidence? A prearranged discovery? Most psychologists would reject the use of psychics, "divining rods," and so forth, in criminal investigation, but some police, at least in "last-resort" cases, will be amenable to any source of possible assistance.

What about lawyers and judges—what determines truth for them? Within the courtroom, for some lawyers, truth may be irrelevant. Probably for more judges and trial lawyers, the assumption is that the adversary system will produce truths or at least fairness. The nature of the adversary system leads some trial lawyers to value conflict resolution over the elusive quest for the truth. Another conception sometimes offered by critics of the legal system (Pulaski, 1980) is that trials are not conducted to find out what happened—the police, the prosecutor, and the defence lawyer all probably know what happened—but as a game to persuade the community that the proof is strong enough to justify punishment.

BOX 1.2
Inductive versus Deductive Methods of Reasoning

Induction and deduction are two contrasting methods used to solve a problem. **Deduction** requires the application of rules or a theory, whereas **induction** requires the generation of rules or a theory. Usually, deduction refers to going from the general to the specific, whereas induction refers to a process of using several specifics to generate a general rule.

In a creative analysis, Bruce Frey contrasted the ways that two popular fictional detectives solved crimes. Sherlock Holmes's investigative procedure was to examine a set of clues, develop a number of possible solutions, and eliminate them one by one. "When you have eliminated all the possibilities but one, that remaining one, no matter how improbable, must be the correct solution"—so goes his credo. (Further examples of Holmes's approach can be found in Chapter 4). Frey (1994) labelled this the inductive process because it examined many possibilities and used observations to create a theory, to infer a conclusion.

In contrast, Miss Jane Marple, the heroine of many of Agatha Christie's mysteries, used quite different,

deductive skills. A polite elderly woman who lived in the village of St. Mary Mead, she possessed an intimate knowledge of human interactions and behaviours among the inhabitants of her hometown. Her procedure when entering a problem-solving situation was to use the model of St. Mary Mead as a template and to apply that model to whatever the specific facts were.

We know that both detectives were quite successful (their authors made sure of that!). And neither procedure has a clear superiority over the other. Do these approaches distinguish between the problem-solving styles of the psychologist and the lawyer? Psychology as a science relies on the deductive method; a general theory leads to specific hypotheses; the testing of these hypotheses leads to results that confirm, disconfirm, or revise the theory. With its emphasis on precedent and previous rulings, the law would seem, in a broad sense, to be inductive. But each discipline is multifaceted, and specific psychologists, legal scholars, and lawyers might follow either procedure.

But if trial lawyers and, especially, judges focus on the assessment of truth in a court-related context, evidence and the law are determinants. Legal authorities rely heavily on precedents in reaching decisions. The principle of **stare decisis** ("let the decision stand") has a weight, for judges, equivalent to that of experimentation for scientific psychologists. This is not to say that the courts always ignore social science research when that research can help clarify or resolve empirical issues that arise in litigation. In fact, Monahan and Walker (1991) concluded that "increasingly in recent decades the courts have sought out research data on their own when the parties have failed to provide them" (p. 571). Tomkins and Oursland (1991), among others, have observed that the historic tension between social science and the law "does not imply that social science has been excluded from the courts" (p. 103).

The Nature of Reality

In the novel *Body of Evidence* (1991), author Patricia D. Cornwell (an expert on medical forensics) has a character express the opinion that "Everything depends on everything else" (p. 13); that is, you can't identify cause and effect, as variables interact with each other in undecipherable ways. To what extent do people give credence to such a view? Psychologists are trained to disabuse this notion; the experimental method emphasizes an analytic nature of the world. Psychologists assume that each quality of a stimulus has a separate, discernible influence on our response or behaviour. None of the other professions or disciplines holds so adamantly to this conception of the world.

Although the psychological field assumes that the world is composed of separable variables that act independently or interactively on other variables, it also is more tolerant of ambiguity than is the legal field. In fact, the approach of psychology can be labelled probabilistic, for several reasons. Psychologists express "truths" as "statistically significant" at a numeric level, for example, the .05 level (which means that if a result occurs in less than 5 out of 100 comparisons it is not signifi-

cant in that it may have occurred by chance or coincidence). Based on the statistics their research yields, psychologists will conclude that there is or is not a likelihood—not a certainty—that a real effect or difference exists.

Even more basic is psychology's assumption that people think in terms of probabilities and likelihoods. If you examine the instruments used by research psychologists, you find that they often will ask subjects, "What is the likelihood that …?" or similar questions. In contrast, the courts, lawyers, and people in general may well think in yes-or-no, right-or-wrong categories.

The research of Kahneman, Slovic, and Tversky (1982; Tversky & Kahneman, 1974, 1983) and a book by Robyn Dawes (1988) provide numerous examples of the lay public's misunderstanding of probabilities and inability to apply probabilistic reasoning; for example, the adherence to the "gambler's fallacy," ignorance of regression-to-the-mean effects, and failure to pay attention to base rates.

In our legal system, proof is based "on showing direct cause and effect: action A caused (or at least in measurable ways contributed to) result B; Jones pulled the trigger and Smith died; Roe violated the contract and as a consequence Doe lost money" (Rappeport, 1993, p. 15). In contrast, psychologists are more concerned with the probability that A is related to B.

The Legal System's Criticisms of Psychology

If psychology wants to make a contribution to the functioning of the legal system, then it is incumbent on psychology to ask what are the criticisms of it and to indicate what it can provide. Some of these criticisms are evaluated in the following paragraphs.

The Lack of Ecological Validity of Psychological Research

The oldest criticism, tracing back to Wigmore's response to Münsterberg's work, involves the

ecological validity of studies, that is, the question of whether results found in controlled or laboratory conditions will also occur in real life. The procedures and subjects of psychological research studies and the procedures and participants in the actual legal system may be dissimilar. For example, jury research has served as a significant source of such criticism, both by lawyers and by some psychologists (Dillehay & Nietzel, 1980; Konecni & Ebbesen, 1981). It is erroneous to assume that because a manipulation has an effect in the laboratory, it will have the same effect on jurors in the courtroom (Tanford & Tanford, 1988). As John Yuille (1989), a founder of one of the first forensic psychology programs in Canada, noted, there are two fundamental problems for psychologists in the role of expert:

> First, the types of assessments clinicians are asked to make (e.g., concerning the accused's mental state at the time of committing the offense) may exceed the capacity of the discipline. Second, the research foundation that psychologists employ in court does not always apply to the court situation in the way experts imply; the application of laboratory research findings to real world contexts is sometimes premature. It is concluded that psychologists should adopt a more conservative response to requests to provide expert evidence. (p. 181)

Going beyond the Data to Make Moral Judgments

Judge David Bazelon (1982), who was one of the strongest supporters of psychology on the American federal bench, chastised psychologists for going beyond their data and venturing beyond their expertise to make moral judgments. Melton, Petrila, Poythress, and Slobogin (1997), in an introductory chapter for a handbook on psychological court evaluations, used this admonition as a springboard to examine what they call the "current ambivalence" about the relationship of mental health and the law. For example, psychologists may be encouraged to testify in court

about theories and findings that lack validity. These and other temptations are examined in detail in Chapter 2. Throughout this book the quality of the scientific evidence supporting the conclusions of forensic psychologists will be examined, as this problem is, perhaps, the most important to be overcome if the relationship between psychology and law is to improve.

Intruding upon the Legitimate Activities of the Legal System

A fear of some lawyers, law professors, and social critics is that the infusion of psychological knowledge into the legal system will somehow change it for the worse and will subvert its legitimacy. An example is the use of psychologists as trial consultants, a common practice in the U.S., which many of us question. Gold (1987) argued that their use has created a set of superlawyers who are able to control the decision making of juries. According to this view, the psychologists' knowledge of persuasion techniques and jury decision making will somehow increase the likelihood of extraneous influences affecting verdicts. For example, Gold fears that, armed with such knowledge, "lawyers can induce jurors to make judgments about the credibility of a speaker through manipulation of the 'powerfulness' of the speaker's language" (Gold, 1987, p. 484).

Gold's detailed critique reflects the fact that many lawyers "fundamentally misunderstand the psychology of jury behavior and the trial process" (Tanford & Tanford, 1988, p. 748). This is regrettable, but is once more an indication that forensic psychology must reach out and seek to correct such false assumptions.

THE FUTURE OF THE RELATIONSHIP BETWEEN PSYCHOLOGY AND THE LAW

Courts have sometimes been sympathetic to psychological research; sometimes they have not.

Can we detect why? Can we predict the future of this relationship?

Tanford (1990) reviewed two types of theories of the interaction between social science and the law. One type predicts that the obstacles to the use of social science research in the courts can be overcome and that science will eventually assume a prominent role in legal policy making. This view notes that modern Western culture has elevated science to a prominent position. In contrast, the other approach predicts that social science will not have much of an impact on the law in the foreseeable future. This position is based on the current reluctance of the courts to rely on empirical research. Tanford (1990) offers six reasons for this reluctance:

1. Judges are conservative and perceive social scientists to be liberal.
2. Judges are self-confident and do not believe that they need any assistance from non-lawyers.
3. Judges are human, and it is human nature to be unscientific.
4. Judges are ignorant of, inexperienced with, or do not understand empirical social science.
5. Judges perceive science as a threat to their power and prestige.
6. Law and social science are rival systems with competing logics (Tanford, 1990, p. 152).

Any of these reasons for reluctance to accept forensic psychology can surface in a specific case. Chapter 2 examines some of the roles for psychologists in the legal system and some of the ways that psychologists may abuse their opportunities, thus contributing to the conflict between the two disciplines.

SUMMARY

Forensic psychology may be broadly defined as any application of psychological knowledge or methods to a task faced by the legal system. This definition implies that forensic psychologists can play many roles: from criminal profiler to child-custody evaluator, from police counsellor to prison psychologist, from expert witness to evaluation researcher. But other definitions of forensic psychology limit it to clinical and professional applications of psychology to the legal system. Current training programs reflect these diverse definitions, and Canada is considered to be a world leader in many areas of psychological research and application in the legal system.

In their attempts to apply their knowledge to the legal system, forensic psychologists need to be aware of the history of the relationship and the conflicting values between the scientific and legal approaches. In the 100-year-old history of the relationship, influences can be traced from criminology and from experimental psychology. Hugo Münsterberg, a professor and director of the Psychological Laboratory at Harvard University in the first two decades of the 20th century, may be considered the founder of forensic psychology because of his research (on such contemporary topics as eyewitness accuracy and memory), his influential articles for the lay public, and his involvement in several prominent trials. But he was only one of a number of experimental psychologists who were active in applying their knowledge to the courts during the period from 1900 to 1920. For various reasons, the relationship between the two fields languished for 50 years, until the mid-1970s. Since that time there has been an explosion of research and also a similar expansion in the application of psychological concepts and findings to such diverse legal issues as the battered woman syndrome, the use of police interrogations to elicit confessions, and the selection of juries.

But psychology has not always had the effect it sought. Court decisions in both Canada and the U.S. illustrate the conflict between psychology and the law with regard to their bases of decision making. Some conflicts are fundamental, dealing with the nature of truth and reality. Others are not necessarily rooted in the philosophy of each discipline; for example, the legal system is uninformed about and hence unsympathetic to the methods used in psychology, and the methods of psychological research are sometimes unsatisfactory when dealing with real-world problems.

KEY TERMS

deduction, p. 18
ecological validity, p. 20
empirical approach, p. 7
forensic psychology, p. 2
induction, p. 18
precedent, p. 17
reliability, p. 7
replicability, p. 7
specialty designation, p. 4
stare decisis, p. 19
values, p. 6

SUGGESTED READINGS

Bartol, C. R., & Bartol, A. M. (1999). History of forensic psychology. In A. K. Hess & I. B. Weiner (Eds.), *Handbook of forensic psychology* (2nd ed., pp. 3–23). New York: John Wiley.

The Bartols' readable history of the field reviews developments in five major topics: courtroom testimony, cognitive and personality assessment, correctional psychology, police psychology, and criminal psychology.

Hess, A. K., & Weiner, I. B. (Eds.). (1999). *Handbook of forensic psychology* (2nd ed.). New York: John Wiley.

This updated collection of comprehensive and detailed reviews of many of the topics explored in this book includes lie detection, hypnosis, testifying in court, assessing competency, and police consultation.

Lyons, A., & Truzzi, M. (1991). *The blue sense: Psychic detectives and crime.* New York: Mysterious Press.

This book analyzes the use by police of psychics to help solve crimes. Although the book exposes the tricks of charlatans, it is sympathetic to the use of paranormal techniques in crime investigation.

Melton, G. B., Huss, M. T., & Tomkins, A. J. (1999). Training in forensic psychology and the law. In A. K. Hess & I. B. Weiner (Eds.), *Handbook of forensic psychology* (2nd ed., pp. 700–720). New York: John Wiley.

This chapter is of special value to those considering further training in forensic psychology. The following models for professional training are described and critiqued: joint Ph.D.-J.D. programs, Ph.D. specialty programs, a Ph.D. minor, and postdoctoral programs. Internship opportunities are also described.

Münsterberg. H. (1908). *On the witness stand.* Garden City, NY: Doubleday.

This book is worth extracting from stuffy library stacks to determine just how prescient it is for the forensic psychology of the 21st century.

Nietzel, M. T., & Dillehay, R. C. (1986). *Psychological consultation in the courtroom.* New York: Pergamon Press.

Written by two forensic psychologists with extensive hands-on experience, this book not only illustrates a number of activities but also considers professional and ethical dilemmas.

2

Roles and Responsibilities of Forensic Psychologists

We can't trust prison shrinks. I got a high score on your fucking test
because the psychologist has a beef against me. He screwed me because in
a group session I said he was full of crap. So now he says I'm a flaming
psychopath, and you can't treat me. So what the fuck do you do with me?
—CANADIAN INMATE QUOTED BY R. HARE (1998, P. 114)

THE MULTITUDE OF ROLES

Chapter 1 was introduced by describing six people whose duties qualify them to be called forensic psychologists, even though their day-to-day activities dramatically differ. The activities of these six psychologists by no means encompass the entire field of forensic psychology. For example, consider two different tasks, reflecting **assessment** as a primary responsibility of many forensic psychologists. Neuropsychologists engage in forensic activities when they examine a defendant to determine whether he or she has damage to the right hemisphere of the brain, affecting judgment and impulse control (Dywan, Kaplan, & Pirozzolo, 1991; Pirozzolo, Funk, & Dywan, 1991). In their forensic capacity, neuropsychologists carry out a comprehensive evaluation of brain functioning, with emphasis on the measurement of deficits in psychological functioning. A number of tests have been developed to assess normal versus impaired brain functioning, and several handbooks and textbooks review these procedures, including those by Lezak (1995), by Kolb and Whishaw (1990), and by Goldstein and Incagnoli (1997).

The assessment of the psychological, as well as the neurological, characteristics of offenders is also a task for forensic psychology. One example is psychopathy. Although perhaps 1 percent of the general population may be classified as psychopaths, they constitute 15 percent to 25 percent of the prison population "and are responsible for a markedly disproportionate amount of the serious crime, violence, and social distress in every society" (Hare, 1996, p. 26). **Psychopathy** reflects the following characteristics: impulsivity, a lack of guilt or remorse, pathological lying and manipulativeness, and a continual willingness to violate social norms. They also perpetrate much of the premeditated, instrumental violence in society, as established by Michael Woodworth and colleagues at Dalhousie University by examining a large sample of homicide offenders (Woodworth & Porter, 2002). Forensic psychologists have sought to develop instruments to assess psychopathy. Among the most prominent is the Hare Psychopathy Checklist-Revised (or PCL-R), developed by Robert Hare, now a professor emeritus at the University of British Columbia and a consultant with the FBI. The PCL-R employs a 20-item rating scale, completed on the basis of a semi-structured interview and on other information about the subject (Hare, 1991, 2003). Sample characteristics to be rated by the psychologist include lack of realistic long-term goals and callous lack of empathy. Each item is rated on a three-point scale, according to specific criteria.

Much of the leading research and theory on psychopathy has been conducted by Canadian researchers at the University of British Columbia, Simon Fraser University, Queen's University, and Carleton University. These researchers have pointed out that because of pressures from the legal system, forensic psychologists must be careful to remain objective when using such assessment tools (e.g., Hare, 1998). Thus, this chapter emphasizes the ethical responsibilities of psychologists as they respond to the demands of the legal system. In doing so, we will investigate specific activities of psychologists, some of which will be further developed in subsequent chapters.

THE TEMPTATIONS OF FORENSIC PSYCHOLOGISTS

Although there are diverse roles for psychologists to play in the legal system, limits have been placed on the application of psychology in this setting by organizations of psychologists, including the Canadian Psychological Association (CPA) and Division 41 of the American Psychological Association (APA), the latter known as the American Psychology-Law Society (APLS). These groups have developed specific guidelines as to what is and is not acceptable behaviour in legal contexts. These guidelines are described later in this chapter. The law itself also limits the contributions of psychologists, whether they are expert witnesses asked to testify at trial or consultants conducting pre-trial assessments.

Despite such guidelines from psychological governing bodies and the legal system, forensic psychologists, for various reasons, may sometimes exceed what is acceptable in their profession and what the law theoretically permits them to do. The following are some of the potential temptations of forensic practitioners described in the rest of this book.

Promising Too Much

Sometimes forensic psychologists who are hired by lawyers or the courts promise a level of success they cannot guarantee. The types of assessments conducted by forensic psychologists include assessment tools that are not infallible. The accuracy of the test results depends on numerous factors beyond the training and abilities of the psychologist; these include the standard error of measurement (the average level of error associated with the test), the honesty of the person being tested, and the setting in which the tests are administered. Psychologists need to concede the potential fallibility of their assessments, while using tools with a strong empirical basis (such as the PCL-R) and describing such strengths for the court. In particular, the psychologists who have developed the tests and other instruments that are used in forensic assessments may be tempted (consciously or unconsciously) to claim a greater level of validity than is warranted in real-life situations.

Some forensic psychologists may become committed to the use of certain tests such as the MMPI-II or the Rorschach even in situations where their applicability is questionable. For example, in institutions run by the Correctional Service of Canada, the MMPI-II is almost always used during intake assessments (assessments that occur soon after incarceration) with criminal offenders, when, in fact, there is little evidence for its predictive validity in that context. While such tests may provide useful "clinical" informa-

tion concerning an offender, the limits on their ability to predict future criminal behaviour should be made clear to everyone reading his or her psychological assessment report.

Substituting Advocacy for Scientific Objectivity

When psychologists become **expert witnesses** in Canada, they are usually hired by one side in an adversarial proceeding. Most psychologists, in such a situation, are conscientious and try to be ethical, to the point of fully describing the limits of their opinion and even empirical evidence that supports the opposite view. But it may be tempting to play the **advocate role**, to take sides, to become sympathetic to the arguments of the side that is paying the psychologist, and to slant the testimony in that direction. The shift toward partisanship may be subtle, even unconscious. Some lawyers contribute to the problem by "shopping around" until they find an expert who will say what they want (Spencer, 1998). Many people, including some judges, see the expert witness as a **hired gun**, willing to say whatever his or her hiring client needs to be said. An apparent example of a hired gun on the stand occurred in the trial of John Demjanjuk, the alleged "Ivan the Terrible," a Nazi concentration camp guard, at his eventual trial in Israel. A handwriting expert who was testifying in Demjanjuk's defence concluded that a signature on a document was probably not Demjanjuk's, but the prosecution confronted him with an earlier public statement of his that had expressed the opposite conclusion. The expert refused to explain the inconsistency on the grounds that he had a "contractual relationship" with the Demjanjuk Defense Fund, which would sue him if he explained further (Spencer, 1998). A recent, widely discussed book by experimental psychologist Margaret Hagen (1997) has served as a broadside attack on psychologists as hired guns; see Box 2.1.

In *R. v. Samra* (1998), the Ontario Court of Appeal considered the issue of "hired gun"

BOX 2.1
Are Psychologists "Whores of the Court"?

With its bright yellow book jacket and its provocative title, *Whores of the Court*, splashed across the entire cover, Margaret Hagen's book was bound to attract attention. But it is the book's contents that have generated the strongest reaction. For Hagen, an experimental psychologist on the faculty of Boston University, the whores are those forensic psychologists, psychiatrists, and social workers who mislead judges and juries about child sexual abuse, criminal responsibility or insanity, psychological disability, and a variety of other topics—hence the book's subtitle: *The Fraud of Psychiatric Testimony and the Rape of American Justice.*

Those concerned with the powerful temptations of forensic psychology will find much to applaud in the book. Hagen expresses the caution that should be the basis of forensic applications when she questions whether mental health professionals can distinguish between real victims of post-traumatic stress disorder and those who fake symptoms. She describes (on p. 262) how a professional staff member at a trauma clinic testified that no one could fake traumatic memories or fool psychiatric tests. She has been justifiably critical of psychologists who serve as hired guns in child custody disputes.

But she weakened her case by overreaction, exaggeration, and stereotyping. Saul Kassin (1998a), in a thoughtful review, summarized:

> Underlying much of Hagen's attack are three underlying themes, or stereotypic portraits, of forensic clinical psychologists. One is that they are simply not competent on the basis of science (not to mention their lack of education in such areas as neuroscience, learning, memory, development, and behavior in social groups) to testify as they do. Second is that many clinical psychologists are driven by missionary liberal motives.... The third theme is that forensic clinical psychologists are economically motivated by the almighty dollar.... This last motive is what gives rise to the image of psychologists as "whores" of the court. (p. 322)

Some of Hagen's statements are wildly divergent from the present authors' experience as expert witnesses; for example, she wrote:

> For the whole clinical psychological profession in whatever guise, the increase in power and prestige in the civil litigation arena has been dizzying. Just think of it. Judges genuflecting before your sagacious testimony, and changing the law to fit your word.... It is a compelling picture of a powerful profession flexing its muscles as never before. (Hagen, 1997, p. 255)

Neither of us can recall a judge "genuflecting"—more likely, when testifying, other types of judicial nonverbal behaviour were pointed in our direction. Thus we agree with another thoughtful review of her book, by Solomon Fulero (1997), that noted that she has committed the same mistakes that she attributed to forensic psychologists:

> I agree here that while Hagen's essential point is well-taken—that is, a number of psychological experts are offered in courts to testify about shaky theories, questionable ideas, and conclusions without solid empirical evidence—the manner in which this point is presented "throws out the baby with the bathwater," obscuring valid comments about the proper types and uses of psychological expert testimony with anecdotes, errors, flaming overgeneralizations, and inflammatory charges. Further, the presentation of the essential point in such a manner will actually make it more difficult to rein in the very excesses Hagen deplores. (p. 10)

Thus, Hagen's book reminds readers that forensic psychologists can succumb to the temptations of exaggeration and falsification when they respond to the pressures of the legal system. But the book fails to acknowledge the more typical efforts of people in our field to represent the field in an ethical and objective manner. Nonetheless, even if "hired guns" are rare, we should carefully consider their potential impact in the courtroom.

---

testimony. On March 18, 1982, the appellant Kuldip Samra entered Courtroom 4 at Osgoode Hall in Toronto armed with a gun and ammunition. Although Samra would later claim that he went into the courtroom to commit suicide, he walked directly to the front of the room, where he shot and killed two men and wounded a third

victim. Samra then left the scene and fled Canada. Eight years later, he was arrested in India and extradited back to Canada in 1992. The defence introduced expert testimony by Dr. Allan Long, a psychologist, and Dr. Jerry Cooper, a psychiatrist. These experts were called to support the theory that Samra was in an "altered state" at the time of the shootings and was incapable of formulating a plan to murder someone.

When the defence lawyer attempted to have Dr. Cooper qualified as an expert, the Crown prosecutor challenged his expertise and was allowed to cross-examine him (in front of the jury) on material from a *Globe and Mail* article. The following parts of the article were read to Dr. Cooper (see *R. v. Samra*, 1998):

[According to Dr. Andrew Malcolm,] some of my colleagues have apparently decided to play the game and become courtesans, court prostitutes, experts of easy virtue. In that case, let themselves be employed by either one of the adversaries and then pack a pile of lies on top of their genuine credentials for all the world to see.

It is hard to find a more flexible expert witness than Toronto psychiatrist Jerry Cooper, who, unlike many of his colleagues who seem to testify with great reluctance, loves the battle as no other.

He says candidly, "When I look at a case, I always ask the lawyer what he wants. When a lawyer is happy and his client is happy, then I'm happy."

But he shudders when it is suggested that sounds like ammunition for the hired gun theory.

Mr. Greenspan says he has noted an "institutional bias": Psychiatrists who work in the world of the mentally ill have a tendency to see mental illness in various degrees wherever they look.

Dr. Cooper appears to give him credence when he says, "Depending on the defence [a lawyer wishes to offer], I can find anyone insane." (para. 70)

Although Dr. Cooper denied telling the reporter that he could find anyone insane, his credibility was greatly undermined by the suggestion from the article that he may be a hired gun. In the end, Samra was convicted of two counts of first-degree murder and one count of attempted murder, and the Ontario Court of Appeal dismissed his appeal.

The proper role for a psychologist as an expert witness is that of a friend of the court— an objective scientist who reports *all* the data and conflicting findings, even if he or she makes a less supportive case for the side that hired the psychologist (Yuille, 1989). But it is hard to avoid the seduction of taking sides. Sometimes, when the advocate role becomes paramount, the psychologist or psychiatrist may create a diagnosis to fit the behaviour when no proof exists for the validity of the diagnostic construct.

Take the example of Karla Homolka, who along with her husband Paul Bernardo took part in the rapes and murders of Leslie Mahaffy and Kristen French. In one of the most notorious plea bargains in Canadian legal history, Homolka entered into a deal with the Ontario Crown on May 14, 1993, in which she agreed to plead guilty to two counts of manslaughter in return for a 12-year sentence (see Galligan Report, 1996). At sentencing, evidence was presented that she had played a direct role in the drugging, sexual assault, and death of her 15-year-old sister Tammy. Prior to the plea bargain, Homolka had been assessed by several mental health professionals. In March 1993, she was admitted into a Toronto hospital where she remained for over six weeks of evaluations by two psychiatrists and two psychologists selected by the Crown prosecutor. Reports from this stay include a mix of various diagnoses and sometimes colourful clinical descriptions, including stress, anxiety, depression, learned helplessness, post-traumatic stress disorder, "psychic numbing" (Galligan Report, p. 152), lack of affect, and other indicators of "battered woman syndrome," whereas no evidence was found for psychosis or sexual deviance. Her domestic abuse and domination by Bernardo supposedly had left her similar to a "concentration camp survivor," and was seen as having contributed to her involvement in the murders (Galligan Report, 1996). In explaining battered woman syndrome, expert witness psychologist Peter Jaffe testified that such women feel powerless and can develop maladaptive behaviour, potentially contributing to the commission of criminal acts.

Battered woman syndrome? Concentration camp survivor? Psychic numbing? Learned helplessness? None of these are psychiatric disorders. Although battered woman syndrome is a valid legal defence, did Homolka really show evidence for such a syndrome? The true extent of Homolka's involvement or culpability in the Mahaffy and French cases was evident from six homemade videotapes later recovered. Her claims of being under Bernardo's control—central to the plea bargain—appeared to be false as she (reportedly) actively conversed with and enthusiastically sexually assaulted the victims with a coy smile on her face. How helpful were the descriptions provided by the psychologists and psychiatrists in facilitating justice in this case?

Letting Values Overcome Empirically Based Findings

Probably none of us can escape our values as influences on the ways that we perceive the world. Sometimes there may be a temptation for our values to determine our conclusions in a court of law. Let's look at some examples.

A forensic psychologist is asked to do an evaluation of a pair of parents who are divorcing in order to assist the judge in making a custody decision that is in the best interests of the child. The psychologist discovers that one of the parents—on rare occasions when the child has uttered an expletive—washes out the child's mouth with soap. There may be nothing illegal about this, and probably nothing physically harmful, but the psychologist is repulsed by the behaviour. No empirical data exist that such an action is related to the general question of appropriateness for custody, but the psychologist's recommendation is affected by it. Or let us assume that one parent smokes and the other does not; should such factors influence a recommendation about custody?

In an American case (*Barefoot v. Estelle*, 1983), two psychiatrists went beyond the research con-

clusions on the difficulty of predicting dangerousness by testifying that they "knew" that the defendant would commit crimes in the future (Lavin & Sales, 1998). In subsequent cases, the courts made explicit their recognition that predictions of future behaviour given by psychologists or psychiatrists are far from infallible. For example, in the Canadian case *Re Moore and the Queen* (1984), Justice Ewaschuk stated:

> I accept the submission that the evidence of a psychiatrist, psychologist or criminologist is at times highly speculative and in certain instances a lay person is in as good a position to make a prediction as to future dangerousness. In the final say, the court, however, must be so satisfied and not the expert witnesses. That is not to say that experts may not assist the court, especially as to whether the offender currently suffers from a psychological disorder, e.g., psychopathy, which may be relevant to the likelihood of future dangerous conduct.

In our view, at all times psychologists must strive to maintain objectivity in the courtroom and to make sure that they do not make statements that move beyond what science has established on any legal issue. Perhaps the legal system would be best served if we fill an "education" role rather than an advocacy role (Porter, Campbell, Birt, & Woodworth, 2003), although some would disagree, as we shall see.

The Problem of Cursory or Unreliable Forensic Assessments

In the Canadian correctional system, we have seen many cases in which the reliability of the forensic assessment is questionable. Problems with the assessment of psychopathy provide a good example. As mentioned earlier, the best-validated tool used to determine whether an offender is psychopathic is the PCL-R (Hare, 1991, 2003), an observer-rated instrument based on a thorough review of collateral information complemented, if possible, by an interview with the offender. Despite the high validity and relia-bility of the PCL-R, problems have occasionally arisen with its use. The PCL-R's creator, Robert Hare, has outlined some of the misuses he has observed (Hare, 1998):

1. *Assessments by unqualified raters.* Hare notes that individuals with insufficient qualifica-tions and training have sometimes utilized and applied the PCL-R in their assessments. He argues that clinicians who apply the PCL-R should possess an advanced degree in the social, medical, or behavioural sci-ences (such as a Ph.D., D.Ed. or M.D.) and have adequate training and experience in the use of the PCL-R. These recommended qualifications were endorsed in the Canadian courts by Justice MacKay in *Pinkney v. Canada (Attorney General)* (1998).

2. *Confusing psychopathy with antisocial personality disorder (APD).* Hare points out that many clinicians continue to confuse these diag-noses and their implications for predicting the behaviour of an offender (e.g., psycho-pathy is much more predictive of future criminal acts than is APD).

3. *Overreliance on "clinical opinion."* Some clini-cians make the mistake of ignoring or downplaying the PCL-R definitions given in the manual in favour of their own clinical opinions ("I know what shallow affect means. I don't need to keep referring to the scoring criteria.").

4. *Unauthorized or blatant misuse.* Occasionally, a PCL-R assessment has been conducted by someone with no credentials to do so what-soever. Hare gives the example of a judge who himself decided to score an offender on the PCL-R and gave a considerably lower score than the score provided by an expert psychiatrist.

Perhaps nowhere could the misuse of the PCL-R have more severe consequences than in the context of a "dangerous offender" hearing. Section 752 of the Criminal Code of Canada has a category of dangerous offenders for those

offenders who are very likely to reoffend vio-lently or inflict severe psychological violence, warranting an indefinite sentence. Typically, during the hearing for such a determination, both the defence and Crown are expected to present reports and/or testimony concerning risk factors from their own psychiatrists or psycholo-gists. Psychopathy is now considered to be one of the most important considerations in this regard due to its strong association with risk for future violence. Very often, the reports for the two "sides" differ in conclusions about PCL-R scores (and the dangerousness of the offender), sug-gesting the possibility of the problems discussed by Hare.

The potential unreliability of psychiatric diagnoses will recur as an issue throughout this book, but the temptation of concern here is being less than thorough and professional in one's work for the courts or other authorities.

Maintaining Dual Relationships and Competing Roles

A psychologist who is evaluating a divorced couple for child custody accepts an invitation to have dinner with the wife. Another psychologist who is seeing a man as a psychotherapy client attempts to initiate a romantic relationship with him. These are examples of **dual relationships**, in this case, a situation that is clearly unethical according to the CPA. A less explicit conflict of interest occurs when the forensic psychologist is engaged in more than one type of professional activity with the same individuals.

When a child reports having been sexually abused, the court may request a local psychologist to do an evaluation. If the psychologist has served as a psychotherapist for the child or someone in the child's family, it is inappropriate for the same psychologist to serve as an evaluator of the claims of abuse. The forensic evaluator has to maintain a stance of absolute impartiality, whereas the thera-pist often serves as an advocate for his or her clients (Lawlor, 1998). A similar temptation to fill two competing roles may occur in child–custody decisions or in situations in which a psychologist treats individual clients in sex offender therapy at a prison, and later is asked to evaluate their risk to reoffend in the community.

SPECIFIC ROLES: THE TRIAL CONSULTANT

To further examine the limits of ethical behaviour, this chapter uses several specific roles for forensic psychologists. For each role, a salient question the forensic psychologist must answer is: "Who is my client?" In this context, forensic psychologists are normally paid by a lawyer and his or her legal client and this team has expectations of the psychologist. But psychologists also have ethical responsibilities to promote human welfare, and, hence, society in general is a "client." Because of these various pressures, conflicts can emerge in each of the roles. Some are illustrated here.

Duties

Increasingly, trial lawyers are relying on psychologists and other social scientists to aid them in preparing for and carrying out a trial. This role has typically been called a **trial consultant** or psycho–legal consultant. Some consultants have doctoral degrees; some have master's degrees or other levels of education. At present, no province licenses or certifies trial consultants, so it is up to the lawyer to decide whom to consult in a trial. As Jeffrey Frederick (quoted by Mandelbaum, 1989, p. 18) noted, "All you need is a client."

What do trial consultants do? The consultant may be hired by a lawyer to assist in identifying the major issues in a case and/or prepare witnesses for trial. Trial consultants also may be asked to comment on the validity of expert reports from the other side and how to effectively cross-examine an opposing expert. In addition, an increasingly common use of trial consultants in Canada is to give an opinion on the quality of the "psychological" evidence available in the case. Was a police interrogation coercive or suggestive? Was an interview by a police officer or social worker with a child leading? Were inappropriate methods used in therapy that may have led to a mistaken "recovered memory" and allegation? Were the psychological tests used by mental health professionals to examine the client valid and appropriate? Is the behaviour of the defendant consistent with someone who commits a particular crime? For example, University of British Columbia psychologist Donald Dutton, a researcher who specializes in spousal violence, was consulted by the prosecution team in the O.J. Simpson case concerning the factors that can lead to spousal homicide (such as previous domestic violence, jealousy, estrangement, stalking, and threats).

In Canada, although there seem to be wide regional differences, trial consulting is becoming an important activity of forensic psychologists. Later chapters describe the duties of trial consultants in more detail.

Clientele

The clientele of proximal concern to the trial consultant is the lawyer or law firm that hires the consultant. A special type of ethical problem emerges because trial consultants are not only social scientists, but are contractors as well. They may advertise and market what they have to offer. Larger firms in the U.S. distribute glossy brochures extolling their various services. These firms also have a number of fixed costs, including support staff's salaries, office rental, and computer costs, which persist regardless of the number of clients they have. In Canada, on the other hand, the trial consultant typically works alone with little advertising and not as part of a large firm. For example, an academic who conducts work in the area of child witnesses might be hired by the defence to discuss how the child's testimony may have been tainted by the improper questioning of police or social workers (and how to cross-examine such witnesses).

Conflicts with the Legal System

Conflicts between trial consultants and their employer-lawyers can be classified as procedural or substantive. With regard to procedures, consultants need always to remember that they are employed by the lawyers and should defer to them with regard to decisions involving the case. For example, a trial consultant may believe that questions about a complainant's history of psychotherapy are necessary to investigate the possibility of a false memory. The lawyer may feel such questions are inappropriate invasions of privacy or could lead to a jury perception of unfair treatment of the complainant. Substantive conflicts can arise over any topic at hand—what is the appropriate "theory" of the case, how witnesses should present themselves, or which witnesses should be presented first.

Again, given that the psychologist–trial consultant is being contracted for paid services by the lawyer, the consultant needs to recognize implications of the conflicts between the two disciplines described in Chapter 1. Trial lawyers often are not impressed by findings generated from laboratory studies, which they consider unrelated to the real world. They may feel threatened by the claims of "interlopers" who imply they know more about witness behaviour or trial strategy than these experienced lawyers do. And they may be right. The relationship should not be adversarial, but collaborative.

Ethical Responsibilities

The dual occupational nature of the consultant—applied scientist plus contractor—makes for challenging ethical responsibilities. As an applied researcher, the consultant must follow the standard guidelines for ethical research, which take the form of a list of moral imperatives:

1. Thou shall not fake data.
2. Thou shall not plagiarize.
3. Thou shall not make false conclusions on the basis of your data.

Further, the consultant has the moral responsibility not to break the law, even if the consultant's client wishes it. The consultant may be faced with a situation in which he or she knows that a witness is lying about important case facts but the lawyer wants the consultant to help the witness appear as credible as possible. As strange as it may sound, lawyers may not even wish to hear the truth from their clients, preferring that a story be maintained even it is a lie. As Winnipeg defence lawyer Greg Brodsky says, "I don't want my client telling me exactly what happened, because I can't put on a defence I know to be perjured in court" (Dotto, 2004, p. 45).

One ethical responsibility might involve informing the lawyer of the client's deception. However, teaching someone how to appear credible on the stand probably would be considered unethical by the CPA. Further, consultants should never suggest that their services will inevitably help win a case for their client, because many events can intervene between preparation for the trial and the jury verdict (Mandelbaum, 1989). In fact, it is a good idea to discuss with a lawyer very early in a consultation that a psychological conclusion rendered about the client may or may not be favourable for their case. For example, if a psychologist is approached by the defence to conduct a risk assessment for a sentencing hearing, he or she should always remind the lawyer that the client may be found to be a high risk.

Confidentiality is a special concern for trial consultants, who need to avoid unreasonable intrusion into the privacy of others. It is essential that trial consultants recognize that all information about a particular case remains private and confidential, unless the consulting lawyer and client have agreed in writing to forego confidentiality.

This is quite different from a forensic psychologist who works in a prison setting and can expect that information collected for a risk assessment will not be kept confidential and will be shared with many relevant parties, including the National Parole Board of Canada, for example. In that context, the paying client is considered to be the Correctional Service of Canada, a government organization representing Canadian society at large. As such, the psychologist has no obligation of confidentiality to the offender and his or her lawyer during any type of pre-release assessment. On the other hand, a psychologist who is providing mental health services (such as treating a depressed offender) should be expected to keep personal information from therapy sessions confidential (unless the material pertains to risk for violence to self or others). This is because the offender is best construed as the client in that context. Obviously, deciding "who is the client" is critical but can be complicated!

SPECIFIC ROLES: THE EXPERT WITNESS

Academic psychologists as well as practising forensic psychologists may be called on to provide expertise in court. A different type of ethical issue may surface in this role. The lawyer, who is paying the psychologist, may want the psychologist to draw conclusions from research or clinical findings that he or she is unwilling to do.

Duties

During a trial, each side may ask the judge to permit expert witnesses to testify as part of its presentation of the evidence. In contrast to other witnesses (called **fact witnesses**), who can only testify about what they've observed or what they know as fact, expert witnesses may express opinions, for they possess special knowledge about a topic, knowledge that the average juror does not have. The judge must be convinced that the testimony that any expert will present is of a kind that requires requisite knowledge, skill, or experience in a certain field and that the testimony will help resolve the dispute and lead jurors toward the truth.

The topics for which a psychology expert may be called as an expert witness are extensive.

Box 2.2, containing examples from Nietzel and Dillehay (1986), describes a number of these topics. Most of these reflect some form of clinical expertise, and many of them (including criminal responsibility, eyewitnesses' identification, and children's custody) are evaluated in detail in subsequent chapters. The purpose of this section is to examine the conflicts and ethical issues that cut across specific topics.

Clientele

In the 19th century, an expert witness served the court rather than the litigants (Landsman, 1995). But almost always, nowadays, expert witnesses are recruited by trial lawyers (and only rarely by the judge). Nevertheless, it is the judge who determines the expert witness's acceptability. In Canada, experts must be formally "qualified" in the court prior to entering evidence. During the qualification process, lawyers from the two sides have the opportunity to examine the credentials (education, training, and experience) of the psychologist as they pertain to the psychological issue at hand. The judge then makes the determination of whether to admit the psychologist as an expert and to give an expert opinion.

As far as the presiding judge is concerned, the expert witness at trial "is cast in the role of a witness, not as one of the advocates and not as a decision maker" (Saks, 1992, p. 191). Like other witnesses, experts must promise to give honest testimony while on the stand. Despite this similarity, some judges are dubious about what experts have to say (Saks & Van Duizend, 1983, cited in Saks, 1992). One decision by the Supreme Court of British Columbia is typical:

The issue of the impugned medical opinions raises a matter of concern which has been addressed by the courts of this Province on numerous occasions. The proliferation of competing expert reports in civil litigation is increasingly becoming a problem of costs to the litigants and delays and cost in the court process. This problem of proliferation is exacerbated by an even greater concern that

BOX 2.2
Examples of Topics for Psychologists as Expert Witnesses

1. Criminal responsibility	What is the relationship between the defendant's mental condition at the time of the alleged offence and the defendant's responsibility for the crime with which the defendant is charged?
2. Competence to stand trial	Does the defendant have an adequate understanding of the legal proceedings?
3. Sentencing	What are the prospects for the defendant's rehabilitation? What deterrent effects do certain sentences have? What is the defendant's level of risk for re-offence?
4. Eyewitness identification	What are the factors that affect the accuracy of eyewitness identification? How is witness confidence related to witness accuracy?
5. Trial procedure	What effects are associated with variations in pre-trial and/or trial procedures?
6. Civil commitment	Does a mentally ill person present an immediate danger or threat of danger to self or others that requires treatment no less restrictive than hospitalization?
7. Psychological damages in civil cases	What psychological consequences has an individual suffered as a result of tortious conduct? How treatable are these consequences? To what extent are the psychological problems attributable to a pre-existing condition? Is post-traumatic symptomology related to another person's behaviour?
8. Trademark litigation	Is a certain product name or trademark confusingly similar to a competitor's? Are advertising claims likely to mislead consumers?
9. Class action suits	What psychological evidence is there that effective treatment is being denied or that certain testing procedures are discriminatory against minorities in the schools or in the workplace?
10. Guardianship and conservatorship	Does an individual possess the necessary mental ability to make decisions concerning living conditions, financial matters, health, etc.?
11. Child custody	What psychological factors will affect the best interests of the child whose custody is in dispute? What consequences are these factors likely to have on the family?
12. Adoption and termination of parental rights	What psychological factors affect the child whose parents' disabilities may render them unfit to raise and care for the child?
13. Professional malpractice	Did defendant's professional conduct fail to meet the standard of care owed to plaintiffs?
14. Social issues in litigation	What are the effects of pornography, violence, spouse abuse, etc., on the behaviour of a defendant who claims that his or her misconduct was caused by one of these influences?

(From *Psychological consultation in the courtroom*, by M. T. Nietzel and R. C. Dillehay, 1986, pp. 100–101. Reprinted by permission of Allyn & Bacon, a division of Pearson Education Inc.)

experts called upon by litigants to assist the court and then given deference by the court often abandon their legitimate and valued role and descend to advocacy. (*Houseman [Guardian of] v. Sewell*, 1997, para. 18)

As noted in Box 2.1 on page 26, it is not only judges who are critical of expert witnesses.

Several advocates of tort reform, including Peter Huber in his book *Galileo's Revenge* (1991), have claimed that **junk science** in the form of scientific "experts" hired by "unscrupulous plaintiffs' lawyers [is] responsible for the awarding of millions of dollars each year against blameless corporations" (Landsman, 1995, p. 131). In the Canadian case *R. v. Lavallee* (1990), the Crown prosecutor brought an application to have expert evidence concerning "battered woman syndrome" withdrawn from the jury. The first reason he gave was that the jury was perfectly capable of deciding the issue and that expert evidence was therefore "unnecessary and superfluous" (the trial judge denied the application, stating that the Crown's concerns could be met through an appropriate charge to the jury).

Conflicts

Conflict is inevitable when expert witnesses are invited into the courtroom. As Saks (1992) observed, experts "control" the knowledge of their fields; they determine how to conceptualize and organize the material and what to emphasize. But judges and lawyers control the case, including just what part of the expert's store of information they consider to be relevant. Thus, "the paradigms of the legal process and virtually any field of knowledge are almost assured to be in conflict with each other" (Saks, 1992, p. 185). If a trial lawyer concludes that his or her preliminary choice for an expert witness is unsatisfactory, that expert can be dismissed prior to trial, and another one selected. Further, expert witnesses learn the "facts" of the case from the lawyers who hired them, teachers who have a very particular agenda (Saks, 1992).

Testimony on Eyewitness Accuracy

Among the various topics in Box 2.2, judges are perhaps most inconsistent in their reaction to the admissibility of psychologists testifying on the accuracy of eyewitnesses (Penrod, Fulero, & Cutler, 1995). In fact, in trials in which the testimony of an eyewitness is potentially pivotal and the eyewitness's accuracy is an issue, psychologists have often been denied the opportunity to testify. Robert Buckhout (1983) reported that in New York, "I have testified before juries in about 10 cases and been kept out too many times to count" (p. 67). Solomon Fulero (1988) concluded that psychologists have been allowed to testify

about eyewitness accuracy for the defence in at least 450 cases in 25 states, but many states still prevent them from doing so.

In Canada, judges have generally disallowed expert testimony concerning eyewitness testimony. For example, in the Toronto robbery case *R. v. McIntosh and McCarthy* (1997), the defence lawyer attempted to have the testimony of prominent University of Guelph researcher Dan Yarmey admitted as evidence. Yarmey was to testify on several aspects of eyewitness identification, including the accuracy of recall, the effect of post-event information, cross-racial identification, and factors at the time of the robbery that could have influenced the memory of the witnesses. When considering this evidence, the judge refused to admit his testimony, stating, "I do not agree, based on the evidence I've heard from Dr. Yarmey, that the science has advanced that far away from the common experience of jurors" (para. 25). A major development since this case challenges this judicial viewpoint. In the 2001 inquiry into Thomas Sophonow's wrongful murder conviction in Manitoba, Justice Cory highlighted that injustices have resulted from errors by "honest, right-thinking eyewitnesses," and strongly advocated the need for a better understanding of eyewitness memory among the judiciary. He stated that he "would recommend that judges consider favourably and readily admit properly qualified expert evidence pertaining to eyewitness identification. This is certainly not junk science. Careful studies have been made with regard to memory and its effect upon eyewitness identification" (Sophonow Inquiry Report, 2001). Therefore, we may see more expert testimony on this issue in coming years.

Why have so few psychologists been permitted to testify in this area in the past? Many judges may fear that an expert witness's testimony will be so powerful that it will usurp the jury's role as the fact-finders in the case. Similarly, many judges feel that the credibility of eyewitness testimony is a matter of "common sense" for legal decision-makers, precluding the need for expert testimony.

A second reason is that judges fear a "battle of the experts," and a third is that, according to judges, psychologists do not possess information beyond the common knowledge of ordinary persons and therefore would not meet the usual criterion for expert witness. These last two reasons can be collapsed together because one of the factors that contributes to the court's suspicion of the quality and reliability of psychologists' testimony is disagreement within the field about psychological phenomena, with respected researchers coming to contradictory conclusions in some areas, and the controversy among psychologists over the appropriateness of testifying in court as an expert witness. Each of these issues is discussed in the following material.

Kassin, Ellsworth, and Smith (1989) surveyed 63 experts on eyewitness testimony. At least 80 percent of these experts agreed that research results on each of the following topics were consistent enough to present in court: the relationship between accuracy and confidence, the lineup instructions, the impact of exposure time, and unconscious transference, as well as other topics. More than 70 percent of the experts believed that the tendency to overestimate the duration of the event, the cross-racial identification bias of white witnesses, and lineup fairness generated consistent research findings. Additionally, leading researchers (Buckhout, 1983; Loftus, 1983; Wells, 1986) have agreed with the above, and they have often testified when asked.

But others, equally adamantly, have proposed that the research is not sufficiently conclusive or applicable (Konecni & Ebbesen, 1986; McCloskey & Egeth, 1983; McCloskey, Egeth, & McKenna, 1986). Some of these psychologists have testified to that effect, thus contributing to the court's concern over a "battle of the experts." As Kassin et al. (1989) have suggested, the legal system is not as tolerant of minority dissenting voices as is psychological science. In one case, upon hearing that 80 percent of experts agreed on a particular issue, the judge responded, "*Only* 80 percent, hmm."

As mentioned, many judges believe that eyewitness memory is within the purview of common sense. The problem with relying on the common sense of the trier of fact in judicial decision making was shown by Yarmey (1986) in his test of the standards outlined by the U.S. Supreme Court for the assessment of eyewitness accuracy. Despite some of the court's "common sense" standards for determining eyewitness accuracy, he found that the accuracy of the witness's description of the accused and the witness's level of confidence at the time of incident were not important predictors of accuracy. In a subsequent review of the role of eyewitness experts in the courtroom published in *Canadian Psychology*, Yarmey (2001) argued that many of the difficulties arising with eyewitness testimony contradict the commonsense beliefs held by lay persons and and lawyers about eyewitness memory. This view was reiterated by Justice Cory in the Sophonow Inquiry (Sophonow Inquiry Report, 2001).

Another conflict concerns the role of the expert witness. We saw in Chapter 1 that Münsterberg did not hesitate to take sides; he played the role of advocate. In contrast, contemporary psychologists have been trained to be impartial scientists. Which role is appropriate? Elizabeth Loftus (Loftus & Ketcham, 1991) posed it this way:

> Should a psychologist in a court of law act as an advocate for the defense or an impartial educator? My answer to that question, if I am completely honest, is *both*. If I believe in his innocence with all my heart and soul, then I probably can't help but become an advocate of sorts. (p. 238, italics in original)

As John Brigham responded, "Loftus's implication that one will become an advocate could prove destructive in the creative hands of an aggressive lawyer who is seeking to destroy an impartial expert witness's credibility" (Brigham, 1992, p. 529). Further, in the survey by Kassin et al. (1989), the experts said that they were as willing to testify for the prosecution as for the defence. In response to an article by Loftus (2003), we recently argued that "it is not our role as psychologists to make policy decisions for the legal system, just as it is not our role to comment on whether recovered memory evidence should be admissible in the courtroom. We argue that this is simply not our question to answer" (Porter, Campbell, et al., 2003, p. 213). On the other hand, our role as researchers should be to provide relevant scientific data to legal decision makers to help them in their cases.

Ethical Responsibilities

In 1986, a psychic testified in court that a CAT scan had caused her to lose her psychic powers, and a physician—testifying as an expert witness—backed up her claim. The jury awarded her US$1 million in damages. (The award was later overturned.) The expert witness in a trial has a great opportunity to influence case decisions that is only accentuated by the fact that "it is virtually impossible to prosecute an expert witness for perjury" (*Sears v. Rutishauser,* 1984, p. 212). Michael Saks concluded that an expert witness who manages to overlook contrary findings or who commits errors "still is likely to remain safe from any formal penalty" (1992, p. 193). This includes protection from civil liability. Testimony given in court is privileged; "a witness may say whatever he or she likes under oath, and no private remedies are available to persons who may be harmed as a result" (Saks, 1992, p. 193). One problem is to decide whether an expert is deliberately deceitful or only incompetent. Unless evidence for dishonesty exists, the court must conclude that the defendant was "only" incompetent.

Suppose that an expert witness, at the end of extended testimony, looks at the jury intently and says:

> "I guess you noticed that I withheld some information from the court, stretched other information, and offered an opinion that sounded more certain than our field's knowledge really permits. I did that because I am committed to making the world a better place, and I think it will be better if the court reaches the outcome I want to see in the case." (Saks, 1992, pp. 187–188)

In actuality, such actions do happen, even if they are not acknowledged by the experts, who may disregard contradictory evidence, or exaggerate their own credentials. Every expert witness must consider the question: Do I tell the court things that will undercut my own seemingly authoritative knowledge (Saks, 1992)? And, as is considered in detail later in this chapter, every expert must make a personal decision about what the standard should be for reporting on a particular finding or the validity of a specific diagnostic tool.

Every expert witness must decide how to resolve the central dilemma of "relating his or her field's knowledge to the cause at stake in the litigation" (Saks, 1992, p. 190). Is one loyal to one's field of expertise or to the outcome of the case? Saks (1992) identified three different ways to resolve this conflict:

1. *The conduit-educator.* As a **conduit-educator**, the expert's own field becomes his or her first priority. The thinking might go like this:

   > "My first duty is to share the most faithful picture of my field's knowledge with those who have been assigned the responsibility to make the decisions. To do this may be to be a mere technocrat, rather than a complete human being concerned with the moral implications of what I say and with the greatest good of society. The central difficulty of this role is whether it is all right for me to contribute hard-won knowledge to causes I would just as soon see lose." (Saks, 1992, p. 189)

2. *The philosopher-ruler/advocate.* If the expert witness views himself or herself as a kind of **philosopher-ruler/advocate**, the oath of telling "the whole truth" is of less concern than it is in the conduit-educator role. Hans described it as follows:

   > Some experts chose a legal-adversary stance, in which they volunteered only research evidence that supported their side, de-emphasized or omitted the flaws in the data,

or refrained from discussing opposing evidence. In the words of one expert: "I understand the partisan nature of the courtroom and I realized that I would be on the stand arguing for a position without also presenting evidence that might be contrary to my … side. But, you see, that didn't bother me, because I knew that the other side was also doing that." (Hans, 1989, p. 312)

3. *The hired gun.* Although somewhat similar to philosopher-ruler/advocates in their bias toward one side, hired guns serve their employer's values rather than advance their own (Saks, 1992). Their motivation is to help the person who hired them. However, the CPA's ethical guidelines assert that psychologists are responsible for attempting to prevent the distortion, misuse, or suppression of psychological data, and that they must present scientific findings in a balanced way.

Saks has suggested one test of how well the expert has assumed the honest educator's role is to ask the witness: "Please tell the court everything you know about this case that the party who called you to the witness stand hopes does not come out during your cross-examination" (Saks, 1992, p. 191).

The courts have, of course, established some standards for admissibility of proposed experts, as we introduced in Chapter 1. The first guidelines were known as the **Frye test** (*Frye v. United States*, 1923), established in the U.S. more than 80 years ago. It stated that the well-recognized standards regarding principles or evidence for any particular field should determine the admissibility of expert testimony. In the U.S., additional guidelines were established in 1975 with the adoption of the Federal Rules of Evidence, which specified, among other determinants, that qualified experts can testify "if scientific, technical, or other specialized knowledge will assist the trier of fact to understand the evidence or to determine a fact in issue" (quoted by Bottoms & Davis, 1993, p. 14).

Thus, the Federal Rules of Evidence focused on the importance of general acceptance but did not limit admissibility on that basis, emphasizing whatever is "relevant." The United States Supreme Court, in the case of *Daubert v. Merrell Dow Pharmaceuticals, Inc.* (1993), sought to clarify the distinction between the Federal Rules of Evidence and the more restrictive Frye test—most state courts were then using the Frye rule. The Court sought to decide the basis for admitting experts as witnesses.

Hence, a central issue in question of expert testimony is the conflict between science and the law: "To what extent should judges be gate keepers, screening out what has come to be known as junk science from naive jurors who might otherwise be misled, overly awed, or moved by compassion for plaintiffs? Conversely, to what extent should juries be permitted to serve their traditional role as fact finders?" (Greenhouse, 1992, p. A9). In *Daubert*, both the state court and the appeals court ruled that certain experts' testimony was inadmissible because the research they discussed was unpublished and had not been evaluated by other scientists (or subjected to **peer review**); that is, in the court's view, their evidence was not generally accepted by the appropriate scientific community. In a U.S. Supreme Court decision announced in 1993, the Court held that the Frye test was unnecessarily restrictive and was superseded by the Federal Rules of Evidence. The Court held that expert evidence had to be grounded in relevant and reliable evidence, with those considerations to be decided by the presiding judge (Bottoms & Davis, 1993). Several criteria were considered as appropriate for judges to use in determining the scientific validity of research; these included (1) whether it had been peer-reviewed (favourably, we assume, as the Court didn't indicate), (2) how testable it was (or how it stacked up on "falsifiability" or "refutability"), (3) whether it had a recognized rate of error, and (4) whether it adhered to professional standards of use of the technique in question (Bersoff, 1993).

In Canada, the classic statement of the role of expert evidence is found in *Kelliher (Village of) v. Smith* (1931), in which the Supreme Court of Canada concluded that in order for testimony to be considered "expert," "the subject matter of the inquiry must be such that ordinary people are unlikely to form a correct judgment about it, if unassisted by persons with special knowledge" (p. 684). As described earlier, in *R. v. Mohan* (1994) the Supreme Court stated that expert evidence must be both *necessary* in assisting the trier of fact and *relevant*. Again, while in some ways these requirements have been interpreted liberally, it is apparent that experts would not be allowed to testify about matters that the court felt were "common sense," such as eyewitness testimony.

SPECIFIC ROLES: THE PREPARATION OF SCIENTIFIC BRIEFS FOR THE COURTS

The efforts of Münsterberg and his contemporaries to bring scientific psychology into the courts sought to produce results that would be influential at the trial level. Münsterberg apparently never tried to influence the decision of an appellate court. This role, specifically the preparation of **amicus curiae briefs** to accompany appeals, has become an important example of the role of forensic psychologists in the U.S. (Acker, 1990). *Amicus curiae* briefs are arguments by a third party (in this case a psychologist or group of psychologists) to the dispute that seek as a "friend of the court," to inform judges on matters relevant to the dispute.

In Canada, the use of *amicus* briefs in this way is rare. However, courts do accept analogous submissions from psychologists about the need for certain information to be disclosed before trial. For example, a lawyer in Halifax recently requested a written submission from a forensic psychologist (the second author of this text) pertaining to the general importance of examining therapy notes in evaluating the credibility of recovered memories, while not speaking to the particular evidence in the case. In addition, in the mid-1990s the CPA adopted a similar role by submitting a report to the federal justice minister recommending that a full judicial inquiry be conducted into all Canadian convictions stemming from recovered memory evidence (this recommendation was ultimately rejected). Nonetheless, such an action is similar in purpose to the American *amicus* brief in that its intention is to alter the legal system through scientific advocacy concerning "psychological" evidence.

The development of *amicus* briefs may in part be a result of the uncertain impact of social science on the law (Roesch, Golding, Hans, & Reppucci, 1991), leading to more activist interventions. But in doing so, psychologists force an issue we visited earlier with expert witnesses: Are we reporters of research or advocates? A second issue is—once again—the lack of agreement among psychologists on the desirability of submitting such *amicus* briefs. Because *amicus* briefs give an example of the strong impact psychologists can have in the legal system, we now turn to a famous historical American case in which an *amicus* brief was used.

Brown v. Board of Education (1954)

In the historic decision that racially segregated schools were "inherently unequal" (*Brown v. Board of Education,* 1954), the U.S. Supreme Court cited research by psychologists Kenneth Clark and Mamie Clark and a statement by a group of prominent social scientists titled "The Effect of Segregation and the Consequences of Desegregation: A Social Science Statement." It is uncertain just how much the justices, in overturning school segregation, were influenced by the social scientists' statement (Cook, 1984). However, consider statements such as "[T]he policy of separating the races is usually interpreted as denoting the inferiority of the Negro group," or: "A sense of inferiority affects the motivation of a child to learn." These statements from the Court's opinion are quite consistent with the conclusions drawn from the well-publicized doll study by Kenneth Clark and Mamie Clark (1952). Consistent with conclusions, yes, but how consistent with results?

The Clarks showed a set of dolls to 134 black children (ages six to nine) in the segregated schools of Pine Bluff, Arkansas, and to 119 black children in unsegregated schools in Springfield, Massachusetts. The children were requested to do certain things, such as:

Give me the doll you like the best.

Give me the doll that looks like you.

Give me the doll that looks bad.

The segregated Southern children, the Clarks wrote, were "less pronounced in their preference for the white doll." When asked to hand their questioner "the doll that looks like you," 39 percent of the unsegregated Springfield children picked the white doll compared with only 29 percent in the segregated Arkansas schools. When asked for the nice doll, 68 percent of the Springfield children chose the white doll, while only 52 percent of the Pine Bluff children did. Which doll "looked bad"? More than 70 percent of the desegregated children chose the black doll, whereas only 49 percent of the segregated children did. What are we to make of these findings? Do they, as the Clarks concluded, show invidious effects of segregation? The straightforward interpretation of the data, for critics of the Clarks' conclusions (see van den Haag, 1960), was that if the tests demonstrate damage to black children, then they demonstrate that the damage is *less* with segregation and *greater* with desegregation.

Kenneth and Mamie Clark's interpretation of the results was, as you might expect, completely opposite. Essentially, they were that "black children of the South were more adjusted to the feeling that they were not as good as whites, and because they felt defeated at an early age, did not bother using the device of denial" (quoted by Kluger, 1976, p. 356). Surely the Clarks' interpretation is not the most parsimonious. Did they predict this finding before the data were collected? The research report does not say so. The Clarks stated that some children, when asked which doll they resembled, broke down and cried. This type of behaviour, they reported, "was more prevalent in the North than in the South"

(1952, p. 560). Research results that are subject to conflicting interpretations—especially when the result is not consistent with a desired explanation—demand that the researchers begin with a theory that produces testable hypotheses. Fortunately, the U.S. Supreme Court in 1954 concluded that school segregation is inherently unequal and did not have to rely on research data to so conclude.

If the data were thus subject to a multitude of interpretations, why did the Court not simply note that school segregation, on the face of it, induced an assumption of inferiority leading to a response of humiliation? It may have been "precisely because the Court knew it was backing a firm precedent and entering a heated debate, that it wished to garner *all* the supporting evidence that was available. Without data, there was a danger that the arguments on both sides might merely have become so much moral posturing and empty assertions" (Perkins, 1988, p. 471). As Thurgood Marshall noted in 1952, the earlier separate-but-equal "doctrine had become so ingrained that overwhelming proof was sorely needed to demonstrate that equal educational opportunities for Negroes could not be provided in a segregated system" (quoted in Rosen, 1972, p. 130).

Turning from Clark and Clark's data to the statement by the social scientists that was part of the *Brown amicus* brief, we should note that some psychologists also disagree about the statement's desirability. Stuart Cook (1979), 25 years later, concluded that the information in it was sound, but Harold Gerard (1983) felt that the statement was based "not on hard data but mostly on well-meaning rhetoric" (p. 871).

Differences between Psychologists

Should a psychologist become an expert witness or aid in the preparation of scientific briefs for the courts? What accounts for the differences in the sometimes-volatile reactions of psychologists on specific issues and specific cases?

Kassin and Wrightsman (1983) proposed that jurors, contemplating evidence in a criminal trial, possessed varying degrees of either pro-prosecution or pro-defence biases. They found that a measure constructed to assess juror bias could predict the direction of the juror's verdict in most types of criminal trials. This analysis may be extended to differences in psychologists' reactions to involvement in the court system. How consistent should a phenomenon be to declare it reliable? And, how is consistency measured: a box score of different studies' results, the percentage of variance accounted for, a meta-analysis? Monahan and Walker (1988) proposed that the same standard should exist for going public as for peer evaluation; there should be no double standard. Elliott sought a high **standard of reliability**, or degree of consistency in research findings—in his view, psychologists should reflect "organized skepticism" (Elliott, 1991, p. 75). Self-labels to describe those who insist on an exceedingly high standard of reliability include "cautious" and "prudent." It would seem that for such psychologists, the state of knowledge must approach certainty. Does this mean that there is no situation in which they would endorse involvement with the courts? Elliott's response: "The claim made here is not that scientific organizations should not or may not (or should or may) take moral positions. Rather, it is that, if they do so, they should not affect to base them on scientific foundations when such foundations are insufficient to bear the argument constructed on them" (1991, p. 74).

In contrast, psychologists who have testified and submitted *amicus* briefs or similar reports, while demanding a clear pattern of research findings, do not have the same standards regarding reliability. Many of them endorse the "best available evidence" argument, which proposes that it is appropriate for psychologists to testify even if their conclusions must be tentative. Dan Yarmey (1986) argued that an expert's statements should conform to the criterion of scientific respectability, but that absolute certainty is not required. He suggested the criterion: Is the evidence clear, convincing, reliable and valid, or is it sufficiently ambiguous

that experts could find support for whatever position they wished to defend?

Other representations of what might be called "the clear and convincing" standard of proof: Phoebe Ellsworth, in response to Elliott, wrote, "to keep silent until our understanding is perfect is to keep silent forever" (1991, p. 77), and "I think we should file briefs when we believe that we have something to say that would improve the quality of the courts' decision making" (p. 89).

Another example: Bersoff (1987) has asked what state of the data would ever be strong enough to persuade critics and skeptics to testify? This question leads to consideration of a second dimension. Psychologists differ in their perception and weighing of conflicting facts, just as jurors do. Bermant (1986) proposed that these assessments of the strength of the available evidence are the basis for any decision about the propriety of expert testimony. Part of the difference in evidence interpretations results from the degree to which psychologists show **sympathy for the defendant** and a concern about avoiding erroneous convictions. The state of mind of the testifying psychologist, of course, varies from case to case, but individual differences in general predispositions may also be present.

As Ring (1971) observed more than three decades ago, most social psychologists are politically liberal, but not all. Social scientists who sympathize with the defendant tend to be skeptical that the defendant truly committed the crime, or that the eyewitnesses' testimony is truly accurate or that the confession was truly voluntary. A major concern of politically liberal psychologists is that some defendants will be wrongfully convicted, imprisoned, and executed. Their critics do not share this concern. McCloskey and Egeth (1983) argue that wrongful convictions from mistaken eyewitness testimony reflected only a "small fraction of the 1% of cases in which defendants were convicted at least in part on the basis of eyewitness testimony" (p. 552). Konecni and Ebbesen approvingly quoted the above, and concluded from it "that in the state of California one person is wrongfully convicted approximately every three years because of mistaken eyewitness testimony" (1986, p. 119).

The second dimension of the differences in psychologists' willingness to intervene is the question: How many errors of omission are we willing to make to avoid making one error of commission? Konecni and Ebbesen (1986) conclude: "One wrongful conviction every three years because of mistaken identification in a state the size of California (if the estimates given above are correct) may be one wrongful conviction too many, but most reasonable people would probably regard it as well within the domain of 'acceptable risk'—acceptable because no workable system of justice is perfect" (1986, p. 119).

Other psychologists would disagree; the magnitude of error, they would say, is much greater. But for politically liberal psychologists one wrongful conviction *really is* too many; it is unacceptable. In that regard, they seek a standard of perfection in some ways similar to the standard of perfect research consistency sought by their critics. Both seek "zero defects." The *amicus* brief directed to the U.S. Supreme Court has been a frequent mechanism by which the American Psychological Association seeks its goals to promote and advance human welfare (Grisso & Saks, 1991). In several instances this device has been effective (Tremper, 1987). But in notable cases the Court decided in a direction contrary to the conclusions supported by psychological theory and findings (*McCleskey v. Kemp*, 1987; *Schall v. Martin*, 1984).

At first it may appear that psychology's intervention was unsuccessful in such cases. But in such cases the court's references to scientific data did not challenge the facts that the psychologists had demonstrated; it simply said that "the psychological data were not sufficient grounds upon which to decide the legal questions" (Grisso & Saks, 1991, p. 207). The Court appeared to listen to the evidence and took it seriously enough to discuss it.

Thus, in Grisso and Saks's (1991) view, these briefs may be making two important contributions to forensic psychology. First, "they may reduce the likelihood that judicial use of spurious, unsubstantiated opinions about human behavior will establish precedent for future cases" (p. 207). Second, the briefs may, to put it crudely, "keep the Court honest," or to quote Grisso and Saks, "psychology's input may compel judges to act like judges, stating clearly the fundamental values and normative premises on which their decisions are grounded, rather than hiding behind empirical errors or uncertainties" (p. 208). In this light, psychology's efforts in these controversial cases appear to be more effective.

When psychology seeks to influence the courts, it needs to go more than halfway. In a study of the court's use of social science research in cases involving children, Hafemeister and Melton (1987) concluded that when secondary social science sources were cited, they typically were works published in law reviews or government reports, not in psychology journals. The moral is clear: If you want to influence judges, publish your conclusions in the periodicals they read.

Ethical Considerations

What is the appropriate stance for psychologists who seek to influence court decisions? We have mentioned some of the dangers. Roesch, Golding, Hans, and Reppucci (1991), a group of Canadian and American collaborators, posed these choices:

> Should social scientists limit themselves to conducting and publishing their research and leave it to others to apply their research findings? Or do they have an ethical obligation to assist the courts and other social groups in matters relating to their expertise? If an activist role for social scientists is appropriate, what are the comparative advantages of brief writing, expert testimony, and other mechanisms of approaching the courts? (p. 2)

When psychology as an organized profession seeks to influence the law through an *amicus* brief to an appellate court, it can do so for a variety of reasons. For example, the APA may perceive a shared interest in the outcome with one of the parties in the litigation—usually this interest relates to economic benefits, powers, or prerequisites for its members (Saks, 1993). For example, in 1993, the APA filed an *amicus* brief in conjunction with a court case involving the confidentiality of unfunded grant applications (Adler, 1993). This "guild" interest is not consistent with the neutral stance of some conceptions of the *amicus* brief. Roesch et al. (1991) noted that this advocacy brief contrasts with the **science-translation brief**, that is, an objective summary of a body of research similar to the one the CPA submitted to the justice minister concerning repressed memories.

The science-translation brief reflects the second role, as an honest broker. It is offered when the psychological body possesses knowledge the court otherwise might not have and that might assist the court in deciding the case before it. Saks argued that taking this role "minimizes the temptation to fudge, maximizes the value of the knowledge to the public interest" (1993, p. 243) and helps protect the integrity of psychology.

Even a science-translation brief will reflect the perspective and values of its writers (Roesch et al., 1991). How much interpretation should a brief contain? Melton and Saks suggested that both the advocacy brief and the science-translation brief:

> can end up misleading a reader, especially a lay reader, which is what judges are when they read these kinds of briefs. The solution, we think, is in approaching the writing with an honest desire to share with the courts a faithful picture of the available psychological knowledge, and to interpret the research only to the extent that doing so will clarify its meaning. (1990, p. 5)

Because controversy is inevitable in science, any science-translation brief will generate some disagreement by social scientists. But "in preparing briefs, social scientists should strive to ensure, at a minimum, that briefs represent a consensual view of social scientists (i.e., what *most* experts in the field would conclude)" (Roesch et al., 1991, p. 6). Alternative explanations should be included, when appropriate.

Guidelines for Forensic Psychologists

As interest in forensic psychology continues to grow, systematic concern about codifying the ethical guidelines has increased. The CPA provides general guidelines concerning issues such as confidentiality (see Box 2.3), dual relationships, and test administration for psychologists working in legal contexts, whereas the American Psychology-Law Society has developed a more specific set of guidelines for forensic psychologists, under the direction of Stephen L. Golding, Thomas Grisso, and David Shapiro, that are generally accepted in Canada. These "Specialty Guidelines for Forensic Psychologists" focus on several aspects of forensic work, including the relationship between psychologists and litigating parties and procedures in preparing forensic evaluations. In another way of certifying competence, the American Board of Professional Psychology offers a diploma in forensic psychology, indicating that the recipient is at the highest level of excellence in his or her field of forensic competence. Many Canadian forensic psychologists have been certified in this manner.

SUMMARY

The roles of forensic psychologists in the legal system are diverse, but they share certain temptations, including promising too much, substituting advocacy for scientific objectivity, letting values overcome empirically based conclusions, doing a cursory job, and maintaining dual relationships and competing roles.

Psychologists differ about the degree to which the field should apply its findings to solutions of legal problems. Some believe that psychologists do not possess findings that are sufficiently reliable to be applied to real-life decisions. Others are critical of the majority of their colleagues, who because of their politically liberal orientations, tend to sympathize with the defendant in criminal cases. Psychologists active in legal intervention respond by noting that the information from that field, although not perfectly consistent, improves the quality of decision making in the legal system.

The courts have entered this controversy by considering just what the standard should be in admitting scientific evidence at trial. In recent decisions, the courts have applied standards of scientific acceptance (i.e., publication in a peer-reviewed journal, replicability) to determine the admissibility of psychologists as expert witnesses.

BOX 2.3
Confidentiality and Psychotherapists

When a person consults with a psychologist, there is an assurance from professional ethics codes that information shared within the meeting will remain confidential. In this context, confidentiality means that nothing will be shared with a third party, except for other medical or mental health professionals (and then only as required). A privileged communication extends even beyond the ethical expectation of confidentiality into a legal obligation. In general, a person involved in the contract of a privileged communication cannot be compelled to disclose the privileged information in the courtroom. Examples of such relationships include lawyers and clients, spouses, doctors and patients, and religious advisors and their followers.

It is noteworthy that there is a recent legal precedent on the matter of duty to warn in the Canadian case *Smith v. Jones* (1999). In this case, Jones underwent a psychiatric assessment (by Smith) requested by the defence for the purpose of sentencing. During the assessment, Mr. Jones disclosed his intent to kidnap, rape, and kill prostitutes. Dr. Smith informed the defence counsel of the threats, and was instructed to maintain confidentiality as the disclosures were bound under the solicitor–client privilege. Dr. Smith pursued a civil action entitling him the legal right to disclose the threat, and to force the lawyer to present this information to the courts in the sentencing hearing. This case was appealed through to the Supreme Court of Canada, which held that lawyer–client privilege is limited in the circumstance that public safety is at risk. The court ruled that a breach of solicitor–client confidentiality was warranted when (1) there is a clear risk to an identifiable class of victims; (2) there is a risk of serious bodily harm or death; and (3) the danger is imminent. However, the dissenting position stated that confidentiality should be maintained in all other circumstances in order to promote confidence in legal and therapeutic relationships. Within this context, dangerous individuals may be more likely to disclose the danger they pose, and seek treatment, rather than acting on these impulses (*Smith v. Jones*, 1999). This case provides the legal backbone requiring Canadian mental health professionals to breach confidentiality and fulfill their ethical duty to warn and protect third parties from harm (Glancy, Regehr, Bryant, & Schneider, 1999).

But what of evidence of past crimes? Is confidentiality provided? Consider the U.S case of Lyle and Erik Menendez, who were charged with killing their parents. In this case, the police were informed by a former lover of the brothers' psychotherapist (Beverly Hills psychologist L. Jerome Oziel) that tapes existed on which the brothers had confessed to their parents' murders. So a further question arose: Can psychologist–client privilege be broken by a third party?

In 1992, two years after the brothers' arrest, the California Supreme Court suppressed the tape from evidence as an invasion of therapist–client privilege. But when (in late 1993) the trial started, the brothers presented their mental state as an issue in the trial. The trial judge then ruled that the client privilege was waived. The judge acknowledged that his ruling had little precedent, that it was "a unique situation not addressed by any other case in any other court" (quoted by Associated Press, 1993, p. A7).

KEY TERMS

advocate role, p. 25

amicus curiae briefs, p. 38

assessment, p. 24

conduit-educator, p. 36

confidentiality, p. 31

dual relationships, p. 29

expert witness, p. 25

fact witness, p. 32

Frye test, p. 37

hired gun, p. 25

junk science, p. 33

peer review, p. 37

philosopher-ruler/advocate, p. 36

psychopathy, p. 24

science-translation brief, p. 42

standard of reliability, p. 40

sympathy for the defendant, p. 40

trial consultant, p. 30

SUGGESTED READINGS

Brodsky, S. L. (1991). *Testifying in court: Guidelines and maxims for the expert witness.* Washington, DC: American Psychological Association.

This relentlessly readable book by one of the United States' most respected forensic psychologists includes a wealth of practical suggestions, succinctly put. An example: "With indifferent attorneys be assertive. With incompetent attorneys, decline the case or educate them" (p. 197).

Bruck, M. (1998). The trials and tribulations of a novice expert witness. In S. J. Ceci & H. Hembrooke (Eds.), *Expert witnesses in child abuse cases* (pp. 85–104). Washington, DC: American Psychological Association.

All forensic psychologists anticipating their first testimony are indebted to Maggie Bruck for painfully portraying the pitfalls of such an activity. She had not been warned about what to expect, but now we know.

Dawes, R. M. (1994). *House of cards: Psychology and psychotherapy built on myth.* New York: Free Press.

The general viewpoint of this book is similar to that of Margaret Hagen's *Whores of the Court;* both books are by psychologists who are critical of their psychotherapist-colleagues whose use invalid psychological tests and substitute intuition for empirical findings.

Hagen, M. A. (1997). *Whores of the court: The fraud of psychiatric testimony and the rape of American justice.* New York: HarperCollins.

A few forensic psychologists love it, more hate it, and some of us say to it, "Yes, but ..." (see Box 2.1 on page 26). Certainly the most talked-about book in recent years.

Ziskin, J. (1995). *Coping with psychiatric and psychological testimony* (Vol. 1–3, 5th ed.). Los Angeles: Law and Psychology Press.

Few of us have had such an impact that our names have become verbs within the lingo of a certain profession, but that is true of the late Jay Ziskin. When trial lawyers "Ziskinize" psychologists or psychiatrists who are testifying, they challenge them by cross-examining them *intensively* with regard to the accuracy of their statements and the validity of the procedures they have used. This three-volume set (earlier editions were prepared with David Faust) assesses the validity of a number of forensic topics; any forensic psychologist who anticipates being an expert witness needs to consult these volumes.

3

The Police: Selection, Training, and Evaluation

Looking in the rear view mirror, I want to state unequivocally that this organization is solidly on the right road and is making excellent progress.
—Royal Canadian Mounted Police Commissioner Giuliano Zaccardelli
(RCMP 2004/2005 Directional Statement)

PSYCHOLOGY'S ROLE IN POLICE WORK

This chapter attempts to show that psychology can play a significant role in many aspects of police work, from the selection of recruits, through the training of police and other law-enforcement officers, to the evaluation of their work performance. Forensic psychologists can assist in responding to the major types of complaints about the police—corruption, racism, and brutality. Further, psychology and the other social sciences have evaluated recent changes in police procedures, such as **team policing,** or the assignment of police officers to particular neighbourhoods, so that they become familiar with local concerns. The purpose of this chapter is to examine what psychology has to offer in reaching our shared goal of improving law-enforcement procedures.

WHO ARE THE CLIENTS?

In 2004, the largest investigation into police corruption in Canadian history was ongoing in Toronto, with allegations of serious criminal activity against at least 12 members (CBC News Online, 2004). In January 2004, the Halifax Police Department publicly apologized to boxer Kirk Johnson for treating him unfairly due to his race. In the U.S., there was the beating of Rodney King in Los Angeles and the arrest of three police officers in Detroit for planning the theft of US$1 million in cash. These and other events have sensitized the public to serious problems in law-enforcement agencies (Cannon, 1998; Fields, 1993). Less acknowledged is the other side of the coin: the acts of heroism by law-enforcement officers and the risk of officers' death or injury. In Canada, 227 police officers were killed in the line of duty between 1879 and 1994 (Canadian Professional Police Association, n.d.). In addition, according to the Canadian Professional Police Association (n.d.), over the

past 23 years, six to eight police and peace officers have been killed in the line of duty each year. Further, stresses on the police can take a terrible toll: According to Loo (1986), 35 RCMP officers took their own lives between 1960 and 1983. Between 1975 and 1999, 22 members of the Toronto Police Service committed suicide, a far higher rate than the general population (Schaer, 1999).

In identifying the possible contributions of psychology to policing, we begin by asking: Who are the **clients**? To whom are forensic psychologists responsible when they seek to apply psychological knowledge to the criminal justice system? A forensic psychologist might be hired by a police department, most often as a consultant although sometimes as a staff member, but the psychologist also has an ethical responsibility to respond to the public's concerns about the police. As we will see, achieving both of these responsibilities at the same time is often challenging.

The Public

What does the public want from law-enforcement officers? Specific responses would differ, but some common desires include fairness, respect, and a lack of prejudice. However, the public does not seem to believe that the police always meet these standards. In the wake of several stories in recent years about alleged incidents of police brutality in British Columbia (especially in Vancouver), the Ipsos-Reid Group polled citizens of the province in October 2003, and found that about 26 percent of residents considered incidents of police brutality "common." A desire for fairness and an equal treatment of all citizens is typical (Tyler & Folger, 1980; Vermunt, Blaauw, & Lind, 1998). A frequent complaint about Canadian police is their discrimination against minority groups such as Aboriginal Canadians, blacks, and other minorities. For decades, members of racial minority groups have perceived themselves to be unjustly victimized by police officers (Decker & Wagner,

1982). Black people believe they are abused by the police far more than are whites in several ways: being roughed up unnecessarily, being stopped and frisked without justification, and being subjected to abusive language. This perception was given obvious credibility in a recent case in Halifax. Heavyweight boxer Kirk Johnson claimed he was discriminated against because of his ethnic background when Halifax police pulled him over and seized his car in 1998. The Nova Scotia Human Rights Commission ruled in Johnson's favour in December 2003, ordering police to pay him $10 000 in damages. It found officers had "acted on a stereotype." Although the officer involved refused to apologize, the Halifax Police Department admitted that some of their members were guilty of "unconsciously" pulling over black drivers in disproportionate numbers (CBC News Online, 2004, January 19).

These concerns are so great that victims have sarcastically developed the crime-classification expression **DWB** ("driving while black") to reflect the tendency of some patrol officers to concentrate on minorities as possible offenders. While until recently the problem was much more apparent in the United States (e.g., in Philadelphia 70 percent of complaints against the police were from blacks, even though the population of the city was at the time 75 percent white; Hudson, 1970), inquiries into policing and the legal system in Nova Scotia, Manitoba, and Ontario have indicated the presence of police bias against various minority groups in Canada. Indeed, the Canadian courts have acknowledged the existence of **racial profiling**. For example, in April 2003, the Ontario Court of Appeal stated in *R. v. Brown* (2003):

> In the opening part of his submission before this court, counsel for the appellant (the Crown) said that he did not challenge the fact that the phenomenon of racial profiling by the police existed. This was a responsible position to take because, as counsel said, this conclusion is supported by significant social science research (note 4 at 165).

A 2003 report by the Ontario Human Rights Commission called "Paying the Price: The Human Cost of Racial Profiling" concluded that a major problem existed with "the entire criminal justice system's" treatment of Aboriginal people (p. 58). The report noted that Aboriginal peoples are vastly overrepresented in the correctional system, from arrest by police to incarceration in prison. While making up only 2.8 percent of Canada's population, Aboriginals comprise 17 percent of the federal offender population. In fact, adult Aboriginal people are incarcerated at more than six times the national rate, and they are denied parole at a higher rate than other offenders.

What can be done to resolve this problem? Does psychology have anything to offer? Although this topic deserves more attention, one intervention is the use of a psychologist to assist in community involvement in **police selection.** Often, the goals in selection by police departments reflect traditional criteria; they fail to recognize the goal of diversity in the makeup of law-enforcement agencies, specifically the hiring of minorities and women.

Members of special interest groups have a desire to put their own agendas on police departments, but many of these departments have "resisted what they consider unwarranted interference from people whom they believe have little understanding of the nature of the job, and are, in fact, hostile to the police and their definition of the nature of their work" (Ellison, 1985, p. 77).

Katherine W. Ellison (1985) is a community psychologist who was invited to develop a new procedure for selecting police officers for a New Jersey police department. In doing so, she capitalized on the concept of **stakeholders**, people who have a special knowledge and interest, or a "stake," in running the department. Stakeholders included, as you would expect, officers from the department, especially patrol officers. Members of the township council and other township officials, as well as members of the local media, the clergy, and other opinion leaders were included as well. But Ellison also solicited interviews from a stratified quota sample of 100 citizens from the community and included community representatives in the specific panel that interviewed candidates for police training. A side benefit, in addition to selecting officers who reflected community demographics, was an increase in the communication between the police and members of the community who traditionally complain about the unresponsiveness of the police.

A second community concern is **police corruption**. Deviant behaviour by police can vary along a continuum of seriousness; a categorization is offered in Box 3.1. Canadians were astonished in January 2004, when six officers in the Toronto Police Department were charged with robbery, assault, perjury, and conspiracy. The officers allegedly concocted informants, stole hundreds of thousands of dollars, and helped to launder money. Court documents also revealed that some officers pretended to get tips from false informants and used this fabricated information to obtain search warrants (CBC News Online, 2004, January 20). Modern corruption by police officers is different from that of earlier times, when some officers were bribed to ignore rampant examples of gambling, prostitution, or liquor violations. Now, the corruption is manifested in

officers who are active participants in the crime; some, in the words of the former police commissioner of New York City, William Bratton, have "truly become predatory figures" (quoted by K. Johnson, 1998, p. 8A).

In some cases, officers who engage in corrupt behaviour do so partly because of conflicts in achieving professional success. Big city police who are given the task of capturing drug dealers must often rely on informants, but when the police slip informants money for information (usually $10 to $20), their supervisors ridicule their requests for reimbursement, telling them that's just part of doing business (Kramer, 1997). But temptations to become lawbreakers are also a part of chasing drug dealers. One police officer, convicted of corruption, told a reporter:

> "So when we hit a place, we'd take some money to reimburse our informant payments. After a while, with so much dough sitting around, you just take more, and then you begin to get used to it. Unless you're completely nuts, you're careful. If you find 10 grand, say, you take only three or four. You can't raid a drug house and come back

---

BOX 3.1

Types of Police Deviance by Category and Example

Higher-Level Corruption

Violent Crimes: The physical abuse of suspects, including torture and nonjustifiable homicide

Denying Civil Rights: Routinized schemes to circumvent constitutional guarantees

Criminal Enterprise: The resale of confiscated drugs, stolen property, and so forth

Major Bribes: Accepting, for example, $1000 to "overlook" contraband shipments and other law violations

Property Crimes: Burglary, theft, and so forth

Lower-Level Corruption

Role Malfeasance: Destroying evidence, offering biased testimony, and protecting "crooked" cops

Being "Above" Inconvenient Laws: Speeding, smoking marijuana

Minor Bribes: Accepting, for example, $20 to "look the other way" on a parking or moving violation

Playing Favourites: Not ticketing friends, family, and so forth

Gratuities: Accepting free coffee, meals, and so forth

(Modified from Schmalleger, Frank, *Criminal Justice Today: An Introductory Text for the 21st Century*, 8th Edition, © 2005. Reprinted by permission of Pearson Education Inc., Upper Saddle River, N.J.)

and not turn in some money. That'd be a sure tipoff." (quoted by Kramer, 1997, p. 83).

Why does such corruption occur, given the extensive screening that is demanded of candidates for training as a law-enforcement officer? Are these behaviours the result of personality characteristics, or do they develop from the presence of a subculture (a local precinct, a squad of officers) prone to corruption? These are important questions that have not received sufficient study. Skolnick (1966) concluded that a process of informal socialization—specifically, interactions with experienced officers—was perhaps more important than police-academy training in determining how rookies viewed their work and the public. In his classic analysis of police life, Niederhoffer (1967) claimed that the police subculture transformed a police officer into an authoritarian personality, and several studies of changes that take place from the recruit to the experienced police officer support such a tendency (Carlson & Sutton, 1975; Genz & Lester, 1976; Hageman, 1979; McNamara, 1967). Role demands may lead to increased authoritarianism and a greater willingness to use force; working in high-crime areas seemed to foster authoritarianism in the police (L. Brown & Willis, 1985). One empirical effort to determine if authoritarianism scores of police officers were related to the number of times they had been disciplined produced no significant relationships (Henkel, Sheehan, & Reichel, 1997), but the approach needs to be extended. Expressions of brutality and corruption may well reflect an interaction between a predisposition to law breaking within the individual officer and being in a subculture that makes such actions easy to do and easy to get away with doing—a subculture that may even have norms that encourage such behaviour.

The Police Department

A second segment of the forensic psychologist's clientele is, of course, the police department itself. A psychologist can assist police departments and other law-enforcement agencies in answering a number of important questions, such as:

- What should be included in the training program for recruits? Does success in a training program predict effectiveness as a police officer?
- Are there ways to prevent or reduce police burnout? What are effective ways to deal with the stresses of police work?
- How effective are different strategies for combating crime? Are foot patrols more effective than police cars? Does saturated patrolling work?

Subsequent sections of the chapter examine psychology's answers to these questions and identify conflicts between the approaches of psychology and the police. More detailed information relevant to these questions can be found in books on the topic of police psychology, including those by Blau (1994) and by Kurke and Scrivner (1995).

THE SELECTION OF POLICE

What should be the goals of a program to select candidates for law-enforcement training? Foremost for police chiefs has been the screening out of mentally ill applicants rather than the selection of those with a desirable profile (Reiser, 1982c). Some psychologists (e.g., Smith & Stotland, 1973) have proposed that we should move beyond this focus on gross pathology. For example, what are the characteristics of an ideal law-enforcement officer, and how best are they measured? Psychology has made strides toward answering these questions over the last 80 years but definitive answers remain elusive, partly because of the lack of agreement about the ideal and partly because some desired traits cannot be reliably measured (Ainsworth, 1995).

Attainment of the goal of selecting desirable police officers for training is especially tantalizing because the initial pool is typically a large one. The selection of recruits for the RCMP in

Canada is rigorous. Each year, there are a large number of applicants (10 000 to 15 000), some of whom are selected to write the **RCMP Police Aptitude Test (RPAT)**, a multiple-choice test (114 questions) designed to evaluate one's aptitude for police work. Seven "psychological" competencies are measured that are seen by the RCMP as "essential" to perform as a police officer: composition (spelling, grammar, and vocabulary), comprehension, memory, judgment, observation, logic, and computation. Applicants who score high enough on the RPAT then must pass a Physical Abilities Requirement Evaluation (PARE). Applicants who succeed in the PARE then must participate in an **interview** to assess their communication and knowledge competencies as well as their potential to obtain a security clearance. Following this stage, candidates undergo a background investigation and, finally, basic cadet training. Obviously, one must be highly motivated to go through such a gruelling application process!

A History of Psychology and Police Selection

Psychologists' involvement in the evaluation of police characteristics extends back, surprisingly, to Lewis Terman, the author of the widely used Stanford-Binet intelligence test. Terman (1917), publishing in the very first issue of the *Journal of Applied Psychology,* tested the intelligence of 30 police and firefighter applicants in San José, California. Finding that their average IQ was 84, he recommended that no one whose IQ fell below 80 be accepted for those positions (Spielberger, 1979).

Several decades later, the emphasis shifted to personality characteristics. In the 1940s an attempt was made to use the Humm-Wadsworth Temperament Scale as a basis to select police applicants in Los Angeles (Humm & Humm, 1950), despite the lack of evidence for its validity (Ostrov, 1986). Since then, a variety of procedures have been employed by psychologists. Personality inventories continue to be used, but

interviews and situational tests have also been employed as tools. Each of these approaches is evaluated in the next sections.

Tools for Psychological Selection

The Interview

As in the selection of persons for most professional positions, the personal interview has been a central part of the selection process for law-enforcement officers throughout North America. In some areas, a clinical psychologist or psychiatrist typically conducts a brief interview, with a traditional goal of searching for pathology (Silverstein, 1985). Are there personality characteristics or traits that imply abnormal behaviour? But more recently, emphasis has shifted to the use of the interview to assess such desirable qualities as social maturity, stability, and skill in interpersonal relations (Janik, 1993). Chandler (1990) viewed the interview as providing answers to questions about "military bearing," sense of humour, and absence of anger. The interview can provide information on characteristics not visible through other procedures; these include body language, appropriateness of emotions expressed by the interviewee, insight into one's own behaviour, and an ability to convey a sense of self (Silverstein, 1985).

Nevertheless, the interview, as a selection device, is fraught with problems. The purpose of the clinical interview has traditionally been not so much to predict behaviour but to gain an in-depth understanding of the individual. Validity was often assessed by comparing one clinician's judgment with that of other clinicians. The literature from industrial/organizational psychology on the use of the clinical interview gives no indication that it is valid as a predictor of job performance (Ulrich & Trumbo, 1965).

Another problem is that there is no agreed-upon format for the interview. Some urge that the interview be standardized so that it always covers issues relevant to the job criteria (Hibler & Kurke, 1995); a structured approach also permits comparisons between applicants. But other psychologists and psychiatrists prefer the opportunity to probe topics of concern as these emerge from the responses of the individual candidate. Regardless of the procedures used, it is essential that the interview be conducted fairly and equitably (Jones, 1995). Members of minority ethnic groups who are applicants are sensitive to possibilities of racial bias by interviewers, and some commentators (Jones, 1995; Milano, 1989) have suggested that a form be prepared, specifying the topics covered in the interview.

An article by Hargrave and Hiatt (1987) cites studies related to psychiatric interviews for selection of police officers. One of the problems they note is the strong tendency for people to portray themselves more positively in face-to-face interviews than on personality tests, resulting in an increase in the number of **false positives** (poor risks who are hired) and no impact on the goal of reducing **false negatives** (those not hired who would have displayed acceptable performance).

Two particular problems obstruct the attainment of validity for interviews in police selection, although each of these problems is characteristic of some other occupations, too (Spielberger, 1979). The first is the lack of criteria against which to judge predictors (Hargrave & Hiatt, 1987). Police and other law-enforcement officers have a great deal of autonomy in their activities; also, the number of activities they carry out daily may be quite diverse. Second, screening of applicants via a clinical interview leads to an elimination of those considered unqualified; the resulting studies thus only have a restricted range of candidates, from whom individual differences in effectiveness are compared with their interview results.

Hargrave and Hiatt (1987) set forth to deal with the second problem, by capitalizing on a rather unusual situation. Two classes of police academy trainees ($N = 105$) were individually tested and interviewed by two clinical psychologists who each rated them on suitability for the job. But these ratings were not used to exclude any candidate from training. They were rated on the following: personality characteristics (anxiety, mood, anger, antisocial characteristics, and ability to

accept criticism), interpersonal effectiveness (ability to communicate, assertiveness, self-confidence, and ability to get along with others), and intellectual characteristics (judgment and verbal skills). The interview used a 5-point rating scale, ranging from 1 = unsuitable to 5 = excellent, in order to assess overall psychological suitability for the job.

The trainees then completed a five-month law-enforcement course at the academy. At the end of training, three performance criteria were examined: (1) attrition during training, (2) ratings of psychological suitability given by the training officers, and (3) peer evaluations. Correlations were determined between each of these and the ratings by each clinician; the correlations follow:

	Clinician A	Clinician B
Academic attrition	.24★★	.14
Instructors' ratings	.19	.27★
Peer evaluations	.09	.13
Composite criterion	.26★★	.24★★

★p < .05
★★p < .01

Although some of these correlation coefficients are statistically significant, the relationships are relatively weak and are certainly too low to make confident predictions about the success of individuals.

An analysis of clinicians' dichotomized ratings of "suitable" versus "unsuitable" with the goal criterion of "successful" versus "unsuccessful" found that Clinician A correctly classified 67 percent of the subjects, and Clinician B 69 percent; an analysis of trainees who were rated by the clinicians as "suitable" but were "unsuccessful" on the composite criterion indicated that all but one were unsatisfactory due to attrition.

Psychological Tests

Administration of psychological tests to police trainees is a frequent selection device. The tests can be group-administered, computer-scored, and easily interpreted. But do they have any validity?

The MMPI and the CPI General personality measures such as the Minnesota Multiphasic Personality Inventory (MMPI) (Hathaway & McKinley, 1983) and the California Psychological Inventory (CPI) (Gough, 1975) are staples of such testing. The **Minnesota Multiphasic Personality Inventory** was originally designed, in the early 1940s, to identify persons with psychotic or neurotic problems. As Blau (1994) observed, it has become the workhorse of paper-and-pencil personality assessment for more than half a century. It consists of 550 true-or-false items and usually takes an hour to complete. In the late 1980s, the MMPI-2 was developed out of a need to update and restandardize the original instrument (Butcher, Dahlstrom, Graham, Tellegen, & Kaemmer, 1989). Whether the MMPI-2 was an improvement over the original MMPI has generated much discussion (see Blau, 1994, p. 83). One study that administered both scales to 166 police officers found that 70 percent of them produced normal profiles on both tests (Hargrave, Hiatt, Ogard, & Karr, 1993). But individual respondents did not always score the highest on the same subscale from one form of the test to the other.

The **California Psychological Inventory** is similar in format to the MMPI, but its subscales reflect personal traits such as dominance, sociability, and flexibility, in contrast to the diagnostic categories (e.g., Psychopathic Deviate, Hypomania) of the MMPI. A survey of 72 major law-enforcement agencies (Strawbridge & Strawbridge, 1990) found that the MMPI was by far the most frequently used instrument—in 33, or 46 percent, of the departments. Next most frequent were the CPI (in 11 of 72 departments) and the Inwald Personality Inventory (used in five departments), which we'll discuss below. The Rorschach Inkblot Technique was used by two departments, and two used a human figure drawings test. Thirty-seven (or 51 percent) of the departments used no test at all. Because this survey is more than ten years old, it is likely that the percentage of departments using tests has increased, as more departments have sought accreditation by the Commission on Accreditation for Law Enforcement Agencies (CALEA) (Blau, 1994). This organization has given accreditation to several Canadian police services, including those in Camrose, Edmonton, and Lethbridge, Alberta; Brandon and Winnipeg, Manitoba; and Brantford, Ontario. Other Canadian agencies (e.g., Alberta Transportation and Inspection Services) have also been accredited by CALEA (CALEA, 2004).

Reviewing the use of psychological tests in police selection, Hargrave and Hiatt (1987) reported studies finding significant relationships between MMPI scales and police officers' job tenure, automobile accidents, supervisors' ratings, and job problems. Although the CPI has been used less often, scale scores were related to trainees' academy performance and to supervisors' ratings. (Specific studies cited are listed in Hargrave and Hiatt, 1987, p. 110, and Bartol, 1991, p. 127). In a more recent review, Bartol (1991) was less sanguine, describing the track record of the MMPI in screening and selection of law-enforcement personnel as "mixed." But despite its limitations, Bartol (1991) concluded that the MMPI continues to be the most commonly used personality measure for the selection of police.

In the study of trainees described earlier that evaluated the predictive validity of the clinical interview, Hargrave and Hiatt also administered the MMPI and CPI to 105 police trainees on their first day of training. The clinicians then interpreted each trainee's scores to classify his or her suitability. These ratings were compared with the same criteria as the interview data, with these results:

	Clinician A	*Clinician B*
Academic attrition	.24**	.15
Instructors' ratings	.25**	.27*
Peer evaluations	.36*	.13*
Composite criterion	.34**	.24**

*p < .05
**p < .01

Clinician A correctly classified 66 percent of the trainees; Clinician B 67 percent. These latter predictions were not different from those by the interview data, although the correlations between test results and individual criteria are somewhat higher than the interview. Again, the results are not strong enough to make decisions about individual applicants.

Although some of these correlations are significant, once more, the relationships are not impressive. In a follow-up study, Hargrave and Hiatt (1989) tested 579 trainees with the CPI and found that CPI profiles distinguished between those suitable and unsuitable for training. These authors concluded that CPI profiles have a more consistent relationship with job performance by police than with police academy variables. In general, the higher-rated police officers scored higher on the measures from the so-called Class II and Class III on the CPI (Class II consists of measures of socialization, responsibility, intrapersonal values, and character; Class III consists of measures of achievement potential). The other two classes of variables on the CPI showed no replicated relationship with police performance; these are Class I (measures of poise, ascendancy, self-assurance, and interpersonal adequacy) and Class IV (measures of intellectual and interest modes).

A second approach by Hargrave and Hiatt (1989) capitalized on the evaluations given to police on the job. A total of 45 officers from three municipal law-enforcement agencies, all of whom had experienced serious job problems, were compared with 45 matched controls who had not received disciplinary notices for serious job problems. (The groups were matched on gender, race, education, and length of employment; their average age was 27 years and most had some college and had been on the job three years.) The kinds of job-related difficulties experienced by the problem group included providing drugs to prisoners, conviction for use of illegal drugs, unnecessary use of force, physical confrontations with other officers, and violations of departmental procedures that resulted in the escape of prisoners. All these police had taken the CPI as part of the job-selection process. Only on

the CPI Class II scales were there significant differences between the two groups; recall that Class II measures maturity, personal values, self-control, and sense of responsibility. Individuals who score higher on the scales in Class II are seen as careful, cautious, controlled, and as having a sense of duty and a reluctance to take risks. Those scoring low (less than 40) are more carefree, but also are opportunistic risk takers.

The non–problem group scored higher on the CPI scales of So (Socialization), Sc (Self-Control), and Wb (Sense of Well-Being). Compared to non–problem officers, there were four times as many problem officers with scale scores at or below a T score of 40 (meaning they scored at least one standard deviation under the mean). Thus, it appears that qualities of impulsivity, risk taking, easy boredom, lack of objectivity, and willingness to break rules contribute to problems among officers (Hargrave & Hiatt, 1989).

These researchers (Hargrave & Hiatt, 1987) used a similar procedure to assess the predictive validity of the MMPI. They followed 55 urban police officers who had received at least one performance evaluation. Those rated as unsatisfactory scored significantly higher on two MMPI scales: Pa (Paranoia) and Ma (Hypomania). Building on this procedure, Bartol (1991) followed 600 police officers from 34 small-town police departments over a 13-year period to determine which officers were terminated. He concluded that an **immaturity index** consisting of a combination of the MMPI scales of Pd (Psychopathic Deviate), Ma (Hypomania), and the L Scale (discussed below) was a strong predictor of termination.

Bartol suggested that an immaturity index cutoff score of 49 (combination of the Pd and Ma scores plus the L score) is "*suggestive* of possible problems" (1991, p. 131, italics in original), especially if the Ma scale is highly elevated. Of the terminated officers, 70 percent received immaturity scores of 49 or above, compared with 23 percent of the retained group. (If an immaturity score of 54 was used as the cutoff, 53 percent of the terminated group would be correctly identified, contrasted with 95 percent of the retained group.)

It should be noted that the typical interpretation given a high Ma score on the MMPI is consistent with a low score on the CPI Class II—impulsive, moody, and having a low frustration tolerance. Bartol wrote: "Police administrators and peers of high Ma officers often describe them as hyperactive individuals who seek constant activity" (1991, p. 131). One terminated police officer reportedly had developed the off-duty habit of locating speed traps and then driving by at a high speed to test other officers' alertness and effectiveness in high-speed chases (Bartol, 1991).

Bartol concluded that the Pd scale from the MMPI, by itself, had limited predictive power; it was more useful when combined with a high Ma score. In general, this combination—in MMPI lingo, a 4-9 code—in individuals reflects "a marked disregard for social standards and values. They frequently get into trouble with the authorities because of antisocial behaviour" (Graham, 1987, p. 109).

The 4-9 code had appreciable predictive power for Bartol's sample only when merged with the **L Scale**. When the MMPI was originally developed, the purpose of the L Scale was to detect a deliberate and unsophisticated attempt on the part of respondents to present themselves in a favourable light (Graham, 1987). (Items scored on the L Scale include the test taker portraying him- or herself as someone who does things such as "read every editorial in the newspaper every day," which most people would like to say they do but in all honesty cannot say they do.) Bartol (1991) noted that "police administrators continually report that high-L-scoring police officers demonstrate poor judgment in the field, particularly under high levels of stress. They seem to be unable to exercise quick, independent, and appropriate decision making under emergency or crisis conditions. They become confused and disorganized" (1991, p. 131). Based on 15 years of working with police supervisors, Bartol considered an L score above 8

(out of 15 items) to be one of the best predictors of poor performance as a police officer. However, he has offered a titillating addition: "More recently, we have also discovered that extremely low L Scale scores (0 or 1) also forecast poor performance, suggesting that the L Scale may be curvilinear in its predictive power" (1991, p. 131).

The Inwald Personality Inventory The MMPI and the CPI are, of course, general instruments. In contrast, the **Inwald Personality Inventory** (IPI) was developed for a more specific and limited purpose: to measure the suitability of personality attributes and behaviour patterns of law-enforcement candidates (Inwald, 1992; Inwald, Knatz, & Shusman, 1983). This instrument is a 310-item, true–false questionnaire consisting of 26 scales (25 original scales and one validity scale) designed to measure, among other matters, stress reactions and deviant behaviour patterns, including absence and lateness problems, interpersonal difficulties, antisocial behaviour, and alcohol and drug use. Suspicious, anxious, and rigid characteristics are also measured by IPI subscales. This test usually takes about 45 minutes to complete.

Another significant difference between the IPI and the MMPI and CPI is that the IPI was developed "with the express purpose of directly questioning public safety/law enforcement candidates and documenting their admitted behaviours, rather than inferring those behaviours from statistically derived personality indicators" (Inwald, 1992, p. 4). As Blau (1994) has noted, it is essentially a "screening out" test that seeks to assess antisocial behaviour and emotional maladjustments that might adversely affect police performance.

The IPI items measure both personality characteristics and behaviour patterns. The scales contain statements that assess both the unusual types of behaviour patterns that reflect severe problems and those that reflect less extreme adjustment difficulties. They are designed to identify, for example, "a highly guarded but naive individual as having hyperactive or antisocial tendencies based strictly on behavioural admissions" (Inwald, 1992, p. 3). The scales also have a goal of differentiating between individuals who express socially deviant attitudes and those who act on them (Inwald, 1992).

The Inwald Personality Inventory contains a validity scale (Guardedness) somewhat similar to some of the validity scales on other inventories. But in contrast to the MMPI L Scale, the 19 statements on the Guardedness scale contain minor shortcomings common to almost all people. Inwald notes: "When a candidate denies such items, a strong need to appear unusually virtuous is indicated" (1992, p. 4).

The IPI items were developed by Inwald after reviewing more than 2500 pre-employment interviews with candidates for law-enforcement positions. Not only did the emerging characteristics include qualities related to effective police functioning, but they also included self-revealing statements made by applicants during actual interviews.

A factor analysis (Inwald, 1992) of the IPI scales, using 2397 male and 147 female police officer candidates, to determine what is common to the responses to different items, found the following:

- Factor 1, for both sexes, measured rigid, suspicious, and antisocial behaviours. It included Rigid Type, Undue Suspiciousness, and Antisocial Attitudes.

- For the males, Factor 2 was composed of two scales, Substance Abuse and Hyperactivity, reflecting risk taking and impulsive behaviour. For the female sample, Alcohol and Depression scales also contributed to this factor.

- For the third factor, even greater sex differences emerged; for the men, Phobic Personality, Lack of Assertiveness, Depression, and Loner Type scales loaded on the factor, but for females, these were replaced with Job Difficulties and Absence Abuse.

An early effort to validate the IPI compared it to the MMPI in a study of 716 male correc-tional officer recruits; criterion measures included job retention or termination, absence, lateness, and disciplinary measures in the first ten months of service (Shusman, Inwald, & Landa, 1984). This study concluded that for most criteria, the IPI scales predicted the status of officers more often than did the MMPI scales and that the combination of IPI and MMPI scales increased accuracy of classification. The improved performance when the two scales are used together is a consistent conclusion of the validation studies reported in the test manual (Inwald, 1992), along with the relative strength of the IPI over the MMPI (Scogin, Schumacher, Howland, & McGee, 1989).

Further validation studies (Inwald & Shusman, 1984; Shusman & Inwald, 1991a) used 329 police recruits and 246 correctional officers; again, it was concluded that more IPI than MMPI scales discriminated successfully. For example, the IPI yielded 82 percent correct classifications for absences, whereas the MMPI produced 69 percent correct classifications. The two scales, when combined, increased the accuracy rate to 85 percent. Especially useful as predictors of problematic behaviour were IPI scales measuring trouble with the law, previous job difficulties, and involvement with drugs.

Another kind of study (Shusman, Inwald, & Knatz, 1987), a cross-validation, studied 698 male police officers who completed six months of training in the police academy. In the validation sample ($N = 421$), the IPI scales assigned from 61 percent to 77 percent of the officers into correct group membership, based on eight performance criteria, whereas the MMPI scales identified only between 50 percent and 70 percent. In the cross-validation sample, slightly more shrinkage (i.e., a lower rate of correct classifications) was observed for the IPI than for the MMPI in regard to most of the criteria. But even with this somewhat greater degree of shrinkage, the cross-validation classification rates for the IPI were equal to or greater than the original validation percentages from the MMPI alone for all but one of the eight criteria.

Several of the IPI items ask for admissions of behaviours that are, at the least, socially unacceptable, and often are violations of laws. Would applicants for positions in law enforcement readily admit to such behaviours? A clever study by Ostrov (1985) provided a provocative answer.

Two groups of approximately 200 applicants each were screened by the Chicago Police Department, using the IPI. Each candidate was also asked to provide a urine sample for analysis of drug use. In the first sample, 43 candidates had positive urinalysis results; in the second sample, 34 did. These subgroups were found to differ from random samples of the other candidates (i.e., those with a negative urinalysis) on several of the Drug Scale items (significant differences on three items for Sample 1 and five items for Sample 2). The particular items referred to both marijuana and hard drug use.

Despite some impressive validation findings, the reliability of the IPI scales is not always strong. Inwald (1992) has reported Cronbach alpha coefficients (measures of internal consistency) of .41 to .82 for male police officer candidates and .32 to .80 for female candidates. An effort to combine the original 26 scales into 12 lengthier scales in order to increase reliability was not successful in any meaningful degree (Shusman & Inwald, 1991b).

Situational Tests

A third approach to screening potential law-enforcement officers uses **situational tests**, that is, placing the testee in a simulated police situation to evoke samples of the behaviour he or she will show on the job. One example of such testing is the work of Dunnette and Motowidlo (1976), who sought to define the critical dimensions of job performance for each of four police jobs: (1) general patrol officer, (2) patrol sergeant, (3) detective (investigator), and (4) intermediate-level commander. Finding little in the way of assessing these specific dimensions when they began their work in the early 1970s, they designed a series of simulations and standardized situational tasks, such as role-playing exercises on

behaviours believed to be representative of critical police tasks. They used these tools to assess how the recruits would respond to activities that form the criteria for effective police work. For instance, they asked recruits to intervene in a dispute between a husband and wife, to carry out a burglary investigation, and to aid a man injured at a hotel. Selection of candidates for police training was based on performance on these and other kinds of tasks.

On other occasions, situational tests have been used in police selection. One example is the work of Mills, McDevitt, and Tonkin (1966), who administered three tests intended to simulate police abilities to a group of Cincinnati police candidates. The Foot Patrol Observation Test required candidates to walk a six-block downtown route and then answer questions about what they remembered having just observed. In the Clues Test, candidates were given ten minutes to investigate a set of planted clues about the disappearance of a hypothetical city worker from his office. They were observed as they performed this task and were graded on the information they assembled. The Bull Session was a two-hour group discussion of several topics of importance in police work.

Performance on the Clues Test correlated significantly with class ranking in the police academy, but the scores from the Foot Patrol Observation test did not. Although independent grades for the Bull Session measure were not derived, it was viewed as an important measure of emotional and motivational qualities. Additionally, Mills and colleagues (1966) discovered that the Clues Test was not correlated with intelligence—indicating the advantage of including a measure of nonintellectual abilities in a selection battery.

Despite the fact that situational tests have an intuitive appeal as selection devices, they have not proven to be superior to the personality tests (MMPI, CPI, and IPI) as predictors of performance. Because they are time-consuming and expensive, they are used mainly to supplement psychological tests.

THE TRAINING OF POLICE

All law-enforcement agencies have some form of training programs for their recruits. What roles do psychologists play in such training programs, and what does our clientele want from psychologists in this regard?

A forensic psychologist with training in organizational psychology can evaluate a police training program to see whether it is consistent with the responsibilities and responses of police as they carry out their tasks. The typical training program has been criticized for emphasizing "narrowly defined aspects of the job dealing with criminal activity, understanding relevant laws, effective firearms training, self-defense, and other survival techniques" (Stratton, 1980, p. 38). Although these skills are important, psychologists are urging departments to include in training the strategies necessary for coping with job-related stress and other interpersonal and communication skills. Police department administrators have become increasingly aware that police need to have human-relations skills, including awareness of diversity and ability to communicate effectively.

The Psychologist's Activities in a Police Department

In Canada, some police forces have a full-time psychologist on the force. However, it is more common for psychologists to be consulted by police on an "as needed" basis. For example, Dr. Mike Webster, a former RCMP officer, is a well-known psychologist in private practice in B.C., who deals almost exclusively with law-enforcement agencies, including the RCMP and the FBI (Webster, 2004). He teaches at the British Columbia Police Academy, the Canadian Police College, and the FBI Training Academy. The Law Enforcement Behavioural Sciences Association (LEBSA), formed by a group of psychologists who work with police, and a section of Division 18 of the American Psychological Association (Division of Psychologists in Public Service), called the Police Psychology Section, were developed to address the concerns of police psychologists. These organizations sponsor presentations and workshops at national conventions and share procedures, experiences, and data with each other.

Martin Reiser was the first full-time police psychologist, beginning his service as department psychologist with the Los Angeles Police Department in 1968. He has observed that psychologists are usually asked to participate in police training programs in two ways: as teachers and as consultants (Reiser, 1972). As teachers they may be asked to instruct recruits on handling mentally ill persons, human relations, criminal psychology, and relationships with authority figures, among other topics. As a consultant, "the psychologist is expected to have some practical know how and expertise about educational processes, teaching techniques, learning systems, and technology" (Reiser, 1972, p. 33).

Psychologists serving as consultants to police departments are generally available and on call to anyone in the department. Requests might include the following:

- The police chief wants a survey of pursuits and shootings.
- A sergeant asks for help in developing a psychologically based program of driver training to reduce police-involved accidents.
- Homicide detectives may want consultation on a bizarre murder.
- A particular officer may need psychological counselling (Reiser, 1982b).

Psychologists acting as consultants to police departments need to be flexible and adaptable; they must modify their frame of reference in order to accommodate the variety of service requests (Reiser, 1982a, 1982b). One of the central problems for the psychologist-consultant is that of identification; is the psychologist a mental health specialist, a social change agent, an organizational staff specialist, or an employee in a hierarchy? Reiser (1982b) has proposed that the level of the organization at which the consultant "gets plugged in" will determine how he or she is seen by other members of the organization, particularly by those in power.

Traditionally, police officers have been wary, if not downright antagonistic, toward psychologists. They likely have come in contact with a psychologist or another mental health professional in one of several ways that inhibit the development of their respect for the psychological profession. White and Honig described these interactions as follows:

1. Watching "do-gooder" psychologists testify on behalf of criminals.
2. Observing psychologists seem to protect police officers who are claiming a disability but are perceived by their fellow officers as weak or abusing the system.
3. Viewing psychologists as the "enemy" who has the power to keep an officer or potential officer off the force through the psychologist's role in police selection or fitness-for-duty evaluations.

Negative perceptions of police psychologists may be somewhat lessened if they have a policing background (such as former police officer Dr. Mike Webster in B.C.). However, an initial task for all police psychologists is to listen and learn. He or she should seek to understand the culture of the police department by participating in **ride-alongs** (in which the psychologist accompanies the officer on patrol), asking questions, and in all ways understanding the world of law enforcement rather than "gathering ammunition to change it" (White & Honig, 1995, p. 259). Police administrators may fear that the psychologist has magical powers and that the consultant may somehow usurp the administrator's control or brainwash the police administrator in some way. Reiser (1982b) has emphasized that the personal attributes of the consultant—being pragmatic, showing adaptability—are crucial for success; what a psychologist is able to achieve is "a function of role expectations of the organization, plus what the individual consultant brings to the situation in the form of his [or her] personal attributes" (p. 28).

Each of these responsibilities may have many manifestations. Like many organizations, police departments are susceptible to adopting innovative and unique programs, partly because they are new and different. Often such programs do not receive an adequate internal evaluation, if any evaluation at all. Psychologists can play a useful role in evaluating the effectiveness of such innovations, whether they are team policing, sensitivity training, or community orientation sessions.

The Curriculum of Training Programs

A new police chief may ask a psychologist to design a training program for recruits. Central questions the psychologist should ask are, What do police do? What do they need to know and be able to do? Studies of policing have consistently found that the police role is to provide services and keep peace rather than attend to crime-related activities (Meadows, 1987). Yet, the training the police get may be inconsistent with their subsequent duties. Germann (1969) has noted that most entry-level police training is devoted to "crook-catching"—as much as 90 percent of the training time—although they spend only 10 percent to 15 percent of their time on these activities. The RCMP seems to be recognizing this traditional problem and focusing more on the realities of police work in their training. For about 120 years, RCMP recruits have been trained at the "depot" in Regina, Saskatchewan. Their current training methodologies emphasize problem-solving exercises, knowledge of the law, cultural diversity and sensitivity, role plays, performance demonstration, lectures, panel discussions, research discussions, and community interaction. The RCMP's training agenda appears to approach the recommendations of the National Advisory Commission on Criminal Justice Standards and Goals (1973, p. 392), who suggested a training program organized around the following six subject areas:

1. *Introduction to the criminal justice system.* An examination of the foundation and functions of the criminal justice system with specific

attention to the role of the police in the system and government.

2. *Law.* An introduction to the development, philosophy, and types of law; criminal law; criminal procedure and rules of evidence; discretionary justice; application of federal legislation; court systems and procedures; and related civil law.

3. *Human values and problems.* Public service and noncriminal policing; cultural awareness; changing roles of the police; human behaviour and conflict management; psychology as it relates to the police function; causes of crime and delinquency; and police–public relations.

4. *Patrol and investigation procedures.* The fundamentals of the patrol function including traffic, juvenile, and preliminary investigation; reporting and communication; arrest and detention procedures; interviewing; criminal investigation and case preparation; equipment and facility use; and other day-to-day responsibilities and duties.

5. *Police proficiency.* The philosophy of when to use force and the appropriate determination of the degree necessary; armed and unarmed defence; crowd, riot, and prisoner control;

physical conditioning, emergency medical services; and driver training.

6. *Administration.* Evaluation, examination, and counselling processes; department policies, rules, regulations, organization, and personnel problems.

The commission recommended a distribution of training time as indicated in Box 3.2. Meadows (1987) surveyed 234 police chiefs and 355 criminal justice educators as to the importance of training in each of these categories. Both groups felt a need for increased training in the law and in written and oral communication, implying that police officers may not be doing a good job of communicating with the public.

On-the-Job Training

Once the police officer is credentialed and is on the job, the need for training does not end. A chapter by White and Honig (1995) on the role of the police psychologist in training activities divided on-the-job training into three categories: wellness training, training that provides information or skills, and training that relates the individual to the organization. Each is described in

---

BOX 3.2
Criminal Justice Standards and Goals
Commission Recommended Distribution of Training Time by Percent by Area

Subject Area	Recommended Percentage of Training Time
Introduction to the Criminal Justice System	8%
Law	10
Human Values and Problems	22
Patrol and Investigation Procedures	33
Police Proficiency	18
Administration	9
TOTAL	100%

(From *Report on Police*, by the National Advisory Commission on Criminal Justice Standards and Goals, 1973, p. 394.)

Box 3.3. In addition, police officers may need training in specialized activities; two types are described in the following sections.

Specialized Training: Responses to Spouse Assault

As we explore further in Chapter 10, research in Canada indicates that nearly a third of ever-married women report that they have been subjected to violence (pushed, grabbed, shoved, slapped, sexually assaulted, hit with an object, or had a gun or knife used against them) by their partner (Statistics Canada, 1998). However, very few incidents of domestic violence ever get reported to the police (Schulman, 1979; Straus, & Gelles, 1986); one reason is that victims do not expect police to be sympathetic or helpful.

These expectations are at least sometimes realistic. Levens and Dutton (1980) found that Canadian police had negative attitudes toward intervening in domestic disputes. In 1979, the Oakland, California, Police Department's training bulletin instructed police that a man should not be arrested for wife assault because he would "lose face" (Paterson, 1979, cited by Jaffe, Hastings, Reitzel, & Austin, 1993). Training of police by psychologists conceivably can improve

---

BOX 3.3
Types of On-the-Job Training for Law-Enforcement Officers

WELLNESS TRAINING

White and Honig stated that the goal of **wellness training** "is assisting the police officer toward improving his or her lifestyle through learning new, health-enhancing behaviours and ideas. Wellness training is based on the concept that how an individual manages his or her life, and the accompanying stressors, will have a significant impact on job performance" (1995, p. 260).

Job stress is recognized as a major problem for law-enforcement officers, and **burnout** may be the result. Training that deals with these issues must take into account the police culture that emphasizes the illusion of invulnerability, the suppression of emotion, and the emphasis on mental and physical toughness (Hogan, 1971; Reiser, 1974). Among the specific topics, in addition to stress management, that are a part of wellness training, are the following:

- *Alcohol and drug abuse.* A tradition in law enforcement is drinking with fellow officers after a shift, often known as "choir practice" (White & Honig, 1995).
- *Relationship with one's spouse.* The literature suggests that police, compared to most other occupational groups, have great difficulties in marital relationships (Kroes, Margolis, & Hurrell, 1974; Singleton & Teahan, 1978).
- *Surviving critical incidents.* It is estimated that 60 to 70 percent of law-enforcement officers leave the force within five years of an episode in which a fellow officer, witness, or suspect is killed or the officer is seriously injured (Reese, Horn, & Dunning, 1991; Simpson, Jensen, & Owen, 1988).

INFORMATIONAL AND SKILL TRAINING

This type of continuing education assists police officers in performing their job duties. All the special topics listed below reflect human-behaviour issues and can benefit from the participation of psychologists.

- Managing persons with mental illness.
- Cross-cultural awareness.
- Improvement of communication skills.
- Working with victims of rape and sexual assault.

Two kinds of specialized topics, responses to spouse assault and negotiating with hostage takers, are considered in this chapter.

ORGANIZATIONAL TRAINING

The goal of organizational-training procedures is to improve the functioning of the organization as a whole; it is especially useful for officers in supervisory and management roles (White & Honig, 1995). For example, like any organization, police departments may face questions of sexual harassment, grief management, racial discrimination, and substance abuse.

how police respond and eventually whether victims choose to call for help. The renowned work by Donald Dutton and his colleagues (Dutton, 1981, 1988; Dutton & Levens, 1977) at the University of British Columbia found that training significantly increased the use by police of mediation and referral techniques.

One review (Jaffe, Hastings, Reitzel, & Austin, 1993) has suggested that training programs for police should include information on the "social costs of wife assault, statistics on prevalence, information on why victims stay or return, and descriptions of local services" (p. 89). The review also suggested that a manual of resources for victims of domestic violence be available to police and that officers carry business cards printed with the phone numbers of 24-hour hotlines or shelters.

Negotiating with Terrorists and Hostage Takers

As September 11, 2001, made shockingly clear, terrorism is now a part of modern industrialized society; every time we go through a metal detector at an airport, we may be reminded of the possibility. Psychologists and other social scientists are beginning to study the phenomenon systematically (Crenshaw, 1986; Friedland & Merari, 1985). As the first line of response, police and other public-safety agencies play a central role (Greenstone, 1995b).

Another serious concern that has become almost commonplace is the taking of hostages. Law-enforcement officers must choose whether to negotiate with the hostage taker or to use force to protect and free the hostages. An example of this occurred recently with the longest hostage situation in Nova Scotia's history. A three-day-long armed standoff, which began on May 19, 2004, in Halifax, finally ended when a couple left a barricaded home with their five-month-old daughter and a deceased elderly woman (the man's mother) and were arrested by police. Larry Finck and Carline VandenElsen left the house without warning and crossed the street carrying the body of the elderly woman on a makeshift stretcher (she had died of natural causes). Several shots were fired from the home by Mr. Finck on the first day of the standoff, but no one was hurt. The standoff had started after Finck refused to hand over his daughter to the Children's Aid Society. Police cordoned off the street and began negotiations with the aid of a local psychologist. The police in this case had made the difficult decision not to use force but to wait things out, thankfully with a peaceful conclusion.

Negotiation with terrorists and hostage takers has become a well-established concept and receives great emphasis in policing throughout North America (Webster, 2004). A survey of 34 police departments found that 31 (91 percent) had a designated negotiation team (Fuselier, 1988). Training courses on hostage negotiation often recommend consultation with a clinical psychologist (Fuselier, 1988). What can the field of psychology offer?

Who Takes Hostages?

Four basic types of **hostage taker** are differentiated in the law-enforcement and clinical literature: the political activist or terrorist, the criminal, the mentally disturbed person, and the prisoner. Hassel (1975, cited by Fuselier, 1988) concluded that the most frequent type of hostage taker is the criminal trapped while committing a crime, and Stratton (1978) has identified political terrorists as the most difficult to negotiate with because of their "total commitment, exhaustive planning, and ability to exert power effectively" (p. 7). Maher (1977) considered the mentally disturbed hostage taker the greatest threat. These contradicting conclusions reflect, for Fuselier (1988), the need for a "systematic nationwide collection or compilation ... of information on hostage incidents" (pp. 175–176) by law-enforcement agencies.

Recently, psychopathy has emerged as an important psychological condition in understanding some hostage takings. Canadian researcher Dr. Hugues Hervé and colleagues (Hervé, Mitchell, et al., 2004) found that among

1200 Canadian federal offenders housed in the Pacific region between the 1960s and 1998, 11.3 percent had committed acts of unlawful confinement. Approximately half of these perpetrators were psychopaths, and the sample scored significantly higher on the PCL-R (Hare Psychopathy Checklist-Revised) than offenders in the general prison population.

Why Do People Take Hostages?

Fuselier (1988) suggested causes why political terrorists take hostages: to demonstrate to the public the inability of a government to protect its own citizens, to ensure increased publicity for their political agenda, to create civil discontent indirectly by causing the government to overreact and restrict its citizens, and to demand release of members of their groups who are in custody.

These reflect planned activities; in contrast, the criminal may spontaneously take a hostage when his or her own freedom is jeopardized, thus reflecting a need for safe passage or a means to escape. Mentally disturbed people take hostages for a variety of reasons, though each stems from the hostage taker's own view of the world. Inmates usually use hostages to protest conditions within the prison.

The Role of the Forensic Psychologist

Does the psychologist have something valuable to offer when hostages are taken? The answer seems to be a qualified yes. Police who are well trained in the procedures of hostage negotiations are more likely to bring about a successful resolution of the incident (Borum, 1988a). Success in such situations is usually defined as "a resolution in which there is no loss of life to any of those involved in the incident including police, hostage taker, and hostages" (Greenstone, 1995b, p. 358). Psychological considerations are central in evaluating progress in the negotiations. For example, Greenstone (1995b) suggested that if the hostage taker is talking more, is more willing to talk about his or her personal life, and reflects less violence in his or her conversation, progress is being achieved. Further, McMains (1988) identified

three roles: the professional, who is a source of applicable behavioural science information; the consultant, who develops training programs, materials, and exercises; and the participant-observer, who makes suggestions but recognizes the authority of the law-enforcement personnel.

Experts are not in agreement, however, and several perspectives can be identified:

1. Powitsky (1979) argued that psychologists might perform some relevant duties, such as gathering information to be used in the negotiating strategy, but "the majority of practicing psychologists, especially those who work outside of the criminal justice system, would not be very helpful (and some would be harmful) in a hostage-taking situation" (p. 30).

2. Poythress (1980), who described himself as a "guarded optimist," has offered that "mental health professionals may have something to offer in the hostage situation, but probably less than the field commanders might hope for" (p. 34). He listed three reasons why the responsible police officer should not enlist a psychologist's opinion on the decision to negotiate rather than attack:

   ■ Psychologists have little formal training on this topic, little research has been done, and few psychologists have had much field experience on it. In the two decades since Poythress wrote this, a modest beginning has occurred in providing assistance to negotiations (e.g., Fowler, De Vivo, & Fowler, 1985; Soskis, 1983; and Yonah & Gleason, 1981). The FBI's training academy at Quantico, Virginia, has developed a 30-hour Basic Hostage Negotiations training module (Greenstone, 1995a).

   ■ Predictors of the probable dangerousness of a given person in a given situation are notoriously bad (Poythress, 1980).

   ■ As Meehl (1954) showed many years ago, statistical (i.e., actuarial) methods are more accurate than clinical judgment in general predictions of outcome.

3. More positive in his view was Reiser (1982a, 1982b), who saw the psychologist contributing as a backup and adviser to the negotiation team, as well as providing training on the topics of assessment of the hostage taker's motives and personality, the development of communication skills, and the challenge of dealing with stress and fatigue.

4. Fuselier (1988), author of a useful review, has accepted the value of psychologists as consultants, but only after they have received training in hostage negotiation concepts. After attendance at a hostage negotiation seminar, the psychologist "can assist in both determining whether a mental disorder exists and deciding on a particular negotiation approach" (p. 177). But he believes that a psychologist should not be used as the **primary negotiator**; instead, being a consultant allows the psychologist "to maintain a more objective role in assessing the mental status and performance of the negotiator" (1988, p. 177).

Psychologists, if not primary negotiators, can then play a role in offering a post-incident critique of the team, as well as counselling the police and victims. The effects on police of participation in a hostage negotiation may be similar to those resulting from other stressful situations: anxiety, somatic responses, and a subjective sense of work overload (Beutler, Nussbaum, & Meredith, 1988; Dietrich & Smith, 1986; Zizzo, 1985).

The Psychologist as Evaluation Researcher

Another role for the psychologist with respect to hostage negotiations is as an evaluation researcher. What works and what doesn't work? Allen, Cutler, and Berman (1993) collected the types of responses used by the police tactical teams to all 130 situations reflecting hostage taking or suicide attempts for five years. They focused on the 48 of these cases in which some form of negotiation was used. Face-to-face negotiation (compared to use of a bullhorn, a public address system, or a telephone) was the least effective method of apprehending the hostage taker. Face-to-face

negotiation is often seen as a "last resort." The analysis also indicated that hostage takers under the influence of drugs were much less likely to come out without violence.

EVALUATING EFFECTIVENESS OF POLICE ACTIVITIES

Many evaluations of police activities and innovations in police policies are carried out by persons not trained in the methodology of psychology and the social sciences, but psychologists can play a major role in the evaluation of police activities. Two examples are provided here: one at the level of the individual police officer (the fitness-for-duty evaluation) and the other at the level of general policy innovation (community policing).

Fitness-for-Duty Evaluations

After participating in critical incidents involving the death of a partner or an injury during a chase or shootout, the law-enforcement officer may display emotional or behavioural reactions such that a **fitness-for-duty evaluation** is requested by his or her supervisor (Inwald, 1990). Complaints against the officer, such as charges of brutality, may also lead to an investigation of the officer's emotional stability. A psychologist may be called on to conduct the evaluation (Delprino & Bahn, 1988). Robin Inwald (1990) has offered a set of guidelines for such evaluations; these include the following:

1. They shall be done only by qualified psychologists or psychiatrists who are licensed in that region.

2. The evaluator should be familiar with research on testing and evaluation in the field of police psychology.

3. As far as possible, the evaluation should *not* be done by a psychologist or psychiatrist who provides counselling within the same department.

4. Issues of confidentiality should be made explicit in writing prior to conducting the fitness-for-duty evaluation, and a consent form should be obtained from the officer.

5. The fitness-for-duty assessment should include at least one interview with the officer, a battery of psychological tests, interviews with supervisors, family members, and co-workers, and a review of any past psychological and medical evaluations.

6. The fitness-for-duty evaluator should provide a written report documenting the findings of the evaluation along with specific recommendations regarding continued employment and rehabilitation. (Two examples of such reports may be found in Blau, 1994, pp. 134–138 and pp. 140–142.)

Community Policing

The decades of the 1970s and 1980s saw increases in drug usage and related crime, along with the continued decay of many inner cities. Like other concerned institutions, law-enforcement agencies sought new ways to deal with these problems. The concept of **community policing** was developed as a response. As the name implies, its goal was to reunite the police with the community (Peak & Glensor, 1996). One definition is that community policing is "an extension of the police–community relations concept which envisions an effective working partnership between the police and members of the community in order to solve problems which concern both" (Schmalleger, 1995, p. 200). In community policing, the police department focuses on improving the quality of life and being responsive (even proactively) to citizens' concerns. For example, residents of a neighbourhood are outraged at the intrusion of "crack houses" on their streets and drug traffickers in the public parks. A community-policing program might respond to this concern by frequently patrolling the parks and establishing surveillance of the "crack houses."

However, community policing has been implemented in different ways in different regions (Skolnik & Bayley, 1986). The RCMP provides community-policing services to all provinces and territories except Ontario and Quebec. The manner in which their services are delivered is based on the individual community's policing philosophy. The RCMP rightfully states that this approach helps to identify the particular social needs of the communities who play a major role in the recognition, development, and determination of their own policing needs. In San Francisco, where police adopted a community policing strategy, officers began riding on city buses; in other cities, police began athletic programs for young people in high-crime areas, established bicycle patrols or re-established foot patrols, or developed neighbourhood police stations.

Anecdotal evidence for the effectiveness of these programs was encouraging, but a more reliable evaluation was more difficult to do. Often communities would establish several changes at once and hence not be able to evaluate the separate impact of each. It was unclear just what was the goal of the change—a quicker response by the police to crimes, reduction of crime rates, higher clearance rates (i.e., the percentage of crimes for which an arrest or a conviction is made) for crimes that were committed, or greater community satisfaction with the police and reduced fear of crime. Some citizens remain suspicious of the police and are not willing to accept a more visible presence of the police in their neighbourhood (Schmalleger, 1995). Also, some police are more comfortable with traditional law-enforcement duties rather than community relations (Sparrow, Moore, & Kennedy, 1990). The forensic psychologist as an evaluation researcher can aid the police department in designing interventions that permit clearer tests of their effectiveness. The evaluation researcher can also clarify what the important outcome measures are—how the community weighs the importance of crime control, citizen satisfaction, or job satisfaction of police.

SUMMARY

Forensic psychologists can contribute to many aspects of police work: to the selecting of candidates for training, to the pre-service and on-the-job training of officers, to the evaluation of the performance of individual officers, and to the creation and evaluation of innovative programs by law-enforcement agencies. In doing so, forensic psychologists have the difficult task of being responsive to the police department as a client, but also recognizing public concerns about police corruption, racism, and brutality.

The selection of candidates for law-enforcement training is usually an involved and extensive process. The psychologist often plays a role in interviewing candidates and in advising the department about instruments to administer to candidates. Among these, the Minnesota Multiphasic Personality Inventory is the most widely used, but the Inwald Personality Inventory is worthy of consideration, as it was designed specifically for selection of law-enforcement officers. The RPAT written examination used in RCMP selection examines a number of psychological competencies including memory and language.

There are both general and specific topics for which psychologists can contribute to the in-service training of police officers. Wellness training is of special importance, given the high rates of stress and resulting alcoholism, burnout, and marital discord among law-enforcement officers as an occupational group. Forensic psychologists have also contributed to specialized training in responding to the taking of hostages and to domestic assaults.

The psychologist acts as evaluation researcher when asked to assess the worthiness of a recently adopted policy, such as community policing.

KEY TERMS

burnout, p. 60
California Psychological Inventory, p. 52
clients, p. 46

community policing, p. 64
DWB, p. 47
false negatives, p. 51
false positives, p. 51
fitness-for-duty evaluation, p. 63
hostage taker, p. 61
immaturity index, p. 53
interview, p. 50
Inwald Personality Inventory, p. 54
L Scale, p. 54
Minnesota Multiphasic Personality
    Inventory, p. 52
police corruption, p. 48
police selection, p. 47
primary negotiator, p. 63
racial profiling, p. 47
RCMP Police Aptitude Test (RPAT), p. 50
ride-alongs, p. 58
situational tests, p. 56
stakeholders, p. 47
team policing, p. 46
wellness training, p. 60

SUGGESTED READINGS

Baker, M. (1985). *Cops: Their lives in their own words.* New York: Pocket Books.

A number of books, available in paperback, chronicle the lives of police in the line of duty. This book reflects interviews with 100 police officers; as you would suspect, the dramatic receives more coverage than the routine, but the book is a useful portrayal of how police describe their jobs.

Blau, T. H. (1994). *Psychological services for law enforcement.* New York: John Wiley.

A comprehensive review by a prominent police psychologist, it contains extensive practical information.

McAlary, M. (1987). *Buddy boys: When good cops turn bad.* New York: G. P. Putnam's.

This exposé was authored by a former investigative reporter of organized criminal activity by officers in the New York City Police Department.

Peak, K. J., & Glensor, R. W. (1996). *Community policing and problem solving: Strategies and practices.* Upper Saddle River, NJ: Prentice-Hall.

The development and implementation of community policing is discussed in this book-length analysis.

Rachlin, H. (1991). *The making of a cop.* New York: Simon & Schuster.

This readable report of the transition of four recruits from the New York City Police Academy to life on the streets contains a detailed description of what is involved in police training.

Reviews of the Inwald Personality Inventory: A number of reviews of the Inwald Personality Inventory are available. The following are worth reading to understand what is involved in developing an effective selection device:

Bolton, B. (1985). Review of Inwald Personality Inventory. In J. V. Mitchell (Ed.), *Ninth mental measurements yearbook* (pp. 711–713). Lincoln, NE: Buros Institute of Mental Measurements, University of Nebraska.

Juni, S. (1992). Review of Inwald Personality Inventory. In J. J. Kramer & J. C. Conoley (Eds.), *Eleventh mental measurements yearbook* (pp. 415–418). Lincoln, NE: Buros Institute of Mental Measurements, University of Nebraska.

Swartz, J. D. (1985). Review of Inwald Personality Inventory. In J. V. Mitchell (Ed.), *Ninth mental measurements yearbook* (pp. 713–714). Lincoln, NE: Buros Institute of Mental Measurements, University of Nebraska.

Waller, N. G. (1992). Review of Inwald Personality Inventory. In J. J. Kramer & J. C. Conoley (Eds.), *Eleventh mental measurements yearbook* (pp. 418–419). Lincoln, NE: Buros Institute of Mental Measurements, University of Nebraska.

4

Criminal Profiling

Profiling is neither a readily identifiable nor a homogenous entity and its status is properly regarded as a professional sideline not amounting to a true science.
—Gisli H. Gudjonsson and Gary Copson
(forensic psychologist and police officer) (1997, p. 76)

CRIMINAL PROFILING AND FORENSIC PSYCHOLOGY

In many countries, such as Canada, police sometimes rely on **criminal profiling** to aid in their investigations. A criminal profiler is a psychological consultant or investigator who examines evidence from the crime scene, victims, and witnesses in an attempt to construct an accurate description of the person or persons who perpetrated the crime. Although criminal profiling may hold potential as an investigative tool, the empirical foundations of profiling and its assumptions remain questionable, as the quotation at the start of the chapter conveyed.

Is criminal profiling an appropriate topic for a book on forensic psychology? On the one hand, many students—some of whom will be the forensic psychologists of the future—are drawn to the field because of their desire to emulate Clarice Starling of *The Silence of the Lambs* or the main characters in television shows such as *Profiler* or *Cracker*. The classification and capture of criminals sounds like a fascinating career.

On the other hand, the quotation at the beginning of this chapter reflects the views of many forensic psychologists who do not include criminal profiling under the rubric of forensic psychology. Here are some of their reasons:

1. Training in criminal profiling has been controlled by the law enforcement, and most graduate programs in forensic psychology do not offer specialized courses on this topic. To date, the only persons who have been eligible for formal training by the FBI are law-enforcement officers. In Canada, the RCMP relies on a small number of senior law-enforcement officers who have received specialized training from the FBI.
2. The number of criminal profiling jobs is extremely small. Even during its period of most frequent activity, the Behavioral Sciences Unit of the FBI was a very small operation, with only a dozen or fewer profilers. Although there are positions in U.S. crime labs and some detectives in large-city police departments may do some profiling, the number of open positions is minuscule compared to the intense level of interest. In Canada, there are few or no openings at any given time.
3. The vast majority of people who do profiling did not do graduate work in psychology; rather, they have advanced through the ranks of law enforcement, starting out as field agents, or they went through police-academy training. Although one current FBI profiler has a Ph.D. in psychology, he is a profiler because of his extensive FBI work experience, not because he has a Ph.D. In Canada, the small number of profilers used by the RCMP (such as Superintendent Glenn Woods, who was mentioned in Chapter 1) and provincial police forces generally do not have Ph.D.s. (The situation is different in Great Britain, where many profilers are psychologists [Gudjonsson & Copson, 1997].)
4. Even experienced profilers such as John Douglas acknowledge that profiling is an art more than it is a science. All profilers are not in agreement about the appropriate methodology, for example, whether to use a statistical analysis of the findings or to use clinical approaches of single cases to make inferences about the perpetrator's unconscious personality processes (Bekerian & Jackson, 1997). Therefore, criminal profiling is a broad, hard-to-pin-down term that covers a variety of procedures and operating assumptions (Woodworth & Porter, 1999).
5. For these and other reasons, expert testimony on profiling is not likely to be admitted in court, as it fails to meet *Mohan* or *Daubert* standards of merit as judged by the scientific community.

Despite these disclaimers, using the broad definition of forensic psychology introduced in Chapter 1, profiling is an application of psychological concepts to the legal system, even while evidence for its effectiveness is less than overwhelming. (In that respect, it shares a quality with topics of some of the other chapters of this book, procedures that are more accepted by many forensic psychologists.) It is hoped that a critical analysis of the current state of the field will increase awareness of readers of both its opportunities and its traps.

WHY DEVELOP CRIMINAL PROFILES?

The Problem of Serial Criminal Behaviour

Serial crimes of a sexual and/or homicidal nature continue to be a major concern to the public. As we know from Canadian cases, violence by serial offenders can escalate to tragic proportions if law enforcement fails to apprehend them quickly. For example, between 1957 and 1981, Clifford Olson was arrested 94 times for both minor and major crimes, including armed robbery and sexual assault (Woodworth & Porter, 1999). After numerous children were found murdered in B.C. between November of 1980 and August of 1981, Olson became a suspect and was arrested. However, he was released and continued to murder children until he was arrested again. Olson, a diagnosed psychopath, was ultimately convicted of eleven counts of murder. Most readers will be aware of another Canadian offender whose crimes increased in severity over many years—Paul Bernardo, known as the "Scarborough Rapist." Bernardo sexually assaulted numerous Ontario women over the course of several years in the early 1990s. Although he was a suspect in the investigation, he was not arrested and his violence escalated until he, along with his partner Karla Homolka, raped and murdered three young women.

Next to crime prevention, crime detection is of the highest priority to the public and to law-enforcement agencies. The types of cases described above have made clear the need for Canadian law enforcement to develop better techniques to help solve serial crimes, especially murders. A common definition of serial murder is the killing of three or more people with a "cooling off" period between the killings (Holmes & Holmes, 1998). There are a number of factors present in serial murder cases that make them especially difficult to solve; notably, there is often no relationship between the killer and victim, whereas in most murder cases a relationship exists (e.g., Correctional Service of Canada, 1995). Further, it may be difficult or impossible to establish a motive in many serial homicide cases (Hazelwood & Burgess, 1995).

People who commit one murder after another are of particular concern; some observers believe these serial killers and spree killers account for one third of all murders (Linedecker & Burt, 1990, p. ix). The FBI has reported that 151 serial killers have been identified and imprisoned since 1970 (Youngstrom, 1991). Estimates of the number of serial killers at large in the United States today vary widely—from 25 (Associated Press, 1992) to 100 (Holmes & Holmes, 1996, p. 62). In Canada, we have had our share of serial killers in the past two decades. In 1998, when this book's second author worked at Mountain Institution, a medium-security prison in British Columbia, at least five serial killers were housed there. There is currently a high-profile serial murder case being investigated in B.C., in which farmer Robert Pickton has been charged in the deaths of at least 22 women. In addition, the RCMP in Edmonton firmly believe they are dealing with a long-time serial murderer who has disposed of at least 13 female victims—many of them sex trade workers—outside of the upscale suburb of Sherwood Park. If we are able to develop profiles of criminals, the process would aid both of the above-mentioned goals—detection and prevention.

But what do we mean by a **criminal profile**? A "profile" of what? Some profilers emphasize the personality and motivations of the offender, including characteristic ways of committing crimes and treating their victims. But certainly physical characteristics are important—the criminal's age, sex, race, height, and weight. Whether the perpetrator is left-handed or right-handed is sometimes easily determined from an analysis of the criminal act. Because these qualities plus other demographic data (e.g., occupation, education) are sought in addition to a personality sketch of the criminal, some investigators (e.g., Holmes & Holmes, 1996) prefer to refer to a **sociopsychological profile** rather than the more common term, **psychological profile**.

Canadian law enforcement might include computer-based profiling, in which the crime scene characteristics or peculiarities of a current crime are matched with past crimes to identify the perpetrator. This computer-based approach is known as the Violent Crime Linkage Analysis System or **VICLAS**. This might also include **geographic profiling,** developed by Dr. Kim Rossmo, a former member of the Vancouver Police Department who received his Ph.D. in criminology from Simon Fraser University. With geographic profiling, the geographic pattern of crimes is used to make a probabilistic estimate of where the offender lives (see Woodworth & Porter, 1999).

Recurring Mysteries

One of the outcomes of criminal profiling, as we shall see in more detail, is matching information from the crime scene—especially physical evidence—with characteristics of a specific suspect, to help determine whether this suspect did commit the crime.

Knowledge generated from criminal profiling may provide insights into some of the unresolved questions about highly publicized crimes. The case of Jeffrey MacDonald provides an example. In February 1970, Jeffrey MacDonald was a hard-working doctor, a graduate of Princeton University who had completed a prestigious residency at Northwestern University Medical School before concluding his obligatory military service as a Green Beret in Vietnam. But on the night of February 16, 1970, Captain MacDonald

allegedly "smashed the skull of his pregnant wife several times with a club, and stabbed her 21 times with an icepick; clubbed his 5-year-old daughter Kimberly with three blows, then stabbed her no fewer than ten times; and finally placed his little (age 2) blond child, Kristen, across his lap, knifed her 17 times, and drove an icepick into her tiny body 15 times" (Noguchi, 1985, p. 61).

MacDonald himself had a superficial knife wound to the ribs. He has steadfastly claimed—for more than 30 years now—that these atrocities were committed by a knife- and club-wielding "hippie cult," screaming, "Acid is groovy; kill the pigs," and that one of the cult members scrawled the word *pig* in blood across the headboard of his bed. Since the crimes occurred on an army base, a military court first processed the case. As a result of this investigatory hearing (which lasted for four months), all charges against MacDonald were dismissed. But nine years later he was tried in a civilian court and convicted of the murders of his wife and children. Despite numerous appeals, MacDonald remains in prison.

The prosecution in the trial argued that MacDonald had staged the crime scene so that it would appear that a violent struggle had taken place that involved him and four intruders. It provided the following explanation: MacDonald had fallen asleep on the living-room couch while watching television; when he awoke and went to the bedroom he found that one of his children had wet the bed. An argument with his wife resulted, escalating into a fight. MacDonald, it was claimed, got a club, became angrier, and lost control. When his older daughter came upon the scene, he attacked her too. Realizing the need for a cover story, he continued the grisly acts, stabbing the children frequently to make it appear to be a cultish, Manson-like murder.

For several reasons, the MacDonald case continues to capture attention (Anson, 1998; Malcolm, 1995; Potter & Bost, 1995). MacDonald is an attractive, personable defendant, who continues to claim he is innocent; further, some of the evidence was destroyed by the police, and it has been argued that the FBI presentation of crucial evidence was misleading (Noguchi, 1985; Wecht, 1994). The widespread publicity about errors in the FBI's laboratory that surfaced in the late 1990s (see, for example, Kelly & Wearne, 1998) included a claim that in MacDonald's trial, an FBI agent misrepresented the results of laboratory analyses of clothing fibres. Cyril Wecht, an internationally recognized forensic pathologist, investigated the case and concluded:

> As I studied his psychological profile—that of a well-educated, successful, balanced person—I found that it did not fit the profile of a person who would suddenly snap, kill his wife and kids, and then regain his composure enough to try to cover it up.... That kind of person is known to slam a fist into a door, throw household objects, or verbally threaten people. But Jeffrey MacDonald had never displayed any of those actions either before or after that night in 1970. (Wecht, 1994, pp. 136–137)

The former chief medical examiner of Los Angeles County, Dr. Thomas Noguchi, reviewed the evidence in detail and has expressed a similar concern: "If MacDonald destroyed his own loving family, then on this one occasion an otherwise normal man behaved with the almost inconceivable rage and cunning of a psychotic" (1985, p. 87). But to the specific question: Is Jeffrey MacDonald innocent? Noguchi's response was "I do not know" (p. 88), and Dr. Wecht chose not to testify at the trial because his examination of the wounds to MacDonald left him uncertain about whether or not they had been self-inflicted.

This case is illustrative because it contrasts conclusions drawn from the physical evidence (forensic evidence) with conclusions drawn from criminal profiling. Physical evidence, such as blood typing and the pattern of knife thrusts through MacDonald's pajama top, is highly influential for jurors. But as Wecht (1994) has noted, physical evidence can be misrepresented or misinterpreted. Such evidence needs to be weighted

against what we know about the character and motivations of Jeffrey MacDonald, including his intelligence, his articulateness, and his decades-long claim of innocence.

False Stereotypes and Simplified Assumptions

The Jeffrey MacDonald case makes us confront our assumptions about human nature. Could someone as engaging and dedicated as MacDonald cold-bloodedly kill his own children? It also sensitizes us to the fact that each of us carries around our own theories about the motivations for criminal acts.

In the novel *Evidence* (Weisman, 1980), an assistant district attorney says to an investigative reporter:

> "Most crime is amazingly simple.... You guys always look for some kind of conspiracy. You're always writing about psychological motivation, about role modeling.... [M]ost perps do what they do because it's all they know. They're stupid. They hate, they want, and they do things to other people because that's what they know how to do. Robbers rob. Muggers mug. Rapists rape. That's what they do best. It's their job. All that talk about sociopathic patterns, the messed-up childhoods, the resentment of the father-authority figure, I think it's a crock. The perp is a perp.... They do what they know best." (p. 221)

Perhaps this oversimplified analysis applies in a few instances. But experienced criminal investigators would argue that a sophisticated psychological analysis is often required. Take, for example, the crime of stalking. In Canada, reported incidents of stalking have been on the rise since the 1990s. A group of police services noted an estimated 16 percent rise in stalking incidents from 1999 to 2000, and about a 50 percent increase since 1996 (Statistics Canada, 2001). Although it is hard to know whether this reflects a real increase in stalking behaviour or a greater awareness and reporting of the crime, it does highlight the societal importance of the problem. But stalkers reflect a variety of motives, behaviours, and psychological traits, making it difficult to develop one psychological profile that covers all, or even a majority, of them (Meloy, 1998). The procedure of profiling needs to be applied to the individual stalker, rather than the group.

Another problem that criminal profiling must overcome is the false stereotypes that many citizens hold about criminals. For example, bank robbers are seen by the public as clever, debonair, skillful, and glamorous; in reality, a study of convicted bank robbers found that most were young, impulsive, high on drugs or experiencing a personal crisis, and desperate (Associated Press, 1986). Most of them repeat the crime until they get caught (and most of them are). In contrast to some other types of major crimes, police solve nearly four out of every five bank robberies.

Similarly, embezzlement, as a crime, carries a false connotation. Many people assume that embezzlers are old, trusted employees who have steadfastly worked for a single firm for many years. But a survey of 23 men and 39 women convicted of embezzling (Pogrebin, Poole, & Regoli, 1986) concluded that the typical embezzler was a 26-year-old, married white woman with a high-school education who earned close to a minimum wage and worked in an entry-level position for less than one year. The most frequent motivation expressed by the embezzlers was a marital or family problem.

When asked to describe what an assassin is like, many people would probably describe a deranged madman, a lonely loser who follows up his threats of violence with an act against his sole target (Dedman, 1998). But an analysis by the U.S. Secret Service of all 83 persons who killed or tried to kill American politicians or other nationally known figures in the last 50 years challenges these stereotypes: "Fewer than half of the assassins showed symptoms of mental illness. Many shifted from one target to another, valuing the act more than the victim. No one had communicated a

direct threat to the target or to law-enforcement authorities" (Dedman, 1998, p. A-15).

We also make assumptions about the backgrounds of murderers. As Ressler and Shachtman (1992) observed, a common myth is that murderers come from impoverished or broken homes. Ressler, Burgess, and Douglas (1988) conducted interviews with 36 convicted male murderers; more than half lived initially in a family that appeared to be intact, with both of the mother and father living together with the son. As a group, they were intelligent children; although 7 of the 36 had IQ scores below 90, almost a third (11 of 36) had IQs above 120, and most were at least in the normal range. (There were dysfunctional aspects of these families—high rates of alcohol or drug abuse, consistent emotional abuse—but the families often appeared to be "normal.")

CURRENT NEEDS FOR PROFILING

Criminal profiling is not appropriate as an aid in detection for every crime. But for certain types of criminals, criminal profiling can be useful.

Arsonists

In 2001, 14 513 incidents of arson were reported in Canada (Statistics Canada, 2001). One of these incidents occurred in Lunenburg, Nova Scotia, when the second-oldest church in Canada (built in 1754) was deliberately torched. A team of 20 investigators was assigned to the still-unsolved case, which has been officially classified as arson. In the fall of 1993, forest fires devastated large sections of Southern California, including Malibu and Laguna Beach; at least five of the 23 fires, it was concluded, were deliberately set, with several others suspected to be arson (Sharn, 1993). The state of California alone has 40 000 suspicious fires a year. In a recent year in New York City, more than 101 000 fires occurred; 246 people died in these conflagrations.

Investigators concluded that 5362 of these fires were deliberately set (Micheels, 1991). As Micheels (1991) noted, "next to war, arson is humanity's costliest act of violence" (p. xv).

What kind of person would do this? Very few arsonists are caught or prosecuted because of few witnesses and little evidence; yet arson takes the lives of hundreds of North Americans every year. Can criminal profiling analysis assist in overcoming these challenges? In their *Crime Classification Manual*, Douglas, Burgess, Burgess, and Ressler (1992) began the profiling process by identifying three types of this crime: serial arson, spree arson, and mass arson. They also classified the motives of arsonists into various types, including vandalism, excitement, revenge, crime concealment, and profit. The FBI's National Center for the Analysis of Violent Crime has interviewed 83 convicted serial arsonists; their most frequently reported motive was revenge (Rider, 1980). Micheels provided an example: "The guy is pissed off that his girlfriend is seeing another man. This type of fire setter is probably one of the most dangerous…. In his rage, he'll try to burn her out, or burn the new boyfriend, with a Molotov cocktail or by squeezing flammable liquids under the door, and he won't really care about who sees him or anything else" (1991, pp. 6–7). One of the most tragic examples of this type was the Puerto Rican Social Club fire on Sunday, October 24, 1975, in the South Bronx, New York. A total of 27 people died, and 22 were seriously injured. The fire was set on the only stairway from ground level to the second-floor club. José Antonio Cordero, who admitted setting the fire, stated that his motive was jealousy. A young woman had attended the dance that night against his wishes. Cordero was sentenced to life in prison.

The profile of the typical arsonist is "a young, white male—most likely a loner with a history of problems" (Sharn, 1993, p. 3A). But as noted above, fires are started for a multitude of reasons. Other characteristics of arsonists are as varied as their motives; a veteran fire investigator observed that "they range from kids to little old ladies, from jilted lovers to Mafia wiseguys, from

teenage crack dealers to lawyers and respectable businessmen. Arson is committed by individuals and by groups" (Micheels, 1991, p. xv).

Serial Bombers

Former P.E.I. chemistry teacher Roger Charles Bell is serving a ten-year sentence for setting off four bombs in Charlottetown, including one in the P.E.I. Supreme Court in 1988 and one in the legislature building in 1995. These and other bombings, such as the Federal Building in Oklahoma City and the World Trade Center in New York, led to instant analyses of the type of persons who commit these acts. This section describes a special type of bomber—the serial bomber—specifically, the so-called Unabomber, who was so named because most of his initial targets were universities, high-tech centres, and airlines (Meddis, 1993). (The actions of another serial bomber, the "Mad Bomber," and how profiling was involved in his arrest are discussed later in this chapter.) The Unabomber was linked to 16 bombings all over the United States, causing three deaths and injuries to 23 others. His attacks began in 1978, but became sporadic with no attempts between 1987 and 1993. After a six-year hiatus, he sent one bomb to a genetics professor at the University of California, San Francisco, in June 1993, and another to a computer science professor at Yale University two days later. Then, the next year, he struck again, with a different kind of victim. On December 10, 1994, Thomas Mosser, an advertising executive, was killed by a mail bomb at his suburban New Jersey home. His final victim, a California forestry executive, was killed five months later, in April 1995.

The variety of intended victims, their locations all over the United States, and the time lapse between bombings posed a tough problem for criminal profilers. However, this serial bomber was considered to be a neat, meticulous individual who spent hours making and polishing bomb components (Fernandez, 1993). Behavioural-science specialists at the FBI theorized that "because there are no links between the victims and because many of them have been on the cutting edge of computer sciences, psychology, and genetics, the bomber may select his targets more for symbolic significance than because of any personal animus" (Labaton, 1993b, p. A10). Federal officials noted that the attacks were growing increasingly violent, with the use of very powerful bombs. Even though it was difficult to connect the deaths of the advertising and forestry executives to earlier victims, these bombs were built with similar materials and had a similar, sophisticated design (Levy, 1994). Like the previous ones, the explosives were made from scratch, without any traceable store-bought parts.

Interestingly, at least four of his targets, including the two in June 1993, had been featured in articles in the *New York Times* that characterized them as leading figures in their fields (Labaton, 1993a). (Another one of these, James McConnell of the University of Michigan, was a psychologist recognized for his successful introductory textbook and his research on memory transfer in invertebrates. Professor McConnell received a large manila envelope at his home; the cover letter—with a Salt Lake City postmark—suggested that McConnell should review "this thesis, which should be of interest" [Reynolds, 1994, p. 148]. McConnell's graduate assistant opened the package, and the blast injured him severely. McConnell, who was not injured, died in 1990 of causes unrelated to a bombing.) The next victim, Thomas Mosser, was featured in a *New York Times* article that appeared five days before he received the deadly bomb; the article described his promotion at the Young and Rubicam advertising agency.

After the attack on Mosser, FBI officials even published a sketch of what they thought the Unabomber looked like, based on reports of a shadowy figure spotted in a Salt Lake City parking lot just after a bomb exploded in 1987. They described him as a recluse, a white man in his late 30s or 40s, who had a high-school education but a familiarity with university life. They

speculated that he mailed his packages from Northern California (Levy, 1994).

In 1994, the FBI suggested it might even know his motivation: a hatred of sophisticated technology, the one link that the FBI saw among his multitude of targets (Perez-Pena, 1994). The investigators stated that the signature that was sometimes used—"F. C."—stood for "an obscene phrase belittling computers" (Perez-Pena, 1994, p. A12), but they didn't say how they had reached that conclusion. As concern mounted in the early 1990s over further attacks, the FBI made some interesting speculations about him. In a magazine article about the Unabomber published six weeks before his December 1994 attack on the advertising executive, an FBI agent was quoted as saying: "I can see him moving away from academic targets. I think he will broaden his horizons and go into a lot of different areas" (Reynolds, 1994, p. 154).

The search for the Unabomber took another turn in the fall of 1995, when the Unabomber promised no further bombings if his 35 000-word manifesto was published in U.S. national newspapers. Analysis of his manuscript led the FBI to conclude the following to be a part of his criminal profile:

1. That he was born and grew up in Morton Grove, Illinois, a northern suburb of Chicago. He almost certainly came from a background of affluence and education. After completing high school in nearby Skokie or Maine Township, he attended Northwestern University but did not graduate.
2. That he was a "meticulous grammarian" who produced his efforts on a manual typewriter made in the early 1960s.
3. That he was then believed to be living in the San Francisco area.
4. That he was a talented machinist who assembled his devices mostly from hand-made parts.
5. That he was "a loner fixated on detail, the son of an overbearing parent, an egomaniac who

is unable to get along with others and probably never married" (Howlett, 1995, p. 2A).

The FBI laboratory is even reported to have a DNA profile of the Unabomber, based on samples of saliva used to mail one of the package bombs. But despite all the information and effort, it took a unique break for a suspect to be located. With the publication of the Unabomber's manifesto, the brother of Theodore Kaczynski noted strong similarities to his brother's writings. After the FBI was contacted, it investigated and eventually arrested Kaczynski in his isolated cabin in Montana. Among his possessions found in the cabin was an old manual typewriter and the materials used for assembling bombs.

As we know, Kaczynski eventually admitted the actions, but we can still ask: How well did the profile fit? He is clearly a loner, never married, who had difficulty relating to other people. And he did grow up in the Chicago area. But rather than being a college dropout, he completed his undergraduate education and then received a Ph.D. from Harvard University. He taught mathematics for several years at the University of California at Berkeley before he voluntarily resigned. And, of course, he was living in the mountains of Montana when apprehended although he had lived in the San Francisco Bay area. So the profile was only partially correct. Would it have aided the FBI in apprehending Kaczynski had his brother not come forward? We cannot say, but certainly the eventual identification of the Unabomber was not a sterling example of the usefulness of profiling.

WHAT *IS* CRIMINAL PROFILING?

The origins of criminal profiling are unclear, but for centuries, elements of society have tried to pinpoint the physical or psychological qualities linked to criminal or deviant behaviour

(Pinizzotto, 1984). Even literary works such as Shakespeare's *Julius Caesar* ("yon Cassius has a lean and hungry look") and Edgar Allan Poe's "The Murders in the Rue Morgue" reflected attempts to profile unacceptable behaviours by use of physical attributes (McPoyle, 1981, cited by Pinizzotto, 1984). The documented history of real-life profiling can be traced at least to the publication of the notorious *Malleus Malificarum*, a book from the 1400s written for the Catholic Church and intended to identify witches based on their behaviours and physical characteristics (Woodworth & Porter, 1999).

The first modern example of criminal profiling occurred in the "Jack the Ripper" case in London, England, in the late 1800s. Dr. George Phillips, the police surgeon involved in the investigation, observed the pattern of wounds on the victims in order to attempt to determine the offender's psychological characteristics. Phillips thought that a careful examination of the evidence could give clues about the personality of the killer (e.g., Turvey, 1999). One of the most famous examples of a successful criminal profile came in 1956 when psychiatrist Dr. James Brussels successfully profiled the New York Mad Bomber (described in greater detail below) for investigators, using a psychoanalytic interpretation of the crime scene and the Mad Bomber's letters (e.g., Wilson, Lincoln, & Kocsis, 1997). In 1972, the FBI Behavioral Science Unit (BSU) was created after several notorious cases of serial and mass homicide in the 1960s (e.g., the Boston Strangler and Richard Speck).

Definitions

Criminal profiling has been described as an educated attempt to provide specific information about a certain type of suspect (Geberth, 1981) and as a biographical sketch of behavioural patterns, trends, and tendencies (Vorpagel, 1982, cited in Douglas, Ressler, Burgess, & Hartman, 1986). The basic premise of criminal profiling is that the way a person thinks directs the person's behaviour. It is important to recognize that profiling does not provide the specific identity of the offender (Douglas et al., 1986).

Similarly, not all types of crimes are conducive to successful criminal profiling. Holmes and Holmes (1996) concluded that crimes such as cheque forgery, bank robbery, and kidnapping are not good candidates for profiling. A single act of murder, especially if it is spontaneous, is more difficult to interpret than a series of crimes that reflect similar actions or locations. In the latter instance, the consistencies in crime scenes and treatment of victims permit the police to get a better handle on the nature of the perpetrator. The nature of the victim's wounds might also give clues to the personality and experience of the attacker. Holmes and Holmes (1996) even have suggested that some serial killers are aware of the "trace" they leave at a crime scene; these psychologists quote the remarkable observations of one such killer, as presented in Box 4.1.

Geberth (1990) stated that the purpose of criminal profiling is:

> to provide the investigator with a personality composite of the unknown suspect(s) that will aid apprehension. By studying the crime scene from a psychological standpoint, the

criminal psychologist is able to identify and interpret certain items of evidence at the scene, which provide clues to the personality type of the individual or individuals who have committed the crime. (p. 492)

Three Approaches to Criminal Profiling

Although the above quotation implies a specific procedure, three different approaches can be included under the rubric "criminal profiling" (or "offender profiling," the term used in Europe to describe this process). Even though each has a different procedure, the general intent is the same. Each is described below.

Profiling Historic and Political Figures

Understanding the behaviour and motivations of individuals who play a role in important events reflects one goal of profiling. In the nine days between his murder of Gianni Versace and his own suicide, spree killer Andrew Cunanan became the target of widespread questions about his motivations and personality (Orth, 1999). Whether a person's effects are broad and perverse, like Hitler's or Stalin's, or futile, like those of Frank Corder (the man who was killed as he

BOX 4.1
A Killer's View of His Own Crimes

R. M. Holmes, a forensic psychologist, has interviewed a number of criminals. The following is the statement of one.

"First of all, any investigative onlooker to my crime scene would have immediately deduced that the offender was extremely sadistic in nature. The visible markers of bondage, and the nature of the victims' wounds—the evidence of unhurried, systematic abuse—would have indicated that sadistic acts were not new to the offender; he had committed such brutality in the past, and would likely continue this pattern of victimization in the future.

"From these points, it could have then been correctly assumed that, although brutally violent, the

offender was nevertheless intelligent enough to attach method to his madness—as well as cautious and aware enough with regard to his surroundings—to make sure he proceeds unseen in the commission of his deeds.

"Further, ... such a brutal offense was unprecedented in this area, it could have been correctly assumed that the offender was very new to the city; if he was a drifter, he was at least someone who very possibly could deem to leave town as suddenly as he arrived (which is exactly what I did)." (Quoted in Holmes & Holmes, 1996, p. 41, from the first author's files)

flew his small plane into the trees surrounding the White House), their actions lead us to ask, Why? When a national leader dies suddenly and is replaced by a newcomer—as in the case of North Korea's long-time dictator Kim Il Sung, who died in 1994 and was replaced by his son Kim Jong Il—the CIA seeks to develop a personality profile that will predict the behaviour of the new ruler while he or she is in power.

Adolf Hitler The practical purposes of profiling a specific person were tested by the World War II effort of the U.S. government's Office of Strategic Services (OSS) to profile the personality of Adolf Hitler. In 1943, a practising psychiatrist, Walter C. Langer, assembled material to provide a psychological description of Hitler's personality, a diagnosis of his mental condition, and a prediction of how he would react to defeat. Almost three decades after the war was over, a book was published, detailing all these conclusions (Langer, 1972). (Hitler's basic nature remains a controversy among scholars; in fact, two recent books, by Lukacs, 1997, and by Rosenbaum, 1998, dealt with the varying conceptions held by other authors of Hitler's motivations and character.)

Langer employed a psychoanalytic profile of Hitler, in which the nature of Hitler's childhood relationship with his parents was seen as quite influential on his future behaviour. Apparently, Hitler saw his father as brutally cold and cruel in his relationship with his wife and children. In contrast, his mother was long-suffering and affectionate; young Adolf developed a strong emotional attachment to her. But, while Hitler was still an adolescent, his mother died a painful death from cancer.

Langer concluded that Hitler could not develop an intimate relationship with others that sustained adversity because he judged people to be untrustworthy. At the same time, he saw himself as infallible and omnipotent. Through his leadership of a powerful Germany, he could somehow prove his manhood to his deceased mother.

With regard to predictions, the analysis by Langer offered several possibilities for Hitler's approach to adversity. It doubted that Hitler would seek refuge in another country; more likely was the possibility that he would lead his troops into a final futile battle. Langer concluded as quite plausible the possibility that in the face of inevitable defeat, Hitler would commit suicide. He noted that Hitler had threatened to take his own life on earlier occasions and had said to an associate, "Yes, in the hour of supreme peril I must sacrifice myself to the people" (quoted by Langer, 1972, p. 216). As we know, Langer was right.

It is unlikely that the profile of Hitler transmitted to the U.S. government had any discernible effect on Allied foreign policy or the outcome of the war; even Langer (1972, p. 25) doubts that it did. It simply came too late.

Saddam Hussein The quest to understand the personality and behaviour of world leaders is never-ending. Recently, the world has focused on the Yugoslavian leader Slobodan Milosevic. During the Iraqi conflicts, the United States government sought to profile Saddam Hussein, who was eventually captured by American soldiers in 2003. Psychiatrist Jerrold M. Post of George Washington University testified on this matter before the U.S. House of Representatives in December 1990, and his testimony was later published (Post, 1991).

Post disabused the government officials of labels for Saddam Hussein such as "madman of the Middle East." He stated: "[T]here is no evidence that he is suffering from a psychotic disorder. He is not impulsive, only acts after judicious consideration, and can be extremely patient; indeed he uses time as a weapon" (1991, p. 283). However, Post concluded that Saddam Hussein was often politically out of touch with reality, that he possessed a "political personality constellation—messianic ambition for unlimited power, absence of conscience, unconstrained aggression, and a paranoid outlook" (1991, p. 285), which made him quite dangerous.

In the wake of the Gulf War of 1991, Post predicted that Saddam Hussein would not "go down to the last flaming bunker" if he had a way out, but that he would "stop at nothing if he is backed into a corner" (pp. 288–289). For a long time, Post's predictions—in light of what has happened in the years since the Gulf War of 1991—seemed accurate. Based on CIA profiles, U.S. policymakers fully expected Saddam Hussein to break under the pressure (Cockburn & Cockburn, 1999), but when he was recently found by American soldiers in a hole in the ground (with a pistol), he seemed meek and offered no resistance whatsoever.

David Koresh The analyses of Hitler and Saddam Hussein were based on a wealth of material about these public figures, developed over extended periods. Sometimes, in contrast, a crisis develops, requiring a quicker decision.

After a 51-day siege of the Branch Davidian compound led by David Koresh, the FBI decided to attack, based on reports that children inside were being abused. The result, as we now know, was a disaster. As many as two dozen cult members, including Koresh, were shot as fire began to consume the 86 persons in the compound on April 19, 1993 (Verhovek, 1993).

The actions of Koresh and the people in the compound have brought questions about the adequacy of the psychological profile of Koresh assembled by the FBI. William Sessions, then director of the FBI, was quoted as saying: "We had been assured, both from our own evaluations of David Koresh, from the psychologists, from the psycholinguists, from a psychiatrist, from his writings, from his assertions himself, repeatedly, that he did not intend to commit suicide" (quoted by Lewis, 1993, p. A19).

One of those to whom Director Sessions apparently referred was Murray S. Miron, then a professor of psychology at Syracuse University and a specialist in psycholinguistics. Miron had done forensic analyses of communication for years—he did a quite accurate profile of David Berkowitz, the "Son of Sam"—and, with John Douglas of the Profiling and Consultation Program of the FBI Academy, had published analyses of threats of violence (Miron & Douglas,

1979). Miron was quoted as telling the FBI that suicide "was not part of his (Koresh's) agenda" (*Los Angeles Times*, 1993).

Profiling Criminals' Common Characteristics

Far different from the focus on specific influential individuals is the second approach, in which the profiler looks for consistencies in the personalities, backgrounds, and behaviours of offenders who carry out similar crimes. Are all bank robbers alike? Do rapists have similar personalities? One benefit of the extensive amount of profiling done in the last 20 years is the generation of new, and sometimes surprising, relationships. For example, as Heilbroner has noted, "serial killing turns out to be an immensely sexual process" (1993, p. 147); for many serial killers—including Ted Bundy and Jeffrey Dahmer—their victims are simply bodies on which they enact their sexual fantasies.

The goal of constructing a descriptive profile of a crime classification is not new; more than 40 years ago Palmer (1960) studied 51 murderers serving sentences in New England. His "typical murderer" was 23 years old at the time of the murder, from a lower socioeconomic group, and unsuccessful in regard to education and occupation. The typical murderer's mother was well meaning but maladjusted, and he had experienced psychological frustrations and physical abuse while a child.

Childhood Experiences Many methods exist for seeking answers to questions about consistency in criminals' backgrounds. One approach is to determine whether similar childhood experiences characterize offenders of a particular type. For example, do sexual murderers have a history of having been sexually abused as children? Unfortunately, many of the highly publicized answers to this question are based on conclusions drawn from self-reports of convicted rapists and pedophiles. For example, Murphy and Peters wrote that "There is a good deal of clinical lore that a history of being sexually victimized is predominant in the backgrounds of sex offenders" (1992, p. 33). When Robert R. "Roy" Hazelwood of the FBI's Behavioral Sciences Unit interviewed 41 men who had raped at least ten times each, he found that 31 of them reported they had been sexually abused as children (reported in Sullivan & Sevilla, 1993).

Ressler, Burgess, Hartman, Douglas, and McCormack (1986) classified 36 murderers as having committed sexually oriented murders, by using such observations as the victim's attire or lack of attire, exposure of sexual parts of the victim's body, positioning of the victim's body in a provocative way, and evidence of sexual intercourse or insertion of foreign objects into the victim's body cavities. When questioned about prior sexual abuse, 43 percent of the sexual murderers indicated they had been the victims of such abuse in childhood, 32 percent in adolescence, and 37 percent as adults. Approximately 75 percent reported having been psychologically abused, and 35 percent witnessed sexual violence as a child. The murderers who had been abused themselves reported a wider variety of symptoms of maladjustment in childhood, including everything from cruelty to animals to rape fantasies. Those who were sexually abused in childhood tended to mutilate the body after killing, as contrasted with the murderers who raped and then killed. The authors of the study speculate that "undisclosed and unresolved early sexual abuse may be a contributing factor in the stimulation of bizarre, sexual, sadistic behavior characterized in a subclassification of mutilators" (Ressler et al., 1986, p. 282). That is, they concluded that murderers with a history of sexual abuse will first kill the victim to achieve control before they carry out sexual intercourse, masturbation, or other sexually symbolic activities. But differences between the two groups only approached statistical significance, and no effort was made to verify these self-reports by the use of independent sources.

Nevertheless, to presume that having been sexually victimized as a child is a predominant cause of becoming a sexual offender is risky. The vast majority of such victimized children do not become offenders as adults (Murphy & Peters, 1992).

MMPI Profiles Another approach, within the search for common characteristics, is the use of personality inventories to develop psychological profiles of offender types.

As noted in chapter Chapter 3, the Minnesota Multiphasic Personality Inventory and its revision, the MMPI-2, are the most widely used assessment devices for detecting psychopathology. A number of studies have looked at the typical MMPI profiles of various types of offenders.

How specific and diagnostically accurate are the results of these studies? Controversy exists. In the study of sex offenders of children, for example, several researchers have found that such offenders have an elevated score on MMPI Scale 4, which measures Psychopathic Deviance (Swenson & Grimes, 1969; Langevin, Paitich, Freeman, Mann, & Handy, 1978); these results suggest that these offenders were rebellious, impulsive, self-centred, and defiant of authority. But other studies (reviewed by Murphy & Peters, 1992) find no differences between types of offenders, or basically normal profiles. A number of problems exist in the quest for useful information from such an approach. Many of the studies use only convicted offenders; often the control groups are nonexistent or unsatisfactory.

We may also question how specific the obtained profiles are to one type of offender. Quinsey, Arnold, and Pruesse (1980) compared child molesters to a number of other groups seen in a psychiatric correctional facility; these other groups included rapists, murderers of non–family members, murderers of family members, arsonists, and property offenders. Each group showed an elevation on MMPI Scale 4 and on Scale 8 (the Schizophrenia Scale). In general, prison populations and a number of psychiatric populations show elevations on Scale 4 alone or on that scale along with Scale 8 or Scale 9, the Hypomania Scale (Dahlstrom, Welsh, & Dahlstrom, 1972).

Another problem is that use of average elevation of each scale may imply greater homogeneity in the group than is actually warranted. Three studies with large groups, reviewed by Murphy and Peters (1992), were consistent in finding the 4-8 profile (indicating that the individual scored high on both Scale 4 [psychopathic deviate] and Scale 8 [schizophrenia]) as the most frequent. But the actual percentage of child molesters with this as the elevated profile were the following:

1. Erickson, Luxenburg, Walbek, & Seely (1987): $N = 498$ offenders, 13 percent
2. Hall, Maiuro, Vitaliano, & Proctor (1986): $N = 406$ offenders, 7 percent
3. Hall (1989): $N = 81$ offenders, 17 percent

Among these 985 sex offenders, almost every imaginable MMPI profile was found—of the 45 possible Scale-2 elevated profiles, 43 different combinations were observed (Murphy & Peters, 1992). A similar study (Duthie & McIvor, 1990), using a cluster analysis of MMPI profiles of child molesters, found eight identifiable clusters.

A more specific instrument than the MMPI is the Multiphasic Sex Inventory, or MSI, developed by Nichols and Molinder (1984) for the evaluation of sex offenders. A study (Clark & Grier, 1993) of 30 men who first denied they were child molesters but then later admitted it found that scores on the L Scale regarding child molestation distinguished between deniers and admitted offenders.

Profiling Criminals from Crime Scene Characteristics

Is it possible to draw a profile of the criminal from the psychological or physical characteristics of the crime scene? Stated another way, does the pattern of behaviours in this crime resemble patterns from other cases? This second question reflects the current application of the term *criminal profiling* by the FBI (Ressler & Shactman, 1992). An example and a description of the procedures are provided in the next section, but first we need to recognize that some characteristics extracted from the crime scene or interviews with victims are more diagnostic than others.

Douglas and Munn (1992) made a distinction between the MO (*modus operandi*, or standard procedure) of a criminal and his or her "signature." A burglar may begin his criminal life by breaking a basement window to gain entry. But realizing the danger of being caught as a result of the noise, in subsequent crimes he brings glass-cutting tools; he refines his MO in order to reduce the risk of apprehension. In contrast, a criminal's **signature** reflects unique, personal aspects of the criminal act, often the reflection of a need to express violent fantasies. (See Box 4.2 for John Douglas's elaboration of the distinction.) For example, a rapist may consistently engage in the same specific order of sexual activities with each of his victims. Douglas and Munn (1992) concluded that "the signature aspect remains a constant and enduring part of each offender ... it never changes" (p. 5).

CRIMINAL-PROFILING PROCEDURES USED BY THE POLICE AND THE FBI

Contemporary law enforcement seeks to do more than describe the typical murderer or child molester. Rather, investigators use the crime scene to generate hypotheses about the type of person who committed the crime and then seek specific individuals who possess those characteristics.

In some ways the modern criminal profilers resemble the legendary detectives of fiction such as Hercule Poirot, Sherlock Holmes, Charlie Chan, and Miss Marple. As Box 4.3 (page 82), which presents an example of the deductive skill of Sherlock Holmes, indicates, attention to detail is the hallmark of these investigators (Douglas, Ressler, Burgess, & Hartman, 1986), and not the smallest clue at the crime scene escapes the attention of the profiler (Douglas & Olshaker, 1995). But, unlike the detectives in novels, criminal pro-

> ### BOX 4.2
> ### Modus Operandi versus Signature

John Douglas offers a vivid description of the difference between a criminal's MO and a signature:

> *MO is what an offender has to do to accomplish a crime. It's learned behavior and gets modified and perfected as the criminal gets better and better at what he does. For example, a bank robber's accomplice might realize after one or two jobs that he ought to leave the getaway car's motor running during the robbery. This would be an aspect of modus operandi. The signature, on the other hand, is something the offender has to do to fulfill himself emotionally. It's not needed to successfully accomplish the crime, but it is the reason he undertakes the particular crime in the first place....*
>
> *I worked on two cases, with two different offenders working in two different states, yet both did a similar thing during [a bank] robbery. In a case in Grand Rapids, Michigan, the robber made everyone in the bank undress—take off everything—and stay that way until he had left with the money. In another case in Texas, the bank robber also made his victims undress, with one variation: he*

> *posed them in degrading sexual positions and then took photographs of them.*
>
> *... [T]he first case is an example of an MO, while the second is an example of signature. In the Michigan case, the robber had everyone strip to make them uncomfortable and embarrassed so they would not look at him and be able to make a positive ID later on. Also, once he escaped, they would be preoccupied with getting redressed before calling the police or reacting in any other way.... So this MO greatly helped the offender accomplish his goal of robbing money from that bank.*
>
> *In the Texas case, having everyone strip so he could take pictures of them had nothing to do with accomplishing the robbery; in fact, quite the opposite, it slowed him down and made him easier to pursue. But it was something he felt a need to do for his own emotional satisfaction and completeness. This is a signature—something that is special (possibly even unique) to that particular offender. (Douglas & Olshaker, 1998, pp. 90–92)*

filers must focus on more than one clue. They analyze all clues and crime patterns. Truly, as Rossi (1982) suggested, criminal profiling can be thought of as a collection of leads.

Onlookers are sometimes bewildered or astounded at the conclusions drawn by profiling specialists, but many of these are simply the result of commonsense inferences. Consider, for example, these conclusions drawn from sets of facts in different cases, examined by John Douglas and other profilers:

- Based on descriptions by her friends and co-workers, the victim was obedient, submissive, and compliant. But the crime scene showed evidence of torture on her body.
   Inference: The offender inflicted pain for its own sake; "that's what he needed to make the crime satisfying" (Douglas & Olshaker, 1998, p. 13).

- A serial rapist was described as wearing work boots.

   Inference: He might be employed at one of the nearby factories. "Since he was able to come and go as he pleased at home (evidenced by the late night/early-morning timing of most [of his] rapes, he was either single, worked shifts, or was the dominant partner in a relationship" (Douglas & Olshaker, 1998, p. 55).

- The victim's body was dumped along the side of a road in a remote location.
   Inference: The offender had access to a vehicle, and the offender was familiar with this specific, isolated area (Oldfield, 1997).

- In a case in which the victim survived, the rapist made himself unidentifiable to the victim.
   Inference: The victim and the offender knew each other (Jackson, van den Eshof, & de Kleuver, 1997).

BOX 4.3
Sherlock Holmes's Deductive Skills

Behaviour is there for everyone to see. But the consummate criminal profiler notices and interprets things that others neglect. Sometimes works of fiction can provide examples more efficiently than can real life. Sherlock Holmes, for example, once remarked that "Perhaps I have trained myself to see what others overlook" (Doyle, 1891, p. 42). In *The Man with the Twisted Lips*, the challenge to Holmes was to determine the status of a missing husband. A clue surfaces in the form of a letter:

Holmes: *I perceive also that whoever addressed the envelope had to go and inquire to the address.*

Mrs. St. Claire: *How can you tell?*

Holmes: *The name, you see, is in perfectly black ink, which has dried itself. The rest is of the grayish color which shows that blotting paper has been used. If it*

had been written straight off, and then blotted, none would be of a deep black shade. This man has written the name, and there has then been a pause before he wrote the address, which can only mean that he was not familiar with it. (Doyle, 1892, p. 89)

A small point, perhaps, but often an accumulation of details permits the investigator to narrow the possibilities to a manageable area of inquiry.

More recent fictional examples of police investigators using criminal profiling in their work include three novels by Thomas Harris—*The Red Dragon* (1981) is more detailed than the more famous *Silence of the Lambs* (1988) and the more recent *Hannibal* (1999)—as well as Caleb Carr's *The Alienist* (1994) and *The Angel of Darkness* (1997) and Lawrence Sanders's *The Third Deadly Sin* (1981).

■ A number of people were found separately murdered on isolated hiking trails in the mountains near San Francisco. Each had been a victim of a sudden attack from the rear.

> *Inference*: In perhaps his most famous (correct) prediction, John Douglas told the local law-enforcement officers that the killer had a speech impediment. He later wrote: "The secluded locations where he wasn't likely to come in contact with anyone else, the fact that none of his victims had been approached in a crowd or tricked into going along with him, the fact that he felt that he had to rely on a blitz attack even in the middle of nowhere—all of this told me we were dealing with someone with some condition that he felt awkward or ashamed about. Overpowering an unsuspecting victim and being able to dominate and control her was his way of overcoming this handicap" (Douglas & Olshaker, 1995, p. 156). When the offender, David Carpenter, was eventually captured, it was found that he had a severe stuttering problem.

The "Mad Bomber"

The highly popular true-crime books by former FBI profilers such as John Douglas, Robert Ressler, and Roy Hazelwood have convinced many readers of the effectiveness of criminal profiling. Often the case of New York City's "Mad Bomber" is offered as a dramatic demonstration of an accurate profile. But as in the case of the Unabomber, the successful resolution of this case was dependent on other factors besides the specifics of the profile.

For 16 years, starting in 1940, someone was detonating homemade bombs in public places around the city. The first bombs were small and ineffective, and hence little noticed, but as they gradually increased in size, the city grew terrified. The police and the city's newspapers came to label the perpetrator as mad, partly because he had sent letters and made phone calls to the local newspapers; these messages conveyed a mixture of emotions from threat to apology. He admitted, "I am not well" (Brussel, 1968, p. 17).

The first bomb was found on a windowsill of the Consolidated Edison Company's building. The second bomb, also unexploded, was found ten months later, lying on the street (stuffed inside a man's woollen sock) five blocks from Consolidated Edison's headquarters. But within three months (in December 1941) the United States was at war, and, amazingly, the police received a letter, printed in block letters, stating: "I will make no more bomb units for the duration of the war—my patriotic feelings have made me decide this—Later I will bring the Con Edison to justice—They will pay for their dastardly deeds—F.P." (quoted in Brussel, 1968, pp. 15–16). During the war (from 1941 to 1946) at least 16 other letters signed "F.P." were received by the electric company, the *New York Times*, and various hotels, theatres, and department stores in Manhattan. But no more bombs were delivered until 1950, when a third unexploded bomb was discovered on the lower level of Grand Central Station. Five more surfaced in the same year, several of which exploded. Miraculously, no one was hurt.

By 1956 the citizenry was petrified, and the police were mystified. In desperation, the police contacted a psychiatrist, James A. Brussel, who had a private practice in New York City and was also the state's assistant commissioner of mental hygiene. Could he provide any suggestions about the type of person who would do this?

Based on his success in this case (and, later, on others), Dr. Brussel came to be referred to as a modern-day Sherlock Holmes. And in some ways his methods were similar to those of the great fictional detective. He described them as "my own private blend of science, intuition, and hope" (Brussel, 1968, p. 3). By looking at the Mad Bomber's deeds, Brussel tried to deduce what kind of man he might be.

Brussel knew from conferences with the police that the bomber had to know something about metalworking, pipe fitting, and electricity. He might have learned such skills on a job, or perhaps as a hobby. If the latter, he might require space and equipment, a situation that neighbours would notice.

Brussel also analyzed the Mad Bomber's phone calls and letters. The terrorist believed that some grave injustice had been done him by Consolidated Edison, "something which, according to his letters, had rendered him chronically ill" (Brussel, 1968, p. 29). A single fixed belief dominated his thoughts, and had for 16 years. Brussel concluded that the Mad Bomber was suffering from paranoia and that it was steadily getting worse. His grudges moved to delusions—unalterable, systematized, logically constructed delusions.

Next, Brussel focused on the Mad Bomber's physical characteristics. He proposed that the man was "symmetrically built; perpendicular and girth development in good ratio; neither fat nor skinny" (1968, p. 32). These conclusions were based on the body typology first developed by Ernst Kretschmer and later systematized by William Sheldon. The relationship of body type and personality has largely been ignored by contemporary criminologists, but Brussel relied on a conclusion of Kretschmer's that roughly 85 percent of paranoiacs have a mesomorphic or athletic body type (Kretschmer, 1925).

Some of Brussel's deductions were considered farfetched by the police. He noticed the odd curved way that the Bomber printed the *W*s in his letters. Brussel also meditated about the way the Bomber slit the undersides of theatre seats to laboriously stuff his bombs in the upholstery. Brussel later wrote:

This slashing of seats, like the misshapen *W*, was an out-of-pattern fact in the Bomber's otherwise careful, tidy existence. Just like the *W*, therefore, it had to represent the welling-up and breaking-through of some powerful emotion within the man. My deduction was that it was the same feeling in both cases—a feeling related in some way to sex.

I studied the photograph of the slashed seat. I wondered: Why would a man take a knife and slash the *underside*? Could the seat symbolize the pelvic region of the human body? In plunging a knife upward into it, had the Bomber been symbolically penetrating a woman? Or castrating a man? Or both? (1968, p. 37, italics in original)

Brussel, through a series of steps, concluded that the Mad Bomber "obviously" distrusted and despised male authority, including the police and his former employers at Consolidated Edison. This suggested to Brussel that he harboured no love for his father, or even hated him. He concluded that the Mad Bomber had never progressed beyond the Oedipal stage of love for his mother, a common pattern, Brussel had found, in paranoiacs. He wrote:

And now, I thought, I had a plausible explanation for his otherwise unexplainable act of slashing theater seats. In this act he gave expression to a submerged wish to penetrate his mother or castrate his father, thereby rendering the father powerless—or to do both.

Farfetched? Perhaps. But nothing else I could think of seemed to fit with the available facts so well. It fitted the picture of a man with an overwhelming, unreasonable hatred of men in authority—a man who, for at least 16 years, had clung to the belief that they were trying to deprive him of something that was rightfully his. Of what? In his letters he called it justice, but this was only symbolic. His unconscious knew what it really was: the love of his mother. (1968, p. 39)

From all these deliberations, Brussel developed a detailed description of the Mad Bomber:

Single man, between 40 and 50 years old, introvert. Unsocial but not anti-social. Skilled mechanic. Cunning. Neat with tools. Egotistical of mechanical skill. Contemptuous of other people. Resentful of criticism of his work but probably conceals resentment. Moral. Honest. Not interested in women. High school graduate. Expert in civil or military ordnance. Religious. Might flare up violently at work when criticized. Possible motive: discharge or reprimand. Feels superior to critics. Resentment keeps growing.

Present or former Consolidated Edison worker. Probably case of progressive paranoia. (1968, p. 47)

Brussel went on to tell the police that the Mad Bomber was "Middle-aged. Foreign-born. Roman Catholic. Single. Lives with a brother or sister. When you find him, chances are he'll be wearing a double-breasted suit. Buttoned" (quoted by Douglas, Ressler, Burgess, & Hartman, 1986, p. 404).

Brussel persuaded the police to put a description of the Mad Bomber in the newspapers, in an effort to prod him out of hiding. And so they did, on Christmas Day 1956. The notice in the newspapers generated a brief, unrevealing phone call from the Mad Bomber to Dr. Brussel and several letters to the papers in which he wrote: "I did not get a single penny for a lifetime of misery and suffering—just abuse ..." (quoted by Brussel, 1968, p. 62). This response betrayed his grudge against his former employer, Consolidated Edison, leading to a frantic search through its personnel records, but the records for the 1930s were quite disorganized.

Finally, on January 18, 1957, the search through the Consolidated Edison records produced a breakthrough. A long-forgotten employee named George Metesky (age 28 at the time) had been injured and felt the company owed him more money than it had agreed to pay. The injury dated back to 1931, and it really didn't differ from a lot of other cases—except for one detail. In one of the vituperative letters written by the employee to the company appeared the words "dastardly deeds."

Metesky had been knocked down by a back draft of hot gases from a boiler. Doctors had found no injuries, but Metesky complained of headaches and other symptoms. For several months the company had given him sick pay while he stayed home. Because follow-up medical examinations by the Consolidated Edison staff found no tangible injuries, he was dropped from the payroll. Two-and-a-half years later he filed a claim for permanent-disability pay with the Workmen's Compensation Board, arguing that the boiler accident had given him tuberculosis, but it was denied. Other, equally bitter letters followed for three years, until 1937, and then he disappeared from view.

Metesky was located, living in Waterbury, Connecticut, about 80 miles (128 km) from New York City. He was 54 years old (slightly older than Brussel envisioned), unemployed, and living with two older sisters, also unmarried. He weighed 170 pounds (77 kg), stood 5 feet 9 inches (1.73 m) tall, and was well proportioned. After he prepared to accompany the police to the police station he was neatly dressed in a blue double-breasted suit. It was buttoned.

He was eventually judged to be mentally ill and was committed to a state institution for mentally ill criminals, where he remained until his release in 1973. He died in 1994, at the age of 90.

Two aspects of the Mad Bomber case are particularly noteworthy:

1. Brussel was remarkably accurate on both major and minor aspects of the case, but he did make an error in predicting what kind of chronic illness Metesky claimed. He said: "There are hundreds of chronic conditions, and if we wanted to we could go through a medical textbook and come up with a list a yard long. But let's stick to the usual. Let's place our bets on chronic conditions that are statistically the commonest. This means heart disease, cancer, and tuberculosis" (Brussel, 1968, p. 43). He chose heart disease. Brussel later acknowledged his "unpardonable error"; he wrote: "I failed to make every possible allowance for the known facts" (1968, p. 42).
2. It is important to note that Metesky was identified not because of the profile per se but because of information in the Consolidated Edison personnel files. It did not require a psychiatrist to propose that the Mad Bomber was possibly a former employee; the very first bomb was wrapped in a note that said, "Con Edison crooks, this is for you."

We should always remember that the goal of criminal profiling is not to pinpoint a specific person, but to identify the type of individual who would perpetrate such crimes.

Procedures

The Mad Bomber example provides some insight into the procedures used in criminal profiling. **Crime scene analysis** is an important part. Detailed analysis generates many specific questions. Dealing with a case in which a 67-year-old woman was found tied up in her bathroom and beaten to death, an FBI agent asked his associates: "Why so many loops in the rope? You don't need that many to control an old woman.... Why is she in the bathroom? It's a closed-in space—is he after security, or is he secretive? ... Were the cuts on the body made before or after she died?" (quoted by Toufexis, 1991, p. 68).

Crime Scene Analysis

The profiling in the Mad Bomber case reflects an emphasis on the psychological. Another approach to criminal profiling places somewhat greater emphasis on the dynamics of the crime scene. The goals of the two are the same, and in both approaches the profilers make hypothetical formulations, or educated guesses, based on their past experience. Douglas, Ressler, Burgess, and Hartman defined a formulation as "a concept that organizes, explains, or makes investigative sense out of information, and that influences the profile hypotheses" (1986, p. 405).

For example, in a rape and murder of a woman, the way that the assailant has left the body will lead the profiler to make certain inferences. If he made no attempt to cover up the victim, he may have felt no respect for her and desired to shock whoever found her. Placing objects inside her mouth and vagina is interpreted as a way of humiliating his victim, but insertion of these after her death would mean he was not motivated by sadism. If no money or possessions were taken, the conclusion might be that the attacker had a stable income (Toufexis, 1991). The fact that the victim was female would suggest to the profiler that the perpetrator was male and about the same age as the victim (Douglas & Olshaker, 1995).

The pattern of blood reveals a lot; for example, the force of a gun bullet sprays blood farther than the swing of a blunt instrument. As Detective Dusty Hesskew observed, with the blood pattern, "we can say, 'Okay, the victim started out here, ran to this point, fell down, and tried to get back up.' We can even determine whether the killer was left-handed or right-handed and where he stood when he did it" (quoted by Dingus, 1994, p. 84).

Generating the Criminal Profile

Despite Brussel's success, use of criminal profiles was infrequent until the FBI established a psychological profiling program within its Behavioral Science Unit in Quantico, Virginia. Since then, investigators at this facility have developed a criminal-profile generating process with five main stages; apprehension of a suspect is the goal and the final step in the process. This **criminal–profile generating process** involves the following steps:

1. A comprehensive study of the nature of the criminal act and the types of persons who have committed like offences in the past.
2. A detailed analysis of the crime scene.
3. An in-depth examination of the background and activities of the victim or victims.
4. A formulation of possible motivating factors for all parties involved.
5. The development of a description of the perpetrator based on overt characteristics from the crime scene and past criminals' behaviour. (Pinizzotto, 1984, p. 33)

Initially, the profiler would acquire evidence from the crime scene, knowledge of the victim, and specific forensic evidence about the crime (cause of death, nature of wounds, autopsy report, etc.). Photographs of the victim and crime scene are included. Efforts are made to understand why this person, in particular, was the victim. Information about possible suspects is not included, so as not to subconsciously prejudice the profilers (Douglas, Ressler, Burgess, & Hartman, 1986).

The next process involves decision making, by organizing and arranging inputs into meaningful patterns. The crime is classified. For example, is the crime a **mass murder** (defined as anything more than three victims in one location and within one event)? Family murders are distinguished from so-called classic murders. John List, an insurance salesperson, killed his entire family (his wife, his mother, and three teenage children) on November 9, 1972. In contrast are the "classic" murders of Charles Whitman, the man who barricaded himself at the top of the University of Texas tower and killed 16 people, wounding 30 others.

As mentioned earlier, two other classifications are the **spree murder** (killings at two or more locations with no emotional cooling-off period between homicides) and the **serial murder** (three or more separate events with a cooling-off period between homicides) (Douglas et al., 1986).

The next procedure is to reconstruct the sequence of events and the behaviour of both the perpetrator and the victim. One important distinction is that between **organized** (or nonsocial) and **disorganized** (or asocial) **criminals**. This classification was first applied by Hazelwood and Douglas (1980) to murders motivated by lust, but since then has been expanded to other types of crimes. In their book *Sexual Homicide* (1988), Ressler, Burgess, and Douglas extended the classification but deleted the terms *asocial* and *nonsocial*.

Organized murderers are those who plan their murders, target their victims (who usually do not know the perpetrator), show self-control at the crime scene by leaving few clues, and possibly act out a violent fantasy against the victim, including dismemberment or torture (Douglas et al., 1986; Jackson & Bekerian, 1997a).

Ted Bundy was a clear example of the organized rapist-murderer; he planned his abductions, usually using a ruse such as feigning a broken arm in order to get assistance. He selected victims who were young and attractive women, similar in appearance. He used verbal manipulation and then physical force. He sexually abused them after he killed them. The disorganized murderer "is less apt to plan his crime in detail, obtains victims by chance, and behaves haphazardly during the crime" (Douglas et al., 1986, pp. 412–413).

Herbert Mullin was an example of the disorganized murderer. Between October 1972 and February 1973, Herbert Mullin killed 13 persons in or near Santa Cruz, California. No pattern existed to the selection of his victims: a homeless person, a hitchhiker, a priest in a church, and four teenage campers (Lunde & Morgan, 1980). Once he was "instructed by voices" to kill a man he had never seen before.

Ressler, Burgess, Douglas, Hartman, and D'Agostino (1986) analyzed the crime scene differences in cases involving 36 convicted serial murderers. Each of those who provided consent was then interviewed extensively by FBI agents. Two-thirds, or 24, were classified by the FBI agents as organized offenders and 12 were placed in the disorganized group. In looking at aspects of the crime scene, the researchers found that organized offenders were more apt to:

■ plan
■ use restraints
■ commit sexual acts with live victims
■ emphasize control over the victim by using manipulative or threatening techniques
■ use a car or truck

Disorganized offenders were more likely to:

■ leave a weapon at the crime scene
■ reposition the dead body
■ perform sexual acts with a dead body
■ keep the dead body
■ try to depersonalize the body
■ not use a vehicle (Ressler et al., 1986, p. 293)

The inclusion of "did not use a vehicle" sounds like an unusual manifestation of the disorganized personality, but Holmes and Holmes (1996) described one murderer whom they profiled as travelling by city bus because he lacked both a car and a driver's licence:

> He killed and assaulted within the immediate area of his home, and his range of travel was restricted to within his own neighborhood. The hunting area was immediate to his personal activities and was determined not only by his daily actions, but also by his personality. He was a disorganized personality who saw visions and heard voices. His restricted comfort zone was defined by his daily activities, limited by the range and mode of his travels and by his own personal inadequacies. (p. 150)

The outcome of the criminal-profile generating process is usually a profile that follows a standard format, including hypotheses about the perpetrator's age, sex, race, educational level, marital status, habits, family characteristics, type of vehicle, and indications of psychopathology.

Research on Convicted Offenders

In 1981 the FBI established the Violent Criminal Apprehension Program, or **VICAP**. The success of this program and that of the Psychological Profiling Program generated U.S. legislation that established a National Center for the Analysis of Violent Crime in 1984. It is based at the FBI Academy as a subdivision of what was originally called the Behavioral Science Unit. The profiling procedures used in other countries, including Canada (VICLAS), Great Britain, and the Netherlands, have reflected the FBI's approach (Jackson & Bekerian, 1997a). Also, advances in computer technology permitted each of these countries to develop databases on characteristics of specific crimes and procedures for the sharing of information between agencies (Stevens, 1997).

One activity of the FBI centre was to interview incarcerated offenders, leading to classifications that aid in future profiling. For example, with regard to child molesters, FBI agent Kenneth Lanning has concluded that "about 90 percent are what we call situational molesters;

they have no real sexual preference for children and have relatively few victims a piece. They may turn to a youngster because an adult woman isn't available" (quoted by Toufexis, 1991, p. 68). Only the remaining 10 percent have a true sexual preference for children, but each may have victimized hundreds of young people. The two types have different patterns of behaviour (Douglas & Olshaker, 1997).

Canadian researchers have examined the relevance of psychopathy in correlating personality and behaviour in incarcerated sex offenders. Porter, Fairweather, and colleagues (2000) found that psychopathic sex offenders were more likely to engage in diverse types of sexually deviant behaviour. For example, they were more likely to rape women and molest children of both genders than were nonpsychopathic offenders, who usually targeted a single victim type. Recently, some of the first research to examine the relation between psychopathy and sexual homicide was conducted by a team of Canadian academic researchers and Correctional Service of Canada psychologists. Porter, Woodworth, Earle, Drugge, and Boer (2003) looked at the types of violent actions used by murderers in the context of the murder and as a function of psychopathy. The main source of information was the detailed file description of the crime known as the criminal profile report, based on police, forensic/autopsy, and court information. Of greatest interest was the level of gratuitous and sadistic violence that the killer had perpetrated on the victim. Evidence for gratuitous violence included torture, beating, mutilation, and the use of multiple weapons at the crime scene. Evidence that the offender obtained enjoyment or pleasure from the violent acts was coded as sadistic violence. It turned out that almost all offenders scored in the moderate to high range on the Psychopathy Checklist-Revised. Murders by psychopaths were more gratuitous and sadistic than those by other offenders. In fact, most psychopaths (82.4 percent) had committed sadistic acts on their victims, compared to 52.6 percent of the nonpsychopaths. This type of empirical research

correlating specific crime scene behaviours with personality pathology in the offender could give profiling a stronger foundation in the future.

How Effective Is Criminal Profiling?

It is a mistake to assume that the solution of a crime is the only indication of the usefulness of criminal profiling. A survey in Great Britain of 184 cases indicated that in only five (or 2.7 percent) did profiling lead to identification of the offender, but police frequently reported other benefits—that it "furthered understanding of the case or the offender" (61 percent of cases), "reassured their own conclusions" (52 percent), and "offered a structure for interviewing" (5 percent). In 32 of these cases, or 17 percent, the police concluded that the profiling information was not useful (Gudjonsson & Copson, 1997).

A profile may lead police in a new direction in their investigation. For example, in the winter of 1981, Atlanta was beset by the acts of a killer of a series of black children. Some commentators believed the crimes were perpetrated by the Ku Klux Klan, but the FBI's John Douglas, on the basis of a crime-scene analysis, announced that they were the acts of a lone black man, between the ages of 25 and 29, a police buff who drove a police-type vehicle. "He would have a police-type dog, either a German shepherd or a Doberman" (Douglas & Olshaker, 1995, p. 204). When Wayne Williams was taken into custody (and later convicted of two of the murders), he "fit our profile in every respect [actually he was 23 years old], including his ownership of a German shepherd. He was a police buff who had been arrested some years earlier for impersonating a law officer. After that, he had driven a surplus police vehicle and used police scanners to get to crime scenes to take pictures" (Douglas & Olshaker, 1995, p. 213).

Profiling generates hypotheses but its conclusions should not be treated as final. One problem is that sometimes police "lock in" to certain characteristics and prematurely apprehend an innocent person because he or she fits the profile. On other occasions, the profile may be misguided, as in the Boston Strangler case described in Box 4.4.

When Can Profiling Be Productive?

As noted earlier, not all murders are alike. Both Woodsworth and Porter (2002) and Wolfgang and Ferracuti (1967) identified two basic behaviours of murderers: (a) premeditated, intentional, planned and rational murder and (b) killing in the heat of passion or slaying with an intent to harm, but without a deliberate intent to kill. Criminal personality profiling is more likely to be productive in cases in which the offenders plan their crimes (and repeat them) or in which some psychopathology is associated with the criminal (Geberth, 1990). A homicide that results from a sudden barroom fight is not as good a candidate for profiling as a homicide that includes sadistic torture or postmortem slashing. According to the FBI analyses, a person with abnormal behaviour patterns becomes more ritualized, displaying a distinct pattern in his or her behaviour (Geberth, 1990). The personality and behaviour scene thus

produce much more in the way of idiosyncratic and useful cues. For profiling efforts to succeed, it is almost essential that the offender's personality or signature be revealed.

Implicit in the above statements are two fundamental assumptions that profilers make about the nature of the criminal's behaviour:

1. The signature of the perpetrator (the unique way in which he or she commits the crimes) will remain the same. For example, in his writings, former FBI agent John Douglas (see Douglas & Olshaker, 1995, 1997) states that such actions do not change.
2. The offender's personality will not change (Holmes & Holmes, 1996, pp. 41–43).

The Dangers of Exaggerating the Benefits of Profiling

We have already seen that it is dangerously inaccurate to use the MMPI or other personality tests to claim that offenders' personalities are homogeneous. Sometimes descriptions of criminal profiling can report too much homogeneity, too. The

---

BOX 4.4
A Profile Gone Awry—The Boston Strangler Case

For a period of a year and a half, from June 1962 through January 1964, the city of Boston was paralyzed by the murders of 13 women—in all cases by strangulation. Most of the first victims were elderly (from age 55 to 75) but most of the later ones were in their 20s or younger. The various crime scenes reflected hate and chaos—and enough general similarities to justify the construction of a criminal profile. For example, 19-year-old Mary Sullivan, the last victim, was found nude in her bed with a broom handle inserted in her vagina. Both breasts were exposed, the murderer had ejaculated on her face, and a card reading "Happy New Year" had been placed next to her left foot.

A profiling committee, composed of a psychiatrist with knowledge about sex crimes, a physician with experience in anthropology, a gynecologist, and others, was established. James Brussel of "Mad Bomber" fame was also a member. The psychiatric profile that they

developed suggested that there were two different perpetrators for different strangulations. According to the majority opinion, one killer was raised by a domineering and seductive mother; he was unable to express hatred toward his mother and thus directed anger toward other women, especially older women. It was predicted that he lived alone. The committee report proposed that the younger victims had been killed by a homosexual man who knew his victims. (Dr. Brussel filed a minority view, that one killer committed all the murders.)

Albert DeSalvo was eventually arrested and convicted, after he confessed to the crimes. Married and living with his wife, DeSalvo had an insatiable sexual appetite, demanding sex from his wife five or six times a day. He was sentenced to life in prison.

He showed no signs of the detailed predictions in the profile—no consuming rage toward his mother, no lack of sexual potency, no Oedipus complex.

(From Frank, 1966; Holmes & Holmes, 1996.)

distinction between organized and disorganized offenders was presented above; the following is Vernon Geberth's evaluation of the general characteristics of the organized offender:

- *Age.* This offender is approximately the same age as the victim.
- *Marital status.* Married or living with a partner. This type of offender is sexually competent and usually is in a significant relationship with a woman. (Most serial murderers are men, and most of the victims are women.)
- *Automobile.* Middle-class vehicle. Maybe a sedan or possibly a station wagon. The auto may be dark in colour and may resemble local police cars. This vehicle will be clean and well maintained (1990, pp. 504–505).

Geberth went on to list 40 "general behaviour characteristics" of organized offenders, including "high birth order status, may be first born son," "methodical and cunning," "travels frequently," and (if unmarried) "dates frequently" (pp. 506–507). A danger exists in giving too much weight to these classifications. For example, police may limit their search to suspects who fit all or most of the characteristics.

Another trap of profiling is to assume that if a person possesses several characteristics of a criminal profile, he or she is necessarily guilty. For example, the profile of drug couriers used by the U.S. Drug Enforcement Administration includes the description of them as dark-skinned; hence, innocent members of minority groups are frequently stopped, searched, and harassed by the police. At the Buffalo, New York, airport in 1989, U.S. federal agents detained 600 people as potential couriers; only ten were arrested (Bovard, 1994). Yet drug courier profiling—which has been approved by the U.S. Supreme Court—allows police to search almost anyone they please.

In Canada, however, the situation is different. In a recent Ontario Court of Appeal decision, the judge ruled that police are not able to detain an individual or search his or her vehicle simply because there is evidence to suggest that the person may be a drug courier (*R. v. Calderon,* 2004). In the case of *R. v. Calderon,* two members of the Ontario Provincial Police observed a vehicle that was exceeding the speed limit and, after determining that the car was a rental, decided to pull it over. This conclusion was based on a course that one of the police officers had completed. After the vehicle was pulled over, the two officers observed two cellular phones, a pager, road maps, fast-food wrappers, and luggage in the back seat instead of the trunk, further confirming their belief that the individuals were drug couriers. After initially consenting to allow the police to search the car, one of the suspects withdrew his consent, but the police officers continued the search, finding 10 kg of marijuana. During the trial, the police officer testified that he had continued the search because there were reasonable grounds to suspect that there were drugs in the vehicle. Although the suspects were originally convicted, on appeal the judge ruled that the Charter rights of the individuals were violated and as such an acquittal should be admitted for the appellants (*R. v. Calderon,* 2004).

FBI agents themselves try not to exaggerate the powers of profiling (Toufexis, 1991). "It's a myth that a profile always solves the case," stated Robert Ressler, former FBI agent and now an author and consultant; "It's not the magic bullet of investigations; it's simply another tool" (quoted by Toufexis, 1991, p. 69). And sometimes police can be misled when they rely too heavily on the conclusions from FBI profiling. In 1993 police on Long Island, New York, searching for the missing ten-year-old Katie Beers, complained that they had been distracted by an FBI profile that said that pedophiles didn't usually hide their victims in their homes (Rosenbaum, 1993).

Are Professional Profilers Better?

Another way to assess the effectiveness of profiling is to determine whether professional profilers do better in a controlled test than do those less experienced in this task. Pinizzotto and Finkel (1990) sought to determine whether the process used by professional profilers and their success rate differs from those of nonprofessionals. They submitted the same materials to 28 persons divided into five categories:

1. Group A, Experts/Teachers ($N = 4$), profiling experts who had trained police detectives in profiling at the FBI Academy in Quantico, Virginia. Each was or had been an FBI agent; they possessed from four to 17 years' profiling experience.
2. Group B, Profilers ($N = 6$), police detectives from different police agencies across the United States who had been specially trained in personality profiling, through a one-year program at the FBI headquarters. These six profilers had from seven to 15 years' experience as police detectives and from one to six years in profiling.
3. Group C, Detectives ($N = 6$), detectives from a large metropolitan police department who were experienced investigators but had no training in criminal profiling. Individual experience in criminal investigation ranged from six to 15 years.
4. Group D, Psychologists ($N = 6$), practising clinical psychologists naïve to both criminal profiling and criminal investigations.
5. Group E, Students ($N = 6$), undergraduate students from a large metropolitan university, naïve to both criminal profiling and criminal investigations. Their average age was 19.

Two actual cases were used, one a homicide and one a sex offence; both cases were "closed" at the time, meaning that an individual had been arrested and convicted of the crime. The materials for the homicide case included 14 black-and-white crime scene photographs, information about the victim, autopsy and toxicology reports, and crime scene reports. For the sex offence, the material included a detailed statement by the victim-survivor, crime scene reports by the first officer on the scene and the detectives, and a victimology report.

The researchers collected a variety of responses from the subjects after the subjects had reviewed the two case materials. Each subject was asked to write a profile of the offender in each case. For both cases the profiles written by the professional profilers were richer than those of the nonprofiler groups of detectives, psychologists, and students. Measures with significant differences between groups included the time spent writing the report, the length of the report, and the number of predictions made. The number of accurate predictions made by the professional profilers was twice as high as that of the detectives, three times greater than that of the psychologists, and almost five times greater than that of the students. However, the sex offence case accounted for the majority of the differences. The accuracy of the predictions and the correctness of lineup identifications did not differ very much between groups with respect to the homicide case materials. In fact, with regard to the homicide case, students on the average got 6.5 questions correct out of 15, whereas the profilers got only 5.3 correct (a nonsignificant difference).

The superiority the profilers demonstrated in this study was certainly a reflection of their expertise, but the level of motivation to do well on the task may also have differed between groups. It is hard to specify just how differently the groups would respond to an actual case because the case materials had been sanitized to protect the identities of the parties involved and the police agencies. Some material ordinarily available to profilers (such as maps of the geographical area and the neighbourhood) was therefore not included. (All of the profilers spontaneously mentioned that some of the usual types of information were missing; no other subjects did.)

The profilers did not appear to process the material in qualitatively different ways from the nonprofilers (Pinizzotto & Finkel, 1990, p. 229) but they did recall more information. The authors concluded that the profilers' greater ability to extract and designate more details is what made the difference in predictive accuracy.

A systematic study of detectives and profilers done in the Netherlands (Jackson, van den Eshof, & de Kleuver, 1997) led to a different conclusion—

one that surprised the investigators, who assumed that the profiling processes of profilers and detectives were similar. They concluded:

> One of the main characteristics of offender profiling is that it is based on inferences drawn from considerable experiences both of and with similar types of case. This experience is achieved by extensively studying the main characteristics of a large number of solved crimes. Solved crimes produce data which can then function as statistical probabilities or testable hypotheses rather than facts. This probabilistic way of thinking is virtually unknown in everyday police practice. For detectives, facts are all-important. (1997, p. 118)

An Evaluation of Profiling

As noted earlier, profiling is an art; Holmes and Holmes (1996) concluded that a good profiler develops a "feel" for certain types of crimes, thus reflecting the intuitive quality of an art. Often, when profilers perceive patterns in behaviour, they can't describe how their processes work; "they just do." No two profilers will necessarily produce the same profile (Bekerian & Jackson, 1997; Stevens, 1997). But deductions that are drawn from a crime scene analysis qualify as legitimate scientific procedures.

The introduction of a profile can result in more efficient use of the detective's time. Cases sometimes overwhelm the detectives with details to be investigated. In the case of the Green River Killer in Washington State in which 49 prostitutes were murdered, police had 18 000 names in their suspect files, and a single television program generated 3500 tips (Rossmo, 1997). The killings seemed to stop in 1984, after Marie Malvar's boyfriend saw her getting into Gary Ridgway's truck and Ridgway became a suspect. He was questioned by detectives that year but passed a polygraph (despite the fact that he was lying). When Ridgway was finally apprehended (and convicted) in 2003, many observers noted that he had some characteristics that were typical of most

serial killers (e.g., age, ethnicity, personality), and others that were atypical. He held a job painting trucks for 32 years and was married. Such stability is rare in serial killers, although not unheard of: Jeffrey Dahmer held a job at a chocolate factory, and Robert Yates of Spokane, Washington, who also preyed on prostitutes, had five children, a wife, and a mortgage.

But profiling (and polygraphy) is not a panacea; rather, it should be viewed as an instrument to facilitate the work of the investigators and detectives, by evaluating suspects and providing useful advice on investigation and interviewing (Jackson, van den Eshof, & de Kleuver, 1997; Stevens, 1997).

PSYCHOLOGICAL AUTOPSIES IN UNEXPECTED OR EQUIVOCAL DEATHS

Profiling, using psychological concepts and procedures to create a profile of a person, can be used in other arenas besides crime detection. Often the cause of a person's death is a matter of forensic concern even if no criminal act is assumed to be involved. Even when the cause of death is certain, issues related to the mental state of the person prior to his or her death may require the application of psychological analysis. Canadian researcher James Ogloff and his colleague Randy Otto (1993) suggested several types of situations:

- The need to determine whether the person was competent to draw up a will (called the decedent's **testamentary capacity**).
- In workers' compensation cases, claims may be made that stressful working conditions contributed to the person's premature death.
- In a criminal case, the defendant, on trial for murder, may claim that his victim was a violent person who instilled such fear in the defendant that his act was truly one of self-defence.

However, probably the most frequent situation in which profiling is applied is to determine whether a death was suicide or homicide. On July 20, 1993, the body of Vincent Foster, deputy White House counsel and a former law partner of Hillary Rodham Clinton, was found in a Virginia park across the Potomac River from Washington, D.C. Law-enforcement officials, including the Park Police, concluded that the death from a gunshot wound was suicide. But speculation about the death persisted, not only about why Foster died but even about where he died. "Who killed Vincent Foster?" the *Washington Times* asked in a front-page story (Ruddy, 1997). Probably the most persistent of the speculations was that the White House aide had been murdered (Isikoff, 1994). Supporters of this view described Foster's body as lying gently on an incline with a .38-caliber revolver in one hand. They claimed that contrary to the usual mess from a suicide by gunshot, only a "thin trickle of blood" came from the corner of Foster's mouth (Ruddy, 1997).

Actions by the White House staff immediately after the discovery of Foster's body—such as controlling and curtailing the search of Foster's office and the discovery several days later of a shredded suicide note—doubtless contributed to the conspiracy theories, despite the fact that a Park Police investigator stated that Foster's shirt was still wet, there was blood on the ground, and black powder burns were found on his hand and mouth.

In early 1995 Kenneth Starr, the special prosecutor handling the investigation of President Clinton's Whitewater land deals, announced that he was reopening some aspects of the investigation of Foster's death, and it was not until July 1997 that Starr announced a reaffirmed conclusion that suicide was the mode of death. This saga only verifies the need to carry out a thorough and competent initial investigation of any suspicious death, including an inquiry into the psychological state of the person before his or her death.

The term **psychological autopsy** refers to the investigative method used by psychologists or other social scientists to help determine the mode of death in equivocal cases (Ogloff & Otto, 1993; Selkin & Loya, 1979). For example, as Shneidman (1981) noted, asphyxiation as a result of drowning in a swimming pool does not tell us whether the victim struggled and drowned (accident), entered the pool with the intention of drowning himself or herself (suicide), or was held under water until he or she drowned (homicide). The cause of death—water in the lungs—is quite clear, but the **mode of death** is not.

As noted above, the range of such cases is broad; for example, an insurance company handling a claim of death wants to know if the cause was an accident or suicide. Was an on-the-job accidental death a result of operator error or equipment malfunction? When a man's car plunges off a bridge and he dies, was it a result of a heart attack, a failure in the steering mechanism, or a desire to kill himself? It is estimated that between 5 percent and 20 percent of all deaths that need to be certified are equivocal deaths.

Selkin (1987) concluded that the most common inquiry in a psychological autopsy questions whether the death was an accident or suicide. A central task of medical examiners is to certify whether a death could reliably be classified as natural, accidental, suicidal, or homicidal (Jobes, Berman, & Josselson, 1986); this classification—the so-called **NASH classification** (Shneidman, 1981)—reflects the four traditional modes in which death is currently reported.

The addition of a psychological autopsy to the standard examination by a coroner or medical examiner may uncover new facts about the case, information that had not been used by the medical examiner. An empirical study (Jobes et al., 1986) demonstrated this. The researchers used as subjects 195 medical examiners drawn from the population of 400 practising examiners in the United States. All were MDs and members of the National Association of Medical Examiners. The examiners were given two kinds of cases, one in which the death was "typical" (i.e., one in which the manner of death was not difficult to certify), and one in which the death was an "equivocal" case (i.e., the mode of death was less clear).

To determine generalizability of results, five different pairs of cases were used, ranging from a single-car accident to the death of a child to a Russian roulette death. For half of the cases, psychological autopsies were provided the medical examiner in addition to the standard information. These psychological autopsies included information about the dead person's lifestyle, personality, and demographics, as well as a psychological interpretation of the death.

As expected, the availability of the psychological-autopsy information did not influence the manner of death certification in most of the typical cases, but it did influence reactions to two of these typical cases (psychotic and Russian roulette cases). But in regard to the equivocal cases, the psychological information had a statistically significant impact on the determination of the manner of death in four of the five types of cases, with a trend toward significance in the fifth (the Russian roulette case).

Consider, for example, the single-car death. In the typical case, examiners were told that a woman had lost control of her car on a mountain road; her blood alcohol content was 0.21 percent. All but one examiner agreed that the case should be certified as an accidental death, and the inclusion of psychological-autopsy information had no effect on these decisions.

But, in great contrast were the results in the equivocal single-car death. Here, a man's car collided head-on with a truck. The incident occurred late at night on a winding road, and the victim's car swerved into the path of the oncoming truck. A few short skid marks were left by the car.

The examiners who received no additional information were about equally divided as to cause of death between accident, suicide, and undetermined (with slightly more favouring suicide). The psychological autopsy added that the victim was depressed, had anxiety attacks, and recently suffered a significant loss. Examiners given this added information almost unanimously (90 percent) ruled that suicide was the cause of death.

Perhaps such results are not surprising. Given the extra information—and especially in the context that these were not real-life cases for these examiners—the outcome may be inevitable. More research is needed to determine the extent of receptiveness by medical examiners to psychological evidence in cases for which they are responsible for the certification. Although the use of psychological autopsies has not been adopted widely in Canada, this situation may change as the science progresses.

RECENT PROFILING ADVANCEMENTS IN CANADA

In recent years, we have witnessed some significant developments in innovative, nontraditional approaches by both law enforcement and psychological researchers. Inspired by the FBI's VICAP approach, the RCMP has developed a profiling technique called VICLAS using computer technology. Geographic profiling, also relying upon computer technology, attempts to profile where the offender may be located.

Violent Crime Linkage Analysis System (VICLAS)

In 1999, one of the this text's authors (S. P.) conducted a psychological assessment on a serial rapist for the National Parole Board. The offender, now incarcerated at Mountain Institution in Agassiz, B.C., had been first arrested after perpetrating a brutal sexual assault on a teenage girl in B.C. A year into his three-year sentence, he was connected to the rapes of other women in Alberta and Saskatchewan over a period of several years. Although he had not been a suspect during the original investigations of these offences, his unique behaviours during his current offence were matched to the others using the VICLAS profiling system.

With VICLAS, police in every province (with each database linked to a main server in Ottawa) record the information for all solved and unsolved homicides, sexual assaults, and unidentified bodies of known or suspected homicide. The investigator completes a booklet covering more than 200 details of the incident. The information is then entered into the computer to look for potential linkages with other crimes in Canada. Although the RCMP have been reluctant to open their VICLAS files for psychological research (for security reasons), they recently created a board of advisory consultants, which includes forensic psychologists and psychiatrists, to advise them on the types of research that could most benefit their investigations.

Geographic Profiling

Another Canadian development in the field of profiling is called geographic profiling, a computer-based system developed by Dr. Kim Rossmo for his Ph.D. in criminology at Simon Fraser University. This approach considers the pattern of documented crime scene locations to provide a statistical estimate of the probable residence or base of operations of a serial offender (Rossmo, 1997). The computer program produces a three-dimensional "map" to highlight the most probable locations of the offender's residence. The main purpose of geographic profiling is to allow law enforcement to focus their investigative efforts in certain regions (Rossmo, 1996). The results of Rossmo's initial research project, based on a large sample of solved serial murder cases, revealed that geographic profiling had considerable validity (Rossmo, 1997). Although it is clear that this technology requires further scientific validation, Rossmo's approach is gaining much attention from law-enforcement agencies around the world.

the psychological makeup of a specific person posing a threat of national security, such as Adolf Hitler in the 1940s or Saddam Hussein more recently, reflect one approach to profiling. Other activities include determining whether people who commit a particular type of crime reflect a common set of characteristics and extracting characteristics from a particular crime or set of crimes in order to identify the criminal. The latter approach is typical of the criminal profiling procedures used by the FBI. Profilers carry out a thorough analysis of the crime scene in search of a "signature" left by the criminal. They have created the categories of organized and disorganized offenders to help them develop more accurate profiles of perpetrators. In the Canadian context, innovative new profiling techniques such as the computer-based VICLAS and geographic profiling have extended the definition and scope of profiling and offer potentially more objective approaches.

The effectiveness of criminal profiling has yet to be firmly established. Some cases reflect remarkable accuracy in predicting specific characteristics of the offender but in other cases, such as that of the Unabomber, much of the FBI's profile was inaccurate. An empirical study of effectiveness found only weak support for a conclusion that experienced profilers generated more information and more accurate information about the perpetrator from an examination of the files than did other types of law-enforcement officials, clinical psychologists, and students. Recently, the Ontario Court of Appeal ruled that "unscientific" criminal profiling should not be allowed as expert opinion evidence (*R. v. Ranger*, 2003). As such, the scientific foundations of profiling must be strengthened if this type of evidence is to move beyond the criminal investigation and into the courtroom.

SUMMARY

Criminal profiling is an educated attempt to provide specific information about a certain type of suspect, but several types of activities fall under the general label. For example, attempts to determine

KEY TERMS

crime scene analysis, p. 85
criminal profile, p. 69
criminal-profile generating process, p. 86

SUGGESTED READINGS

Brussel, J. A. (1968). *Casebook of a crime psychiatrist.* New York: Bernard Geis Associates.

This work includes a readable description of the Mad Bomber case plus others by an early forensic psychiatrist.

Douglas, J. E., & Olshaker, M. (1995). *Mindhunter: Inside the FBI's elite serial crime unit.* New York: Scribner.

The first of several books describing some of John Douglas's classic cases of criminal profiling, this one is especially valuable because it also serves as an autobiography that describes how Douglas became a highly regarded profiler.

Fowler, R. D. (1986, May). Howard Hughes: A psychological autopsy. *Psychology Today,* pp. 22–33.

After the death of Howard Hughes, the flamboyant millionaire-turned-recluse, numerous persons claimed to be inheritors of his estate. Raymond Fowler, the chief executive officer of the American Psychological Association, was asked to complete a psychological autopsy of Hughes, especially focusing on his testamentary capacity.

Harris, T. (1981). *The red dragon.* New York: G. P. Putnam's.

This novel's hero, a criminal profiler, is based on famed profiler John Douglas.

Jackson, J. L., & Bekerian, D. A. (Eds.). (1997). *Offender profiling: Theory, research and practice.* New York: John Wiley.

This thorough, critical evaluation of criminal profiling includes chapters written by experts from the United Kingdom, the Netherlands, and Canada. Chapter 2 provides a classification of crime motives, with case histories; the final chapter describes criticisms of profiling. Highly recommended.

Meloy, J. R. (Ed.). (1998). *The psychology of stalking: Clinical and forensic perspectives.* San Diego: Academic Press.

Research psychologists, clinicians, and other experts in the field contributed the 15 chapters of this work dealing with classifications of stalkers, victims, explicit and implicit threats, and other related topics.

Michaud, S. G., with Hazelwood, R. (1998). *The evil that men do: FBI profiler Roy Hazelwood's journey into the minds of sexual predators.* New York: St. Martin's Press.

This very readable description of many of the cases investigated by former FBI profiler Roy Hazelwood, who developed the organized/disorganized crime classification, includes descriptions of the fatal explosion on the USS Iowa and the Atlanta child murders. The book also includes some controversial conclusions, not shared by all psychologists, about the effects of pornography.

Ressler, R. K., & Shachtman, T. (1992). *Whoever fights monsters.* New York: St. Martin's Press.

This book offers a vivid description of how Robert Ressler used interviews with convicted serial killers to develop the procedure now known as criminal profiling.

5

Deception Detection in the Legal System

Both Mr. Corkum and Mr. Jabarianha were less than believable as they gave much of their evidence.... Each was evasive at times or his eyes shifted around. Thus in certain points of the story each by the story and his demeanour, displayed signs of untruthfulness.

—HONOURABLE MADAM JUSTICE M. KOENIGSBERG (*R. v. Jabarianha*, 1997).

FORENSIC PSYCHOLOGY AND INVESTIGATIVE TECHNIQUES

Traditionally, courts of law have assumed that judges and juries are able to determine whether someone is telling the truth on the stand. However, several notorious wrongful convictions in Canada have brought this assumption into question. In fact, many injustices have resulted directly from the inability of legal decision-makers to recognize lying or mistaken recollections. The judge quoted at the beginning of this chapter believed she could determine honesty by paying attention to someone's demeanour and mannerisms on the stand. But was she right?

Long before the trial, police must apprehend suspects and, in the process, generate evidence that may be used to convict the person. Further, they may question victims and other witnesses in order to determine just what they know about the crime and the suspect. In gathering their evidence, police use a variety of techniques to determine the credibility of these individuals. When victims have been traumatized by an event, they may report little or no memory for the event; on rare occasions this may represent **dissociative amnesia** that cannot be attributed to head injury or intoxication (Scheflin, Spiegel, & Spiegel, 1999). Sometimes, even perpetrators of extreme violence experience dissociative amnesia for their actions (Porter, Birt, Yuille, & Hervé, 2001). If victims or suspects are not able to recall as much as the police had hoped, the police may suggest hypnosis as a way of improving their recall. Additionally, when the police have identified suspects who claim innocence, they may ask them to take a polygraph examination to determine whether they are lying. But are the police really able to enhance someone's memory or determine whether someone is telling the truth?

Both hypnosis and polygraphy have their advocates (not only among the police but among some psychologists) and are widely used in some jurisdictions, but they have major limitations. These common approaches used in the area of **credi-bility assessment** serve as a focus of this chapter. The questioning of witnesses and victims continues as the topic of Chapter 6, and the further interrogation of suspects is the topic of Chapter 7.

A common theme of all three chapters is that forensic psychologists must try to balance the desire of the legal system to apprehend and prosecute criminals with a caution regarding questionable procedures. For example, in their understandable desire to increase the conviction rate, police may fail to evaluate the accuracy of procedures that seem to produce positive results. Thus, an objective of each of these chapters, beyond evaluating the techniques described, is to seek ways that forensic psychologists can improve credibility assessment practices. Some of the suggestions in these three chapters may elicit resistance from investigators, who—like any occupational group—object to interference from outsiders.

CAN POLICE OFFICERS AND JUDGES ACCURATELY DETECT DECEPTION?

Before we consider specific credibility assessment techniques such as polygraphy, let us first turn to the issue of the ability of the police, judges, and other legal staff to determine when someone is lying in general. Given their level of relevant experience, one might expect that they would do a good job at catching liars. Judges, in particular, must often decide who is lying as part of their job in order for justice to be served.

Unfortunately, although the triers of fact try to remain objective, there is considerable evidence that their decision making is subject to significant biases (e.g., Kahneman & Tversky, 1982). Judges form impressions of credibility from a witness's **demeanour** that influence decisions, even though there is little evidence for the validity of this process. In fact, there are suggestions that both judges and police are poorly equipped to identify deceit. In a classic study,

Paul Ekman and Maureen O'Sullivan (1991) found that judges, police officers, and other groups performed only around the level of chance in determining who among a group of videotaped speakers were telling the truth. Although this may come as a surprise to many judges, Justice Rooke of the Court of Alberta (1996) recognized the problem and stated (at a judicial conference) that judges are probably no better than laypersons in judging credibility. Are lawyers any better at detecting lies? Probably not. As well-known criminal lawyer Clayton Ruby of the Toronto firm Ruby and Edwardh recently observed, "We're terrible. That's in part because people hear what they want to hear. You want to believe your client's version of events" (Dotto, 2004, p. 45). Wells, Lindsay, and Ferguson (1979) had mock jurors watch witnesses being questioned and then judge their testimony. Both accurate and inaccurate witnesses were believed about 80 percent of the time, leading the authors to conclude that observers are unable to determine the truth from listening to testimony.

A major problem in detecting lies by legal staff is a widespread reliance on stereotypical cues to lying that are not valid. Porter, Woodworth, and Birt (2000) found that a group of Correctional Service of Canada parole officers performed at below the level of chance in deciding whether videotaped speakers were lying or telling the truth. Many of their mistaken judgments were associated with their reliance on questionable cues and strategies. For example, when they relied upon on a single dominant cue to lying or their "gut instinct," they tended to make mistakes. Research indicates that people tend to associate lying with signs of nervousness such as speech errors, gaze aversion (the person refuses to "look you in the eye"), body movements, and shifting positions. In fact, research shows that liars often behave in the completely opposite manner (e.g., Vrij, 2000)! The fact that judges may use such misguided beliefs in evaluating credibility is apparent from their own statements. At the start of this chapter, we quoted the judge who thought that the suspects were lying

because each was "evasive at times or his eyes shifted around." In the case of *Laurentide Motels v. Beauport* (1989), Supreme Court Justice L'Heureux-Dubé stated that judges should consider "the movements, glances, hesitations, trembling, blushing" of witnesses. Such remarks reflect a faulty approach to credibility assessment.

Obviously, there is a need for the development of better techniques to detect deception!

HYPNOSIS IN CRIMINAL INVESTIGATIONS

The RCMP and regional police forces in Canada frequently use hypnosis in the course of their investigations, mainly with victims and witnesses (Royal Canadian Mounted Police, 2004). The use of hypnosis by police grew rapidly during the 1970s, in part because the rules in most regions at that time permitted wide admissibility of hypnotically induced memories (Steblay & Bothwell, 1994). Martin Reiser (1980), the LAPD psychologist mentioned in Chapter 3, started the Law Enforcement Hypnosis Institute (LEHI) in the mid-1970s so that police officers could be trained as forensic hypnotists. His 32-hour course taught law-enforcement officers to become what he called "hypno-technicians" (Scheflin & Shapiro, 1989, p. 67). Within its first seven years, more than 1000 police officers received training at LEHI (Serrill, 1984).

In reality, hypnosis has been used by the legal system for more than 100 years (Spiegel & Spiegel, 1987), but the topic has always been fraught with mystery and controversy. The early enthusiastic claims were reminiscent of Hugo Münsterberg's promise that psychology "could pierce the soul"; they were eventually renounced. Yet even today experts continue to disagree about whether hypnosis is effective in recovering memories and whether it is unduly suggestive (Hibler, 1995; Scheflin, Spiegel, & Spiegel, 1999).

Advocates and Skeptics

Reiser reported in 1985 data from more than 600 major crime cases at the LAPD, claiming that interviews using hypnosis had enhanced "investigatively useful recall in approximately three-fourths of the cases" and that "accuracy levels of the hypnotically elicited information were around 90%" (1985, p. 515). But other experts were not nearly so sanguine or positive. In his book *Multiple Identities and False Memories: A Sociocognitive Perspective* (1996), the late Nicholas Spanos, director of the Laboratory for Experimental Hypnosis at Carleton University from 1975 to 1994 (when he died in a plane crash), rejected the notion of a special "hypnotic state" and, instead, argued that hypnosis is learned "role-playing" behaviour. In a fascinating earlier experiment, Spanos and colleagues (1991) found that when people are hypnotically "age regressed," some come to accept and believe suggestions that they were abused in a past life. This and other evidence indicated that hypnosis can result in bizarre, implausible memories.

Hypnosis is only possible with the most suggestible individuals (e.g., Spiegel, 1994), who are especially prone to **false memories** following exposure to misleading information (e.g., Lynn & Nash, 1994). When such false memories happen, they can be held very confidently by the person (e.g., Loftus, 2003; Porter, Yuille, & Lehman, 1999). Accordingly, Martin Orne, a psychologist and psychiatrist, urged judges to use caution when considering the admissibility of hypnotically assisted testimony (cited in Scheflin & Shapiro, 1989). Orne's own research led him to conclude that the probative value of such testimony was overcome by the risks of false confidence and distorted recollection (see, for example, Orne, Soskis, Dinges, & Orne, 1984, for an illustration).

Despite this skepticism from many researchers, police assume that in most instances what is recalled under hypnosis is "the truth," at least as the person remembers it. But this kind of "truth" (i.e., what the person believes happened) and accuracy are not the same thing. Despite this distinction, some observers can become convinced that whatever hypnosis generates is, in and of itself, accurate. Such trust fails to recognize that the reports of witnesses may be influenced by later events, including the way they are questioned. An even greater danger is that an expert who is convinced about the efficacy of hypnosis will come to believe a "hypnotically induced" testimonial that actually is an elaborate deception. One such example comes from the "Hillside Strangler" case (O'Brien, 1985).

The "Hillside Strangler" Case

The benefits and dangers of using hypnosis with victims and witnesses to uncover more information about a crime is the primary focus of this chapter. Although the use of hypnosis with Kenneth Bianchi does not fit this category, as he was a suspect rather than a victim, his case is illustrative of the dangers of assuming hypnotically induced testimony is accurate. Bianchi's ability to manipulate psychologists and psychiatrists who were hypnosis experts was so powerful that his story is truly a cautionary tale about relying too heavily on the powers of hypnosis.

Between October 1977 and February 1978, ten young women were raped, tortured, and strangled to death; their bruised and stripped bodies were found on various hillsides northeast of downtown Los Angeles. In January 1979 a suspect was arrested in Washington State, but he denied everything. Then, under hypnosis, the suspect—Kenneth Bianchi—began to display the classic manifestations of **multiple personality**. In addition to his normal-state "Ken" personality emerged an alter ego, "Steve," who took responsibility for having committed the murders. A third personality later emerged, and possibly a fourth and fifth. Kenneth Bianchi claimed that he knew nothing of the murders, and thus his lawyers filed a plea of not guilty by reason of insanity.

A psychiatrist, Glenn Allison, and a psychologist, John Watkins, separately hypnotized Bianchi; each was convinced of the legitimacy of a multiple-personality diagnosis in this case, and each supported Bianchi's claim that he was not responsible for his actions. But other people, including the police detectives, were dubious. They recruited Martin Orne, another expert on forensic hypnosis, to examine Bianchi. Orne tricked Bianchi and found that while the suspect was supposedly hypnotized, he overreacted; Bianchi did things during his "hallucination" that were clearly inconsistent with actual reactions of persons while in a hypnotized state. Orne concluded that Bianchi was malingering; his demonstration led to Bianchi's pleading guilty to five of the hillside rape-murders (as well as two in Washington). In exchange for his plea of guilt prior to a trial, Bianchi avoided the death penalty; he is now serving a life sentence in a California prison.

How could experts on hypnosis be so misled by Bianchi's performance? The author of a book on this case offers the following:

> A key lies in Dr. [John] Watkins' comment to the skeptical BBC producer that Bianchi could not have possibly known enough about hypnosis and psychology to fake multiple personality syndrome. Dr. Watkins said Bianchi would have to have had "several years of study in Rorschach [tests] and graduate study in psychology for him to be able to do that." So great is the belief of some professionals in the intricacy and obscurity of their specialty that they can become blind to the obvious. Nor was Dr. Watkins impressed by Bianchi's library of psychology texts. After all, Bianchi did not have a degree. (O'Brien, 1985, pp. 274–275)

Spanos, Weekes, and Bertrand (1985) created an experiment based on the Bianchi case to examine whether participants could readily produce a second "personality." Undergraduate students were asked to play the role of an accused murderer who had pled not guilty, despite overwhelming evidence. They were told they would participate in a psychiatric interview for the court that could involve hypnosis. In the

"Bianchi condition," participants were hypnotized and instructed to allow a second personality to emerge. In the "hidden part condition," participants were hypnotized and told that they may have "walled off" a part of themselves. Control participants were not hypnotized. Participants receiving the explicitly suggestive interview (Bianchi condition) were more likely than the other groups to manifest symptoms of multiple personality disorder, in both the interview and in subsequent psychological testing. Although they had been explicitly instructed to simulate an accused criminal, the results show that diagnostic interviews often contain cues that convey the types of behaviours sought by a clinician.

The moral of the Bianchi case: Self-recognition as an expert may lead the forensic psychologist to forget that even lay people often have access to the same knowledge and insights, or at least enough to make a convincing case. Our expertise always must be tempered by skepticism and common sense. In fact, the Supreme Court of Canada has criticized psychiatrists and psychologists for sometimes not demonstrating this attribute. In *R. v. Gruenke* (1991), the court reviewed the lower court's instruction to the jury:

> In commenting on the evidence of a defence psychiatrist, Dr. Shane, who had questioned the appellant about her involvement in the murder under hypnosis and sodium amytal, Judge Krindle (presumably referring to Dr. Shane's statement that he was impressed with Ms. Gruenke's credibility under hypnosis) stated: "He is not a lie detector machine. He is not an expert on who is telling the truth. He should not have commented before you on his opinion on credibility. He has no expertise in that area. I ask you to disregard any comments he may have made in that connection."

The theme of this passage is a common one in the Canadian court system. Judges frequently admonish psychologists and psychiatrists for commenting on ultimate issues, in this case, the honesty of the accused based on evidence from a hypnosis session. Further, forensic psychologists need to be aware of their own limitations in determining whether someone is lying to them.

Hypnosis of Suspects, Witnesses, and Victims

The use of hypnosis with suspects is not limited to the Bianchi case. Traditionally it has been used—and abused—in order to get information from a defendant about a crime. Well-known Canadian cases in which hypnosis was used by police to elicit a confession from a suspect include *Horvath v. The Queen* (1979) and *R v. Clark* (1984). However, more recently the RCMP appear to have changed their view on hypnosis with suspects. They now maintain that "since subjects can confabulate during a hypnotic session, the accuracy of all information obtained through hypnosis must be verified and/or corroborated through careful investigation. Hypnosis is not used in relation to suspects or accused/charged persons for the noted reasons" (Royal Canadian Mounted Police, 2004). Today it is much more common for police to attempt to help a witness remember more about a crime. Some victims of a violent crime—such as a rape or a mugging—may not recall important details about the incident or perpetrator. Can more information be recalled under hypnosis? As noted, police have long assumed that it can and will offer anecdotal support for their expectations. Similarly, psychotherapists using hypnosis report many cases where, "within a therapeutic relationship, they were able to elicit many new and apparently valid memories through hypnosis" (Watkins, 1989, p. 80). But within the scientific community there remains great skepticism over the accuracy of material recalled during a hypnosis session. In the following sections, the claims are presented and evaluated.

Supportive Research Reviews

Reiser (1989) has reviewed the research on the utility of hypnosis as an investigative tool. One of the problems is the variability in the quality of the research. He judged that many of the studies had not "adequately addressed such important questions as the meaningfulness and level of emotional arousal of the event, the utilization of retrieval for relevant information cues, the use of real police interviewers, and the testing of the claims of hardening of memory and the impossibility of cross-examination of witnesses after hypnosis interviewing" (Reiser, 1989, pp. 167–168). But he concluded that the studies possessing great degrees of ecological validity were "more likely to yield results comparable to those found with witnesses in real crime cases" (p. 177). John Watkins, another advocate of forensic hypnosis, took another position: "The critical issue is the hypnotic *state/relationship*, not an isolated, abstract, altered state of consciousness by itself" (1989, p. 80, italics in original). But other reviews of the literature have not been as optimistic, as we will see in the next section.

When Is Hypnosis Beneficial?

The profusion of laboratory and field research in the last 30 years has led to several reviews and evaluations beyond that by Reiser. For example, Brown, Scheflin, and Hammond's (1998) book included a 60-page review that was generally supportive of the usefulness of hypnosis in aiding recall. In contrast, Smith's (1983) review was "unable to document an improvement in memory for hypnotized subjects, but did find a clear demonstration that such subjects are more suggestible" (cited by Steblay & Bothwell, 1994, p. 637). Another review, by Geiselman and Machlovitz (1987), examined 38 experiments from 30 articles published between 1930 and 1985; this review offered a conclusion only mildly encouraging to those who advocate the admissibility of hypnotically refreshed memories. Of these 38 experiments, 21 concluded that the use of hypnosis generated more correct information, 13 reported no effect from hypnosis, and four reported significantly less correct information when the subjects were hypnotized. As

Reiser (1989) notes, these were laboratory studies with—usually—poor ecological validity. Further analysis by the reviewers, Geiselman and Machlovitz, identified three factors that elicited additional correct information under hypnotic recall: an interactive interview with a skilled interviewer, longer-delayed tests of recall, and the use of realistic materials that had arousal effects. They noted that "The five studies where clear success was reported with hypnosis recall (those showing memory facilitation without an increase in errors) are more analogous to the forensic use of hypnosis (as a group) than are most of the other studies that were examined" (1987, p. 43).

Since the publication of that review, Steblay and Bothwell (1994) identified 19 more recent studies—three found hypnotized subjects to be more accurate than nonhypnotized subjects, five studies reported the opposite conclusion, and 11 studies found no statistically significant difference. Steblay and Bothwell carried out a **meta-analysis**, that is, a procedure that statistically combines the results of various studies and determines an overall probability of statistical significance in order to determine whether certain moderator variables explained the variety of outcomes. They concluded:

> The hypothesized increase in recall accuracy for hypnotized subjects has not been substantiated by research to date. Even with the most straightforward scenario, in which nonleading prepared questions were asked of the eyewitness, hypnotized subjects show only a minimal, unreliable edge over control subjects. When leading questions are used, the research evidence in fact demonstrates the reverse: a (nonsignificant) recall deficit in hypnotized subjects compared to controls. The recall performance of hypnotized subjects shows wide variability, suggesting that any gains in recall that might be achieved through hypnosis are easily compromised by moderator variables.
>
> Unfortunately, at this time, the research has not presented a clear identification of the moderator variables which, when implemented in the hypnosis procedure, might guarantee the success of hypnosis in a forensic setting. A statistically significant difference between hypnotized and control subjects was found when the time delay between a subject's viewing of the event and subsequent recall event was considered.... [H]ypnotized subjects do show greater recall accuracy for delays of 24 hours or more. However, the strength of this finding must be tempered with three considerations: (1) Leading questions even in the delay condition reduce the effect size and eliminate the significant difference between groups. (2) The confidence intervals for these effect sizes are quite large and encompass zero; thus there is substantial variability in effect size yet accounted for. And (3) although an increased interval between event and recall attempt does appear to favor hypnotized subjects, this benefit is limited to delays of 1 to 2 days. Even a 1-week delay reverses the effect to favor control subjects. (Steblay & Bothwell, 1994, p. 648)

Other dependent variables analyzed in Steblay and Bothwell's meta-analysis were the following:

1. Unstructured free recall as a procedure found the performance of hypnotized subjects to be better than control subjects, but only three studies evaluated this procedure.
2. Identification of the perpetrator from a lineup did not appear to be aided by hypnosis. In fact, control subjects more accurately identified perpetrators in a lineup, and hypnotized subjects identified more individuals incorrectly.
3. Preliminary evidence suggested that hypnotized subjects commit more recall errors and that they generate significantly more intrusions of uncued errors and experience higher levels of pseudo-memory.
4. Among the clearest of conclusions from the meta-analysis was that hypnotized subjects are more confident about the accuracy of

their recall. An even more convincing reason for skepticism about the use of hypnosis was the fact that confidence and susceptibility to hypnosis were found to be related (Steblay & Bothwell, 1994).

Hence the earlier optimism generated by the Reiser and Geiselman-Machlovitz reviews was not supported in this more recent analysis. Methodological variations such as interactive interviews, longer retention intervals, and realistic stimuli don't aid hypnotically refreshed recall.

Conclusions

The conservative conclusion at this time is that the costs of using hypnosis to aid in memory recall outweigh the benefits, and its use in a court of law to convict someone is not defensible. Authorized reviews by panels from professional organizations on the issue of hypnotically refreshed memory are consistent with this conclusion. The Education Council of the Canadian Psychiatric Association (1996) concluded that great care should be taken to avoid the inappropriate use of leading questions, hypnosis, narcoanalysis (an interview that is conducted while the individual is under the influence of a drug such as sodium pentathol), or other memory-enhancement techniques to generate lost material (Blackshaw, Chandarana, et al., 1996). Similarly, Orne argued that the use of hypnosis can "profoundly affect the individual's subsequent testimony" and "since these changes are not reversible, if individuals are to be allowed to testify after having undergone hypnosis to aid their memory, a minimum number of safeguards are absolutely essential" (1979, p. 335). Porter and colleagues (2003) concluded that the use of suggestive techniques such as hypnosis during forensic investigations should immediately raise concerns about the validity of the allegation in question.

Court Decisions

Given the above cautions, what is the position of the courts on the admissibility of hypnotically refreshed memories? One might assume that they would prohibit them completely as evidence. However, in Canada, the courts decide to allow or disallow such evidence on a case-by-case basis. The Quebec Court of Appeal in *R. v. Taillefer and Duguay* (1995) specifies what a judge should consider before admitting evidence obtained through hypnosis: (1) the competence of the expert who elicited the evidence; (2) the reliability of hypnosis as a technique to revive memory and the safeguards required to ensure its reliability; and (3) whether the conditions under which the technique was employed with respect to the witness met these safeguards. The guidelines for evaluating these safeguards were established in *R. v. Clark* (1984), a decision of the Alberta Court of Queen's Bench:

1. The person conducting the hypnotic interview must be a qualified professional with training both in the use of hypnosis and expertise in psychiatry or psychology.
2. The hypnotist must be independent of the party who requires his or her services. That is, the hypnotist must be free to conduct the hypnotic interview in accordance with his or her professional standards rather than in concert with the party who employs him or her.
3. The hypnotist should be given only the minimum amount of information necessary to conduct the interview.
4. The entire interview between the hypnotist and the potential witness should be recorded, preferably on video.
5. The interview should be conducted with only the hypnotist and the subject present.
6. Before the hypnosis of the subject, the hypnotist should conduct a lengthy interview focused on medical history (including information about the present or past use of drugs). The judgment and intelligence of the subject should be evaluated.
7. Prior to hypnosis, the hypnotist should elicit from the subject a detailed description of the facts surrounding the subject matter of the hypnosis session, as the subject is able to recall them at that point in time.

8. The hypnotist should pay careful attention to the form and manner of his or her questions, the choice of words and the avoidance of body language so that the hypnotist is not either intentionally or inadvertently providing the subject with information.

In the *Clark* case, the accused was charged with first-degree murder. He had no memory of the events surrounding the killings until it was revived through hypnosis. The court was highly critical of the use of hypnosis in that case, stating:

> [T]he great danger of using hypnosis to refresh the memory of potential witnesses is the phenomenon of "memory-hardening," that is, in the opinion of some experts, a person in a hypnotic state has a reduced critical judgment capability and consequently if a person being questioned under hypnosis fantasizes, or lies or responds to suggestions by the hypnotist, he will be unable to distinguish between these "memories" and his actual memories, once the hypnosis session has been completed. (para. 120)

Thus, although hypnotically refreshed testimony is allowed as evidence, the judge in the *Clark* case recognized the potential fallibility of memories elicited under hypnosis. After that case, it was much more difficult for lawyers to convince judges to allow such evidence. For example, the judge in the B.C. murder case *R. v. Savoy* (1997) ruled inadmissible the evidence of eyewitness Jolynne Point who had undergone a hypnosis interview by Dr. Lee Pulos to enhance her memories. In dismissing this evidence, the judge cited the expert evidence of University of British Columbia psychologist Dr. John Yuille, who had given a scathing critique of the investigative interview, calling it a "travesty." The judge found it apparent that the interview had not met the standards set out in *Clark*.

Guidelines

Given the concerns about the accuracy of **hypnotically assisted memory**, a prime function of the forensic psychologist is to offer and encourage guidelines for the use of hypnosis. For example, if memories produced by hypnosis should not be used as evidence in court, can the police seek them during the early stages of a crime investigation? As noted above, the Canadian courts have placed restrictions on the use of hypnosis in crime investigations. Several reviewers offer guidelines similar to those set out in *Clark*, including Spiegel and Spiegel (1987), who provided the following:

1. *Qualifications of the person using hypnosis.* Traditionally, police officers have conducted the hypnosis of witnesses, but the Society for Clinical and Experimental Hypnosis has proposed that only trained psychiatrists or psychologists—independent of the police department should conduct forensic hypnosis and questioning. One benefit of this approach is a possible reduction in the use of leading or suggestive questions.

2. *Pre-hypnosis records.* It is important to keep separate what the witness knew before the hypnosis from what he or she remembered as a result of it.

3. *Electronic recording of hypnosis session.* All the interactions between the examiner and the subject should be recorded electronically, preferably on videotape. If the latter is used, focus should be on both the subject and the hypnotist, in order to try to detect any possible subtle influences in the interaction.

4. *Measurement of hypnotizability.* One guideline suggested by Spiegel and Spiegel (1987) has not been made explicit in Canadian court decisions; it is that the level of **hypnotizability** of the subject should be determined by use of one of the standardized hypnotizability scales, in order to document the subject's degree of responsivity, if any. These scales include the Hypnotic Induction Profile (Spiegel & Spiegel, 1978), the Stanford Hypnotic Susceptibility Scales (Weitzenhoffer & Hilgard, 1959), the Stanford Hypnotic Clinical Scale (Hilgard & Hilgard, 1975), or the Barber Creative

Imagination Scale (Barber & Wilson, 1978–1979). If the subject does not show any hypnotic responsivity during pre-testing, Spiegel and Spiegel suggested that "the person conducting the session would be well advised to forgo any further hypnotic ceremonies since the subject is unlikely to respond, and the problems inherent with the appearance of having induced hypnosis can be avoided" (1987, p. 501).

What about the subjects at the other end of the continuum, the subjects who are highly hypnotizable? This small group of subjects should receive special concern, because they may be highly responsive to manipulation, to leading questions and suggestions, whether or not hypnosis has been used. Procedures described in Chapter 6, for questioning of witnesses by police, are especially relevant for such subjects.

5. *Pre-hypnosis briefing.* The hypnotist should not give the subject any indication that the subject will recall new information or that the memory of the relevant experience will be any clearer. An effort should be made to determine exactly what memories were held before hypnosis (Scheflin, Spiegel, & Spiegel, 1999).

6. *Management of the hypnotic session.* Spiegel and Spiegel suggest that the person conducting the session should provide "a setting in which the subject can remember new facts if there are any, but in which none is introduced in the questioning" (1987, p. 501). They propose that initially, the person should be allowed to review the events as they occurred, with little prompting. Prompting is best done through nonleading questions such as "And then what happens?"

7. *Selective use.* Spiegel and Spiegel note that forensic hypnosis should never be used as a substitute for routine investigative procedures.

Recall that these are guidelines for the use of hypnosis during the **crime-investigation stage**. The inherent dangers in hypnotically assisted memories mean that if the police choose to hypnotize a victim at this early stage, the authorities should exert great caution in allowing this same person to testify at the trial, because of the suggestibility involved in the procedure and the risk of producing false memories.

THE COGNITIVE INTERVIEW

Because of the concerns with the use of hypnosis to retrieve memories, psychologists have developed a procedure, called the **cognitive interview**, that has the same goals without requiring the subject to be hypnotized (Fisher, 1995; Fisher & Geiselman, 1992; Geiselman, Fisher, MacKinnon, & Holland, 1986). The cognitive interview seeks **context reinstatement**; victims are asked to re-create the crime scene mentally, report every single aspect they can remember, and even recall the events in reverse order. The questioning of witnesses, described in the next chapter, can greatly benefit from the procedures used in this approach, as the procedure has been found to improve eyewitness accuracy (Cutler & Penrod; 1988; Fisher, 1995).

THE POLYGRAPH TECHNIQUE

Police at times use devices to question suspects and other persons. Primary among these is the **polygraph** technique, also called the lie-detector test. In fact, when you hear the term "lie detection" you probably think of the polygraph. Two typical uses of the polygraph are to assess the honesty of exculpatory statements given by criminal suspects and to periodically review the status of employees whose work involves international security. Iacono and Patrick (1987, 1999) listed other uses, including determining the truthfulness of claims by both parents in child-custody decisions during divorce proceedings and the use of successful responses to a polygraph test in the appeal of a conviction.

Using the Polygraph to Interrogate Criminal Suspects

When suspects are questioned by the police, they may be asked to complete a polygraph examination if they maintain their innocence. Polygraph examiners assume that changes in physiological reactions in response to incriminating questions are indications that the suspect is lying (Bull, 1988). Police believe in the accuracy of the polygraph, but are their assumptions verified by empirical research findings?

The Forensic Psychologist and the Polygraph Technique

One of the functions of the forensic psychologist in consulting with the police is to serve as an evaluator of interrogative techniques, including the polygraph. The forensic psychologist must question the police assumption of polygraph accuracy. If it is found that the polygraph examination has limitations (see the discussion in the next section), the forensic psychologist may testify before the legislature to encourage ameliorative legislation or appear before the court during an appeal.

Scientific Conclusions

The scientific conclusions about the polygraph do not encourage its use. According to a review by Anthony Gale (1988), the truth of the matter is "that we do not know the full truth about polygraph lie-detection" (p. 2). The British Psychological Society, the leading organization of research and applied psychologists in that country, authorized a study of available research literature and concluded that the evidence supporting the use of the polygraph test was "very slender," its reliability and validity were in question, and a need existed for more research on the topic, since much of the existing research was inadequate.

Criticisms of Polygraph Procedures

More specifically, the British Psychological Society's report criticized the typical polygraph procedure on the following grounds:

- It involved the use of nonstandardized procedures.
- Examiners often misled subjects about how accurate the test was.
- Sometimes efforts were made to create anxiety in subjects in order to encourage confessions.
- The subject's privacy was violated. Very personal questions about a subject's sexual, political, or religious preferences may be asked (Lykken, 1998).

The report concluded: "In such circumstances, it is difficult to see how members of the Society could engage in work as polygraphic interrogators and claim that their conduct is consistent with the Society's current Code of Conduct" (British Psychological Society, 1986, p. 93).

Differing Goals

At this point we need to distinguish between the usual procedures and goals of the professional polygraph examiner and the research psychologist who uses the polygraph technique in the laboratory. For example, the professional polygrapher will usually begin an interview with a suspect with some biographical questions. The examiner will then tell the subject the nature of the actual questions to be asked in the lie-detection procedure. Bull pointed out that many polygraph examiners will use this first phase "to obtain an initial impression of the testee and to judge whether the individual seems to be more of an honest, upright citizen than a deceiver" (Bull, 1988, p. 12). In contrast, the research psychologist is interested either in determining the validity of the polygraph procedure or in understanding its physiological basis.

A Psychological Analysis of the Polygraph Procedure

The use of the "lie-detecting machine" generates strong and varied reactions from the public. So, too, is the professional psychological community divided with regard to the appropriateness of polygraph testing. Before reviewing the literature, we will examine the arguments for each position.

Inferences and Assumptions in the Polygraph Test

First, it is useful to evaluate the entire process. The procedure is well known: a subject is strapped to a machine that includes electrodes attached to the subject's body. The examiner then asks the subject a variety of questions. Depending on the type of polygraph technique employed, some questions may be irrelevant to the issue at hand or some may deal with other potentially emotional issues for the subject. Always, some of the questions deal with the issues at hand, the crime that was committed.

The responses that the examiner evaluates are not the verbal responses, but rather the physiological changes that occur as the subject answers. The measures of various responses—heart rate, breathing rate, blood pressure, and galvanic skin response—traditionally were recorded by ink pens as a series of lines on a chart or by a visual display unit. Computer monitors have replaced the ink pens in contemporary equipment, with the digitally stored data plotted by a printer (Iacono & Patrick, 1999). This equipment can even provide a probability statement of the likelihood that the subject is telling the truth.

Sources of Inaccuracy

Two potential sources of inaccuracy emerge. First, the physiological measures do not directly measure lying; their changes only reflect shifts in emotional reactivity. Thus any conclusion about lying is an *inference*. It is essential that responses to the critical questions (e.g., "Did you steal the car?") be compared with responses to some other type of question. Two types of polygraph testing, described next, use different contrasts.

The Control Question Technique The **Control Question Technique** (CQT) typically consists of about ten questions. Relevant questions deal with the issue at hand; control questions deal

with possible past behaviours that might generate emotion on the subject's part (Iacono & Patrick, 1987). An example: "Before the age of 24 did you ever try to hurt someone to get revenge?"

Note the crucial assumption that if the subject is guilty or not telling the truth, the questions on the issue at hand will generate more emotional reactivity than will the control questions. The control questions provide a baseline measure for that person's level of reactivity. Control questions must be chosen with care and pre-tested with the individual subject; it is essential that the questions chosen for the actual examination will elicit lying by the subject, and hence a physiological response.

The rationale behind the Control Question Technique is that an innocent person will respond as much to the control questions as to the crime-related ones (or will react even more to the control questions). In contrast, the guilty person will show more physiological responses to the crime-related questions than to the control questions. Any score (a "score" represents a numerical value that combines the extremity of various physiological reactions) that emerges from this procedure is thus a **difference score**.

The Relevant-Irrelevant Test The **Relevant-Irrelevant Test** was the first widely used polygraph test of deception. Here, the relevant questions are similar in form and content to the relevant questions in the Control Question Technique, but the irrelevant questions reflect a different type. They are essentially innocuous; "Are you sitting down?" or "Is your birthday in April?" The basic assumption of the Relevant-Irrelevant Test is that:

> a person who is deceptive in answering the relevant questions will be concerned about being discovered, which will cause involuntary autonomic reactions to occur with greatest strength in response to questions that one answered deceptively. Thus, guilty individuals are expected to show their strongest reactions to relevant questions, whereas truthful subjects are expected to show no difference in their

reactions to relevant and neutral questions. Therefore, the polygraph examiner looks for heightened reactivity to the relevant questions, and the presence of such patterns of reactions leads to the conclusion that the subject was practicing deception on the relevant issues. If no difference in reactions to relevant and neutral questions is observed, the examiner concludes that the subject was truthful in answering the relevant questions. (Raskin, 1989, pp. 250–251)

The assumptions reflected in procedures such as the Relevant-Irrelevant Test are simplistic and naïve (Podlesny & Raskin, 1977). Most polygraph examiners have discarded this procedure, recognizing that "even an innocent person is much more likely to display more physiological activity when (truthfully) responding to the relevant questions than to the irrelevant ones" (Bull, 1988, p. 13). That is why the preferred technique, the Control Question Technique, employs as its unrelated questions ones that will generate emotion and lead to a response that denies culpability.

In addition to the problem of inference, a second problem of polygraph examination confounds its proponents: How can physiological responses (as operationalized by sweeping waves of recordings) be translated into quantified measures. How can the examiner classify the subject's set of responses as "truthful" or "deceptive" (or "inconclusive" in cases of uncertainty)?

Many polygraph examiners are former police officers; few are trained as psychologists in measurement procedures (Bull, 1988). Some simply look at the charts and base their conclusions on global, or "eyeball" impressions. Even those who are more precise may still be quite subjective; many polygraph examiners "decided which questions had occasioned the largest responses by merely looking at the charts without bothering to measure each response" (Bull, 1988, p. 17). They might even use their expectations based on the pre-examination interview, along with the examinee's physiological reactivity, as determinants of their global classification. This type of subjectivity is the very antithesis of the scientific measurement model by which psychology seeks objective, replicable observations.

Even when the polygraph examiner attempts to quantify the physiological responses, the task is far from completely reliable. Raskin (1989) stated that in the procedure he developed, a score is assigned for each of the physiological parameters for each question-pair; the score can range from −3 to +3, and "it represents the direction and magnitude of the observed difference in the reactions elicited by the relevant question and its nearby control question" (p. 260). If the observed reaction is stronger in response to the relevant question, a negative score is given; positive scores are assigned when the reaction is stronger to the control question. A value of 0 is assigned to comparisons where no difference is observed, 1 to a noticeable difference, 2 to a strong difference, and 3 to a dramatic difference. Raskin noted that most assigned scores are 0 or 1; scores of 2 are less common, and scores of 3 are "unusual." After this evaluation is made for the first pair, it is repeated for other pairs of questions so that a total score can be obtained. Just how different do the reactions to the two types of questions have to be in order to conclude that the subject is deceptive? That is a matter for debate.

Note that these scores are subjectively based on a visual inspection of graphic data; certainly there is room for error. Raskin (1989) reported that the correlations among the total numerical scores assigned by the original examiner and by blind raters "tend to be very high" (p. 261). In both laboratory studies using mock crimes and in field studies, his inter-rater reliabilities (the degree of agreement in ratings given by different observers) were typically greater than .90. But, as we will see in the case of Floyd Fay (discussed below), these consistencies don't always hold up in real-world cases. Furthermore, a psychometrically oriented psychologist would react negatively to Raskin's procedure for a variety of reasons, not the least of which is its reliance on difference scores. Difference scores—and in its broadest sense, the polygraph output is a difference between responses to two types of questions—are notoriously less reliable than are the scores on which they are based because of the error or unreliability of each separate score.

But for Ray Bull (1988) even greater faults exist. In the Control Question Technique "it is extremely difficult to devise control questions that ensure the eliciting of stronger reactions in an innocent person than would the relevant questions relating to the crime of which they had been accused" (p. 14). He noted that professional polygraphers try to minimize this problem, but for many subjects it may defy a satisfactory solution. This difficulty in selecting adequate control questions may be a reason for the Control Question Technique leading to more **false positives** (classifying truthful people as liars) than **false negatives** (classifying liars as truthful) (Carroll, 1988). Both types of errors can have major consequences. For example, as mentioned in Chapter 4, Gary Ridgway had been a suspect in the Green River Killer investigation in the early 1980s but passed a polygraph examination and was eliminated as a suspect (false negative error), after which he killed several more women.

Despite these cautions, some psychologists are professional polygraphers and hence are advocates for their use. Others who have studied the phenomenon are quite critical of it, as we have seen in some of the above observations. These differences are illustrated in the variety of reactions to the Floyd Fay case.

The Floyd Fay Case

This case illustrates the problems in using the polygraph technique to determine whether a suspect is lying. On March 28, 1978, at 9:30 P.M., in a small town in Ohio, a man named Fred Ery was shot and killed by a large man in a blue ski jacket and full ski mask. One witness was present during the attack, but her back was toward the attacker; she was sitting at the counter as Ery, standing behind the counter, was killed with a blast from a sawed-off shotgun.

As Ery lay dying, he said something like, "It looked like 'Buzz' but it couldn't have been." He and Floyd "Buzz" Fay had argued earlier. Fay was arrested at his trailer at 4:30 A.M. the same night; he denied committing the crime. The murder weapon and the ski mask were never found. But the police took Fay's ski jacket from his trailer and put it in a lineup of ski jackets (probably a first in the annals of eyewitness identification!). The witness, Debra Koehler, was unable to identify it as having been worn by the gunman.

Fay had only one previous arrest, for drunk driving, but he was charged with aggravated murder and thrown into jail, as he could not afford bail. He had been waiting in jail for two months when the district attorney came up with an unusual deal:

1. Take a polygraph test, administered by the government.
2. If Fay came out as truthful, all charges would be dismissed.
3. If Fay's responses were judged to be deceptive, a second, privately administered, test would be given.
4. If the results of the two polygraph tests were in conflict, the case would proceed to trial without any of the results being used as evidence.
5. If both tests indicated deception, Buzz Fay would plead guilty to the lesser charge of murder, rather than aggravated murder.
6. If he refused to plead guilty, he would be tried for the original charge of aggravated murder and the results of the polygraph tests would be admitted into evidence.

Fay contemplated the offer and decided to agree to take the polygraph test. He desperately wanted out of jail and, after all, he knew he was innocent. He took the first test and failed it. A second test produced the same conclusion. Fay refused to plead guilty and so, as a result of a jury trial, he was found guilty of aggravated murder and sentenced to life in prison.

A year later, while in prison, he wrote several psychologists who were experts on the polygraph, asking them to rescore his polygraph records. David Lykken, a critic of lie-detector tests, felt the test was useless and refused to. David Raskin, however, agreed to; he concluded that Fay's score was a +7, that he was telling the truth (the original test result was a −6, or "deceptive"). A third expert, Gordon Barland, scored him +1, or "inconclusive"; a fourth expert, Frank Horvath, also concluded the record was inconclusive (Raskin, 1981). These inconsistencies had no practical effect—Fay was not released because of them (although a year and a half later he was released, because the real killers were apprehended and confessed)—but they reflect the serious problems in drawing conclusions from testing procedures that may be unreliable.

RESEARCH EVALUATION

Examiners who make their living by administering polygraph tests do not question the validity of what they are doing (Bull, 1988). An experienced examiner once testified that he had administered more than 20 000 polygraph examinations in his career and never once had been proven to be wrong (Lykken, 1981). David Raskin and Robert Hare have stated that "the accuracy of lie detectors on hardened criminals behind bars is 95.5%" (1978, p. 133).

In contrast, the polygraph examination received extensive unfavourable publicity when it was claimed in 1994 that Aldrich Ames, the CIA official charged with spying for the Russians since 1985, had passed polygraph examinations on two occasions five years apart (1986 and 1991). The false sense of security given the CIA by the apparently truthful test results permitted Ames to continue his spying. In a conflict between two U.S. federal agencies, the FBI later claimed that Ames gave deceptive answers in 1991 when he was asked whether he was a spy,

but the CIA failed to follow up, giving Ames a second chance by rephrasing questions (Weiner, 1994). And just to cloud the issue further, a professional writer and expert on the FBI (Kessler, 1994) claimed that Ames had failed three polygraph tests but CIA higher-ups neglected to act on this fact. At the end of 1994, R. James Woolsey, director of the CIA, resigned, partly as a result of the Ames case.

Criticisms of the Polygraph's Supposed Validity

The psychologist most critical of the polygraph test is David Lykken (1981, 1985, 1988, 1998). Part of his criticism centres on his position that the lie detector is stressful and intrusive; furthermore, he has noted that polygraph examiners often rely on deceit to convince the subject that the test is accurate (Lykken, 1988, p. 112). But his central claim—and our focus here—is whether it is, in actuality, an acceptably valid instrument.

Two types of studies have been used to evaluate the accuracy of the polygraph. Laboratory studies have the advantage of knowing whether subjects are actually lying or not, but they are limited in their ecological validity. This problem can more specifically be articulated as "the difficulty of inducing in subjects the degree and type of emotional concern experienced by guilty or by innocent suspects being tested in real life" (Lykken, 1988, p. 114). Lykken concluded that the laboratory studies that ask volunteer college students to "commit a crime" and lie during an interrogation are creating in such subjects more of a state of excitement than a state of guilt.

A better way of assessing accuracy is through a field study, but certain criteria must be met:

1. The study must include a representative sample of polygraph tests administered under real-life circumstances.
2. The charts must be independently scored by polygraph examiners who only have the charts to guide their decisions (i.e., blind

scoring). As Carroll (1988) noted, the apparently straightforward question: "How accurate is polygraph lie detection?" is subject to several interpretations. Proponents of lie detection have interpreted the question to mean "based on polygraph records plus all other available information" (Carroll, 1988, p. 19).

3. The scores must be compared with a criterion that is independent of the polygraph findings (that is, it is necessary to be able to know which subjects actually did commit a crime).

Lykken concluded that many field studies did not meet these criteria; in fact, only three did (Barland & Raskin, 1976; Horvath, 1977; and Kleinmuntz & Szucko, 1984). The results of each of these studies will be described later, but, overall, 84 percent of the guilty subjects were judged to be lying; only 53 percent of the innocent subjects were judged to be truthful. Is this "accurate enough?" With these studies as our guide, our conclusion must be that the procedure is seriously biased against the truthful subject (Lykken, 1988, p. 124).

What if a psychologist or other expert is called on to testify and bases his or her testimony on these studies? Following the Supreme Court of Canada guidelines for expert testimony in the *Mohan* case, does the research qualify? This chapter has noted the limitations in the polygraph procedure: the lack of standardized testing procedures, the unreliable error rate, and the lack of general scientific acceptance.

One of the most comprehensive reviews of the other type of validity check, the laboratory experiment, was carried out by the Office of Technology Assessment of the U.S. Congress (1983). It found that on the average, 88.6 percent of the guilty were correctly classified, and 82.6 percent of the innocent were correctly classified. But a more ecologically valid review used the results of only those laboratory studies whose methodology closely resembled the use of the Control Question Technique in the field (Carroll, 1988); these studies are summarized in Table 5.1. The first three of these studies had guilty subjects engage in a mock crime. The Waid, Orne, and Orne (1981) study had guilty subjects conceal certain code words from the examiner, and Barland (1981) had guilty subjects lie about a biographical detail. (The last scenario is closer to a pre-employment examination than to a crime-detection one.) The average success rate at detecting guilt was 85.4 percent, but the average for correctly detecting the innocent was lower—76.9 percent. However, these results reflected the examiners' use of data beyond those provided by the polygraph. When blind scoring was used (i.e., only the polygraph records were reviewed), the accuracy rate dropped some, particularly for innocent subjects.

Field studies produce more of a challenge, as Lykken (1998) noted. How does one find a criterion of guilt or innocence independent of a polygrapher's judgment? Two procedures have been used. Barland and Raskin (1976) asked five experienced lawyers to ascertain guilt or innocence based on evidence in the files; then Barland conducted the polygraph examination, and Raskin, blind to the case files, analyzed the charts. Of the 92 original cases, the lawyers agreed sufficiently for the cases to be used on 64. Of these, Raskin found the polygraph results to be inconclusive in 13 cases; the data are based on the remaining 51 cases.

The second type of criterion was, for guilt, a confession of guilt, and for innocence, a confession of guilt by another person. Horvath (1977) located 28 examples of each type from police files and gave the polygraph charts to ten trained polygraph examiners for a blind evaluation. Five of these examiners had more than three years' experience; five had less, but the experience levels of the examiners did not significantly affect their accuracy. Kleinmuntz and Szucko (1984) also used actual suspects—the polygraph charts of 50 confessed thieves and 50 innocent persons who, though originally suspects in these crimes, were cleared because of the confessions of the actual thieves. Six professional polygraph examiners made blind evaluations of guilt or innocence.

Table 5.2 on page 114 summarizes the findings of these three field studies. Average accuracy

Table 5.1	Laboratory Studies of Polygraph Accuracy				
Study	Status of subjects	Number of subjects	Percent accuracy	Percent guilty classified innocent (false negative)	Percent innocent classified guilty (false positive)
Barland and Raskin (1975)	Guilty	26	88.5	11.5	28.6
	Innocent	21	71.4		
Raskin and Hare (1978)	Guilty	21	100.0	0	8.7
	Innocent	23	91.3		
Hammond (1980)	Guilty	24	95.8	4.2	33.3
	Innocent	18	66.7		
Waid, Orne, and Orne (1981)	Guilty	40	72.5	27.5	23.5
	Innocent	34	76.5		
Barland (1981)	Guilty	26	80.8	19.2	23.8
	Innocent	21	76.2		
Average accuracy[a]			85.4 76.9	14.6	23.1

[a]These averages were computed taking into account the different sample sizes.

(From "How accurate is polygraph lie detection?" in *The Polygraph Test* edited by Anthony Gale, p. 22, Sage Publications, 1988. Reprinted by permission of Sage Publishing Ltd.)

in identifying guilty subjects was 83 percent, but for innocent subjects only 57 percent. Carroll (1988) summarized these results as follows:

These data largely speak for themselves; overall accuracy is generally low, and the rate of false positive judgments staggeringly high. Thus polygraph data per se would seem to be remarkably insensitive, particularly to a suspect's innocence. Expressed another way, the "blind" evaluation studies strongly imply that the polygraph contributes nothing of worth to traditional means of establishing innocence. In fact, the data it provides probably mislead. (p. 27)

Carroll concluded that whatever accuracy the polygraph examination provides in field tests comes from conclusions by the examiner of the subject's general demeanour rather than his or her chart responses. This evaluation is a harsh one; we prefer to frame the question of the forensic applicability of the polygraph examination within the legal instruction for determining guilt. Fact-finders—juries, judges—are not to

rule for guilt unless they are convinced "beyond a reasonable doubt." Although judges are loathe to translate this instruction into a percentage figure, usually it is seen as an 85-to-90-percent likelihood. Therefore, although the assignments of guilt or innocence based on polygraph examinations produce results that are above chance, they do not achieve this standard.

The Current Legal Status

The pivotal Canadian court decision pertaining to polygraph evidence occurred in the case *R. v. Béland* (1987). In that case the Supreme Court of Canada ruled that polygraph evidence related to a crime would not be allowed into the court under any circumstances. The court stated that "the results of a polygraph examination are not admissible as evidence. The polygraph has no place in the judicial process where it is employed as a tool to determine or test the credibility of witnesses" (*R. v. Béland*, 1987, para. 5). The presiding justices were Chief Justice Dickson, Justice Beetz, Justice La Forest, Justice Lamer, Justice Le Dain, Justice

Table 5.2	Summary of Results of Field Studies That Involved Blind Assessment of the Polygraph Records				
Study	Status of subjects	Number of subjects	Percent accuracy	Percent false negative	Percent false positive
Barland and Raskin (1976)	Guilty	40	97	3	55
	Innocent	11	45		
Horvath (1977)	Guilty	28	79	23	49
	Innocent	28	50		
Kleinmuntz and Szucko (1984)	Guilty	50	76	24	37
	Innocent	50	64		
Average accuracy[a]			83	17	43
			57		

[a]These averages were computed taking into account the different sample sizes.

(From "How accurate is polygraph lie detection?" in *The Polygraph Test* edited by Anthony Gale, p. 26, Sage Publications, 1988. Reprinted by permission of Sage Publishing Ltd.)

McIntyre, and Justice Wilson. Five of these judges formed the majority and deciding judgment, while two of them dissented. The latter were Justice Lamer and Justice Wilson, who argued strongly that polygraph examination results should be deemed admissible in court. In a recent Supreme Court of Canada case, *R. v. Oickle* (2000), Justice Iacobucci, writing for the majority, reviewed the legal status of the polygraph and concluded that: "As many sources have demonstrated, polygraphs are far from infallible.... Similarly, the court recognized in *Béland* that the results of the polygraph are sufficiently unreliable that they cannot be admitted in court" (para. 95).

Thus, at present, the use of the polygraph in Canada must be limited to the police investigation stage in formulating suspects; evidence generated through a polygraph examination will generally not be allowed in our courts.

THE ROLE OF THE PSYCHOLOGIST AS A PSYCHOMETRIC EXPERT

If polygraph examiners want their examinations to produce accurate results, psychologists can provide expertise regarding the psychometric qualities of adequate testing instruments. Particularly important are the phenomena of reliability, validity, and freedom from bias; as we have seen, the polygraph procedure often falls short of the standards for these (Blinkhorn, 1988). Bull (1988) noted that many polygraphers have "at best only a rudimentary understanding of all the physiological and psychological factors involved" (p. 18).

Another role for the psychologist is as an evaluation researcher. For example, controversy exists over the claim that subjects can be trained to engage in thoughts or acts that affect the validity of the polygraph responses. Most examiners don't think they can. What does the research conclude about the use of **counter-measures** (attempts to prevent the polygraph technique from revealing untruthful answers)?

What if a subject wants to present a false self-picture; will he or she be able to influence the responses by using one or more counter-measures during the examination? The most thorough review of this issue is by Gisli H. Gudjonsson (1988), a researcher and clinical psychologist and former police officer experienced in the use of the lie detector in criminal investigations.

What kinds of deliberate counter-measures might be used by subjects? Gudjonsson (1988) identified three different physical ways that have been offered in order to "fool" the polygraph technique:

1. Suppressing physiological responses to relevant questions.
2. Augmenting physiological responses to control questions, thereby increasing the baseline measure of the subject's emotional response. Gudjonsson observed that it is usually easier for subjects to augment responses to this type of question than to suppress responses to the crime-related questions.
3. Suppressing the overall level of physiological activity by, for example, taking drugs.

One study found that ingestion of 400 milligrams of the tranquillizer Meprobamate significantly reduced the detection rate (Waid, Orne, Cook, & Orne, 1981), but this study did not employ a realistic mock crime, but instead used a more innocuous memorization task. Gudjonsson expressed doubt that drugs are generally effective as a counter-measure; perhaps when the level of arousal or concern is low they might be. And it is unlikely that a drug would differentially affect responses to the crime-related and control questions, and that difference is central to the diagnosis of truth telling or lying.

In addition to taking tranquillizers or other drugs, subjects may use other physical means such as inducing either physical pain or muscle tension. Gudjonsson wrote: "For example, biting one's tongue in response to the control questions may create sufficient pain or discomfort to elicit an artificial physiological response indistinguishable from that of a genuine one. Similarly, pressing the toes against the floor or the thighs against the chair the individual is sitting in have been shown to be effective techniques under certain circumstances" (Gudjonsson, 1988, p. 129).

Do these procedures work? Early research was inconsistent in its conclusions; more recent laboratory studies (reviewed by the Office of Technology Assessment, 1983, and by Gudjonsson, 1988) suggest that:

1. Counter-measures may result in an "inconclusive" diagnosis, rather than the "truthful" diagnosis aspired to by the deceptive subject using the physical counter-measures (Honts & Hodes, 1982a).
2. Using several physical counter-measures at the same time is more effective than using only one (Honts & Hodes, 1982b).
3. Special training and practice in their use are necessary; simply providing subjects with information about such counter-measures is ineffective (Honts, Raskin, & Kircher, 1984).
4. Some of the physical counter-measures used by deceptive subjects are not easily detected by visual observation or the equipment ordinarily available to polygraph examiners; they require special electromyograph recordings (Honts, Raskin, & Kircher, 1983). Some polygraph examiners can monitor gross bodily movements through the use of pneumatic sensors built into the back and the seat of the subject's chair (Reid, 1945), but these don't detect subtle responses.

A potentially fruitful way of detecting gross bodily movements stems from the fact that some physiological responses are easier to augment by self-stimulation than others; Gudjonsson noted that the galvanic skin response is more sensitive than are cardiovascular responses to minor stimulation. He reported that in some circumstances, cardiovascular responses may be difficult to fake (Gudjonsson & Sartory, 1983).

In addition to these, certain kinds of mental counter-measures may be employed; these usually reflect deliberate attempts by subjects to change their pattern of thinking during the polygraph examination (Gudjonsson, 1988, p. 130). Specifically, three types of practices can be distinguished:

1. Artificially producing responses to control questions (e.g., by thinking of an earlier erotic or painful experience).

2. Attenuating responses to relevant questions, perhaps by trying to calm themselves down when this type of question is posed.

3. Mental dissociation, often by attempting to distract themselves, focusing their attention on some irrelevant object or thought. They may try to answer questions "automatically" in a uniform way.

For subjects who wish to be deceptive, the advantage to the use of mental counter-measures rather than physical ones is that they cannot be detected by observation or even sensitive equipment. But Gudjonsson concluded they are less effective: "The available evidence suggests that mental counter-measures are generally less effective in defeating polygraph tests than physical counter-measures, although some subjects can successfully apply such techniques" (Gudjonsson, 1988, p. 131). The most effective of the mental counter-measures seems to be for deception-motivated subjects to think of emotionally arousing thoughts while being asked the emotional-baseline–generating questions.

Gudjonsson further observed that all of the scientifically acceptable studies he has used in his review were carried out under controlled laboratory conditions and used a mock-crime paradigm. No field studies were available. Bearing that in mind, he offered the following tentative conclusions:

> The use of different classes of counter-measures has been reported in the literature. The available evidence shows that mental counter-measures and the use of pharmacological substances (such as tranquillizers) are only moderately effective at best, whereas physical counter-measures can be highly effective under certain conditions. Two conditions appear important to the effective use of physical counter-measures. First, employing multiple counter-measures simultaneously improves the person's chances of defeating a polygraph test, at least as far as the control question technique is concerned. Second, physical counter-measures appear relatively ineffective unless people are given special training in their use. It is generally not sufficient to provide people with instructions about polygraph techniques and counter-measures.
>
> Although there are clear individual differences in the ability to apply counter-measures effectively, training by experts in the use of physical counter-measures poses a potentially serious threat to the validity of the polygraph techniques. For this reason it becomes very important that the use of counter-measures is readily identified by polygraph examiners. Unfortunately subtle and effective counter-measures are not readily observable without special expertise and equipment which are not generally available to field examiners. (Gudjonsson, 1988, pp. 135–136)

SUMMARY

When crime victims or witnesses cannot recall many details of a crime, the police may use hypnosis as an aid in improving their recollections. Additionally, after a suspect has been identified, he or she may be asked to take a polygraph examination if the suspect claims innocence. These two techniques reflect the use of psychological procedures in crime investigation and are the focus of this chapter.

Psychologists differ as to whether hypnosis, as a crime investigation tool, offers benefits beyond its costs. Under hypnosis, some victims and witnesses may be able to recall some information they could not remember in a waking state, but being in a hypnotized state makes one quite suggestible and can lead to the production of false memories. Given the concerns about the accuracy of hypnotically assisted memory, a contribution of the forensic psychologist is to suggest guidelines for its use, especially with respect to the qualifications of the person doing the hypnosis and the procedures followed during the hypnosis session.

When a suspect claiming innocence is administered a polygraph, it is usually done by an employee of the police department, not by a psychologist. Although the specific procedures may vary, a common one, the Control Question Technique, compares the subject's physiological responses to questions about the crime with his or her responses to other questions (called control questions) designed to create guilt in the subject. If there is a difference in physiological response such that a more extreme response is made to the crime-related questions, it is concluded that the suspect is lying. But these responses are by no means perfectly reliable, and research findings conclude that the success rate of the polygraph procedure in detecting guilt is above chance, but not so high as to achieve the legal goal of guilt beyond a reasonable doubt.

KEY TERMS

cognitive interview, p. 106
context reinstatement, p. 106
Control Question Technique, p. 108
counter-measures, p. 114
credibility assessment, p. 98
crime-investigation stage, p. 106
demeanour, p. 98
difference score, p. 108
dissociative amnesia, p. 98
false memories, p. 100
false negatives, p. 110
false positives, p. 110
hypnotically assisted memory, p. 105
hypnotizability, p. 105
meta-analysis, p. 103
multiple personality, p. 100
polygraph, p. 106
Relevant-Irrelevant Test, p. 108

SUGGESTED READINGS

Gale, A. (Ed.). (1988). *The polygraph test: Lies, truth, and science.* London: Sage.

This set of contributed chapters by psychologists on the polygraph reflects the views of the British Psychological Society.

Hammond, D. C., Garver, R. B., Mutter, C. B., Crasilneck, H. B., Frischholz, E., Gravitz, M. A., Hibler, N. S., Olson, J., Scheflin, A. W., Spiegel, H., & Webster, W. (1995). *Clinical hypnosis and memory: Guidelines for clinicians and for forensic hypnosis.* Des Plaines, IL: American Society of Clinical Hypnosis Press.

This work contains a detailed set of guidelines for forensic hypnosis, authorized by the American Society of Clinical Hypnosis.

Iacono, W. G., & Patrick, C. J. (1999). Polygraph ("lie detector") testing: The state of the art. In A. K. Hess & I. B. Weiner (Eds.), *The handbook of forensic psychology* (2nd ed., pp. 440–473). New York: John Wiley.

This work presents a recent, critical examination of claims of accuracy for the polygraph.

Lykken, D. T. (1998). A tremor in the blood: Uses and abuses of the lie detector. New York: Plenum.

This extensively revised version of a book first published in 1981, by one of the leading critics of the use of the polygraph to determine guilt, contains a history of attempts at lie detection, plus reviews of the Control Question Test, the Relevant-Irrelevant Test, and voice stress analysis. Highly recommended.

O'Brien, D. (1985). *Two of a kind: The hillside stranglers.* New York: New American Library.

This account, available in paperback, of the Hillside Strangler case is a highly readable example of the "true crime" genre.

Scheflin, A. W., & Shapiro, J. L. (1989). *Trance on trial.* New York: Guilford Press.

This volume presents an erudite examination of the history and contemporary forensic uses of hypnosis.

Scheflin, A. W., Spiegel, H., & Spiegel, D. (1999). Forensic uses of hypnosis. In A. K. Hess & I. B. Weiner (Eds.), *The handbook of forensic psychology* (2nd ed., pp. 474–498). New York: John Wiley.

This chapter on the uses of hypnosis in law enforcement was written by experts who support the use of hypnosis but recognize the necessity that it be done only by well-trained clinicians.

6

Improving Eyewitness Identification and Interviewing Procedures

The Trial Judge should stress that tragedies have occurred as a result of mistakes made by honest, right-thinking eyewitnesses. It should be explained that the vast majority of the wrongful convictions of innocent persons have arisen as a result of faulty eyewitness identification.

—JUSTICE PETER DE C. CORY (*Sophonow Inquiry Report*, 2001)

GATHERING USEFUL INFORMATION FROM EYEWITNESSES

A goal of the police is to solve, or "clear," crimes. But one reason that fear of crime is so widespread today is that the **clearance rate** for major crimes is quite low. For example, according to the Canadian Centre for Justice Statistics (2000), Vancouver had a 16 percent clearance rate (the lowest for a major Canadian city), followed by Halifax (22 percent) and Ottawa (23 percent). In their goal of solving crimes, police are more likely to be successful if at least one eyewitness was present.

Fisher (1995) cited a 1975 Rand Corporation study of the process of crime investigation that concluded that the major factor determining whether a case would be solved was the completeness and accuracy of the eyewitness's account. In fact, the crimes that were most likely to be cleared were those in which the offenders were captured within minutes or those in which an eyewitness provided a *specific* relevant piece of information—a licence plate number, a name, an address, or a unique identification. If one of these was not present, the chances that the crime would be solved were less than 10 percent (Greenwood & Petersilia, 1976).

But the importance of the eyewitness accurately reconstructing events from the past does not end with the arrest of a suspect. At a trial, the testimony of an eyewitness who incriminates the defendant is—along with the presence of a confession—usually the most influential evidence. If a jury or a judge believes eyewitnesses who have testified in good faith (and why doubt their credibility?), the belief leads to a conclusion of guilt. Alibis, circumstantial evidence, even masses of physical evidence favouring the defendant's innocence wither away in light of an eyewitness's courtroom identification.

Unfortunately, as we mentioned in Chapter 5, judges and juries have a difficult time determining whether an eyewitness is giving accurate testimony. In the 2001 inquiry into Thomas Sophonow's wrongful murder conviction in Manitoba, Justice Cory observed that injustices in Canada often have resulted directly from mistakes by "honest, right-thinking eyewitnesses." Nowhere is the problem and significance of accurate eyewitness testimony more clear than in the increasingly common "he said, she said" historical cases. As highlighted by researchers at Simon Fraser University and Dalhousie University, in such cases, allegations often go back years or decades with little evidence other than contradictory reports (Connolly & Read, 2003; Porter, Campbell, Woodworth, & Birt, 2003a). Take, for example, the case involving the former premier of Nova Scotia, Gerald Regan (*R. v. Regan*, 1999, 2002). In 1995, Regan was charged with 18 counts of sexual offences (from sexual touching to rape) against 13 women, dating as far back as the 1950s. The complainants were 14 to 24 years of age when the incidents were alleged to have occurred. Regan denied all wrongdoing. After he was acquitted on several of the original charges, the Crown prosecutor decided not to pursue prosecution on any of the remaining counts. In this type of case, a determination of guilt or innocence hinges on the accuracy of the complainants' recollections and the perceived credibility of both the witnesses and the accused. In light of the difficulties in assessing the credibility of witnesses in historical cases, some legal experts have called for a statute of limitations in Canada for sexual assault cases (we will explore this issue later in the chapter).

As pointed out by Justice Cory, eyewitnesses clearly are not infallible. In a review of 205 cases of defendants who had been wrongfully convicted, Rattner (1988) discovered that 52 percent included testimony from eyewitnesses who had made mistaken identifications. Wells (1993) concluded that eyewitnesses' errors provide the single most frequent cause of wrongful convictions; an examination of the first 40 persons in the United States who were convicted of crimes but later exonerated on the basis of DNA testing found that in 36 of these cases (or 90 percent), one or more eyewitnesses falsely identified the innocent person (Wells, Small, Penrod, Malpass, Fulero, & Brimacombe, 1998). An estimated 4500 people are convicted each year in the United States as a result of mistaken eyewitness identifications (Cutler & Penrod, 1995). As noted by Yarmey (2003), although corresponding estimates have not been made for Canada, numerous well-known wrongful convictions here have established that mistaken witnesses pose a major problem in our legal system.

Can forensic psychology contribute to reducing the error rate? As Chapter 1 described, the field of experimental psychology has had a long history of the study of memory and especially errors in memory, as far back as the work by Hermann Ebbinghaus and Hugo Münsterberg more than a century ago. But in the last 30 years there has been an explosion of research on forensic aspects of memory. The first scholarly conference devoted to eyewitness testimony took place in Edmonton in 1980, organized by Gary Wells (see Yarmey, 2003). A group of eyewitness researchers from Canada and the United States came together to discuss their work, and the result was the first special issue of a scientific journal (*Law and Human Behavior*) focused on the psychology of eyewitness testimony. As a result of literally hundreds of studies, psychologists now possess extensive information on how accuracy of memory can be improved in actual cases. Some implications of a century's worth of memory research are described in this chapter.

The act of a witness describing or identifying a suspect involves more than memory alone; included are reasoning processes, suggestibility and social influence, self-confidence, authoritarian submission, and conformity. Wells (1995) has pointed out that "*memory testimony* and *memory* are not identical twins. **Memory testimony** is the witness's statement of what he or she recalls of a prior event. These statements can be influenced by more than just memory processes" (p. 727, italics in original, boldface added).

The examples of questionable police interrogation procedures—to be described in the next section—illustrate the distinction between memory and memory testimony and some of the determinants of problematic eyewitness evidence. A goal of forensic psychology is to make an eyewitness's identification a product of his or her memory rather than a product of the identification procedures used by the police. Studies in the psychological laboratory or controlled field studies that simulate a crime and then determine the degree of accuracy of eyewitnesses indicate the fear that false identifications by bystanders occur with considerable frequency (Brigham, Maass, Snyder, & Spaulding, 1982; Buckhout, 1974; Cutler, Penrod, & Martens, 1987; Ellis, Shepherd, & Davies, 1980; Leippe, Wells & Ostrom, 1978; Wells, 1984b; Wells, Lindsay, & Ferguson, 1979). In crime simulations in which participants believed the crime was real and their identification would have consequences for the accused, high rates of false identification still occurred (Malpass & Devine, 1980; Murray & Wells, 1982). How high a rate of inaccuracy? In some studies, as many as 90 percent of responses were false identifications; in others, only a few participants erred. The extreme variation exemplifies a central theme of this chapter: The degree of accuracy of eyewitness identification can partially be determined by the specific procedures used in the criminal investigation.

System Variables versus Estimator Variables

In fact, a point emphasized by Gary Wells and his colleagues who study eyewitness identification is that rather than being satisfied simply to point out that the reports of eyewitnesses are often inaccurate, we should recognize that the degree of accuracy is often influenced by the procedures used by the police and other members of the criminal justice system (Wells & Seelau, 1995). Wells (1978), then at the University of Alberta, referred to these as **system variables**; they include the type of questioning done by the police, the nature of the lineup or photo arrays, and the presence or absence of videotaping of procedures. These are the focus of this chapter, because when they contribute to eyewitness inaccuracy, they are *preventable* errors (Wells, 1993); in fact, psychologists can aid in the construction of lineups and the development of interviewing procedures that reduce inaccuracy.

The other type of determinant of an eyewitness's accuracy—what Wells called **estimator variables**—is not controllable by the criminal justice system and hence not reviewed in detail in this chapter, given that the chapter's topic is working with the police to improve their crime investigation. Estimator variables include environmental factors (e.g., the amount of lighting at the crime scene, length of exposure of the criminal to the witness) and within-the-person variables (the witness's psychological state, physical condition, etc.). Estimator variables are determined before the police respond. For example, the presence of a weapon or degree of violence that is a part of a crime may affect the witness's ability to recall the event. Clifford and Scott (1978) reported that participants who witnessed a nonviolent act were able to remember aspects with more detail and correctness than were those who witnessed a violent act. However, the relation between violence and memory accuracy is controversial. Some naturalistic research suggests that witnesses to violence can hold accurate memories for the event.

In a landmark field study, John Yuille and Judith Cutshall (now Judith Daylen) (1986) of the University of British Columbia examined the recollections of 13 eyewitnesses several months after they had witnessed a murder and an attempted murder in Burnaby, British Columbia. Results indicated that the witnesses' memories generally remained accurate, detailed, and resistant to the effect of misinformation. Although there was no "nonviolent" control condition, their results suggested that under some circumstances memory for violence can be

enduring. But the occurrence of violence during a crime is an estimator variable, and there is nothing the police can do to change the characteristics of the criminal incident to increase or decrease the accuracy of this aspect.

Thus the distinction of importance between these two types of variables is that errors in system variables can often be reduced and can sometimes be prevented. We can do nothing about poor lighting conditions or the brevity of exposure to the criminal, but police can eliminate practices that lead to further inaccuracies in reports.

Improper Police Procedures

Wells (1995) has observed that police use great caution and care when collecting physical evidence at the crime scene, but "these same police … do not seem to accept the premise that memory traces can also be contaminated" (p. 727). Yarmey (2003) has traced the development of guidelines for use by police in eyewitness identification. A major development occurred in the early 1980s when the Law Reform Commission of Canada commissioned Osgoode Hall law professor Neil Brooks to prepare a paper entitled "Police Guidelines: Pretrial Eyewitness Identification Procedures." For the first time several psychologists from Canada (Tony Doob at the University of Toronto, Don Read at the University of Lethbridge, Gary Wells at the University of Alberta, and Yarmey himself) and the United States (Elizabeth Loftus) were asked to act as consultants. Many of their recommendations echoed a 1929 Royal English Commission Report, intended to instruct police officers in optimal lineup procedures. One of the report's recommendations was that lineup "foils," or fillers in a lineup, should be matched to the suspect on the basis of their physical characteristics.

Yet police in Canada have often ignored such recommendations. Yarmey brings up the 1959 case of *R. v. Armstrong*, in which child witnesses were shown a live lineup containing the Asian suspect and a group of Caucasian foils. In more recent years, there have been numerous cases (such as the Thomas Sophonow case described later in the chapter) in which police practices have deviated greatly from accepted standards. In the recent Court of Queen's Bench of Alberta case, *R. v. Redbreast* (2004), the judge observed that the police detectives had exhibited a "rather unique" photograph of the defendant in the photo array, which was strongly distinguishable from all of the other photographs in the group of 15 shown. One witness testified that the defendant's photograph with long, untied hair "jumped out" at the viewer from the group (para. 109). Obviously, the recommendations by the Royal English Commission Report from nearly 80 years ago still are not being consistently followed in Canada.

Variations from acceptable procedures in questioning witnesses identified by Wells (1995, p. 727) included the following:

1. Asking witnesses poorly constructed questions immediately upon discovering the crime.
2. Allowing one eyewitness to overhear the responses of other eyewitnesses.
3. Taking "spotty" notes of witnesses' answers (and not recording the actual questions asked).
4. Failing to use any theory of a proper memory interview.
5. Using investigators who have little training in interviewing or the psychology of memory (or as Fisher, 1995, noted, generalizing interviewing procedures from those they use to interview *suspects*).

Further compounding the problem is the fact that, as Fisher (1995) noted, many interviews with eyewitnesses are conducted under the worst conditions imaginable: witnesses who are agitated and/or injured, time pressures that demand rapid-fire questioning, and background conditions characterized by distractions, confusion, and noise. On top of this, police officers are often pressured by their supervisors to file their reports rapidly.

An even broader concern is the motivation of police in questioning witnesses. A temptation of police investigators is to act prematurely in forming a conclusion about the likely perpetrator; this too-early hunch then guides the investigator toward questions and procedures that validate the belief (Fisher, 1995). For example, in the 2004 Cecilia Zhang murder investigation in Ontario, Peel Region Police Chief Noel Catney was widely criticized for this description of suspect Min Chen at a press conference: "Ladies and gentlemen, this is not just a murderer. This is the most despicable of criminals. This is a child murderer" (CBC Online News, July 23, 2004). Obviously, Catney did not hold a presumption of innocence for Chen, having already come to his own conclusion about guilt. So, in interviewing eyewitnesses, police may be tempted to ask leading questions or offer subtle confirmation of their hunches; they may construct biased **lineups** or **photo arrays** to aid in identifying whom they consider the "correct" suspect, as observed by leading lineup researcher Rod Lindsay at Queens' University (R. Lindsay, 1994).

In a decision almost 60 years ago (*R. v. Smierciak*, 1946), the Canadian courts recognized that there are great risks associated with certain practices that police sometimes use lineups and photo arrays to question victims and witnesses. In that case, the accused was charged with attempting to pass a forged cheque by presenting it to a bank teller. When the teller asked for a registration card, the accused searched his pockets and stated that he must have left it in his car. He then exited the bank and did not return. Although the teller did not take any special care to observe the accused at the time of the interaction, the court noted that the conditions for observation were excellent. The police subsequently showed her a single photo of a suspect, whom she identified as the perpetrator, and he was convicted. In later overturning the conviction, the judge stated that:

> of the utmost importance, is the method
> used to recall or refresh the recollections of

a witness who is to be relied upon to identify a person suspected of wrongdoing or who is under arrest. If a witness has no previous knowledge of the accused person so as to make him [or her] familiar with that person's appearance, the greatest care ought to be used to ensure the absolute independence and freedom of judgment of the witness. His [or her] recognition ought to proceed without suggestion, assistance or bias created directly or indirectly.... Anything which tends to convey to a witness that a person is suspected by the authorities, or is charged with an offence, is obviously prejudicial and wrongful. (*R. v. Smierciak*, 1946, para. 177)

In his written judgment, the judge stated that the police procedures had rendered the teller's evidence valueless and, in the absence of any other evidence, "it would be unfair and unsafe to convict him" (*R. v. Smierciak*, 1946, para. 180).

But, subsequently in important cases before the Canadian Supreme Court with regard to eyewitness identification, the court decided—rather than to reject police practices as improper—to try to deal with the problem by considering and warning the jury about the possible frailties of the eyewitness evidence. For example, in *Mezzo v. the Queen* (1986), the court ruled that in determining whether to convict in cases hinging on eyewitness testimony, the trial judge should first consider the factors that have affected the quality of the identification evidence (such as police procedures). Then, it was argued, the frailties in the evidence can be "remedied" by a caution to the jury, and the judge should leave the matter in their hands.

In other words, rather than ruling against the use of improper police procedures, the court concluded that judges and juries could make up their own minds about whether testimony is tainted. But why not try to prevent those practices from occurring at all, as well as attempting to protect defendants' rights if damage is still done?

The following are two cases where errors by the police have been documented; they provide raw material for guidelines advocated by forensic psychologists.

The Thomas Sophonow Case

Barbara Stoppel was a vivacious 16-year-old who was murdered on December 23, 1981, in Winnipeg. Thomas Sophonow was charged with her murder and eventually went through three trials. The first was declared a mistrial, as the jury was unable to reach a unanimous verdict, while in the second and third trials he was convicted. The Court of Appeal finally acquitted him. The case largely hinged on the eyewitness testimony of John Doerksen.

In the **Sophonow Inquiry** (*Sophonow Inquiry Report,* 2001, [Online]), the problems with the main eyewitness in the case were outlined by Justice Cory:

Sometime after 8:15 P.M. on December 23rd, John Doerksen went to the Ideal Donut Shop to get a coffee. The door was locked and he saw a person inside the shop. He saw that person at the cash register take a cardboard box. He saw the murderer leave the shop with a box, unlock the door, close it behind him and then move rapidly towards the Norwood Bridge.... Later that evening, he gave a description of the man he followed to the police.

Sometime later, Mr. Doerksen agreed to a session with a hypnotist at the University of Manitoba where he again described the murderer with some variations from his first description. The questionable nature of Mr. Doerksen's identification became readily apparent in the following weeks. On the 6th of January 1982, Mr. Doerksen called the police from the Norwood Hotel. He reported that the killer was in the hotel at that moment. He said that, if he was not the killer, he was certainly his twin brother. This was an identification of Mr. Dubé [an innocent bystander] as the killer and he was quickly exonerated by the police. Shortly thereafter, Mr. Doerksen identified a *Sun* reporter as the killer and he too was speedily exonerated.

He reported that he was seeing the killer everywhere and that every tall man resembled the killer. Most significantly, he attended a line-up on March 13th, which included Thomas Sophonow. The line-up was conducted by Sergeant Biener. Although Thomas Sophonow stood out as the tallest person in that line-up, Mr. Doerksen was unable to identify anyone as the man he struggled with on the 23rd of December…. Mr. Doerksen testified that Sergeant Shipman was in the room with him while the identification parade was held. He stated that Sergeant Shipman suggested that he should consider number seven, which was the number that Thomas Sophonow had been given for this parade. He also stated that Sergeant Shipman told him that those in the line-up could change articles of clothing with any other member of the line-up. Sergeant Shipman vehemently denied these suggestions.

The evidence relating to Mr. Doerksen becomes even more troublesome. At approximately 9:30 A.M. on Monday the 15th, Constable Foster saw John Doerksen on the street and picked him up for a spot check. Constable Foster was unable to tell the Commission why he picked up Mr. Doerksen. In any event, he found that there was a warrant for Mr. Doerksen for unpaid fines. He took him to the Public Safety Building. While he was waiting for his father to pay the fines, Mr. Doerksen came face to face with Thomas Sophonow. He had with him a copy of a Winnipeg newspaper, which contained a picture of Thomas Sophonow. He spoke to Mr. Henley, a custodial officer at the Remand Centre, and asked if he could see Thomas Sophonow. He was directed by Mr. Henley to the area of Thomas Sophonow's cell. There, he again saw Thomas Sophonow. I wonder how many people would have been directed to

Thomas Sophonow simply because they had a picture of him published in a recent edition of a Winnipeg newspaper. In any event, as strange and disturbing as this apparent chance meeting may be, there is no evidence of any arrangement or conspiracy on the part of the Winnipeg police to have Mr. Doerksen meet Thomas Sophonow. Mr. Doerksen explained that his ability to identify Thomas Sophonow when he saw him in a cell at the Remand Centre was because he was clean-shaven whereas he had not been at the time that he viewed the line-up on the 13th. However, Exhibits 52 and 53 are photos of the line-ups of the 13th and 15th of March in both of which Thomas Sophonow appears to be clean-shaven. His appearance was just the same on the 13th as it was on the 15th, when he was seen and purportedly identified by Mr. Doerksen. There really is no basis for the statement that there was any difference in Thomas Sophonow's appearance from the time that he was seen in the line-up on March 13th and the time that he was seen in the Remand Centre on the 15th of March.

On the 24th of March at the Public Safety Building, he met Sergeants Wawryk and Paulishyn and advised them that he had seen Thomas Sophonow in court that day and he was now "90% sure" that Thomas Sophonow was the man even though he had not been able to pick him out at the line-up.

Prior to the preliminary hearing, Sergeant Biener prepared a "can say" report which indicated that, although Mr. Doerksen was unable to identify Thomas Sophonow at the time of the line-up on March 13th, after seeing him at the Provincial Remand Centre he was now 90% sure that Thomas Sophonow was the killer. (Inquiry, Exhibit 149—Police Supplemental Report, Vol. 16B, page 812). It is, indeed, strange that, by the time he testified at the preliminary hearing, he was certain of the identity of Thomas Sophonow and he had no reservations whatsoever. He testified with the same certainty that Thomas Sophonow was the killer at each of the three trials.

This situation becomes even more troublesome. Mr. Doerksen advised the Winnipeg Police, when they were reinvestigating the case, that in 1982 he required glasses and he had trouble with his eyes at night and in poor lighting conditions (Inquiry, Vol. 22, page 2254). Further, Mr. Doerksen had developed a friendship with the Stoppel family, particularly Mr. Fred Stoppel. He met with him on numerous occasions and it may be that the friendship that he developed affected his opinion with regard to the identification of Thomas Sophonow.

Lastly, Sergeant Biener noted that Mr. Doerksen came to court during the first and second trials on the days that he was to testify with "quite a shine on" (Inquiry, Exhibit 149—Police Supplemental Report, Vol. 16B, page 924). In light of all these circumstances, it is apparent that little, if any, weight can be attached to the evidence of Mr. Doerksen.

(Reprinted by permission of Manitoba Justice.)

It should be apparent to the reader that this eyewitness and the use of ill-advised police practices created a nightmare for the legal system and for Mr. Sophonow. From Justice Cory's report, three major problems with the police evidence-gathering procedures with Doerksen become apparent:

- The use of hypnosis to "refresh" Doerksen's memory for the perpetrator.
- The use of foils who differed on an important physical attribute from the main suspect: during the original lineup, Mr. Sophonow was taller than the foils.
- Leading a witness to choose a particular person in the lineup as the perpetrator: Doerksen reportedly was led by police to choose Mr. Sophonow from the lineup.

The John Demjanjuk Case

In the 1980s John Demjanjuk was a retired automobile worker living in Cleveland, Ohio, but he was accused of having been "Ivan the Terrible," a Nazi collaborator who was a guard at a concentration camp where thousands of German and Polish Jews were annihilated during World War II. With the cooperation of the United States government, he was deported to the nation of Israel, where he was put on trial as a war criminal in February 1987.

Incredibly, several survivors of the concentration camp at Treblinka identified him after examining his 1951 visa photo; note that these identifications reflect the assumption of accurate memories of interactions that occurred more than 30 years before. For example, Yossef Czarny survived the Treblinka camp and later was freed from the camp at Bergen Belsen; when he examined a photo album of Ukrainian suspects, he immediately pointed to Demjanjuk's photo and exclaimed:

> "This is Ivan, yes. It is Ivan, the notorious Ivan. Thirty years have gone by, but I recognize him at first sight with complete certainty. I would know him, I believe, even in the dark. He was very tall, of sturdy frame, his face at the time was not as full and fat from gorging himself with food, as in the picture. However, it is the same face construction, the same nose, the same eyes and forehead, as he had at that time. A mistake is out of the question." (quoted by Wagenaar, 1988, pp. 110–111)

Czarny and other survivors testified at Demjanjuk's trial, but cross-examination of the Israeli police investigator, Miriam Radiwker, revealed that she did not think it was wrong to direct the survivors' attention to one particular photo during the questioning. She admitted having used this very suggestive procedure. Furthermore, the photos of **foils** (persons who are not suspects in the crime at hand) presented to the survivors did not fit the description of "Ivan the Terrible"; his picture was the only one that could be described as balding, with a round face and short neck (Wagenaar, 1988, p. 133). Also, in their report to the court, investigators failed to mention that some survivors failed to recognize Demjanjuk.

Even though Demjanjuk was convicted of war crimes in April 1988, the Supreme Court of Israel five years later overturned the conviction, basing its conclusion on the inconsistency of evidence that created a reasonable doubt as to the identity of Demjanjuk as "Ivan the Terrible."

Whereas most eyewitness studies have focused on memory for relatively benign events, researchers are now paying more attention to emotional or traumatic events (e.g., McNally, 2003; Read & Lindsay, 1997). The use of improper police procedures in cases such as Demjanjuk is particularly problematic when one considers the body of research showing that traumatic memory can be very accurate over long periods under the right circumstances (as we saw in the Yuille & Cutshall, 1986, study of murder witnesses). Wagenaar and Groenewed (1990) compared the memory reports of 78 World War II concentration camp survivors from the trial of Marinus De Rijke in the 1980s with statements given to Nuremberg investigators shortly after the war. The eyewitness accounts were accurate and detailed despite the passage of time. For example, the accounts of the camp, camp registration numbers, malicious treatment, daily activities, labour, housing, and main guards were "remarkably consistent" over four decades. Dalhousie University doctoral student Kristine Peace examined the reliability of the traumatic memories in 52 people who had recently gone through a violent or nonviolent experience (Peace & Porter, 2004). After three months, the details of the traumatic experiences remained highly consistent and had changed far less than memories for positive experiences by the same participants.

Clearly, it is possible for memories of crime to be reliable. The onus is on investigators to ensure that they do not taint eyewitness evidence through their own evidence-gathering practices.

QUESTIONING WITNESSES (INFORMATION GENERATION)

Police conduct a variety of activities as a part of a crime investigation. This section focuses on the task of eliciting descriptions from victims and bystander witnesses; no distinction is made between these two types of eyewitnesses, although it is clear that victims and bystanders sometimes recall the same event quite differently (e.g., Yuille, Davies, Gibling, Marxsen, & Porter, 1994).

As in Fisher's (1995) useful article, the goal of this section is to propose methods that improve the quality of the methods police use to interview witnesses. In doing so, it is necessary to assess the current state of police interviewing techniques. Unfortunately, the picture is a rather bleak one.

Lack of Training

First, police receive surprisingly little instruction on how to interview cooperative witnesses (Fisher, 1995, p. 733). Only the larger departments and major training centres offer what Fisher called "reasonably adequate training" (p. 733). Further, the handbooks and textbooks used in police training "either omit the issue of effective interviewing techniques or provide only superficial coverage" (Fisher, 1995, p. 733).

Interview Content

Despite this lack of training, the interviews carried out by different police officers possess some consistencies (Fisher, Geiselman, & Raymond, 1987):

1. After an introduction, the interviewer asks the witness to describe, via a narrative, what happened in the crime.
2. Police then tend to ask brief, direct questions that elicit equally brief responses ("How tall was he?").
3. Other than ending the interview with a broad request for additional information ("Is there anything else you can remember about the event?"), the police interviewer gives

little or no assistance to enhance the witness's recollection (Fisher, 1995).

Three types of errors occurred almost universally: interrupting the witness, asking too many short-answer questions, and an inappropriate sequencing of questions (Fisher, Geiselman, & Raymond, 1987). The average interview had three open-ended questions and 26 direct ones; the latter were asked in a staccato, rapid-fire style, usually a second or less after the witness's answer to the previous question.

Failure to Recognize the Dynamics of the Interview

Police appear to be insensitive to the dynamics of the situation when an eyewitness is interviewed by a police officer. The witness is often seeking confirmation or justification. The **demand characteristics** (cues that suggest what response is expected from the witness) of the situation may elicit pressures to give a "right answer" to an authority figure, or at least to avoid appearing ignorant when asked a specific relevant question. Thus, when asked, "Was he wearing jeans?" a victim may be reluctant to acknowledge not noticing. (Even more serious is the failure by the police to evaluate whether a victim-witness might be lying.)

Psychologists are probably more aware of the dangers of post-event suggestion (e.g., asking "What colour was his coat?") than are police investigators (see discussion below). Less clear is the frequency with which police ask **leading questions** or make subtle suggestions during the questioning of witnesses. Martin Reiser (1989), long-time psychologist with the Los Angeles Police Department, has concluded that the phenomenon is seen more often in laboratory studies than in real-world questioning. Fisher (1995) acknowledged that the empirical evidence about actual use of leading questions "is meager and, at best, difficult to interpret" (p. 740). A laboratory study (Geiselman, Fisher, MacKinnon, & Holland, 1985) found very few leading questions offered, but a field study that tape-recorded actual interviews by British police officers concluded that one out of every six questions was leading (George & Clifford, 1992). Fisher's conclusion: "[A] cautious approach is to assume that leading suggestions do occur with some regularity" (1995, pp. 740–741).

Police also seem to be unaware that a witness's previous exposure to the photograph of a suspect can increase the eyewitness's likelihood—when shown the photograph again at a later time—to identify the suspect as the culprit. Brown, Deffenbacher, and Sturgill (1977) carried out an experiment that manipulated this experience, using a one-week time interval between viewings. Approximately 20 percent of subjects who had been shown an earlier photograph wrongly identified a suspect. That is, people may remember a face but forget where they saw it—an example of the phenomenon called **unconscious transference**.

Also, police officers seem to be insensitive to types of errors in their own interviews. Although most recognized that it was a poor interviewing technique to interrupt a witness repeatedly and denied that they did so in their own interviews, many of these same officers made this error at an alarmingly high rate (Fisher, Geiselman, & Amador, 1989). Fisher (1995) observed: "I have witnessed countless times in training workshops detectives who claim at the outset that they already know the principles of effective interviewing from earlier training programs, only to make the same interviewing mistakes as those who have never had any formal training" (p. 757).

Another interviewing technique fraught with potential danger is to ask the same question several times or more during the same interview (Fisher, 1995). If the witness failed to answer the question the first time, the repeated questioning may create a demand characteristic to respond *in some way*, even if it means that the witness lowers his or her standard of confidence. If the witness did answer the first time questioned, the repetition may communicate that the answer was not satisfactory to the police–authority figure, creating social pressure to substitute another response (Fisher, 1995). The latter result is especially likely with witnesses who are young children (Geiselman & Padilla, 1988). Memorial University researcher Carole Peterson and her colleagues interviewed children four times about an injury that required hospital emergency room treatment, namely at one week, six months, one year, and two years after the incident. Although new details that were introduced after six months were more likely to be accurate than inaccurate, new information introduced at one or two years following the injury was as likely to be wrong as right (except for 12- and 13-year-olds) (Peterson, Moores, & White, 2001). Although we do not know how often police use repeated questions, laboratory research concludes that such a procedure increases a witness's mistakes in recollection (Poole & White, 1991).

Similarly, the use of multiple-choice questions may encourage guessing. Unless witnesses are clearly told that they shouldn't respond unless they are sure—an admonition rarely offered by the police—such a procedure may lead to an increase in information apparently uncovered, but at a cost in accuracy (Lipton, 1977). (See Fisher, 1995, pp. 748–749, for a discussion of the difficulty in comparing the accuracy levels of open-ended and forced-choice questions.)

Leading Questions and False Memories

Before we examine some ways in which police might improve the accuracy of witnesses' information, it is important to give a brief background concerning the effect of leading questions on memory. Distortion in eyewitness memory has become a major focus of research in cognitive psychology and neuroscience. Consistent with a constructive memory framework, research findings show that memory is greatly affected by the conditions of encoding and retrieval (e.g., Loftus, 2003). In the case of a crime, encoding would refer to how the witness or victim experienced the event, and retrieval would refer to the act of recalling the event privately or to another person such as a police officer. Although **false memories** have been studied for more than 70 years (Bartlett, 1932), the catalyst for the enormous level of interest in the phenomenon at present

was Elizabeth Loftus's **post-event misinformation paradigm**, developed in the 1970s.

In the original paradigm, participants were shown a slide presentation of a crime or accident (e.g., Loftus, Miller, & Burns, 1978). Some witnesses then received misinformation after which they answered questions about the event. For example, in studies using a slide sequence depicting a car accident, experimental witnesses were provided misinformation such as "Did the car stop at the stop sign?" when, in fact, there had been a yield sign. On a recognition test, misled witnesses chose a stop sign far more often than did control witnesses.

Another advance in the area was the Deese-Roediger-McDermott (DRM) paradigm (e.g., Roediger & McDermott, 1995), inspiring numerous false memory studies since the 1990s. This work established that after participants encode related words (e.g., rest, bed, awake), many later misremember a related word (e.g., sleep) that was not presented. The premise of the DRM is that memory is associative; when items are associated semantically, processing one tends to activate the other in recall.

Building upon these experiments, recent studies have established that it is not only minor details that can be altered in memory. With misleading questions and other suggestive techniques sometimes used by police, false memories are possible for major details in a scene or even entire personal experiences. By enlisting the aid of participants' family members, Loftus and Pickrell (1995) attempted to convince adults that at the age of five they had been lost in a shopping mall and later rescued. Participants were given brief descriptions of three real events and a false event of being lost in a shopping mall. In later interviews, a quarter of participants came to generate false memories. Using a similar approach, Hyman, Husband, and Billings (1995) found that 20 percent of their participants experienced false memories for other childhood experiences, such as an eventful birthday or the loss of a pet.

Porter, Yuille, and Lehman (1999) investigated whether false memories were possible for more negative, stressful events. Parents of the partici-pants were asked to provide information about several negative events (e.g., medical procedure, animal attack) that may have happened to their child. Participants then were questioned about a real and false event in three suggestive interviews over two weeks. Results indicated that 26 per-cent of participants came to fully recall the false event, while another 30 percent recalled some-thing about it. Such findings have been used to challenge the validity of many "recovered" mem-ories of alleged crimes, as discussed in Chapter 1. Evidence suggests that many such "recollections" were false memories generated during question-able police interviews or psychotherapy (e.g., Loftus, 2003).

Clearly, eyewitness memory is highly mal-leable in the face of misleading questions and social pressure. As such, investigations in which such system variables are present can lead to questionable evidence and, ultimately, equivocal legal decisions.

Improving the Accuracy of Witnesses' Information

Ronald Fisher's (1995) thorough review details a number of procedures specific to the questioning process that can either increase the memory retrieval of a witness or improve the witness's conversion of a conscious recollection into a statement to the interviewer. Many of these sug-gestions are quite straightforward; for example:

- *Slow down the rate of questioning.* When asked a specific question, witnesses may need to search through their memory store; police should not impatiently interrupt the search with another question.
- *Re-create the original context.* A staple of the **cognitive interview**, this principle pro-poses that, before answering any questions about the crime, witnesses should be told to re-create, in their own minds, the environ-ment that existed when the crime hap-pened. They should focus on how things

looked and sounded and smelled, what they were doing, how they felt, and what was happening around them.
- *Tailor questions to the individual witness.* Many police routinely plod through a standardized checklist of questions (Fisher, Geiselman, & Raymond, 1987). Instead, Fisher encourages the investigation to be sensitive to each wit-ness's unique perspective.
- *Make the interview witness-centred not inter-viewer-centred.* Too often, the interview is structured so that the witness sits passively waiting for the police officer to ask question after question (Fisher, Geiselman, & Raymond, 1987). Investigators even apply their aggressive, controlling, intimidating style for questioning suspects to the inter-viewing of cooperative witnesses. For the latter, police should use more open-ended questions and tell the subject that he or she should do most of the talking. Similarly, police officers need to convey what they need from the witnesses more explicitly than the typical "Tell me what happened," because the detailed, extensive responses wanted from witnesses go beyond the level of precision typical of ordinary discourse. For example, witnesses should be told not to edit their thoughts, but rather to pour forth all of them.
- *Be sensitive to the distinction between correct and incorrect responses.* How do we know when someone is giving us false information? Common sense suggests that when a witness is slow to respond, is less confident in his or her answers, or is inconsistent in answering from one situation to another, the response is less likely to be an accurate one. Psychological research has confirmed that subjects who take longer to respond make incorrect responses (Sporer, 1993).
- *Be sensitive to temptations to form premature conclusions.* At the beginning of the chapter it was noted that one problem with police interviewing techniques is the bias of the police interviewer who has already formed a

conclusion about the identity of the perpetrator. Several ways of dealing with this bias have been suggested; these will be described in detail later in the chapter. For example, Wells (see Fisher, 1995, p. 754, n. 5) proposed that police interviewers be given only general knowledge about the crime (e.g., that a bank was robbed) before doing their witness interviews. A second suggestion is to videotape interviews and provide them to both the prosecution and the defence (Fisher, 1995; Kassin, 1998b).

The most basic suggestion is to provide proper training for police interviewers (Yuille, Marxsen, & Cooper, 1999). Although it is true that some police have better interviewing skills than others do, psychologists have been able to improve the skills of both recruits and experienced detectives (Fisher, Geiselman, & Amador, 1989; George & Clifford, 1992).

University of British Columbia forensic psychologist Dr. John Yuille and his colleagues developed one of the most highly regarded forensic interviewing approaches for use with victims and witnesses, known as the Step-Wise Interview (Yuille, Hunter, Joffe, & Zaparniuk, 1993). The Step-Wise Interview attempts to minimize any trauma the witness may experience during the interview, maximize the amount and quality of the information obtained from the witness, minimize any contamination of the reported information, and maintain the integrity of the investigative process for the agencies involved. Following rapport building, the steps in this approach begin with the most open, least leading, least suggestive form of questioning (free narrative) and, if necessary, proceed to more specific questioning. For more than 15 years, Yuille has been active in training police, prosecutors, defence lawyers, and child protection staff in Canada and other countries in this approach. The Step-Wise Interview has been adopted as the standard for child abuse interviews in many jurisdictions. Not only does such training act as a highly effective bridge between forensic psychology and policing, it may contribute to better legal decision making.

LINEUPS AND PHOTO ARRAYS

When the police have a suspect, they usually ask any victim or other eyewitness to identify him or her through the use of a lineup (called a **parade** in Great Britain) or a photo array (also called a photo spread). The use of photo arrays is now more frequent than the use of live lineups, perhaps because the suspect has no right to counsel when witnesses look through a "mug book" (in contrast to suspects' rights to have a lawyer present when they are placed in a lineup). Then, too, it is easier for the police to assemble a photospread than arranging for a live lineup including four to seven innocent persons who bear some resemblance to the suspect (Wells & Seelau, 1995). Despite an assumption that live lineups should be more effective than photo arrays, a meta-analysis of research findings indicates no consistent difference (Cutler, Berman, Penrod, & Fisher, 1994), and the conclusion of prominent researchers is that the principles governing the responses of the eyewitness are the same (Wells, Seelau, Rydell, & Luus, 1994). Box 6.1 presents a comparison of lineups and photo arrays.

A special mention should be made of the procedure called the **showup**—essentially a lineup composed of only one person. Both psychologists, as a group, and the courts, when faced with the procedure, have assumed that showups are inherently more suggestive than lineups that include four, five, or six foils (*Stovall v. Denno*, 1967, p. 302); these views are amplified later in the chapter. In fact, experimental psychologists who study the accuracy of memory are quite strong in their belief that the procedure is prejudicial (Malpass & Devine, 1983; Wells, Leippe, & Ostrom, 1979; Yarmey, 1979). Yet the limited research on this procedure comes up with conflicting conclusions. A set of studies by Richard

BOX 6.1
Lineups versus Photo Arrays

The greatest threats to the accuracy of identifications—regardless of which procedure is used—may come from the actions of the police questioner. But the medium is still worthy of study. Cutler, Berman, Penrod, and Fisher (1994) have noted that an inherent distinction between a lineup and a photo array is image quality: "common sense tells us that live lineups produce the clearest image" (p. 163). Further, photo arrays do not provide information about the behaviour of the criminal, including his or her voice and gait. But the other side of the picture is that many advantages exist for the photo array or photospread approach (Cutler et al., 1994):

1. Its immediate availability and selection of foils.
2. Its portability.
3. The control over the behaviour of lineup members. (In a live lineup a possibility always exists that a suspect will act in some way to draw the eyewitness's attention. This can invalidate the lineup.)
4. The opportunity to examine a photo array repeatedly and over extended lengths of time.
5. Anxiety of eyewitnesses is probably lessened when they use a mug book, in contrast to viewing their potential attacker through a one-way glass.

The careful analysis by Cutler and his colleagues of studies using different procedures concluded that "given the apparent comparability of lineups and photo arrays, it is not worth the trouble and expense to use live lineups" (Cutler et al., 1994, p. 180). However, a newer development may offer promise. Videotaping lineups is increasingly popular in police departments. Cutler and his colleagues noted that the use of videotaped lineups has advantages not present in either live lineups or photospreads:

> With the use of large monitors, faces can be blown up larger than life. With the use of jog-and-roll dials, lineup members can be shown moving in slow motion, even on a frame-by-frame basis. Videotaped lineups can be paused on a specific frame, showing a lineup member in a specific bodily position. In addition, videotaped lineups can be shown repeatedly and for an unlimited amount of time. The equipment is simple enough to use that eyewitnesses can be placed in control of some of the features, such as the jog-and-roll dial. (Cutler et al., 1994, p. 179)

Gonzalez and his colleagues (Gonzalez, Ellsworth, & Pembroke, 1993; Davis & Gonzalez, 1996) found that showups resulted in no greater number of mistaken identifications than did lineups and that showup witnesses were more likely to say that the perpetrator was "not there" than were lineup witnesses. Gonzalez and his colleagues concluded on the basis of their research that the showup is *not* the equivalent of a lineup with a functional size of one; instead, the witness uses a different mode of processing information when viewing a showup. Witnesses "appear to approach showups more cautiously; they are more reluctant to say that the person they see is the perpetrator, even when he or she is" (Gonzalez et al., 1993, p. 536). In fact, in a replication of the original study, Davis and Gonzalez (1996) found that 82 percent of the subjects were willing to identify one of the persons in the lineup as the perpetrator, but in the showup only 48 percent were willing to do so.

However, the above results may not be as applicable in real-world settings; there, the implementation of a showup reflects other differences from that of a lineup besides the sheer number of persons involved. The showup is more likely to be carried out right after the apprehension of a suspect filling the witness's description; it may even occur at the crime scene. If the latter is the case, the suspect's clothes (are they the same as the perpetrator's?) and other qualities contribute to the decision by the witness. In contrast, lineups usually come later, when the police have a definite suspect. In which situation is the danger of suggestion strongest? Gonzalez and his colleagues argue that contrary to popular belief, the pressures on the witness to make an identification may actually be greater in a lineup procedure. The important point for police is to be aware that in each of these situations there are pressures on the witness to "help the police" and so specific instructions are necessary to try to mitigate the effects of suggestion.

The conclusion that showups produce fewer inaccurate identifications than lineups has not gone unchallenged. A University of Guelph study by Yarmey, Yarmey, and Yarmey (1996) drew the opposite conclusion, finding that six-person lineups were superior to showups over a 24-hour retention period; innocent suspects were significantly less likely to be identified in the six-person lineup. The latter study differed from those by Gonzalez and his colleagues in several respects. The Yarmeys' study tested witnesses individually and used a successive lineup procedure. In Gonzalez's laboratory experiments, a staged crime before a class and a videotaped staged crime before groups of subjects served as stimulus materials.

The majority of psychologists who are experts on eyewitness memory remain dubious that the showup's convenience can overcome its potential for error, as Box 6.2 illustrates (see page 137), and on the basis of their research, Yarmey and his colleagues recommend that showup encounters not be used, except in life-or-death circumstances. Further research is needed to determine whether, as Gonzalez and his colleagues have proposed, the showup procedure does not elicit as much suggestibility as its critics believe.

Common Errors

Ellison and Buckhout (1981), psychologists who have testified frequently about witness-identification issues, reported that the most biased lineup they ever encountered "was composed of five white men and one black man in an actual murder investigation in which a black suspect had been arrested. The excuse given was that the police wanted to make the lineup representative of the town's population, which had few black people! Another 'justification' was that there were no other people in the building" (p. 115). Certainly, improper procedures used by the police can have the same effect on witnesses' reactions, regardless of whether the witness is viewing a lineup or scanning a mug book (Lindsay, 1994). We can summarize the frequent kinds of errors as follows:

1. Implying that the criminal is definitely one of the stimulus persons (as apparently occurred in the Sophonow case).
2. Pressuring the witness to make a choice (i.e., creating a demand characteristic).
3. Asking the eyewitness specifically about the suspect while not asking those same questions about the foils (or what Wells and Seelau [1995] call a **confirmation bias**).
4. Encouraging a loose recognition threshold in the eyewitness.
5. Leaking the police officer's hunch, by making it obvious to the eyewitness which is the suspect (Wells & Seelau, 1995, pp. 767–768).
6. After an eyewitness's selection, telling the eyewitness that his or her choice is the "right" one. This increases witnesses' confidence that they are accurate when they later testify. Luus and Wells (1994, Luus, 1991) have shown that the confidence level of witnesses' reports can be manipulated by telling them that another witness identified the same person.

The fact that eyewitnesses are highly susceptible to the powers of suggestion from police is admirably demonstrated in a study by Wells and Bradfield (1998), who showed undergraduate-student participants a grainy videotape made by a Target store surveillance camera; it portrayed a man entering the store. Participants were told to notice the man as they would be asked questions about him later. After viewing the tape, they were informed that the man had engaged in a robbery that went wrong and that a store security guard had been killed. Each participant was then shown a five-person photospread, which did not contain the photograph of the man who had been seen in the surveillance tape. Each individual participant selected someone from the photospread as the person in the video. Upon making this response, the participant was either told, "Good, you identified the actual suspect" (called confirming feedback), or "Actually, the suspect is No.___" (disconfirming feedback); a third of the subjects were given no feedback. Immediately thereafter, each participant answered a long set of questions, some of which assessed the effect of the feedback. Those who had been told, "Good, you identified the actual suspect" were far more confident in their choices than were those who were told the suspect was someone else; the latter feedback had a moderate detrimental effect on the subject's confidence. The mean confidence ratings were Confirming feedback, 5.4; No feedback, 4.0; Disconfirming feedback, 3.5. In addition, those given positive feedback felt they had a better view of the perpetrator, reported paying greater attention to the videotape, had an easier time making the identification, and were more willing to testify about their identification. Clearly, the nature of feedback from an authority distorts the witness's reports, across a wide variety of phenomena.

The use of such responses by police questioners is particularly disturbing, given the emerging conclusion from psychological research that the act of lineup identification is largely governed by a **relative judgment process** (Wells, 1984b, 1993); that is, the witness selects the stimulus person who most resembles, in the witness's memory, the perpetrator of the crime. If the real culprit is present, this procedure is effective, but if the lineup contains only foils, an innocent person who resembles the perpetrator is likely to be chosen. For example, Malpass and Devine (1981) carried out a study in which they staged a crime and then asked eyewitnesses to pick out the culprit from a lineup. When the actual culprit was *not* in the lineup and when witnesses were *not* warned of this, 78 percent of the subjects chose one of the innocent persons. When warned about the possibility of the perpetrator's absence, only 33 percent chose someone from the culprit-absent lineup. The latter figure is important. In fact, other research (Wells, 1993) confirmed that about one-third of witnesses or more select an innocent person in a culprit-absent photospread or lineup, even when told that the culprit might not be present. The problem with the relative judgment process, in the words of Wells and his colleagues, is "that it includes no mechanism for describing that the culprit is none of the people in the lineup" (Wells et al., 1998, p. 614).

Operational Rules

It is clear that the procedures used by some police have the potential of increasing the rate of false identifications (Loftus, 1993a; Yarmey, 2003). Wells and his colleagues (Wells & Seelau, 1995; Wells et al., 1998) have suggested that the application of four straightforward rules can reduce such errors.

Rule 1. "The person who conducts the lineup or photospread should not be aware of which member of the lineup or photospread is the suspect" (Wells et al., 1998, p. 627). Customarily, the detective who has handled the case administers the lineup. The problem is that this officer, knowing the identity of the suspect, may communicate this knowledge, *even without intending to do so.* A variation in eye contact with the witness, a subtle shift in body position or facial expression, may be enough to communicate feedback to the witness (who often is unsure and hence seeks guidance and confirmation from the detective). And, as we know, some detectives are not reluctant to tell witnesses when their choices identified the suspect or even explicitly draw attention to the suspect. But if a **double-blind procedure** is used, in which the lineup administrator is unaware of the "correct" answer, neither subtle nor overt communication would be made, and a purer estimate of the witness's confidence level could be determined.

Rule 2. "Eyewitnesses should be told explicitly that the perpetrator might not be in the lineup or photospread and therefore eyewitnesses should not feel that they must make an identification. They also should be told that the person administering the lineup does not know which person is the suspect in the case" (Wells et al., 1998, p. 629). Consider the reaction of an eyewitness when he or she is shown a lineup; it probably is something like this: "They wouldn't have gone to this trouble unless they have a sus-pect. So one of these guys must have done it." (Given a book containing several hundred mug shots, the eyewitness is less likely to have this reaction, but in contrast, the witness faced with a mug book usually assumes that everyone in it is a previous offender.) Thus it is essential to emphasize that the culprit might not be in the photo array or lineup. Empirical studies, analyzed by Steblay (1997), find that an explicit warning reduces the rate of incorrect identifications when the offender is not in the lineup.

Rule 3. "The suspect should not stand out in the lineup or photo array as being different from the distractors based on the eyewitness's previous description of the culprit or based on other fac-tors that would draw extra attention to the sus-pect" (Wells et al., 1998, p. 630). In previous lineups the ways that the suspect stood out included:

1. He or she was the only one who fit the verbal description that the eyewitness had given to the police earlier (Lindsay & Wells, 1980).
2. He or she was the only one dressed in the type of clothes worn by the perpetrator (Lindsay, Wallbridge, & Drennan, 1987).
3. The suspect's photo was taken from a dif-ferent angle than the foils' photos (Buckhout & Friere, 1975, cited by Wells & Seelau, 1995).

Wells and his colleagues emphasize that distrac-tors should not necessarily be selected to look like the police detectives' prime suspect; instead, they should be chosen to match the description of the criminal given by the witness. Note that this recommendation goes against the common police procedure: Police choose foils to resemble the suspect, rather than resembling the witness's description of the offender.

Rule 4. "A clear statement should be taken from the eyewitness at the time of the identifica-tion and prior to any feedback as to his or her confidence that the identified person is the actual culprit" (Wells et al., 1998, p. 635). Repeated

questioning by authorities (police, investigators, prosecutors) may increase the confidence of the witness's answers (Shaw, 1996; Shaw & McClure, 1996). By the time witnesses reach the witness box at the actual trial, their behaviour may be quite different from their initial response. The initial levels of confidence should be recorded.

In response to the above guidelines (and especially Rule 4), Saul Kassin (1998b) has sug-gested one more rule: that the identification process (especially the lineup and the interaction between the detective and the witness) be video-taped, so that lawyers, the judge, and the jury can later assess for themselves whether the reports of the procedure by police are accurate.

CHILDREN AS EYEWITNESSES

Because of beliefs and research findings about their heightened suggestibility, children as eyewitnesses pose particular challenges to investigators who seek information from them about the nature of perpetrators (Bruck & Ceci, 1999; Ceci & Bruck, 1993; Ceci, Toglia, & Ross, 1987; Lindsay, Pozzulo, Craig, Lee, & Corber, 1997; Yuille et al., 1993). The recommendations noted above in questioning adult eyewitnesses would, of course, apply to the questioning of children also. Special problems with respect to the questioning of children and proce-dures for reducing suggestibility are covered in Chapter 12, which deals with forensic responses to sexual abuse of children.

PUBLIC POLICY ISSUES

In Chapter 1 it was noted that psychology and the law are often in conflict and that psychology's attempts to have an impact on the legal system have frequently failed. Some have argued that neither the police nor the courts at present have been very responsive to input from psychological research. Wells concluded: "To date, the scientific literature on witness memory has not been a driving force behind the legal system's assumptions, procedures, and decisions regarding witness memory" (1995, p. 730). On the other hand, as mentioned in Chapter 1, influential agencies like the National Judicial Institute based in Ottawa have been inviting psychological researchers (such as lineup researcher R. C. L. Lindsay of Queen's University) to train members of the judiciary in recent years. Further, training in forensic interviewing by people such as John Yuille is being welcomed by some police forces. Hence the situation may be changing for the better. Two ways to continue to influence this situation are to change legislation and to educate jurists. This section discusses three approaches to changes in public policy: recent statute-of-limitation laws, trial judges' decisions on admitting psychologists as expert witnesses, and relevant Supreme Court decisions.

Statute-of-Limitation Laws

Traditionally, crimes such as sexual violence were "hidden" in that most victims chose not to report their experiences for years (if ever), because of embarrassment, fear of the offender, fear of being disbelieved, or fear of being blamed for the incident (Porter et al., 2003). In fact, most victims of sexual assault still do not report a recent sexual assault experience (e.g., Kennedy & Yuille, 1999). It is only recently that Canadian courts began to recognize that many crime victims remain silent about the incident for a lengthy period of time, if they report it at all (as noted by the Supreme Court of Canada in *R. v. W. [R.]*, 1992). As such, Canada has no **statute of limitations** to forestall the prosecution of historical offences. This perspective encouraged people to report historical crimes and brought many guilty perpetrators to justice. On the other hand, in the United States, legislative decisions concerning the statute of limitations in child sexual abuse cases have disregarded the complexity of psychological viewpoints on recovered memories. As discussed earlier in this text, some alleged victims of abuse as children do not recall the abuse until much later in life; previously, such claims had to be brought forward within a specific period of time after the act in order to be responded to by the criminal justice system. Legislators and judges have accepted the concept of "**delayed discovery**" (Bulkley & Horwitz, 1994; Boland & Quirk, 1994). The goal of this liberalization of the statutes of limitation was to provide opportunities for the delayed but legitimate claims of child abuse to be reported. But in light of the recent heightened concern about such cases (e.g., Loftus, 2003), the legal changes may encourage false reports to be brought forward. Some psychologists (Ernsdorff & Loftus, 1993; Bulkley & Horwitz, 1994) have proposed several changes, ranging from complete exclusion of cases based on claims of recovered memory to an imposition of a higher burden of proof in civil cases.

Thus, an absence of a statute of limitations in Canada and jurisdictions within the United States allows victims to report crimes long after their occurrence. On the other hand, the American legislative changes in this direction arguably were inspired by a questionable understanding of human memory.

Judges' Decisions on the Admissibility of Expert Testimony

Chapter 1 recounted the efforts of Hugo Münsterberg almost 100 years ago to educate trial judges about the relevance of psychological expertise when fact-finders evaluated how accurate eyewitnesses were. But consider that Münsterberg also arrogantly wrote, "It seems indeed astonishing that the work of justice is ever carried out in the courts without ever consulting the psychologist and asking him for all the aid which the modern study of suggestion can offer" (1908, p. 194). It is not surprising that the legal community (e.g., Wigmore, 1909) treated such advocacy with disdain then, and—if not disdain—at least ambivalence now. Despite these conflicts, expert witnesses do have something to offer with respect to witness interview system variables and how witness interviews can be conducted to reduce bias (Seelau & Wells, 1995).

Expert testimony about the determinants of eyewitness accuracy is an example of what Monahan and Walker (1988) have called **social framework testimony**; that is, it presents "general conclusions from social science research" in order to assist the fact-finder (whether that is judge or jury) "in determining factual issues in a specific case" (Monahan & Walker, 1988, p. 470). As noted in Chapter 2, a judge's decision to admit or exclude scientific testimony in Canada is usually based on a combination of four criteria: the relevance of the evidence, the necessity of the evidence (and the extent to which the expert might unduly influence the jury), the absence of any exclusionary rule, and qualification of the expert. But in real life, matters are not so straightforward: "From a legal and public policy perspective … there is a problem to the extent that the variation in admissibility decisions is attributable more to ambiguity in the criteria for admissibility, the idiosyncratic views of the trial judge, or the characteristics of the jurisdiction than it is to the specific characteristics or needs of the case" (Wells, 1995, p. 729).

Also noted in Chapter 2, the Canadian courts have been reluctant to allow expert testimony on eyewitness testimony (recall that Dr. Yarmey's evidence was excluded in *R. v. McIntosh and McCarthy*, 1997). How can psychologists convince trial judges of the importance of their findings? Two relevant issues are reviewed here: the tendency for fact-finders not to be adequately informed on the topic and the high level of consistency in conclusions among experts.

How Accurate Is the Knowledge of Jurors?

Until the mid-1970s, expert testimony in cases involving the testimony of eyewitnesses was rarely admitted; among reasons given by judges were that "jurors already know all this" and that experts would "waste the court's time" (Leippe, 1995, p. 912). But jurors are often in error in two respects: They overestimate the level of accuracy of eyewitnesses and they do not appreciate the impact of environmental factors on reducing accuracy. They fail to consider the impact of

system variables such as those described in this chapter. People usually begin with the assumption that the memory of an adult eyewitness is accurate (Leippe, 1995) and hence they expect a far greater percentage of witnesses to be accurate than are found in the field studies that create a mock crime and determine levels of eyewitness accuracy (Brigham & Bothwell, 1983; Wells, 1984a; Wells & Leippe, 1981; Lindsay, Wells, & Rumpel, 1981).

An assumption that "jurors already know all this" is clearly unwarranted. Four different surveys came to the same conclusion: "that much of what is known about eyewitness memory—that eyewitness experts might talk about in court—is not common sense" (Leippe, 1995, p. 921). Specific findings of these surveys documented this conclusion, as follows:

1. Deffenbacher and Loftus (1982) gave a set of multiple-choice questions on variables associated with eyewitness accuracy to university students and nonstudents with and without jury experience. At least half the respondents chose the wrong answer (i.e., an answer in conflict with the direction of empirical findings) on questions about the confidence-accuracy relationship, cross-racial bias in identification, and weapon focus (the victim's tendency to pay attention to the gun pointed at him or her and to ignore every other stimulus).

2. Using as participants law students, legal professionals, undergraduate students, and adults, Yarmey and Jones (1983) found that respondents did not recognize the empirically derived relationships between level of accuracy and such factors as eyewitness's confidence, the presence of a weapon, and the status of the witness (i.e., that police are no better at identification than are other witnesses).

3. Using the 13 empirical findings deemed by experts to be reliable enough to testify about, Kassin and Barndollar (1992) found that significantly fewer students and adults than experts considered the findings as reli-

able. In four of the 13 reliable findings, the majority of the students and adults disagreed with the experts.

4. Brigham and Wolfskeil (1983) surveyed trial lawyers and found, not surprisingly, that prosecutors were much more likely to believe that eyewitnesses were accurate than were criminal defence lawyers.

But this wealth of empirical findings is not enough. As Leippe (1995) has pointed out, even though the empirical relationships may not fit "common sense" when they are presented to jurors, the reaction of the jurors is often that "we knew these things all along." This **hindsight bias** (Slovic & Fischhoff, 1977) may create problems for the admissibility of expert testimony, and Leippe (1995) wisely suggests that requests to admit expert testimony must speak explicitly about the possibility of hindsight bias in trial fact–finders.

A second argument to be used in trying to persuade judges to admit psychological testimony is the consistency of agreement among experts on the phenomenon. A survey by Kassin, Ellsworth, and Smith (1989, 1994) of 63 active psychological researchers determined just which specific phenomena, in their opinion, were reliable enough to testify about in court. Box 6.2 describes those findings that at least 70 percent of this sample felt were reliable.

These are not idle speculations; they are based, for most of the findings, on a multitude of studies using a variety of methods and types of subjects. As Leippe observed: "in matters of reliability, a number of eyewitness research findings score highly. They are replicable, the opposite findings (as opposed to

---

BOX 6.2
What Is Reliable Enough to Testify About?

The following are the findings that at least 70 percent of the researcher-experts surveyed by Kassin, Ellsworth, and Smith (1989) rated as reliable enough to include in courtroom testimony. (Note: percentages of experts rating the statement as "reliable enough" are given in parentheses beside each statement.)

1. Wording of questions: An eyewitness's testimony about an event can be affected by how the questions put to that witness are worded. (97 percent)
2. Lineup instructions: Police instructions can affect an eyewitness's willingness to make an identification and/or the likelihood that he or she will identify a particular person. (95 percent)
3. Post-event information: Eyewitness testimony about an event often reflects not only what they actually saw but information they obtained later on. (87 percent)
4. Accuracy-confidence: An eyewitness's confidence is not a good predictor of his or her identification accuracy. (87 percent)
5. Attitudes and expectations: An eyewitness's perception and memory for an event may be affected by his or her attitudes and expectations. (87 percent)

6. Exposure time: The less time an eyewitness has to observe an event, the less well he or she will remember it. (85 percent)
7. Unconscious transference: Eyewitnesses sometimes identify as a culprit someone they have seen in another situation or context. (85 percent)
8. Showups: The use of a one-person showup instead of a full lineup increases the risk of misidentification. (83 percent)
9. Forgetting curve: The rate of memory loss for an event is greatest right after the event, and then levels off over time. (83 percent)
10. Cross-racial/white: White eyewitnesses are better at identifying other white people than they are at identifying black people. (79 percent)
11. Lineup fairness: The more the members of a lineup resemble the suspect, the higher is the likelihood that identification of the suspect is accurate. (77 percent)
12. Time estimation: Eyewitnesses tend to overestimate the duration of events. (75 percent)
13. Stress: Very high levels of stress impair the accuracy of eyewitness testimony. (71 percent)

(From Leippe, 1995, p. 914). Copyright © 1995 by the American Psychological Association. Reprinted with permission.

simply null findings) are seldom reported, the research has high internal validity, and the settings and measures often have high mundane realism in terms of approximating certain eyewitness situations. A strong argument can be made for reliability and validity" (Leippe, 1995, p. 918).

Not all experts agree with the above statement. Some psychologists, including Rogers Elliott (1993), Vladimir Konecni and Ebbe Ebbesen (1986), and Michael McCloskey and Howard Egeth (1983; Egeth, 1993) have been critical for several reasons, including their conclusion that the findings have not reached a level of consistency necessary for application in the courts. But these psychologists are in the minority, and sometimes the issue of dispute is how high the standard should be for the admissibility of psychological research findings.

Court Decisions and Recommendations

In Canada, the 2001 Sophonow Inquiry should be considered the major milestone in the court's agreement with and advocacy of research-based practices by police with eyewitnesses. Justice Cory's recommendations concerning lineup procedures, for example, virtually mirror the major conclusions of psychologists in the area. Further, Justice Cory recommended that trial judges must emphasize the potential frailties of eyewitness testimony. A critical development in the U.S. was a 1999 report to the Department of Justice commission by the Office of the Attorney General. This report authored by a group of police officers, eyewitness researchers, defence lawyers, and prosecutors provides national guidelines concerning the gathering of eyewitness evidence at all stages of criminal investigation (see Wells, Malpass, Lindsay, Fisher, Turtle, & Fulero, 2000, for a description of the psychological foundations of the report).

But the Sophonow Inquiry and U.S. Department of Justice reports were a long time coming. Traditionally, many of the major legal decisions that exemplify legal assumptions vastly different from the empirical findings of psychol-

ogists come from the U.S. Supreme Court. One dealt with the question of when suggestion becomes so strong that it intrudes on the right of defendants to fair treatment. In the case of *Stovall v. Denno* (1967), a man named Paul Behrendt was stabbed to death in the presence of his wife; she was so severely wounded that her survival was questionable. Stovall, a suspect, was brought to Ms. Behrendt's hospital room in handcuffs, two days after the crime, and in this showup circumstance, the victim identified him as the perpetrator. This procedure was justified by the authorities because it was uncertain whether the victim would survive, and, under such conditions, the victim could not come to the police station. Stovall appealed his conviction, but the U.S. Supreme Court ruled that the procedure was not a violation of due process because—although the procedure was suggestive—it was not "unnecessarily" suggestive. That is, a showup procedure would be excluded if it were "unnecessary"—if the circumstances had permitted the use of a lineup as a viable alternative. Although we may be able to agree about the justification in this case, the Court has not taken a position on how suggestive procedures can be reduced or avoided; in fact, as Wells and Seelau (1995) observed: "The Court has not articulated some simple and effective minimal requirements for lineups and photospreads for the vast majority of cases for which there is no necessity for suggestive procedures" (p. 785).

The second difference between the U.S. Supreme Court and experimental psychology deals with the relationship of eyewitnesses' accuracy levels and their levels of confidence. In *Neil v. Biggers* (1972), the Court concluded that even the pressure of unnecessarily suggestive procedures by the police didn't mean that the testimony of the eyewitness had to be excluded from the trial *if* the procedure did not reflect a substantial possibility of a mistaken identification. (In this case, a rape victim identified her attacker in a showup seven months after the crime occurred.) The criteria that the Court, in the above decision and in *Manson v. Braithwaite* (1977), felt increased the likelihood of an accurate identification were the following:

1. The opportunity for witnesses to view the criminal at the time of the crime.
2. The length of time between the crime and the later identification.
3. The level of certainty shown by the witnesses at the identification.
4. The witness's degree of attention during the crime.
5. The accuracy of the witness's prior description of the criminal.

For example, if little time had passed since the crime, even a suggestive procedure should not have had an impact and it could be assumed that the witness was on target. Most of these reflect plausible assumptions, but they are questionable, for several reasons. Leading questions (e.g., "You had a pretty long time to look at him, didn't you?") can alter the witnesses' responses about their degree of attention and opportunity to view the criminal—and, indirectly, can then alter their level of confidence. Second, the initial relationship between different witnesses' levels of accuracy and their levels of confidence about their own accuracy is quite low (Cutler & Penrod, 1989, 1995). In a comprehensive review, Bothwell, Deffenbacher, and Brigham (1987) completed a meta-analysis of 35 studies that used staged crimes to assess eyewitnesses' accuracy and confidence; the average correlation was only an r of .25, suggesting that "witnesses who are highly confident in their identifications are only somewhat more likely to be correct as compared to witnesses who display little confidence" (Penrod & Cutler, 1995, p. 823).

A third reason for concern about the U.S. Supreme Court's criteria is that—contrary to the assumptions of most jurors—the confidence of a witness is malleable; that is, events that happen after the initial identification can cause the eyewitness to become more or less confident (Wells et al., 1998). It was found in the studies by Luus and Wells (1994) and by Wells and Bradfield (1998) that certain suggestive procedures used by police can increase the confidence of eyewitnesses without changing their accuracy (Wells, Rydell, & Seelau, 1993). If a police officer tells an eyewitness that her choice from the lineup is "the guy we think did it," such a reaction quite likely increases her confidence, without affecting her accuracy. And once the confidence of the witness is heightened by the feedback, the witness's assessments of some of the other criteria are endangered; recall that the Wells and Bradfield (1998) subjects who received positive feedback reported that they had paid more attention to the video; such feedback could colour witnesses' self-reports about several of the *Neil v. Biggers* criteria.

Thus, witness confidence should be considered a system variable (i.e., police questioning procedures can affect it) as well as being an estimator variable. But jurors are ordinarily not aware of this; in fact, "jurors appear to overestimate the accuracy of identifications, fail to differentiate accurate from inaccurate eyewitnesses—because they rely so heavily on witness confidence, which is relatively nondiagnostic—and are generally insensitive to other factors that influence identification accuracy" (Wells et al., 1998, p. 624).

SUMMARY

This chapter attempts to demonstrate that the field of psychology has much to offer police officials who wish to reduce bias in eyewitness interviews. Some of the suggestions in this chapter stem from the conclusions of empirical research; others are commonsense principles derived from the observation of police investigations. Some police detectives will object to representatives from another discipline "telling them how to run their business," and psychologists always need to remember the pressures and constraints on police conducting crime investigations. In fact, the field of psychology needs to do feasibility studies to determine what factors affect the level of receptivity of police to suggestions from psychologists.

Psychologists must remember that the goals for the forensic application of their findings may differ from the goals of testing a theory in the laboratory. The results of laboratory studies may not generalize to the real world of crime victims and eyewitnesses, who may have high levels of stress and concerns about the impact of their testimony (Kebbell & Wagstaff, 1997; Yuille, 1989, 1993). Criticisms by some experimental psychologists that high levels of stress inhibit accuracy of memory may conflict with the experience of police officers, who find that real eyewitnesses often have good recall for many of the details of armed robberies, such as the weapons used and statements made by the criminals (Christianson & Hubinette, 1993) (not to mention conflicting with the finding of field studies by Yuille and others that stress does not necessarily impair memory). Although stress may have an adverse effect on overall performance, it may improve the recall for specific relevant information (Kebbell & Wagstaff, 1997; Peace & Porter, 2004).

Further, the oft-repeated conclusion that a witness's high degree of confidence may not reflect an equivalent level of accuracy fails to distinguish between types of information elicited in police questioning. For example, Kebbell, Wagstaff, and Covey (1996) found that the relationship between witnesses' confidence and accuracy was high when straightforward and easy questions were asked (such as basic descriptive qualities of the perpetrator) but the relationship deteriorated when more detailed, and hence more difficult, types of information were sought.

The research findings described in this chapter are only a beginning to the task of helping police improve their procedures. For example, the effects of police officers' provision of feedback to witnesses about the "correctness" of their identifications, as illustrated in the study by Wells and Bradfield (1998) described earlier, needs to be extended to other types of subjects in other types of situations, and particularly to actual crime victims who are given disconfirming feedback by the police investigator.

The **evaluation research** role of psychologists also is relevant concerning other approaches that police use to generate information from eyewitnesses. Victims and eyewitnesses may be asked to describe the perpetrator, after which a sketch artist will draw the criminal based on this description. Traditionally, police have used the **Identikit**, a collection of various facial characteristics from which witnesses can choose to put together the lips, eyes, and hair of the criminal. More recently, computer-generated faces have replaced the Identikit.

The problem with these procedures is that it is much harder than we think to recall individual facial features of a person, especially after only a limited opportunity to observe them. Furthermore, features interact; when using the Identikit, a nose will look different when the witness changes the eyes. Wells (1993), in reviewing the literature on this issue, concluded that the identification of faces by an eyewitness is a **holistic process** rather than an analysis of component features, meaning that face recognition is an act in which the relationship of features and the general appearance serve as determinants so that piecemeal analyses are not productive. Psychologists should continue to evaluate such procedures and advise police departments on their effectiveness.

KEY TERMS

clearance rate, p. 119
cognitive interview, p. 129
confirmation bias, p. 132
delayed discovery, p. 135
demand characteristics, p. 127
double-blind procedure, p. 133
estimator variables, p. 121
evaluation research, p. 140
false memories, p. 128
foils, p. 125
hindsight bias, p. 137
holistic process, p. 140
Identikit, p. 140
leading questions, p. 127

SUGGESTED READINGS

Cutler, B. L., & Penrod, S. D. (1995). *Mistaken identification: The eyewitness, psychology, and the law*. New York: Cambridge University Press.

This comprehensive account presents psychological research on eyewitness accuracy, and a good description of errors in estimator variables (not covered in this chapter) as well as system variables.

Devenport, J. L., Penrod, S. D., & Cutler, B. L. (1997). Eyewitness identification evidence: Evaluating common sense evaluations. *Psychology, Public Policy, and Law, 3*, 338–361.

This useful review evaluates the safeguards developed by the legal system to protect defendants from being convicted falsely on the basis of mistaken identifications. The article concludes that many of these safeguards are not as effective as the legal system assumes them to be.

Fisher, R. P. (1995). Interviewing victims and witnesses of crime. *Psychology, Public Policy, and Law, 1*, 732–764.

The definitive article on the ways that psychologists can assist the police to improve the quality of their interviews with crime witnesses.

Loftus, E. F., & Ketcham, K. (1991). *Witness for the defense: The accused, the eyewitness, and the expert who puts memory on trial*. New York: St. Martin's Press.

This immensely readable work recounts some of the cases (including those of Steve Titus, Ted Bundy, and Ivan the Terrible) for which Elizabeth Loftus, premiere researcher–expert witness, was asked to testify for the defence regarding the inaccuracy of eyewitnesses' testimony.

Sporer, S. L. (1993). Eyewitness identification accuracy, confidence, and decision times in simultaneous and sequential lineups. *Journal of Applied Psychology, 78*, 22–33.

In contrast to the standard lineup procedure, a sequential lineup procedure has the witness view only one person at a time, deciding whether that person is the offender before seeing the remaining members of the lineup. This article is one of several that find that sensitivity to the presence or absence of the culprit in the lineup is greater when the sequential procedure is used rather than the traditional simultaneous procedure.

Steblay, N. M. (1997). Social influence in eyewitness recall: A meta-analytic review of lineup instruction effects. *Law and Human Behavior, 21*, 283–297.

This review and analysis of 18 studies assesses the impact of biased police lineup instructions; it contains a useful bibliography.

Wells, G. L., & Seelau, E. (1995). Eyewitness identification: Psychological research and legal policy on lineups. *Psychology, Public Policy, and the Law, 1*, 765–791.

Among the many authoritative articles by Gary Wells, this one applies what forensic psychologists know to the recent court decisions and legislative acts.

Wells, G. L., Small, M., Penrod, S., Malpass, R. S., Fulero, S. M., & Brimacombe, C. A. E. (1998). Eyewitness identification procedures: Recommendations for lineups and photospreads. *Law and Human Behavior, 22*, 603–647.

The first scientific review paper of the American Psychology-Law Society, this article provides a detailed rationale for its four recommendations for improving the construction and administration of lineups and photo arrays. In October 1999, the U.S. Department of Justice published a manual for police and prosecutors, titled *Eyewitness Evidence: A Guide for Law Enforcement*, that supported most of the recommendations of this review paper.

7

Police Interrogations and Confessions

The voluntary Confession of the Party in Interest is reckoned the best Evidence.
—Lord Chief Baron Gilbert (1754)

THE IMPORTANCE OF A CONFESSION

A **confession** by a defendant—an admission of guilt—is the most damaging evidence that can be presented at the defendant's trial (Kassin, 1997), as acknowledged by the Supreme Court of Canada in *R. v. Hodgson* (1998, para. 14). Because of its impressive impact, the courts need to be wary about the circumstances under which a confession was obtained. In the ground-breaking case **R. v. Oickle** (2000), the Canadian Supreme Court recently stated: "In sum, because of the criminal justice system's overriding concern not to convict the innocent, a confession will not be admissible if it is made under circumstances that raise a reasonable doubt as to voluntariness."

In the *Oickle* case, during an investigation of eight fires around Waterville, Nova Scotia, the police interrogators misled Richard Oickle by telling him he "failed" a polygraph examination and that it was an infallible technique. Before the polygraph, Oickle was informed of his rights to silence, to legal counsel, and to leave the interview at any time. He also was told that while the interpretation of the polygraph results was not admissible in court, anything he said during the examination was admissible. At the end of the examination, the polygrapher informed Oickle that he had failed the exam. After nine hours of further questioning, he confessed to setting most of the fires. The trial judge in Nova Scotia ruled that his statements were admissible and convicted him on all counts. However, the Court of Appeal excluded the confessions and entered an acquittal. Finally, the Supreme Court of Canada restored the conviction. Six of the seven Supreme Court justices ruled that the confession by Oickle was acceptable:

> The police conducted a proper interrogation. The accused was fully apprised of his rights at all times. The police questioning, while persistent and often accusatorial, was never hostile, aggressive, or intimidating. In this context, the alleged inducements offered by the police do not raise a reasonable doubt as to the confession's voluntariness (*R. v. Oickle*, 2000, summary para. 6).

Apparently, the Court was not fazed by the police trickery. Nonetheless, the dissenting judge, Madame Justice Louise Arbour, strongly disagreed with her colleagues. She seemed shocked by what she viewed as unfair deception, threats, and inducements. In her dissenting opinion, she wrote that "a failed" polygraph test is likely to be perceived as simply a confession by another name: "Given the unparalleled weight attributed to confessions, I believe that the prejudicial effect that flows from an accused's reference to his 'failed' polygraph test is overwhelming" (*R. v. Oickle*, para. 146). Clearly, she felt that the confession should have been ruled inadmissible.

The quest for a confession from a suspect by police and prosecutors can be fierce. In their zeal to obtain an admission of guilt, police may intimidate innocent suspects. Not all confessions represent the truth, and one of the tasks of the forensic psychologist—one of the most difficult ones—is to try to convince law-enforcement authorities to re-examine their interrogation procedures, and as a result, perhaps reduce their clearance rate. In fact, the Supreme Court of Canada has described situations in which "police trickery … is so appalling as to shock the community" and confessions obtained in this fashion should be excluded (*R. v. Oickle*, 2000, para. 67). The police can never act in a way that contravenes the Canadian Charter of Rights and Freedoms (1982), which requires that suspects be informed of their right to retain and instruct counsel (section 10), and the common law right to remain silent and not make incriminating statements. The Newfoundland Provincial Court case *R. v. McLean* (2003) gives an example. On September 19, 2002, a dog was found hanging with a chain around its neck from a tree on a path in Corner Brook. Raymond McLean was charged with unlawfully killing the dog, contrary to section 445 of the Criminal Code. McLean gave two separate confession statements to detectives with the Royal Newfoundland Constabulary. The Crown planned to introduce the two statements as evidence at trial. However, the defence argued that his statements should be considered inadmissible because they were false confessions resulting from false promises by police (that he would not get jail time) and in violation of his right to contact counsel in accordance with section 10(b) of the Charter. Judge P.C.J. Gorman agreed with the defence, concluding that both statements made by McLean were induced by the two factors above.

This chapter deals with one of the most acrimonious topics that can divide psychologists and police officers. We examine how police use interrogations in order to obtain confessions, what the courts permit police to do and prohibit them from doing, and what psychology has to offer this part of the police detective's job.

THE DARRELLE EXNER AND PAUL INGRAM CASES

When people confess to crimes, sometimes questions persist about the accuracy of the confession; false occasions occur for a number of reasons, as this chapter illustrates. Perhaps the suspect was overly suggestible, or simply too fatigued or anxious. Perhaps excessive pressure was placed on the suspect to confess. We must also realize that it is not always easy to separate false confessions from authentic ones; some confessions are proven to be false whereas others are equivocal. Two notorious cases—one a murder case and one a ritual abuse case—will highlight the complexities of evaluating confession evidence.

The Darrelle Exner Murder

On October 25, 1996, 14-year-old Darrelle Exner left a restaurant in Regina and started walking home. Tragically, she ended up being raped, beaten, and murdered before her body was found by one Kenneth Patton. After several weeks, the police still had no suspect and they began to canvass the neighbourhood. They finally encountered a 17-year-old male (who cannot be named) who said that he knew Darrelle and that he had started walking her home that night, along with his two friends, 23-year-old Douglas Firemoon and 20-year-old Joel Labadie. The police proceeded to interview the suspects and each, independently, confessed to the girl's murder. It turned out, however, that all three confessions were completely false; DNA evidence established that Kenneth Patton had raped Darrelle and he pled guilty to her murder.

As documented in the CBC documentary series *Disclosure* (2003, January 28a), Firemoon and the 17-year-old had produced different versions of how Darrelle had been killed during the interrogations. Whereas Firemoon reported that they had stabbed her, the 17-year-old confessed to hitting her over the head. However, the police knew that Darrelle had been strangled. Regarding Labadie, the police had convinced him that he must have "blacked out," so he was unable to remember committing the murder but still confessed. Interrogation approaches taken from the "Reid technique" (described in detail later in this chapter) were implicated in the false confessions. The three suspects spent nearly four-and-a-half months in jail following their confessions. Although the Crown prosecutor in the case later acknowledged that the three original suspects were innocent, according to the CBC documentary (*Disclosure,* 2003, January 28b), some of the officers from the investigation still believe that the three men were involved in the murder.

Interviewed for the CBC documentary (*Disclosure,* 2003, January 28b), Joel Labadie later stated, "I'm not even sure how to explain it, 'cause I'm not sure how it happened to me. All I know is for hours on end I said, 'No, I had nothing to do with it.' Next thing you know I'm sitting here going 'Sure, why not? I did it.' More or less its [sic] like they kill your spirit or something."

The Paul Ingram Case

In 1988 Paul Ingram was serving as a deputy sheriff in the state of Washington, a position he had held for almost 17 years. He was married, the father of five, and a central member of a local Pentecostal church. Apparently the paragon of mainstream U.S. values, he was even the chair of the Thurston County Republican Party. He spent many of his working hours in schools, warning children of the dangers of drug use (Wright, 1994).

But suddenly his life changed, as he was charged with a number of heinous crimes: sexual abuse, the rape of his own daughters, and participation in hundreds of satanic cult rituals that included the slaughter of some 25 babies. Even more amazingly, these charges stemmed from allegations by his eldest daughter Ericka, age 22 at that time, who claimed that her father had repeatedly molested not only her but also her sister. The abuse had ended in 1979, Ericka said, when she was nine and her sister Julie was five. But Julie later reported that she had been molested as recently as five years before, when she was 13.

Ericka first made the charges public in the summer of 1988 at a church camp where she served as a counsellor. As she talked to police later, the allegations grew in extremity and detail: she had caught a disease from her father; he had led satanic rituals in which live babies were sacrificed; a fetus had been forcibly removed from her body when it was almost full-term. Contrary to her first revelations, Ericka now told the police that the last incidents of abuse had happened just two weeks earlier.

After Ericka came forward with these claims, Julie provided further allegations; the police acquired two letters that Julie had written a teacher five or six weeks before. One stated:

> I can remember when I was 4 yr. old he would have poker game [sic] at our house and a lot of men would come over and play poker w/ my dad, and they would all get drunk and one or two at a time would come into my room and have sex with me

they would be in and out all night laughing and cursing. I was so scared I didn't know what to say or who to talk to. (quoted by Wright, 1994, p. 36)

Even though he was a law-enforcement officer, Paul Ingram had no experience with interrogations (Ofshe & Watters, 1994). After his arrest, he was kept in jail for five months and interrogated 23 times during that period. At first, he denied any knowledge of the claims. He was hypnotized and given graphic crime details; mystified by his inability to remember any details of these acts, he was told by a Tacoma forensic psychologist, Richard Peterson, that sex offenders often repress memories of their offences because they were too horrible to acknowledge. His pastor—who urged him to own up to the claims—told him the charges were probably true, because children did not make up such things. Even while Ingram's response was that he could not remember having ever molested his daughters, he added, "If this did happen, we need to take care of it" (Wright, 1994, pp. 6–7).

Leading questions by the police and the psychologist were used to cause Ingram to visualize images of scenes involving group rapes and satanic cult activities. His response began to change from "I didn't do it" to "I don't remember doing it" (Ofshe & Watters, 1994, p. 167). After further questioning, he told the police:

> I really believe that the allegations did occur and that I did violate them and abuse them and probably for a long period of time. I've repressed it, probably very successfully from myself, and now I'm trying to bring it all out. I know from what they're saying that the incidents had to occur, that I had to have done these things … my girls know me. They wouldn't lie about something like this. (Ofshe & Watters, 1994, p. 167)

Yet, at that point he could not recall any specific incidents of abuse.

But later Ingram was able to visualize scenes the detectives had suggested, and he did confess in detail, but in a rather detached and almost remorseless manner; for example, he would describe events by saying "I would have …" rather than "I did …" The admissions—given after relaxation exercises by the psychologist—were devastating; they included having sex with each of his daughters many times (beginning when Ericka was five years old) and having taken Julie for an abortion of a fetus he had fathered, when Julie was 15. For a time, he came to believe the accuracy of the charges. He "recalled" the crime scenes in detail and admitted guilt; for example, he reported seeing people in robes kneeling around a fire and cutting out a beating heart from a live cat, as well as watching another of the sheriff's deputies having sexual intercourse with Ingram's own daughter.

A social scientist, as an expert witness, played a unique role in this case. Richard Ofshe (1992) is a social psychologist and professor of sociology at the University of California at Berkeley. Even though he was called as a witness by the prosecution, he came to conclude—after interviewing Ingram—that through hypnosis and "trance logic" Ingram had been "brainwashed" into believing that he had been part of a satanic cult. Ofshe decided to try a daring experiment with Ingram. He suggested that Ingram had forced one of his sons and one of his daughters to have sex with each other and watched them while they did. (No one had ever brought that accusation against Ingram before.) After repeated questions and suggestions by Ofshe, Ingram began to "remember" and acknowledged that he had done that, too, and even embellished details of the act. He prepared a three-page, excessively detailed description of the incestuous act. Thus Ofshe (1992) began to have serious doubts "that Ingram was guilty of anything, except of being a highly suggestible individual with a tendency to float in and out of trance states and a … rather dangerous eagerness to please authority" (Wright, 1994, p. 146); Professor Ofshe became an advocate of Ingram's innocence.

But it was too late. Ingram had not only pleaded guilty but had plea-bargained to six counts of third-degree rape. There was no trial.

He began serving a 20-year term in prison, with the possibility of parole after 12 years.

Yet no physical evidence exists that he was a Satanist or a child abuser. Ingram no longer believes that he was, and his lawyers have appealed, unsuccessfully, to withdraw his guilty plea. The Washington State Supreme Court rejected his appeal in September 1992. Ingram was finally released from prison on April 8, 2003.

THE FORENSIC PSYCHOLOGIST AND POLICE INTERROGATIONS

What is the appropriate role of the forensic psychologist when asked to evaluate the procedures or results of a police interrogation? The short answer is that there are many roles. Richard Ofshe, first asked to be an expert witness by one side, came to play an active role for the other. This chapter examines possible roles by considering the clients to whom the psychologist might be responsive. For example, acting as a consultant or employee of a police department, a psychologist might seek to educate police detectives about the possibility of false confessions. If the client is a lawyer or the judiciary, the psychologist could serve as an expert witness or author of a consultation report about how the use of coercion and trickery by the police contributes to false confessions. And last, the forensic psychologist may feel that his or her ultimate responsibility is to society in general and attempt to educate the public about the dangers of misleading interrogations. This chapter considers each of these roles, but first we examine why false confessions occur.

THE PSYCHOLOGY OF FALSE CONFESSIONS

People assume that most confessions are spontaneous and that almost all are truthful. In reality, many confessions are negotiated, and 20 percent are **recanted**; that is, the suspect who has made an incriminating statement to the police later states that it was false. Among the reasons that people confess is the desire to escape further interrogation. They may say to themselves at some level: "I'll tell the police whatever they want, to avoid this terrible situation and deny it later." Sometimes they may come to believe what the police have told them, as some observers concluded had temporarily occurred with Paul Ingram.

Three Types of False Confessions

Recanted or disputed confessions are not necessarily false confessions. With regard to those that are, Kassin and Wrightsman (1985; Wrightsman & Kassin, 1993) identified three types of false confessions: voluntary, coerced-compliant, and coerced-internalized.

Voluntary

Voluntary false confessions are offered willingly, without elicitation. They may be instigated by a desire for publicity or by generalized guilt, or they may reflect some form of psychotic behaviour. Most highly publicized crimes inspire people to come forward and claim to have committed the crime. When the baby son of the Lindberghs was kidnapped in 1932, more than 200 people falsely confessed (Note, 1953).

Saul Kassin (1997) described a case in which he was contacted as a possible expert witness by the defence lawyer: A young woman had falsely implicated herself and a group of bikers in a murder case. She later told the police that she had lied about participating in the murder because she craved the notoriety and attention.

Coerced-Compliant

Coerced-compliant false confessions are those in which the suspect confesses, even while knowing that he or she is innocent. Coerced-compliant confessions may be given to escape further interrogation, to gain a promised benefit, or to avoid a threatened punishment. For example,

Raymond McLean in the Newfoundland case described above may have given a coerced-compliant confession. In such cases, the person does not privately believe that he or she committed the criminal act. In general, **compliance** refers to an inconsistency between one's public behaviour and one's private opinion, a phenomenon reflected in Asch's (1956) classic study of the impact of others' false estimates in a line-judging task.

In the fall of 1974 the Irish Republican Army (IRA) placed bombs in two public houses in Guildford (in the county of Surrey) and Birmingham, England. In one bombing five people were killed, 21 were killed in the other, and more than 150 were injured in total. Police, under great pressure to make arrests, questioned four Irishmen about one bombing and six other Irishmen about the other. After intense questioning, the four men questioned in the Guildford bombing and four of the six men interrogated about the other bombing made written confessions, although they all recanted their confessions at trial. They said that their confessions had been beaten out of them (Mullin, 1986). One, Paddy Hill, claimed that he had been kicked, punched in the side of the head, and kneed in the thigh. "We're going to get a statement out of you or kick you to death," was the threat that he later reported (Mullin, 1986, p. 100). Those claims were rejected by the jury, which found the Irishmen guilty; they were sentenced to life in prison.

One of the Irishmen convicted in the Guildford bombing (who came to be known as the Guildford Four), Gerry Conlon, was the subject of a 1993 movie—*In the Name of the Father*. Both sets of defendants spent close to 15 years in prison before their convictions were overturned because the English courts acknowledged that the police had coerced the defendants to confess by subjecting them to psychological and physical pressure (Gudjonsson, 2003).

Gisli Gudjonsson (1992, 2003) was able to later interview and administer suggestibility scales to one member of the Guildford Four and each of the Birmingham Six. The most dramatic finding from the responses of the Birmingham Six was the difference in personality test scores between the two defendants who did not confess and the four who did. Thirteen years after their interrogations, the two who didn't make written confessions "scored exceptionally low on tests of suggestibility and compliance" (Gudjonsson, 1992, p. 273). Gudjonsson concluded that all eight of the defendants who made self-incriminating written statements reflected the coerced-compliant type.

Certainly the **third-degree tactics** that were commonplace all over the world 100 years ago—such as extreme deprivation, brutality, and torture—led to many coerced-compliant confessions (see *Brown v. Mississippi*, 1936, for an example). But do they still today? The 2004 revelations of widespread physical and sexual abuse of incarcerated detainees in Iraq by American and British soldiers establish that they certainly occur in modern wartime. What about in more commonplace, everyday interrogations? In at least some jurisdictions and at least with selected suspects, they may still take place. In the mid-1980s, four New York City police officers were arrested and accused of extracting confessions from suspects by jolting them with a stungun; one of the victims was found to have 40 burn marks on his body (Huff, Rattner, & Sagarin, 1996). Lawyers for Barry Lee Fairchild, a black man with an IQ score of 62, have claimed that he confessed to the murder of a white nurse only after Pulaski County (Arkansas) sheriff's deputies "put telephone books on the top of his head and slammed downward repeatedly with blackjacks" (Lacayo, 1991, p. 27). Such actions cause excruciating pain but leave no marks as evidence of coercion. The sheriff of Pulaski County denied Fairchild's claims, but 11 other black men brought in for questioning about that time reported almost equally intimidating procedures. Three said that pistols were placed in their mouths, with officers pulling the triggers of the unloaded guns (Lacayo, 1991). A former sheriff's deputy even came forward and testified that he had seen the sheriff and some deputies abuse various suspects (Annin, 1990).

More common are procedures that more subtly seduce suspects. Now popular among police interrogation procedures are psychologically oriented ploys, such as apparent solicitousness and sympathy, the use of informants, and even lying to suspects (Leo, 1992). When a bomb exploded during the 1996 Summer Olympics in Atlanta, the FBI brought in for questioning a man named Richard Jewell because he fit their criminal profile of someone intrigued with law enforcement. Although Jewell was certainly a suspect, the FBI got his initial cooperation by telling him they needed his help in preparing a training film. He willingly came in; the next thing he knew, FBI agents, with a search warrant, were going through his apartment and plucking hair from his head (Brenner, 1997).

When the two sons of Susan Smith were found in the family car, drowned in a South Carolina lake, Mrs. Smith first told the sheriff that a black man had hijacked her car and had kidnapped her children. The Union County sheriff, Howard Wells, noted inconsistencies in her story and her behaviour, doubted her story, and—after extensive questioning—tricked Mrs. Smith by telling her that his deputies had been working a drug stakeout at the very same crossroads at the time Susan Smith claimed the abduction had occurred. "This could not have happened as you said," he told her, upon which she broke down in tears and confessed to driving the car into the lake (Bragg, 1995, p. A1).

Richard Jewell was innocent and did not falsely confess; Susan Smith was guilty and did eventually confess, truthfully, to the murder of her two children. In fairness, it must be acknowledged that in both of these cases "the system worked," but the willingness on the part of law-enforcement authorities to mislead suspects in the hopes of eliciting a confession still creates problems for a society in which many members of the community distrust and fear the police.

In the 2000 *Oickle* case, the Supreme Court of Canada confirmed that police deception is justifiable. Specifically, the Court concluded that a confession should only be excluded if the police deception "shocks the community" or even if not rising to that level, the use of deception is a relevant factor in whether the confession was voluntary. Many legal experts disagreed (as with Madame Justice L'Heureux-Dubé) or expressed outrage. Noted Toronto defence lawyer Clayton Ruby wrote in a October 17, 2000, *Globe and Mail* article:

> Such treatment sets Canada's standards at the lowest common denominator of civilized behaviour. Our values are revealed. They are these: Lie, cheat, mislead if you must. Ignore tears and repeated protestations of innocence. But get a confession from whomever you have in your hands. That's the message the Supreme Court has just sent to police forces across our land. We're playing with fire.

Coerced-Internalized

In the **coerced-internalized false confession**, the innocent suspect confesses and comes to believe that he or she is guilty. Interrogation by the police is a highly stressful experience that can create a number of reactions, including a state of heightened suggestibility in which "truth and falsehood become hopelessly confused in the suspect's mind" (Foster, 1969, pp. 690–691). In this type, Gudjonsson concluded that "after confessing for instrumental gain, the persistent questioning continues and the accused becomes increasingly confused and puzzled by the interrogator's apparent confidence in the accused's guilt" (1992, p. 273). In such cases, the suspect may even come to "remember" committing the crime, a type of false memory discussed in Chapter 6 (e.g., Loftus, 2003; Porter et al., 1999). Richard Ofshe and some other observers of his case concluded that Paul Ingram—reflecting an extreme state of **suggestibility**—should be placed in this category (Wright, 1994), and case reports exist of other coerced-internalized false confessions (Gudjonsson & Lebegue, 1989). It appears that suspects who cannot recall their actions at the time of the crime of which they have been accused (due to a drinking binge, for example) may be especially susceptible to such false memories (Porter, Birt,

Yuille, & Hervé, 2001). Joel Labadie in the Darrelle Exner murder case in Regina may have provided this type of confession.

At times, it is difficult to classify a specific person's response as compliant or internalized; this is especially true of the responses of children to interrogations. They will later say things like, "I was so confused; I couldn't separate what happened from what they told me happened." In Chicago in 1998, two boys—ages seven and eight—were arrested and charged with the sex-related murder of a young girl. They had confessed to the murder during an intensive interrogation. Later, however, the authorities concluded that the boys were not physically mature enough to produce the semen found on the victim's body, and they were released. Although no recording was made of the questioning, it appears that the boys repeated back what the detectives had told them (Kotlowitz, 1999). The validity of the responses of children to questioning by authorities—whether the children are suspects, as in the Chicago case, or victims—is a matter of great concern and is described in more detail in Chapter 12.

How Many Confessions Are False?

Clearly, in at least a few isolated cases, false confessions may occur. But how extensive is the problem?

Wrongful Convictions

It is not possible to determine conclusively how many people confess falsely. In fact, estimates of the number of convictions that are a result of a false confession vary widely (e.g., Cassell, 1996a; Huff, Rattner, & Sagarin, 1996). As Kassin (1997) has observed, determining the number is difficult for two reasons: (1) Even if it was coerced and the accused retracts it, a confession may be true and (2) "a confession may be false even if the defendant is convicted, imprisoned, and never heard from again" (Kassin, 1997, p. 224). But independent evidence exists that some confessions are false.

Several cases of persons wrongfully convicted of crimes are known to have been caused by an erroneous confession (Bedau & Radelet, 1987; Borchard, 1932; Rattner, 1988). For example, Rattner (1988; Huff, Rattner, & Sagarin, 1996) analyzed 205 cases of known wrongful convictions and concluded that 16, or 8 percent, were the result of coerced confessions. Although this percentage is low, false confessions more often occur in highly publicized cases dealing with major crimes because police devote more effort to solving high-profile cases.

People's Self-Expectations

Does questioning by the police lead to false confessions, even if intimidation is absent? Sometimes people admit to the police that they committed a crime when they are in fact innocent. This conclusion is hard for most of us to apply to ourselves; many even ask, "Why would anyone confess to something they didn't do?" Curious about the extent of this belief, Fellhoelter, Posey, and Wrightsman asked 347 students in an introductory psychology class the following:

> Let us say that the police are questioning you about a certain crime. You know that you did not commit this crime. Are there any circumstances under which you would confess to the police that you committed a crime, when you actually didn't?
>
> Please check one.
>   Yes, I might confess. __
>   No, I wouldn't confess to a crime I didn't commit. __
>   My answer depends on the circumstances. __
>
> Responses were as follows:
>   Yes, I might confess: 9 or 2.6%
>   No, I wouldn't: 220 or 63.4%
>   My answer depends: 118 or 34.0%.

If combined, the "yes" and "it depends" choices garner about 37 percent of the responses. What is most provocative is the gender difference

in responses. Do men or women more frequently acknowledge that they might confess to a crime they didn't commit? The data are as follows: Combining "Yes" (seven men and two women) with "My answer depends," 43 percent of men (70 of 161) but only 31 percent of women (57 of 186) reflected some possibility of a false confession; this is a statistically significant difference at the .05 level. Why this gender difference occurs remains an unanswered question; perhaps women hold stronger convictions or perhaps men more often consider the possibility of being coerced into a confession.

These results, indicating a general disbelief in the possibility of false confessions, are relevant to jury decisions in trials involving contested confession evidence. As Wakefield and Underwager wrote: "Widespread overconfidence in personal ability to resist coercion may lead jurors to give undue and erroneous weight to a coerced confession" (1998, p. 424).

False Confessions in the Laboratory

If we assume that on occasion, at least, a confession was a result of suggestibility and pseudo-memories and that the suspect did not commit these crimes, the question remains: Is this an isolated case? Is there any evidence that under controlled conditions, in the psychological laboratory, people can be convinced that they committed undesirable acts that, in fact, they did not commit?

To study such a question under controlled conditions, and still protect subjects' rights and act in an ethical manner, is a challenge for research psychologists. Ethical guidelines (both internal and institutional) prevent most researchers from placing research participants in a situation in which they may succumb to a belief that they committed a criminal act. The solution to the challenge, described here, may strike some as contrived and not generalizable to real crime-related interrogations. Yet it is a beginning.

Kassin (1997; Kassin & Kiechel, 1996) developed the following paradigm to test the proposal that people can be convinced that they did undesirable acts even when they didn't. He and Kiechel had pairs of students (one participant and one confederate) participate in a reaction-time task on a computer, with the subject typing the letters on a keyboard. Before beginning the session, the participants were instructed on how to use the computer and were specifically told not to press the ALT key near the space bar. If they did, the program would crash and the data would be lost. But during the experiment, the computer did crash and the seemingly distressed experimenter accused the participant of hitting the forbidden key.

When this happened, all 75 of the participants denied the experimenter's charge, but in half of the cases the confederate sheepishly "admitted" that she saw the participant accidentally strike the ALT key. (This procedure was designed to reflect the use by police of false incriminating evidence, a topic described later in this chapter.) Participants were given a chance at that point to sign a confession of wrongdoing prepared by the experimenter. Not to sign the confession would cause a confrontation with the professor supervising the study. Perhaps not surprisingly, all participants in the crucial condition (that is, the case in which the confederate informed on the subject) agreed to sign the confession. But as each was leaving the experimental area, a waiting "participant" (actually another confederate of the experimenter) asked the participant what had happened. Two-thirds of the participants in the crucial condition indicated that they had erred and hit the wrong button; they didn't say, "He said I hit the wrong button" but rather things like "I hit the wrong button and ruined the program." Thus, even under laboratory conditions, not just compliance but **internalization** occurs, and people can come to believe that they committed acts that they did not, in fact, commit. Further, some participants even manufactured explanations for how they had made the "mistake." These results are consistent with those of Stanley Milgram's (1974) obedience studies (in which some adult participants were willing to administer painful electric shocks

to other subjects) in that—despite their protestations beforehand—many people conform to an authority figure when in a coercive environment.

THE ROLE OF POLICE INTERROGATIONS IN GENERATING CONFESSIONS

Throughout history every society has been concerned with violations of its laws, customs, and social expectations. Those who were suspected of such violations were often subjected to interrogations in hopes that they would confess. In fact, many did so during ancient investigations, through the trials by ordeal in Europe, torture of "witches," and in modern-day interrogations around the globe. The first pictures ever drawn of police—found in 12th dynasty Egyptian tombs of about 2000 B.C.—show them administering the third degree to a suspect. In light of the videotape of the treatment given Rodney King by the Los Angeles police, it is provocative to note that in one of the drawings, "a man is being beaten with a stick by one of the policemen, while his legs and arms are being held by three others; a fifth officer looks on, supervising the proceedings" (Franklin, 1970, p. 15).

Most police officers recognize that intimidating actions like those claimed by Barry Fairchild (noted above) are illegal and often counterproductive, as "confessions" created by such coercion will usually not stand the scrutiny of a judge in a preliminary hearing. Police and legal experts differ about whether the warnings that inform suspects of their rights to a lawyer and to remain silent (in accordance with the Charter of Rights and Freedoms in Canada and the Miranda warning in the U.S.) are a good idea. It is claimed that the requirement that police use such warnings has decreased the conviction rate and that more criminals are on the street (Cassell, 1996a; 1996b; Cassell & Hayman, 1996). Leo (1996a) has argued that the requirements that police use such warnings has had a civilizing effect on police practices and has increased the public's awareness of defendants' rights. But some police officers may ignore such rules, viewing themselves as members of a profession with an agreed-upon set of practices deriving partly from the law, partly from common sense, and partly from tradition. The guidelines for these practices are systematized in several handbooks developed for use by police and are described in Box 7.1. Also, police are briefed about new laws and court decisions that have impact on what is and is not acceptable procedure.

Police must recognize that suspects confess for a variety of reasons, some of which may be unreliable. The greatest value of obtaining a confession may be that it leads to other incriminating evidence. But even false statements are useful, because "the subject who lies is then committed to the psychological defence of a fantasy" (Royal & Schutt, 1976, p. 25).

If the goal of the forensic psychologist is to improve the accuracy rate of confessions, it is appropriate to examine just what procedures the police use in questioning suspects.

The Goals of Interrogation

Police question suspects for two reasons: to get more information about the case and to induce suspects to confess. Contrary to the stereotype held by some, police handbooks state that the main goal for the **interrogation** of suspects by the police is to gain information that furthers the investigation; "interrogation is not simply a means of inducing an admission of guilt," wrote O'Hara and O'Hara (1980, p. 111), who included a number of other specific goals, including the location of physical evidence, the identity of accomplices, and details of other crimes in which the suspect participated. Royal and Schutt have

BOX 7.1
Police Guidelines for Interrogations

Many police interrogators are very experienced and skilled at their trade (Leo, 1996c). After spending a year with homicide detectives in Baltimore, Simon described the typical interrogator as "a salesman, a huckster as thieving and silver-tongued as any man who has ever moved used cars or aluminum siding, more so, in fact, when you consider that he's selling long prison terms to customers who have no genuine need for the product" (1991, p. 213). One reason they are so effective is the wealth of information available to them.

It is not difficult to find advice from police experts about how their colleagues ought to conduct interrogations. Among the numerous books with guidelines on criminal investigation are the following:

1. *The Gentle Art of Interviewing and Interrogation*, by Royal and Schutt (1976). This is an informal and readable manual that concentrates on interviewing and interrogation. Some of the procedures proposed by the authors are controversial and may be surprising, but the authors cannot be faulted for failing to express their opinions.

2. *Fundamentals of Criminal Investigation*, by O'Hara and O'Hara (1980). In its fifth edition, this 900-page handbook devotes almost 100 pages to interrogations, confessions, and appropriate procedures by the police.

3. *Criminal Interrogation and Confessions*, by Inbau, Reid, and Buckley (1986). In its third edition, this widely quoted text falls between the above two books in its length and style. It contains a detailed set of steps for questioning and eliciting confessions from suspects. Its authors facilitated the development of the polygraph, and the senior author was the John Henry Wigmore Professor of Law, Emeritus, at Northwestern University.

4. *The Confession: Interrogation and Criminal Profiles for Police Officers*, by Macdonald and Michaud (1987). The authors of this manual are a psychiatrist and a police detective. Containing a number of fascinating examples, it concentrates on interrogations leading to confessions.

5. *Police Interrogation: Handbook for Investigators*, by Walkley (1987). This book is the first manual designed for police officers in the United Kingdom.

agreed: "The real objective of interrogation is the exploration and resolution of issues, not necessarily the gaining of a written or oral confession" (1976, p. 25). Inbau, Reid, and Buckley (1986) advised: "Avoid creating the impression of an investigator seeking a confession or conviction. It is far better to fulfill the role of one who is merely seeking the truth" (p. 36). That may well be, but if a suspect does confess, the police do not look a gift horse in the mouth.

As Irving and Hilgendorf (1980) observed, sometimes a police manual conflicts with itself about the primary goal of interrogation. Lloyd-Bostock (1989) summarized this viewpoint:

> Inbau and Reid are working with a dual notion of the causality of confessions and therefore are sometimes inconsistent in their advice. On the one hand they see confession as resulting from the suspect coming to believe that confession is the reasonable course of action but, on the other, they also sometimes view confession more in terms of ["breaking"] the suspect. But overt threats, a build up of stress and pressure, and displays of force tend to be counterproductive as a means of extracting a confession. There is a danger that the suspect will become over-aroused and this can produce a boomerang effect. When people (or animals) become very frightened, they respond by retreating or attacking. Similarly, an over-aroused suspect may withdraw cooperation in panic, or aggressively defy the interrogator. (p. 28)

Sometimes, experts have advocated keeping the pressure on suspects who, close to the point of deciding to confess, begin to fidget and show confusion. But on other occasions they have proposed what Lloyd-Bostock calls a more promising approach to dealing with the suspect's conflict over making a decision; in these situations, they have suggested that the interrogator lead the suspect away from the ultimate choice and thus take the pressure off, so that the suspect is not faced with making the critical choice until the optimal point in the questioning.

What Police Can and Can't Do

As noted, the police handbooks emphasize the need to be professional in conducting investigations and interrogations. Beyond the previously described reasons for restraint, too much pressure may put the accused in such an emotional state that his or her capacity for rational judgment is impaired. Some manuals suggest opening with a positive statement: "We're investigating an armed robbery and we think you can help us" (Macdonald & Michaud, 1987, p. 19). But the question remains: What other kinds of tactics do police use in questioning suspects? What are the limits?

The public has very limited knowledge about the broad powers given to police during interrogations; we will return to this point later when we consider the forensic psychologist's role in working with society in general as a client. Police can use trickery, they can lie to suspects, and can otherwise mislead them. Box 7.2 outlines the rules on using confessions as evidence.

Methods of Interrogation

The term *interrogation* was traditionally used to describe all questioning by police, regardless of whether it is conducted in custody or in the field, before or after arraignment. The term was preferred over *interviewing* because it implies a much more active role by the police detective (Macdonald & Michaud, 1987). On the other hand, many police officers now prefer the more general term *interviewing* because of the powerful, negative connotations of the term *interrogation*. Here we use the term *interrogation* simply to refer to an interview with a suspect. Despite the persistence of controversy surrounding this aspect of criminal investigation, surprisingly little exists in the way of empirical documentation of interrogation practices.

Back in 1931, the U.S. National Commission on Law Observance and Enforcement published a report of its findings and confirmed the worst fears about police abuse, noting that the use of severe third-degree tactics to extract confessions was at that time "widespread" (p. 153). As examples, the

BOX 7.2
Confession Evidence in the Canadian Legal System

As mentioned earlier, in Canada the Charter of Rights and Freedoms describes what police must do prior to attempting to elicit a confession. However, courts have long relied on a higher-level "confessions rule," which states that "no statement made out of court by an accused to a person in authority can be admitted into evidence against him [or her] unless the prosecution shows, to the satisfaction of the trial judge, that the statement was made freely and voluntarily" (*Erven v. The Queen*, 1979, para. 931). The court must consider two main factors in deciding whether to admit a confession:

1. *The voluntariness of the statement.* A statement is said to be voluntary when is it is made "without

fear of prejudice or hope of advantage" (*Boudreau v. The King*, 1949) and must be the product of an "operating mind" (*Ward v. The Queen*, 1979). This principle assumes that when people freely incriminate themselves, the statement is probably true. However, when a confession follows threats or promises by an authority figure, the truthfulness of the statement can no longer be presumed.

2. *Whether the recipient of the statement was a person in authority.* This requires the recipient to be a person involved in "the arrest, detention, examination, or prosecution of the accused" (*Horvath v. The Queen*, 1979).

commission cited as commonplace the use of physical violence, methods of intimidation that capitalized on the youth or mental abilities of the accused, refusals to give access to counsel, fraudulent promises that could not be fulfilled, and prolonged illegal detention. In an effort to find out if and how the interrogation process had changed, the U.S. Supreme Court in its *Miranda v. Arizona* (1966) decision—lacking direct observational or interview data—turned for information to reported cases involving coerced confessions and to reviews of the most popular manuals then available for advising law-enforcement officials about successful tactics for eliciting confessions (see Aubry & Caputo, 1965; Inbau & Reid, 1962; O'Hara & O'Hara, 1956). Essentially, the Court concluded from its inquiry that "the modern practice of in-custody interrogation is [now] psychologically rather than physically oriented" (p. 448), but that the degree of coerciveness inherent in the situation had not diminished. The Court's opinion in *Miranda* in 1966, noted "the use of physical brutality and violence is not, unfortunately, relegated to the past" (p. 446). The well-known case of Iraqi detainees being systematically abused by American soldiers during the Iraq war gives extreme evidence that they still remain. But what about questionable psychological tactics?

Manipulative Tactics Inbau and Reid (1962) described in considerable detail 16 overlapping strategies by which confessions could be elicited from initially recalcitrant suspects. From these, three major themes emerge:

1. *Minimization.* The tactic of **minimization** is reflected in "soft sell" techniques in which the interrogator offers sympathy, face-saving excuses, or moral justification (Kassin & McNall, 1991). Thus the detective reconceptualizes for the suspect the attributional implications of his or her crime by seemingly belittling its seriousness (e.g., "It's not all that unusual" or "I've seen thousands of others in the same situation"), or by providing a face-saving external attribution of blame (e.g., "on the spur of the moment you did this"). The interrogator might, for example, suggest to the suspect that there were extenuating circumstances in his or her particular case, providing such excusing conditions as self-defence, passion, or simple negligence. Or the blame might be shifted onto a specific person such as the victim or an accomplice. Often the suspect is asked whether the act was precipitated by the victim. Sometimes, as in the *McLean* case in Newfoundland discussed earlier, the officer

might tell the suspect that there is "no chance" he or she will receive jail time, in return for a confession.

Inbau and Reid (1962) offered the following example of how such attributional manipulation has been used successfully as bait: A middle-aged man, accused of having attempted sexual intercourse with a ten-year-old girl, was told that "this girl is well-developed for her age. She probably learned a lot about sex from boys … she may have deliberately tried to excite you to see what you would do." In another documented instance, a detective told a breaking-and-entering suspect that "the guy should never have left all that liquor in the window to tempt honest guys like you and me" (Wald, Ayres, Hess, Schantz, & Whitebread, 1967, p. 1544).

2. *Maximization.* The opposite strategy is to use "scare tactics" to frighten the suspect into confessing (Kassin & McNall, 1991). One way to accomplish **maximization** is by exaggerating the seriousness of the offence and the magnitude of the charges. In theft or embezzlement cases, for example, the reported loss—and the consequences for a convicted defendant—might be exaggerated. Another variation of the scare tactic is for the interrogator to presume to have a firm belief about the suspect's culpability, based on independent, supposedly factual evidence. A variation of this procedure, advocated by Inbau and Reid (1962), is to falsify the magnitude of the crime in the hopes of obtaining a denial that would implicate the suspect—for example, accusing the suspect of stealing $80 000 when only $20 000 was taken.

Police manuals are replete with specific suggestions about how to use what is referred to as the **knowledge-bluff trick**. The interrogator could pretend to have strong evidence, such as the suspect's fingerprints at the crime scene or DNA; the interrogator might even have a police officer pose as an eyewitness and identify the suspect in a rigged lineup. Another technique is

to focus the suspect on his or her physiological and nonverbal indicators of an apparent guilty conscience, such as dryness of the mouth, sweating, fidgety bodily movements, or downcast eyes.

In the Alberta case *Dix v. Canada (A.G.)* (2002), it was established that police had lied about nonexistent evidence in numerous other ways. The use of lying with suspects and witnesses by the RCMP came under intense scrutiny. Jason Dix was awarded $764 863 in damages in a malicious prosecution lawsuit brought against police officers and prosecutors. Dix had spent 22 months in jail before the charges against him for an execution-style double murder were dismissed. The Court of Queen's Bench Justice Keith Ritter slammed police tactics in the investigation as "reprehensible," including police lies to Dix and his ex-wife that he had failed a polygraph examination. In the lawsuit, Dix gave 23 allegations of the RCMP lying to witnesses during the investigation. These included that Dix had failed the polygraph, that he had a "dual personality," that he often picked up prostitutes, that he may have killed before, that "medical evidence" existed that he was a homosexual, and that the police "would not lie to you" (para. 287). The judge agreed with Dix, concluding that, in fact, "many of them were lies" (para. 288).

Baiting questions are sometimes employed if this approach is chosen. These are not necessarily accusatory in nature but still convey to suspects that some evidence exists that links them to the crime. For example, the detective may ask: "Jim, is there any reason you can think of why one of Mary's neighbours would say that your car was seen parked in front of her home that night?" Without waiting for an answer, the interrogator would then say: "Now, I'm not accusing you of anything; maybe you just stopped by to see if Mary was at home" (Inbau, Reid, & Buckley, 1986,

p. 69). Sometimes baiting questions carry the strong implication that the answer is already known to the police, when in fact it is not.

3. *Building rapport.* The third type of approach is based on the development of a personal rapport with the suspect. Referring to **rapport building** as the emotional appeal, police manuals advise the interrogator to show sympathy, understanding, and respect through flattery and gestures such as the offer of a drink. Having then established an amicable relationship, the interrogator might then try to persuade the suspect that confessing is in his or her own best interests. In a more elaborate version of this strategy, two detectives use the **Mutt-and-Jeff tactic** (also called playing "good-cop, bad-cop"), in which one comes across as hostile and relentless, while the other gains the suspect's confidence by being protective and supportive. This technique is quite common (Zimbardo, 1967). Rachlin (1995) described a New York City detective as using a combination of rapport building and minimization: "He appealed to his human feelings, he occasionally made gentle body contact, he tried to make Turner believe that, yes, people do make mistakes sometimes and the detectives understood and wanted to help him" (1995, p. 182). Police detectives emphasize the need to maintain pressure on the suspect. One told Rachlin (1995):

> You put your suspect on a rail…. You push him forward, then back up a little. But once you get any kind of statement, he is committed to that statement. You back off a little, but stay on the rail. If your suspect feels he's losing control, he'll back off. You let that aspect go for a while, go on to something else, then come back. And ask another question that will incriminate him. He'll finally put the pieces together and realize you've nailed him. (p. 183)

Observational Data on Interrogation Methods

Are such examples an accurate depiction of the everyday interrogation process or do they portray only the most atypical and extreme forms of coercion? David Simon's year-long observations of Baltimore detectives (the inspiration for the TV series *Homicide*) led him to characterize such tactics as routine, "limited only by a detective's imagination and his ability to sustain the fraud" (1991, p. 217). In an empirical study, Wald, Ayres, Hess, Schantz, and Whitebread (1967) observed 127 interrogations over the course of 11 weeks in the New Haven, Connecticut, Police Department. In addition to recording the frequency with which various tactics were used in these sessions, the investigators interviewed the police officers and lawyers involved as well as some former suspects.

Overall, this research revealed that one or more of the tactics recommended by Inbau and Reid (1962) were employed in 65 percent of the interrogations observed and that the detectives used an average of two kinds of tactics per suspect. The most common approach was to overwhelm the suspect with damaging evidence, to assert a firm belief in his guilt, and then to suggest that it certainly would be easier for all concerned if the suspect admitted to his or her role in the crime. This last appeal was often accompanied by a show of sympathy and concern for the suspect's welfare. Most of the other methods cited in the manuals were also used with varying frequency, including the Mutt-and-Jeff routine, playing off suspects against each other, minimizing the seriousness of the offence, shifting the blame for the crime to external factors, and alerting the suspect to his or her signs of nervousness that reveal a guilty conscience. The researchers reported that no undue physical force was used by the detectives, but they did observe the frequent use of promises, such as offers of decreased bail, reduced charges, and judicial leniency, plus vague threats about harsher treatment. In three instances, suspects were told that the police would make trouble for their families and friends if they refused to cooperate.

Wald et al. (1967) concluded from their observations that detectives employed most of the persuasive techniques listed by Inbau and Reid. When these tactics were combined with a generally hostile demeanour and lengthy interrogation, they often appeared to be successful. Moreover, it is perhaps reasonable to speculate that because the mere presence of observers at the sessions could have inhibited the use of stronger forms of pressure, these results might even underestimate the coercion employed during interrogation.

In the United Kingdom, Barrie Irving and Linden Hilgendorf (1980) carried out a similar study, by observing interrogations carried out by law-enforcement officials at Brighton. They classified police interviewing techniques on the basis of how well they altered the suspect's view of the consequences of confessing or not confessing. These consequences can be considered utilitarian, social, or affecting the suspect's self-esteem. For example, if interrogators choose to downgrade the seriousness of the crime, it could make the suspect believe that the punishment for the crime will be less severe, thus affecting the practical, or utilitarian, consequences of confessing. In one case in the U.K. study, interrogators were observed telling suspects that if they made a clean breast of things, it would increase the likelihood of their receiving lenient treatment in court (Irving & Hilgendorf, 1980).

In other studies, police interrogators have been observed skillfully developing a relationship with a suspect, so that the interrogator's own approval had social consequences for the suspect. The police officer might express sympathy, understanding, or empathy with the suspect's actions, thus downplaying the negative social outcomes that might follow a conviction (Lloyd-Bostock, 1989). Or, the interrogator may attempt to alter the way a suspect views himself or herself, by emphasizing the suspect's good sense or likable nature or by pointing out how much better it would feel to get things off one's chest,

thus attempting to have an effect on the suspect's self-esteem (Irving & Hilgendorf, 1980).

Leo (1996b) observed 182 interrogations, either live or videotaped, in three police departments, all in the state of California. Typically, five or more different tactics were used in an interrogation; detectives would note contradictions in the suspect's statements and confront the suspect with incriminating evidence (some of it faked), but they also used minimization and positive incentives such as praising the suspect. Leo's observations led him to characterize the interrogation as a **confidence game** that involved the well-developed use of deception and manipulation, and thus the betrayal of trust (Leo, 1996c).

What Is Allowed?

The discussion above reveals that the police have much greater leeway in the interrogation of suspects than most people assume. As recently confirmed in the *R. v. Oickle* (2000) case, police are allowed to misrepresent certain facts of the case, use techniques that take advantage of the emotions or beliefs of the suspect, and fail to inform the suspect of some important fact or circumstance that might make the suspect less likely to confess. One of the most common forms of acceptable deception used is making false claims about evidence pointing to the accused, such as a "failed" polygraph test, as in the Jason Dix case. As established in *Oickle*, the court determined that police deception is only unacceptable when it is "so appalling as to shock the community."

The Canadian Supreme Court has decided that imminent physical threats by a police officer are sufficiently shocking, and bans confession evidence obtained in this manner. The types of tactics that are illegal include physical force, abuse, and torture; explicit threats of harm or punishment; prolonged isolation or deprivation of food or sleep; promises of leniency; and failure to notify the suspect of his or her right to counsel (e.g., Kassin, 1997). However, surprisingly, the Canadian Supreme Court has argued that the use of "veiled threats" requires close examination. While the police are allowed to offer certain inducements to obtain a confession, they are not allowed to offer "quid pro quo" offers, regardless of whether they are in the form of threats or promises. Trial judges have been instructed to assess whether a suspect was questioned aggressively for a long period and/or was confronted with fabricated evidence and police trickery. Whereas either of these practices on its own may be acceptable in some forms, the judge must decide whether, collectively, they may have contributed to false self-incriminating statements (*R. v. Oickle*, 2000).

Why Isn't Police Trickery Uniformly Prohibited?

Two reasons lie behind a court's decision when it rules that a confession is inadmissible because it was coerced: As described by Judge Gorman (cited above in *R. v. McLean*, 2003), such confessions violate the Charter of Rights and Freedoms and they may be unreliable because of the possibility of false confession. When the police lie to a suspect, the courts apparently assume that such lying would be counterproductive with truly innocent suspects. That is, if suspects are told that they were seen at the crime location, and the suspects know that they have never been there, the suspects would recognize that the police are lying to them and refuse to confess. But human behaviour is not that simple, and forensic psychologists can try to educate the police about the power of the interrogation process to convince innocent suspects that the false information they received is true. Further, false evidence presented to suspects by the police might cause them to doubt the likelihood of their receiving a fair trial and lead them to plea-bargain.

WHAT CAN PSYCHOLOGISTS CONTRIBUTE?

The responsibilities of the forensic psychologist with respect to the use of police interrogations are diverse and often conflicting.

The Police as Client

Police and psychologists maintain a complex relationship, as the previous two chapters have illustrated. Psychologists want to assist police in improving their interrogation procedures when they lead to authentic confessions, but at the same time, many psychologists are appalled by the coercive procedures often used and are concerned that the use of manipulation and falsehoods leads to false confessions. How may the two professions work together to achieve common goals? Some of the ways suggested in this section, such as psychologically strengthening the interrogation process, reflect an effort to better achieve police goals; others, such as videotaping of interrogations, reflect psychologists' concern about the validity of confessions.

The Role of Interrogative Suggestibility

Police tend to believe that almost all suspects are guilty and that they confess only if they are guilty; thus interrogators may extract confessions that are false without realizing it (Leo, 1996a). Psychologists need to introduce to police the concepts of coerced-internalized and coerced-compliant false confessions. The forensic psychologist also must help police understand that some suspects are subject to **interrogative suggestibility**; that is, the idea that because suspects are anxious or lack a strong self-concept or for other reasons they actually come to believe what the police are telling them. Gisli Gudjonsson (1984, 1989, 1992, 1997, 2003) developed a procedure to identify subjects high in interrogative suggestibility. The subject first is read a narrative paragraph; then he or she is asked to provide a free recall of the story and to answer 20 memory questions, 15 of which are misleading. After being told—in a firm voice—that he or she made several errors, the subject is then retested, and shifts in the subject's answers are studied. A distinction is made between the number of shifts in memory and the number of responses that reflect a yielding to the misleading questions. Subjects who score high on interrogative suggestibility also tend to have high levels of anxiety, low self-esteem, poor memories, and a lack of assertiveness (Gudjonsson, 2003). Among criminal suspects, those who confessed to the police but later retracted their statements scored higher than the general population (Gudjonsson, 1991). While in the above description interrogative suggestibility is portrayed as a trait, it also may be a temporary state; for example, sleep deprivation increases scores on interrogative suggestibility (Blagrove, 1996).

How to make police aware of such problems is a challenge. First of all, police don't consider these to be "problems," and police detectives do not routinely solicit advice from psychologists to improve the accuracy of their interrogation techniques. Police detectives don't necessarily see the use of false evidence during the interrogation as unfair (Skolnick & Leo, 1992), because most of them believe that if the suspect is innocent, he or she won't "bite" on the false information. Such techniques, for Inbau, Reid and Buckley, are not "apt to make an innocent person confess" (1986, p. xvii). And as noted earlier in the chapter, the actual number of innocent persons who confess under such an inducement remains controversial (Cassell, 1998; Ofshe & Leo, 1997; Slobogin, 1997).

Prior Planning of Interrogations

Police are always interested in ways to improve their ability to get suspects to cooperate and reveal information. Part of the prevalent stereotype of police interrogation is the belief that the criminal is usually driven to confessing after having been trapped by the piercing brilliance of the police interrogator (Deeley, 1971). "In reality," states a Scotland Yard detective, "there is no sudden blinding shaft of light. You pick a villain [the British word for a suspect] up on something he said yesterday…. Usually it's a matter of wearing a person down. You may consider that a form of duress, but that's what it amounts to—wearing them down by persistence, like water dripping on a stone. Not brilliance" (quoted by Deeley, 1971, p. 139).

Prior planning is one facilitator of a successful crime investigation. Psychologists can aid by encouraging detectives to ask themselves if the questioning of a suspect is potentially the most valuable means of getting the desired information under the existing circumstances (Royal & Schutt, 1976). If it is decided to question suspects, the police officer should first read all the investigation reports and statements already taken, as well as visiting the scene of the crime, checking out suspects' alibis, examining any previous criminal records of suspects, and making inquiries of other people who may have relevant information (Macdonald & Michaud, 1987; Royal & Schutt, 1976). One detective commented: "The more you know about the man you are going to interrogate the better position you are in to know his weak points. I had a case where I could have talked till hell froze over and this guy wouldn't have confessed. But another policeman had supplied me with a tiny scrap of information beforehand which opened him up" (quoted by Deeley, 1971, p. 142).

The Physical Setting of the Interrogation

Whether police like it or not, social psychologists have a number of concepts and research findings that are helpful to them as they seek to generate confessions. Consider, for example, what we know about the effects of the physical setting on behaviour. Police manuals agree with social psychologists in urging officials to employ a specifically constructed room that is psychologically removed from the sights and sounds of everyday existence and to maintain rigid control over the ecology of that room. The novelty of this facility serves the function of promoting a sense of lack of control and social isolation and hence gives the suspect the illusion that the outside world is withdrawing further and further away (Aubry & Caputo, 1980). Inbau, Reid, and Buckley (1986) go so far as to conclude that privacy—being alone with the suspect—is "the principal psychological factor contributing to a successful interrogation" (p. 24).

To further minimize sensory stimulation and remove all extraneous sources of distraction, social support, and relief from tension, the manuals recommend that the interrogation room be acoustically soundproofed and bare, without furniture or ornaments—only two chairs and perhaps a desk (see, for example, Macdonald & Michaud, 1987, p. 15). Also critical, of course, is that the accused be denied communicative access to friends and family. Finally, the interrogator is advised to sit as close as possible to the subject, in armless, straight-backed chairs, and at equal eye level. Such advice reflects the psychological hypothesis that invading the suspect's personal space will increase his or her level of anxiety, from which one means of escape is confession.

Establishing Authority during the Interrogation

In keeping with the above constraints, psychological principles would advise police interviewers to avoid letting the suspect establish the ground rules. The most common procedure is the **stipulation,** in which the detectives attempt to stifle attempts by the suspect to set down ground rules for the questioning. A suspect may say, "I will answer any questions about 'X' or 'Y' or 'Z' but not others" (Royal & Schutt, 1976, p. 67). Some suspects may use seductive behaviours or may cry in order to try to control the situation. In response, the interviewer must display firmness and authority without reflecting arrogance.

Emphasis in the police manuals on establishing authority is consistent with the findings of psychological research. As Lloyd-Bostock (1989) observed, the relationship between an individual and someone in authority can generate quite dramatic psychological effects. As mentioned earlier, Stanley Milgram's (1974) series of studies showed the appalling degree to which ordinary people would obey instructions to administer painful shocks—instructions that came from an experimenter who had established a position of authority. Many subjects in Milgram's studies were willing to follow instructions to administer painful and dangerous shocks to other participants. Lloyd-Bostock (1989) concluded that subjects being interrogated can become, like Milgram's subjects, just as acquiescent to the

demands of the interrogator who has carefully established control over the situation.

The Police's Ability to Detect Deception

Psychologists have carried out extensive research on the accuracy of persons in detecting deception in others and in the cues that indicate deception. These research findings can be applied to the task of the police detective in assessing the truth telling of a suspect.

Police Assumptions about Their Own Accuracy
Police believe they can spot the liar in the interrogation room. Inbau and his colleagues (1986) claimed that it is possible, using a variety of cues from the suspect, to distinguish between guilt and innocence. For example, they proposed that the innocent suspect will give concise answers because "he has no fear of being trapped" (p. 48). In contrast, guilty suspects wouldn't make "direct eye contact" (p. 51) and would be "overly polite" (p. 47).

Rachlin (1995) was given permission by the New York City Police Department to observe police detectives at work. He has provided information about how these detectives formed impressions of suspects immediately:

> Detectives often wanted to appraise how compliant their subject would be, and there was one simple method that gave them a good clue right from the start. When the detective shook hands with the subject at the time of introduction, in grasping the subject's hand, the detective pivoted his own around clockwise. If the subject's hand followed [quite] easily, it could be interpreted to mean he would be tractable and forthcoming; if not, it was an indication he might be resistant … (1995, p. 180)

Interrogators also had their strategies for detecting deception:

> The so-called **scan technique** involved asking the subject to describe his activities the day of the crime, covering a period from

several hours before to several hours after. The detective would listen to the entire recital without interrupting, paying attention to the degree of denial. If the person provided explicit particulars of events up until the time of the actual crime, then glossed over what he was doing at the time of the crime and concluded with a detailed post-crime accounting of events, it was a signal to the detective that the subject was trying to conceal the criminal behaviour that was the focus of the interview. (Rachlin, 1995, p. 181, boldface added)

Research on the Ability to Detect Deception

Much research in Canada, the U.S., and the U.K. suggests that law-enforcement and other legal professionals cannot generally tell whether someone is lying, even though they believe that they can. In a study by Ekman and O'Sullivan (1991), customs officials, police officers, judges, FBI agents, forensic psychiatrists, and other groups were no better than chance at judging the honesty of videotaped speakers. Only the Secret Service performed significantly above what would be expected from guessing alone (64 percent correct). Dalhousie-based researchers Porter, Woodworth, and Birt (2000) found that parole officers performed significantly below chance at detecting deception prior to participating in a deception-detection training workshop.

Videotaping Interrogations

Given that police often use manipulation and trickery in interrogations and that some suspects are susceptible to making false confessions, it is essential that an independent record of the proceeding be made available to the judge and jury (Cassell, 1996b; Gudjonsson, 2003; Kassin, 1997; Leo, 1996a). In Great Britain the Police and Criminal Evidence Act requires that all interrogations be taped. The courts of Minnesota and Alaska have ruled that defendants' statements obtained without taping are generally inadmissible (Leo,

1996a). A U.S. survey (Geller, 1993, cited by Kassin, 1997) estimated that one-third of all large police and sheriff's departments do some video-taping of interrogations, but often what is shown to jurors is only the defendant's final confession. In Canada, there is no formal legal requirement that interrogations be taped, although in many municipalities, such as Toronto, police agencies expect their detectives to record interrogations if possible.

Further, the way the interrogation is video-taped can affect jurors' reactions to it. Judgments of the voluntariness of videotaped confessions were systematically affected by the camera angle (Lassiter & Irvine, 1986). Participants watched a tape of an interrogation from one of three angles: one in which the interrogator was visually salient, one in which only the suspect was, and one in which both participants were. Judgments that coercion had been used were lowest when the suspect was salient, highest when the interrogator was salient, and intermediate when the two were equally visible. The research results are consistent with social-psychological tests of **correspondent inference theory** (Jones & Davis, 1965; Jones & Harris, 1967), which deals with the decision to infer whether a person's actions reflect (or "correspond to") an internal characteristic. A camera focused on the suspect increases the attribution by observers that the suspect's response was determined by his or her internal predispositions rather than by any coercive nature of the situation.

The Courts as Client

On the matter of suspects' confessions, the forensic psychologist can play a role in advising trial judges as well as the police. Courts have, over the years, made a number of decisions relevant to the admissibility of confession evidence; these are reviewed in this section.

What Do the Courts Want to Know?

In determining whether to admit a confession into evidence, the fundamental question asked by judges is whether it was voluntary. Involuntary confessions, usually generated by coercion, are seen as false by the courts and hence are inadmissible. But where do we draw the line between involuntary and voluntary? We may agree that physical brutality or torture contribute to an involuntary confession, but often the police and the defendant will disagree as to whether such actions by the police took place. With increased recording of interrogations, this situation will undoubtedly improve. But what about less obvious "psychological" coercion? In general, judges rarely conclude that the police trickery was so severe that it undermined voluntariness (Young, 1996). Research by Kassin and Wrightsman (1980, 1981; Wrightsman & Kassin, 1993) suggests that judges need to exert more caution in admitting such disputed confessions into evidence. When told that a suspect confessed, mock jurors do not always consider the circumstances or give much weight to the possibility that coercion caused the confession; rather, they tend to reflect an application of the **fundamental attribution error**, accepting a dispositional attribution of a person's actions without fully accounting for the effects of situational factors (E. E. Jones, 1990).

Forensic psychologists can serve the court by pointing out how judicial assumptions about juries are sometimes in conflict with the findings of psychological research. For example, the conclusion of the research program by Saul Kassin and his colleagues (see especially Kassin & Sukel, 1997) is that "confession evidence is inherently prejudicial and that people do not discount it even when it was logically and legally appropriate to do so" (Kassin & Neumann, 1997, p. 471).

It is true that when a defence lawyer attempts to introduce the testimony of a psychologist regarding the circumstances that lead to involuntary confessions, the trial judge may not admit such testimony. But the effort needs to continue, if for no other reason than it establishes grounds for an appeal. Sometimes such appeals have been successful. For example, in *United States v. Hall* (1996),

the court reversed a trial judge's decision not to admit the testimony of Dr. Richard Ofshe. The court ruled that:

> Once the trial judge decided that Hall's confession was voluntary, the jury was entitled to hear the relevant evidence on the issue of voluntariness.... This ruling [by the trial judge] overlooked the utility of valid social science. Even though the jury may have had beliefs about the subject, the question is whether those beliefs were correct. Properly conducted social science research often shows that commonly held beliefs are in error. Dr. Ofshe's testimony, assuming its scientific validity, would have let the jury know that a phenomenon known as false confessions exists, how to recognize it, and how to decide whether it fits the facts of the case being tried. (*United States v. Hall,* 1996, pp. 1344–1345)

Judges also need to be exposed to the psychological perspective that has concluded, in the words of Kassin (1997), that "for all intents and purposes, [techniques of minimization and rapport building] circumvent laws designed to prohibit the use of coerced confessions" (p. 224). The most recent edition of the police manual by Inbau et al. (1986) throws down the gauntlet to judges; it advises its readers that "although recent [U.S.] Supreme Court opinions have contained derogatory statements about 'trickery' and 'deceit' as interrogation devices, no case has prohibited their usage" (p. 320).

Society as Client

The typical layperson does not think very much about confessions of suspects until a highly publicized case brings a claimed confession into question. But people have expectations and standards for how the police should behave when interrogating suspects, and some people are concerned when judges permit the admission of evidence that unfairly convicts a defendant.

Lying to Suspects by the Police

Deceit is generally viewed negatively in our society. Police manuals differ about its acceptability during interrogations. Macdonald and Michaud (1987) advise police: "Do not make any false statements. Do not tell him his fingerprints were found at the scene if they were not found at the scene. Do not tell him he was identified by an eyewitness if he was not identified by an eyewitness. If he catches you in a false statement, he will no longer trust you, he will assume that you do not have sufficient evidence to prove his guilt, and his self-confidence will go up" (p. 23).

But, as we have seen, *many police interrogators disregard such admonitions.* Further, some police manuals conclude that without the use of some trickery—leading the suspect to believe that the police have some tangible or specific evidence of guilt—many interrogations would be totally ineffective. Documented cases exist of police telling the kinds of lies admonished by Macdonald and Michaud; such behaviour may even be the norm (Aronson, 1990).

Do people subscribe to such tactics? Research (Engelbrecht & Wrightsman, 1994) indicated that when mock jurors were told that police carried out improper activities during an interrogation, they were less likely to find the defendant guilty than were mock jurors who were told that the police acted appropriately. The effect of the improper police tactics on verdicts was just as strong whether or not the suspect had confessed during the interrogation. Similarly, Skolnick and Leo (1992) asked university students to respond to a brief vignette that described a suspect who was confronted with false evidence by the police; only 36 percent of the students felt that the tactic was fair. The addition of a fabricated scientific report reduced the sense of fairness; only 17 percent of the students then rated the procedure as fair.

At a broader level, betrayal in the interrogation room not only taints the police but our society in general, a society built on relationships of trust (Paris, 1996; Slobogin, 1997). A general distrust of police interrogators creates an unwillingness on the part of innocent law-abiding citizens to cooperate with law-enforcement authorities (Stuntz, 1989).

SUMMARY

The goals for police when interrogating suspects are the elicitation of information about the crime and a confession of wrongdoing by the suspect. Confessions, as evidence at trial, are extremely influential; however, an uncertain number of confessions are false. These can be of three types: voluntary, coerced-compliant, and coerced-internalized. Of these, the coerced-compliant type is probably the most frequent; suspects confess—perhaps to get relief from the persistent questioning—even though they know they are innocent.

Police use a number of techniques during interrogations that reflect psychological principles; these include maximization and minimization, "baiting questions," and rapport building. Courts have been reluctant to prohibit the use of lying and trickery by the police, apparently on the assumption that innocent suspects would not succumb to such ruses and confess falsely.

One contribution that can be made by forensic psychologists is to emphasize to police that their procedures can produce false confessions and that some suspects are susceptible to what has been called interrogative suggestibility, in which suspects will sometimes come to believe false information about their role in the crime. It is recommended that police videotape the entire interrogation, so that judges and jurors can observe the procedures used by the interrogators and the style and content of the suspect's responses.

Psychologists can be called by defence lawyers to testify as expert witnesses with regard to the coercive effects of certain interrogation techniques. Forensic psychologists also serve society as a client by evaluating the public's reaction to the use of trickery in interrogations. General distrust of police interrogators erodes the willingness of innocent citizens to cooperate in investigations.

KEY TERMS

baiting questions, p. 155
coerced-compliant false confession, p. 147
coerced-internalized false confession, p. 149
compliance, p. 147
confession, p. 143
confidence game, p. 157
correspondent inference theory, p. 161
fundamental attribution error, p. 162
internalization, p. 151
interrogation, p. 152
interrogative suggestibility, p. 158
knowledge-bluff trick, p. 155
maximization, p. 155
minimization, p. 154
Mutt-and-Jeff tactic, p. 156
R. v. Oickle, p. 143
rapport building, p. 156
recanted confession, p. 147
scan technique, p. 160
stipulation, p. 160
suggestibility, p. 149
third-degree tactics, p. 148
voluntary false confession, p. 147

SUGGESTED READINGS

Ekman, P. (1985). *Telling lies: Clues to deceit in the marketplace, politics, and marriage.* New York: Norton.

Can people tell when someone else is lying? Most cannot, using customary procedures. But psychologist Paul Ekman has developed a system that analyzes brief, specific muscle movement such a fleeting grimace that may momentarily precede a liar's smile; these are quite difficult to fake.

Gudjonsson, G. (2003). *The Psychology of interrogations and confessions: A handbook.* London: Wiley.

This updated comprehensive review of the interrogation process was written by one of the world's leading authorities.

Inbau, F. E., Reid, J. F., Buckley, J. P. (1986). *Criminal interrogation and confessions* (3rd ed.). Baltimore: Williams and Wilkins.

This guide is the most frequent source for what police are told about how to conduct an interrogation of a suspect.

Kassin, S. M. (1997). The psychology of confession evidence. *American Psychologist, 52,* 221–233.

Many of the issues introduced in this chapter are discussed in this outstanding article.

Kotlowitz, A. (1999, February 8). The unprotected. *New Yorker,* pp. 42–53.

A disturbing account of the threats to validity when children are interrogated as crime suspects.

McCann, J. T. (1998). A conceptual framework for identifying various types of confessions. *Behavioral Sciences and the Law, 16,* 441–453.

This article proposes a fourth type of false confession, called the coercive-reactive type, that reflects coercion from sources other than the police; for example, a teenager who is threatened with death by his gang members unless he admits responsibility for a crime actually committed by the gang leader.

Shuy, R. W. (1998). *The language of confession, interrogation, and deception.* Thousand Oaks, CA: Sage.

Many examples from actual cases are provided in this examination of criminal confessions through the use of linguistic analysis. Highly recommended.

Wakefield, H., & Underwager, R. (1998). Coerced or nonvoluntary confessions. *Behavioral Sciences and the Law, 16,* 423–440.

This recent article covers a number of topics from this chapter, including types of false confessions, police interrogation procedures, and the admissibility of psychologists as expert witnesses. Specific cases are described in detail.

Young, D. (1996). Unnecessary evil: Police lying in interrogations. *Connecticut Law Review, 28,* 425–477.

This law review article documents how courts have had shifting standards over the years regarding the admissibility of confessions elicited in interrogations that involved questionable police tactics.

8

Jury Selection and Research

Researchers cannot carry out studies involving real Canadian juries to
gain more insight into the mechanics of the jury process and the effect of
judicial instructions upon the deliberations and verdict of the jury.
—Supreme Court of Canada Justice Louise Arbour (*R. v. Pan; R. v. Sawyer,*
2001, para. 100)

INTRODUCTION

Like many aspects of the Canadian legal system, our jury system is founded in English traditions and practices from the United States. However, the process of jury selection in Canada is very different from that of the U.S. In Canada, the kind of litigation consulting and jury "manipulation" that is witnessed to our south does not occur. In the first section of this chapter, the basis of and process of selecting juries in Canada is described. Next, we introduce the important role of forensic psychologists in conducting research on and making observations about jury decision making. As you will see, our current laws offer particular challenges to conducting research on Canadian juries that do not exist in some other countries. The rest of the chapter explores the significant role played by psychologists in jury-selection practices in the U.S., and looks at the controversies arising from jury manipulation.

JURY SELECTION IN CANADA: THE "RANDOM" IDEAL

In Canada, the Charter of Rights and Freedoms (1982) provides the overriding principles by which juries are to be selected. The Supreme Court interprets these principles and directs lower courts in their application. Section 11(d) of the Charter requires that an accused person receive a fair trial by an independent and impartial judge or jury. The selection of a jury is based on the idea that an accused person should have his or her charge judged by a random, unbiased sample of his or her peers. When it is established that a jury was not impartial, the Charter rights of the accused have been violated.

In line with this principle, the Supreme Court of Canada has been careful to try to ensure that juries judging the guilt of accused persons are always unbiased. However, as the Supreme Court outlined in *R. v. Bain* (1992, para. 93), the court takes a conservative approach in deciding whether a person's Charter rights have been violated in this way. So, interestingly, in order for an infringement of the Charter to occur, a jury does not actually have to be biased. The test for whether a jury is biased is whether it may be "reasonably perceived" as such by the courts. For example, if, for some reason, either the defence or Crown has too much influence on the selection of jurors, the judge needs only to have a reasonable perception or suspicion of a biased jury.

The Supreme Court has decided that the best way to create an impartial jury is by taking a **random sample of jurors** from citizens in society. As such, the information about potential jurors during the selection process generally is limited to name, gender, age, and occupation. Despite this ideal, jury selection in our country is not purely random. A proper jury also must be *competent* to make a decision of guilt or innocence. Similar in some ways to the criteria for judging whether an accused person is competent to stand trial (discussed in Chapter 9), all jurors must have a basic understanding of the trial, their role in the process, and the evidence that is offered. As noted in *R. v. Bain* (1992), "Some trials are more complex and complicated, however, and a tampering with randomness may be appropriate to achieve a minimal ability to understand the evidence and issues" (para. 96). The Crown in particular must work toward the "random" ideal, while sometimes "tampering" to ensure that jurors are unbiased, representative, and competent. As such, the Crown is expected to exclude jurors who do not meet any of these criteria. For example, numerous members of motorcycle gangs in Quebec have been tried and convicted of various serious offences in the past two decades. If a potential juror in such a case enters the court wearing a Hell's Angels jacket, the wise Crown prosecutor would probably make a challenge. However, unlike jury selection in the U.S., no fishing expeditions are allowed in Canadian courts.

Thus, the Supreme Court recognizes that randomness is not a "panacea" and the Criminal Code offers both sides a means of challenging prospective jurors. Specifically, section 634 of the Criminal Code states that the Crown prosecutor and the accused each are entitled to 20 challenges if the charge is high treason (not exactly one of our more common crimes) or first-degree murder, 12 challenges if the charge is another offence for which the accused may be sentenced to a term of over five years, or four challenges if the charge involves any other offence.

The challenges can be based on any of the following:

1. The identity of the potential juror is not the name stated on the list.
2. The juror has already formed an opinion about guilt.
3. The juror has been convicted of an offence for which he or she was sentenced to a term of imprisonment exceeding 12 months.
4. The juror is an alien (i.e., not a Canadian citizen).
5. The juror, even with the aid of technical, personal, interpretative, or other support services is physically unable to perform properly the duties of a juror.
6. The juror does not speak an official language of Canada or the language in which the accused can best give testimony.

In practice, it is common for neither side to oppose the first 12 jurors whose names have been randomly generated from the voters' list. However, often a judge may decide that a juror can be excused from jury service, even if neither side has offered a challenge. Jurors can be excluded from duty if they have any personal involvement in the case or any relationship with the defendant, the judge, the prosecutor, the defence lawyer, or any potential witness in the case. They also can be excluded if serving on a jury is likely to cause any personal hardship, such as losing their job or experiencing health problems. Further, although the court seeks to maintain "12 good men and women and true" on

each jury, occasionally a juror will die or be dismissed during the course of a trial. As such, as long as there are at least ten jurors remaining, the trial shall proceed and the remaining jurors will decide on a verdict.

One reason that a juror might be dismissed during a trial or that a trial verdict might be challenged is a revelation of a **conflict of interest** or outright unethical behaviour. Shakespeare observed the fallibility of individual jurors in *Measure for Measure*: "I not deny, The jury, passing on the prisoner's life, May in the sworn twelve have a thief or two Guiltier than him they try."

A notorious example of a conflict of interest that was not identified until after the verdict occurred in the 1995 Vancouver murder case involving Peter Gill (who was on bail during the trial). The jury in the case acquitted Gill and five other men accused of the first-degree murder of Ron and Jimmy Dosanjh, who had been gunned down execution-style during a drug war in Vancouver. However, the decision was later appealed after one of the jurors—a 40-year-old single mother named Gillian Guess—was convicted of willfully attempting to obstruct the course of justice. It was revealed that Guess was having sex with the accused during the time of his trial. At Guess's own 1998 trial, evidence was presented that she had flirted with Gill early in his trial, and, ultimately, they began a secret sexual relationship during his six-month trial. For the first time in the history of North America or the British Commonwealth, a juror was charged with having an affair with an accused killer during a trial. Guess was sentenced to 18 months in jail (but served only three). Gill himself was eventually convicted of obstruction of justice and received a 70-month sentence.

Jury selection occurs in a very different way in the United States. There, lawyers have been given broad powers to generate a group of jurors with particular characteristics. Potential jurors typically undergo extensive questioning before trial to allow the two sides to gain sufficient information for their challenges. These questions can address the potential jurors' attitudes toward the accused, criminals in general, and their views on certain issues such as the death penalty. In addition, the types of reasons for which a juror can be excluded are almost limitless. Often, psychologists or other consultants are hired to form the right jury. In fact, there is now an entire cottage industry or sub-specialty of psychologists who perform as "litigation consultants" in American cases.

JURY RESEARCH IN CANADA: NOT SO IDEAL

A considerable amount of research on jury decision making has been conducted in Canada. One prominent group, Regina Schuller and her colleagues at York University, has conducted many important studies of various influences on juror decisions, including knowledge of a complainant's sexual history (Schuller & Hastings, 2002) and the victim's self-defence behaviour in battered spouse cases (e.g., Schuller & Rzepa, 2002). For example, she has found that jurors view battered women who have fought back or behaved aggressively toward their abusers' violence more negatively than more passive victims.

However, existing laws in Canada offer a limitation on the type of research that can be conducted. Generally, researchers such as Schuller use a **mock jury approach** in which people (usually undergraduates) are asked to pretend they are jurors and are presented with fictitious or real case materials to come up with an appropriate verdict or sentence. At present, it is not possible for researchers to observe jury decision making in real cases or interview jurors about their decisions after the trial. In fact, section 649 of the Criminal Code states that if a juror discloses any information relating to the proceedings of the jury during its deliberations (that was not subsequently disclosed in open court), he or she is guilty of a criminal offence.

Because of differences between actual and mock juror decision making (such as the consequences of the decisions), the generalizability of mock jury studies can always be questioned. James Ogloff, previously a psychology professor at Simon Fraser University (now at Monash University in Australia) and past president of the Canadian Psychological Association, has published widely on the psychology of juries (e.g., Chopra & Ogloff, 2000; Ogloff & Vidmar, 1994). He has outlined his concerns with the current legislation that does not permit researchers to discuss jury decisions with actual jurors (Ogloff, 2001). In addition to this prohibition making research on juries impossible, he describes the problem of juror stress in cases involving violent, heinous crimes. The current law does not permit jurors to discuss their deliberations with anyone (including their spouse, a researcher, or a psychologist), which can lead to long-term psychological difficulties such as post-traumatic stress disorder (PTSD). He felt that the state of affairs was so problematic that he and a CPA Board known as the Committee on Legal Affairs in 2000 (unsuccessfully) attempted to intervene in two Supreme Court cases. In these cases, former jurors revealed that the juries had engaged in serious misconducts during their deliberations (such as coercing one juror into agreeing with the majority). However, the Supreme Court continues to insist that the confidentiality of what happens in the jury room is paramount and there are no exceptions.

Thus, at present, we must continue to rely largely on mock jury research or research from other countries to understand how juries make their decisions. Hopefully, the Canadian courts will revise the laws on juries in the coming years. For example, the laws could be changed to become more flexible in allowing jurors to discuss their experiences with certain others, such as mental health professionals and researchers in a confidential interview setting.

PSYCHOLOGICAL CONSULTANTS IN JURY SELECTION OUTSIDE CANADA

In some jurisdictions, the role of psychological consultants in jury selection is a major one. In some cases, there is disagreement between the lawyer and the consultant concerning the "best" jury composition for the case. In one famous case, it was the lawyer who won—but only in the short run. This refers to the decision about who would be "ideal jurors" for the prosecution in the first O. J. Simpson trial. Were certain types of individuals more likely to find the defendant guilty? Donald Vinson, founder of the large trial-consulting firm Litigation Sciences, offered his services pro bono to the prosecution for the Simpson trial, and for a while Los Angeles County Deputy District Attorney Marcia Clark accepted them. Litigation consultants on both sides, on the basis of their surveys and focus groups, concluded that black women, as a group, were sympathetic to the defence, so Vinson strongly urged the prosecution lawyers to use some of their **peremptory challenges** to dismiss them from the jury pool. But Marcia Clark firmly believed that she could convince these women; she had a gut feeling that black women, if on the jury, would commiserate with the victim and accept the prosecution's contention that the murder of Nicole Brown Simpson was related to the pattern of domestic violence she had experienced while married to O. J. Simpson. As the lead lawyer, Clark prevailed; in fact, the prosecution did not even use all 20 of its peremptory challenges (Toobin, 1996a). Vinson came to have "zero credibility" in Clark's eyes (Clark, 1997, p. 118), and so she summarily dismissed him after only a day and a half of jury selection (Toobin, 1996b). The 12-person jury that found Simpson not guilty included eight black women and one black man.

Conflicts in Styles and Values

A theme of this book is that forensic psychologists—whatever their duties—must ask: "Am I acting ethically?" and "Who is the client?" Although psychologists serving as jury consultants outside Canada must be responsive to the ethics code of their national psychological association, they also must be aware that they are advocates, hired by lawyers, and conflicts between the two professions and perspectives may occur. Sometimes the only resolution of such clashes is for the trial consultant to disengage from the relationship.

In her book about the O. J. Simpson trial, Marcia Clark (1997) was candid that she did not like Donald Vinson from their first meeting. She had been urged by her supervisor to accept Vinson's **pro bono** offer (i.e., that he would assist the prosecution free of charge). However, it is clear that Marcia Clark does not like trial consultants: "As far as I'm concerned they are creatures of the defense. They charge a lot, so the only people who can afford them are wealthy defendants in a criminal trial or fat-cat corporations defending against class-action suits" (p. 138). (This, despite the fact that Vinson had offered his services free to the *prosecution*.) She only agreed to the trial consultant's participation against her better judgment and in deference to her boss's insistence. Additionally, Clark was opposed to many of the staples of trial consultants' practices: "I don't feel that the government should be in the position of market-testing its arguments" (1997, p. 138).

In many ways, the above example is not typical of the relationship between litigation consultants and lawyers. Few lawyers turn down an offer of free professional help. The example also is unusual in that consultants are much more likely to be hired by the defence than by the prosecution. But conflict can occur in even the most congenial of relationships between a psychologist-consultant and a lawyer, and nowhere can the conflict between the law and psychology become more intense than in the task of **jury selection**. (Actually, *deselection* would be a better term, as lawyers cannot select jurors; they can only prevent some from being chosen. Nevertheless, the common expression will be used here.) Most psychologists are committed to procedures that reflect an empirical approach; whether litigation consultants use community surveys, focus groups, or mock juries, they are exemplifying a belief that it is not enough "to fly by the seat of one's pants" or to rely on intuitions or "gut feelings." As a group, trial lawyers are harder to characterize. A few are not particularly concerned with which individuals are on the jury; some of these lawyers are so self-assured that they believe they can persuade anybody, while others may be convinced that their side will prevail, regardless of the obstacles. Some lawyers are so confident that they fail to exercise all their opportunities to dismiss prospective jurors.

Other trial lawyers in the U.S. increasingly rely on consultants and empirical methods to advise them in making jury selection decisions. These procedures are a main focus of the remainder of this chapter. But most lawyers have their own ingrained assumptions about who makes a good or bad juror (Fulero & Penrod, 1990). If they cannot hire the expertise of a trial consultant, these lawyers will employ their assumptions and stereotypes in their choices. Thus it can be argued that the goals of trial consultants, despite their negative reputation in the eyes of the public, aren't any different from those of trial lawyers—they both seek a jury composed of persons who will be open-minded about (or, better, sympathetic to) their side's set of facts and arguments. The difference is that litigation consultants use what is called **systematic jury selection**, or scientific procedures, rather than rely on intuition, as do many lawyers.

Examples of Lawyers' Stereotypes

Examples of trial lawyers' stereotyped beliefs about jurors are the stuff of legend. Jeffrey Toobin recounted, "Early in my career as a prosecutor, when I first began selecting juries, a senior colleague warned me about men with beards. 'Guys with beards are independent and iconoclastic,' my mentor said. 'They resist authority. Get rid of them'" (Toobin, 1994, p. 42). The master lawyer Clarence Darrow believed that, as a defence

lawyer, he was better off with jurors of an Irish background; he avoided Scandinavians, who—he presumed—had too much respect for the law. The celebrated contemporary lawyer Gerry Spence has said: "Women are more punitive than men by a score of about five to one" (quoted by Franklin, 1994, p. A25). And the lawyer Keith Mossman (1973) has reported that "a nationally known trial lawyer once told me he would not accept any left-handed jurors" (p. 78). The second author of this text was once told by an Ontario lawyer at a judges' conference that the lawyer distrusted the judgment of any juror of Guyanese descent because he felt that that culture encouraged manipulation and lying (which they apparently would use on other jurors).

Such stereotypes may be specific to the individual lawyer. But the problem is more pervasive than that; general stereotypes are taught in law school trial advocacy courses, as well as passed down to neophyte lawyers on the job. Toobin described how, as a new member of the staff of federal prosecutors, he learned that "[W]e preferred jurors who were old rather than young; married rather than single; employed rather than jobless.... We sought jurors smart enough to understand the evidence but not so clever that they would overanalyze it; educated, but not to excess" (1994, p. 42). Stereotypes also abound for the defence bar, for whom the ideal juror was a member of the helping professions—a teacher, a social worker, a psychologist—because such people had sympathy for the underdog. Despite the lawyer mentioned above, members of racial minorities were also seen as pro-defence jurors in criminal trials, because of their more frequent conflicts with police and other authorities in the legal system.

Should such stereotypes be dismissed as lame folklore? Or is there some basis for their evolution? Early in the psychological study of racial stereotypes, a position was advanced, which came to be called the **kernel-of-truth hypothesis**, that group stereotypes may be unwisely generalized, but that some basic distinctions exist between groups. A review by Brigham (1971) concluded that ethnic and racial stereotypes could have such a "kernel of truth" in the sense that different groups of respondents agreed on which traits were associated with a particular object group; for example, respondents may all associate Newfoundlanders with being down-to-earth, light-hearted, and forgiving. (But we often lack the information to know whether the object group actually possesses the traits.) Even if the kernel-of-truth proposal is accepted as a general proposition, do these stereotypes have enough predictability to be used in selecting or rejecting individual jurors? Usually not.

What Do Psychologists Do?

Psychologists have sought to determine whether group differences (including racial and ethnic classifications as well as broad personality characteristics and attitudes) are predictive of verdicts. Their conclusion is not a simple one, for the verdict of an individual juror is the product of a wealth of factors, not only that juror's gender and race, attitudes and personality, but also the weight of the evidence in the case, the responses to the pressures on the juror to vote one way or another, and other factors specific to the situation. At the broadest level, we can say that jurors' verdicts can be affected by their biases, but how their biases are manifested may depend on specific aspects of the trial. For example, jurors who are relatively authoritarian *tend* to go along with the prosecution, but what if the defendant is an authority figure, such as a police officer or a physician? Then, the relationship may shift, and the authoritarian juror may side with the defence.

TWO APPROACHES TO JURY SELECTION

Given the fragile relationship between jurors' demographic classifications or internal qualities and their verdicts, psychologists have followed two pathways in advising and evaluating jury selection. These approaches, described further later in this section, reflect disagreement about the wisdom of a search for generality. Illustrative approaches that fit either the general or the case-specific approach are discussed in the following sections.

Broad Attitudes and Traits

A fundamental principle of social psychology is that each of us perceives the world in an idiosyncratic way. It is very difficult for us to look at a stimulus without evaluating it at the same time that we perceive it. Two different jurors will interpret the same stimulus differently, based on their past experiences and training. The phenomenon of **juror bias** refers to the assumption that each of us makes interpretations based on past experience and that these interpretations can colour our verdicts.

In criminal trials, jurors' biases can be classified as favouring the prosecution or favouring the defence. That is, some prospective jurors—without knowing anything about the evidence—may assume, for example, that the defendant is guilty. Pro-prosecution bias reflects, in some jurors, the aforementioned trust of authority figures; in others, a belief in a just world; in others, perhaps an acquiescent response set (i.e., a tendency to agree with what has been said), regardless of its content. In contrast, a pro-defence bias often stems from a sympathy with the underprivileged or an opposition to or suspicion of those in power.

In general, civil cases are hardly ever decided by juries in Canada. In fact, some provinces never allow juries to decide such cases. Nova Scotia, on the other hand, has liberal rules regarding the participation of juries in civil trials; in this province, they are allowed in any civil case. When juries make decisions in civil cases, biases can also occur. Here the biases are more varied, and it may not be possible to identify a single dimension of bias that applies to every civil suit. Some complainants who sue resemble defendants in criminal trials, in that they are (sometimes powerless) individuals in opposition to a powerful organization. Consider, for example, a parent whose child was injured in a car wreck who claims that the child seat in the car was defective. A suit by an individual against a major corporation with seemingly limitless resources evokes from some jurors a sympathy bias that resembles a pro-defence bias in criminal trials, but here, in civil trials, it reflects a **pro-plaintiff bias**. But other jurors may manifest **pro-defendant bias** (or at least **anti-plaintiff biases**); for example, some jurors feel strongly that society is too litigious and that many lawsuits are without merit. By identifying with powerful corporations, some pro-defendant jurors in civil cases may possess some of the authoritarian orientations that pro-prosecution jurors show in a criminal case.

Several instruments have been developed to attempt to measure the basic biases. A later section reviews and evaluates these instruments. But recall that some trial consultants prefer to relate jury selection to specific issues in the case at hand, rather than trying to assess general biases.

Case-Specific Approaches

If the broad-attitude/trait approach may be said to approach jury selection with a preconceived theory about how certain traits of jurors relate to their verdicts, the **case-specific approach** works in the opposite way. In this approach the litigation consultant looks at the particular facts and issues of the case and then develops a list of measurable characteristics of jurors who will decide one way or the other. In its purest form, the case-specific approach is coldly empirical; it uses the reactions of mock jurors and focus groups to identify the variables likely to be important in the actual jurors' decisions. In the end the trial consultants develop a list of characteristics that they hypothesize to be important. These characteristics, however, are not as broad as those described in the other approach. For example, if a criminal defendant is a member of a minority group, the racial identifications or racial attitudes of jurors may be considered as case-specific variables. If a hospital patient is suing a surgeon for medical malpractice, attitudes

toward the medical profession become salient. Later in the chapter, the use of scientific jury selection in several actual trials will be described to illustrate this approach.

MEASUREMENT OF JUROR BIAS

As indicated earlier, the general attitudes that may be related to jurors' verdicts in criminal trials differ from the attitudes relevant to responses in civil trials; thus different instruments have been developed to assess each type of attitude.

Criminal Trials

Two concepts have provided the structure for the measure of criminal juror bias—authoritarianism and the distinction between a pro-prosecution and a pro-defence orientation. Attitude scales have been developed to measure each.

The Legal Attitudes Questionnaire

The Legal Attitudes Questionnaire (LAQ) was apparently the first systematic measure developed to assess jurors' biases; it was published by Virginia R. Boehm in 1968. As a pioneering instrument it had worth, but it was also burdened with some of the problems characteristic of attitude scales of that period. The LAQ contained 30 statements, arranged in ten sets of three items. In each of these triads, one statement reflected **authoritarianism**, one reflected **equalitarianism**, and one reflected, to use Boehm's term, **anti-authoritarianism**. (The instructions for the LAQ and a sample item are reprinted in Box 8.1; because the scale has been revised to reflect more contemporary measurement procedures, the entire scale is not included in this box.)

According to Boehm (1968), the authoritarian items reflected one of three topics; they either "expressed right-wing philosophy, endorsed indiscriminately the acts of constituted authority, or were essentially punitive in nature" (p. 740). In con-

BOX 8.1
LAQ Instructions and Sample Item

The Legal Attitudes Questionnaire was the first instrument to attempt systematic measurement of jurors' general predispositions. However, it was cumbersome to complete and to score, as is illustrated by its instructions below.

Instructions: On the following pages are ten groups of statements, each expressing a commonly held opinion about law enforcement, legal procedures, and other things connected with the judicial system. There are three statements in each group.

Put a plus (+) on the line next to the statement in a group that you agree with most, and minus (–) next to the statement with which you agree the least.

An example of a set of statements might be:

+ A. The failure of a defendant to testify in his own behalf should not be taken as an indication of guilt.

  B. The majority of persons arrested are innocent of any crime.

– C. Giving an obviously guilty criminal a long drawn-out trial is a waste of the taxpayer's money.

In this example, the person answering has agreed most with statement A and least with statement C.

Work carefully, choosing the item you agree with most and the one you agree with least in each set of statements. There is no time limit on this questionnaire, but do not spend too much time on any set of statements. Some sets are more difficult than others, but please do not omit any set of statements.

Set 1

__ A. Unfair treatment of underprivileged groups and classes is the chief cause of crime.

__ B. Too many obviously guilty persons escape punishment because of legal technicalities.

__ C. The U.S. Supreme Court is, by and large, an effective guardian of the Constitution.

(From Kravitz, Cutler, and Brock, 1993, p. 666; reprinted by permission of Springer, the language of science; the other sets of statements may be found in Boehm, 1968.)

trast, anti–authoritarian items "expressed left–wing sentiments, implied that the blame for all antisocial acts rested with the structure of society, or indiscriminately rejected the acts of constituted authority" (p. 740). The more moderate third type, equalitarian items, "endorsed traditional, liberal, nonextreme positions on legal questions or were couched in a form that indicated the questions reasonably could have two answers" (p. 740). Answering reflected a type of forced-choice procedure; for each triad, respondents assigned a plus (+) to the statement with which they most agreed and a minus (–) to the statement with which they least agreed. In scoring, these responses were treated as ratings, with the positively marked statement receiving a rating of 3, the unmarked statement a rating of 2, and the negatively marked statement a rating of 1. Then the ratings for each of the three subscales were totalled separately; no total score was determined. Thus, every respondent could have a score ranging from 30 (high) to 10 (low) on each of the three dimensions: authoritarianism, anti-

authoritarianism, and equalitarianism. Boehm theorized that jurors with high scores on authoritarianism had a tendency to convict, that high scores on anti-authoritarianism were associated with a verdict of acquittal, and that scores on equalitarianism were not related to verdicts.

More recently, researchers have systematically examined the validity of the LAQ and have proposed revisions. As part of a meta-analysis of the effects of authoritarian attitudes on mock jurors' verdicts, Narby, Cutler, and Moran (1993) reviewed studies using the original LAQ; the results of these studies are summarized below:

■ Boehm (1968) gave the LAQ to 151 undergraduate respondents and then presented each with one of two written versions of a murder trial. In a case in which the weight of the evidence leaned toward innocence, the respondents who voted guilty had significantly higher authoritarian subscale scores than did respondents who voted not guilty. In a case in which the evidence was in the direction of guilt, the anti-authoritarian subscale score for individual subjects predicted the verdict for the group of adult respondents (age 21 and older). Among younger respondents (under age 21) the difference was in the same direction but was not statistically significant. The author did not report whether the equalitarian subscale scores were related to verdicts.

- Jurow (1971) asked 211 employed adults to complete the original LAQ and then listen to tapes of two simulated murder cases. An examination of the verdicts given by the respondents found that, in both trials, those who voted to convict the defendant scored higher on the authoritarian subscale. Scores on the anti-authoritarian subscale distinguished between mock jurors who voted guilty and not guilty for one case, but not the other.

- Cowan, Thompson, and Ellsworth (1984) had 288 jury-eligible adults complete the LAQ and then watch a videotaped re-enactment of a murder trial. The choice of verdict options by individual mock jurors was related to their scores on the authoritarian subscale; the authors did not report whether the other two subscales had any predictive validity.

These studies (plus others, to be reported later, that altered the format and scoring of the original LAQ) indicated that subscale responses (at least for the authoritarian subscale) had predictive validity; that is, they were related to eventual verdicts. But this conclusion reflected **group differences**, not results that were so precise that you could, with assurance, predict an individual's verdict on the basis of his or her authoritarian score. Furthermore, the original version of the LAQ had several problems (Kravitz, Cutler, & Brock, 1993), one of which was the cumbersome scoring structure, in which the three forced-choice response format prevented an independent assessment of the dimensions. The format and instructions were also difficult for

some respondents to understand and follow, leading to frequent invalid responses. For those and other reasons, a revised version of the LAQ was developed.

The Revised Legal Attitudes Questionnaire

The Revised Legal Attitudes Questionnaire (RLAQ) was constructed by Kravitz, Cutler, and Brock (1993), who created 30 items with statements from the original LAQ. (The items on the RLAQ may be found in Box 8.2.) Further item analyses reduced the number of scored items to 23. (In Box 8.2 items that were included in the final 23 are marked with an F.) This version can be administered with the usual Likert-scale response options (that is, strongly agree, agree somewhat, etc.).

Several types of evidence for the general validity of this revised scale are available:

- Several studies converted the format of the original LAQ to that of the RLAQ, dropped some items, and related scale responses to verdicts. Using 24 of the items, Moran and Comfort (1982) administered the scale to 319 persons who had served as jurors in felony trials; they found that legal authoritarianism scores were significantly related to jurors' verdicts in female jurors but not male jurors. Moran and Cutler (1989) dropped three more items and compared responses to mock-juror verdicts in another sample of persons with jury experience; again, those with higher scores on the attitude scale were more likely to convict.

- Cutler, Moran, and Narby (1992), in their second study, used all 30 items in a Likert-type response format with 61 undergraduate respondents, who also watched a videotaped simulation of a murder trial in which the defendant claimed he was not guilty by reason of insanity. Again, high scorers (i.e., relatively authoritarian subjects) on this revised LAQ were significantly more likely to vote guilty than were low scorers. This version of the LAQ had greater predictive

BOX 8.2
Items of the Revised Legal Attitudes Questionnaire

The statements in the Revised Legal Attitudes Questionnaire are the following:

1. Unfair treatment of underprivileged groups and classes is the chief cause of crime. (AA, R, F)

2. Too many obviously guilty persons escape punishment because of legal technicalities. (A, F)

3. The Supreme Court is, by and large, an effective guardian of the Constitution. (E)

4. Evidence illegally obtained should be admissible in court if such evidence is the only way of obtaining a conviction. (A, F)

5. Most prosecuting attorneys have a strong sadistic streak. (AA, R)

6. Search warrants should clearly specify the person or things to be seized. (E, R, F)

7. No one should be convicted of a crime on the basis of circumstantial evidence, no matter how strong such evidence is. (AA, R, F)

8. There is no need in a criminal case for the accused to prove his innocence beyond a reasonable doubt. (E, R, F)

9. Any person who resists arrest commits a crime. (A, F)

10. When determining a person's guilt or innocence, the existence of a prior arrest record should not be considered. (E, R, F)

11. Wiretapping by anyone or for any reason should be completely illegal. (AA, R, F)

12. A lot of recent Supreme Court decisions sound suspiciously Communistic. (A)

13. Treachery and deceit are common tools of prosecutors. (AA, R)

14. Defendants in a criminal case should be required to take the witness stand. (A, F)

15. All too often, minority group members do not get fair trials. (E, R, F)

16. Because of the oppression and persecution minority group members suffer, they deserve leniency and special treatment in the courts. (AA, R, F)

17. Citizens need to be protected against excess police power as well as against criminals. (E, R, F)

18. Persons who testify in court against underworld characters should be allowed to do so anonymously to protect themselves from retaliation. (A)

19. It is better for society that several guilty men be freed than one innocent one wrongfully imprisoned. (E, R, F)

20. Accused persons should be required to take lie-detector tests. (A, F)

21. It is moral and ethical for a lawyer to represent a defendant in a criminal case even when he believes his client is guilty. (E, R, F)

22. A society with true freedom and equality for all would have very little crime. (AA, R, F)

23. When there is a "hung" jury in a criminal case, the defendant should always be freed and the indictment dismissed. (AA, R, F)

24. Police should be allowed to arrest and question suspicious-looking persons to determine whether they have been up to something illegal. (A, F)

25. The law coddles criminals to the detriment of society. (A, F)

26. A lot of judges have connections with the underworld. (AA, R)

27. The freedom of society is endangered as much by zealous law enforcement as by the acts of individual criminals. (E, R, F)

28. There is just about no such thing as an honest cop. (AA, R)

29. In the long run, liberty is more important than order. (E, R, F)

30. Upstanding citizens have nothing to fear from the police. (A, F)

Note: Identification of subscales (A = authoritarian, AA = anti-authoritarian, E = equalitarian) is given immediately following each item. Items that were reverse-coded (scored in the opposite direction) on the overall RLAQ scale are indicated with an R following the subscale identification. Items included in the final RLAQ23 scale are indicated with an F.

(From Kravitz, Cutler, & Brock, 1993, p. 666. Reprinted with permission.)

validity than the Juror Bias Scale (described below).

- Construct validity of the RLAQ was assessed by comparing respondents of different ethnic groups (black versus Hispanic versus white) and political parties. As expected, lower legal authoritarianism scores were found among blacks and among Democrats (those supporting the more left-wing of the two major U.S. political parties).

The Juror Bias Scale

In seeking to uncover attitudes that would predict jurors' verdicts, Kassin and Wrightsman (1983) chose another dimension, the bias to favour the prosecution or the defence. They noted that virtually all models of juror decision making (cf., Pennington & Hastie, 1981) assume that jurors make decisions in criminal cases that reflect the implicit operation of two judgments. The first of these is an estimate of the **probability of commission**; specifically, how likely is it that the defendant was the person who committed the crime? Though jurors will base their estimates of this probability mainly on the strength of the evidence, their previous experiences will influence their interpretation of the evidence. For example, if a police officer testifies that she found a bag of heroin on the person of the defendant, some jurors, trusting police, would use this to increase their estimate that the defendant did commit a crime, but other jurors, given the same testimony, would discount or reject it based on their prior experiences and beliefs that police witnesses are dishonest.

A second judgment by the juror concerns his or her use of the concept of **reasonable doubt**, or the threshold of certainty deemed necessary for conviction. Judges always instruct jurors in criminal trials that they should bring back a verdict of not guilty if they have a reasonable doubt about the defendant's guilt. But the legal system has great reluctance to operationalize reasonable doubt, and when juries, during their deliberations, ask the judge for a definition, the judge usually falls back on the prior instruction, or tells

them that it is a doubt for which a person can give a reason. Left to their own devices, different jurors apply their own standards for how close they must be to certainty in order to vote guilty. Some jurors may interpret "beyond a reasonable doubt" to mean "beyond any doubt," or 100 percent certainty. Others may interpret it quite loosely (Dane, 1985; Kagehiro & Stanton, 1985).

Kassin and Wrightsman proposed that judgments of guilt arise when a juror's probability-of-commission estimate exceeds his or her reasonable-doubt criterion; they thus used these two factors to classify jurors as having a pro-prosecution or pro-defence bias. To determine whether bias affected one's verdicts, they constructed a 17-statement Juror Bias Scale (JBS). (The statements, and filler items, are reprinted in Box 8.3.) The JBS gives scores on each of the two factors of probability of commission and reasonable doubt.

Two methods of validation of the Juror Bias Scale have been used:

1. Kassin and Wrightsman (1983) had university students and jury-eligible respondents complete the JBS scale and later watch videotapes of re-enacted actual trials or read transcripts of simulated trials. Four types of criminal trials were used, dealing with offences ranging from auto theft to conspiracy to assault and rape. After being exposed to the trial, each mock juror was asked to render an individual verdict about the defendant's guilt or innocence. These verdicts were then related to the respondents' scores on the JBS. On three of the four cases, mock jurors with a pro-prosecution bias significantly more often voted to convict the defendant than did mock jurors with a pro-defence bias. The differences were large; the average rate of conviction for prosecution-biased jurors was 81 percent, compared to 52 percent for defence-biased ones. Thus, in most cases, scores on the JBS have predictive validity.

   But with regard to the trial for rape, mock jurors generally predisposed to favour

BOX 8.3
The Juror Bias Scale

The second measure of general juror attitudes is the Juror Bias Scale. The instructions and scale items are listed here. (Note: On the version of the scale administered to respondents, each statement is followed by five choices: 1. Strongly agree, 2. Mildly agree, 3. Agree and disagree equally, 4. Mildly disagree, and 5. Strongly disagree. In order to conserve space these are deleted here.)

Instructions: This is a questionnaire to determine people's attitudes and beliefs on a variety of general legal issues. Please answer each statement by giving as true a picture of your position as possible.

1. Appointed judges are more competent than elected judges.

2. A suspect who runs from the police most probably committed the crime.

3. A defendant should be found guilty if only 11 out of 12 jurors vote guilty.

4. Most politicians are really as honest as humanly possible.

5. Too often jurors hesitate to convict someone who is guilty out of pure sympathy.

6. In most cases where the accused presents a strong defence, it is only because of a good lawyer.

7. In general, children should be excused for their misbehaviour.

8. The death penalty is cruel and inhumane.

9. Out of every 100 people brought to trial, at least 75 are guilty of the crime with which they are charged.

10. For serious crimes like murder, a defendant should be found guilty if there is a 90 percent chance that he or she committed the crime.

11. Defence lawyers don't really care about guilt or innocence, they are just in business to make money.

12. Generally, the police make an arrest only when they are sure about who committed the crime.

13. Circumstantial evidence is too weak to use in court.

14. Many accident claims filed against insurance companies are phony.

15. The defendant is often a victim of his or her own bad reputation.

16. If the grand jury recommends that a person be brought to trial, then he or she probably committed the crime.

17. Extenuating circumstances should not be considered—if a person commits a crime, then that person should be punished.

18. Hypocrisy is on the increase in society.

19. Too many innocent people are wrongfully imprisoned.

20. If a majority of the evidence—but not all of it—suggests that the defendant committed the crime, the jury should vote not guilty.

21. If the defendant committed a victimless crime like gambling or possession of marijuana, he should never be convicted.

22. Some laws are made to be broken.

Scoring procedures: The following are filler items and are not scored: Items 1, 4, 7, 18, and 22.
   The following nine items are part of the Probability of Commission subscale: Items 2, 6, 9, 11, 12, 13 (reversed scoring), 14, 15 (reversed scoring), and 16.
   These eight items are part of the Reasonable Doubt subscale: Items 3, 5, 8 (reversed scoring), 10, 17, 19 (reversed scoring), 20 (reversed scoring), and 21 (reversed scoring).

(Adapted from Kassin & Wrightsman, 1983.)

the defence were just as likely to find the defendant guilty as were jurors who favoured the prosecution. It is possible that pro-defence jurors, who are relatively liberal in their political views, are especially sympathetic with the victim when the crime involves a sexual assault; that is, their usual bias is balanced by a concern for the victim.

2. Lecci and Myers (1996; Myers & Lecci, 1998) sought, through the use of factor analysis, to determine whether the two theoretical dimensions, reasonable doubt and probability of commission, were verified empirically. Two samples, each consisting of 301 university students, completed the JBS, and several factor analyses were done. (A **factor analysis** is a statistical procedure that examines relationships between responses to different items and thus identifies which items are related to each other; factors are theoretical labels for what is common to the item statements that cluster together.) The reasonable doubt concept survived the empirical analysis fairly intact; results produced a six-item empirically driven reasonable-doubt factor, but the original eight items also achieved a reasonable fit with the data in a cross-validation (Lecci & Myers, 1996, p. 6). Lecci and Myers recommend the six-item empirically based scale; the items from Box 8.3 on this scale are items 3, 5, 10, 17, 20 (reversed), and 21 (reversed).

The dimension of probability of commission was not supported empirically as one factor. Three items—numbers 2, 12, and 16—formed one factor, which could keep the "probability of commission" label. Three other items from this scale—items 6, 11, and 14—emerged on another factor, which seems to reflect cynicism about the legal system.

To determine the predictive validity of the empirically derived scales, Lecci and Myers administered the JBS scale to 406 university students and had them watch a videotape of a simulated rape and murder trial; the videotape included opening and closing statements by the prosecution and defence, direct and cross-examination of eight witnesses, and the judge's instructions, which included an explanation of reasonable doubt; the tape lasted 60 minutes.

Participants were classified as either prosecution-biased or defence-biased, on the basis of their responses to the original 17 items on the JBS. Consistent with previous results, prosecu-

tion-biased respondents were more likely to find the defendant guilty than were defence-biased ones. Although the difference was statistically significant, it was not as large as in the previous validation: 54 percent of the prosecution-biased respondents voted guilty, compared to 46 percent of the defence-biased respondents. A similar analysis was done with the empirically based scales—essentially 12 of the original 17 items—and similar results were found: 52 percent of the prosecution-biased respondents convicted the defendant, compared to 47 percent of the defence-biased respondents, a difference that was also statistically significant. The reasonable-doubt items accounted for the bulk of the predictive validity, as was the case in the original validation.

Of what use are the Revised Legal Attitudes Questionnaire and the Juror Bias Questionnaire to the trial consultant faced with aiding a lawyer in jury selection for a criminal trial? Individual items can serve as the basis for questions to individual prospective jurors during the **voir dire** (or jury-selection phase), or if there is an opportunity to administer a supplemental juror questionnaire (to be described subsequently), prospective jurors can be asked to respond to all the statements. But the trial consultant should always remember that general traits, as measured here, have a very limited relationship to verdicts in specific cases. They are better than nothing, and they are probably better than most people's intuitions, but their predictive accuracy is low when it comes to verdicts by individual jurors.

Civil Trials

Most of the published work on assessment of jurors' pre-trial biases has dealt with criminal trials. But it can be argued that the issue of civil law is most susceptible to the effects of bias by individual jurors. Traditionally, criminal cases come to trial because the prosecution believes there is a chance for conviction. The defendant may feel there is little chance of acquittal but, having refused to plea-bargain, he or she is faced with only one last resort. In civil cases, however, it is necessary that *both* the plaintiff and the defendant be reasonably assured of a favourable decision. A litigant who is not so assured will, most likely, settle the issue out of court. Given this aspect of civil jury trials, in many cases the amount of evidence favouring each side will be nearly equal. But what are the basic dimensions or qualities of a pre-trial bias in a juror in a civil trial? Though such trials can differ in the nature of the claim, the types of parties involved, and other specifics, it may be useful to examine some general attitudes.

General Attitudes

Biases in civil trials may not be as easily verbalized as those in criminal cases, but they can include several possible attitudes, which together can be collapsed into a distinction between pro-plaintiff and pro-defendant jurors. These differing attitudes are outlined below.

Attitudes about the "Litigation Explosion" Whether or not there has truly been an increase in the amount of civil litigation in recent years, there has been ample publicity for those who claim there has (Huber, 1988; Olson, 1991). Some prospective jurors—believing media claims of a **litigation explosion**—may have adopted beliefs that too many lawsuits are frivolous and that people are too quick to sue, thus reflecting an anti-plaintiff bias.

Attitudes about Risk Taking Risk, as a concept, is central to Anglo-American jurisprudence (Carson, 1988), but it has not received the analysis it deserves. In law, **risk** means a danger of harm or loss from a plaintiff's action or behaviour. Traditionally, the law has said that "a plaintiff who voluntarily encounters a known risk cannot recover" (Cox, 1991, p. 24). But in real life things are not that simple, as demonstrated by the attempts to classify the allocation of blame implicit in contributory negligence. For example, in one case a man sued Sears and Roebuck because he had a heart attack while trying to get his Sears lawnmower started (Cox, 1992), and

everyone is familiar with the elderly woman's lawsuit against McDonald's for the too-hot cup of coffee.

Jurors can differ in their attitudes toward the **assumption of risk**. Assumption of risk can be thought of as a continuum ranging from no risk to 100 percent risk. Particular actions by plaintiffs can be assigned values along this continuum. For example, a person who buys a package of Tylenol and takes several tablets assumes very little risk; a patient undergoing double-bypass heart surgery assumes some risk; a person who mixes drugs whose interactive effects are unknown takes a higher risk. But the same action may be rated differently by different jurors.

Attitudes about Standard of Care How stringent a standard do jurors hold with regard to the manufacture of products or the providing of services? Should a drug be 100 percent free of serious side effects before it is approved for sale? The availability of Viagra made its use instantly popular, but it apparently contributed to the sudden death of several men. How much should a new car be tested to determine whether its design is faulty before it is placed on the market? How risk-free should a surgical procedure be before a doctor uses it?

Attitudes about Personal Responsibility The public has stereotyped civil juries as pro-plaintiff—that is, sympathetic to claims of misfortune and willing to tap into the **deep pockets** of rich defendants. The empirical evidence challenges this view (see Vidmar, 1995) and even leads to a conclusion that an anti-plaintiff bias often emerges in jury decisions. Several causes for this doubtless exist. When talking to jurors after civil trials, this text's first author got the impression that they had a strong belief in personal responsibility; these jurors lack sympathy for people with unhappy outcomes and (sometimes justified) grievances against a manufacturer, physician, or governmental organization. Feigenson, Park, and Salovey (1997) noted "evidence of a specifically antiplaintiff bias in responsibility judgments" (p. 600) and refer to interviews with actual jurors (Hans & Lofquist,

1992) and experimental research (Lupfer, Cohen, Bernard, Smalley, & Schippmann, 1985) supporting a conclusion that jurors often attribute the behaviour of plaintiffs to undesirable motives, such as greed, rather than to legitimate grievances.

Corporate Responsibility

Attitudes toward corporations are related to some of the general attitudes detailed above, but they deserve special concern (Hans, 1990). Some potential jurors are anti-business, standing up for the powerless individual against the monolithic corporation. But others believe that businesses are hampered too much by government regulations. Should we hold corporations to higher standards of responsibility than individuals? Who deserved the blame when the Exxon tanker *Valdez* ran aground off the coast of Alaska, the captain or the oil company?

Hans and Lofquist (1992) constructed an attitude scale to measure potential jurors' attitudes toward business regulation. The 16 items on this scale tap attitudes about civil litigation, the benefits and costs of government regulation of business, and standards for worker safety and product safety. After reviewing this work, Wrightsman and Heili (1992) formulated additional items that might reflect jurors' biases in civil trials. These items, called the Civil Trial Bias Scale, were administered along with Hans and Lofquist's items, to 204 undergraduate students, and the responses were factor-analyzed to determine what constructs underlay the responses. The first factor that emerged in this analysis was to favour business and the easing of stringent requirements for safety. For example, the highest loading item (the one that correlated the highest with the factor), #16 from the Hans and Lofquist set, states: "Requiring that products be 100 percent safe before they're sold to the public is just too expensive." The other factors emerging from this analysis also covered a variety of attitudes.

A separate analysis of the Hans and Lofquist items produced clearer results than the factor analysis of the two scales together. What emerges is one set of attitudes opposed to government regulation and another dealing with what are the proper safety standards. But other dimensions may also be present; the separate factor analysis of the Civil Trial Bias Scale, not detailed here, found that jurors differed on assigning responsibility for bad outcomes, the inexplicability of bad events, and the value of risk taking.

A recent instrument that shows promise here is the Attitudes Toward Corporations (ATC) scale (Robinette, 1999). It contains five subscales that measure product safety, government regulation, treatment of employees by corporations, and anti-plaintiff and anti-corporation attitudes. The original pool of items from which the ATC emerged capitalized on the items developed by Hans and Lofquist (1992), described above, but other items were constructed, and then the early versions of the scale were subjected to item analyses so that a 15-item scale resulted.

CASE-SPECIFIC APPROACHES

Some litigation consultants seek to determine the criteria for jury selection by "working from the inside out" rather than beginning with hypothetical determinants. The goal is to determine characteristics of the **ideal juror** or, if that is not possible, the ideal juror to avoid. Two examples of trials illustrating this approach are described. But recall that the procedure does not permit one to compose an "ideal jury" without restrictions. First, the procedure is to remove the supposedly undesirable jurors rather than to select the desirable ones; second, there is no way to prevent the other side from dismissing those whom your side considers most desirable. As we will see, this often happens.

The Harrisburg Seven Trial

The trial of the "Harrisburg Seven," in 1972, was the first highly publicized application of social-science techniques, or scientific jury selection. Despite its age, it remains an illustrative standard for several reasons, including the comprehensiveness of the procedures and the availability of a detailed account of what the trial consultants did (Schulman, Shaver, Colman, Emrich, & Christie, 1973).

The "Harrisburg Seven" is actually something of a misnomer; the trial took place in Harrisburg, Pennsylvania, but otherwise the defendants had nothing to do with that city. Catholic priests and nuns who had protested against the Vietnam War by pouring blood over draft-board records were charged by the U.S. government with a conspiratorial plan to carry out a number of other anti-war activities, including blowing up the heating tunnels under Washington, D.C., and the kidnapping of Henry Kissinger, then U.S. Secretary of State. The government persuaded the presiding judge to move the trial to Harrisburg because it was considered the most conservative area in that judicial district.

Capitalizing on a number of volunteers who were opposed to the war, Jay Schulman and the other social scientists carried out a number of studies prior to the trial:

1. Suspecting that the original jury pool was not representative of the population, they compared the demographic characteristics of those drawn in the jury pool with a random sample of voters and found that the average age of the jury pool members was somewhat older. This caused the judge to order the drawing of a second, more representative jury pool.

2. They sought to discover what background and demographic characteristics were related to potential jurors' biases in favour or against the defendants. They surveyed 250 people from the Harrisburg area (not members of the jury pool) to assess their degrees of tolerance toward dissidents and war protesters. These attitudes were related to a number of demographic characteristics, including age, education, religion, and gender, and some surprises emerged. For example, contrary to their expectation, the more educated members of the community were less sympathetic to the defendants. These results permitted the social scientists to develop a profile of the ideal juror—a female Democrat with no religious preferences who held a skilled-labour or white-collar job.

3. Armed with this information, the social scientists and the defence lawyers rated each of the 46 prospective jurors who survived the earlier winnowing process. On the basis of their demographic characteristics, the way they responded to questions during voir dire, and their nonverbal behaviour, these jurors were classified on a five-point scale, with 5 = very good for the defence, 4 = a good defence juror, 3 = neither good nor bad, 2 = undesirable, and 1 = very undesirable. Of the 46, only eight were rated as very good, and the prosecution used its six peremptory challenges to remove six of these eight. So the defence team was left with two "very good" jurors, five "good" ones, and five whom they had rated as neither desirable nor undesirable. (The defence had been given 28 peremptory strikes, compared to the prosecution's six.)

Did the strategy work? Yes and no. The jury ended up deadlocked, with ten jurors voting to acquit and only two to convict. The judge declared a mistrial, and the U.S. government decided not to retry the defendants. In that sense, the jury selection was successful. But the social scientists missed completely on the two jurors who voted to convict; each of these two had been rated rather positively by the trial consultants.

The de la Beckwith Retrial

Late one summer evening in 1963, at the height of the civil rights protest in the southern U.S., Medgar Evers was shot and killed as he returned to his home in Jackson, Mississippi. Evers had been leading the drive to register black Americans to vote in Mississippi, and it was a particularly heinous crime—someone, crouched in a honeysuckle bush 60 metres away, fired a shot into Evers's back as his wife and children watched from the front porch. A gun was abandoned at the crime scene; it was later traced to Byron de la Beckwith.

De la Beckwith was a white supremacist, active in the Ku Klux Klan and other pro-segregation organizations. He was known for his intense hostility to Jews and blacks. In addition to his fingerprints on the gun, there was some other evidence that linked de la Beckwith to the crime; several cabdrivers came forward to report that some days earlier he had been inquiring as to where Evers lived. De la Beckwith denied committing the crime and claimed that the rifle had been stolen from him two days before the killing; yet, at the same time he seemed to revel in his sudden celebrity as a prime suspect (Morris, 1998; Vollers, 1991).

De la Beckwith was put on trial for murder in January 1964; the jury was all white and all male. The prosecution presented strong circumstantial evidence pointing to de la Beckwith; in his defence, his lawyers produced several white police officers who testified that he had been seen in his hometown, 230 kilometres away, at the time of the murder. The jury could not reach a unanimous verdict. After deliberating 11 hours, the jurors were deadlocked, six to six.

A second trial was held three months later, still in 1964, with a similar outcome—again deadlocked (the vote was eight to four for acquittal). De la Beckwith was released and allowed to return to his home in Greenwood, Mississippi.

But reports persisted that de la Beckwith had committed the crime; people even came forward describing how he had bragged about doing it. Meanwhile, in 1973, de la Beckwith was suspected of planning the bombing of an office of the Anti-Defamation League, a Jewish organization, in New Orleans. He served five years in prison in Louisiana for illegal possession of dynamite.

Early in the 1990s, the district attorney in Jackson, Mississippi, decided to reactivate the case. (There is no statute of limitations for murder.) At this point, several psychologists at the University of Kansas offered their services pro bono to the prosecution, to aid that side in its jury selection. Professor C. K. Rowland spear-headed the effort; he knew the district attorney and had worked with him on earlier cases. Rowland, then a doctoral student in psychology, was assisted by Amy Posey, Andrew Sheldon, and Lawrence Wrightsman in the preparation of a jury questionnaire that included questions about due process, racial attitudes, and items from the Juror Bias Scale.

This case presented unique challenges in the selection of jurors. It is true that racial relationships had dramatically changed in Mississippi in 30 years; blacks and whites went to school together, worked side by side, and ate in the same restaurants. But were racist attitudes still below the surface in some prospective jurors? And what was the reaction of the jury pool to the decision to retry de la Beckwith *30 years* after the murder had taken place; he was now 73 years old, frail, and not in good health. Would that affect some jurors? In considering who would be the "ideal juror" for the prosecution, the obvious choice would seem to be a black person, but preliminary surveys indicated that not all blacks thought alike. Members of some black fundamentalist churches believed "judge not, that ye are not judged"—that it was God's job to determine guilt and punishment; they were reluctant to play the role of jurors deciding the fate of another.

The trial judge permitted a change of venue; jurors for the third trial were from Panola County (county seat: Batesville), a rural county about 240 kilometres from Jackson. The social scientists assisting the prosecution learned several things about residents of this county that were helpful in identifying potential jurors who might be racist and hence likely to sympathize with de la Beckwith; these included:

- In Batesville, there were two softball leagues; one was racially integrated, while the other was all white.
- In the wake of public school desegregation, a number of private (translation: all white) "academies" had been established. These were a haven for parents who didn't want their children mingling with children of other races.

■ Political party identification was potentially diagnostic; if a person was Republican and financially well-off, that was of little use as an indicator, but poor Republicans were likely to be racist (Rowland, 1994).

The judge did not permit the administration of the 80-item questionnaire developed by the social scientists; the court clerk had said it would be too much trouble to copy and collate them. But the judge did institute a **sequestered voir dire**, in which each of the potential jurors was questioned individually in the judge's chambers. This questioning facilitated a sometimes-frank revelation of racial attitudes, and prosecutors found the younger whites to be candid; some straightforwardly said, "I don't like integration." But it was harder to pin down the racial attitudes of older middle-class whites. The second issue of concern by the prosecutors was potential sympathy for the defendant. On the advice of the social scientists, the lawyers asked: "What was your first thought when you heard that Byron de la Beckwith was to be retried?" Again, many prospective jurors were open about their feeling that it was hard to accept the idea of a retrial. Some were even **challenged for cause** because their answers reflected that they had already formed an opinion, or because they knew trial participants, and they were dismissed by the judge.

The social scientists were not permitted in the judge's chambers while individual jurors were questioned, but they were able to provide questions to the lawyers. One of the contributions was to urge the prosecution lawyers to move away from their usual style (similar to cross-examination) of asking closed-ended, yes-or-no questions to the prospective jurors and instead use open-ended ones like the question above. The answers to these are much more informative.

The successful challenges for cause shifted the racial composition, from an original pool that was composed about equally of the two races to a jury of eight blacks and four whites. A 70-year-old black minister was chosen as foreperson.

Exactly 30 years after his first trial, de la Beckwith's third trial began, in late January 1994.

Testimony lasted only six days; de la Beckwith did not testify. The jury deliberated six hours before unanimously finding the defendant guilty. Byron de la Beckwith was sentenced to life in prison; his appeal of his conviction was rejected by the Mississippi Supreme Court late in 1997.

DOES SCIENTIFIC JURY SELECTION WORK?

The examples in this chapter—Marcia Clark rejects a trial consultant's advice and her side loses; in the Harrisburg Seven and de la Beckwith trials the side with the trial consultants wins—may leave the impression that jury outcomes can routinely be successfully "rigged" by the use of trial consultants' techniques. And some consultants are not reluctant to claim high rates of success (Strier, 1999).

In actuality, the effectiveness of trial consultants in jury selection is more difficult to assess. For instance, we may ask: Jury selection is effective compared to what? To dismissing jurors by chance? To the traditional methods used by lawyers? The latter, as a comparison, is full of problems, because lawyers differ in how they "select" juries. A further difficulty is that real-life trials are not susceptible to an experimental manipulation, in which they are repeated with an alteration of the method for selecting the jury. One study did follow that procedure, but it was a laboratory study using mock jurors recruited from the community and using law students who role-played the lawyers (Horowitz, 1980). The study compared scientific jury selection with a traditional method; in the latter, lawyers used their past experience, conventional wisdom, and beliefs about jurors to make their choices. Four different criminal trials were simulated. The results indicated that scientific jury selection was sometimes more effective, but not in all trials. In fact, its effectiveness seemed to be limited to trials in which a strong correlation existed between jurors' personality or demographic variables and their votes.

Legal psychologists remain divided about the appropriateness or effectiveness of scientific jury selection (Diamond, 1990; Moran, Cutler, & DeLisa, 1994; Saks, 1976, 1987); Shari S. Diamond, after reviewing the research, concluded: "There is good reason to be skeptical about the potential of scientific jury selection to improve selection decisions substantially" (1990, p. 180). But Gary Moran and his colleagues (Moran, Cutler, & DeLisa, 1994) have noted that studies that fail to find a relationship often have not used real jurors; these researchers also concluded that case-specific attitudes are better predictors of verdicts than are broad demographic variables.

In summary, as Strier (1999) has concluded, "empirical studies testing the predictive value of scientific jury selection have produced inconclusive findings" (p. 101). Reid Hastie's (1991) review of his own and other studies observed:

> It remains unclear exactly which types of cases will yield the greatest advantage to the "scientific" selection methods.... "Scientific" jury selection surveys or [lawyer] intuitions occasionally identify a subtle, case-specific predictor of verdicts. It is difficult, however, to cite even one convincingly demonstrated success of this type, and these methods frequently suggest the use of completely invalid, as well as valid, predictors.... The predictive power of these [juror] characteristics invariably turned out to be subtly dependent on specific aspects of the particular case for which they proved valid. Due to their subtlety, prospective identification of any of these factors under the conditions that prevail before actual trials remains doubtful. (pp. 720, 723–724)

The quality of the evidence remains the clearest determinant of jury verdicts (Visher, 1987); the side with the stronger evidence *usually* wins. However, as noted, especially in civil trials the evidence for the two sides may be close to equal. In such "close cases" scientific jury selection might be able to predict 10 percent or 15 percent of the variance in jurors' verdicts (Penrod

& Cutler, 1987). Trial lawyers seek every edge they can obtain; this might be enough for them to justify the use of a trial consultant.

IS IT ETHICAL FOR PSYCHOLOGISTS TO AID IN JURY SELECTION?

Obviously, psychologists working in Canada do not have to be concerned about whether aiding in jury selection is ethical, since the courts do not allow such a practice anyway. However, psychologists elsewhere must reflect on this issue. Further, it is certainly possible for Canadian forensic psychologists to be asked to consult in American cases. As a student of forensic psychology, how do you feel about the ethics of this practice?

John Grisham's highly entertaining novel *The Runaway Jury* (1996) begins with the surveillance of a young man who works at the computer store at the local mall. He's surreptitiously photographed by the observers; they know he doesn't smoke from watching him at his lunchtime breaks; they also know he claims to be a part-time university student but checking with every university within 500 kilometres revealed no one enrolled under his name.

Why is he being watched? A potential security risk? A drug courier? No. Nicholas Easter is on a jury panel for an important case and he is being investigated by a trial consulting firm in the employment of the defendants, a consortium of tobacco companies. Is this what trial consultants do in real life? And regardless of whether they do or not, what ethical dilemmas surface for psychologists who assist in jury selection? Several are perplexing.

Juror Investigation

Although the activities described in *The Runaway Jury* are an exaggeration of what usually happens in the real world, citizens clearly have their privacy invaded when they become prospective jurors. The courts have accepted certain procedures because they subscribe to the goal that voir dire can identify prospective jurors whose biases prevent them from being open-minded. But how far can the inquiry go?

Trial consultants do, on occasion, use out-of-court investigations to determine the attitudes and values of prospective jurors. Public records, such as house appraisals, may be consulted; the trial consultants' team may drive by the prospective juror's house, note its condition and the quality of its neighbourhood, and search for any "diagnostic" bumper stickers on the juror's car. Friends and neighbours may be interviewed.

In the U.S., there are limits to such activities. Clearly, prospective jurors cannot be contacted outside the courtroom; **jury tampering** is illegal, and the courts have held persons to be in contempt of court for communicating with jurors even though it was not clear that they sought to influence the jurors. But would such rules apply to investigation of *prospective* jurors? Herbsleb, Sales, and Berman thought not; they have written that "it seems unlikely that [such jury tampering laws as the above] will be applied today to hold social scientists in contempt for gathering jury information, unless some communication with the sworn jurors has occurred in or near the courtroom" (1979, p. 206).

But the dangers of out-of-court investigations remain. As Herbsleb and colleagues (1979) suggested, "Suppose that as social scientists are establishing their network, one of the people contacted becomes suspicious of the investigators' motives and of the propriety of their actions…. [H]e may contact the prospective juror to inform him that persons of questionable character and motives are conducting an investigation into his personal affairs. The prospective juror in turn may well feel threatened or intimidated by the knowledge that someone is 'checking up' on him" (pp. 207–208).

What is the solution to this problem? To seek court approval for such inquiries? To inform prospective jurors that such information will be used only to exercise challenges? Although the above have been suggested as remedies, they fail to recognize that out-of-court investigations by psychologists may violate ethical guidelines about participants' rights to decline or withdraw from research participation. Herbsleb and colleagues (1979) offered one solution: "Have the court announce the presence of the social scientists and ask jurors if they object. If objections are voiced, the judge orders the social scientists to discontinue their research; if no objections are voiced, it is assumed that the jurors are participating voluntarily" (p. 211). But the "compliance" in this situation may be a rather coerced one, not well thought-out. And invasions of privacy, whether "voluntary" or not, are still invasions of privacy.

Use of Supplemental Juror Questionnaires

Perhaps a better solution to the above problem is to avoid out-of-court investigations and substitute for them the use of a **supplemental juror questionnaire**, an extensive set of questions that prospective jurors answer in writing before the jury selection begins. Such questionnaires can cover a number of topics that might have been answered by out-of-court investigations—what newspapers and magazines the prospective jurors read, what television shows they watch, whether they own any guns. Further, attitude statements like those in the above-described juror-predisposition measures can, with the approval of the judge, be included. The validity of information now rests on the honesty of the prospective jurors; some invasion of their privacy remains, but this problem seems inevitable, given the defendant's right to a fair trial by impartial jurors.

In fact, prospective jurors have a real dilemma if the trial judge is unconcerned about the psychologist's ethical responsibility to obtain consent from participants. If the judge has approved the administration of the questionnaire to prospective jurors, they may be punished if they refuse to answer. This happened to a Texas prospective juror, who refused to answer 12 questions (out of 100) that dealt specifically with her religion, income, and political-party affiliation. The judge cited her for contempt and sentenced her to three days in jail.

The rules in most jurisdictions do not specifically address the use of questionnaires prior to voir dire, and so the judge has discretion to permit them. However, the U.S. courts have recommended the use of pre-screening questionnaires in highly publicized cases, and they were used in the trials of William Kennedy Smith, General Manuel Noriega, and Susan Smith, as well as O. J. Simpson's criminal trial (Fargo, 1994). When such questionnaires have been approved, they are, in some jurisdictions, distributed by the clerk of the court at the beginning of jury selection, and jurors fill them out in the jury assembly room. Completed questionnaires are available for review by lawyers on either side. The amount of time allowed the lawyers to examine them depends on the judge and may be as brief as a couple of hours, although often the lawyers are given overnight to review them. Responses not only help the lawyers and trial consultants to make preliminary decisions about peremptory challenges, but also to identify prospective jurors who might be challenges for cause.

The use of supplemental juror questionnaires may save time during the voir dire, in that many of the questions would have been asked orally and individually during that process. They also add to the goal of fairness by giving both sides equal access to information.

Several commonsense suggestions can be made for the preparation and administration of such questionnaires (Fargo, 1994):

1. Keep the questionnaires as short as possible. It is suggested that four to six pages will suffice. Follow-up questions may be allowed during voir dire.
2. The introduction to the questionnaire should explain its purpose; Fargo suggested the following:

> This questionnaire will be used only to assist the judge and the [lawyers] in the jury selection process. The information requested is strictly confidential and will not be used for any other purpose. Please read all questions carefully, answer them fully, and notify court personnel if you need any assistance or have any questions. Do not discuss the questions or answers with fellow jurors. It is very important that your answers be your own. You are sworn to give true and complete answers to all questions. (1994, p. 1)

3. Questions should be clustered by topic and arranged in a logical sequence.
4. Topics to be covered should include the prospective juror's experience with legal matters and the courts, his or her experiences related to the case at hand, and the juror's exposure to media coverage about the case. On all these topics, the experiences of the juror's immediate family and close personal friends are also relevant. Questions on these topics often work better as open-ended ones, rather than yes-or-no types.
5. At the end of the questionnaire, statements reflecting general attitudes and opinions, such as those from the instruments described in this chapter, may be included.

All the above implies that the trial consultant, working with the lawyer, needs to be proactive in the preparation of such questionnaires. Such instruments require some time to prepare, and sometimes obstacles to scheduling may delay preparation of a final draft, especially if both sides contribute questions to the questionnaire.

The O. J. Simpson criminal trial was an extreme case; the supplemental juror questionnaire covered more than 60 pages, reflecting questions contributed by both sides. In selecting questions for inclusion, the trial consultant for the defence, Jo-Ellan Dimitrius, used public opinion polls and focus groups (Gordon, 1997). (See Box 8.4 for some examples.)

BOX 8.4
The O. J. Simpson Questionnaire

The supplemental juror questionnaire for O. J. Simpson's criminal trial contained 294 questions, on 61 pages. Both sides contributed questions. For the prosecution, the questions were developed by the district attorney's office. Marcia Clark (1997) has stated that their trial consultant, Donald Vinson, submitted only one question. Jo-Ellan Dimitrius, the defence team's trial consultant, supervised the preparation of questions from the defence. Although prospective jurors were instructed that "Each question has a specific purpose," respondents must have wondered about the relevance of some, like the following:

143. Have you ever asked a celebrity for an autograph? (p. 33)

165. Have you ever had your spouse or significant other call the police on you for any reason, even if you were not arrested? (p. 37)
201. Do you have a religious affiliation or preference? (p. 44)
210. Have you ever given [a] blood sample to your doctor for testing? (p. 45)
212. Do you believe it is immoral or wrong to do an amniocentesis to determine whether a fetus has a genetic defect? (p. 46)
248. Have you ever written a letter to the editor of a newspaper or magazine? (p. 54)
257. Are there any charities or organizations to which you make donations? (p. 55)

(Daily Journal Court Rules Service, 1994)

Fairness in Jury Selection

What if one side employs a psychologist or a trial consulting firm and the other does not? Is this fair? Should the psychologist be concerned? The position of the courts is that no legal violation has occurred when one side and only one side uses a trial consultant. A generally recognized principle of the law is that the counsel on the two sides are "never perfectly equal in abilities or resources" (Herbsleb, Sales, & Berman, 1979, p. 201). In fact, a justification of the early participation of psychologists and other social scientists on the defence team was that the U.S. government, as prosecutor, had many unfair advantages in its efforts to convict war protesters. Strier (1998a) has summarized the current situation as follows:

> [U]ntil clear and convincing evidence of the ability of scientific jury selection to affect verdicts surfaces, there appears no sustainable argument that its use threatens the Constitutional right to an impartial jury or the court-mandated injunction to seek cross-sectional juries. The law seeks jury representativeness. Scientific jury selection will still result in unfairly excluding some Americans from jury service; it will merely substitute exclusions based on scientific analysis for those derived from stereotypes and intuition. (p. 11)

Even if the use of scientific jury selection and trial consultants does not violate American laws, psychologists always have—as one of their clients—society in general. We need to ask: Is the "institutionalization" of jury selection in the best interests of society? Should Canadian psychologists be communicating disagreement with this practice to their American colleagues? Advocates of scientific jury selection will say that the process is only a more systematic version of what most trial lawyers do in a more subjective, less precise and thorough manner. But it is true that the inclusion of these procedures may move actual juries further away from the goal of a representative sample of the populace.

It remains that in criminal trials, the defence is much more likely to use a trial consultant than the prosecution (the Simpson and de la Beckwith cases were unusual, and recall that in both of these the services of the trial consultant were offered pro bono). Although no law prevents the prosecution from doing so, there is some merit to Marcia

Clark's view, expressed earlier in the chapter, that the government has no business doing market surveys to test the strength of its arguments. In a criminal trial, the prosecution is constrained in ways that the defence is not; it must base its argument on the evidentiary facts at its disposal. Thus, it is likely that defence lawyers will continue to use assistance in jury selection more than prosecutors will.

SUMMARY

In Canada, the way in which juries are selected is governed by the Charter of Rights and Freedoms, which says that everyone accused of a crime is entitled to a fair trial by an impartial jury. Canadian courts attempt to ensure a jury that is "as random as possible," while requiring jurors to be unbiased and competent to do their job. We do not see the type of jury manipulation that is witnessed in other countries, particularly the United States. Psychologists in Canada have conducted important work on jury decision making, while working within the constraints of laws preventing jurors from speaking about their deliberations after trials. As such, much of the research on juries has used a mock jury approach in which people are asked to act as if they are jurors in an actual case.

Some American lawyers believe that trials can be won or lost on the basis of the specific jury "selected" for the trial. In actuality, jury "selection" is a misnomer, because lawyers on each side can dismiss prospective jurors but cannot ensure that any one juror is chosen, as the other side also has the opportunity to "strike" or dismiss jurors through the use of peremptory challenges. Trial lawyers are increasingly relying on psychologists as trial consultants. In such jurisdictions, in advising the lawyer about jury selection, the psychologist uses information based on mock trials, focus groups, community attitude surveys, and sometimes out-of-court investigations.

Two approaches have been used. The use of broad traits or general attitudes reflects an assumption that certain predispositions of jurors may predict their verdicts in a wide variety of trials. With regard to criminal trials, two attitude scales have some limited general utility in predicting juror verdicts: the Revised Legal Attitudes Questionnaire Scale, which measures authoritarianism, and the Juror Bias Scale, which measures biases regarding probability of commission and reasonable doubt. With regard to general characteristics that may predict verdicts in civil suits, measures of risk taking, beliefs in personal responsibility and corporate responsibility, and attitudes toward the "litigation explosion" are promising. Psychologists are in disagreement about whether scientific jury selection is appropriate or useful. One laboratory study found that it was more effective than the traditional method in some trials, but not all trials. A conservative conclusion is that the use of such procedures may account for a small degree of variance in jurors' verdicts—perhaps 10 percent, thus not enough to conclude that trial consultants can "rig" juries, but enough of an edge to make them useful to some trial lawyers.

The second approach works from the inside out, identifying specific aspects of a particular case and then assessing prospective jurors on those characteristics (such as racial attitudes or attitudes toward protesters). Two examples, the Harrisburg Seven trial and Byron de la Beckwith's retrial, illustrated the procedures used in this approach.

A number of ethical issues surface when forensic psychologists assist in jury selection. Investigations of prospective jurors may violate their right to give consent and to privacy. Another concern is the inequality between prosecution and defence of the utilization of trial consultants. Use of supplemental juror questionnaires may lessen this concern.

In Canada, we have a unique and diverse society. Research examining actual jury decision making in this context is essential. It remains to be seen whether Canadian laws will advance to become more flexible in allowing jurors to discuss their experiences with mental health professionals and researchers.

KEY TERMS

anti-authoritarianism, p. 172
anti-plaintiff bias, p. 172
assumption of risk, p. 179
authoritarianism, p. 172
case-specific approach, p. 172
challenging a juror for cause, p. 183
conflict of interest, p. 167
deep pockets, p. 179
equalitarianism, p. 172
factor analysis, p. 178
group differences, p. 174
ideal juror, p. 180
juror bias, p. 171
jury selection, p. 169
jury tampering, p. 185
kernel-of-truth hypothesis, p. 170
litigation explosion, p. 179
mock jury approach, p. 168
peremptory challenge, p. 169
probability of commission, p. 176
pro bono, p. 169
pro-defendant bias, p. 172
pro-plaintiff bias, p. 172
random sample of jurors, p. 166
reasonable doubt, p. 176
risk, p. 179
sequestered voir dire, p. 183
supplemental juror questionnaire, p. 185
systematic jury selection, p. 170
voir dire, p. 178

SUGGESTED READINGS

Adler, S. J. (1994). *The jury: Trial and error in the American courtroom.* New York: Times Books.

This critique of the jury system pays close attention to the role of trial consultants (or as Adler calls them, "jury consultants"). Chapter 3 illustrates how the plaintiff's strategy was completely altered by the input from his trial consultant.

Bennett, C., & Hirschhorn, R. (1993). *Bennett's guide to jury selection and trial dynamics in civil and criminal litigation.* St. Paul, MN: West.

Two of the most experienced and successful trial consultants have contributed this practical description of jury selection procedures.

Krauss, E., & Bonora, B. (1983). *Jurywork: Systematic techniques* (2nd ed.). St. Paul, MN: West.

This indispensable reference for the professional trial consultant contains many examples of supplemental juror questionnaires, community opinion surveys, post-trial interviews with jurors, and other procedures.

Kravitz, D. A., Cutler, B. L., & Brock, P. (1993). Reliability and validity of the original and revised Legal Attitudes Questionnaire. *Law and Human Behavior, 17*, 661–677.

The steps in constructing and validating a scale to measure prospective jurors' general attitudes are presented in this research article.

Rose, V. G., & Ogloff, J. R. P. (2001). Evaluating the comprehensibility of jury instructions: A method and an example. *Law and Human Behavior, 25*, 409–431.

In a series of five experiments using typical Canadian legal instructions on criminal conspiracy and the co-conspirator exception to hearsay, the authors show that it is relatively simple to test for the comprehensibility of jury instructions.

Saks, M. J. (1987). Social scientists can't rig juries. In L. S. Wrightsman, S. M. Kassin, & C. E. Willis (Eds.), *In the jury box: Controversies in the courtroom* (pp. 48–61). Thousand Oaks, CA: Sage.

A distinguished psychologist and legal scholar suggests that trial lawyers should use psychologists to help structure the evidence to be presented at trial rather than as "jury selectors."

Schulman, J., Shaver, P., Colman, R., Emrich, B., & Christie, R. (1973, May). Recipe for a jury. *Psychology Today*, pp. 37–44, 77–84.

This report of the trial that initiated "scientific jury selection" was authored by the social scientists who aided the defence. Highly recommended.

Strier, F. (1999). Whither trial consulting: Issues and projections. *Law and Human Behavior, 23*, 93–115.

This comprehensive article on the current status of the trial-consulting field describes many of the profession's techniques, including the use of community surveys, focus groups, mock trials, and jury selection at voir dire. Also examined are the effectiveness of consultants and the ethical issues they face.

Vidmar, N. (1995). *Medical malpractice and the American jury.* Ann Arbor: University of Michigan Press.

A thorough analysis of the behaviour of jurors in medical malpractice trials, this book deflates claims that jurors are usually biased against "deep-pocket" defendants.

9

Criminal Responsibility and Competency to Stand Trial

He stated that The Holy Father has punished his mother, a local Anglican priest and an RCMP officer, all of whom he believes to be involved in the reported conspiracy against him, by giving his mother, the priest's wife and the officer's mother cancer and that "maybe they'll see the light." He also believes that crows warn him of danger by cawing.

—JUSTICE P. C. GORMAN IN THE PROVINCIAL COURT OF NEWFOUNDLAND AND LABRADOR (*R. v. Normore*, 2002, PARA. 13)

OVERVIEW

- A mother drowns her infant son in the bathtub to save him from an imagined threat of physical and sexual abuse.
- A man who believes that he has an electronic device implanted in his neck kills his elderly mother with an axe in their home.
- A woman stabs her husband 200 times because she thinks he plans to steal her money and run off with another woman.

These are all cases in Nova Scotia in which a person was ultimately found to be not criminally responsible by the courts (*Chronicle Herald*, 1999, 28 April). From 1987 to 1997, eight homicides in Nova Scotia were perpetrated by people with mental illnesses who were found by the courts to be either insane, or—after the Criminal Code of Canada was revised—**not criminally responsible by reason of a mental disorder (NCRMD)**. In all cases, the killer and victim knew or were related to one another. Psychiatrists and psychologists who assessed the defendants found that five of the eight had experienced delusions or hallucinations that led them to kill. Two specifically heard voices telling them to kill the victim.

When someone is found to be NCRMD in Canada it can incense the public, who may see such a determination as the defendant "getting off." Melton, Petrila, Poythress, and Slobogin (1997) have highlighted some of the major public misperceptions of the insanity defence: (1) that it is used by a large number of defendants; (2) that when used it is often successful; (3) that those acquitted with this defence are usually released; and (4) that such individuals are extremely dangerous. In fact, whereas the public estimates that the defence is used in 33 percent to 42.7 percent of cases, it is actually used about nine times in 1000 cases. Whereas the public estimates that the "success" of the defence is between 36 percent and 45 percent when it's used, in reality the success rate is less than 20 percent.

Criminal defendants who are found to be not criminally responsible are usually committed to a psychiatric hospital and remain there as long as they—in the judgment of the psychiatric staff—fit the criteria for having serious psychiatric disorders. Most spend extended periods of time in confinement, sometimes longer than if they had been found guilty and sentenced to prison (Borum & Fulero, 1999; Rodriguez, LeWinn, & Perlin, 1983).

As we will see, a key issue concerning whether a defendant is NCRMD is whether he or she had a mental illness at the time that caused his or her criminal actions. This is an extremely complicated matter. In fact, the determination of a person's psychological state at the time of an offence is one of the most challenging tasks given to the forensic psychologist. As indicated above, the NCRMD and insanity defence are rare. However, the presence of a mental illness among those who have committed offences is not. For example, according to a 2000 report, 32 percent of all inmates in British Columbia have a mental disorder (Hall, 2000). How do we decide whether some offenders' illnesses caused them to commit crimes while others did not?

In addition to advising the court and lawyers as to whether a defendant has the features of someone who is NCRMD, the forensic psychologist is frequently asked to make competency assessments. Does the defendant understand what it means to be on trial and is he or she competent to stand trial? The issue of predicting the dangerousness of offenders who have been hospitalized because of mental illness, now called risk assessment, exemplifies a more specialized task for the psychologist, but still a vital one. And throughout the above assessments underlies the question: Is the person malingering? That is, is the defendant simulating a serious mental disorder in order to avoid a guilty verdict or a prison sentence?

DETERMINING CRIMINAL RESPONSIBILITY/SANITY

One of the most important tasks facing forensic psychologists is assisting the courts in making a determination of criminal responsibility. And some might argue that it is the most difficult—or even impossible. In this chapter, we will examine the process of evaluating criminal responsibility/insanity by considering some recent cases and matching the behaviour of defendants with the definitions of NCRMD used in the courts.

Why Is Evaluating Criminal Responsibility Difficult?

The sources of difficulty when evaluating NCRMD are many. First, criminal responsibility is a legal concept, to be decided by the triers of fact, and not a psychological or medical one decided by psychologists or psychiatrists. A person may demonstrate psychotic behaviour and still not fulfill the legal definition of NCRMD. Additionally, the forensic psychiatrist or psychologist faced with the task of assessing criminal responsibility must make a retrospective assessment of the person's psychological state at the time of the offence, several months or years before. Often this can only be done on the basis of the person's present status.

A Brief History of the Insanity Defence

It is part of Western moral and legal tradition that a person who is unaware of the meaning of his or her acts should not be held criminally responsible for them. For thousands of years, the presence of *mens rea*, or "guilty mind" (in addition to the *actus reus* or "criminal action"), has been essential to the classification of an illegal act, according to many societies. A determination of guilt and an appropriate punishment, as evaluations and responses, should ensue only if there is free will and intent to do harm. **Guilt** requires not only the commission of an illegal act but also a state of mind reflecting awareness of its implications. The Canadian Supreme Court reasoned in *R. v. Chaulk* (1990) that the insanity defence is based on the principle that an accused person has no capacity for criminal intention because his or her psychological condition has created a skewed frame of reference. As such there is no capacity for *mens rea*.

As outlined by Quen (1981), Aristotle reasoned that free will was essential in evaluating blameworthiness, a capacity lacking in animals, children, and insane individuals. The first milestone concerning insanity in the British court system occurred in 1724. Edward Arnold, known locally as "Crazy Ned," had shot and wounded Lord Onslow. The evidence indicated that Arnold believed that Onslow had "bewitched" him and entered his body to torment him. Justice Tracey instructed the jury that in order for a man to be acquitted on the grounds of insanity he could not have known what he was doing any more than an infant, brute, or wild beast. (Interestingly, Arnold was found guilty and sentenced to death but Lord Onslow intervened and the sentence was reduced to life imprisonment). This came to be known as the "Wild Beast Test," the first formal legal definition of insanity.

The next landmark in the history of the insanity plea occurred in an 1834 trial in England. The accused in this case was Daniel McNaughton (also spelled M'Naghten and a multitude of other ways), who was found not guilty by reason of insanity after making an assassination attempt on British Prime Minister Robert Peel. The **McNaughton Rules** established by the judge in that case have been the foundation for the insanity criteria in many jurisdictions around the world. This definition contains three elements—a person should, according to the definition, be judged insane if:

1. The defendant was suffering from "a defect of reason, from a disease of the mind."
2. As a result, the defendant did not "know" the "nature and quality of the act he was doing."
3. An inquiry has been carried out to determine whether the defendant knew "what he was doing was wrong" (Ogloff, Roberts, & Roesch, 1993).

The McNaughton test is called a **cognitive test of insanity** because it emphasizes the quality of the person's thought processes and perceptions of reality at the time of the crime (Low, Jeffries, & Bonnie, 1986).

The Irresistible Impulse Standard Criticism of the McNaughton standard for its narrow focus on the defendant's cognitive knowledge led to its being supplemented—temporarily—by what was called the **irresistible impulse exception**. If a defendant demonstrated cognitive knowledge of right or wrong, he or she could still be found not guilty by reason of insanity if his or her free will was so destroyed or overruled that the person had lost the power to choose between right and wrong (Ogloff, Roberts, & Roesch, 1993). When referring to this loss of ability to control one's behaviour, the courts sometimes refer to the **volitional aspect of insanity**.

The Durham Test Continued criticism of the McNaughton standard's cognitive focus caused the courts to abandon reliance on the irresistible impulse exception and to seek broader definitions. In the case of *Durham v. United States* (1954), Judge David Bazelon developed a new definition, which came to be called the Durham rule; it stated that the accused was not criminally responsible if his or her unlawful act was a product of mental disease or defect. First seen as a progressive step because it moved the legal definitions closer to psychiatric concepts, the Durham rule soon became a problem. Mental health experts, who increasingly were testifying in trials involving the insanity plea, interpreted the term *mental disease* to mean any familiar clinical-diagnostic label (Ogloff, Roberts, & Roesch, 1993). The Durham standard is currently used in only one U.S. state, New Hampshire.

The ALI Standard, or Brawner Rule Further development stemmed from criticisms of the Durham rule. The American Law Institute developed a new definition that received acceptance in the case of *United States v. Brawner* in 1972; this innovation, now called the **ALI standard**, sought comprehensiveness. It stated: "A person is not responsible for criminal conduct if at the time of the action, as a result of mental disease or defect, he [or she] lacks substantial capacity either to appreciate the criminality (wrongfulness) of his [or her] conduct or to conform his or her conduct to the requirements of the law" (American Law Institute, 1962, p. 401). As used in this statement, the term "mental disease or defect" does not include an abnormality manifested only by repeated criminal or otherwise antisocial conduct.

There are several aspects worth noting in this attempt at a comprehensive definition. First, note it states "substantial" rather than total incapacity. For example, a five-year-old can know that it is wrong to kill someone but not fully appreciate the wrongfulness of it. Second, the use of "appreciate" wrongfulness rather than to "know" it connotes volitional or affective as well as cognitive understanding and fits better with modern psychiatric perspectives (Ogloff, Roberts, & Roesch, 1993). Thus, the ALI standard includes two aspects, or prongs, one cognitive ("can't appreciate the wrongfulness") and one volitional ("can't conform his conduct"). Currently, 21 U.S. states use the ALI standard. Wisconsin, the site of Jeffrey Dahmer's trial, has a unique procedure that combines elements of the McNaughton and ALI standards.

Another development in the history of the insanity defence is the "guilty but mentally ill" (GMBI) verdict. This decision combines a recognition of mental illness in defendants while still holding them guilty. Thirteen U.S. states provide for this type of verdict (Borum & Fulero, 1999). After such verdicts, the defendant is provided treatment at a state psychiatric hospital until he or she is declared to be sane; then the defendant is sent to prison, to serve the same term as those not mentally ill who have been convicted of similar offences. Some jurisdictions (such as Idaho, Montana, Nevada, Kansas, and Utah) do not have a provision for an insanity defence, although the defence lawyer can introduce evidence of the defendant's psychological status to try to disprove the *mens rea* element of the charged offence (Borum & Fulero, 1999). In the U.S., the jury's verdict that John Hinckley—charged with the attempted assassination of President Reagan—was not guilty by reason of insanity not only incensed the public but motivated Congress to radically overhaul the federal laws regarding the determination of insanity (Caplan, 1984). U.S. Congress passed the Insanity Defense Reform Act of 1984, removing the volitional prong of the ALI rule, leaving it substantially like the McNaughton rule, with focus on the accused's cognitive "appreciation." Congress also removed "substantial" as a modifier, so that the U.S. federal insanity test now instructs the fact-finder to decide whether or not the defendant "lacks capacity to appreciate the wrongfulness of his conduct."

The Canadian Approach: NCRMD

In Canada we have a unifying set of guidelines concerning mental disorder and criminal responsibility that have been incorporated in the Criminal Code. Section 16 of the Criminal Code used to describe the "not guilty by reason of insanity" (NGRI) defence, reformulated to reflect the concept of NCRMD. The Criminal Code legislation was revised on February 4, 1992, following the introduction of Bill C-30. The changes were initiated by the Supreme Court of Canada in the *R. v. Swain* (1991) case. The Court decided that the existing Criminal Code law requiring that a person found NGRI be automatically detained violated the Charter of Rights and Freedoms. At present, if the judge or jury decides that the accused committed the offence but it was caused by a mental disorder, he or she will be found NCRMD and will not go to prison.

The Criminal Code dictates that all accused persons are presumed *not* to suffer from a mental disorder and allows an NCRMD defence only when the mental disorder is proved on the "balance of probabilities." In Canada, unlike many American states, the burden of proof in establishing NCRMD is on whomever raises the issue, either the defence or Crown prosecutor.

Section 16 of the Code now states that "no person is criminally responsible for an act com-mitted or an omission made while suffering from a mental disorder that rendered the person incapable of appreciating the nature and quality of the act or omission or of knowing that it was wrong." The elements of this definition suggest that the accused person must have had a mental disorder which prevented him or her from understanding the criminal action or knowing that it was wrong; that is, the mental disorder had to justify the action. The courts have often had to grapple with what "knowing that it was wrong" means. Does this mean knowing that the criminal action was legally wrong, morally wrong, or both? In *R. v. Chaulk* (1990), the Supreme Court of Canada established that knowing that something is legally wrong does not result in a finding of NCRMD (or "insanity" at the time). The Crown must show that the accused person knew that what he or she was doing was morally wrong: "A person may well be aware that an act is contrary to the law but by reason of disease of the mind is at the same time incapable of knowing that the act is morally wrong in the circumstances according to the moral standards of society" (*R. v. Chaulk*, 1990, summary para. 10).

Take, for example, the Provincial Court of Newfoundland and Labrador case *R. v. Normore* (2002), which is cited at the start of the chapter. In this case, evidence indicated that on May 29, 2001, Alex Normore had threatened to burn down a pigpen that was being constructed close to his mother's residence. On that day, he approached an RCMP officer with a loaded, unlicensed 30-30 rifle on the front seat of his vehicle and live rounds in his pocket. He told police that the pigpen constituted a health hazard, and that he was in possession of the gun to protect himself from oil companies who meant to kill him. Other evidence indicated that he had long believed the RCMP were conspiring against him, stemming from a 2001 incident in Deer Lake in which he thought they had attempted to drown him in a bathtub. Justice P. C. Gorman concluded that Mr. Normore had a profound delusion. He noted that Mr. Normore had appreciated that his actions with the weapon were illegal. However, he decided that Mr. Normore was not capable of understanding that his actions would have been viewed as morally condemned by reasonable members of society. As such, he found the accused to be NCRMD on the weapons offences (but guilty on others).

There is a specific type of defence in the Criminal Code that can lead to a finding of NCRMD, known as **automatism**. In the British Columbia case *R. v. Stone* (1999), the Supreme Court of Canada defined this defence, noting that there are two distinct forms of the defence, non-insane and insane automatism. Noninsane automatism refers to an involuntary action that is not caused by mental disorder and will lead to a verdict of complete acquittal. For example, if a person was struck on the head or had an adverse reaction to medication immediately prior to committing a criminal action, the defence might argue non-insane automatism. Another example is someone who commits a criminal action while sleep-walking. In an infamous Ontario case, Kenneth Parks from Toronto was sleepwalking when he killed his mother-in-law and tried to kill his father-in-law. He had been suffering from severe insomnia before the attack. Early in the morning on May 23, 1987—according to the evidence, while he was sleeping—he drove 23 kilometres to the victims' home where he proceeded to stab them. The jury accepted expert evidence that his actions were involuntary and he was acquitted, a finding upheld by the Ontario Court of Appeal and Supreme Court of Canada (*R. v. Parks*, 1992).

The second type of this defence is insane automatism, used if an involuntary action was caused by a disease of the mind. If the court agrees with this defence, the accused person is found to be NCRMD. This disease of the mind can be in the form of mental disorder caused by a "psycho-logical blow" in which the person experiences psychiatric symptoms following an extremely stressful experience. For example, in the Halifax case *R. v. Lomax* (2002), the judge rejected the insane automatism claim made by the defence that Lomax had robbed a gas station following a psy-chological blow. The psychological blow described by the defence was the accused being told by his wife that "the neighbour was fucking me with a dildo and we had a good time." In many cases, however, courts have accepted similar arguments and found the accused to be NCRMD (see Porter, Birt, Yuille, & Hervé, 2001).

Characteristics of NCRMD Individuals

In a study entitled "A Follow-up Study of Persons Found Not Criminally Responsible on Account of Mental Disorder in British Columbia," Livingston, Wilson, Tien, and Bond (2003) looked at information about people found NCRMD between 1992 (when Bill C-30 was introduced) and 1998. Some of their key findings were the following:

- In the six years after the Criminal Code changes, a much higher number of people were found NCRMD in B.C., compared with those found NGRI in the years before the change. The difference was apparently due to a much higher frequency of minor charges leading to a finding of NCRMD after 1992.
- The average length of hospitalization for the NCRMD group was only 9.8 months, much shorter than the average for the NGRI group (49.9 months).
- Very few NCRMD individuals were con-victed of new criminal charges following their discharge into the community, but most required rehospitalization.
- Of the 276 NCRMD individuals in B.C., 85.5 percent were male and 14.5 percent were female.
- Prior to committing their offence, 76.5 per-cent of the NCRMD group had been treated in a psychiatric inpatient facility. Further, 51.8 percent of the patients had been admitted to a psychiatric facility on at least four occasions.

The authors concluded that the "Bill C-30 provisions have made the NCRMD defence an attractive option for defendants and legal counsel" (Livingston et al., 2003, p. 408). Overall, the effects of the legal changes seemed to be positive in that they reduced the length of time that a person is initially detained in custody. Unfortunately (but perhaps not surprisingly), a high proportion of those who were found NCRMD but later conditionally discharged required lengthy rehospitalizations.

A finding of NCRMD typically follows expert testimony from psychiatrists and psychologists concerning the accused. Often, within the context of the same assessment, the mental health professionals will consider whether the accused is competent to stand trial and whether the accused was, at the time of the commission of the alleged offence, suffering from a mental disorder so as to be NCRMD.

PSYCHOLOGISTS' ROLES IN NCRMD/INSANITY CASES

The forensic psychologist may play several roles when NCRMD is used by a defendant as a defence. Prior to trial, the psychologist may be asked to assess the defendant; then at the trial, the psychologist may testify about his or her findings.

Assessment of Criminal Responsibility

As mentioned earlier, assessing criminal responsibility is a difficult task. The first thing the psychologist must do is understand the Criminal Code definition of the NCRMD defence and realize that it is not equal to the presence of psychosis or a mental disorder. It is certainly possible for someone with a mental disorder to commit a crime and be fully responsible for his or her actions.

In deciding whether offenders were aware of the implications of their actions, psychologists have traditionally used interviews; often these were unstandardized and unstructured. A more reliable procedure was needed. Developed for this purpose, the Rogers Criminal Responsibility Assessment Scales (R-CRAS) have as their goal the application of the logic of diagnostic structured interviews to the forensic assessment of criminal responsibility (Rogers, 1984, 1986;

Rogers & Cavanaugh, 1981; Rogers & Ewing, 1992; Rogers, Wasyliw, & Cavanaugh, 1984). They attempt to transfer the ALI definition of insanity into 25 quantifiable variables, grouped into five topics of psycho-legal relevance: organicity, psychopathology, cognitive control, behavioural control, and the reliability of the report. Each R-CRAS item requires the examiner to rate a specific psychological or situational variable on the delineated criteria; Box 9.1 gives examples of these items.

The authors have reported high interjudge reliabilities (the degree of agreement between raters) for assignment of scores to the five topics and for a final judgment of insanity; the mean rate of agreement was more than 90 percent (Nicholson, 1999; Rogers, Dolmetsch, Wasyliw, & Cavanaugh, 1982). Also there is a high correspondence between the examiners' ratings and the final legal adjudications (Rogers, Cavanaugh, Seman, & Harris, 1984), although these data are derived from examiners who "work closely with one another in specialized forensic evaluation centres, and whose reports and testimony are well known to and influential in local courts" (Ogloff, Roberts, & Roesch, 1993, p. 171).

The review of the R-CRAS by Canadian researcher James Ogloff and his colleagues (1993) concluded that it is a useful device; these reviewers saw one of its benefits as the requirement that forensic psychologists be comprehensive and explicit about what the contributing factors are in their judgments about the presence of insanity/NCRMD. Other reviewers have not been as accepting of the R-CRAS; Golding and Roesch (1987) were quite critical and questioned whether the interjudge reliabilities of the R-CRAS were any higher than those resulting from unstructured interviews. Robert Nicholson (1999), in evaluating various reviews of the R-CRAS, noted that its variable rate of acceptance may partly reflect differences of opinion about just what is the goal of forensic assessment; specifically, does it seek to provide an *ultimate opinion* regarding the criminal responsibility of the individual?

BOX 9.1
Sample Items from the R-CRAS

Two of the 25 items from the Rogers Criminal Responsibility Assessment Scales are the following:

ITEM 10. AMNESIA ABOUT THE ALLEGED CRIME.

(This refers to the examiner's assessment of amnesia, not necessarily the patient's reported amnesia.)
- (0) No information.
- (1) None. Remembers the entire event in considerable detail.
- (2) Slight; of doubtful significance. The patient forgets a few minor details.
- (3) Mild. Patient remembers the substance of what happened, but is forgetful of many minor details.
- (4) Moderate. The patient has forgotten a major portion of the alleged crime but remembers enough details to believe it happened.
- (5) Severe. The patient is amnesic to most of the alleged crime, but remembers enough details to believe it happened.
- (6) Extreme. Patient is completely amnesic to the whole alleged crime.

ITEM 11. DELUSIONS AT THE TIME OF THE ALLEGED CRIME.

- (0) No information.
- (1) Absent.
- (2) Suspected delusions (e.g., supported only by questionable self-report).
- (3) Definite delusions, but not actually associated with the commission of the alleged crime.
- (4) Definite delusions, which contributed to, but were not the predominant force in the commission of the alleged crime.
- (5) Definite controlling delusions, on the basis of which the alleged crime was committed.

(From Rogers, Wasyliw, & Cavanaugh, 1984, p. 299.)

A second instrument for assessing criminal responsibility, the Mental Screening Evaluation, or MSE (Slobogin, Melton, & Showalter, 1984), has a more modest goal: to "screen out" defendants whose law-breaking actions clearly were not caused by a mental disorder. The MSE includes questions about the defendant's general psychological history, questions about the alleged offence, and an evaluation of his or her present mental state. For example, in the first section, the psychologist is asked, "Does the defendant have a history of prolonged bizarre behaviour (i.e., delusions, hallucinations, looseness of association of ideas … [or] disturbances of affect?" (Slobogin, Melton, & Showalter, 1984, p. 319).

A purpose of the MSE is to sensitize psychological examiners to the kinds of information required when addressing the legal question of the defendant's mental state at the time of the law-breaking behaviour. But there is neither a standardized administration nor a formal scoring procedure for the test's use, and empirical evidence on its validity is limited (Grisso, 1986; Nicholson, 1999).

Testifying as an Expert Witness

In making decisions on issues beyond their knowledge, jurors often pay attention to the testimony of expert witnesses. But the forensic psychologist who testifies for the defence that the defendant meets the definition of NCRMD faces several challenges. First, the Crown is likely to have an expert witness of its own, with conflicting conclusions. Second, any expert witness is likely to face a withering cross-examination. On this last point, the volumes prepared by the late forensic psychologist Jay Ziskin (1995) and a highly publicized article in *Science* by Faust and Ziskin (1988) provide a compendium of material that challenges the claim that the assessments done by clinical psychologists and other mental health professionals possess adequate levels of validity and reliability for use in court (see Nicholson, 1999, pp. 125–131, for a critique of Ziskin's efforts). Many recent trials illustrate the concerns about expert witness testimony, especially the differing assessments by defence and prosecution experts of the defendant's psychological state. Two familiar murder cases from the U.S. will be used to exemplify the "battle of the experts" problem.

The Hinckley Trial

The trial of John W. Hinckley, Jr., utilized expert psychiatrists on each side. When Hinckley went on trial 15 months after shooting President Reagan, his lawyers didn't dispute the evidence that he had planned the attack, bought special bullets, tracked the president, and fired from a shooter's crouch. But he couldn't help it, they claimed, for he was only responding to the "driving forces" of a diseased mind. Their claims were supported by the testimony of psychiatrist William Carpenter, that Hinckley did not "appreciate" the consequences of his act: he had lost the ability to control himself and was suffering from process schizophrenia. The defence also tried to introduce the results of a CAT scan of Hinckley's brain to support its contention that he was schizophrenic.

The psychiatrists testifying for the prosecution conceded that Hinckley had strange fantasies but said he did not have schizophrenia, but only a few relatively mild and commonplace mental disorders. They stated that he had no delusions or psychoses and that he was always in touch with reality, including the reality that Jodie Foster would never feel affection for him. The real motives, they said, had been to win fame and to give Ms. Foster and his parents a jolt (Caplan, 1984).

A prominent forensic psychiatrist testifying for the prosecution, Park Dietz, diagnosed Hinckley as having a borderline personality disorder with depressive neurosis. He concluded that Hinckley's goal of making an impression on Jodie Foster was indeed reasonable, because he accomplished it (Caplan, 1984). Even though his were not the reasonable acts of a completely rational individual, no evidence existed that he was so impaired that he could not appreciate the wrongfulness of his conduct or conform his conduct to the requirements of the law.

The decision by the jury that found Hinckley not guilty by reason of insanity appears to have been strongly influenced by the judge's instruction that the burden of proof was on the prosecution to prove that Hinckley was sane.

The Dahmer Trial

The 1992 trial of Jeffrey Dahmer is unusual for more than the reason that he had admitted killing and dismembering 17 young men over a ten-year period. Some bodies he cannibalized; others he tried to turn into "zombies" who could remain with him for companionship (Berlin, 1994). The purpose of the trial was to determine whether Dahmer could be absolved of responsibility by reason of insanity rather than to determine guilt, as he had already conceded that he had committed the acts. Hence, the jury was given two different characterizations of the defendant. His lawyer told the jury: "This is not an evil man; this is a sick man." The prosecuting lawyer disagreed, claiming that Dahmer "knew at all times that what he was doing was wrong."

The trial was also unusual in that in addition to the expert witnesses introduced by each side, the presiding judge asked two experts to testify, one psychiatrist and one psychologist. The defence experts, who testified first (in Wisconsin the defence had the burden of proof to prove that Dahmer was insane), included the following:

■ Dr. Fred S. Berlin, a psychiatrist from Johns Hopkins University School of Medicine, who diagnosed Dahmer's psychiatric disorder as **necrophilia** (a type of **paraphilia** or abnormal sexual behaviour), reflecting sexual urges that caused him to kill young men and then preserve their body parts, in an effort to maintain sexual intimacy. Dahmer used such terms as "overpowering" in describing the strength of his cravings; hence Berlin felt that he lacked "substantial capacity" to control his actions. In a subsequent article (1994), Berlin concluded that Dahmer came to believe it was his destiny to kill, even though he often felt miserable, alone, and despairing. Berlin also testified that Dahmer would become erotically aroused by thoughts of having sex with dead male bodies. He was frequently impotent and unable to sustain an erection when relating to those who were still alive (Berlin, 1994).

In his article on the case, Berlin stated: "I did not feel uncomfortable defending the position that an individual who recurrently experiences much more powerful urges to have sex with a corpse than with a living human being is an individual who is afflicted with a mental disease or defect" (1994, p. 14). Of all the expert witnesses, he came closest to the layperson's view when he said, "If this isn't mental illness I don't know what is."

■ Dr. Judith Becker, a clinical psychologist and professor at the University of Arizona, who offered a sexual history of Dahmer and described Dahmer's fantasies about capturing young men and building a kind of "temple" in his apartment from the body parts, skulls, and skeletons of his victims (Norris, 1992). She, too, felt that Dahmer suffered from a sexual disorder of necrophilia and that he lacked control of his urges. She did not diagnose him as psychotic, although she felt that some of his behaviour was "psychotic-like."

■ Dr. Carl Wahlstrom, a psychiatrist who, on cross-examination, acknowledged that he had not yet passed his board certification and that this was his first defence testimony (Norris, 1992). He proposed that Dahmer killed in order to avoid abandonment; Wahlstrom was the only defence witness to conclude that Dahmer had a borderline personality and was psychotic, even though he lacked hallucinations.

The prosecution countered with two experts:

■ Dr. Frederick Fosdal, a forensic psychiatrist from the University of Wisconsin Medical School, who noted that Dahmer's were not brutal, sadistic acts and, further, that Dahmer was able to refrain and had some control as to when he followed through on his sexual desires.

■ Dr. Park Dietz (who had testified in the Hinckley trial also), formerly on the faculty at the University of Virginia but now a full-time forensic psychiatrist. (Box 9.2 elaborates on Dietz's background.) Perhaps the most effective of the expert witnesses, Dietz pointed to Dahmer's capacity to exert methodical control as an indicator of his sanity and premeditation (Norris, 1992). Further, "the mere fact that Dahmer disposed of his bodies efficiently, planned different methods of disposal, was able to control his murderous urges for years between crimes, and was able to fool his probation officer and policemen on different occasions proved that the man knew exactly what he was doing" (quoted by Norris, 1992, p. 281). He offered two diagnoses: alcohol dependence, of a mild to moderate nature, and paraphilia (sexual deviation). These two interacted; Dahmer would drink to overcome his inhibitions against killing and dismemberment. Thus Dietz concluded that Dahmer did not meet the Wisconsin standard of insanity.

The two court-appointed expert witnesses were the following:

■ Dr. George Palermo, a psychiatrist, who read his report to the jury. For several reasons, he

BOX 9.2
Park Dietz—Expert Witness for the Prosecution

Among forensic psychiatrists who testify in murder cases in which the defence is a claim of insanity, Park Dietz is clearly the most consistently effective as an expert witness for the prosecution. Always meticulously prepared, he is able to provide jurors with plausible explanations of defendants' behaviour that do not involve insanity or psychosis. In both the Hinckley and the Dahmer trials, Dietz effectively related the specifics of the defendant's behaviour to show qualities in conflict with the local definition of insanity.

In another highly publicized trial, Dr. Dietz testified in the trial of Joel Rifkin, a New York landscape gardener who picked up 17 prostitutes whom he later strangled and dismembered. The psychiatrist interviewed Rifkin extensively prior to the trial, and Rifkin told him that at times he would speak to the corpses, "saying reassuring things as he drove with them" (McQuiston, 1994, p. B16); he said "whispers" had told him to strangle his victims. Are these whispers hallucinations? Do they indicate psychosis? Do they contribute to a judgment of insanity? On the stand, Dietz characterized the whispers as nothing more than an "internal dialogue" (p. B16). Under intense cross-examination, he remained unwilling to call them hallucinations or symptoms of paranoid schizophrenia.

Dietz characteristically testifies for the prosecution. He holds little sympathy for defence lawyers—in discussing his own experience with them, he wrote:

"Criminal defence lawyers routinely withheld evidence of their clients' guilt, at least until confident that the government has the evidence" (1996, p. 159). In contrast, he noted, "I have known the prosecution to withhold important evidence on only one occasion, and it was in the context of a court-ordered evaluation" (Dietz, 1996, p. 159).

To what extent is Dr. Dietz's interpretation of behaviour related to his political ideology? While an undergraduate at Cornell University he was president of the Conservative Club (Johnson, 1994). He has no clinical caseload. Defence lawyers, not surprisingly, believe that he sees things through the eyes of the prosecutor. When he agrees to take a case, Dietz warns the prosecutor that he might well end up forming an opinion that would prevent him from testifying against the defendant. But in the cases of John W. Hinckley, Jr., Jeffrey Dahmer, Betty Broderick, Arthur Shawcross, Joel Rifkin, and others, he has always concluded that the behaviour did not meet the definition of insanity. In the opinion of one observer, "[I]n his view, when criminal charges are heavy, truth is rarely to be found on the side of a defence [lawyer's] client. Dietz's predilection for the prosecutor's side does not seem unconnected to his conservative politics or to his profound alienation from the physician's role in traditional psychiatry" (Johnson, 1994, p. 48).

---

was not an effective witness. He concluded that Dahmer was not insane, that he had a serious personality disorder and was driven by obsessive fantasies, but that he knew what he was doing.

■ Dr. Thomas Friedman, a psychologist in independent practice, who, in response to a question, waxed philosophical about the nature of mental illness. Friedman agreed with Dietz and Palermo that Dahmer had a personality disorder and that he was not psychotic. In that respect, his testimony aided the prosecution, but he probably was not very effective because of his self-deprecatory manner ("My understanding of

the literature is not the most sophisticated" [Court TV, 1992]).

In Wisconsin a unique version of the ALI rule is used to define insanity; consequently, to have found Dahmer insane, the jury would first have had to conclude that he had suffered from a mental disorder or defect that made him unable to know right from wrong and, second, whether, as a consequence of that, he lacked substantial capacity to control his conduct, as required by the law. In a split decision, acceptable by Wisconsin rules, the jury concluded that Dahmer was not an individual who suffered from mental disease, perhaps because of the evidence that Dahmer was careful to kill his victims in a manner that minimized his chances of getting caught—such a degree of cautiousness suggested that he appreciated the wrongfulness of his behaviour *and* could control this behaviour when it was to his advantage to do so. Thus, Dahmer was sentenced to 999 years in prison, where he was bludgeoned to death by another inmate in 1994.

Ultimate-Issue Testimony

As noted earlier, one of the roles of the expert is "to explore carefully, and to explain to the court, how psychopathological processes at the time of the crime might have influenced the defendant's then-existing perceptions, motivations, cognitions, intentions, and behaviours" (Ogloff, Roberts, & Roesch, 1993, p. 172). This retrospective evaluation has to be expressed in terms of likelihood rather than finality, and it is subject to several sources of error, including examiner bias, possible malingering, and undetected defensive covering of genuine paranoid pathology, among other factors (Ogloff, Roberts, & Roesch, 1993).

How far should a psychologist or psychiatrist be allowed to go, when testifying in a case involving an NCRMD defence? Is it proper for an expert to express an opinion about whether the defendant was criminally responsible at the time of the offence? Psychologists are divided on this issue; some strenuously oppose the court's questioning of mental health experts about the status of the specific defendant, while others do not (Bonnie & Slobogin, 1980; Morse, 1978). Some of the concerns stem from a belief that it is the role of the jury, not the psychiatric expert, to determine the criminal responsibility of the defendant. In keeping with the issues that introduced this chapter, we need to remember that the judgment of responsibility is a legal one, not a psychological one, and that psychologists, as experts, should stop at the limits of their expertise. But some psychologists have gone further in their criticisms, questioning whether psychology and psychiatry have any valid viewpoints on such issues, and have challenged their colleagues to provide supporting evidence for their

claims of accuracy in forensic opinions (Dawes, Faust, & Meehl, 1989; Hagen, 1997; Ziskin & Faust, 1988; Ziskin, 1995).

One resolution to this conflict is to prevent the expert from expressing an opinion on the ultimate issue of legal criminal responsibility/insanity itself. In Canada, **ultimate-issue testimony** by experts was once not allowed in the court. While current rules of evidence are more liberal, the *Mohan* case (see Chapter 1) determined that if an expert's testimony speaks to the ultimate issue, "the criteria of relevance and necessity are applied strictly, on occasion, to exclude expert evidence as to the ultimate issue" (*R. v. Mohan*, para. 24). In the U.S., ultimate-issue or ultimate-opinion testimony was one of the targets of the Insanity Defense Reform Act of 1984, passed by Congress after John Hinckley's trial. It modified U.S. federal law specifically to prohibit mental health experts from testifying about ultimate legal issues. As amended, Federal Rule of Evidence 704(b), which allows ultimate-issue testimony in other types of cases, now states:

> No expert witness testifying with respect to the mental state or condition of the defendant in a criminal case may state an opinion or inference as to whether the defendant did or did not have the mental state or condition constituting an element of the crime charged or of the defence thereto. Such ultimate issues are matters for the trier of fact alone.

Note that this proscription applies to U.S. federal cases only; Jeffrey Dahmer's trial, as are the vast majority of trials using the insanity plea, was a state matter. Some state courts have permitted experts to testify as to the ultimate issue of insanity but have instructed jurors that they may give such testimony as much or as little weight as they wish. Similar to Canada, some other countries (including the United Kingdom and South Africa) permit ultimate-opinion testimony, at least in some types of cases (Allan & Louw, 1997).

This ruling has led to consternation and confusion in the U.S. federal courts. Supposedly, the expert could describe a defendant's psychological condition and the effects it could have had on his or her thinking and behavioural control, but the expert could not state conclusions about whether the defendant was sane or insane. But some commentators have speculated that this exclusion may lead to the omission at the trial of clinical information quite relevant to the case (Braswell, 1987; Goldstein, 1989; Rogers & Ewing, 1989, cited by Ogloff, Roberts, & Roesch, 1993). For example, Canadians Ogloff, Roberts, and Roesch have observed:

> If the revised rule were applied strictly, an expert could not testify as to whether a given defendant was legally sane or insane *and* whether he or she had a "mental disease," "intended" to do great bodily harm, "knew" the probable consequences of his or her act, "knew" what he or she was doing, "appreciated" the criminality of his or her conduct, and so forth. Yet the same expert is literally being asked by the courts to give testimony that bears directly on such psychological constructs. (1993, p. 172, italics in original)

Further, forensic psychologists, whose expertise is in evaluating policy changes, need to ask whether this prohibition solves any problems, or whether it is, in the words of Rogers and Ewing (1989), merely a "cosmetic fix" that has few effects. (Similarly, Fulero, 1998, sees it as a "semantic" issue, only.) A study by Fulero and Finkel (1991) was designed to answer this question. Mock jurors read one of several versions of a murder trial, in which the defendant claimed that he was insane at the time of the offence. Some mock jurors were told that expert witnesses had testified, but only that they had given diagnostic testimony, specifically that the defendant suffered a mental disorder at the time of the offence; other jurors were told about the effects of this disorder on the degree to which the defendant understood the wrongfulness of his act; and a third group of jurors heard ultimate-opinion testimony about whether the defendant was sane or insane at the time of the act. In this study, the type of information the mock jurors heard from the expert witness did *not* significantly

affect whether they found the defendant guilty or not guilty by reason of insanity. Does this mean the prohibition is unnecessary? Further research is needed. Let us say that a psychologist testifies that the defendant did not know the difference between right and wrong and was not able to appreciate the wrongfulness of his or her actions. If the expert is allowed to testify thus (and stops there), the jury probably has a good idea of the expert's opinion on the ultimate question.

ASSESSING COMPETENCY

A fundamental principle of the criminal justice system in Canada is that criminal proceedings should not continue against any person who is not able to understand their nature or purpose. To have a fair trial, criminal defendants must be able to understand the nature of the proceedings and assist counsel, as noted by Patricia Zapf, Ronald Roesch, & Jodi Viljoen (2001). If an accused person is unable to contribute to the defence due to a mental disorder, he or she may be found unfit to stand trial, and proceedings will be delayed until fitness is regained. It is estimated that at least 5000 criminal defendants are referred for evaluation of their competency to participate in legal proceedings annually in Canada (Roesch, Webster, & Eaves, 1984). The criterion in the determination of competency is the present level of ability of the defendant, not his or her state at the time of the offence; thus the focus drastically differs from the evaluation of the defendant's criminal responsibility. Nonetheless, the typical presence of a mental disorder is the strongest commonality of NCRMD and "not competent to stand trial" findings.

Traditionally, the disposition for a defendant found incompetent or "not fit" to stand trial was committal to a psychiatric facility for an indeterminate period until fitness was regained. However, with revisions to the Criminal Code of Canada in 1992, the definition of fitness and the dispositions following such a finding changed (e.g., Zapf et al., 2001). The Criminal Code now defines "unfit to stand trial" as:

> Unable on account of mental disorder to conduct a defence at any stage of the proceedings before a verdict is rendered or to instruct counsel to do so, and, in particular, unable on account of mental disorder to (a) understand the nature or object of the proceedings, (b) understand the possible consequences of the proceedings, or (c) communicate with counsel.

Forensic psychologists as well as psychiatrists assist in assessing competency of defendants who come before the court. In general, **competency** (or "competence") refers to the person's ability to understand the nature and purpose of court proceedings, and it is applicable at every stage of the criminal justice process, from interrogations and pre-trial hearings to trials and sentencing hearings. Competency or fitness is especially an issue when a defendant goes to trial or when he or she plea-bargains a guilty plea.

Although the subsequent emphasis in this section is on assessing competency of defendants facing criminal charges, competency is also a relevant question in some types of civil suits. For example, in a civil case it may be necessary to evaluate the testamentary capacity of a person when he or she makes out a will. Also, when issues of guardianship are raised, the courts want to know whether the individual does or does not possess the necessary mental ability to make decisions regarding his or her health care, living conditions, and finances. These and other types of civil cases provide expanding demands for competency assessments by forensic psychologists and other mental health professionals.

Defence lawyers express concerns about their clients' fitness to stand trial in about 10 percent to 15 percent of their cases (Hoge, Bonnie, Poythress, & Monahan, 1992; Poythress, Bonnie, Hoge, Monahan, & Oberlander, 1994). If, as in the case of competency to plead, a question is raised about the defendant's fitness to stand trial, the judge will order an evaluation of the defendant. One review (Roesch & Golding, 1980) estimated that in 30 percent of these referrals, the defendant was actually found to be incompetent, though more recent estimates reduce this to 10 percent (Melton, Petrila, Poythress, & Slobogin, 1997). Most evaluations are completed on an inpatient basis, although some psychologists have questioned the necessity of this costly procedure and have recommended that it be done on an outpatient basis (Melton, Weithorn, & Slobogin, 1985; Roesch & Golding, 1987).

The judge, of course, makes the decision of whether the defendant is fit to stand trial. But studies consistently find that judges often defer to the opinion of the examining psychologist or psychiatrist, with judge-examiner rates of agreement at 90 percent or higher (Hart & Hare, 1992; Reich & Tookey, 1986; Williams & Miller, 1981, reviewed by Skeem, Golding, Cohn, & Berge, 1998).

The basic question to be answered in such an evaluation is: If the defendant has an impairment, does it affect his or her ability to participate knowingly and meaningfully in the trial and to cooperate with the defence lawyer? The procedure in the competency evaluation is subject to the usual problems of subjectivity of clinical examinations. Thus psychiatrists and psychologists have designed competency assessment instruments that seek greater objectivity. Five of these are described below; though some call themselves "tests," they serve as semi-structured interviews.

The Fitness Interview Test-Revised (FIT-R)

The Fitness Interview Test-Revised (originally named the Interdisciplinary Fitness Interview), now one of the most widely used fitness assessment tools in Canada, was developed by Ron Roesch and Steven Golding (1980; Golding, Roesch, & Schreiber, 1984). The revised version includes questions on three main topics adhering to the Criminal Code criteria: understanding of the proceedings, understanding of the consequences of the proceedings, and the defendant's ability to communicate with counsel (Roesch,

Webster, & Eaves, 1994; Roesch, Zapf, Eaves, & Webster, 1998; Zapf & Roesch, 1997; Zapf, Roesch, & Viljoen, 2001). The FIT involves a semi-structured interview, which takes about 30 minutes to administer to the accused person. Each of the 16 items is rated on a three-point scale (0–2), with 0 indicating no impairment on the criterion and 2 indicating definite of serious impairment. The revised version responded to criticisms of the earlier version and reflected the 1992 changes made to the Criminal Code. It appears to work very well as a screening device to assess fitness to stand trial in Canada (Nicholson, 1999). Zapf and colleagues (2001) compared decisions about fitness to stand trial based on FIT results with the findings of institution-based decision makers on the same male patients. They found that the FIT had excellent utility as a screening instrument that can reduce the number of remands to an inpatient facility.

The Competency Screening Test (CST)

This 22-item sentence-completion task, developed by Lipsitt, Lelos, and McGarry (1971), serves as an initial screening test for incompetency. The CST is reproduced in Box 9.3.

Each answer by the defendant is scored as a 2 (a competent answer), a 1 (a marginally competent answer), or a 0 (an incompetent answer); thus the range is from 0 to 66. A score of 20 or below indicates that the respondent should be given a more comprehensive evaluation.

This procedure is an improvement over the traditional, rather unstructured interview that led to subjective conclusions and a global, unquantified indication of competency (Golding, 1990). But the CST still has some subjectivity, especially in the scoring of responses (Roesch & Golding, 1987). For example, for the statement "Jack felt that the judge …," a response of "was unjust" receives 0 points. The CST had the lowest predictive validity index of the instruments reviewed by Melton, Petrila, Poythress, and Slobogin (1997). Even though the inter-rater reliability coefficients on the CST appear to be high—generally .85 or better—these are apparently

derived from raters who have had extensive training and have used the instrument frequently (Melton et al., 1987). Studies that seek to identify a factor structure have found inconsistent results (Ustad, Rogers, Sewell, & Guarnaccia, 1996). Of greater concern is the outcome of a study (Felchlia, 1992) that sought to determine whether there was a relationship between the constructs that the CST claimed to assess and measures of parallel psychological constructs. The results were disappointing. For example, assessments of the defendant's ability to cope with events in the trial, as indicated by CST responses, were not significantly related to psychological measures of adaptive and coping potential.

The Competency Assessment Instrument (CAI)

The Competency Assessment Instrument is a structured interview, lasting about one hour, that seeks to explore 13 aspects of competent functioning (Laboratory of Community Psychiatry, 1974). The defendant's response is rated with a score from 1 (total incapacity) to 5 (no incapacity). In the CAI the mental health worker is asked to appraise where the defendant stands on a number of qualities, including how he or she relates to the lawyer, the defendant's ability to testify relevantly, his or her appreciation of the charges and the possible penalties, and his or her ability to realistically assess the outcome of the trial. Many of these characteristics are, of course, similar to those in the CST.

Little research exists on the reliability of this system; in a review of research done between 1991 and 1995, Cooper and Grisso (1997) reported no published articles on the CAI. The administration and scoring are not standardized. A revision of the CAI has been developed by John A. Riley (1998), along with colleagues Craig Nelson and John Gannon, at Atascadero State Hospital, in California. It assesses 14 aspects of functioning and takes about 30 to 45 minutes to administer. These aspects include understanding of the charges against the accused, appreciation of the penalties, ability to cooperate with counsel, and capacity to cope with

---

BOX 9.3
Competency Screening Test

1. The lawyer told Bill that _____
   _____

2. When I go to court, the lawyer will _____
   _____

3. Jack felt that the judge _____
   _____

4. When Phil was accused of the crime, he _____
   _____

5. When I prepare to go to court with
   my lawyer _____
   _____

6. If the jury finds me guilty, I _____
   _____

7. The way a court trial is decided _____
   _____

8. When the evidence in George's case
   was presented to the jury _____
   _____

9. When the lawyer questioned his client
   in court, the client said _____
   _____

10. If Jack had to try his own case, he _____
    _____

11. Each time the DA asked me a question, I _____
    _____

12. While listening to the witnesses testify
    against me, I _____
    _____

13. When the witness testifying against Harry
    gave incorrect evidence, he _____
    _____

14. When Bob disagreed with his lawyer on his
    defence, he _____
    _____

15. When I was formally accused of the crime,
    I thought to myself _____
    _____

16. If Ed's lawyer suggests that he plead guilty, he
    _____
    _____

17. What concerns Fred most about his
    lawyer is _____
    _____

18. When they say a man is innocent until
    proven guilty _____
    _____

19. When I think of being sent to prison, I _____
    _____

20. When Phil thinks of what he is
    accused of, he _____
    _____

21. When the jury hears my case, they will _____
    _____

22. If I had a chance to speak to the
    judge, I _____
    _____

(From Lipsitt, Lelos, and McGarry, 1971.)

---

incarceration while awaiting trial. The subject's responses are evaluated for their adequacy on a 1-to-4 scale.

Georgia Court Competency Test (GCCT)

The Georgia Court Competency Test or GCCT (Wildman et al., 1978) consists of 21 questions.

Although it is more limited in coverage, its reliability appears to be good (Bagby, Nicholson, Rogers, & Nussbaum, 1992). It has demonstrated the same factor structure in two samples (Nicholson, Briggs, & Robertson, 1988)—specifically, general legal knowledge, courtroom layout, and specific legal knowledge, although a more recent study suggests that the two legal knowledge factors can be combined into one (Ustad, Rogers, Sewell, & Guarnaccia, 1996).

The original form of the GCCT was modified by psychologists at Mississippi State Hospital by adding four questions, changing the weighting of some answers, and making scoring criteria more explicit (Johnson & Mullett, 1987). Studies using this revision, the GCCT-MSH, have found significant correlations with independent criteria of competency (Nicholson, 1999). One of these validity studies concluded that performance on the GCCT-MSH "made a significant, independent contribution to prediction of competence status beyond that based on diagnosis, intellectual functioning, offence type, and background characteristics" (Nicholson & Johnson, 1991, quoted in Nicholson, 1999, p. 139).

The MacArthur Competence Assessment Tool-Criminal Adjudication (MacCAT-CA)

The most recently developed competency-assessment device is the MacArthur Competence Assessment Tool-Criminal Adjudication, abbreviated MacCAT-CA (Hoge et al., 1997). Its purpose is to measure the person's competence to proceed to adjudication—that is, his or her ability to plead guilty as well as the ability to go to trial. It is a more structured measure than the CAI and uses an objective, theory-based scoring system. In keeping with four kinds of abilities seen as relevant to the competency evaluation, questions are grouped into four categories:

- Understanding of charges and trials (including understanding of general trial issues, competence to assist counsel, understanding whether to plead guilty, and understanding whether to waive a jury and request a bench trial).
- Appreciation of the relevance of information for a defence.
- Reasoning with information during decision making, or an assessment of logical problem-solving abilities.
- Making a choice.

Most of the MacCAT-CA contains hypothetical situations about which the defendant is questioned. (See Box 9.4.) Administration time is from 25 to 55 minutes. The instrument discriminates well between adult defendants the court has judged to be incompetent and those whom competence was never an issue (Hoge et al., 1997), and it possesses construct validity in that it shows the expected patterns of relationships with cognitive ability, psychopathology, and judgments

---

BOX 9.4
The MacArthur Competence Assessment Tool-Criminal Adjudication

The MacArthur instrument uses hypothetical situations and asks the defendant questions about them. For example:

Two men, Fred and Reggie, are playing pool at a bar and get into a fight. Fred hits Reggie with a pool stick. Reggie falls and hits his head on the floor so hard that he nearly dies. (quoted by Melton, Petrila, Poythress, and Slobogin, 1997, p. 146)

Defendants are asked a number of specific questions; for example, to measure understanding, the subject is told the following:

Fred may plead not guilty and go to trial, or Fred may plead guilty. Now, if Fred pleads guilty to

attempted murder, he would give up some legal rights and protections. What are they? (quoted by Melton et al., 1997, p. 146)

To measure the defendant's ability to identify relevant information, the defendant is asked to decide which of the following is relevant:

A. At the bar, there was a country and western band playing in the room next to the pool room.

B. Fred himself called the ambulance because he could see that Reggie was hurt very badly.

Thus the MacArthur instrument strives to provide an objective assessment of competency.

by clinicians of the degree of impaired competency (Otto, Edens, Poythress, & Nicholson, 1998). Its results show strong agreement with those of the FIT-R (Zapf, 1998).

The MacCAT-CA clearly reflects a "new generation" of instruments. Melton, Petrila, Poythress, and Slobogin (1997) were quite positive about its promise:

> It taps legal domains related to both the general capacity to assist counsel and competence for discrete legal decisions, simultaneously examining multiple competence-related abilities such as understanding, reasoning, and appreciation, both before and after competency instruction. It retains the relative efficiency of existing measures, yet it offers standardized administration and, for most of its submeasures, objective, criterion-based scoring that should minimize the subjectivity that plagues existing comprehensive measures. (pp. 149–150)

Much work needs to be done by forensic psychologists to improve the process in judging competency to stand trial. Research indicates that many lawyers do not follow through when they have fears about their clients' passivity and failure to understand (Hoge, Bonnie, Poythress, & Monahan, 1992; Poythress, Bonnie, Hoge, Monahan, & Oberlander, 1994). We grant that lawyers often face a dilemma; if they raise the question of their client's competency, they may sacrifice their client's trust (Gould, 1995).

RISK ASSESSMENT

Persons are committed to psychiatric hospitals because they are judged to be in danger of harming themselves or others. Sexual offenders are sentenced to a period in a correctional institution but eventually come before a parole board or release review board. Can forensic psychologists predict which individuals within these groups will engage in violence against others or predict which will attempt suicide?

Predicting Suicide

Answers to such questions have been put within the context of the accuracy of clinical prediction. The term **clinical prediction** usually refers to the process by which the psychologist reviews all the information about an individual and, combining this information in an intuitive—or at least, an unspecified—way, then makes a prediction about the individual's actions or outcome, such as, "If released, this person will become violent toward others." Traditionally, such clinical predictions have not fared well when compared with what are called **actuarial predictions**, or those that combine information based on pre-specified, empirically established decision rules (Dawes, 1994; Grove & Meehl, 1996; Meehl, 1954). One cause of the difference in accuracy, according to critics of clinical prediction, is that clinicians fail to consider **base rates** fully; for example, they may predict that a higher percentage of depressed patients will commit suicide than the actual rate in the population, which is very low.

For example, Pokorny (1983) studied the progress of 4800 persons who were psychiatric inpatients in U.S. Veterans Administration hospitals. During a five-year period, 67 of the 4800 persons committed suicide, a base rate of 1.4 percent. Given this base rate, the predictive task for the clinician would be a nearly impossible one: Which one out of every one hundred patients you see is most likely to commit suicide? A review of the literature (Garb, 1998) has concluded that predictions of suicide generally have not been valid; even predictions of suicide risk seem to have no validity (Janofsky, Spears, & Neubauer, 1988). But the statistical prediction of suicidal behaviour has also been unsuccessful, because of the infrequency of the behaviour.

Predicting Danger to Others

Is there a relationship between mental disorder and a tendency to be violent toward others? Certainly the public believes there is. Psychologists have been more skeptical, although prominent psychologists (see, for example,

Monahan, 1992) now believe that a consistent but small relationship may be present.

If such a relationship exists, can forensic psychologists specify which persons are at risk of harming others? Monahan (1992) has concluded that only people who are experiencing psychotic symptoms are at an increased risk of violence; he wrote: "Being a former patient in a mental hospital—that is, having experienced psychotic symptoms *in the past*—bears no direct relationship to violence" (1992, p. 519, italics in original).

Second, the vast majority of persons who have mental disorders to a significant degree are not violent. With a low probability that any one individual in a population will commit a violent act against another, it becomes very difficult to assess risk, because of the base rate problem described above. In fact, the validity of such assessments has been described by reviewers as "modest." One recent review concluded that the validity of these assessments was only slightly above chance (Steadman et al., 1996). Another (Garb, 1998) concluded that clinical psychologists make "moderately valid" short-term and long-term predictions of violence; a third review (Mossman, 1994) asserted that the accuracy rates of psychologists' predictions remain below those using statistical prediction.

Rejuvenated interest in risk assessment, spurred by the MacArthur Foundation's financing of a massive study, has allowed **dangerousness** to be divided into component parts (Heilbrun & Heilbrun, 1995), specifically, **risk factors** (or the variables used to predict violence), **harm** (the amount and type of violence being predicted), and **risk level** (or the probability that harm will occur). Further, better methodology in more recent studies has increased the rate of accuracy. For example, older research studies often used only limited resources for assessing violence (e.g., only arrest records), while more recent research relies also on self-reports and other outcome variables. The increased use of actuarial methods has also improved the accuracy of predictions (Monahan & Steadman, 1994). An example of contemporary risk assessment reflecting this approach is the pro-

gram of work by Ontario researchers Vernon Quinsey, Grant Harris, Marnie Rice, and their colleagues (Quinsey, Harris, Rice, & Cormier, 1998; Rice & Harris, 1995). For example, Harris, Rice, and Quinsey (1993) used 12 variables coded from institutional files of 618 men at a maximum-security forensic hospital in Canada. These variables included scores on the Hare Psychopathy Checklist (Hare, 1991), separation from parents before the age of 16, never having been married, early reports of maladjustment, presence of alcohol abuse, injuries to victims, and DSM classifications. The criterion for subsequent violence was any new criminal charge for a violent offence or return to the institution for such acts, with the typical follow-up period being seven years. The actuarial combination of predictor variables led to a correlation of .46 with violent recidivism. The use of actuarial procedures is improving prediction, but current estimates are that predictions may still be inaccurate as much as 40 percent to 50 percent of the time (Slobogin, 1996).

Psychopathy

As we first described in Chapter 1, psychopaths are manipulative, callous, remorseless, impulsive, irresponsible individuals (e.g., Hare, 1996, 1998), as defined by the well-validated Psychopathy Checklist-Revised (PCL-R; Hare, 1991, 2003). So defined, psychopathy is one of the best predictors of future violence, and must be a consideration when a psychologist is conducting a risk assessment. As reviewed by Porter and Woodworth (2004), research has established a strong link between psychopathic traits and future aggressive behaviour in adult offenders, antisocial children and adolescents, and civil psychiatric patients. Some findings were as follows:

■ *Adult offenders.* Numerous studies have demonstrated that the presence of psychopathy is associated with violent behaviour in adults. In one of the first studies of this relationship, Hare and Jutai (1983) found that adult psychopaths had been charged with violent crimes about twice as often as nonpsychopaths. And virtually all of them had committed at least one violent crime compared to about half of the nonpsychopaths. Within a large sample of Canadian offenders, Porter, Birt, and Boer (2001) found that psychopaths had been convicted of an average of 7.32 violent crimes, compared to 4.52 violent crimes for other offenders. Knowledge of the psychopathy–violence link greatly aids in the prediction of future violent behaviour in adult offenders (e.g., Harris, Rice, & Quinsey, 1993; Hemphill, Hare, & Wong, 1998; Rice & Harris, 1997; Salekin, Rogers, & Sewell, 1996). For example, Serin and Amos (1995) found that psychopaths were about five times more likely than nonpsychopaths to engage in violent recidivism within five years of their release. Recent meta-analyses show that PCL–R scores show an overall correlation of $r = .27$ to .37 in predicting violence (e.g., Hemphill, Templeman, Wong, & Hare, 1998; Salekin et al., 1996).

- *Young people with conduct problems.* Porter and Woodworth (2004) note that growing evidence suggests that psychopathy is related to aggression much earlier in life. It appears that precursors to psychopathy emerge in early childhood in the form of "callous/unemotional" traits (e.g., Frick, Bodin, & Barry, 2000; Frick & Ellis, 1999; Lynam, 2002; Porter, 1996), which seem to map onto adult psychopathy. These features can signal a pattern of persistent antisocial and violent behaviour (e.g., Dodge, 1991; Frick, 1998; Frick, O'Brien, Wooton, & McBurnett, 1994; Lynam, 2002; Waschbusch, Porter et al., 2004). Additionally, during adolescence, psychopathic traits are associated with convictions for violent offences (e.g., Campbell, Porter, & Santor, 2004; Forth & Mailloux, 2000), a high level of institutional aggression (Edens, Poythress, & Lilienfeld, 1999; Murdock, Hicks, Rogers, & Cashel, 2000; Rogers, Johansen, Chang, & Salekin, 1997), and a high level of violent reoffending (Brandt, Kennedy, Patrick, Curtain, 1997; Gretton, et al., 2001).

- *Psychiatric patients.* Very few civil psychiatric patients are psychopathic, compared to the proportion within the criminal offender population (e.g., Douglas, Ogloff, Nicholls, & Grant, 1999). Yet, psychopathy can still help predict future violence in this population. In a study of 1136 psychiatric patients, Skeem and Mulvey (2001) found that psychopathy scores predicted future serious violence, despite a psychopathy base rate of only 8 percent. During a one-year follow-up, 50 percent of psychopaths and 22 percent of nonpsychopaths had committed violence. In addition, there was a 73 percent chance that a patient who became violent had scored higher on psychopathy than one who did not become violent (see also Douglas et al., 1999).

MALINGERING

A special problem in assessing the mental state of individuals is to determine whether their statements are truthful or are the result of **malingering**. In the *Diagnostic and Statistical Manual of Mental Disorders, 4th edition* (or DSM-IV) (American Psychiatric Association, 1994), malingering is defined as the conscious fabrication or gross exaggeration of physical and/or psychological symptoms, done in order to achieve external goals such as avoiding prison or receiving monetary compensation.

Richard Rogers and his colleagues (Rogers, 1990; Rogers, Sewell, & Goldstein, 1994) have distinguished three types of malingerers:

1. The pathogenic: Persons who are motivated by underlying pathology. These people are genuinely disturbed, and Rogers and his associates assume that "the voluntary production of bogus symptoms will eventually erode and be replaced by a genuine disorder" (Rogers, Sewell, & Goldstein, 1994, pp. 543–544).
2. The criminological: Persons with an antisocial or oppositional motivation; they may

feign mental disorders in order to obtain outcomes they do not deserve.

3. The adaptational: The type of person who makes "a constructive attempt, at least from the feigner's perspective, to succeed in highly adversarial circumstances" (Rogers, Sewell, & Goldstein, 1994, p. 544).

Individuals may be tempted to fake mental illness at several points in the criminal justice process, including determining competency to stand trial, pleading NCRMD, and attempting to influence the sentence (Iverson, Franzen, & Hammond, 1993). But detection of malingering is also central to a variety of other forensic psychological tasks. Claims of injuries and disabilities, such as lower back pain, head injury, or post-traumatic stress disorder, may require a check for malingering. Claims of amnesia or other kinds of memory impairment have increasingly involved the assessment by neuropsychologists of malingering (Arnett, Hammeke, & Schwartz, 1993; Bernard & Fowler, 1990; Lee, Loring, & Martin, 1992; Wiggins & Brandt, 1988).

There are indications that psychologists are poor at detecting malingering during forensic evaluations. Silverton, Gruber, and Bindman (1993) cite the classic study done by David Rosenhan (1973) as an example. Rosenhan and seven other persons free of mental abnormalities gained admission to various mental hospitals by complaining that they heard voices repeating the word "one." No other complaints were reported. Seven of the eight were diagnosed as schizophrenic, the other as manic-depressive. Immediately after being admitted, the pseudo-patients stopped saying they heard voices. None of the pseudo-patients were detected as malingerers by the hospital staff; in fact, the only persons who sometimes recognized the pseudo-patients as normal were the other patients.

As a result of dissatisfaction with traditional procedures, psychologists have begun to use scales and other assessment procedures to try to effectively detect malingering. Two strategies

have been used: applying existing measures and developing new ones.

As a traditional measure, the Minnesota Multiphasic Personality Inventory (MMPI) has an L scale of 15 items measuring social desirability, but this is a rather unsophisticated measure of malingering. Further, the person who "fakes" on these items is attempting to communicate an unduly *favourable* impression, whereas the malingering of concern to the courts is often of the opposite type. The original MMPI also included an F scale, designed to assess inconsistent or deviant answering. On the newer MMPI-2, the Fb scale seeks to detect malingering or a "fake bad" response style. This procedure seems promising in differentiating between persons instructed to malinger and actual psychiatric patients (Iverson, Franzen, & Hammond, 1993), but research needs to move beyond such analogue designs.

A second approach is to construct new instruments; a number of these have been developed in the last 20 years. Some, including the Malingering Probability Scale, by Silverton and Gruber (1998), are available only through commercial publishers.

Frequently used is the Structured Interview of Reported Symptoms, or SIRS (Rogers, 1988), a 16-page structured interview covering signs of malingering. Although this procedure has produced some encouraging results (Rogers, Gillis, Bagby, & Monteiro, 1991), it requires an extended administration time and the need for a trained examiner (Smith & Burger, 1993).

A self-report measure, the M test (Beaber, Marston, Michelli, & Mills, 1985) is a 33-item inventory composed of three separate scales: the Confusion Scale, the Schizophrenia Scale, and the Malingering Scale. The last of these is composed of 15 items tapping unusual or rare symptoms that would be expected to be endorsed only by malingerers (e.g., atypical hallucinations and delusions or extremely severe symptoms).

Another type of assessment device is the Malingering Scale (MS) (Schretlen, 1986). It is lengthy (150 items) and requires judgment calls on the part of the test administrator (Smith & Burger,

1993). A replication is needed to confirm the high detection rates reported in the initial study.

SUMMARY

One of the most important tasks of the forensic psychologist is to aid the court in its determination of the mental state of individuals who come before the court; this chapter reviews four relevant concepts: the legal term *criminal responsibility*, competency, risk assessment, and malingering.

Although criminal responsibility is a legal concept and not a psychiatric one, forensic psychologists and psychiatrists may be called on to make judgments related to the NCRMD (or insanity) defence. The difficulty in achieving consistent diagnoses is illustrated by the trial of Jeffrey Dahmer, in which seven psychiatrists and psychologists gave conflicting judgments about whether Dahmer's state of mind met the definition of insanity.

A related activity of the forensic psychologist is assessing the fitness or competency of those who come before the court. In general, *competency* or *fitness* refers to the person's ability to understand the nature and purpose of court proceedings. Competency is relevant to the decision to stand trial and the decision whether to plead guilty. Several tools are available for assessing competency, including the Fitness Interview Test-Revised and the recent MacArthur assessment procedure.

Predictions of dangerousness have long been a challenge to forensic psychologists. Predictions of suicide are not always accurate, partially because of the base-rate problem—that is, the small percentage of mentally ill or depressed persons who actually commit suicide. The prediction of dangerousness to others, now called risk assessment, has had a rejuvenated research interest; here, predictions of individuals' behaviour are often closer to accuracy than in suicide prediction, but such forensic estimates are far from perfect. One thing, however, is clear—psychopathy should be a critical consideration in evaluating an offender's or patient's risk for future violence.

When assessing the mental state of persons appearing before the court, the possibility of malingering is always a concern. Several instruments are available for the assessment of malingering.

KEY TERMS

actuarial prediction, p. 207
actus reus, p. 192
ALI standard, p. 193
automatism, p. 195
base rate, p. 207
clinical prediction, p. 207
cognitive test of insanity, p. 192
competency, p. 203
dangerousness, p. 208
guilt, p. 192
harm, p. 208
irresistible impulse exception, p. 193
malingering, p. 209
McNaughton Rules, p. 192
mens rea, p. 192
necrophilia, p. 199
not criminally responsible by reason of a
    mental disorder (NCRMD), p. 191
paraphilia, p. 199
risk factors, p. 208
risk level, p. 208
ultimate-issue testimony, p. 201
volitional aspect of insanity, p. 193

SUGGESTED READINGS

Borum, R., & Fulero, S. M. (1999). Empirical research on the insanity defence and attempted reforms: Evidence toward informed policy. *Law and Human Behavior, 23*, 117–135.

This very useful article examines many of the myths and current misconceptions about the use of the insanity defence. Various reforms, including the authors' proposal of carefully developed, intensively monitored release programs for defendants found NGRI, are described and evaluated.

Nicholson, R. (1999). Forensic assessment. In R. Roesch, S. D. Hart, & J. R. P. Ogloff (Eds.), *Psychology and law: The state of the discipline* (pp. 121–173). New York: Kluwer Academic/Plenum Publishers.

Nicholson presents an up-to-date, detailed evaluation of instruments for assessing competency, criminal responsibility, and child custody.

Rosenberg, C. E. (1968). *The trial of the assassin Guiteau: Psychiatry and the law in the Gilded Age*. Chicago: University of Chicago Press.

The trial of the assassin of U.S. President Garfield in 1881 included the use of 24 expert witnesses who debated the nature of insanity. It reminds us that concerns over a self-defeating "battle of the experts" are not just a modern phenomenon.

Sales, B. D., & Shuman, D. W. (Eds.). (1996). *Law, mental health, and mental disorder*. Pacific Grove, CA: Brooks/Cole.

This collection of contributed reviews by legal scholars includes several of relevance to this chapter:

the article on the insanity defence by Michael L. Perlin, on competency by Bruce J. Winick, on dangerousness by Christopher Slobogin, and on expert witnesses by Maureen O'Connor, Bruce D. Sales, and Daniel W. Shuman.

Swartz, M. (1997, November 17). Family secret. *New Yorker*, pp. 90–107.

Swartz has crafted a readable description of the life of convicted killer John Salvi, relevant to the question: What is the proper disposition of a lawbreaker who has the mental state that Salvi had?

Woychuk, D. (1996). *Attorney for the damned: A lawyer's life with the criminally insane*. New York: Free Press.

This first-person account by a lawyer who represented a variety of patients at a mental hospital for the dangerously mentally ill in New York City includes useful examples of competency evaluations, assessments of risk, and the temptation to form a false conclusion.

Battered Woman Syndrome and Domestic Violence

> By continuing to adhere to the faulty reasoning inherent within syndrome evidence, courts have managed to avoid answering the difficult and disturbing question that lies within all domestic homicide cases: is the defendant's killing of an abusive partner after continuous, brutal physical assaults a justifiable homicide?
> —DAVID FAIGMAN AND AMY WRIGHT (1997, P. 70)

THE NATURE OF DOMESTIC VIOLENCE

Domestic violence can take many forms, including adolescent-to-parent, sibling-to-sibling, or spouse-to-spouse (Dutton & McGregor, 1992). The focus of this chapter is on husband-to-wife assault, with particular emphasis on the woman's reactions to the violence. Some of the women who are victims of prolonged domestic assault respond by killing their abusers, and psychologists differ as to how (and whether) they should be involved in the defence of battered women who have done so.

An example of abuse in a relationship that led to the woman's killing of her abuser is presented in Box 10.1. This case is not necessarily typical in some ways, but it reflects a common theme: continuing abuse by the more powerful against the less powerful individual, including a death threat. In this example, it led to the less powerful individual killing the abuser. It is also typical in that if the woman who is the victim of the battering does resort to killing her batterer, she is usually found guilty of at least manslaughter, if not murder.

What Characterizes an Abuser?

Who are the men who physically abuse their spouses? Not all men who assault their companions are psychologically similar, just as they all do not display the same patterns of violence (Dutton, 1995b). Using a sample of 182 wife assaulters referred for treatment because of their severe violence, Saunders (1992) administered a number of personality, behaviour, and attitude measures and then completed a statistical analysis to determine whether distinct subgroups of batterers existed. This procedure led to three classifications:

1. The generally violent men, who were described as antisocial and impulsive; Donald Dutton (1995a) at the University of British Columbia calls them **psychopathic abusers**. As implied by the label, they were assaultive both inside and outside the home. They used alcohol frequently.
2. The overcontrolled men, who could not express feelings, including anger, and whose reaction to conflict was to suddenly explode.
3. The emotionally volatile men, who were characterized as being angry, jealous, or depressed. They were only violent toward

---

BOX 10.1
An Example of Abuse in a Relationship and Its Aftermath

The case of Jane Stafford (later Jane Whynot) in Nova Scotia was detailed in the 1986 book by Brian Vallee and the 1993 film *Life with Billy*, produced by Salter Street Films in Halifax. It stands as one of the most disturbing cases of domestic violence and its aftermath in recent Canadian history.

Jane's husband, Billy Stafford, terrorized her and her son throughout their marriage, inflicting severe beatings upon them, and constantly humiliating and degrading her. For example, on at least one occasion, he forced her into sexual relations with the family dog. Billy threatened to kill all of the members of her family, one by one, if she tried to leave him (in fact, he was widely suspected of having murdered a co-worker by throwing

him from a boat). When Jane spoke with police officers, they belittled the danger she was in and considered her abuse to be a "family matter." On the night of his death, Billy had made threats about killing Jane's son. After Billy passed out in his pickup truck from drinking, Jane obtained one of his many shotguns and killed him by shooting him in the head as he slept.

Although she pled self-defence and was acquitted at her trial (*R. v. Whynot*, 1983), the Crown appealed, arguing that the self-defence plea should not have been considered since Jane was not being assaulted and was in no immediate danger before she killed him. Jane ultimately pled guilty to manslaughter and served six months in prison. Several years later she committed suicide.

their wives and showed a build-up of tension leading to battering. Dutton's (1995a) analysis of batterers focused on this group. He described them as Jekyll-and-Hyde types, men whose abusive personality stemmed from a childhood characterized by an ambivalent attachment to the mother, experiencing abuse in the home, and being shamed by the father.

Work is under way that seeks to predict violence in men who are at risk. Randall Kropp, Stephen Hart, Christopher Webster, and Derek Eaves—a collaborative team of academic and government researchers in British Columbia—have developed the Spousal Assault Risk Assessment (SARA, 1994, 1995, 1998) instrument. The SARA is a 20-item set of empirically based risk factors for use in the assessment of risk for spousal assault. The SARA seeks to determine which assaulters are likely to commit violent acts in the future (Kropp & Hart, 1997; Kropp, Hart, Webster, & Eaves, 1998). Kropp and Hart (2000) examined the usefulness of the SARA in assessing risk for violence in 2681 male offenders. The SARA ratings were significantly different among offenders with and without a history of spousal violence in one subsample, and between reoffending and non-reoffending spousal assaulters in another. Although more research is needed, the SARA is a promising tool with some research validation and is becoming widely used in practice.

Roles for the Forensic Psychologist

One goal of this chapter is to examine the roles of forensic psychologists in cases in which a person who has killed his or her spouse claims a defence of having persistently been abused and finally reacted by killing the antagonist. In both the field of psychology and the legal system, this has been called the **battered woman defence**. No one denies that men in relationships have been physically abused by their partners, although experts differ as to the extent to which wives are the abusers in a battering or physically abusive relationship.

Marilyn Kwong, Kim Bartholomew, and Donald Dutton—a group of researchers at Simon Fraser University and the University of British Columbia—examined gender differences in patterns of relationship violence in a representative sample of 356 men and 351 women from Alberta. The respondents reported on whether they had been the victim or perpetrator of violent acts in the year before the survey. The results indicated that men and women, respectively, reported similar rates of husband-to-wife violence (12.9 percent and 9.6 percent) and wife-to-husband violence (12.3 percent and 12.5 percent). However, there were some gender differences. On average, men reported that they and their female partners were equally likely to engage in violent acts and to start them. Women, however, reported lower levels of victimization than perpetration of violence, and they reported less male-only and male-initiated violence than did men. The majority of respondents in violent relationships reported a pattern of violence that was bi-directional or "went both ways." However, women reported more negative consequences when they experienced violence.

These findings corroborate a growing body of research showing that men perpetrate more *severe* violence against their wives than vice versa. For example, in one large-scale study, of the participants who reported being the victim of spousal violence, 3 percent of the women, and only .4 percent of the men, required medical care for resulting injuries (Stets & Straus, 1990). In Canada in 2002, females accounted for 85 percent of all victims of spousal assaults reported to police. Further, between 1993 and 2002, women were far more at risk than men of being killed by their spouse (eight homicides per million couples versus two homicides per million couples, respectively) (Canadian Centre for Justice Statistics, 2004). Thus, although both men and women use violence in relationships, the consequences often are much more severe for women. As the next section indicates, women in Canada are battering victims with high frequency and severity, leading to this chapter's emphasis on battered women.

When a woman is charged with the murder of her spouse or partner, the forensic psychologist can play several roles—an evaluator of myths about family violence, an assessor of battering in the particular case, an expert witness at the trial, or a consultant at the sentencing hearing. In all these roles the psychologist must navigate between being a skeptical scientist and a zealous advocate. Some psychologists have applied the concept of a *syndrome* to define the state of a battered woman, whereas others have questioned the applicability and the validity of this concept. Since the publication of Lenore Walker's widely read book *The Battered Woman*, in 1979, the use of a syndrome as an aid in the defence of women who have killed their partners has become more commonplace. This development has been both good and bad; among the benefits are that the lay public has become more aware of the pervasive nature of domestic violence throughout North America. Also, the writings and testimony of Walker and other psychologists have made judges and legal scholars more aware of the limitations of traditional legal definitions of self-defence, which assume equal strength and power between adversaries (Faigman & Wright, 1997). But the use of a syndrome to describe women who kill their batterers has been challenged on two grounds: the image of women it reflects and the empirical basis for its central concept. This chapter considers these issues.

THE EXTENT OF DOMESTIC VIOLENCE

How extensive is the problem of domestic violence in Canada and elsewhere? Advocates offer alarming statistics, although some of their conclusions about incidence rates are generalized from small and unrepresentative samples.

Nonetheless, it is clear that domestic violence is a pressing social issue.

Reports of Incidence Rates

Among evidence of the severity of the problem are the following:

1. A 1993 telephone survey of 12 300 Canadian women indicated that 29 percent of respondents who had ever married reported that they had been subjected to violence (i.e., they had been pushed, grabbed, shoved, slapped, sexually assaulted, hit with an object, or had a gun or knife used against them) by their partner (Statistics Canada, 1998).
2. Fifty-nine percent of women over the age of 16 in British Columbia report having experienced at least one incident of physical or sexual violence by a partner. This is the highest rate in the country (B.C. Ministry of Women's Equality, 2001). More than 14 000 women and their children were admitted to women's shelters in B.C. between April 1, 1999 and March 31, 2000 (Statistics Canada, 2001a).
3. Serious, repetitive violence such as battering and the use of weapons occurs in a significant minority of marriages (5.2 percent, Dutton, 1998).
4. In Canada, 21 percent of women abused by a marital partner were assaulted during pregnancy; 40 percent of these women stated that the abuse began during their pregnancy (Statistics Canada, 1999).
5. Spousal violence contributes to one-fourth of all suicide attempts by women (Jones, 1994a).
6. Women have a heightened risk of homicide after marital separation. Between 1991 and 1999, separated Canadian women were killed by former partners at a rate of 39 per million couples (Statistics Canada, 2001b).

These statistics sometimes reflect self-reports by victims, whereas others use official crime reports. Some of the conclusions are based on small and unrepresentative samples. Others reflect conclusions that when the records fail to state the cause of a facial injury, the case should be classified as "probable" domestic violence. The extent of abuse against spouses is serious enough without its being exaggerated: In 1998, 57 out of 70 adults who were killed by a spouse (or an ex-spouse) in Canada were women. Forty-six of these women victims were killed by a current spouse and 11 by a former spouse (Fedorowycz, 1999).

Lenore Walker (1992, p. 332) has estimated that between a third and half of all women will be abused at some point in their lives. However, other estimates are somewhat lower, with some form of physical aggression occurring in one-quarter to one-third of all couples (Straus & Gelles, 1988). The latter conclusion was based on a systematic survey, and it is important because Straus and Gelles made a distinction between types of violence. In the 16 percent of families that do experience violence, it usually takes the form of slapping, shoving, and grabbing. In 3 percent to 4 percent of all families the dangerous violence exists—kicking, punching, and use of a weapon (Brott, 1994).

The Official Response

Despite these disturbing statistics, many myths about battered women still abound and many elements of society have been slow to respond. This is reflected in a continuing lack of support for people who have suffered abuse. For example, in a research "snapshot" taken on April 17, 2000, 89 Canadian shelters had to turn away 476 people (254 women and 222 children). The majority (71 percent) of these shelters turned women and children away because their facility was full (Locke & Code, 2001). Further, the mass media sometimes glosses over or minimizes the violence. In fact, society displays dangerous signs of victim blaming:

1. Doctors treat battered women but often fail to ask questions about what happened (Jones, 1994b; Sugg, 1992, cited in M. A. Dutton, 1993).
2. Police traditionally have rarely arrested abusers (Sherman & Berk, 1984).
3. Violent husbands and boyfriends often ignore orders of protection taken out against them.
4. When they represent battered women on trial, lawyers sometimes behave in condescending ways to their own clients.
5. Judges are sometimes insensitive. For example, in one case, the presiding judge, discussing the matter of a severely battered woman who appeared before him on narcotics charges, proposed that "she could have left her husband" (quoted by Aron, 1993, p. 14). Even more extreme, judges sometimes sympathize with the man and blame the woman for a man's violent overreaction. In Maryland, a local judge sentenced Kenneth Peacock to a mere 18 months in prison (and recommended a work-release option) for killing his wife, Sandra, after he discovered her in bed, naked, with another man (Lewin, 1994). The media have described his act as occurring "in the heat of passion" but Peacock spent two hours drinking and arguing with his wife before he picked up his deer rifle and shot her in the head. The judge, Robert Cahill, was quoted as justifying the light punishment by saying, "I seriously wonder how many men married five, four years would have the strength to walk away without inflicting some corporal punishment" (quoted by Associated Press, 1994a, p. C19).
6. Family therapists are often not responsive. Mary Ann Dutton (1993) reported one study in which family therapists were given a written description of an actual case involving domestic violence, and 40 percent failed to address the issue at all (99 percent of the sample were psychologists; 71 percent were male). The description noted that the man had repeatedly been physically violent with both his wife and their children, and on the day before, he had grabbed her and

thrown her on the floor in a violent manner and then had struck her. Walker (1984b, p. 125) concluded that therapists are "inadequately trained and poorly informed" when it comes to the special needs of the battered woman.

Are there any grounds for optimism? In the Canadian context, there are reasons for optimism in the response against domestic violence. In 1983, Solicitor General Robert Kaplan urged police chiefs across Canada to implement aggressive charging policies in spousal assault cases. Thus, domestic violence, which before that year had been considered a social issue, now was considered a serious crime. Since then, the Canadian legal system has introduced several pieces of legislation that validate the seriousness of spousal assault (described in the section "Domestic Violence Law in Canada" on page 226). For example, Bill C-41 amended the Criminal Code of Canada to require the courts to consider the abuse of a spouse or a child to be an aggravating factor (making the crime more serious) for sentencing purposes. Additionally, spouses and children can now seek monetary restitution from the parent offender for expenses incurred because they had to leave home to avoid being harmed. Similarly, in the United States, the Violence Against Women Act, adopted by the Congress in 1994, allows victims of rape and domestic violence to sue their attackers in federal court for compensatory and punitive damages.

MYTHS ABOUT THE BATTERED WOMAN

Despite some grounds for optimism, experts continue to emphasize the prevalence of invidious **myths about the battered woman**. Diane Follingstad (1994b, p. 15) listed the following false assumptions:

1. Battered women are masochists.
2. They provoke the assaults inflicted on them.

3. They get the treatment they deserve.
4. They are free to leave these violent relationships at any time they want to.
5. The physical abuse of women is not at all common.
6. Men who are personable and nonviolent in their dealings with outsiders must be the same in their dealings with their intimates.
7. Middle-class and upper-class men don't batter, and middle-class and upper-class women don't get beaten.
8. Battering is a lower-class, ethnic-minority phenomenon, and such women don't mind because it is part of their culture.
9. "Good" battered women are passive and never try to defend themselves.

Walker (1979) has provided an even more extensive list, summarized in Box 10.2. How widely are these ideas held by the public? Are jurors' beliefs and verdicts influenced by such myths?

Walker concluded that such myths are extensively held by the public, but other psychologists (cf. Acker & Toch, 1985) have questioned this assumption. For example, Acker and Toch then argued that Walker may well have been wrong with regard to the prevalence of these myths about battered women:

Absent evidence to the contrary, the most reasonable and charitable assumption is that the public (and members of juries) may have more awareness, more open-mindedness and less prejudice than the court (or Walker) implies. (p. 140)

Empirical Evaluation of the Myths

Several studies sought to determine the pervasiveness of these myths. Relying on responses to a hypothetical scenario that they developed, Ewing and his colleagues (Ewing & Aubrey, 1987; Ewing, Aubrey, & Jamison, 1986) found that a clear majority of their adult-age subjects subscribed to some of the myths and about a third of the subjects subscribed to most of them.

BOX 10.2
Some Myths about the Battered Woman

In introducing her study of battered women, Walker (1979) described 21 myths about these women, their batterers, and the relationship among them.

Myth No. 1:	The battered woman syndrome affects only a small percentage of the population.
Myth No. 2:	Battered women are masochistic. The prevailing belief has always been that only women who "liked it and deserved it" were beaten … (p. 20).
Myth No. 3:	Battered women are crazy. This myth is related to the masochism myth in that it places the blame for the battering on the woman's negative personality characteristics (p. 21).
Myth No. 4:	Middle-class women do not get battered as frequently or as violently as do poorer women.
Myth No. 5:	Minority-group women are battered more frequently.
Myth No. 6:	Religious beliefs will prevent battering.
Myth No. 7:	Battered women are uneducated and have few job skills.
Myth No. 8:	Batterers are violent in all their relationships.
Myth No. 9:	Batterers are unsuccessful and lack resources to cope with the world.
Myth No. 10:	Drinking causes battering behaviour.
Myth No. 11:	Batterers are psychopathic personalities.
Myth No. 12:	Police can protect the battered woman.
Myth No. 13:	The batterer is not a loving partner.
Myth No. 14:	A wife beater also beats his children.
Myth No. 15:	Once a battered woman, always a battered woman.
Myth No. 16:	Once a batterer, always a batterer.
Myth No. 17:	Long-standing battering relationships can change for the better.
Myth No. 18:	Battered women deserve to get beaten. The myth that battered women provoke their beatings by pushing their men beyond the breaking point is a popular one … (p. 29).
Myth No. 19:	Battered women can always leave home … (p. 29).
Myth No. 20:	Batterers will cease their violence "when we get married."
Myth No. 21:	Children need their father even if he is violent—or, "I'm only staying for the sake of the children."

(Adapted from Walker, 1979, pp. 19–30.)

(See Box 10.3 for elaboration.) These authors concluded that their results supported recommendations that expert testimony be admitted at trial because many of the facts were "beyond the ken" of respondents.

Another study (Greene, Raitz, & Lindblad, 1989) produced indications that not everyone subscribed to these myths. This study also exposed subjects, acting as mock jurors, to scenarios about spousal violence. Dutton and McGregor (1992) commented on this study's results:

Jurors seemed to understand that once violence was used in a relationship the potential for its use again constitutes an ever-present threat, and that women so threatened suffer anxiety and depression, feel helpless, believe their spouses might kill them, and believe that leaving will result in further harm. (p. 334)

In summary, some people hold such myths but perhaps not to the degree that Walker assumed. But we would expect that as publicity about family violence has increased, so too has a more accurate understanding of the phenomenon by the public.

Why These Myths?

Two trends in the criminal justice system may contribute to the acceptance of these myths by some persons. Jones (1994b) proposed that a deep

BOX 10.3
Ewing's Scenario and Results

THE SCENARIO

Robert and Francine were married in 1970. For the first eight years of their marriage, Robert worked as a steelworker while Francine stayed home to raise their three children. In February 1978, Robert was laid off from his job. For the first time since their marriage, Francine was forced to go to work while her husband remained at home. As the months passed by, Francine noticed a gradual change in Robert. He became moody and argumentative. Hoping things would improve, Francine continued working and hoped that Robert would get a lucky break.

In March of 1979, Francine was promoted to a managerial position. That evening, after work, she celebrated with a few friends. When she arrived home, she found Robert waiting for her. Before she had a chance to announce the good news, Robert accused her of cheating and threw her to the floor. As she lay there stunned and ashamed, Robert became tearful and apologetic and swore that he would never hurt Francine again. Francine forgave Robert.

Tables 10.1 and 10.2 present the results of Ewing's survey.

TABLE 10.1 Percentage of Participants Who Agreed with Each Statement

Statement	Percent of Participants Who Agreed
1. Robert and Francine have serious marital problems.	67.9
2. Robert's battering of Francine is an isolated event unlikely to be repeated.	31.3
3. Francine probably bears at least some responsibility for Robert's assaultive behaviour.	38.3
4. If Francine is really afraid for her future safety, she could simply leave Robert.	63.7
5. If Francine remains with Robert and continues to be beaten, she is probably at least somewhat masochistic.	41.8
6. If Francine remains with Robert and continues to be battered, she is probably an emotionally disturbed woman.	44.9
7. Francine could stay with Robert and probably prevent further battering by seeking counselling.	83.5
8. Francine could stay with Robert and probably prevent further battering by relying on the police and the courts to protect her.	16.4

TABLE 10.2 Percentage of Agreement by Gender

Statement	Percent of Participants Who Agreed	
	Males	Females
1. Couple has "serious marital problems."	62.0	73.8
2. Battering is an "isolated event."	39.8	26.6
3. Female victim "bears at least some responsibility."	46.7	29.9
4. Battered woman could "simply leave" her battering husband.	56.5	71.0
5. Battered woman who stays is "somewhat masochistic."	34.0	49.5
6. Battered woman who stays is "emotionally disturbed."	39.8	50.0
7. Woman can prevent battering by seeking counselling.	85.8	81.1
8. Woman can rely upon police to protect her.	17.6	15.1

(Adapted from Ewing & Aubrey, 1987, pp. 150–152.)

MYTHS ABOUT THE BATTERED WOMAN

uneasiness and even hostility exists toward victims. People have a desire to believe "I'm O.K., we're O.K.," and if some women have problems, it is because they are pathological doormats or obsessive delusional people crying "wolf."

Some would argue that the criminal justice system is far from gender neutral in its judgments (MacKinnon, 1987; Rafter & Stanko, 1982). Browne (1987) concluded that women receive harsher sentences for homicide than do male offenders. Recall the case of Kenneth Peacock, who killed his unfaithful wife and received an 18-month sentence. The same month, in the same state, Patricia Ann Hawkins was given a three-year sentence for killing her sleeping husband by setting a fire near him. The judge, a woman, was aware that the wife had been abused and threatened for years, and even the prosecuting lawyer would have accepted a one-year sentence (Jurgensen, 1994).

But these are single cases, and it is hard to evaluate the claim of gender disparity, because the circumstances surrounding the crimes are often different for women and men. For example, Jenkins and Davidson (1990) intensively analyzed the court records of ten battered women charged with the murder of their abusive partners between 1975 and 1988; all pleaded guilty or were found guilty at trial. Sentences ranged from five years' probation to life in prison, but half did get the latter sentence. We need data on the punishments given men charged with or convicted of killing their wives in the same period to make a comparison.

Several other samples of battered women charged with killing their partners are available. Walker, Thyfault, and Browne (1982) reported on the disposition of 28 of 50 cases they studied in which battered women had killed their batterers. A total of 15 of the 28 women went to trial; eight were convicted, and seven were acquitted. For the eight who were convicted, the sentences ranged from six months in jail to 25 years in prison. In most of the cases that did not go to trial, the woman pleaded guilty to reduced homicide charges; some of these women received pro

bation but others were sentenced to as much as eight years in prison. Charges against one woman were dropped.

Browne (1984) reported the disposition of 41 of the 42 women she studied; all these women had killed the man whom they alleged had been abusing them. A total of 33 had been charged with murder, six with attempted murder, and three with conspiracy to commit murder. Most were convicted (31 of 41, or 76 percent), nine were acquitted, and charges were dropped against the remaining one before she went to trial. Of the 31 convicted, 11 were placed on probation or given suspended sentences, while the remaining 20 were given prison sentences ranging from six months to 50 years.

Jones (1981) reviewed the disposition of 33 women who killed their batterers: eight were acquitted, three had their charges dropped, one was found not guilty by reason of insanity, and the other 21 were either convicted or pled guilty. Two of the latter received life sentences; the punishments for the others convicted ranged from five to 25 years.

The Correctional Service of Canada studied a larger number of women—181 Canadian women who had been convicted of a homicide offence. Of these women, 26 percent had killed their spouse (Hoffman, Lavigne, Dickie, & Women Offender Sector, 1998). The following is the breakdown of the sentence lengths of the spousal murderers: two to six years less a day, 22.1 percent; six to ten years less a day, 6.6 percent; ten to 20 years, 15.5 percent; life in prison 55.6 percent. The numbers were not dissimilar from those for homicide during a theft or child homicide. However, women convicted of spousal homicide were more likely to have received a conviction for first-degree murder than women who were convicted for "defence against a sexual assault" homicide. However, it was unclear how previous abuse from the victim had contributed to sentencing.

We cannot say from these figures whether women are treated more harshly than men. What is most striking is the variability, both in judgments of guilt and in the punishments given to those found guilty. More basic than severity may be a pervasive ideology about gender roles, which in some cases may lead to leniency or paternalism and in others to harsher dispositions of cases—"all reflecting an intrinsic gender inequality within the criminal justice system" (Jenkins & Davidson, 1990, p. 162).

BATTERED WOMAN SYNDROME

The most controversial aspect of the defence of battered women who kill their abusers is the use of the battered woman "syndrome." Though the claimed presence of this syndrome is not a legal defence in and of itself, it can be used as a justification for arguing, as a defence, either self-defence or being not criminally responsible.

What Is a Syndrome?

A **syndrome** is usually defined as a group of symptoms that occur together and characterize a disease. **Battered woman syndrome** (BWS) is defined as a woman's presumed reactions to a pattern of continual physical and psychological abuse inflicted on her by her mate (Walker, 1984b). The choice of the term *syndrome* assumes that the symptoms or responses are consistent from one woman to another. But are they?

Mary Ann Dutton (1993) noted that we need to recognize that battered women's psychological realities vary considerably from each other and, in fact, do not fit only one profile. In a study of abused women seeking help at a counselling program, five distinct profile types generated from the MMPI were identified, indicating different patterns of psychological functioning among them, including some profiles that were considered "normal" (Dutton-Douglas, et al., 1990). Confusion about just what battered woman syndrome means has resulted from testimony by expert witnesses that is not typically limited solely to the psychological reactions to domestic violence. Often the expert witness testifies about the nature of physical violence and offers explanations of puzzling behaviour by the victim and behaviour that may have been introduced by the prosecution to suggest that the battered woman is not the "typical" battered woman (e.g., prostitution, abuse of her children, her violent reactions). On other occasions, evidence might be offered after a trial to bring into question the accuracy of the expert testimony. For example, as we discussed in Chapter 2, expert evidence suggested that Karla Homolka had battered woman syndrome. However, this later was brought into question after videotapes of the rapes and murders of two girls showed her to be an enthusiastic participant.

Components of Battered Woman Syndrome

Despite the conclusions that victims may show different symptoms, some psychologists have proposed the existence of a common set of components to BWS. These include (Walker, 1984b):

1. **Learned helplessness**, or a response to having been exposed to painful stimuli over which one has no control and finding that no avenue readily exists for escape.
2. Lowered self-esteem or an acceptance of continued feedback from the abuser about one's worthlessness.
3. Impaired functioning, including an inability to engage in planful behaviour.
4. Loss of the assumption of invulnerability and safety. Previous beliefs that "things would turn out all right" or "this wouldn't happen to me" dissipate in the onslaught of abuse and violence.
5. Fear and terror, as reactions to the batterer, based on past experiences.
6. Anger/rage.
7. Diminished alternatives. Of 400 battered women interviewed by Walker (1993), 85 percent felt they could or would be killed at some point. Also, as a part of the diminished-

alternatives reaction, battered women focus their energies on survival within the relationship rather than exploring options outside (Blackman, 1986).

8. The **cycle of abuse** or cycle of violence. The Jekyll-and-Hyde nature of batterers has been proposed as a contribution to the battered woman syndrome. Men may be loving, nurturing, giving, and attentive to the woman's needs during courtship and perhaps early in the marriage. But then there is a **tension-building phase**—more criticism, verbal bickering, increased strain, and perhaps minor physical abuse. This is followed by the violent step in the cycle: an **acute battering incident**, in which the batterer explodes into an uncontrollable rage, leading to injuries to the woman.

When this dark side appears, the woman may be too involved with the man to break off the relationship. Also she may remember the good times and believe if she can find the right thing to do, he will revert to his earlier behaviour; thus, she often blames herself for his actions. As reflected in her list of myths (see Box 10.2 on page 219), Walker (1992) proposed that "Research has demonstrated that this is a **contrite phase** in which the batterer's use of promises and gifts increases the battered woman's hope that violence occurred for the last time." The batterer expresses regret and apologizes, perhaps promising never to lose control again. But eventually the cycle starts all over once more (Walker, 1984b).

According to the theory of the cycle of violence, the woman feels growing tension during phase one, develops a fear of death or serious bodily harm during phase two, and anticipating another attack, defends herself by retaliating during a lull in the violence (Walker, 1984b). Not all battering follows this cycle (M. A. Dutton, 1993); in fact, of the 400 women interviewed by Walker (1979), involving 1600 battering incidents, only two-thirds reflected this cycle.

9. Hypervigilance to cues of danger. Other components of the battered woman syndrome are less obvious; **hypervigilance** is one of the more important. As a result of being battered, women notice subtle things—things that others don't recognize as dangerous. The woman may notice her husband's words come faster, or she might claim that his eyes get darker. She may make a pre-emptive strike before the abuser has actually inflicted much damage.

10. High tolerance for **cognitive inconsistency** (Blackman, 1986). Battered women often express two ideas that appear to be logically inconsistent with each other. "For example, a battered woman might say, 'My husband only hit me when he was drunk,' but later describes an episode during which he was not drunk and yet abusive. I believe this tolerance for inconsistency grows out of the fundamental inconsistency of a battered woman's life: that the man who supposedly loves her also hurts her" (Blackman, 1986, pp. 228–229).

The Relationship of BWS to Post-Traumatic Stress Disorder

What is the relationship of battered woman syndrome to **post-traumatic stress disorder** (PTSD)? PTSD is included in DSM-IV as a clinical diagnosis. Walker (1992) viewed BWS as a subcategory of the generic PTSD. She wrote:

A good many of the reactions battered women report are similar to those of catastrophe victims. Disaster victims generally suffer emotional collapse 22 to 48 hours after a catastrophe. Their symptoms include listlessness, depression, and feelings of helplessness. Battered women evidence similar behaviour. They tend to remain isolated for at least the first 24 hours, and it may be several days before they seek help. (1979, p. 63)

But Lenore Walker and Mary Ann Dutton seem to disagree about the usefulness of PTSD.

BOX 10.4
Data to Collect for Elements of Self-Defence

Diane Follingstad (1994b) has provided a detailed listing of issues to be considered when preparing a battered woman defence:

I. Seriousness of threatened harm
    Past history of abuse.
    Types of abuse previously occurring.
    Worst episodes in terms of type of force and injuries—hospital records, doctors' records.
    Extent of threats—content of these; whether he has carried out threats in the past; believability of threats.
    Man's reputation for assaulting others in the past.
    Specific cues that signalled severe episodes.
    The woman's reactions and thought processes that led her to believe this episode could be lethal or cause grievous bodily harm.
    Whether man has ever killed anything before, e.g., pets.
    Changes in recent times that signalled that this was a more dangerous period of time.
    Pattern of escalation of abuse over time.

II. Imminence
    Content of the threats.
    Specific cues signalling a dangerous episode was going to occur.
    Changes in the man's behaviour/reactions recently that signalled that this was a more dangerous period of time.
    Changes in the man's behaviour/reactions recently that signalled that the man's behaviour felt unpredictable.

Past patterns of abuse that would make an episode appear imminent.
Likelihood that the man would remain dangerous for hours/days based on history.
If the man was killed while his back was turned or he was sleeping, find out if and why the woman felt that this was the only available time to defend herself.
Determine whether the woman had difficulty in knowing exactly when the man would carry out a threat.

III. "Overt act" as necessary for self-defence response
    Careful detailing of incident.
    Specific content of verbal threats.
    Specific description of nonverbal cues used in intimidation and signals that violence was at hand.

IV Rule of retreat
    (This area of information should be established specifically for the incident in which the woman killed the man as well as generally regarding why the woman remained in the relationship.)
    Prior escape attempts and results of these.
    Prior use of community resources and results of contacts with societal agents.
    Likelihood the man would come after her.
    Analysis of her options that night and her thought processes about those options.
    Specific threats as to dire consequences for leaving.
    Factors preventing leaving that night, e.g., not daring to leave young children behind with the

---

Walker (1992) wrote: "In presenting the BWS to a judge or jury it is often useful to demonstrate using the PTSD criteria chart.... Most battered women easily meet these criteria" (p. 329). But Dutton (1993) has emphasized the variety of reactions, as has Blackman (1986): "For example, it is entirely possible for a battered woman to have a constructive, effective work style outside the home—for her to show no signs of learned helplessness" (p. 230). Also there is the objection that such women will be misclassified as mentally ill. These experts urge psychologists not to "over-clinicalize" the victims of abuse.

The Role of the Forensic Psychologist in the Assessment of BWS

An important role for clinical forensic psychologists is the careful assessment of the responses of a woman who has killed her spouse. What symptoms does she report; is there corroborating evidence for them? Follingstad (1994b) has identified several procedures to be followed by forensic psychologists who assess the status of women who report abuse and battering and are charged with homicide. First, there should be a thorough psychological examination that man, lack of transportation and isolated rural location of the home, no money to go anywhere, nowhere to go.

Whether woman was paralyzed by fear, too scared to run.

Likelihood that the man would remain dangerous for hours/days.

Woman's sense of isolation/learned helplessness.

Woman's perceived alternatives and resources if she did leave.

View of the man as omnipotent.

Beliefs as to why she should not leave.

Psychological dilemmas regarding leaving.

V. Freedom of any responsibility for provoking the confrontation

History of the woman's use of physical force in the relationship.

Reasons for any use of physical force in the relationship.

Careful detailing of everything leading up to the killing.

VI. Equal force rule

If the man was unarmed, get history of extent of injuries and force man could inflict just using hands, feet.

Man's personal history outside the relationship that supports the idea of the extent of his aggressiveness without using weapons.

Size of the man as compared to size of the woman.

Physical strength of the man as compared to physical strength of the woman.

Any formal fight training for the man (e.g., military training, martial arts).

Man's knowledge of the use of guns and any history of collecting guns.

VII. Force not to exceed force necessary to disable the attacker

Woman's awareness of shooting more than one shot.

Woman's thought processes of what it would mean if the man was only injured, that is, what would happen to her.

Woman's knowledge of firearms and whether woman had any idea what would be necessary to stop the man versus killing him.

VIII. Reasonableness

Abuse in history.

Woman's perceptions of what was likely to happen to her.

Patterns of abuse.

Man's threats and history of carrying them out.

Woman's past ability to keep abuse episodes from occurring.

Man's reputation for aggression.

Woman's thought processes leading up to the situation.

Likelihood that the man would cause grievous bodily injury or kill her.

Woman's level of fear during the killing incident.

(From Follingstad, 1994b, Appendix A of the March 10, 1994 Forum. Reprinted by permission of Diane Follingstad.)

explores the history of the relationship, the history of abuse, the attempts to leave the relationship, and the woman's feelings about the deceased. The examination needs to be carried out in a nonjudgmental manner. Box 10.4 gives a detailed outline.

The psychologist should seek verification of self-reports through medical records and interviews with others. He or she may use a survey instrument to systemize the nature of the abuse. One possible measure is Mary Ann Dutton's (1992) Abusive Behaviour Observation Checklist.

It is an interviewer-administered listing of specific physical, sexual, and psychological actions that incorporates psychological abusive items from the Power and Control Wheel (Pence & Paymor, 1985) and physical violence items from the Conflict Tactics Scale (Straus, 1979).

The **Power and Control Wheel** lists eight categories of psychological abuse:

1. Coercion and threats (threat to kill, to injure wife or children, to burn the house down, or to steal the car).

2. Intimidation (displaying weapons, giving a look that instills fear).
3. Emotional abuse (humiliating name-calling, insults, restriction from personal hygiene [bath, toilet], forced nudity).
4. Isolation (restricting access to mail, TV, phone, friends, family; demanding an accounting of wife's whereabouts).
5. Minimization, denial, and blaming (denying that abuse happened, blaming victim for abuse).
6. Use of children to control the woman (threatening to kidnap or abuse, relaying of threatening messages through the children).
7. Use of "male privilege," that is, that the man always gets what he wants, that his preferences overrule those of the woman, that his demands cannot be questioned.
8. Economic/resource abuse (requiring that the partner "beg" for money, stealing money from partner, destroying credit cards, controlling access to transportation).

BWS IN COURT

The next section of this chapter describes the use of battered woman syndrome as part of a defence. In other words, the focus is now solely on women who have killed their abusers.

Battered Women Who Kill Their Abusers

The first known case of a battered woman killing her spouse in Canada occurred in Sault Ste. Marie, Ontario. On April 16, 1911, Angelina Napolitano, a 28-year-old immigrant mother of four, killed her husband with an axe while he slept. Although she was found guilty of murder, an international clemency case on her behalf was later successful as a result of the years of severe spousal abuse she had experienced (Regehr & Glancy, 1995).

According to Statistics Canada (2001), the number of men accused of killing their current wife or ex-wife rose from 52 in 2000 to 69 in 2001, with virtually all of this increase occurring in Ontario. The number of women accused of killing their husbands (16) was unchanged from 2000. One homicide was committed by a same-sex spouse. About 4 percent of the homicides in Canada are committed by women (Motiuk & Belcourt, 1995), and a significant percentage of such women have killed an abusive partner (Browne & Williams, 1989; Jones, 1981). Most of the women in prison for murder convictions are abuse victims. For example, of 181 Canadian women convicted of murder, 82.3 percent of them reported experiencing some form of abuse, either physical (beatings and assault), sexual (sexual assault and molestation), or emotional abuse (verbal attacks and neglect) (Hoffman et al., 1998).

Domestic Violence Law in Canada

The pivotal Supreme Court of Canada case to deal with the issue of battered woman syndrome was **R. v. Lavallee** (1990). Twenty-two-year-old Angelique Lyn Lavallee shot and killed her partner, Kevin Rust, with whom she had been living for three or four years and who had a history of assaulting her. On August 30, 1986, their home was the scene of a party. After most guests had departed, Lavallee and Rust had a loud argument in the upstairs bedroom during which Rust had threatened to kill her after all the guests had departed. After he told her that if she did not kill him, he would kill her, she shot him in the back of the head as he was walking away from her.

Although she did not testify in her trial, her statement to the police read:

> Me and Wendy argued as usual and I ran in the house after Kevin pushed me. I was scared, I was really scared. I locked the door. Herb was downstairs with Joanne and I called for Herb but I was crying when I called him. I said, "Herb come up here please." Herb came up to the top of the stairs and I told him that Kevin was going to hit me, actually beat on me again. Herb said he knew and that if I was his old lady things

would be different, he gave me a hug. OK, we're friends, there's nothing between us. He said "Yeah, I know" and he went outside to talk to Kevin leaving the door unlocked. I went upstairs and hid in my closet from Kevin. I was so scared.… My window was open and I could hear Kevin asking questions about what I was doing and what I was saying. Next thing I know he was coming up the stairs for me. He came into my bedroom and said "Wench, where are you?" And he turned on my light and he said "Your purse is on the floor" and he kicked it. OK then he turned and he saw me in the closet. He wanted me to come out but I didn't want to come out because I was scared. I was so scared. [The officer who took the statement then testified that the appellant started to cry at this point and stopped after a minute or two.] He grabbed me by the arm right there. There's a bruise on my face also where he slapped me. He didn't slap me right then, first he yelled at me then he pushed me and I pushed him back and he hit me twice on the right hand side of my head. I was scared. All I thought about was all the other times he used to beat me, I was scared, I was shaking as usual. The rest is a blank, all I remember is he gave me the gun and a shot was fired through my screen. This is all so fast. And then the guns were in another room and he loaded it the second shot and gave it to me. And I was going to shoot myself. I pointed it to myself, I was so upset. OK and then he went and I was sitting on the bed and he started going like this with his finger [the appellant made a shaking motion with an index finger] and said something like "You're my old lady and you do as you're told" or something like that. He said "wait till everybody leaves, you'll get it then" and he said something to the effect of "either you kill me or I'll get you" that was what it was. He kind of smiled and then he turned around. I shot him but I aimed out. I thought I aimed

above him and a piece of his head went that way. (R v. Lavallee, 1990)

An expert witness, Dr. Fred Shane, was hired by the defence to testify regarding Angelique Lavallee's state of mind at the time of the killing. Using Walker's "battered woman syndrome" description, Dr. Shane gave the opinion that because of her continuing abuse, Lavallee had reasonably believed that Rust was going to kill her later that night. He testified:

I think she felt, she felt in the final tragic moment that her life was on the line, that unless she defended herself, unless she reacted in a violent way that she would die. I mean he made it very explicit to her, from what she told me and from the information I have from the material that you forwarded to me, that she had, I think, to defend herself against his violence. (R v. Lavallee, 1990)

At her original trial, Lavallee was acquitted. However, the Manitoba Court of Appeal overturned the acquittal. Ultimately, the Supreme Court restored the acquittal; its recognition of the battered woman defence was widely viewed as a significant victory for women.

Since the Lavallee decision, there have been several important reforms in the Canadian legal system in dealing with the problem of spousal violence. Examples of recent legislative reforms include the following:

- Bill C-15, reintroduced on March 14, 2001 (previously Bill C-36), proposed to change the Criminal Code to increase the maximum penalty for criminal harassment from five to ten years in prison.
- Bill C-79 (December 1, 1999) changed the Criminal Code to facilitate the participation of victims and witnesses in the criminal justice process, and to prevent their revictimization by the system. For example, bail decisions must take the safety of victims into account, and publication bans are now permitted to protect the identity of any victim or witness.

- As will be discussed further in Chapter 15, Bill C-27 (May 26, 1997) amended the Criminal Code to strengthen the criminal harassment (stalking) provisions. The bill also requires the courts to consider a breach of a no-contact order to be an aggravating factor in sentencing for criminal harassment.
- Bill C-41 (introduced on September 3, 1996) led to Criminal Code changes requiring the courts to take into account the abuse of a spouse or a child as an aggravating factor in sentencing.
- Bill C-42 (introduced on February 1, 1995) changed the Criminal Code to make it easier to obtain peace bonds (no-contact orders). Police and others can now apply for a peace bond on behalf of a person at risk of harm. The maximum penalty for violation of a peace bond was increased from six months to two years.
- Bill C-126 (introduced on August 1, 1993) created the new anti-stalking offence of criminal harassment.

Possible Defences for a Woman Who Has Killed Her Batterer

It is important to recall that BWS is not a legal defence (Aron, 1993). As the Supreme Court of Canada has stated in *R. v. Malott* (1998):

> "Battered woman syndrome" is not a legal defence in itself, but rather is a psychiatric explanation of the mental state of an abused woman which can be relevant to understanding a battered woman's state of mind. The utility of such evidence is not limited to self-defence situations, but is potentially relevant to other situations where the reasonableness of a battered woman's actions or perceptions is at issue. (summary para. 5)

In Canada, in cases in which the battered woman kills her spouse or partner, she must show the need for self-defence or at least provocation.

Self-Defence

The **battered woman self-defence**, as it is called, rests on the justification of the act as necessary to protect the woman or someone else (usually the children) from further harm or death (Walker, 1992). **Self-defence** is defined in Canada and in most U.S. states as the use of equal force or the least amount of force necessary to repel danger when the person reasonably perceives that she or he is in **imminent danger** of serious bodily harm or death. Its key items include a reasonable perception of imminent danger and a justified use of lethal force.

One of the Supreme Court of Canada's most recent considerations of battered woman syndrome is found in *R. v. Malott* (1998) and is relevant to understanding its stance on self-defence in this context. In this case, Margaret Ann Malott was charged with the murder and attempted murder of her common-law husband Paul Malott and his girlfriend Carrie Sherwood, respectively. Her husband had abused her physically, sexually, psychologically, and emotionally, but then he left Margaret to live with Sherwood. Several months after the separation, Malott shot her husband after he drove her to a medical centre to assist him in his illegal drug trade. After shooting him, she took a cab to his girlfriend's home where Malott shot her and stabbed her with a knife (this victim survived).

At the trial, Malott testified about her extensive abuse at the hands of her husband, a fact with which the Crown had no disagreement. Expert evidence was admitted to demonstrate that Malott had experienced battered woman syndrome. However, she was found guilty by the jury of both second-degree murder and attempted murder, but they recommended that she receive the minimum sentence in light of battered woman syndrome. These convictions were upheld by the Ontario Appeal Court in 1996. Malott finally appealed her conviction for second-degree murder to the Supreme Court of Canada, which also dismissed her appeal, finding that the imminence of danger requiring self-defence was not present.

How Widely Should the Self-Defence Defence Be Applied?

In the last two decades the breadth of application of the self-defence defence has been provocative. Walker (1992) wrote:

> In the late 1970s and early 1980s, what became known as the *battered woman self-defense* achieved acceptance within the case law of numerous states. As this defense gained in popularity, [lawyers] and mental health professionals became more familiar with the dynamics of battering and its psychological impact on victims. Its use broadened to include battered children who killed abusive parents, battered men who killed their partners (usually male), battered women who killed their women partners, rape victims who killed their attacker, and even battered roommates! Soon the expert testimony was applied to cases where other criminal acts were committed by victims of abuse under duress from their abusive partners. Participation with a violent co-defendant in homicides involving strangers also have been explained, in part, by the duress the woman was under to comply with the man's demands. Testimony has also been introduced in cases of child abuse that resulted in the violent man's killing the child (often called "murder by omission" because of the battered woman's inability to protect the child). Crimes involving money and property such as embezzlement, forgery, burglary, robbery, and those that are drug related may well have been committed by a woman at the demand of her batterer. (p. 322, italics in original)

Justification of the Self-Defence Defence

Thus, to justify a self-defence defence and therefore acquit the woman, the laws of Canada and most U.S. states require that the judge or jury be convinced that at the time of the incident she had a reasonable apprehension of imminent life-threatening danger. Although such a defence is the primary one chosen by such defendants, it faces several obstacles. The first is the "masculine" nature of the defence.

The legal concept of self-defence developed in response to two basic kinds of situations in which men found themselves: a sudden assault by a murderous stranger (e.g., a robbery attempt with a threat to kill) or a fist fight or brawl between two equals that gets out of hand and turns deadly. Thus, "classic" self-defence action is stranger-to-stranger assault between two males (Blackman, 1986).

But self-defence cases certainly vary from this scenario, and research findings have led some researchers (Finkel, Meister, & Lightfoot, 1991) to conclude that more community support exists for the self-defence defence by battered women than the above would imply. Consider the following case: In the mid-1970s Inez Garcia was raped by two neighbourhood men who told her they were going to come back and rape her again. She went home, got a gun, and after several hours had passed, she found one of the men and shot him dead. She was acquitted at her second trial, a trial in which the court permitted evidence of self-defence even though the actual rape had taken place several hours earlier and there was an intervening time between the act and her responses. The court decided that the threat of further abuse was sufficient to raise her perception of danger to the imminence standard (Bochnak, 1981; Schneider, 1986).

The most fundamental element of the self-defence claim is that at the time of the killing, the defendant honestly and reasonably feared unlawful bodily harm at the hands of her assailant:

> In this regard, proof of violent acts previously committed by the victim against the defendant as well as any evidence that the defendant was aware of specific prior violent acts by the victim upon third parties is admissible as bearing upon the reasonableness of defendant's apprehension of danger at the time of the encounter. (*People v. Torres*, 1985, p. 360)

Psychological Self-Defence

As we have seen, many battered women who kill their abusers are convicted, even though they use the self-defence defence, because requirements of the current self-defence law equate "self" with only the *physical* aspects of personhood (Ewing, 1990, p. 580). That is, most do not kill at the moment they are being battered or directly threatened. Ewing's survey of well-documented homicides by battered women found only about one-third took place during an act of battering. Thus, he has proposed a new concept, the **psychological self-defence** defence; he has written:

> In brief, my position is that failure to meet these narrow legal requirements does not mean that a battered woman did not kill in defense of self. I argue that many, perhaps most, battered women who kill their batterers do so in *psychological* self-defense—that is, to protect themselves from being destroyed *psychologically*—and that under certain circumstances the law should recognize psychological self-defense as a justification for the use of deadly force. (Ewing, 1990, p. 581, italics in original)

Ewing, a psychologist, lawyer, and law professor, wrote further:

> Should a battered woman—or anyone else—who uses deadly force to prevent that result, to avert what reasonably appears to be the threat of psychological destruction, be branded a criminal and sent to prison? I think not, but that is precisely what is happening in many cases under current self-defense law. Contrary to current law, I suggest that the use of deadly force to avoid such a dire fate is a legitimate form of self-defense and should be recognized as such by the criminal law. In short, I believe that, under certain circumstances, psychological self-defense should be a legal justification for homicide.
>
> The legal doctrine I am proposing is not a battered woman defense. Such a defense

would not only arguably violate constitutional guarantees of equal protection, but would be unsound as a matter of public policy. Attaining the status of battered woman or even battered person is not and should not by itself be justification for homicide. Stated most simply, the proposed doctrine of psychological self-defense would justify the use of deadly force where such force appeared reasonably necessary to prevent the infliction of extremely serious psychological injury. *Extremely serious psychological injury* would be defined as gross and enduring impairment of one's psychological functioning that significantly limits the meaning and value of one's physical existence. (1990, p. 587, italics in original)

The major criticism of the use of psychological self-defence as a defence comes from Morse (1990). His major objections are the following:

> The proposal to justify homicide by psychological self-defense rests on an insecure scientific foundation and would be legally mischievous. The core concepts are unacceptably vague and lack rigorous empirical support. The proposed defense is better characterized as an excuse than as a justification because rational victims of purely psychological abuse do have socially preferable alternatives to homicide, and the proposal is inconsistent with modern criminal law that limits justifications for homicide. The defense would create substantial administrative problems and would facilitate adoption or expansion of related undesirable doctrines. The best response to abhorrent physical and psychological abuse is not unnecessary further violence, but the creation of adequate deterrents and alternative solutions for victims. (1990, p. 595)

The psychological self-defence defence remains untested in Canadian courts.

CROSS-EXAMINATION OF THE BATTERED WOMAN

Regarding the Crown's strategies in trials in which a battered woman is on trial for homicide, it is typical to try to discredit the opposing case by characterizing the defendant as "unfeminine or man-like," "not a good mother," or "promiscuous" (Basow, 1986). Gillespie (1989) observed: "The trial courtroom provides a forum for a biased or cynical prosecutor to trot out every myth and stereotype and his [or her] misconception about women that could conceivably inflame a jury against the defendant and that could encourage the jurors to ascribe the worst possible motive to her actions" (p. 22).

One example cited by Jenkins and Davidson (1990) came from the cross-examination of the defendant:

Q. How old was Scott when you married him?
A. 20
Q. And how old were you?
A. 28
Q. You'd been divorced twice before?
A. Yes
Q. Did you tell Scott you were pregnant before you married him?
A. I was not pregnant.
Q. Huh?
A. I was not pregnant.
Q. Did you tell Scott you were pregnant before you married him?
A. I was not pregnant ... No. (p. 164)

The authors observed that three aspects of this exchange—that she was older than her husband, that she was a divorced woman, and the suggestion that she lied to entrap him in marriage—produce for the jury a stereotypically negative connotation of the woman defendant.

Also the Crown may try to minimize the injuries of the accused. Jenkins and Davidson (1990) quoted one closing argument:

[An eyewitness] gets up on the witness stand and she tells you [she] witnessed him beating her in the Tarver Pancake Kitchen. These beatings once a week that she suffered for five years, I don't know. If you've ever seen a boxer that's been in the game too long, it gets punch-strong [sic], and the movements get slower, the speech gets slower, and he can't get around.... If that woman incurred a beating a week for five years, that's the way she would look. She wants you to believe that she was beat that bad because that's her only chance.... That didn't happen. (p. 167)

USING A PSYCHOLOGIST AS AN EXPERT WITNESS ON BWS

Testimony by an expert witness on battered woman syndrome was first introduced in United States courts in 1979 (*Ibn-Tamas v. United States*). Several years ago Walker (1993) estimated that witness experts on BWS had been allowed to testify in at least 500 trials in the United States. She wrote:

My own work as an expert witness in almost 300 of these trials in the United States began in 1977 when I was asked to evaluate Miriam Griegg, a Billings, Montana, woman who had been seriously assaulted during most of her marriage. One night she shot and killed her husband with six hollow point bullets from his own Magnum .357 gun. During an argument, he threw the gun at her and ordered her to shoot him or else, he threatened, he would shoot and kill her. When the police arrived, Miriam Griegg warned them to be careful as she knew her husband would be very angry. Obviously, her emotional state caused her to be unaware that he was dead; any one of the six bullets would have killed him instantly. She made it perfectly clear, however, that she shot him because she believed that he would have killed her otherwise, a straightforward self-defense argument. After listening to her testimony and mine—I explained the context of the relationship and how Miriam Griegg knew in her own mind that she would die if she did not do what he ordered her to do—the jury agreed that she was not guilty. (1993, pp. 233–234)

But, as described in detail later in this chapter, the empirical research on the effect of an expert witness does not lead to a solid conclusion about overall effectiveness of psychologists who testify for the defence.

Reasons for Using an Expert Witness

Basically, the purpose of the expert witness is to provide fact-finders with another perspective, or a "social framework" (Walker & Monahan, 1987) for interpreting the woman's actions. Mary Ann Dutton (1993) described different purposes for testimony by a psychologist:

> Typically, expert testimony concerning the battered woman's psychological reactions to violence has been used to address a number of different issues. Within a criminal context, the testimony is used to bolster a standard defense, (e.g., self-defense or duress) not provide a separate defense, *per se*. Issues toward which the psychological testimony is applied include, for example, whether the victim's perception of danger was reasonable (e.g., self-defense), the psychological damage resulting from domestic violence (e.g., civil tort), the basis for sole custody or restriction of child visitation (e.g., child custody), and why the battered woman engaged in seemingly puzzling behaviours (e.g., remained with or returned to the battering partner, expressed anger toward the batterer in public, left children alone with batterer, recanted testimony regarding occurrence of past violence).
>
> It is, of course, necessary to establish that the particular aspects of a battered woman's

experience of violence (and its aftermath) toward which the testimony is addressed are directly relevant to specific legal issues at hand in order for its application to be both helpful and admissible. It is essential that this link be made explicit to the factfinder, otherwise the relevance of the expert witness testimony may not be clearly understood or missed altogether. (p. 1216)

The expert witness can describe three types of reaction to trauma (described further in Chapter 11):

- psychological distress or dysfunction
- cognitive reactions
- relational disturbances

One of the most important contributions is to confront questions that jurors might be phrasing in their heads. For example, jurors want to know "Why didn't she leave?" This question, one frequently asked, assumes that there are viable options for alternative behaviour; that is, it assumes that leaving will stop the violence. The law is explicit: You have no obligation to rearrange your life in order to avoid a situation in which the need to act in self-defence might arise. The expert witness needs to deflect the assumption that if she didn't leave after the abuse, she wasn't bothered by it. The witness can bring out strategies the woman has used to stop the violence (Follingstad, 1994b). These form three types:

1. Personal strategies.
   Compliance with the batterer's demands in order to "keep the peace."
   Attempt to talk with abuser about stopping the violence.
   Temporarily escaping.
   Hiding.
   Physical resistance.
2. Informal help-seeking efforts.
   Soliciting help from neighbours and others in escaping from the batterer.

Asking others to intervene in an attempt to get him to stop.

3. Formal help-seeking efforts.

Legal strategies—calling the police, prosecuting, getting a lawyer, going to a shelter.

The expert can point out that the lack of her economic resources makes it impossible for the woman to leave. But the expert also needs to alert the jury to the fact that different victims use different strategies and to *why* any one option is not frequently used.

A second question jurors ponder is "Why did she attack when he was asleep?" The expert witness can inform the jury of the reasonableness of the battered woman's perception of danger. Walker has argued: "Many women know that their abusive partner is still dangerous even while he is asleep, frequently forcing his sexual demands upon waking and immediately beginning another attack. Often these men do not sleep for long periods of time, waking early, especially if she is not right by his side as he frequently orders" (1992, p. 325).

In further support of this position, Crocker (1985) suggested:

> The battered woman perceived an imminent danger of physical injury even though there was no overt act of violence. Defendants offer battered woman syndrome expert testimony to explain why their perception of danger was reasonable—why they acted in self-defense after a "reasonable man" would have cooled off or before he would have acted. The testimony may demonstrate how repeated physical abuse can so heighten a battered woman's fear and her awareness of her husband's physical capabilities that she considers him as dangerous asleep as awake, as dangerous before an attack as during one. (p. 141)

A 2004 study by York University researchers Regina Schuller, Elisabeth Wells, Sara Rzepa, and Marc Klippenstine, entitled "Re-thinking Battered Woman Syndrome Evidence," suggested that lawyers should consider dropping the terminology of BWS and focus on the woman's situation and lack of options, because of jurors' misconceptions about battered women. The authors found that when the woman's homicide had been committed outside of a direct confrontation (as her husband was asleep), mock jurors were less likely to believe her claim of self-defence and more likely to render a verdict of guilty. Further, expert evidence concerning BWS was only beneficial to jurors in the confrontational condition; expert testimony in the nonconfrontational condition was ineffective in influencing juror verdicts.

PROCEDURAL AND ETHICAL ISSUES REGARDING THE USE OF EXPERT WITNESSES

The use of a psychologist as an expert witness in cases in which battered woman syndrome is introduced is fraught with both procedural and ethical questions.

Admissibility of Expert Testimony

The rationale for many court decisions to admit expert testimony is that it bears upon a crucial issue of fact that is beyond the knowledge of the average layperson or jury member (Ewing, Aubrey, & Jamieson, 1986).

A decision by the Supreme Court of Canada is illustrative. In *R. v. Malott* (1998), the court wrote:

> To the extent that expert evidence respecting battered woman syndrome may assist a jury in assessing the reasonableness of an accused's perceptions, it is relevant to the issue of unlawful assault.... The Court accepted the need for expert evidence in order to dispel the myths and stereotypes inherent in our understanding of a battered woman's experiences. (para. 18 and summary para. 6)

JURORS' REACTIONS TO BWS AS DEFENCE EVIDENCE

But what is the effect of expert testimony? Does it change jurors' verdicts? If so, how? Several jury-simulation studies are relevant (Blackman & Brickman, 1984), keeping in mind the limitations to this approach described in Chapter 8. Regina Schuller and her colleagues have completed several such studies (Schuller, 1992; Schuller, Smith, & Olson, 1994). In the first, 108 mock jurors (Canadian university students) read about a homicide trial in which a battered woman had killed her husband. The transcript, based on an actual case, was 50 pages in length. Three versions of the trial were used. In one, an expert witness presented only general research findings on battered woman syndrome. In the second version, the expert went further, concluding that the defendant's behavioural and emotional characteristics fit the syndrome. A third group of participants read a transcript in which no expert testimony was presented. Compared to the control condition, jurors exposed to the transcript with the specific expert gave interpretations that were more consistent with the woman's account of what occurred, and more lenient verdicts.

Schuller's (1992) second study—which substituted an hour-long audiotape for the transcript—had the jurors deliberate. (A total of 131 participants were divided into 30 juries.) In this study, compared to the control condition, each expert-witness condition led to a moderate shift in verdicts from murder to manslaughter. If they had heard the testimony of an expert witness, the jurors—during deliberations—discussed the defendant and her actions in a more favourable light.

A third study in Schuller's program of research (Schuller, Smith, & Olson, 1994) collected participants' beliefs about sexual abuse two months prior to their participation as mock jurors in a study that used the same audiotape as the prior study. The presence of testimony by an expert witness again influenced verdicts but especially for the mock jurors whose earlier responses had reflected more informed attitudes about domestic abuse. These jurors attributed less responsibility to the defendant and more responsibility to the alleged abuser, compared to control subjects.

A jury simulation by Greenwald, Tomkins, Kenning, and Zavodny (1990) sought to evaluate Ewing's "psychological self-defence" defence. A total of 196 undergraduate participants read two trial vignettes. The instructions given to the jury were varied: psychological self-defence only, physical self-defence only, psychological and physical self-defence, or none of these. Instructions were given after the vignettes, so that elements of self-defence were the last thing given to the jurors. Only the psychological self-defence instructions significantly influenced verdict patterns, primarily by shifting would-be voluntary manslaughter convictions to acquittals.

However, not all studies have concluded that testimony by a psychologist-expert is that effective. A study by Follingstad and her colleagues (Follingstad et al., 1989) varied the level of force directed by the husband prior to his wife's killing him, as well as the presence or absence of an expert witness (who testified about the relationship of the defendant's actions to battering relationships in general). The presence of the expert witness had no direct influence on the jurors' verdicts, although 80 percent of the jurors in the expert-witness condition reported that it was influential. The factor that had the greatest impact was the level of force used by the batterer; that is, jurors were more sympathetic with the defendant in the condition in which the batterer used the most force (where the husband was described as advancing toward the woman with a weapon).

Similarly, a study by Finkel, Meister, and Lightfoot (1991) manipulated the degree of threat posed by the husband, as well as the presence or absence of expert testimony. As in Schuller's first study, two types of expert testimony were offered; either the expert diagnosed the defendant as having BWS and described the symptoms of the syndrome, or the expert supplemented the diagnosis with an opinion about the woman's perceptions at the time of the killing. As in the study by Follingstad and her colleagues, the only variable that influenced the mock jurors' verdicts was the level of force used by the husband; that is, verdicts of guilt were rendered more often when the woman acted without direct provocation from the man.

Thus the research results give no consistent answer to the question of effectiveness of expert testimony. Methodological differences among the studies described above may account for the differences in results. Schuller (1994) has suggested that it may be necessary for the woman's account of what happened to be challenged (as it is in a real-life trial) for the expert witness to have any impact.

CRITICISMS OF THE USE OF BWS AND THE BATTERED WOMAN DEFENCE

Both battered woman syndrome and the battered woman defence have received criticism from within and outside the field of psychology. The defence has been challenged as portraying women in an unfavourable light, while BWS has been questioned with regard to its validity as an empirically established concept.

Perpetuating the Battered Woman Stereotype as a Passive, Helpless Woman

Psychologists view the use of the battered woman defence as a mixed blessing. Crocker wrote: "The fundamental problem with the battered woman stereotype is that it allows the legal system to continue considering the defendant's claim based on *who she is*, not on *what she did*" (1985, p. 149). The "who she is" manifested by the use of a syndrome is a sufferer of a disability; that is, it can be argued

that the use of BWS "pathologizes" battered women, many of whom have reacted justifiably to their plight (Browne, 1987).

The Scientific Validity of BWS

Criticisms of the validity of BWS have centred on the quality of the empirical basis for the cycle of violence theory and the application of the concept of learned helplessness. In order to test the theory of a cycle of violence, Walker and her colleagues (Walker, 1984b) conducted interviews with 400 "self-identified" battered women. Each was asked about four battering incidents: her first, her second, one of her worst, and the most recent. No control group was used. Faigman (1986; Faigman & Wright, 1997) has described the following as among the flaws of this study:

1. The interview technique permitted the participants to guess easily what the hypotheses of the study were.
2. Interviewers knew the "correct" answer.
3. Interviewers did not record the subjects' answers, only their interpretations of the participants' answers.
4. The research did not give any time frame to the cycle; it could be a few minutes, several hours, or many weeks.
5. In only 65 percent of the cases was there evidence of a tension-building phase prior to the battering; in only 58 percent of the cases was there evidence of loving contrition afterward (Walker, 1984b, pp. 96–97). It is not clear from the report how many women reported all three phases of the cycle.

With regard to learned helplessness, scholars (cf. Schuller & Vidmar, 1992) have questioned the application of Martin Seligman's (1975; Seligman & Maier, 1967) original theory and research on dogs to battered women. Seligman's dogs were rendered helpless and immobile by receiving noncontingent electric shocks; therefore, "one would predict that if battered women suffered from learned helplessness they would not assert control over their environment; certainly, one would not predict such a positive assertion of control as killing the batterer" (Faigman & Wright, 1997, p. 79).

SUMMARY

In recent years, the extent and seriousness of domestic violence in Canada has been increasingly publicized. Useful typologies of men who abuse have been developed. Further, there is accumulating research to suggest that risk prediction tools such as the SARA (Kropp & Hart, 2000) can help us predict whether an abuser is likely to reoffend. Some psychologists have proposed that the responses of women who have been continually abused by their partners are consistent enough to qualify as a syndrome, called battered woman syndrome. Among these reactions are learned helplessness, lowered self-esteem, loss of a feeling of invulnerability, a sense of diminished alternatives, and hypervigilance. Walker proposed that the interaction between the batterer and his partner goes through a set of observable phases—a tension-building phase, an acute battering incident, and then a contrite phase; she called this the cycle of abuse or cycle of violence.

Psychologists can play several roles when a battered woman reacts by killing her abuser. Assessment of the presence of battered woman syndrome includes a comprehensive interview and the collection of medical records and court reports. At the trial, the forensic psychologist may be permitted to serve as an expert witness. It should be noted that battered woman syndrome is not a legal defence in and of itself; usually the woman's defence is to claim that she acted out of self-defence. The psychologist, at trial, can deal with many of the myths about battered women and their batterers and can also respond to the prevalent concerns of jurors, such as "Why didn't she leave?" and "Why did she act when he was asleep?" However, empirical studies on the effectiveness of such expert testimony are inconsistent.

Criticisms of the use of battered woman syndrome take two forms: first, that it portrays women as emotional, passive, and helpless and, second, that it lacks the proper theoretical and research background to justify its admissibility at trial.

KEY TERMS

acute battering incident, p. 223
battered woman defence, p. 215
battered woman self-defence, p. 228
battered woman syndrome, p. 222
cognitive inconsistency, p. 223
contrite phase, p. 223
cycle of abuse, p. 223
hypervigilance, p. 223
imminent danger, p. 228
learned helplessness, p. 222
myths about the battered woman, p. 218
post-traumatic stress disorder, p. 223
Power and Control Wheel, p. 225
psychological self-defence, p. 230
psychopathic abusers, p. 214
R. v. Lavallee, p. 226
self-defence, p. 228
syndrome, p. 222
tension-building phase, p. 223

SUGGESTED READINGS

Barnett, O. W., & LaViolette, A. D. (1993). *It could happen to anyone: Why battered women stay*. Thousand Oaks, CA: Sage.

The layperson's most frequent question is "Why doesn't she leave?" This book examines contemporary theories about why women remain in abusive relationships.

Browne, A. (1987). *When battered women kill*. New York: Free Press.

This text analyzes the causes for the actions of 42 women charged with killing or seriously injuring their partners. Case studies are sensitively presented. Recommended.

Dutton, D. G. (1995). *The domestic assault of women: Psychological and criminal justice perspectives* (Rev. ed.). Vancouver, BC: U.B.C. Press.

This comprehensive examination of the causes and effects of spousal assault includes a detailed classification of types of violent men and an analysis of the dynamics of the victim–abuser relationship.

Ewing, C. P. (1987). *Battered women who kill: Psychological self defense as legal justification*. Lexington, MA: Lexington Books, D. C. Heath.

Ewing presents a thorough review of the psychological plight of the battered woman as well as an exposition of his proposal for the psychological self-defence defence.

Walker, L. E. A. (1979). *The battered woman*. New York: Harper & Row.

This detailed analysis of the components of the battered woman syndrome and the cycle of violence includes examples from the author's interviews and case studies.

11

The Trauma of Sexual Assault

I remember his hands as he was choking me. I thought he was going to kill me. The whole event is just ingrained in my brain, I can remember it all so clearly.

—RESEARCH PARTICIPANT/RAPE VICTIM (CITED IN PEACE AND PORTER, 2004, P. 1153)

A "TYPICAL" SEXUAL ASSAULT CASE

A young woman—a university student—leaves a bar with a man whom she met an hour and a half and two drinks earlier. After accompanying him to his apartment, the woman is forced to engage in oral and vaginal intercourse. Because she resists, she is threatened with death unless she complies. After returning to her home, she informs the police, and she is taken to a hospital. A laceration is found near the opening of her vagina, but no other bruises or marks are noted (Bristow, 1984).

After the woman reports her victimization to the police, they press charges against her attacker (which are approved by the Crown prosecutor); he refuses to plead guilty. A jury trial is held; he is convicted of aggravated sexual assault. However, this type of "he said, she said" case often does not get prosecuted or, if it does, it results in a jury conclusion that there is insufficient evidence to convict the defendant (Porter, Campbell, Birt, & Woodworth, 2003). In the opinion of one observer (Bristow, 1984), what made the difference in the outcome in the above case was the testimony of an expert witness, psychiatrist Herbert Modlin, that the woman suffered from rape trauma syndrome.

PURPOSE OF THE CHAPTER

The purpose of this chapter is to examine the different roles of the forensic psychologist in cases involving the charges of sexual assault. (Chapter 12 examines the sexual abuse of children.) Emphasis in this chapter is placed on testimony about the effects of sexual assault, especially with regard to the admissibility of expert testimony by psychologists and the cross-examination of these witnesses when testimony is admitted. The nature of a "rape trauma syndrome" is sometimes elusive, and forensic psychologists called to testify for the prosecution

may be tempted to conclude on the basis of limited evidence that the person who was attacked shows signs of the syndrome.

BACKGROUND

Sexual violence is a significant problem in our society. About one in eight males and one in four females report having been sexually victimized in childhood (e.g., Finkelhor, Hotaling, Lewis, & Smith, 1990), and 10 percent to 25 percent of women report an adulthood rape experience (Koss, 1993). According to the *Canadian Violence Against Women Survey* (Johnson, 1996), 39 percent of Canadian women experienced at least one incident of sexual assault after the age of 15.

Historically, victims of sexual violence were not treated well within our legal system. In fact, Canadian rape laws served to protect men accused of the crime. For example, before legal reforms in the 1980s, husbands could not be prosecuted for sexually assaulting their wives. In addition, Canadian laws provided safeguards for men accused of rape. Prosecutors were allowed to present information about a complainant's sexual history to undermine her credibility, and judges instructed jurors about the dangers of convicting a defendant on the uncorroborated testimony of a complainant. Traditionally, it was unusual for courts to convict in a rape case in the absence of corroboration (e.g., Yuille, 1988).

These trends were problematic and discouraged crime victims from reporting offences. Fortunately, in the late 1970s and early 1980s the traditional rape laws and doctrines underwent major changes in the Canadian legal system. Under our current Criminal Code, we do not have a "rape" offence per se, but a broad category of "sexual assault," encompassing a wide range of crimes with a sexual component. Sexual assaults with a weapon or those that cause bodily harm (aggravated sexual assaults) have more severe sentences than other forms of sexual assault. Unlike many U.S. states, Canada has no statute of limitations, so charges can be laid at any time in an offender's lifetime after an offence takes place. Further, there are now important limitations on the kind of evidence about a complainant's sexual history that a defence lawyer can bring up in court. Before the last decade, the defence often obtained subpoenas that forced physicians, schools, therapists, and other third parties to produce their confidential files on a complainant, without even having to demonstrate they had any relevance in the case.

However, a 1995 Supreme Court judgment in the British Columbia case of Bishop Hubert O'Connor (*R. v. O'Connor*, 1995) led to stricter controls on the defence having access to such private records in sexual assault cases. The *O'Connor* decision established that the accused must first convince the judge that information in the files is likely to be relevant to the case. The judge can then review the files, and weigh the positive and negative consequences of their being entered as evidence. In October 2000, the Supreme Court of Canada unanimously upheld the constitutionality of the Criminal Code provisions that deal with the exposure of the sexual histories of complainants in trials. In two cases—*R. v. Darrach* (2000) and *R. v. Mills* (1999)—the Supreme Court concluded that the legal system must be committed to balancing the right of an accused to a fair trial with the privacy rights of the sexual assault complainant (who is, invariably, called as a witness at the trial).

The approach adopted by the Canadian legal system encouraged more victims to report sexual offences, as reflected in the increasing number of sexual assault convictions in Canada in the past two decades (e.g., Motiuk & Belcourt, 1997). There also has been an explosion of research on sexual violence and its psychological aftermath, in Canada and elsewhere. It is clear that the experience of sexual assault can have major psychological consequences. In fact, rape is among the most traumatic experiences one can go through, and it frequently leads to mental health problems (Foa & Rothbaum, 1998). Further, such symptoms may constitute a "syndrome."

WHAT IS THE RAPE TRAUMA SYNDROME?

As Chapter 10 described, a **syndrome** is a set of symptoms that may co-occur, such that they may be considered to imply a disorder or disease. Not all the symptoms have to exist in every subject, and, in fact, the criteria for how many must be present are unclear.

About 30 years ago, a psychiatric nurse and a sociologist, Burgess and Holmstrom (1974), coined the term **rape trauma syndrome** (RTS) to describe the collection of responses reported by 92 women who had been raped or subjected to other sexual abuses. Each of these survivors was interviewed within 30 minutes of her admission to a hospital and re-interviewed a month later. Burgess and Holmstrom were struck by the fact that a variety of sources—self-reports by those raped, descriptions by psychotherapists and trained social service workers, and reactions by friends and family of those who have been attacked—showed great uniformity of responses. Some typical self-descriptions of those who survived a rape are reported in Box 11.1. (Because the vast majority of those raped are women, the clinical and empirical literature has focused on their reactions, and much less information is available on male survivors [Koss & Harvey, 1991].)

It should be noted that not all rape survivors suffer from the same severity of symptoms. In support of this finding, Koss and Harvey (1991) used an ecological model of response to having been raped that emphasized that a variety of personal, event, and environmental factors could influence the recovery from a sexual assault. They wrote:

> Person variables of particular relevance include the age and developmental stage of the victim; her or his relationship to the offender; the ability of the victim to identify and make use of available social support; and the meaning that is assigned to the traumatic event by the victim, by family and friends, and by others including police, medical per-

BOX 11.1

Self-Descriptions of the Reactions of Sexual Assault Survivors

Each person who has been raped has a different story to tell, but they all share reactions of personal intrusion and lifelong impact. Each has to come to terms with being assaulted; here are some reactions:

- "Early on, I realized the way to make the pain less was to separate my mind from my body and not permit myself to feel" (quoted by Kraske, 1986, p. 8A).

- "I can recall many landmarks in my recovery, beginning with the moment I picked myself up off the kitchen floor and got myself to a hospital. There was the first night, weeks after the attack, when I didn't wake up crying or screaming. I remember the first time I said to someone—outside of my close friends and family who knew me when the assault occurred—'I was raped.' And the first time I disclosed 'my secret' to a man with whom I was beginning a relationship" (Kaminker, 1992, p. 16).

- "For a long time I thought I could deal with my anger and hostility on my own. But I couldn't. I denied that it had affected me, and yet I was so frantic on the inside with other people: I needed to be constantly reassured. It wasn't until I started seeing myself self-destructing that I realized I needed help. To realize how angry I was and to ask for help—those were the stepping stones. There's a part of me that wants to be stoic and very strong. I had to realize that the attack wasn't directed at me, as Kelly. It was random. I was at the wrong place at the wrong time. That was the first step toward getting rid of all those hostile feelings I had about it. Still, when you're a victim of a violent crime—when somebody has taken control over your life, if only for a moment—I don't think you ever fully recover" (actress Kelly McGillis, quoted by Yakir, 1991, p. 5).

sonnel, and victim advocates with whom the victim has had contact in the immediate aftermath of trauma. Relevant event variables include the frequency, the severity, and the duration of the traumatic event(s) and the degree of physical violence, personal violation, and life-threat endured by the victim. Environmental variables involve the setting where the victimization occurred, including home, school, workplace, or street. Other environmental variables are the degree of safety and control that are afforded to victims post-trauma; prevailing community attitudes and values about sexual assault; and the availability, quality, accessibility, and diversity of victim care and victim advocacy services. (p. 45)

A middle-class college student who has been raised in a family that values daughters as much as sons and who is well-informed about rape and able to avail herself of the supportive resources of an active feminist community may respond to sexual assault quite differently than will a teenage girl whose pre-rape beliefs involved victim blaming and whose key support figures continue to believe that "an unwilling woman can't really be raped." Similarly, individuals who experience violence and abuse in isolation from others and who feel obliged to recover from their experience in continued isolation will adjust differently over time than will those individuals whose suffering has been shared and/or those who have access to and are able to make use of helpful support figures. (p. 44)

Burgess and Holmstrom (1974) divided RTS into two phases, an **acute crisis phase** and a **long-term reactions phase**. The first phase may contain reactions that last for days or weeks, and these are likely to be quite severe. They can affect all aspects of the survivor's life, including physical, psychological, social, and sexual aspects. The second phase is a more reconstructive one, which includes survivors' coming to terms with their reactions and attempting to deal with the hurt and sadness in an effective way.

Phase I: Acute Crisis Phase

Initiated immediately after the act, the acute crisis phase is characterized by great disorganization in the survivor's life. It is often described by survivors as a state of shock, in which they report that everything has fallen apart inside. Many re-experience the attack over and over again in their minds. Even sleep, when it finally comes, does not re-energize; instead, it serves as a vehicle for nightmares about the rape. Those raped in their own beds are particularly affected by insomnia (Burge, 1988).

When victims are asked to complete a check-list of their reactions only two or three hours after having been raped, interviewers found high degrees of similarity in responses: 96 percent reported feeling scared, a similar percentage were anxious or worried, and 92 percent said they were terrified and confused (Veronen, Kilpatrick, & Resick, 1979). "Thoughts were racing through my mind," said more than 80 percent of those who had been attacked.

Cognitive accounts of anxiety were not the only frequent reactions; physiological exemplars of fear or anxiety often included the following:

- shaking or trembling (reported by 96 percent of respondents)
- a racing heart (80 percent)
- pain (72 percent)
- tight muscles (68 percent)
- rapid breathing (64 percent)
- numbness (60 percent)

Although these manifestations of fear and anxiety are the most frequent, a number of other consequences appear. Nearly one-half of survivors scored as moderately or severely depressed on the Beck Depression Inventory (Frank & Stewart, 1984). One study reported suicide attempts by 19 percent of a community sample of women who had been raped (Kilpatrick, Best, Veronen, Amick, et al., 1985b). The person's previous sense of invulnerability dissipates in a decrease of self-esteem. Allison and Wrightsman (1993), in reviewing reports, classified these phase-one reactions with the following characteristics.

Denial, Shock, and Disbelief

"This couldn't have happened *to me*" was a common response. One victim, later recounting her thoughts during the attack, said: "Thoughts pounded through my head as I tried to understand what was happening. Was this a joke? Was this someone I know being cruel? It couldn't be real" (Barr, 1979, p. 18). Survivors may question their family and friends about how the rape could have happened.

Disruption

Changes in sleeping and eating patterns are typical. To varying degrees, survivors may display personality disorganization (Bassuk, 1980). Some may appear to be confused and disoriented, whereas others do not exhibit such easily observable behavioural symptoms, but the latter type may be dazed and numb, and hence unresponsive to their environment.

Guilt, Hostility, and Blame

When learning that a friend has been raped, others may react by **blaming the victim**, by assuming that the rape could have been avoided, or by otherwise attributing responsibility for the rape to the person who was raped. Psychoanalytic theory unfortunately proposed that the essence of femininity included masochism, and the belief that women not only invite, but enjoy, sexual aggression still persists (Bond & Mosher, 1986). Thus it is not surprising that victims, too, respond with guilt and self-blame.

Janoff-Bulman (1979) has suggested that a **self-blaming response** may be the second most frequent one after fear. "If only I had locked that window" or "If only I had taken an earlier bus home" are examples of reactions in which the survivors blame their own actions for the rape, or at least imply that different behaviours on their part could have avoided it. A distinction has been made between this type of self-blame; behavioural self-blame; and characterological self-blame, which refers to attributions by the survivor to stable and uncontrollable aspects of the self and may be characterized by statements such as "I'm just the kind of person who gets raped" (Frazier, 1990; Janoff-Bulman, 1979). In some victims, self-blame can be so strong that they believe the rape was their fault or that the man cared for them. Cases are reported of survivors who even married the men who raped them (Warshaw, 1988).

Other survivors may direct their aggression and blame at men in general, or at society for permitting sexual assaults to occur. Meyer and Taylor (1986) reported that 11 percent of rape victims reacted in this manner, by agreeing to statements like "Men have too little respect for women" or "There is never a policeman around when you need him." In this sample of survivors, only a little more than half (56 percent) assigned blame to the rapist.

Regression to a State of Helplessness or Dependency

Persons who have been raped often report the feeling that they no longer are independent persons. A sense of autonomy or competence is replaced with one of self-doubt. Survivors are overwhelmed with feelings that they no longer have control over their lives and what happens to them. They have to rely on those close to them to make even the most insignificant decisions. One told Warshaw (1988): "Deciding what to wear in the morning was enough to make me panic and cry uncontrollably" (p. 54).

Distorted Perceptions

Distrust and pessimism—and even paranoia—are frequent reactions to being the recipient of a sexual assault. The world becomes a scary place in which to live. In one survey, 41 percent of a sample of college students who were acquain-tance-rape survivors believed that they would be raped again (Koss, 1988).

Phase II: Long-Term Reactions

In the second phase of RTS, survivors face the task of restoring order to their lives and re-establishing a sense of equilibrium and the feeling of mastery over their world (Burgess & Holmstrom, 1985). This task is not an easy one; if, indeed, completion of the task occurs, it usually takes anywhere from a few months to years. Most of the improvement occurs somewhere between one and three months after the rape (Kilpatrick, Resick, & Veronen, 1981), but only 20 percent to 25 percent of survivors reported no symptoms one year after the attack. Burgess and Holmstrom (1985) reported that 25 percent of the women they studied had not significantly recovered several years after the rape. Regression can occur, with some reporting being worse on some measures one year after the rape, compared to six months afterward. Among the responses that may reoccur are specific anxieties; guilt and shame; catastrophic fantasies; feelings of dirtiness, helplessness, or isolation; and physical symptoms (Forman, 1980).

Thus, often life activities are resumed, but they are "undertaken superficially or mechanically" (Koss & Harvey, 1991, p. 54). One of the challenging quests during this phase is for survivors to understand what has happened to them and what they are feeling as a process of psychological healing moves forward (Bard & Sangrey, 1979). Their cognitive development may be impeded by being "constantly haunted" by vivid, traumatic memories (Neiderland, 1982, p. 414). One survivor reported, "I can't stop crying … and sometimes I feel a little bit overwhelmed. All these things flashing, all these memories" (quoted by Roth & Lebowitz, 1988, p. 90). It is not uncommon for rape survivors to experience contradictory feelings: fears, sadness, guilt, and anger all at the same time. A temptation is to assume "Once a victim, always a victim." Four months after having been raped, a woman wrote, "I am so sick of being a 'rape victim.' I want to be me again" (Barr, 1979, p. 105). Following a cognitive explanation, Koss and Harvey (1991) noted a change of schema, or organizing structure, as the rape led to shifts in beliefs about trust, safety, and intimacy.

Allison and Wrightsman (1993) described the following as among the major symptoms of this second phase.

Phobias

A **phobia** is an irrational fear, the possession of which interferes with affective adaptation to one's environment. A one-year follow-up of women who had been raped found frequent reports that they were still expressing phobias and other manifestations of fear and anxiety (Kilpatrick, Resick, & Veronen, 1981). A rape can be viewed as a **classical conditioning stimulus**, and thus anything associated with the rape will come to be feared, as a result of the association (Kilpatrick et al., 1981). The phenomenon of stimulus generalization means that if a knife was used in the attack, the survivor may develop a negative reaction to all types of knives. Survivors of sexual assaults may become afraid of being alone, or of going out at night.

As Allison and Wrightsman observed:

> These fears may force the victim into what seems to be a no-win situation. If she stays home alone, she is afraid. If she goes out, she is also afraid. Many victims leave the lights on in their homes 24 hours a day. Clearly the nature of the conditional associations to the rape leads victims to alter their lives in many ways. (1993, p. 156)

Disturbances in General Functioning

Carrying out routine aspects of life is often a challenge during the second phase. Changes in eating patterns and sleeping patterns remain a problem. For some, the quality of intimate relationships may deteriorate, as the survivor restricts opportunities to take advantage of what previously were seen as positive experiences. One survivor wrote:

> Jon and I had known for months that he would have to make a business trip to California in December. Originally, before things had changed, we had all planned to go. I loved California, I wanted to go away with Jon, I didn't want to be left alone, but as the trip approached we had to face the reality … I didn't think I could leave the little security I found in my house, for strange motels. Camping was out of the question. We gave up the idea and I tried to think about how I would survive a week without Jon. (Barr, 1979, p. 83)

Sexual Problems

Having been sexually assaulted has a strong negative effect on the survivor's sexual life. But several studies concluded that the difference between women who had been raped and a comparable group who had not was not the *frequency* of sexual activities but rather the subjective quality of such experiences (Feldman-Summers, Gordon, & Meagher, 1979; Orlando & Koss, 1983). Sexual assault survivors reported that they did not enjoy sex with their partner as much as they had before they were raped, and this level of satisfaction was not as high as that of the control group for almost every type of intimate relationship. The only exceptions were of two types: activities considered primarily as affectional rather than sexual (such as hand holding or hugging) and masturbation; frequency and satisfaction for both of these types of activities was unaffected by the rape. But survivors reported less desire to engage in sexual activity (Becker, Skinner, Abel, Axelrod, & Treacy, 1984).

Changes in Lifestyle

Some survivors of a sexual assault may restructure their activities and change their jobs and their appearance (Warshaw, 1988). Changing their phone numbers is typical. Moving to another residence or even another city is not unusual.

The Relationship of Rape Trauma Syndrome to Post-Traumatic Stress Disorder

Many people in society live and deal with painful recollections of a horrific traumatic experience, often with severe consequences for their mental health (e.g., Peace & Porter, 2004). Psychological "trauma" is an emotional experience resulting from exposure to an event that involved actual or threatened death or serious injury, or a threat to the physical integrity of self or others. The most extreme psychological outcome of a traumatic experience is **post-traumatic stress disorder** (PTSD), affecting about 9 percent to 15 percent of the population (e.g., Breslau et al., 1991). People with PTSD live with painful recollections of a horrific experience, typically characterized by extremes of recall: intrusive memories combined with avoidance of thoughts or feelings about the event. PTSD often occurs following experiences such as military combat, natural disasters, serious accidents, witnessing violent death, or violent personal attacks.

In Canada, PTSD has received a great deal of attention of late because of high-profile cases in the media. Roméo Dallaire, who commanded Canadian peacekeeping forces during the 1990s mass genocide in Rwanda, suffered extreme PTSD symptoms after he returned to Canada. He has since written about his continuing ordeal with PTSD symptoms in his book *Shake Hands with the Devil—The Failure of Humanity in Rwanda* (Dallaire, 2003). When the SwissAir Flight 111 went down near Peggy's Cove, Nova Scotia, in September 1998, all 229 onboard were killed, leaving nothing but a scattering of body parts and debris in the ocean. Over the next few days, military and civilian personnel launched a massive effort to recover the remains of the victims from open waters and the nearby beaches. Dalhousie University psychologist Sherry Stewart and her colleagues (Stewart, Mitchell, Wright, & Loba, 2004) found that 46 percent of a sample of these volunteer workers met the criteria for PTSD several years later.

The type of horrific experience studied by Stewart and colleagues may be exceeded by few types of human experience in causing PTSD. However, one such experience is rape (e.g., Foa & Rothbaum, 1998). Several researchers have documented that PTSD is often present in survivors of rape, and some have concluded that survivors of rape are the largest single group of PTSD sufferers (Foa, Olasov, & Steketee, 1987, cited by Koss & Harvey, 1991; Steketee & Foa, 1987). Foa and Rothbaum (1998) estimate that the incidence of PTSD symptoms in rape victims is upward of 50 percent.

A number of researchers have pointed to many possible parallels between RTS and PTSD (Follingstad, 1994a). The third edition of the *Diagnostic and Statistical Manual of Mental Disorders-Revised,* often referred to as "DSM-III-R," first recognized the presence of a psychological disorder that was a direct result of a stressful event; this disorder, termed post-traumatic stress disorder, was defined as "the development of characteristic symptoms following a psychologically distressing event that is outside the range of usual human experience" (American Psychiatric Association, 1987, p. 247). The DSM-III-R further suggested that PTSD is "apparently more severe and longer lasting when the stressor is of human design" than if it were a disaster of nature or war combat (1987, p. 248). The major symptoms used to demonstrate the presence of PTSD are (1) a repeated experiencing of the traumatic event (e.g., intrusive thoughts or recurrent nightmares) or, in contrast, an avoidance of situations, ideas, and feelings that were related to the traumatic event and (2) a **psychic numbing** or reduced responsiveness to the environment.

In addition to these primary symptoms, the DSM-III-R diagnosis specified that a person must be experiencing at least two of the following:

1. Difficulty falling or staying asleep.
2. Irritability or outbursts of anger.
3. Difficulty concentrating.
4. Hypervigilance.
5. Exaggerated startle response.
6. Physiological reactivity upon exposure to events that symbolize or resemble an aspect of the traumatic event (American Psychiatric Association, 1987). (The fourth edition of the DSM has maintained this description of PTSD.)

Horowitz, Wilner, and Alvarez (1979) developed the Impact of Event Scale (IES) to measure the first primary symptom associated with PTSD. Later, Kilpatrick and Veronen (1984) administered this scale to survivors whose rapes had occurred earlier (six to 21 days, three months, six months, one year, two years, or three years before). Regardless of the length of time since the rape, most survivors reported experiencing aspects of both primary symptoms. With regard to the second symptom, the numbed responsiveness and reduced involvement with the environment, Kilpatrick et al. (1981) found in a longitudinal study that fear stemming from having been raped caused survivors to restrict their daily activities and lifestyles dramatically.

With respect to the other six PTSD criteria listed above, several studies have identified some or all these symptoms in specific survivors of rape (Burgess & Holmstrom, 1985; Kilpatrick, Veronen, & Best, 1985). More frequently, the symptoms are avoidance behaviours, hypersensitivity, difficulties in maintaining concentration, and intensification of symptoms whenever exposed to rape-related cues.

In 1991, the Supreme Court of Canada explicitly recognized the traumatic consequences of sexual assault in *R. v. McCraw* (1991). The Court observed:

> The psychological trauma suffered by rape victims has been well documented. It involves symptoms of depression, sleeplessness, a sense of defilement, the loss of sexual desire, fear and distrust of others, strong feelings of guilt, shame and loss of self-esteem. It is a crime committed against women which has a dramatic, traumatic impact.... To ignore the fact that rape frequently results in serious psychological harm to the victim would be a retrograde step, contrary to any concept of sensitivity in the application of the law (para. 84).

Why do some people who are sexually assaulted develop debilitating PTSD while others recover relatively quickly? Foa and Rothbaum (1998) proposed that PTSD is the outcome of a fear memory that contains mistaken evaluations, whereas a normal trauma memory that does not result in PTSD reflects evaluations that are closer to reality. In particular, those who develop PTSD come to recall their emotional responses and actions during the experience in a way that promotes an increasingly negative view of themselves ("I am a bad person"), thus interfering with their psychological recovery. As such, a rape victim who blames herself for what happened is more likely to develop the disorder. Another probable factor contributing to whether someone develops PTSD or RTS after a sexual assault is whether the traumatic experience is shared with others. The importance of discussing traumatic experiences such as rape in leading to positive health outcomes is widely recognized (see Foa & Rothbaum, 1998). Several studies have compared outcomes of victims who had written about their trauma to control trauma groups who wrote about unrelated events (e.g., Pennebaker & Beall, 1986). These studies consistently found more positive health outcomes (e.g., fewer doctor visits, self-reported health problems) in disclosure versus control groups. Pennebaker (1993) found that the simple act of writing out a traumatic memory had positive effects on physical and mental health.

WHAT CAN A PSYCHOLOGIST DO?

When a person reports having been sexually assaulted and becomes a witness in a criminal trial against the alleged attacker, one task for a forensic clinical psychologist is an assessment of the survivor's claims and responses. Later, at the trial, a forensic psychologist may be called on to testify about the presence of RTS in order to support the complainant's claim of sexual assault, especially if there is no corroborating evidence to support the claim (Follingstad, 1994a).

As an example, consider the Ontario Court of Appeal case *R. v. Fagundes* (1997). In the original case, José Fagundes was convicted of breaking into a woman's home and brutally sexually assaulting her. Forensic psychologist Dr. Lana Stermac was asked by the Crown to give expert testimony with respect to PTSD and, specifically, rape trauma syndrome. The Crown argued that such evidence was necessary to help the jury to understand the victims' inability to identify the accused until some time after the attack, and to explain her "unusual" psychological reactions following the attack. The trial judge considered these reactions:

> She also testified about three other occurrences. She visualized the assailant as a blank styrofoam head. The type that would be in a store window with a hat or a wig on it. She was unable to visualize the particular features of her assailant. Another was that she would view the incident at times as a third party, as if she was viewing the rape that was perpetrated on her. Another was that, she visualized that during the period of the rape she had been tied up although her memory is clearly that did not occur. She said it was almost as if she was watching a movie, that is how she would reflect upon it. Another circumstance is the fact that the threat that the complainant now testifies to was not disclosed until eight or nine months after the event. (*R. v. Fagundes*, 1997, para. 12)

The judge believed that the pattern of her memories was not something that jurors could easily understand. As such, he allowed expert testimony on PTSD and RTS as possibly beneficial, and in line with the requirements for admitting an expert set out in *R. v. Mohan* (1994).

In Canada, this type of expert testimony during the trial may be less common than during sentencing or in civil hearings. Here, victim impact statements, which may indicate the presence of RTS or PTSD, are often entered prior to sentencing to inform the judge's decision about an appropriate sentence. During civil hearings, the presence of RTS or PTSD can influence the nature of the financial settlement and whether the victim is entitled to counselling.

The potential roles of psychologists in the process are described in the next sections.

ASSESSMENT

Follingstad (1994a) has identified a number of activities for the psychologist in this role:

1. Document the survivor's level of psychological, social, and physical functioning both before and after the sexual assault.
2. Assess the survivor's changes in identity, including loss of self-esteem and dignity, increased difficulty in decision making, and changes in feeling about her appearance.
3. Interview the survivor and administer self-report measures to determine the presence of phobias as well as generalized and specific fears.
4. Determine social adjustment, level of sexual functioning, coping mechanisms, and also identify other stressors around the time of the rape.
5. Interview others (family members, friends, roommates, spouse or significant other) to corroborate the survivor's report, as well as obtain their evaluations of the survivor's truth telling.

6. Determine whether the survivor has experienced previous sexual assaults.

Great care needs to be given to the manner in which rape survivors are questioned. Dean Kilpatrick (1983) has urged that the psychologist not be judgmental and that an effort be made to normalize the experience. That is, recognizing that often survivors are reluctant to disclose or describe the assault, psychologists should give them support when interviewing them. Suggested introductory statements include "Sometimes very bad things happen to good people—sometimes bad sexual things."

A number of rating scales and self-report measures are available to document the victim's level of trauma. Follingstad (1994a) and Koss and Harvey (1991) have described the following instruments:

- Sexual Assault Symptoms Scale (Ruch, Gartrell, Amedeo, & Coyne, 1991): This 32-item self-report scale is administered to the survivor as soon as possible after the rape. It measures four factors, including Disclosure Shame, Safety Fears, Depression, and Self-Blame. A difficulty is that many survivors are unable to complete the scale because of their emotional state, exhaustion, or intoxication.

- Clinical Trauma Assessment (Ruch, Gartrell, Ramelli, & Coyne, 1991): This rating scale, completed by the clinical psychologist is useful in assessing the severity of the trauma. The survivor first participates in a structured interview; then the psychologist rates her or him on each of 16 specific trauma symptoms. Examples include depression, tension/rigidity, and loss of trust in people. A factor analysis revealed three main factors, labelled as Controlled Emotional Trauma Style, Cognitive Trauma, and Expressed Emotional Trauma Style.

- Rape Trauma Syndrome Rating Scale (DiVasto, 1985): This scale is designed to assess the severity of eight symptoms of the trauma of sexual assault; ratings are done by the interviewers after they ask open-ended questions about each symptom (e.g., "Has your appetite changed in any way?"). The scale distinguishes between survivors and a control group of women who had not been raped.

- Impact of Event Scale (Horowitz, Wilner, & Alvarez, 1979): Previously mentioned, this is a 15-item self-report scale, separated into two subscales, designed especially to measure symptoms of intrusion and avoidance. Respondents think of the last week and rate the items according to how much trouble they have had. The IES was able to detect changes in distress in rape survivors after treatment (Kilpatrick & Amick, 1985).

Also, a number of clinical instruments are available to assess PTSD, including scales developed from the MMPI; these are reviewed by Wilson and Keane (1997).

TESTIMONY AS AN EXPERT WITNESS

One justification for the testimony of a psychologist as an expert witness in a rape trial is that jurors do not fully understand the nature of rape; they may misinterpret the reactions of the survivor, and they may subscribe to a number of **rape myths**, or incorrect beliefs about the causes and consequences of rape. Although a number of specific myths abound, they may take three general forms: (1) women cannot be raped against their will, (2) women secretly wish to be raped, and (3) most accusations of rape are faked (Brownmiller, 1975). Specific knowledge about rape trauma syndrome is often lacking. A survey about rape and post-traumatic stress disorder, completed by laypersons and by psychologists, found that the laypersons were not well informed on many relevant issues (Frazier & Borgida, 1988).

Consider a typical set of circumstances: A woman reports to the police that she has been raped and identifies her attacker. The prosecutor concludes that enough evidence exists to proceed to a trial. The defendant's position is that sexual intercourse occurred between the two parties but it was consensual. This set of events is fairly typical; most rapes are acquaintance rapes, not rapes by strangers. Thus, when the case goes to trial, the jury essentially must answer the question "Whom do you believe?" Given such circumstances, a forensic psychologist as an expert witness may be helpful to the prosecution with regard to several issues (Block, 1990), discussed next.

The Issue of Consent

Is a complainant's behaviour consistent with having been raped? Faigman, Kaye, Saks, and Sanders (1997) concluded that "by far the most accepted use of RTS in rape prosecutions" was to demonstrate that the alleged victim's behaviour was "consistent with that of victims in general" (p. 406). A number of courts have permitted psychologists and other mental health professionals to testify about trauma in the survivor as evidence of a lack of consent, or to refute defence claims that the alleged victim's behaviour was inconsistent with that of someone who had been raped. One of the first such cases in which admissibility was granted was the American case *State v. Marks* (1982). The defendant met a woman at a bar and persuaded her to return to his home, where—she later alleged—he drugged her, raped her, and forced her to have oral sex with him. The prosecution introduced the expert testimony of a forensic psychologist who had examined the survivor two weeks after the encounter and concluded "that she was suffering from the PTSD known as rape trauma syndrome" (*State v. Marks,* 1982, p. 1299). The defendant was convicted.

Questions about the Behaviour of the Alleged Victim

As noted earlier, some jurors may subscribe to myths or incorrect beliefs about the nature of rape and survivors of rape. Survivors may delay in reporting the attack, and thus, when they testify, they may make inconsistent statements or exhibit a lack of memory. The defence lawyer may use these behaviours to attack the credibility of the alleged victim; hence the testimony of a psychologist about the presence of RTS in the witness may educate the jury about the real reactions and feelings of rape survivors as well as disabusing them of misconceptions (Block, 1990). Thus, here, the expert would testify as a rebuttal witness, after the survivor's credibility has been challenged, either on cross-examination or during the defence's direct examination (McCord, 1985).

Supporting a Claim of Damages in a Civil Suit

In an increasing number of cases, a sexual assault survivor may sue an alleged attacker in a civil suit in order to recover damages, or a third party may be sued for failure to provide protection. As outlined by Kevin Douglas and his colleagues, Canadian civil courts have begun to acknowledge that someone who suffers psychological injuries because of another person may be entitled to financial compensation (Douglas, Huss, Murdoch, Washington, & Koch, 1999). For example, in one of the first such cases, a woman sued her father for damages arising from years of sexual assaults, and the infliction of mental distress. A jury found that the accused had sexually assaulted his daughter and inflicted psychological distress, and assessed tort damages of $50 000. This finding was reversed but later upheld in the Supreme Court of Canada (*M.[K.] v. M.[H.],* 1992).

However, in general Canadian courts have been reluctant to award damages for psychological harm in the absence of physical injury (Samra & Connolly, 2004). Joti Samra at the University of British Columbia and Deborah Connolly at Simon Fraser University have examined the legal compensability of sufferers of PTSD in Canada. They describe four main concerns of the courts concerning the practice of compensating for psychological injuries:

1. There is a greater degree of diagnostic uncertainty in psychological versus physical injury cases.
2. The prospect of financial gain may have an unconscious motivating effect on potential claimants.
3. By expanding the scenarios in which psychological injury may be compensated, the "floodgates" of litigation may be opened.
4. Liability for purely psychological harm may result in a widened burden of liability on civil defendants.

Despite these concerns, Canadian courts are increasingly willing to award compensation for psychological damages to victims of sexual crimes, even in the absence of physical injuries. Numerous Aboriginal people who suffered sexual abuse during their forced attendance at residential schools have been so compensated, for example. In other cases, parents have been successfully sued by their children whom they sexually victimized. Some recent case examples include the following:

1. *Y. (S.) v. C. (F. G.)* (1997): This is a leading British Columbia case pertaining to damages in sexual assault cases. A stepfather had sexually assaulted his stepdaughter over a seven-year period. Overturning a jury award of $350 000, the judge awarded the stepdaughter $250 000 for general and aggravated damages. The judge described aggravating factors (making the crime more severe and leading to higher compensation) in such cases, including the nature, duration, number, and frequency of the assaults; the relationship between the plaintiff and the defendant; the defendant's level of remorse; and the physical pain and psychological suffering associated with the sexual abuse.
2. *A. B. v. T. S.* (2000): In this case, sexual abuse had been perpetrated on a young girl by a family friend. The judge noted (para. 28) that although there was no violence, there was a very close relationship between the defendant and the plaintiff. The abuse took place over a period of approximately nine years, from infancy to early adolescence. The abuse involved fondling of her genitals and digital penetration of her vagina and anus, along with oral sex. In considering the psychological damages, the judge awarded the plaintiff $165 000.
3. *W. M. Y. v. Scott* (2000): In this case, a man alleged that he was sexually assaulted by his soccer coach about 15 times over three years, starting when he was nine years of age. A psychologist gave his expert opinion that the plaintiff did not meet the full criteria for PTSD, but was left with major psychological problems, such as low self-esteem, relationship difficulties, and substance abuse problems. The judge awarded the man $110 000 in general and aggravated damages.

Thus, Canadian courts have established that physical injuries are not necessary to award compensation in sexual assault cases. Further, whereas it is perhaps the most common diagnosis in such cases, PTSD is not a necessary diagnosis. Psychological damages have been interpreted liberally and, certainly, RTS is applicable.

When a civil claim for psychological damages does occur, a psychologist's testimony will typically be introduced to support the claim. Samra and Connolly (2004) describe several guidelines for psychologists who conduct assessments of PTSD in a civil litigation case. These include:

1. Use well-established diagnostic schemes, such as the DSM-IV.
2. Clearly address the issue of causation (i.e., the relation between the defendant's actions and the plaintiff's psychological problems).
3. Document specifically the functional limitations of PTSD on the specific individual.
4. Document the impact the disorder has on the person's quality of life.
5. Give an opinion of the severity of the disorder and prognosis.
6. Address the person's personality problems and how the traumatic event(s) are related to them.

7. Include an assessment of possible malingering and deception.

As Frazier and Borgida (1992) noted, one problem is that "rape trauma syndrome" refers to a loose collection of symptoms. Some critics have already argued that its generality removes any meaning from the term (Lawrence, 1984). Further, it is a term that may have several specific definitions. Careful review of the scientific literature led Frazier and Borgida to conclude that the recent literature, which has used standardized assessment measures and carefully matched control groups, has established that "rape victims experience more depression, anxiety, fear, and social adjustment problems than women who have not been victimized … [and] that many victims experience PTSD symptoms following an assault" (1992, p. 301).

At the same time, experts need to be careful to limit their testimony to verifiable statements. One problem of expert testimony is that it sometimes is not an accurate reflection of the state of scientific knowledge. Expert witnesses have described symptoms that have not been documented empirically, and on occasion they have generalized findings from adults to children (Faigman et al., 1997). Frazier and Borgida also cited several examples of experts' claims that have not been found in research—for example, that it is "very common" for a victim to ask the rapist not to tell anyone about the rape. Boeschen, Sales, and Koss (1998) classified possible testimony into five levels. These are summarized in Box 11.2 and serve as a useful summary for the limits of testimony.

THE SCIENTIFIC STATUS OF RESEARCH ON RTS

Given the sometimes-misleading testimony and inconsistent court decisions, what is the current status of research on rape trauma syndrome? Frazier and Borgida, in a section of the relevant chapter in the Faigman, Kaye, Saks, and Sanders (1997) handbook on scientific evidence, have provided a useful review of recent research. The two central questions are: "What symptoms do rape victims experience?" and "Do rape victims exhibit a different set of symptoms than do nonvictims?" The reviewers identified several symptoms, with the following conclusions:

- *Depression.* As noted earlier, depression is one of the most commonly reported psychological disorders in rape victims. The review identified seven studies that compared depressive symptoms of groups of rape victims and nonvictims, with depression assessed through the highly regarded Beck Depression Inventory. All seven studies found the average scores of the rape victims to be significantly higher than those of the nonvictims. Across studies, between 18 percent and 45 percent of the victims were moderately to severely depressed, whereas only 4 percent to 23 percent of the subjects in the nonvictim control groups were (Faigman et al., 1997).

- *Fear.* Self-report studies using the Veronen-Kilpatrick Modified Fear Survey found differences between victims and nonvictims up to one year after the rape. One study found that recent rape victims were more fearful than victims of other crimes. However, the duration of the fear was unclear, with some studies reporting differences several years after the rape, whereas other studies concluded that victims' fear had subsided by then.

- *Anxiety.* Difficulties in concentrating and avoidance of certain situations because of anxiety were present more often in rape victims than in nonvictims, for at least one year after the rape. In one study, 82 percent of the rape victims met the criteria for a diagnosis of generalized anxiety disorder.

Despite the consistent findings for these specific symptoms, the question remains whether there is virtue or even validity to suggest the

BOX 11.2
Levels of Testimony by an Expert Witness

Boeschen, Sales, and Koss (1998) proposed five levels of testimony in evaluating the appropriateness of admitting scientific testimony on the trauma of having been raped.

- *Level 1: Testimony on specific behaviours of rape survivors that are described as "unusual" by the defence.* "Testimony at this level is used by the victim's counsel in both criminal and civil trials to rebut the perpetrator's argument that a victim exhibited an unusual behavior following a rape" (Boeschen et al., 1998, p. 424). The courts generally have found this testimony helpful; it counteracts stereotypes held by some jurors, and empirical work has confirmed that such behaviours (delay in reporting a rape, failure to identify the attacker) are not that unusual.

- *Level 2: Testimony on the common reactions to rape and the general diagnostic criteria of RTS or PTSD.* The expert describes common reactions; he or she has not examined the alleged victim and does not discuss the specific victim's behaviours. This type of testimony is generally considered to be appropriate, with the qualifier that the term *rape trauma syndrome* is sometimes excluded because of its prejudicial nature.

- *Level 3: Expert gives an opinion about the consistency of a victim's behaviour or symptoms with RTS or PTSD.* Boeschen and her colleagues noted: "This type of testimony is much more controversial than

that of Level 1 or 2 because it permits the expert to go beyond the general, educational information and apply it to a specific case" (1998, p. 426). Some courts have found it too prejudicial, but these authors believe that it is a valid use of expert testimony, since the psychologist "does not appear to unfairly comment on the victim's credibility" (p. 427).

- *Level 4: Testimony stating that the victim suffers from RTS or PTSD.* The expert describes the complainant's symptoms and states that these meet the criteria for a diagnosis of PTSD, but the expert does not state that she was raped. Some courts have permitted this level of testimony, noting that the defence is allowed to cross-examine this witness or provide its own expert witness. But resolution of the issue remains difficult, especially with RTS testimony. Any psychologist who is allowed to testify has the ethical obligation to state the limitations of the concepts he or she introduces.

- *Level 5: Expert opinion that goes beyond a diagnosis.* At this level, the expert testifies that the victim is telling the truth and that she was raped. This level of testimony will be generally excluded. As noted in Chapter 9 with regard to testimony on criminal responsibility, this is ultimate-opinion testimony that may trespass on the role of the fact-finder.

presence of a "syndrome." The next section offers a substitute for the use of RTS in expert testimony.

SUBSTITUTING PTSD FOR RTS

As we have seen, the concept of rape trauma syndrome was originally based on the commonly shared experiences of rape survivors interviewed in hospital emergency rooms. Its original purpose was to aid psychotherapists in treatment. Some careful reviewers (see Frazier & Borgida, 1992) believe that the evidence is sufficient that certain reactions differentiate women who have been raped from those who have not. But is this

strong enough to justify introduction of RTS testimony in the courtroom?

Recently Boeschen, Sales, and Koss (1998) have proposed that post-traumatic stress disorder be substituted for rape trauma syndrome in the courtroom. PTSD has the following advantages:

1. It is the primary trauma–related diagnosis included in the *Diagnostic and Statistical Manual of Mental Disorders*. (The term *RTS* is not found in the DSM–IV or in any earlier editions.)
2. As described earlier, a diagnosis of PTSD reflects six rather specific criteria, each with an understandable, operational definition.

3. The PTSD criteria reflect "the intense fear that many rape survivors experience, as well as the desire to avoid situations that are reminders of the rape experience" (Boeschen, Sales, & Koss, 1998, p. 418).

4. A variety of tools are available to assess PTSD, including objective tests, structured diagnostic interviews, and trauma-specific self-report measures (Wilson & Keane, 1997).

5. The use of PTSD in the courtroom avoids employing the word *rape* in the diagnosis. As noted, some courts have considered admitting testimony on RTS as too prejudicial.

However, it should be noted that many of the reactions common to sexual assault survivors—depression, anger, sexual dysfunction, and disruption of basic values—are not included in the PTSD criteria (Faigman, Kaye, Saks, & Sanders, 1997). Some have suggested a "complex PTSD categorization" (Herman, 1992) that would create a consolidated diagnosis for those reacting to rape.

the forensic psychologist may be called on to testify about the presence of rape trauma syndrome in order to support the survivor's claims, especially if there is no corroborating evidence to support the claim and the defendant counterclaims that consensual sexual intercourse occurred. Specifically, as an expert witness, the psychologist may testify about the presence of RTS, which is indicative of lack of consent, or in a civil suit the psychologist may testify to support a claim of psychological damages. At sentencing hearings, victim impact statements are used by judges in deciding upon appropriate sentences for sexual offenders, and RTS can play a role.

Because of problems with the conceptualization of RTS, it has been suggested that, instead, psychologists testify about the applicability of post-traumatic stress disorder, which overlaps some with RTS but contains more clearly defined criteria. On the other hand, Canadian civil courts have adopted a liberal approach with the types of psychological problems that can warrant financial compensation.

SUMMARY

The term *rape trauma syndrome* was first developed more than 20 years ago to account for the relative uniformity of responses by survivors of rape. Burgess and Holmstrom divided the RTS into two phases, an acute crisis phase and a long-term reactions phase. The first phase included cognitive and physiological reactions, including denial, disruption of normal activities, guilt, and regression to a state of helplessness or dependency. The second phase dealt with restoration to a sense of equilibrium and mastery over the world, but many problems continued or reoccurred in this second phase.

Two roles for psychologists are salient with regard to the use of rape trauma syndrome. First is the assessment of the complainant's claims and responses. In doing so, the psychologist interviews the survivor and others, and administers several self-report measures. Second, at the trial,

KEY TERMS

acute crisis phase, p. 241
blaming the victim, p. 242
classical conditioning stimulus, p. 244
long-term reactions phase, p. 241
phobia, p. 244
post-traumatic stress disorder, p. 245
psychic numbing, p. 245
rape myths, p. 248
rape trauma syndrome, p. 240
self-blaming response, p. 242
syndrome, p. 240

SUGGESTED READINGS

Boeschen, L. E., Sales, B. D., & Koss, M. P. (1998). Rape trauma experts in the courtroom. *Psychology, Public Policy, and Law, 4,* 414–432.

This recent review explores the scientific legitimacy of using expert testimony on rape trauma syndrome in the courtroom.

Brekke, N., & Borgida, E. (1988). Expert psychological testimony in rape trials: A social-cognitive analysis. *Journal of Personality and Social Psychology, 55,* 372–386.

These empirical studies describe the limits of the impact of an expert witness testifying about RTS on jury deliberations and verdicts.

Faigman, D. L., Kaye, D. H., Saks, M. J., & Sanders, J. (1997). *Modern scientific evidence: The law and science of expert testimony.* St. Paul, MN: West.

Chapter 10, "Rape Trauma Syndrome," includes a section on legal issues by the volume's authors and a section on the scientific status of the concept by Patricia A. Frazier and Eugene Borgida. Highly recommended.

Frazier, P. A., & Borgida, E. (1992). Rape trauma syndrome: A review of case law and psychological research. *Law and Human Behavior, 16,* 293–311.

Organized around the legal issues of scientific reliability, helpfulness, and prejudicial impact, this review considers the psychological research findings relevant to each of these concerns.

Pekkanen, J. (1976). *Victims: An account of a rape.* New York: Popular Library.

Based on one case, this book traces a rape from the attack, through hospital procedures, the survivor's delayed reactions, the rapist's background, his trial, and the outcome of the case.

12

The Sexual Abuse of Children

The time is right to open a dialogue between professionals from different
walks and exposures to childhood sexual abuse to illuminate exactly what
the issues are.

—STEPHEN J. CECI AND HELENE HEMBROOKE (1998B, P. 3)

THE EMERGENCE OF CONCERN ABOUT SEXUAL CHILD ABUSE

The sexual abuse of children is a significant problem in Canada and internationally. Definitive work in the 1990s by David Finkelhor and his colleagues established that approximately one in eight males and one in four females report having been sexually victimized in childhood (e.g., Finkelhor, Hotaling, Lewis, & Smith, 1990). The 2001 *Canadian Incidence Study of Reported Child Abuse and Neglect* (Trocmé et al., 2001) made the following conclusions about child abuse in Canada:

- Approximately 135 600 (22 per 1000 children) child maltreatment investigations were conducted in 1998. Forty-five percent of the reports were substantiated.
- Approximately 10 percent (more than 13 000) of these investigations involved sexual abuse allegations.
- Touching and fondling of the genitals were the most common form of substantiated child sexual abuse (68 percent). Attempted and completed intercourse together accounted for 35 percent of the cases.
- Overall, 93 percent of the alleged perpetrators were related to the children (usually parents).

Despite these statistics, for decades, society was most concerned about non–family members sexually assaulting and/or killing their children, such as the 2003 murders of ten-year-old Holly Jones and nine-year-old Cecilia Zhang in Ontario. But such cases are very rare. The possibility that children may be sexually abused by their parents or caretakers was largely ignored and even denied in our society. Slowly, awareness of the problem has increased, first as a result of parental claims of abuse by daycare providers and, soon thereafter, as a result of claims of victims and alleged victims. Sometimes these reports were made only when the alleged victim had reached

adulthood. Because of these reports, public concern has increased, motivating forensic psychologists to develop methods for evaluating abuse claims from children and for facilitating the adjustment of children who have been abused.

THE MARTENSVILLE AND MCMARTIN CASES

In the past 20 years, allegations have come forward about the sexual abuse of children while being cared for in daycare centres in Canada, the United States, and Europe. The Martensville case in Saskatchewan and McMartin case in California serve to illustrate the complexities that can arise in evaluating such allegations.

The Martensville Case

In 1992 in Martensville, Saskatchewan, members of the Sterling family (Ron, Linda, and their 25-year-old son Travis, along with an unidentified female minor), and five other men were charged with 190 counts of physical and sexual abuse against two dozen children at their baby-sitting service. Several of the male defendants were police officers; one was a prison deputy director. After a report of an infant's diaper rash, suspicions of child abuse arose and interviews with more children at the service were conducted. Some of the allegations included oral and anal sex, a child being locked in a cage, and anal penetration with an axe handle. One child testified that he had witnessed Mrs. Sterling cut off a boy's nipple and eat it. During the interviews, children reported that they had been taken to "the devil's church" where they were forced to drink urine, consume feces, and submit to abuse. During and after the investigation, rumours of Satanism circulated throughout the community. All charges were dismissed but one.

The interviews used by investigators with the child complainants came under great criticism. The Saskatchewan Court of Appeal (*R. v. Sterling*, 1995, para. 277) noted that: "the use of coercive or highly suggestive interrogation techniques can create a serious and significant risk that the interrogation will distort the child's recollection of events, thereby undermining the reliability of the statements and subsequent testimony concerning such events." In 1994, one of the accused police officers, John Popowich, launched a lawsuit against the government for malicious prosecution. The province fought back tenaciously with countersuits, but Popowich eventually received a $1.3 million settlement from the Saskatchewan government.

Another Saskatchewan case remarkably similar to the Martensville case in many ways surfaced around the same time. In 1991, 16 adults (several members of the Klassen family and others) were arrested and charged with over 70 counts of sexual assault, incest, and gross indecency. The reports made by three foster children against these adults included bizarre child–adult orgies, baby sacrifices, ritual abuse, and bestiality. Eventually, the children who made most of the allegations of sexual and physical abuse recanted all of their allegations (saying that they made up the stories in response to interviewers' demands) and these recantations were publicized in the media.

The McMartin Case

On August 12, 1983, the mother of a two-and-half-year-old boy called the local police to tell them that she believed that her child had been molested by a teacher, Raymond Buckey. (Buckey also was the grandson of the school's 82-year-old founder, Virginia McMartin.) According to the child's mother, the child reported that he was forced to drink blood, he witnessed the head of a live baby being chopped off, and that "Mr. Ray" was able to fly.

Shortly thereafter, the Manhattan Beach police sent a letter to 200 parents, asking whether their children had reported any incidents of molestation at the school. The letter indicated that the police investigation had discovered possible criminal acts including oral sex, sodomy, and fondling of genitals. Raymond Buckey was even named in the letter as a prime suspect.

As you would expect, receipt of the letter created panic in many of the parents; many sent their children for assessment to a social service agency under contract with the prosecutor's office, the Children's Institute International (CII). Of the 400 children interviewed by CII staff, at least 350 were judged as having been abused. A grand jury subsequently indicted Raymond Buckey, his mother (Peggy McMartin Buckey), and five other teachers on charges of sexually abusing children. In June 1984 (almost a year after the initial charges) a preliminary hearing was begun; it lasted an incredible 17 months. After another year's delay, charges against five of the teachers were dropped, but in April 1987 jury selection was begun for the trial of Raymond Buckey and his mother (*People v. Raymond Buckey et al.*, 1990).

The jury reached its verdicts in January 1990, after the longest criminal trial in United States history. The Buckeys were acquitted on 52 of the counts; the jury was deadlocked on 13 other counts against Raymond Buckey. Five months later, the state began a second trial against Raymond Buckey on those 13 counts. Mercifully, this second trial was a shorter one, and in July 1990 the second jury announced its verdicts: not guilty on all counts. An investigation that began with a single complaint in July 1983 was resolved almost seven years later.

Although this type of daycare case receives widespread publicity, there is a second type of charge that is far more frequent: the claim that a child has been sexually abused by a parent, another member of the family, or a family friend. What can forensic psychologists provide in the way of expertise in understanding both types of claims?

ROLES FOR PSYCHOLOGISTS

This chapter describes several roles for forensic psychologists in research and practice relating to child sexual abuse. Each role is introduced in this section and then described in detail in the remaining sections of this chapter.

Research and Assessment on Sexual Offenders

Most of this chapter is focused on research and practice with the child complainant or victim of a sexual offence. Equally important is the task of carrying out systematic research on the nature of sexual offenders. Offenders known to have committed sexual offences are increasing in number; by 1996, 21 percent of offenders in the Canadian federal correctional system had been convicted of at least one sexual offence (Motiuk & Belcourt, 1997). Here we offer a brief sampling of some recent findings in this area (for a more comprehensive review, see Quinsey and Lalumière, 2001).

Sexual predators are a diverse group of offenders. Sexual violence/abuse is a varied set of behaviours, with diverse patterns of motivation, *modus operandi*, and personality traits (see Porter, Fairweather, et al., 2000; Porter, Campbell, Woodworth, & Birt, 2001). Some sexual crimes are highly premeditated and controlled, while others are impulsive and situational (e.g., Knight & Prentky, 1993). Some sex offenders have a **paraphilia,** a recognized mental disorder that involves deviant sexual attraction (recall from Chapter 9 the expert testimony concluding that Jeffrey Dahmer fit such a diagnosis), such as pedophilia. But other offenders do not exhibit a paraphilia, and not all child molesters are pedophiles. Whereas offenders with a paraphilia usually have a single preferred victim type (such as girls aged eight to ten), other offenders perpetrate sexual violence against multiple types of victims (Rice & Harris, 1997).

The most basic classification system of sex offenders distinguishes child molesters and rapists. In general, child molesters tend to be motivated more than rapists by the sexual aspects of their crimes (e.g., Malcolm, Andrews, & Quinsey, 1993). In contrast, anger is more likely to drive the sexual offending of many rapists (e.g., Barbaree, Seto, Serin, Amos, & Preston, 1994). Second, child molesters often focus their criminal behaviour in a sexual manner, whereas the criminal behaviour of rapists usually includes nonsexual offences as well (Prentky, Lee, Knight, & Cerce, 1997; Proulx et al., 1997), and rapists tend to have longer criminal histories than child molesters (e.g., Hanson & Bussière, 1998; Quinsey, Rice, & Harris, 1995; Rice & Harris, 1997). This broad distinction between child molesters and rapists has its limitations, however. For example, it does not take into account offenders who victimize both children and adults, a group associated with a high risk for sexual violence.

In fact, one critical task for forensic psychologists is the assessment of future risk in sexual offenders. In Canada, most sex offenders are conditionally released well before the end of their sentences (called the "warrant expiry date"). Further, only a small number of sex offenders are expected to benefit from treatment (in terms of reducing their reoffending potential; e.g., Furby, Weinrott, & Blackshaw, 1989; Hall, 1995), and in general, their reoffending rate is high (e.g., Doren, 1998; Prentky, Lee, Knight, & Cerce, 1997). For example, Prentky et al. (1997) examined the reoffending patterns of 115 child molesters and rapists over a 25-year period. By the end of the 25-year study period, 52 percent of the molesters and 39 percent of the rapists in the sample had been charged with new sexual offences. Thus, the accurate evaluation of risk for sexual reoffending is crucial. In Canada, legislation relating to dangerous and long-term offenders is sometimes applied to repeat sexual offenders who are deemed to remain at risk of reoffending over the long term. The consequences of such a finding are major for the offender; if "D.O.'d" (i.e., labelled a "dangerous offender"), an offender can be given an indeterminate sentence, only to be released when it is deemed by mental health professionals that it is safe to do so (if ever).

Who among the large group of sexual offenders is most likely to reoffend? In their widely cited meta-analysis (a method in which the researcher combines the findings of a large number of studies), Department of the Solicitor General of Canada researchers Karl Hanson and

Monique Bussière (1998) found that one of the strongest predictors of sexual reoffending was a history of diverse sexual offences. Marnie Rice and Grant Harris (1997) found that sex offenders in Ontario who offended against multiple types of victims were the most dangerous, as indexed by their faster rate of violent reoffending.

In recent years, the relevance of psychopathy in contributing to sexual offending has been highlighted (e.g., Porter & Woodworth, 2004; Seto & Barbaree, 1997). The psychopath seems to lack the emotional resources (such as empathy or remorse) that could otherwise inhibit an urge to sexually assault someone. A number of studies have looked at the relationship of psychopathy and sexual **recidivism** (the rate of reoffending). Vernon Quinsey and his colleagues at Queen's University (1995) found that psychopathy predicted both sexual and violent recidivism among a forensic sample of 178 rapists and child molesters. Psychopathic traits also predict sexual aggression in university students (e.g., Kosson, Kelly, & White, 1997). In addition, a combination of psychopathy and deviant sexual arousal is one of the strongest predictors of sexual reoffending (Rice & Harris, 1997).

To examine the association between psychopathy and sexual offending, Porter, Fairweather et al. (2000) examined the files of more than 300 sex offenders incarcerated in Canada. There was a much higher base rate of psychopathy (64 percent) among sex offenders who targeted both child and adult victims than those who "specialized," such as child molesters.

In addition, psychopaths may commit the most severe forms of sexual assaults against their victims. There is evidence that psychopaths often are sadistic (i.e., they enjoy inflicting pain on others) and that this may be reflected in their violence. Holt, Meloy, and Strack (1999) found that psychopaths more often have sadistic personality traits compared to other violent offenders. A small number of studies even suggest a link between psychopathy and deviant sexual arousal (Barbaree, Seto et al., 1994; Quinsey et al., 1995; Serin et al., 1994). Porter, Woodworth,

et al. (2003) focused on violent behaviour by a sample of 38 sexual murderers currently incarcerated in Canadian prisons. Their results showed that the sexual murders by psychopaths contained significantly more sadistic violence than murders by nonpsychopaths. Overall, 82.4 percent of the psychopaths had engaged in sadistic violence compared to 52.6 percent of the nonpsychopaths.

What about the backgrounds of sexual predators? Becker and Murphy (1998) have reviewed the backgrounds of these individuals and have concluded that the literature does not concur on what causes them to become sexual offenders. This is a research area in great need of attention.

For the remainder of the chapter we focus on the child complainant of sexual abuse and the forensic psychologist's role in the assessment process.

Evaluating the Child

Sometimes, in the midst of a contested child custody case, one of the child's parents may claim that the other parent abused the child. Or, as in many daycare cases, a parent may tell authorities of abuse at school. Evaluating claims, whatever their source, is an exceedingly difficult task (see Bruck, Ceci, & Hembrooke, 1998; Yuille, 1988). No one feels comfortable discussing acts that invaded his or her privacy, and some young children may be limited in their ability to communicate what happened. However, if carefully interviewed, children are as capable of providing accurate accounts as are adults (e.g., Yuille, 1988; Yuille, Marxsen, & Cooper, 1999). Investigators, psychologists, and social workers have used various approaches to assess the presence of abuse. Some of these approaches, such as the Step-Wise Interview technique developed by John Yuille and colleagues (Yuille et al., 1993), have much validity in this context, as we discussed in Chapter 6. Other common approaches, such as the use of **anatomically detailed dolls,** are much more questionable (see Bruck, Ceci, & Francoeur, 2000; Ceci & Bruck, 1993; Samra & Yuille, 1996).

Assessing Competency to Testify

Traditionally, it was assumed that children were not sufficiently competent witnesses to testify in court (see Ceci & Bruck, 1993; Yuille, 1988). Based on British common law, it was believed that children could not distinguish fact from fantasy and were inherently unreliable. Beginning in the 1980s, new legislation in Canada (notably Bill C-15 and changes to the Canada Evidence Act) instituted progressive practices with child witnesses. For example, no longer was corroboration needed when a child made an allegation, and children could now provide evidence via closed-circuit television. As the Supreme Court of Canada noted in *R. v. W. (R.)* (1992):

> First, the notion, found at common law and codified in legislation, that the evidence of children was inherently unreliable and therefore to be treated with special caution has been eliminated. Thus various provisions requiring that a child's evidence be corroborated have been repealed. Second, there is a new appreciation that it may be wrong to apply adult tests for credibility to the evidence of children. While the evidence of children is still subject to the same standard of proof as the evidence of adult witnesses in criminal cases, it should be approached not from the perspective of rigid stereotypes, but on a common sense basis. (summary para. 3)

Thus, at present, if a conclusion is made by police and the Crown prosecutor that sexual abuse likely did occur and charges are laid, the child may be called upon to testify at the preliminary hearing and trial.

In Canada, children under the age of 14 are interviewed by the judge in a case to determine whether they have the intelligence and moral capacity to give evidence. The law requires that a child witness must show that he or she understands the meaning of telling the truth, a lie, and an oath before being considered competent to testify. However, some researchers have criticized these requirements, because of the difficulty many child witnesses experience with them in court (Bala, Lee, Lindsay, & Talwar, 2001; Park & Renner, 1998). Queen's University researcher Nicholas Bala and his colleagues (2001) found that many complex moral and social issues are raised with children during this process, and that the questions are often abstract and beyond their cognitive abilities.

Preparing the Child to Testify

Some children face testifying, especially about abuse, with trepidation. (Other children may find that testifying is a source of catharsis or vindication.) The Crown prosecutor may ask a psychologist to assist in making the apprehensive child as comfortable as possible. On a broader front, innovative procedures have been developed, such as closed-circuit television, to lessen the stress when a child testifies about sexual abuse. Psychologists can evaluate the strengths and limitations of these innovations, with regard to their stated goal of reducing trauma.

The importance of psychologists' involvement in the process of helping children prepare to act as witnesses is exemplified at the Centre for Children and Families in the Justice System of the **London Family Court Clinic** in Ontario (London Family Court Clinic, 2002). This service is internationally renowned for its work with over 1000 child abuse victims and child witnesses. Staff members working at the clinic are experienced therapists who first conduct a thorough intake assessment focused on the child's particular situation, special needs, and concerns about testifying in court. In addition to the child interview, parents are interviewed and standardized psychometric tests are employed to evaluate the child's emotional functioning. Child witnesses are then given information about court procedures, taking an oath, and the meaning of various legal terms. The child witness is also trained in relaxation. The clinic states that there are two main goals for this type of court preparation with the child:

- To help the child witness to provide a full and candid account of the experience (without compromising a defendant's right to a fair trial).
- To ensure that child witnesses are not traumatized further by the legal process itself.

Testifying as an Expert Witness

Either the defence or prosecution could conceivably use a psychologist as an expert witness in a trial involving the sexual abuse of children. A Crown prosecutor could employ a psychologist to testify about research on the validity of children's memories in order to try to overcome the reluctance of many jurors to believe the testimony of children. The defence lawyer could use a psychologist to testify about the problems of eyewitness accuracy and the suggestibility of children. Each of these roles is described in subsequent sections of this chapter.

ASSESSING ALLEGATIONS BY A CHILD

Virtually any time parents report that they suspect their child was sexually abused by a teacher, relative, or other person, police will bring in psychologists or social workers to interview the child as part of the investigation.

Interviewing Techniques

One of the temptations in interviewing young children is the use of **leading questions**, or questions that assume a particular answer (as discussed in Chapter 6). The dilemma is that without the use of such questions, the child may be reluctant to respond at all, but the nature of the question may cause the child to answer in the suggested way, even if the answer does not reflect the child's real feelings or beliefs. On the other hand, the Step-Wise approach advocated by John Yuille offers a

compromise—the initial use of completely non-leading questions, followed by progressively leading inquiries, but only as necessary.

The interviewing procedures used by the staff of Children's Institute International in the McMartin Preschool case have been criticized severely by several psychologists and social workers (Ceci & Bruck, 1995; Mason, 1991), and the availability of the transcripts of these interviews (thanks to the Department of Psychology at McGill University) has permitted the identification of specific problems. The following five procedures have been identified as questionable by James M. Wood, Sela Garven, and their colleagues (Wood et al., 1997; Garven, Wood, Malpass, & Shaw, 1998).

1. *The use of suggestive questions.* This problem encompasses more than simply asking the child a set of leading questions. The technique of **suggestive questions** consists of "introducing new information into an interview when the child has not already provided that information in the same interview" (Garven et al., 1998, p. 348). For example, a CII interviewer asked a McMartin preschooler "Can you remember the naked pictures?" when no picture taking or nudity had been mentioned (quoted by Garven et al., 1998, p. 348). Suggestive questions reduce the accuracy level of children's reports (Ceci & Bruck, 1993); even the responses of adults are susceptible to being altered by such questions (Loftus, 1975).

2. *The implication of confirmation by other people.* What Wood et al. (1997) called the technique of "Other People" involves telling the child that the interviewer has already obtained information from another child or children regarding the topic at hand. For example, as one interview began, the CII staff member told the child that "every single kid" in a class picture had already talked to her about a "whole bunch of yucky secrets" from the school (quoted by Garven et al., 1998, p. 348). Such actions

create conformity pressures in the respondent, just as do similar police interrogation techniques, used with suspects and described in Chapter 7. As in the above, the memory of adults as well as that of children can be substantially affected by the purported statements of another witness (Shaw, Garven, & Wood, 1997).

3. *Use of positive and negative consequences.* Wood et al. (1997) noted frequent use of positive and negative reinforcement in the McMartin interviewing. The psychologists labelled the technique of giving or promising praise and other rewards as "Positive Consequences." For example, after a series of suggestive questions led to one child agreeing that a teacher had photographed some children while they were naked, the interviewer responded: "Can I pat you on the head … look at what a good help you can be. You're going to help all those little children because you're so smart" (quoted by Garven et al., 1998, p. 349). The technique called "Negative Consequences" reflected criticism of a statement by a child or a general indication that the child's statement was inadequate or disappointing. Wood, Garven, and their colleagues found striking examples in the transcripts. For example, one child denied any wrongdoing by the McMartin staff, and the interviewer's response was: "Are you going to be stupid, or are you going to be smart and help us here?" (quoted by Garven et al., 1998, p. 349). Although these psychologists noted that the effects of positive or negative reinforcement on children's accuracy have not been explored in forensic settings, wide acceptance exists for their general impact.

4. *Repetitious questioning.* Imagine if you were a child and the interviewer kept asking you a question you had unambiguously answered a few minutes before. Would this procedure cause you to change your answer? Wood and his colleagues called this the "Asked-and-Answered" procedure. Research generally

has found that children will change their answers to repeated forced-choice questions but not to repeated open-ended questions; the interpretation is that children assume that their first answer to a forced-choice question was incorrect and so they change it to please the interviewer (Siegal, Waters, & Dinwiddy, 1988).

5. *Inviting speculation.* In the procedure that Wood et al. (1997) called "Inviting Speculation," the child was asked to "pretend" or "figure something out"; this technique was used by interviewers when other procedures had failed to produce confirmations of wrongdoing. (Again, it is remarkably similar to a technique used by police detectives with suspects, when they ask the suspects to role-play or answer a question such as, "Assume you did kill her—how *would* you have done it?") In effect, this procedure lowered the threshold for producing incriminating statements that later could be "confirmed" by the use of some of the earlier-described procedures, especially positive reinforcement and repeated questioning.

Garven et al. (1998) investigated the impact of these techniques in a field experiment, using children ages three to six. While at their daycare centre, the children had a visit from a story teller; they were interviewed about these happenings a week later. Even though the interview was brief (two to five minutes long), responses of many of the children were influenced by the use of reinforcement and social influence techniques. In fact, close to 60 percent of the children's responses reflected errors as a result of these interview techniques. Garven et al. concluded that techniques that effectively elicit false statements from children and adults "fall into four overlapping but distinguishable categories, represented by the acronym SIRR: (a) suggestive questions, (b) social influence, (c) reinforcement, and (d) removal from direct experience" (Garven et al., 1998, p. 355). The last of these refers to such procedures as "Inviting Speculation" (described above) and the interviewer's use of a puppet and a "pretend" instruction to question the child. The latter may provide the child an "escape hatch" when pressured to make false allegations; that is, the child can comply with the interviewer's insistence and still feel that he or she did not tell a lie.

In a classic study by Leichtman & Ceci (1995), the authors examined the memories of 176 children for a visit from a strange man named Sam. Three- to six-year-olds were interviewed on several occasions about the visit in one of the following conditions:

1. *Control*: no interviews contained suggestive questions.
2. *Stereotype*: participants were given information about the stranger before the visit.
3. *Suggestion*: interviews contained misleading suggestions about misdeeds committed by the man.
4. *Stereotype plus suggestion*: both pre- and post-visit manipulations were used with the child participants.

The authors found that ten weeks later, control participants provided accurate reports, children exposed to the stereotypes gave a modest number of false reports, and misleading suggestions resulted in a substantial number of false reports. The children in the combined stereotype-plus-suggestion group made very high levels of false reports.

On the issues of children's understanding and memory of events, extensive research exists; it has been reviewed by several groups of psychologists (Goodman et al., 1999; Melton et al., 1995). Of special concern is the degree to which children are suggestible, because many judges and jurors assume that children are telling the truth when children on the witness stand are questioned. The following conclusions seem appropriate:

1. Children are more susceptible to suggestion than adults, at least under some circumstances (Ceci & Bruck, 1993). But children are not as suggestible as many adults believe them to be, especially when questioned about salient events in their lives.

2. Qualities that lead to increased **suggestibility** in adults—a relatively weak memory to begin with, or a high-status interviewer—also lead to increased suggestibility in children (Ceci, Ross, & Toglia, 1987).
3. When initial memory is strong, age differences in suggestibility diminish or may not be a factor; even three-year-old children are quite capable of resisting false suggestions when their memory is solid (Goodman et al., 1999).

As mentioned, in optimal circumstances children can provide detailed, accurate accounts of their traumatic experiences. For example, Terr (1979) investigated the memories of 25 children, aged five to 14, who had been kidnapped on a school bus, driven around for 11 hours, and then buried underground in a tractor-trailer. After more than a day, part of the roof collapsed and the children dug their way to freedom. These children had intact and detailed memories of the incident after 13 months (Terr, 1979). In a follow-up study, Terr (1983) found that the children's memories for the event remained detailed four years later.

Nonetheless, while adults can certainly produce false memories when exposed to suggestive techniques and misleading information (e.g., Loftus, 2003; Porter et al., 1999), young children are even more susceptible to such influences. As such, both investigators and counsellors must use nonleading interview techniques with children whenever possible.

The Criterion-Based Content Analysis Technique

Often the purpose of the interview with a child who has alleged abuse appears to be getting the child to provide more information about the abuse, which the interviewer may assume to have happened. We need to step back and acknowledge that allegations can be truthful or entirely manufactured (or something in between) (e.g.,

Yuille, Tymofievich, & Marxsen, 1995). For example, the Nova Scotia government recently awarded various sums of money to former residents of the Shelburne School for Boys after former residents made claims of sexual and physical abuse by staff. Many of these claims were later investigated as probable false allegations. In fact, it is possible for a child's account to be accurate, mistaken, or intentionally falsified (Porter, Campbell et al., 2003). Do psychologists have procedures to distinguish between children's truthful statements and false ones?

Psychological researchers have attempted to find a way of discriminating true from false memories in the absence of corroboration (which is frequent in sexual abuse cases) (e.g., Loftus & Pickrell, 1995; Payne, Neuschatz, Lampinen, & Lynn, 1997; Pezdek et al., 1997; Porter et al., 1999). Most of the literature has focused on adults recalling false events, sometimes from childhood. Pezdek and Taylor (2000) reviewed the literature and concluded that mistaken reports tend to contain less perceptual or sensory detail concerning the event, are described with more words, and tend to be held with less confidence. Porter et al. (1999) compared true and false childhood memory reports using a detailed coding procedure called the Memory Assessment Procedure (MAP). It was found that false memories tended to contain fewer details, were less coherent, and were recalled less confidently than true memories. A strong trend was also noted for false memories to be described from a "participant" perspective (own eyes), whereas most true reports were described from an "observer" perspective (like watching a video). However, true and false memories were similar on several content features, making them difficult to identify without a careful analysis. Collectively, these findings suggest that false memories may be distinguishable from true ones. However, as noted by Loftus (2003), much more research is needed in this area before we apply these criteria in practice.

The **criterion-based content analysis technique** (CBCA) was developed as a clinical procedure in Germany to distinguish between children's truthful and fabricated allegations (Undeutsch, 1982, 1984, 1989; see Vrij, 2001). The CBCA is one component of a more comprehensive procedure, called **statement validity assessment** (SVA), consisting of three parts: a structured interview with the child witness, the CBCA, and the application of the Statement Validity Checklist, which assesses other characteristics of the interview process, the witness, and the investigation (Raskin & Esplin, 1991). A description of these processes is as follows:

> The structured interview portion consists of an extensive interview with the alleged child victim, without the use of leading questions. The purpose of this portion of the SVA is to create rapport and assess the child's cognitive, behavioral, and social skills. The second portion of the SVA consists of the CBCA. In this portion, a set of criteria is applied to the verbal content of the child's statement and used to provide an estimate of the statement's veracity. The presence of a criterion is an indication that the child is telling the truth. During this analysis, it may be important to consider the child's age, experience, and skill level when applying the criteria (e.g., younger children's verbal statements may contain less detail, which is one of the CBCA criteria)....
>
> The last portion of the SVA consists of applying the Statement Validity Checklist, which contains statement-related factors that assess the validity of several other characteristics related to the interview, the witness, and the investigation.... These characteristics include, for instance, the child's psychological status and things about the interview that may have influenced the content. On the basis of the integration of the results of these three parts of the SVA, an overall evaluation is made of the statement's veracity. (Ruby & Brigham, 1997, p. 708)

A list of the criteria typically used is found in Box 12.1. The procedure has been used in more than 40 000 cases in Germany, where it is carried out by psychologists appointed as expert witnesses by the trial judge, it has been used in courts in the United States (Honts, 1994), and a version of statement analysis is currently used by the RCMP (RCMP, 2004). Some prominent psychologists, including Americans Charles Honts (1994) and David Raskin (Raskin & Esplin, 1991), and Canadian John Yuille (1988; Yuille, Marxsen, & Cooper, 1999), have encouraged its wider use, but two reviews of research on its validity, done by Steller and Koehnken (1989) and by Ruby and Brigham (1997), sug-

gest the need for caution. The latter reviewers concluded that the technique "shows some promise in enabling raters to differentiate true from false statements" (Ruby & Brigham, 1997, p. 705) but that its validity still needs to be proved before it is applied to decisions about individual cases.

There is some empirical evidence that certain CBCA criteria tend to be present more in truthful than untruthful accounts (e.g., Porter & Yuille, 1996; Vrij, Akehurst, Soukara, & Bull, 2002). However, there also is evidence that knowledge of the criteria can help liars—both

---

BOX 12.1
Criteria for Analyzing the Validity of Children's Accounts of Abuse

University of British Columbia researchers David Marxsen, John Yuille, and Melissa Nisbet (1995) have suggested that 19 criteria are more likely to be found in truthful than untruthful statements. The first five below are considered essential; the remaining 14 add to the credibility of the child's report. They stated that "A common rule of thumb is that a credible statement must include the first 5 and any 2 of the remaining 14" (1995, p. 455). The criteria are the following:

1. Coherence: Does the statement make logical sense?
2. Spontaneous reproduction: Does the child's presentation of the account seem rigid and rehearsed, or is it reasonably natural?
3. Sufficient detail: Does the child give as much detail in discussing the abusive incident as he or she does in describing a nonabusive incident?
4. Contextual imbedding: Is the account embedded in a distinct spatial-temporal context?
5. Descriptions of interactions: Is there an account of interactions with other persons present during the event?
6. Reproduction of conversation: Is verbatim dialogue reported spontaneously?
7. Unexpected complications during the incident: Did an interruption or complication arise during the abuse?
8. Unusual details: Does the child spontaneously supply any details that would be considered unusual for a child to have made up?
9. Peripheral details: Does the child spontaneously include details peripheral to the abusive incident?

10. Accurate reported details misunderstood: Does the child spontaneously incorrectly describe a detail he or she misunderstood during the incident (e.g., saying that the abuser "peed white and sticky and that must have hurt 'cuz he groaned when it happened")?
11. Related external associations: Does the child spontaneously include something from outside the abusive event that is somehow connected to that event?
12. Accounts of subjective mental state: Does the child spontaneously describe his or her emotion and thought during the abusive event?
13. Attribution of perpetrator's mental state: Does the child spontaneously infer the abuser's emotion and thought during the abusive incident?
14. Spontaneous corrections: Does the child make any spontaneous corrections in his or her account?
15. Admitting lack of memory: Does the child spontaneously admit that he or she does not recall some details of the abusive event?
16. Raising doubts about one's own testimony: Does the child spontaneously express the unlikelihood of his or her own story?
17. Self-depreciation: Does the child spontaneously suggest that she may have some responsibility for the abuse taking place?
18. Pardoning the perpetrator: Does the child spontaneously attempt to excuse the abuser?
19. Details characteristic of the act: Does the child spontaneously describe the details of child sex abuse that may not be common knowledge? (Marxsen, Yuille, & Nisbet, 1995, p. 455)

children and adults—be more convincing in their stories. Vrij et al. (2002) had children of various ages and adult participants take part in a "rubbing the blackboard" event. In a subsequent interview, they either told the truth or lied about the experience. Some participants were taught about CBCA criteria prior to the interview while others were not. Overall, the CBCA scores discriminated between liars and truth-tellers in both children and adults. However, liars who were informed about CBCA got scores similar to those of truth-tellers.

Using Anatomically Detailed Dolls

In seeking to evaluate the reports of sexual abuse by children, psychologists and other mental health professionals have sought to use procedures beyond the usual interview, including the use of puppets, drawings, doll houses, and—especially—anatomically detailed dolls (sometimes called "anatomically correct dolls") (Conte, Sorenson, Fogarty, & Rosa, 1991; Samra & Yuille, 1996). Dolls were introduced in the late 1970s and eventually became "*the* assessment tool" (White, 1988, p. 472). They even received endorsement from the American Psychological Association's Council of Representatives to the effect that they "may be the best available practical solution" (Fox, 1991, p. 722) to the problem of validating allegations of abuse.

Anatomically detailed dolls include, typically, a mature male with a penis, scrotum, and pubic tresses; a mature female with developed breasts, a vagina, and pubic hair; a young male with a penis and scrotum but no pubic hair; and a young female with a vagina but without developed breasts and pubic hair (Skinner & Berry, 1993). Several companies have manufactured these dolls. The justification for the use of anatomically detailed dolls reflects not only a belief that they permit children to reveal aspects of abuse that they wouldn't reveal verbally, but also an assumption that sexually abused children will manifest "inappropriate" sexual behaviour when playing with such dolls—especially precocious play, that

is, play that reflects an awareness that usually occurs only to older children—that is a result of abuse (Skinner & Berry, 1993, p. 401).

The research tests of this latter assumption have led to mixed results (Skinner & Berry, 1993). On one hand, the doll play of 25 nonabused children was found to differ from that of 25 sexually abused children; the latter were more likely to comment about specific sexual acts and demonstrate such acts (White, Strom, Santilli, & Halpin, 1986). Several studies indicated that the use of anatomically detailed dolls increased the reporting of genital contact when such contact had occurred. Gail Goodman and her colleagues (Goodman, Quas, Batterman-Faunce, Riddlesberger, & Kuhn, 1997) used the setting of a medical examination to determine whether three- to ten-year-olds who had been touched during the exam would indicate so when later questioned with the dolls. The researchers found that the children were more likely to disclose the touching with the dolls than when posed a free-response question. Another study that also used the setting of a medical examination found that use of the dolls increased reporting of touching of private parts but that some children who had not been touched reported that they had been when questioned with the dolls (Saywitz, Goodman, Nicholas, & Moan, 1991). Further, a study of two- to three-year-olds found that questions using the dolls did not generate more accurate responses than did questions that asked the children to demonstrate the touching on their own bodies (Bruck, Ceci, Francouer, & Renick, 1995). Some comparisons of abused children and those who had not been abused found no differences in response to the dolls (Cohn, 1991; McIver, Wakefield, & Underwager, 1989).

A further limitation is demonstrated when the dolls are evaluated as a measuring instrument. The APA's Committee on Psychological Testing and Assessment has concluded that anatomically detailed dolls are "a psychological test and are subject to the standards [of test construction and validation] when used to assess individuals and make inferences about their behavior" (Landers, 1988, p. 25). How well does the doll procedure stack up psychometrically? Not well at all. For example, any valid test should be standardized; that is, the materials, testing conditions, instructions, and scoring procedures should remain constant. However, wide variation exists in the specific design of the dolls; as they became widely used, more than 15 firms began to manufacture and distribute them (White & Santilli, 1988). Furthermore, some psychologists use other dolls—genitally neutral dolls, such as Barbie dolls, or incompletely modified ones (e.g., Cabbage Patch dolls with breasts or a penis sewn on) (Skinner & Berry, 1993).

An additional problem is that no standardization exists in administration of the dolls—for example, whether to present them dressed or undressed, how to introduce them into the interview, and just when to use them. No manual is available to provide scoring procedures. One study (Boat & Everson, 1988) found wide variation among examiners as to what was meant by particular types of responses (especially, avoidance and anxiousness). It follows that no norms exist that permit psychologists to know the likelihood of certain types of responses.

It should be clear that if anatomically detailed dolls are to be used at all, they should be used only with the greatest of caution (Everson & Boat, 1994). After reviewing a number of studies, Ceci and Bruck (1995) wrote:

> Although the data, taken together, do not present persuasive evidence for the value of dolls in forensic and therapeutic settings, there are small pockets of data that would appear to provide some support for the validity of doll-centered interviews.... However, we feel that these types of studies are not very relevant ... because these interviewing procedures bear little relationship to the procedures used in actual interviews with children suspected of sexual abuse. In the latter situation, children are rarely observed for over an hour in a free play situation, nor are these children merely asked to undress a doll and name its body parts. Rather, children are asked direct, leading, and misleading questions about abuse with the dolls, and they are often asked to reenact alleged abusive experiences. (p. 174)

Guidelines for the use of dolls include the following:

1. The dolls should not be used to make an initial diagnosis of abuse.
2. Mental health professionals who use the dolls should first be trained about proper interview techniques and the limitations of the procedure.
3. Investigators should be aware of the interpersonal factors, including the age of the child, his or her cultural background, and socioeconomic status, that can affect responses (Goodman et al., 1999; Koocher et al., 1995).
4. Videotaping interviews with the child and the administration of the doll technique has been suggested, so that independent fact-finders can assess whether suggestive procedures were used.

Ultimately, anatomically detailed dolls are probably unnecessary as investigative aids, considering all the potential problems associated with their use, and since there are excellent interview techniques (such as the Step-Wise approach) available to ask children about their allegations.

Suggestions for Improving Procedures

Each of the above procedures has been criticized, but what can be done to improve them? Interviewing techniques that have not received the above criticisms are available (Saywitz, Geiselman, & Bornstein, 1992; Saywitz & Snyder, 1996; Yuille, Hunter, & Harvey, 1990). A number of suggestions for an acceptable procedure have been offered by Saywitz and Dorado (1998):

1. Interviewers must talk to children in language they understand; thus they should

listen to a sample of the child's speech to determine the language level. Subsequent questioning should reflect this language level.

2. Documentation is essential; if not taped, questions and answers should be recorded verbatim whenever possible. The CBCA categories *are* useful here, in judging the validity of the child's statements.

3. Questioning should begin with general open-ended questions. If a narrative results, interviewers can prompt children to elaborate, but highly leading questions should be avoided.

CHILDREN'S RIGHTS WHEN TESTIFYING

It can be argued that for *any* victim of sexual abuse or rape, whether an adult or a child, the experience of facing your alleged attacker in court is potentially stressful or even traumatic. The legal system, in recent years, has become increasingly concerned about the possible traumatic effects upon children as witnesses in court. The trauma is compounded if opposing lawyers view children as especially susceptible to intimidation during cross-examination and judges remain oblivious to efforts to "break down" the child on the witness stand. Some defence lawyers may use questions with complex grammatical structure in order to confuse the child; they may accuse the child of having been coached or use other "dirty tricks" to discredit the child. In the McMartin trial, one child who had been questioned for a half hour by the prosecutor was turned over to a defence lawyer for cross-examination, and then questioned for *15-and-a-half hours* by the defence. Trial judges have great discretion to terminate or restrict cross-examination, yet this child was subjected to more than two days of questioning before being released from the witness box.

Do children possess any special rights to protection against these stresses? And if they do, can the defendant's rights to a fair trial still be preserved? Can psychologists who are advocates for children advise the courts about ways to preserve the child's self-esteem? In addressing these questions, many courts have instituted innovative procedures to protect children from undue traumatization. For example, courts have used child-sized witness chairs and have even permitted children to testify while sitting on the floor (N. E. Walker, Brooks, & Wrightsman, 1998). Dolls or drawings have been allowed to supplement the child's oral testimony; screens have been introduced to shield the child from the defendant, and children have testified over closed-circuit television. Section 486 of the Criminal Code of Canada (2003) provides that a judge may permit a complainant under the age of 18 years to testify behind a screen if the judge is of the opinion that the use of a screen is "necessary to obtain a full and candid account of the acts complained of from the complainant."

PSYCHOLOGISTS AS EXPERT WITNESSES

In light of the recent publicity regarding numerous claims of sexual abuse—either within families or by child-care providers—the testimony of children probably does not receive the degree of skepticism it once did (Goodman, 1984). Yet publicity about such cases can vary; in the early 1980s a dominant theme was that children are victims, but more recent portrayals have once more cast doubt on the accuracy of memories, at least in cases of adults reporting recent awareness of abuses during their childhood (Berliner, 1998; Loftus, 2003). Psychologists can play an important role as expert witnesses by being knowledge brokers in the courtroom and providing reviews of the scientific literature on topics of relevance (see Porter, Campbell et al., 2003). This is an important function, as potential jurors have been found to disagree significantly with psychological research findings on many items in a questionnaire designed to determine knowledge about sexual abuse (Morison & Greene, 1992). These include the greater tendency for jurors to assume that children generally tell the truth, can separate fact from fantasy, and avoid suggestions to answer as expected.

Testimony for the Prosecution

Berliner (1998) has identified several types of testimony by psychologists as expert witnesses in sexual abuse cases.

Social Frameworks Testimony

Social frameworks testimony is the "use of general conclusions from social science research in determining factual issues in a specific case" (Walker & Monahan, 1987, p. 570). (Such testimony can also be given in other types of cases covered in other chapters of this book, including rape trauma, battered woman syndrome, and racial discrimination.) This type of testimony provides a context for evaluating the evidence in the case; it can "tell jurors something they do not already know or disabuse them of common but erroneous misconceptions" (Walker & Monahan, 1987, p. 583). Examples suggested by Berliner (1998) included the nature of sexual abuse of children, the reactions of victims, and the memory abilities and suggestibility of children. A law review article by J. E. B. Myers and his colleagues amplified on these issues (Myers et al., 1989). Courts have accepted as admissible this type of testimony in the interest of educating jurors or correcting misapprehensions.

Testimony about Similarities between the Child Witness and Sexually Abused Children

As Berliner noted, "Although the expert may rely on general social science knowledge, the opinion is specifically linked to the child witness" (1998, pp. 13–14). Here things get more questionable, as the following indicates.

Margaret Kelly Michaels was charged in June 1985 with sexually abusing 20 children at the Wee Care daycare centre in Maplewood, New Jersey, where she had worked, first as a teacher's aide and then as a teacher of a pre-kindergarten class. At her trial, several children testified to the following:

> … having blades of knives inserted into their rectums, vaginas, and penises. Children also reported having had sticks and wooden spoons inserted into their various orifices. One child said that Michaels put a light bulb in her vagina. Others told of the tine end of forks being inserted into their vaginas while the back end of the silverware was inserted into their rectums. (Rosenthal, 1995, p. 252)

As part of the prosecution's case, Eileen Treacy, an expert witness described as an authority in child psychology and the treatment of sexually abused children, testified, despite objections by the defence. Treacy's letterhead stated that she provided "psychological and consultation services," but she did not have a doctoral degree and was not licensed to practise psychology (Rosenthal, 1995). She testified about an elaboration of **child sexual abuse accommodation syndrome,** which included five phases, or characteristics common to many situations of abuse—engagement, sexual interaction, secrecy, disclosure, and suppression. She told the jury that if those five characteristics could be identified in cases in which abuse was suspected, the abuse had in fact occurred (Rosenthal, 1995). She based her testimony on her interviews with 18 of the Wee Care children and a checklist of 32 "behavioural symptoms" for each child. She told the jury that the existence of 5 to 15 of her indicators established the existence of sexual abuse. When she was asked by Michaels's defence lawyer how she had arrived at the "5 to 15" figure, the trial judge refused to allow the question (Rosenthal, 1995).

For Treacy the behavioural symptoms were evidence for the presence of the five phases of child sexual abuse accommodation syndrome; for example:

[W]here children denied that abuse occurred, Treacy instructed the jury that the denials were exhibitions of the "suppression phase." In fact, she found that all 19 of the children who testified at trial exhibited the suppression phase as well as the other four "phases." That the children initially told investigators and their parents that they liked Michaels, Treacy said, was evidence of the "engagement phase," during which the abuser ingratiates herself with the children. Statements elicited from the children regarding the alleged pile-up games and sexual contact between Michaels and the children were evidence of a "sexual interaction" phase. The "secrecy phase," she testified, was found in the absence of complaints or indications of abuse at Wee Care until the interviews with the children began. And, the statements elicited from the children during and about the interviews constituted the exhibition of the "disclosure phase." Treacy testified that, on the basis of her theories, every child's denials, recantations, and unresponsive answers were proof of victimization. (Rosenthal, 1995, pp. 259–260)

Treacy concluded that in all the children but one, the indicators were "consistent with" having been sexually abused. Although she acknowledged that other factors in children's lives could have caused some of the behavioural symptoms—for example, birth of new siblings, severe illness of family members, a turbulent relationship between parents—she was able to conduct a "confounding variable analysis," the results of which led her to conclude that for all but one of the children, these "confounding variables" could not have been responsible for the appearance of the "behavioural indicators."

Although Kelly Michaels was found guilty of 155 counts of sexually abusing these children and sentenced to 47 years in prison, her conviction was later negated by a New Jersey appellate court, which ruled that the expert went beyond acceptable limits in leaving an impression with the jury that particular children had been abused

(*State v. Michaels,* 1993). After some delay, the district attorney decided not to retry Michaels, and she was released from custody. An *amicus* brief by a group of social scientists played a role in the appeal of the conviction (see Box 12.2).

Is the type of testimony exemplified in this case effectively different from ultimate-opinion testimony? Psychologists Gary Melton and Susan Limber (1989) have taken the position that a psychologist testifying that a child has been abused is the same as testifying that the child is telling the truth. Similarly, the New Hampshire Supreme Court ruled that "We see no appreciable difference between [a statement that the children exhibited symptoms consistent with those of sexually abused children] and a statement that, in her opinion, the children were sexually abused" (*State v. Cressey,* 1993, p. 699).

Ultimate-Opinion Testimony

As in the case of determination of criminal responsibility, courts have generally been reluctant to admit **ultimate-opinion testimony** about the credibility of a particular witness—in this case, a child who has reported having been sexually abused. Still, Myers (1992) has distinguished between testifying on the ultimate legal issue and on the ultimate factual issue, which may be permitted. In *R. v. Marquard* (1993), the Canadian Supreme Court ruled that "while expert evidence on the ultimate credibility of a witness is not admissible, expert evidence on human conduct and the psychological and physical factors which may lead to certain behaviour relevant to credibility, is admissible, provided the testimony goes beyond the ordinary experience of the trier of fact. This is particularly the case with evidence of children." (summary para. 11) But it remains very difficult for psychologists to assess whether sexual abuse took place; even physical evidence, such as a ruptured hymen, can occur in young girls through natural causes. No checklist of automatic indicators exists. In fact, a review of the literature found that no symptom was reported to be present in more than half of sexually abused children (Kendall-Tackett, Williams, & Finkelhor, 1993).

BOX 12.2
The Amicus Brief in the *Michaels v. New Jersey* Appeal

The conviction of Kelly Michaels was seen as an injustice by some journalists (Nathan, 1987; Rabinowitz, 1990) and by a number of social scientists. The journalists brought the public's attention to the case by publishing articles in widely read periodicals. The social scientists, led by Maggie Bruck and Stephen J. Ceci (1993), prepared an *amicus* brief accompanying Michaels's appeal. The brief presented a summary of research findings on children's suggestibility and cited examples from interviews with the Wee Care children that increased the risk that the children's responses were more a function of suggestibility than reflective of accuracy. For instance, interviewers often began the interview with an assumption of guilt. Here are some other examples:

- "There's a couple of things I'd like to let you know before we start. Alright? That is, Kelly said a lot of

things to scare kids and I think she might have said them to you, too."

- "All your friends that I told you about before were telling us that Kelly, the teacher we are talking about, was doing something they didn't like very much. She was bothering them in a kind of private way and they were all pretty brave and they told us everything, and we were wondering if you could help us out too, doing the same thing."

- "Some of your friends were hurt and they told us just about everything." (Bruck & Ceci, 1993, p. 284)

The procedures used by the interviewers in this investigation capitalized on intimidation and social influence, just as the ones in the McMartin case did.

Testimony for the Defence

Most of the testimony by psychologists in child sexual abuse cases has been offered in support of the prosecution (Mason, 1998), but several aspects of such cases cause psychologists to be expert witnesses for the defence. Among these are the following:

1. An expert can testify about the suggestive nature of the questions in the interview, as illustrated in the description of types of questions asked by the Martensville interviewers. The expert could inform jurors about the influence of misleading information on the accuracy of the child's self-report (McAuliff & Kovera, 1998).

2. Psychologists can testify about research findings on the causes and extent of suggestibility in children and the sometimes-vulnerable nature of memory. In cases claiming repressed or recovered memory, a defence witness can testify about demonstrations of how false memories can be implanted in children and adults (Loftus, 1993b; Loftus & Hoffman, 1989; Loftus &

Ketcham, 1994; Loftus & Rosenwald, 1995; Pezdek & Banks, 1996).

3. Psychologists can refute the testimony of prosecution witnesses, and, particularly, they can question whether the procedures used by prosecution experts meet the standards for admissibility of scientific testimony. For example, even the psychiatrist who first introduced child sexual abuse accommodation syndrome questioned its use to "prove a child was molested" (Summit, 1992, p. 160), and Treacy's use of "behavioural symptoms" and her procedure of doing a "confounding variable analysis" did not meet scientific standards of verifiability and validity.

General Guidelines for the Evaluation of Credibility in Child Sexual Abuse Cases

Porter, Campbell, and colleagues (2003) have provided a series of four major guidelines for the courts in evaluating the credibility of a complainant in a sexual abuse investigation. In general, they argue that psychologists can provide useful information about memory and the assessment of credibility that can help judges and juries interpret the evidence before them. Further, they argue that psychological or psychiatric testimony concerning memory for trauma would prove useful to inform legal decision making. They offer the following guidelines (for use with both children and adults):

1. The *context* in which the memory was recalled should be evaluated. Suggestive interviewing or other suggestive techniques (e.g., hypnosis) should raise suspicions about the validity of the allegation in question.
2. The *content* of the memory should be evaluated. As discussed, content differences have been found between real and mistaken memories.
3. *Individual differences* should be considered. The authors note that false memories are more likely in people with a greater susceptibility to suggestion in general and with a tendency towards dissociation.
4. *Corroboration* of the alleged event. A critical aspect of the evaluation process should focus on gathering evidence that either refutes or supports the claim based on the complainant's report.

the child to testify and, especially, make recommendations to the judge about whether the trauma of testifying justifies innovations in courtroom procedures; and they can testify as expert witnesses, either for the prosecution or the defence.

In assessing the validity of claims of abuse, psychologists face a challenging task. Sometimes, in order to gain information through interviews with the children, suggestive questions and other procedures are used that inspire legitimate questions about the accuracy of the children's answers. Although designed with good intentions, the use of anatomically detailed dolls lacks the precision required of psychometric instruments and should not be used to diagnose the presence of abuse.

Psychologists have testified on either side in trials of alleged abusers of children. For the prosecution, testimony in general is in support of the validity of claims of abuse, although ultimate-opinion testimony is usually not permitted. Psychologists testifying for the defence may focus on the inadequacies of interviews with children, the suggestibility of young children, or the limitations in the procedures used by the psychologists who concluded that abuse had occurred.

SUMMARY

Charges of the sexual abuse of children usually take one of two forms: that a number of children have allegedly been abused by a daycare provider or that an individual child has been abused by a member of the child's family or a close friend. In the latter type, sometimes adults reported that they only recalled the childhood attack much later.

Psychologists can participate in several ways when charges of sexual abuse of children are advanced. They can assess the nature of the abuse (including whether, in fact, it did occur); they can advise the court about the child's competency to testify; they can assist the prosecutor in preparing

KEY TERMS

anatomically detailed dolls, p. 259
child sexual abuse accommodation syndrome, p. 269
criterion-based content analysis technique, p. 264
leading questions, p. 261
London Family Court Clinic, p. 260
paraphilia, p. 258
recidivism, p. 259
social frameworks testimony, p. 269
statement validity assessment, p. 264
suggestibility, p. 263
suggestive questions, p. 261
ultimate-opinion testimony, p. 270

SUGGESTED READINGS

Bruck, M., Ceci, S. J., & Hembrooke, H. (1998). Reliability and credibility of young children's reports: From research to policy and practice. *American Psychologist, 53,* 136–151.

Some of the leading experts in the field authored this succinct review of the issues and research findings with regard to interviewing young child witnesses.

Ceci, S. J., & Hembrooke, H. (Eds.) (1998). *Expert witnesses in child abuse cases.* Washington, DC: American Psychological Association.

This review includes a number of valuable contributed chapters, all devoted to issues relevant to the psychologist called to serve as an expert witness in child sexual abuse cases. It contains chapters by Michael Lavin and Bruce D. Sales, Margaret Bull Kovera and Eugene Borgida, Lucy McGough, and others. Highly recommended.

Kuehnle, K. (1996). *Assessing allegations of child sexual abuse.* Sarasota, FL: Professional Resource Press.

This text provides a comprehensive model for assessing multiple sources of information in assessing claims of sexual abuse.

Perry, N. W., & Wrightsman, L. S. (1991). *The child witness: Legal issues and dilemmas.* Thousand Oaks, CA: Sage.

This review gives a comprehensive account of the research and legal issues when children are called as witnesses in court.

Pezdek, K., & Banks, W. P. (Eds.). (1996). *The recovered memory/false memory debate.* San Diego: Academic Press.

Both sides of the debate about the existence and frequency of repressed memories or recovered memories of childhood sexual abuse are reviewed in this collection of contributed chapters. The text covers childhood memory and suggestibility also.

Sales, B. D. (Ed.). (1995, June). [Special issue]. *Psychology, Public Policy, and Law, 1* (2).

This journal issue concentrates on the case of Margaret Kelly Michaels, charged with the sexual abuse of children at the Wee Care daycare centre in Maplewood, New Jersey. Included are the *amicus* brief prepared by a committee of concerned social scientists, headed by Maggie Bruck and Stephen J. Ceci; a chronology of the case by Michaels's defence lawyer; and commentaries by psychologists, lawyers, and social workers.

13

Child Custody Decisions

Mental health professionals who conduct child custody evaluations must remain objective and provide compassionate yet unbiased and thorough investigations into the psychological needs of the child.
—Jonathan W. Gould (1998, p. 5)

EXTENT OF THE PROBLEM

In 2001, 387 documented parental abductions occurred in Canada, compared to 48 stranger abductions, according to the National Missing Children Services' (2001) annual report. In the U.S., about 350 000 parental abductions of children occur each year, according to the National Center for Missing and Exploited Children (Lopez, 1998). The problem is so extensive that at least some police departments have established sections dedicated to discovering children abducted by their parents. In addition, forensic psychologists have begun to identify factors that increase the risk of an abduction (Plass, Finkelhor, & Hotaling, 1997). Parents who kidnap tend to have strong ties with their children, to view the other parent as incompetent, and to doubt the ability of child-protection agencies or courts to render justice (Greif & Hegar, 1993). Men comprise the majority of abductors.

THE INTENSITY OF CHILD CUSTODY DISPUTES

We first mentioned Dr. David Fairweather in Chapter 1. Fairweather is a forensic psychologist working in British Columbia. Part of his private practice involves conducting assessments in the context of child custody and access disputes. Although this type of work is important and can be rewarding, it is also among the most challenging for a practitioner in our field.

Dr. Lenore E. Walker has worked extensively with many types of clients, including battered women and rape victims. Speaking at a large psychology convention, she told the audience that "No area in forensic psychology requires more skills than child custody. It is my least favourite area. Psychologists are treated with the greatest disrespect in Children's Court" (Walker, 1998). Frequently it is a thankless job, because, in part, of the overwhelming desire of each parent to maintain custody of the children. Two examples,

although not typical cases, reflect the intense feelings that child custody cases can provoke:

1. After a bitter divorce from his wife a year before, in October 1979, Stephen Fagan kidnapped his two young daughters, moved to Palm Beach, Florida, from suburban Boston (where he held a part-time job at Harvard's Legal Aid Clinic), and took on a new identity as "Dr. William Martin," supposedly a Harvard-educated psychiatrist. He told his daughters—then ages four and two—that their mother had died in a car crash. He maintained this charade for almost 20 years, until May 1998, when a relative told the authorities of his true identity. His daughters, ages 23 and 21 when he was apprehended, maintained loyalty to their father and denied that they desired to see their mother (Parker, 1998). After he was identified, Fagan said that everything that he had done for the last 20 years was for his girls and that their mother was unfit to care for them because of her abuse of drugs and alcohol. Nonetheless, he was transported to Massachusetts, where he later pleaded guilty to several counts of kidnapping and was given a sentence of probation and a US$100 000 fine.

2. After he was found not guilty of the murder of his former wife and Ronald Goldman, O. J. Simpson sought the custody of his children, 11-year-old Sydney and eight-year-old Justin. During the trial the children were kept by the parents of Nicole Brown Simpson, but in December 1996 a judge ruled that the Browns had to relinquish the children to their father. Central to Judge Nancy Wieben Stock's decision was a 16-page court-ordered report by psychologist Jeffrey M. Lulow, who (it is reported) wrote: "Remaining at the home of their grandparents is likely to reinforce the impression [that] their father is either dangerous, uncaring, inadequate or emotionally distant from them" (quoted by Associated Press, 1997, p. 5A). This psychologist also analyzed

O. J. Simpson's test results and concluded that he could be impulsive but that his capacity for empathy was higher than that of either Louis or Juditha Brown. However, two years later a California appeals court overturned the judge's custody decision and ordered a new trial under a different judge, who considered evidence regarding O. J. Simpson's culpability in the murder of the children's mother. This followed a plea by an international group of psychologists for judges to consider the complete history of an abusive spouse in evaluating fitness for custody. This team included Dr. Peter Jaffe, director of the London Family Court Clinic (described in Chapter 12) and the University of British Columbia's Dr. Don Dutton, well known for his work on spousal assaulters. Nonetheless, Simpson eventually gained custody of his two children.

WHAT ROLES CAN PSYCHOLOGISTS PLAY?

When a marriage begins to disintegrate, or completely fails, a psychologist can play a number of roles in working with one member of the couple, with the couple together, or with the children. But only some of these roles reflect actions of a *forensic* psychologist. Nevertheless, for a complete picture of the process of determining child custody, each role is briefly identified in this section.

Marriage Counsellor

Many psychotherapists, whether they are psychologists, psychiatrists, or social workers, work with troubled couples. If a couple has sought help for their marriage but then decides to divorce, their marriage counsellor should not be given the responsibility of advising the judge about the best custody arrangements for the couple's children. The reason for this ruling is that it creates a conflict of interest; the psycho-

gist would have a **dual relationship**, in that the psychologist has had a therapeutic relationship with the couple and now is asked to be an objective evaluator of their personalities and lifestyles. Our ethical obligations as psychologists dictate that matters revealed in the privacy of the counselling relationship should remain there.

Mediator

After a couple decides to divorce, they face the task of deciding custody for the children. If the parents cannot agree on custody, a court may order mediation. As an alternative to litigation, mediation provides several attractions:

1. It is more informal; rules of evidence do not have to be followed, and court personnel and adversarial lawyers are not present (however, specially trained lawyers may serve as mediators).
2. The sessions are usually held in private, and the proceedings are confidential.
3. Participants in mediation are more satisfied with the process and the outcome than parents who use the courts (Gould, 1998).
4. Cases are settled more quickly than if they were to go through court (Emery, 1994; Katsh, 1998).

Psychologists as well as lawyers have become mediators in a variety of disputes (Emery & Wyer, 1987). The allocation of material resources in a divorce proceeding is an important matter, and whatever decisions are made have implications for child custody decisions. For example, if the husband is the sole wage-earner and the wife is granted custody, is the allocation of income sufficient to provide for the children?

The job of the **mediator** is to try to help the parties resolve their differences through an agreement. The mediator explores options with the couple and provides a safe environment for communication; many mediators believe confidentiality to be a necessity if the mediation is to succeed (Stahl, 1994). Mediators ensure that the parents focus on the needs of their children and not on their own individual needs. They seek agreements about plans for the children that can be put in writing, even though mediators do not have the power to enforce rulings. The goal of such mediation often is to develop an acceptance of the nature of the co-parenting relationship: that is, each parent must agree to cooperate with the other parent in raising the children, regardless of his or her feelings about the other parent (Stahl, 1994).

Psychologists can facilitate the realization of several benefits through mediation; for example:

1. The mediator can distinguish between demands and needs. Melton, Petrila, Poythress, and Slobogin (1997) have noted: "In performing custody evaluations, we have been struck by the number of times the spouses' disagreements—on which they are expending substantial time and money—are objectively rather insignificant (e.g., a difference of one or two hours a week in how much time each parent has the children)" (p. 485). An examination of underlying needs sometimes can resolve these disputes.
2. As noted above, mediation provides the opportunity, in a less charged atmosphere, to discuss how property will be divided, how custody will be structured, and how visitations will be implemented (Lemmon, 1985; Friedman, 1993).
3. The process may increase the emotional acceptance of divorce by the two parties (Wallerstein & Kelly, 1980).
4. Mediation may be able to establish an atmosphere that helps the former spouses to establish a new working relationship that is essential for the co-parenting of their children.

In situations in which one parent is passive and not standing up for his or her parental rights, achieving the goals of mediation becomes more challenging. Although it has been suggested that the mediator can assist in balancing the power in a couple (Haynes, 1981, pp. 122–123), the mediator cannot become an advocate for one side. In such families, litigation may be necessary.

On the general question of the effectiveness of mediation in such disputes, the thorough review by Melton and his colleagues is less optimistic than are advocates of the process; these authors concluded:

> [M]ediation (especially when compulsory) is not necessarily beneficial. It has been asserted that, relative to litigation, mediation will likely reduce competition between parents, improve children's adjustment, reduce relitigation, and increase compliance with agreements.... Although the majority of studies on particular hypothesized benefits of mediation have confirmed the hypotheses, research to the contrary is also available on virtually every point. No study has shown mediation, relative to litigation, to have the hypothesized ultimate benefit: better post-divorce adjustment by children. Indeed, mediation—especially when conducted in a high-conflict divorce—may actually increase the strength of association between parental and child problems. (Melton et al., 1997, p. 486)

Despite this less-than-encouraging evaluation, these commentators see the movement toward compulsory mediation of custody disputes as likely to continue, because of one powerful reason—it reduces the workload of the courts.

Child Therapist

Another role for the psychologist is as a psychotherapist for children experiencing the trauma of family conflict and incipient divorce. For example, Stahl (1994) has posed the following dilemma:

> Johnny, age 11, is your client in psychotherapy. You have seen him for a year for school problems and difficulties in his family relationships. During the course of therapy, you have had frequent contact with Johnny's mother but little contact with his father. His parents have had a tumultuous marriage and have finally decided to get a divorce.

Johnny's mother and her lawyer ask you to make a statement to the court about Johnny's poor relationship with his father and to recommend rather limited visitation with him. What do you do? (p. 2)

The answer is simple; you refuse. Again, as in the first role, the psychologist serves as a counsellor, and to ask this person to serve also as an evaluator in court places an undue burden on the psychologist. However, it is possible that the psychologist could testify as a **fact witness** (not as an expert witness). That is, it might be appropriate for the psychotherapist to testify about Johnny's mother's commitment to his mental health, while avoiding any recommendation about custody.

Court-Appointed Evaluator

When custody of children emerges as an issue in a divorce settlement, a judge may ask a clinical or counselling psychologist to serve as a **court–** **appointed evaluator** to make an evaluation of and a recommendation as to the best custody arrangement. In Canada, in making a custody order, the court must look to the **best interests of the child**. In making the order, relevant issues are the health and emotional well–being of the child, the love and affection between the child and parents, the education of the child, the capacity (including financial) of each parent to look after the child, and, if appropriate, the views of the child (typically more important as the child gets older). Do the two parents differ in their expression of good and bad parenting behaviours? Which parent is more competent to respond to the needs of the children? Because the final matter to be decided is which parent will retain legal authority over the child, the judge makes the ultimate determination. Although this is an area in which mental health professionals feel that they could be very useful to the courts, psychologists and other mental health professionals are not routinely consulted by judges (Melton et al., 1997). Box 13.1 provides an elab-

BOX 13.1
Why Don't Judges Consult Psychologists?

Should clinical or counselling psychologists be involved in the resolution of most child-custody disputes? Melton and his colleagues (1997) conclude no, for several reasons. At present, most custody decisions are made during a period of mediation or bargaining between the spouses and do not require a Solomon-like judge to make the decision (even though the judge must ratify whatever decision is made by the parents). But even when the decision goes to trial, only a few judges include evaluation by a mental health professional. In a large-scale survey, summarized by Melton et al. (1997), about half of the judges reported that they consulted mental health experts in fewer than 10 percent of the custody cases they decided; none reported eliciting such evidence in more than 75 percent of their cases. In another survey (Felner, Rowlison, Farber, & Primavera, 1987), only 2 percent of the judges included the opinions of mental health professionals among the five leading factors in their custody decisions.

Melton and his colleagues go on to offer a provocative explanation: "Mental health professionals may have little expertise that is directly relevant to custody disputes" (1997, p. 483). Their arguments for this conclusion include the following:

1. Psychologists have no special expertise with respect to some of the factors related to the child's best interests, including moral guidance and parental "responsibility" (Lowery, 1981).
2. The amount of scientific evidence on some issues to be decided by the judge is limited. One example is the relative benefit of various custody arrangements, a topic evaluated in Box 13.4 (see page 294).
3. In the past, some psychologists have not endeared themselves to judges by testifying and drawing conclusions from clinical data that are irrelevant to the legal questions in dispute (Melton et al., 1997, p. 484). In fact, one of the most distinguished forensic psychologists, Thomas Grisso, has written, "Mental health professionals do not have reason to be proud of their performance in this area of forensic assessment" (1984, pp. 8–9).

oration of this conclusion and some reasons for it. Nevertheless, the role is a crucial one, and a subsequent section of this chapter explores the activities of the evaluator in depth.

Despite occasionally succumbing to the temptations to oversell their offerings, psychologists do have something to offer judges. For example, Melton et al. (1997) noted that "clinical impressions about alliances and conflicts within the family and their bases might present judges with a useful framework for consideration of which child goes where" (p. 485). Similarly, an investigation of the level of marital conflict might aid in the judge's success in predicting whether, for the couple, joint custody might work.

Thus, if appointed to do a **custody evaluation**, the psychologist must approach the task "unburdened by any particular point of view or preset conclusions" (Schutz, Dixon, Lindenberger, & Ruther, 1989, p. 50). The prime duty of the evaluator is to investigate, to gather facts for the judge; the clinical or counselling psychologist's strength is "talking with children and families under stress and gathering information from diverse sources about the life of the family" (Melton et al., 1997, p. 485). The psychologist as evaluator then prepares a report for the judge. In some jurisdictions—but not all—copies of the report are available to the lawyers for each parent, and in some jurisdictions even family members get copies. In Canada, according to the Children's Law Reform Act (1990), when an evaluation is completed, a copy is filed with the clerk or the registrar of the court. The clerk or registrar then gives copies of the report to both parties and to the child's lawyer (if there is a lawyer representing the child). Stahl (1994) has listed the desired characteristics of such a report; it should:

- focus on the issues and problems of the family,
- be credible, well-reasoned, clear, and thoughtful,
- be fair, balanced, and neutral, avoiding advocacy of one parent and accentuating positives when possible,

- avoid jargon and diagnosis, yet remain behaviourally focused, and
- contain recommendations that are focused and that clearly flow from the material in the report (p. 75).

Expert Witness

After providing an evaluation to the court, the psychologist usually participates as an **expert witness** in a hearing. Sometimes the psychologist is hired by one side, rather than appointed by the court. The examination of the psychologist by lawyers representing each of the two parents is likely to be intense; hence a later section of this chapter deals with the trials and tribulations of the expert witness.

Psychologists may serve other functions as expert witnesses. For example, a psychologist may be called upon to testify about the effects on child-rearing if a divorced parent is a gay man or a lesbian, a topic also discussed later in this chapter.

Applied Researcher

A separate role exists for the forensic psychologist as an **applied researcher** in evaluating general claims and assumptions about the nature of custody. As we know, in the past mothers typically received custody of the children, but in recent years joint custody has come into vogue. Is the latter a better arrangement with regard to the adjustment and satisfaction of children? And standing back from the effectiveness of various custody arrangements, the applied researcher also asks: What are the long-term effects of divorce on children?

If the child's wishes are a factor in determining custody, at what age are children competent to participate in the decision making? Forensic psychologists can provide the research findings to guide judges. One study (Garrison, 1991) found that even elementary-school–age children were able to give adult-like reasons, at least in response to hypothetical questions about preferences for custody arrangements.

SERVING THE NEEDS OF THREE DIFFERENT TYPES OF CLIENTS

Throughout this book, an organizing question is: Whose interest is the forensic psychologist serving? The answer depends on the particular role. With regard to child custody evaluations, there are three: the children, their parents, and the presiding judge. What does each want, and have a right to expect, from the forensic psychologist?

The Children

As often-powerless pawns in a dispute, children deserve empathy and concern. The psychologist can help children examine their feelings about their parents and divorce. But the primary responsibilities of the forensic psychologist are to be fair, thorough, and professional. The psychologist should enter into an evaluation free of biases favouring one parent and make a recommendation about the best interests of the child based on an objective evaluation of a variety of data.

The Parents

In the often-acrimonious child custody dispute, parents want to "win." In only 10 percent of divorces do the two parents contest custody, and only a minority of these contested cases go to trial (Hedrick, 1998). Thus, those parents with whom the psychologist interacts are an extreme, intense group. They want vindication in that they want the experts to conclude that they are better parents—even that they are better human beings!—than their ex-spouses, that the other is at fault for the family's problems. Needless to say, a psychologist cannot provide satisfaction to most parents entrenched in emotional disputes. But disputants also seek procedural justice, whether they win or not; that is, they want to have assurance that they have been treated fairly, that all those contributing to the decision have listened to their side with openness and fairness (Thibaut & Walker, 1975; Lind & Tyler, 1988).

A field study of 71 couples who either mediated or litigated their child custody disputes (Kitzmann & Emery, 1993) found that the relative fairness of the proceedings influenced the overall satisfaction felt by the participants, especially by those who felt that they were in a disadvantaged position (usually, the fathers).

The Judge

Some judges feel poorly trained with regard to understanding the dynamics of family relationships (Stahl, 1994). As noted earlier, judges seek relevant information about family dynamics from the psychologist. But like the other participants, judges also want fairness and objectivity, and they also expect from the psychologist an awareness of the court's role and the limits of the law with regard to the resolution of custody disputes. In a word, judges expect the psychologist always to act in a professional manner.

But sometimes judges may not realize what is unprofessional and unethical for a psychologist. Some judges will quiz psychotherapists about what is best for the child they are treating, inadvertently pressuring the psychologist into a dual relationship. Especially in small communities, where "everybody knows everybody else," psychologists need to remind others of their professional limits.

THE COURT-APPOINTED EVALUATOR ROLE

The most "forensic" of the various activities described above are the evaluations of the parents and the children and the formulation of recommendations for the judge. Thus, a major portion of this chapter examines the role of the court-appointed evaluator.

Standards for Resolution of Custody Disputes

Two hundred years ago, if a married couple decided to divorce, the rights of their children were irrelevant to the decision to assign custody to one parent or the other. Until the early 1900s, only one person in a family had any legal rights (Drinan, 1973); only the husband had the right to make a contract or have legal status. Children were treated as property and, like the rest of the property, were automatically assigned to their fathers. In fact, in William Blackstone's influential 18th century commentaries on the law, children were considered as "prized possessions" of their fathers. But early in the 20th century sentiment shifted, advocating a belief that mothers were better caregivers, so that typically the child was placed in the custody of the mother, unless strong countervailing factors prevailed.

The Best Interests of the Child Standard

Around 1970, another shift occurred, placing the best interests of the child at the forefront. In Canada, a child is now treated as a distinct person and is to be accorded, by law, individual rights in child custody proceedings. At present, neither parent is presumed to have a superior right to the child (Wyer, Gaylord, & Grove, 1987). Section 24 of the Family Relations Act, passed in British Columbia in 1996, describes the following as among the factors a judge may consider in reaching a custody decision:

(a) the health and emotional well being of the child including any special needs for care and treatment;

(b) if appropriate, the views of the child;

(c) the love, affection and similar ties that exist between the child and other persons;

(d) education and training for the child;

(e) the capacity of each person to whom guardianship, custody or access rights and duties may be granted to exercise those rights and duties adequately

The legislation outlines some broad characteristics but largely leaves it to the judges to operationalize the terms. The Supreme Court of Canada described the need to keep the terms broad in *Young v. Young* (1993):

> The best interests of the child cannot be equated with the mere absence of harm: it encompasses a myriad of considerations. Courts must attempt to balance such considerations as the age, physical and emotional constitution and psychology of both the child and his or her parents and the particular milieu in which the child will live. One of the most significant factors in many cases will be the relationship that the child entertains with his or her parents. Since custody and access decisions are pre-eminently exercises in discretion, the wide latitude under the best interests test permits courts to respond to the spectrum of factors which can both positively and negatively affect a child. What may constitute stressful or damaging circumstances for one child may not necessarily have the same effect on another. (*Young v. Young,* 1993, summary para. 15)

The conflict between law and psychology once more surfaced; psychologists were used to working with operational definitions, whereas many of the standards that emerged seemed to be based on preconceived notions or intuition. For example, Melton, Petrila, Poythress, and Slobogin (1997) have asked: Is the best interests standard present-oriented or future-oriented? Judges have great discretion when it comes to evaluating the lifestyle of each competing parent. A provocative example of how judges' values can affect their decisions was shown in two 1993 Canadian cases (see Box 13.2).

With respect to the child's preferences, Canadian courts permit children beyond a certain age to express their preference for living arrangement to the "extent that the child's views and preferences ... can be reasonably ascertained." Some U.S. states specify an age, typically 12 or 14; others consider the maturity of the

BOX 13.2
Canadian Supreme Court Justices: Values in Conflict

In 1993, the Supreme Court of Canada heard appeals from two remarkably similar cases. *Young v. Young* and *P. (D.) v. S. (C.)* both involved disputes between a mother who had been given custody of and a father who had been granted access to their children. Further, in both cases, the parental disagreement centred on the father's desire to indoctrinate the children into the Jehovah's Witness religion. Each mother wanted the court to disallow this indoctrination. The Supreme Court, with one judge dissenting, rejected the notion that freedom of religion under the Charter of Rights and Freedoms (1982) includes a parent's right to determine a child's faith. Such a right, the Court argued, would conflict with the reli-gious freedom of a child. Instead, the Court found that the only relevant consideration in these cases was the best interests of the child. From here, however, the Court split into two factions, one adhering to the child's religious freedom principle and the other, led by Justice McLachlin, emphasizing the importance of contact with the access parent in the best interests of the child. In *Young v. Young* the McLachlin argument was upheld. However, in *P. (D.) v. S. (C.)*, Justices Cory and Iacobucci switched their votes. The Court ruled that the child would benefit from knowing her father fully, including an awareness of his religious values.

child's cognitive and emotional development. But consensus is lacking about how much weight is to be given to the child's preferences. For example, the highly publicized American case of "Gregory K," who decided to "divorce" his parents and was allowed to do so, is a very specialized one and should not be taken as any legal landmark (see Walker, Brooks, & Wrightsman, 1998, pp. 96–97, for a description).

One observer has noted that "In all matters where children are involved, courts have said with tedious regularity that the welfare of the child is the supreme goal to be obtained" (Drinan, 1973, p. 40). As a moral principle, the best interests of the child would seem to be a step forward over previous rationales for custody determination. But who determines what is in the child's best interests? Rarely is the child given the final choice in the exercise of his or her rights (Sales, Manber, & Rohman, 1992).

The Tender-Years Doctrine

Another phenomenon that impedes the impact of children's preferences upon custody determinations is the widespread acceptance of the **tender-years doctrine**, which presumes that the best interest of all young children regardless of their gender and the best interests of girls of any age are best served by awarding custody to the mother,
assuming she is fit (Okpaku, 1976). The assumption that "a mother is the natural custodian of a child of tender years" (*B. v. B.*, 1978, p. 251) was based on the theory that the father was unable to provide "that tender care which nature requires, and which it is the peculiar province of the mother to supply" (*Miner v. Miner*, 1849, p. 49). With its presumption that the mother was best for rearing the young child, the tender-years doctrine put the burden of proof on the father to show that the mother was unfit (Wyer, Gaylord, & Grove, 1987). In Canada, mothers are still far more likely than fathers to be granted custody of their children by the court. In 1994–95, the following were the court-ordered custody arrangements: 79.3 percent mothers exclusive custody, 6.6 percent fathers exclusive custody, and 12.8 percent shared physical custody (1.2 percent other) (Marcil-Gratton & Le Bourdais, 1999).

Custody Determinations in Mixed-Race Cases or Cases Involving a Homosexual Parent

As noted, judges have great discretion in awarding or dividing custody. Although psychologists are sometimes consulted by the courts and asked to carry out evaluations about the child's best interests, the judge is not required to follow them.

Judges' decisions may reflect their own biased thinking and stereotyped beliefs about what is in the child's best interests, and these may or may not agree with conventional wisdom or with empirical findings. The American case of *Palmore v. Sidoti* (1984) provides an example. The trial judge transferred the custody of a Caucasian child from her mother to her father because her mother had married a black man. Upon appeal, the judge's decision was upheld by the Florida Circuit Court, which concluded that a child in a mixed marriage would "inevitably" be vulnerable to "social stigmatization." It required an appeal to the U.S. Supreme Court to get the judge's decision overturned.

In two types of cases, divorce in a mixed-race family and custody when a parent is homosexual, conflicts are likely to surface.

Custody Involving a Mixed-Race Couple

What if a husband and wife of different ethnic backgrounds, who have had children together, decide to divorce? Some judges have assumed that such children's interests are best served by "placement with the potential custodian whom the child most closely resembles in terms of physical racial attributes" (Sales, Manber, & Rohman, 1992, p. 31). But some commentators have been critical of this determination. In their extensive review, Sales et al. (1992) found no empirical studies on this specific topic, but they concluded from the findings on adoptions by Caucasian families of nonwhite children that the procedure does not jeopardize the nonwhite child's racial awareness or identity.

Custody Involving a Homosexual Parent

Sharon Bottoms was openly homosexual; she lived with another woman and with her child, Tyler. But in 1993 Sharon Bottoms's mother sued for custody of Tyler, claiming that her daughter's sexual orientation made her unfit as a mother. A judge in Virginia agreed, citing a 1985 state law saying that a parent's homosexuality is a valid reason for losing custody, and awarded custody of the two-year-old child to his grandmother.

As noted by one Canadian commentator (Casey, 1994), traditionally, the best interest of the child standard was not applied equally to heterosexual and homosexual parents. From Casey's perspective, Canadian courts have long assumed that homosexual parents were worse parents. In her analysis, some flawed reasons for judicial discrimination against homosexual parents have included (1) greater likelihood of sexual molestation of the child, (2) injured psychosexual development of the child from exposure to a homosexual lifestyle, (3) harassment and stigmatization of the child, and (4) fear of exposure to AIDS.

Such common myths need to be dispelled through the effective use of expert testimony in custody cases. However, the trial judge in the Bottoms case ruled the way he did despite testimony by a psychologist as expert witness that children suffer no negative effects from growing up in a family in which the caregivers are homosexual. Available research supports the conclusion by the psychologist (APA, 1995; Patterson, 1992, Tasker & Golombok, 1995). A review of relevant research by Cramer (1986) concluded that "the evidence to date suggests that gay parents raise children who are emotionally and sexually similar to those raised by heterosexual parents" (p. 506). No research has found that the sexual orientation of a lesbian couple significantly influences the sexual orientation of any children in the home (Sales, Manber, & Rohman, 1992; Buxton, 1999).

The decision in the Bottoms case was the first known instance in which a judge awarded a third person the custody of a child because the parent was gay (Howlett, 1993). In contrast, an increasing number of lesbian mothers are being given custody by the courts (e.g., *Doe v. Doe*, 1981). The situation is improving in Canada. In 1997, British Columbia passed amendments to the Family Relations Act, which extended the provisions of the law equally to same-sex couples. The new act defines the term "spouse" to include a person in a same-sex relationship. Therefore, homosexual and heterosexual individuals have the same obligations to pay support to a partner, to pay child support, and presumably to have custody of or access to a child.

Like Canada, many jurisdictions in other countries now have statutes or case law holding that homosexuality should not be a factor in determining custody. But it is certainly possible that judges may sometimes still deny custody to a gay person, with the unspoken reason that the other parent is heterosexual and/or because the judge anticipates that the child might encounter future prejudice by a disapproving society.

Ethical Issues and Temptations

As psychologists increasingly are called upon to make child custody evaluations, the potential for making mistakes and taking unethical actions increases. This section discusses some of the potential problems in doing these evaluations and suggests ways to overcome them.

Recognizing One's Limits and Biases

Each of us has biases; for some of us, these have a potential to influence custody and access evaluations in significant and possibly detrimental ways. Does the psychologist have a strong preference for, say, joint custody over mother-only custody? Sometimes the biases of the evaluating psychologist may be more subtle; he or she may look unfavourably upon a parent who lives in a trailer, or one with a low IQ. If the psychologist cannot keep his or her biases from playing a determinative role, the psychologist should withdraw from the case.

Marsha Hedrick (1998), who has conducted more than 300 divorce custody evaluations, has suggested that potential evaluators need to know what their hot buttons are. What behaviours cause knee-jerk reactions in the psychologist: domestic violence, being lied to by a client, sexual abuse? They also need to recognize that if they are "people-pleasers," carrying out such evaluations may not be their activity of choice. "You must tolerate people hating you," she has said; "if you say one negative thing about some parents, you're scum."

Avoiding Dual Relationships

This chapter has described the various roles for the psychologist as a part of the child custody process. The Canadian Psychological Association's code of ethics notes the strong likelihood of an ethical violation when the same psychologist carries out several roles. Morris (1995) has put it succinctly: "[A] psychologist should avoid conducting a custody evaluation involving a family when he or she has seen a member(s) of the family at some previous time in individual psychotherapy or family therapy" (p. 6). But is it improper for a psychologist to enter into a therapeutic relationship with a parent he or she has previously evaluated? Although this type of dual relationship seems problematic to us, other psychologists have argued that sometimes the previous contact may be helpful in therapy, and that the ethical issues need to be reviewed on a case-by-case basis (L. Greenberg, 1998).

Violating Confidentiality and Informed Consent

Both the CPA and APA ethics codes require psychologists not to reveal any information conveyed to them by their clients, without their expressed written consent. However, in child custody evaluations, the very nature of the evaluation means that the information will be shared with others—at the very least with the judge responsible for the decision (Morris, 1995). The legal tradition of admitting evidence into court runs counter to the confidentiality privilege (Knapp & Vandecreek, 1985). Given these circumstances, parents need to be fully informed of the fact that the information they provide will *not* remain confidential; Morris (1995) recommends written permission from the parents reflecting their awareness of which parties will be assessed or interviewed and who will receive the report.

In informing parents and gaining their consent, Morris (1995) has proposed that parents should be told about each step in the evaluation process, including the tests that will be administered to each person, who will be interviewed, whether observations will include home visits, the legal or medical documents that will be examined, and the expected length of the evaluation. Informed consent should also be extended to each child being evaluated. Even if it is a court-ordered evaluation, all parties need to sign a consent form (Gould, 1998).

Custody Evaluations versus Psychological Evaluations

Clinical psychologists, when doing custody evaluations, need to avoid framing them as psychological evaluations. The goal is to determine a course of action that serves the best interest of the child, not to describe all the shortcomings of each parent. Assessing parenting skills is relevant, but too often the evaluation assesses the lifestyles of each parent rather than focusing on the wants and needs of the child (Melton, Petrila, Poythress, & Slobogin, 1997). If the evaluator insists on evaluating the personality traits or pathologies of the parents, he or she needs to be explicit about how they relate to their parenting skills. To say that a mother has a personality disorder is not enough; the psychologist should be explicit that the disorder, in her case, means that it will negatively affect her parenting ability, such as an inability to manage routines or consistently respond to the child's needs (Hedrick, 1998), or even that she may be a risk for violence against her child. Grisso's (1984) critique elaborated this point:

> Too often we still evaluate the parent but not the child, a practice that makes no sense when the child's own, individual needs are the basis for the legal decision. Too often we continue to rely on the assessment instruments and methods that were designed to address *clinical* questions, questions of psychiatric diagnosis, when clinical questions bear only secondarily upon the real issues in many child custody cases. Psychiatric interviews, Rorschachs, and MMPIs might have a role to play in child custody assessments. But

these tools were *not* designed to assess parents' relationships to children … [or their] child rearing attitudes and capacities, and *these* are often the central questions in child custody cases. (pp. 8–9, italics in original)

But judges can also be faulted here. Lowery (1984), after her survey of judicial practices, wrote: "According to the results of this study, the court, on its own, is more likely to ask, 'Which parent is the better adult?', using relatively apparent and verifiable indices of competence such as health, financial status, and reputation in the community" (p. 379). Psychologists need not only to move beyond their own biases, but also to educate judges about the needs of the child and appropriate parenting skills.

Techniques of Custody Evaluation

Not all forensic psychologists carry out custody evaluations in the same way, and certainly they do not completely agree on what specific procedures should be used. Most make sure to interview each parent and each child and to observe each child in interaction with each parent; many include the administration of psychological tests. But a typical characteristic of poor-quality evaluations is the failure to be comprehensive. The most common complaint is that the psychologist failed to evaluate someone but made a recommendation about that person. For example, the negligent psychologist may write a report saying, "the father needs domestic violence therapy" without ever observing or interviewing the father (Hedrick, 1998).

Scope of Evaluation

The scope of the evaluation should reflect a functional assessment of the skills and values of the parents and their congruence with the assessed needs of the child. CPA and APA guidelines note that this necessarily requires a wide range of information sources and methods of gathering data. Thus, the psychologist needs to obtain a picture from all perspectives. Psychologists should attempt to

BOX 13.3
Steps in the Evaluation Process

The clinical inquiry in custody evaluations should include an assessment of each parent and each child. Specifically, the following should be evaluated:

- Parent's description of marital relationship and family structure.
  - Parent's attitude and concerns regarding the other parent, his or her access to the children, nature of visitation, and so on.
  - Discussion with children about the separation and divorce.
  - The parent's communications with the children about the other parent.
  - The parent's goals for visitation and decision making should he or she be awarded custody.
- Parent's prior and current relationship with the children and responsibility for care-taking.
  - Reaction to pregnancy and childbirth and impact of these on relationship and functioning outside the family.
  - Early care-taking.
  - Current care-taking.
  - Punishment.
  - Leisure and social activities.
  - Interactional style.
  - Allegations of abuse/neglect.
- Parent's current and anticipated living and working arrangements.
  - Who is living in the home.
  - Significant others.
  - Daycare, babysitting.

- Schools and school districts.
- Parent's emotional functioning and mental health.
  - Prior or current substance abuse/dependence and treatment.
  - Prior or current mental health problems and treatment.
  - Emotional response to the divorce.
  - History of domestic violence (several jurisdictions now have laws that discourage awarding custody to persons with a history of spouse-battering, Drozd, 1998).
- Child's attitude and preference regarding the parents, current living arrangements, visitation, and future placement.
- Child's depictions and conceptualization of relationship with each parent.
  - Punishment.
  - Leisure and social activities.
  - Interactional style.
  - Allegations of abuse/neglect.
- Child's emotional functioning and mental health.
  - Prior or current substance abuse/dependence and treatment.
  - Prior or current mental health problems and treatment.
  - Emotional or behavioural responses (i.e., problem behaviours) to the divorce.
- Child's social, academic, and vocational functioning prior to and after divorce.

(Adapted from Melton, Petrila, Poythress, & Slobogin, 1997, Table 16.1, and from Otto, 1996.)

interview all parents and guardians alone as well as together. But many other sources should be consulted in a *comprehensive* evaluation procedure; see Box 13.3 for a listing.

Observation Procedures

Observation by a trained eye is critical in child custody and access disputes. Observation of a child interacting with each of his or her parents has the attraction of being a slice of "real" behaviour, and forensic psychologists have used observation techniques in child custody evaluations,

while recognizing the potential for error (Marafiote, 1985). Some might doubt that the interactions under the scrutiny of an observing psychologist are really that "real," but most parents and especially most children soon accommodate to the presence of an observer. Sometimes what happens in real life is surprising. Psychoanalyst Robert M. Galatzer-Levy (1997) has written:

> As a part of a clinical assessment in custody evaluations I have been impressed by how much information is often readily apparent

in observed interactions and incidentally how convincing material from such interactions can be to finders of fact. What is often astonishing is how blatant some of the behavior can be, including being unresponsive to the child, striking the child, the child's unresponsiveness to reasonable attempts at interaction, etc. When blatant interactions occur, they are so striking that issues of validity and reliability or concerns that the difficulties of the situation brought them on are of little relevance. The behavior speaks for itself.

As a structured observation technique, Campagna (1998) has suggested the following:

What I do is buy a math workbook and an English workbook from the local school supplies store. They're cheap enough (usually about $3.50 each) so that I can have one for whatever age child I'm evaluating. (They have different workbooks for each age.) Then I choose a workbook that's a year or so beyond where the child is in school and ask the parent to teach the child one of the pages in each workbook. Since the subject matter is beyond what the child's already learned, I get a nice snapshot of how the parent teaches the child new material, how they interact in a stressful situation, etc.

Such procedures may generate useful hypotheses, but observations by a single individual may lack inter-observer reliability. Nevertheless, experienced custody evaluators often rely on them.

Nims (1998) has a systematic procedure, the NIMS Observation Checklist, which he uses in his home visits. Five aspects of the situation are broken down into specific behaviours that are rated. The five general characteristics are the following:

- Safety and environment
- General behaviour toward the child
- Teaching and training
- Control
- Child-initiated behaviour

Within each category, Nims rates more specific aspects on a 1-to-5 scale. For example, within "General behaviour toward the child," the parent is rated on the degree to which he or she has eye contact, strokes the child, is patient with the child, smiles, cuddles, and hugs appropriately. The rating, Nims states, is done according to *his* value system, and there are no norms. He assumes that the behaviour is reliable and consistent but recognizes that it is not always true. Nevertheless, he reports that judges appreciate his system, doubtless because the characteristics he rates are clearly important and Nims has a solid, no-nonsense manner about him.

Psychological Tests and Scales

If an evaluation is going to be comprehensive, why not include scales to assess the behaviours and attitudes of parents and of children? This sounds like a good idea, but achieving such goals well is not so easy to do (Heinze & Grisso, 1996). The most widely used test administered to parents in custody evaluations is one not designed for that purpose: The Minnesota Multiphasic Personality Inventory, now updated as the MMPI-2 (Butcher, Dahlstrom, Graham, Tellegen, & Kaemmer, 1989). Other instruments that are also frequently administered to each parent, such as the Rorschach Inkblot Technique, the Millon Inventories (another personality inventory), and projective techniques involving drawings, were developed without custody determinations in mind. Their main purpose is the assessment of the likelihood of neurosis or psychosis; some claim to measure neurological malfunctioning. We agree with Stahl's (1994) conclusion: "The Rorschach can provide a good understanding of the adult's affect, organization skills, and reality testing, but, except for the most dysfunctional parent, it will not do much to answer questions about day-to-day parenting" (p. 55).

Despite these reservations, some of these instruments are used almost as frequently as interviews with the parents. LaFortune and Carpenter (1998) surveyed 165 practitioners; among the information solicited was a listing of the procedures used in custody evaluations. Respondents rated the frequency of their usage of each on a scale of 1 = Never to 5 = Always. Mean ratings for interviewing significant parties were, as expected, quite high: Interview mother = 4.98; Interview father = 4.91; Interview younger child = 4.65; Interview older child = 4.91; Observe mother with child = 4.82; Observe father with child = 4.80. But the *next most frequent* activity was to administer the MMPI-2 to the parents; its average rating of 4.19 meant that it was used quite frequently. The scales specifically developed to assess parenting—to be described in this section—were used only about half the time (average rating of 3.28, although there was wide variation among respondents in their reported use). Thus the survey supports the conclusion of reviewers Randy K. Otto and Robert P. Collins (1995) that "the MMPI/MMPI-2 is the psychological assessment instrument most significantly used [with parents] in child-custody evaluations today" (p. 246).

Is it a good idea to rely on an instrument not designed for the specific purpose? Does the degree to which each parent's responses conform to the scales of, for example, schizophrenia or some form of neuroticism, say much about what is best for the child? Otto and Collins's (1995) review concluded that the Minnesota instruments can play a role in a much broader inquiry by the psychologist. They can:

> assess the emotional functioning and adjustment of the parents, other persons who may significantly affect the child (e.g., stepparents, live-in relatives, or others), and (adolescent) children. The MMPI-2/MMPI-A [a version of the MMPI for children] will also prove of some relevance to child custody evaluations to the degree that they offer a description of, and inform the court about, the parents' (or other potential caretakers') and (adolescent) child's traits and behavior. Finally, the MMPI/MMPI-2 also may prove to be of some value with respect to assessing the overall test-taking set that parents, other potential caretakers, and (adolescent) chil-

dren have adopted with respect to the evaluation process. To the degree that minimization or denial of problems and shortcomings is a potential concern in child custody evaluations, the Minnesota tests' validity scales may also prove of some value. (Otto & Collins, 1995, pp. 234–235)

As noted above, several devices have been developed specifically to assist psychologists in making child custody evaluations. The following section reviews five that have received attention in the various books published within the last 20 years on child custody evaluations (Ackerman, 1994; Bricklin, 1995; Gould, 1998; Kissel & Freeling, 1990; Schutz, Dixon, Lindenberger, & Ruther, 1989; Skafte, 1985; Stahl, 1994; and Weithorn, 1987). Most of these scales are distributed by commercial test publishers.

The ASPECT Procedure The first, the Ackerman-Schoendorf Scales for Parent Evaluation of Custody (ASPECT), is really more than a scale or even a set of scales; it is a comprehensive procedure that uses testing, observation, and interviews with each parent and child. Thus the ASPECT procedure (Ackerman & Schoendorf, 1992; Ackerman, 1994) receives good marks for its thoroughness. In addition to a set of 68 questions (mostly open-ended) responded to by each parent, it includes a consideration by the evaluating psychologist of the parents' responses on various standard psychological tests, and the psychologist's own responses to evaluations of each parent. The Parent Questionnaire is composed of questions about custody arrangements, living arrangements, child-care arrangements, the children's development and education, and the relationship between the two parents and between each parent and the children. It also seeks information about the parents' background, including substance abuse, psychiatric treatment, and legal problems. Based on the variety of information, the psychologist answers a series of questions about each parent, leading to scores on three subscales: the Observational Scale, the Social Scale, and the Cognitive-Emotional Scale. The first assesses the quality of each parent's self-presentation during the evaluation process. The Social Scale seeks to measure the quality of each parent's interpersonal relationships and concerns about the family, while the Cognitive-Emotional subscale evaluates each parent's affective and cognitive capabilities in relation to childrearing. These lead to an overall score on a Parenting Custody Index (PCI), considered to be a global measure of parenting effectiveness.

The psychologist is encouraged to assess the quality of each parent's interaction with the child and the manner in which each parent communicates with the child. Also, does the parent recognize the present and future needs of the child? Can the parent provide adequate discipline?

Each parent thus emerges with an ASPECT score, and if one of the parents' score is ten points higher or lower than the other parents' score, the scale authors believe that there exists a significant difference in custodial effectiveness. Among 30 couples who had a ten-point difference or greater, in 28 of these (93 percent) the ASPECT results were consistent with the judge's decision about custody (Ackerman, 1994).

In a chapter reviewing the use of the MMPI in child custody evaluations, Otto and Collins (1995) evaluated the ASPECT because the ASPECT procedure includes items from the MMPI-2. They were not favourable in their review; they wrote:

> The authors' presentation of validity data on the ASPECT is confusing and incomplete. The authors report that predictive validity was assessed by comparing recommendations made on the basis of the ASPECT with the parents in the normative study to their judges' final custody decisions. Although the test manual is unclear, apparently, in 59 of the 100 sample cases, results of the ASPECT were conclusive enough to recommend custody for one parent or the other and this recommendation was offered to the court. The authors report that the ASPECT correctly "predicted" the judges' custody deci-

sions in about 75% of the cases (Ackerman & Schoendorf, 1992, p. 53). This, of course, is not true predictive validity because the results of the ASPECT presumably formed the basis of the examining psychologists' opinions that were presented to the court. (Otto & Collins, 1995, pp. 231–232)

The Parent–Child Relationship Inventory (PCRI) The PCRI (Gerard, 1994) includes 78 items that form seven content subscales and two validity subscales. The content subscales are titled Satisfaction with Parenting, Autonomy, Limit Setting, Involvement, Communication, Parental Support, and Role Orientation, and the two validity scales are called Social Desirability and Inconsistent Reporting. Each parent independently responds to the items, using four-point Likert-type choices. The PCRI provides information about the parents' disciplinary styles and feelings of competence, self-esteem, and social support. Clinicians who have administered the PCRI report that in about half of the couples, the scores do not differentiate between the two parents (Gerard, 1994), a finding consistent with this chapter's belief that often the task of the evaluator is not an easy one, if the evaluator sees his or her role as making a distinction between the desirability of the two parents.

The Bricklin Scales Bricklin (1994) has developed an interlocking set of scales, including the Bricklin Perceptual Scale (BPS), Perception of Relationships Test (PORT), Parent Awareness Skills Survey (PASS), and the Parent Perception of Child Profile (PPCP). As described in his handbook (Bricklin, 1995, Chapters 4–7), these have the following purposes:

- *BPS.* In this scale, 64 items (32 about the mother and 32 about the father) are posed to the child. The child is asked how well each item describes each parent. The author considers it appropriate for use with children over six years of age. The goal is to assess the child's perceptions of each parent on each of four characteristics: competence, supportiveness, follow-up consistency, and possession of admirable character traits. Not only does the child provide an oral response about how well each parent performs each activity, but the child is also instructed to use a nonverbal response (pushing a stylus through a black line with end points of "very well" and "not so well"); the latter procedure, according to the author, reflects "unconscious mental sources" (Bricklin, 1995, pp. 77–78). It is only this latter non-verbal response that is scored. Bricklin believes that children's verbal expressions are often defensive or distorted (Schutz, Dixon, Lindenberger, & Ruther, 1989).

- *PORT.* With the goal of assessing the degree of closeness the child feels toward each parent, this measure primarily uses projective drawings by the child. Bricklin has designed this measure for administration to children three years of age and older.
- *PASS.* This scale measures each parent's awareness of factors important in determining his or her response to 18 issues related to child-care. The scoring indicates the interviewer's assessment of the quality of the parent's answers to questions, including follow-ups that probe the parent's feelings.
- *PPCP.* This procedure asks for information from each parent about his or her perceptions of each child. More than 120 questions (plus probes) are used.

As can been seen, some of the above measures use responses from the child, some from the parents; some are self-report questionnaires, some structured interviews, and some use projective techniques. To varying degrees the psychologist makes his or her own interpretation of the responses and behaviours of the participants. The whole collection makes for a lengthy evaluation, and, unfortunately, no norms exist. However, Bricklin (1994) has reported an 89 percent agreement rate between the "preferred parent" based on the BPS measure and the judge's even-

tual choice of the primary caretaker. A recent survey (Ackerman & Ackerman, 1997) found that the BPS was the test most frequently administered to children.

Parenting Stress Index The fourth measure reflects a different goal—one that is less direct. Its purpose is to assess the type and severity of stresses associated with the childrearing role (Abidin, 1990, 1998). Its author has made a candid disclaimer: "I would like to make it clear that I am not a forensic psychologist and that in developing the PSI I never envisioned that it would be used for forensic purposes" (1998, p. 1). Both a 101-item self-report scale, used by parents of children ages three months to ten years, and a 36-item short form exist. Various subscales are related to the child or children in the family (e.g., the children's adaptability, mood, demandingness, and hypersensitivity) and to the parent's feeling of his or her own competence, social isolation, depression, attachment, and relationship with spouse.

Parenting Satisfaction Scale Another, relatively new scale that focuses on parenting is the Parenting Satisfaction Scale (Guidubaldi & Cleminshaw, 1998), which consists of 45 self-report items, in three domains: satisfaction with the parenting done by the spouse or ex-spouse, satisfaction with one's own parent–child relationship, and satisfaction with one's own performance as a parent. Sample items include the following:

- "I wish I did not become so impatient with my children."
- "My spouse has sufficient knowledge about child development that makes him/her feel comfortable as a parent."

One application of the scale is to assess judgments of compatibility for shared parenting.

Evaluating These Scales The various books on child custody evaluations differ in how much enthusiasm they express for using these measures.

The published reviews of the psychometric properties of these scales are, in contrast, almost uniformly critical. Among the limitations cited are the following:

- Inclusion of unrealistic or untested assumptions, including the reduction of complex constructs to narrow behaviour samples (Melton, 1995; Shaffer, 1992).
- Use of small samples, inappropriate clinical samples, or inadequate descriptions of the sample (Carlson, 1995; Hagin, 1992; Hiltonsmith, 1995).
- Frequent absence of norms (Carlson, 1995).
- Lack of evidence of reliability or validity (Arditti, 1995; Bischoff, 1995; Conger, 1995; Hiltonsmith, 1995).

A more detailed critique of these devices may be found in the review by Heinze and Grisso (1996); see also Borum (1998b) and Melton, Petrila, Poythress, and Slobogin (1997, pp. 503–504). The best use of these may be reflected in the summary by Melton and his colleagues:

> We join with other reviewers who recommend caution in the use of these commercially available "child custody" measures. Although some of these measures may facilitate gathering useful responses regarding parents' attitudes, knowledge, or values with respect to raising their children, the lack of adequate reliability and validity studies counsels against use of formal indices they yield. Certainly these indices do not identify "scientifically" the parent of choice or indicate other dispositional conclusions, matters which are properly reserved for the court. (p. 504)

THE EXPERT WITNESS ROLE

A judge who handles many child custody cases, Samuel G. Fredman (1995), has offered the following specific advice to psychologists who are testifying:

1. *Be prepared.* Be ready to give the judge your point of view. Show the judge you know your subject. "Convince me … that some of my long-held thinking should fall by the wayside because of your testimony" (p. 4).
2. *Provide your expert opinion.* "We want to know, having satisfied ourselves as to your background and experience and knowledge, what you think we ought to do in a given situation" (p. 4).
3. *Reflect objectivity.* "When the court appoints a psychologist, the court expects the neutrality which such designation underscores. We would like to feel we are getting that same kind of objectivity" (pp. 4–5).

Ultimate-Opinion Testimony

Psychologists need to recognize that judges differ to the degree that they want **ultimate–opinion testimony**. Some judges are explicit about wanting a recommendation regarding the custody determination and will not reappoint a psychologist who won't give such an opinion (Gould, 1998). On the other hand, for some judges, their authority and rule making is paramount. Judge Fredman, in speaking to psychologists, stated: "*You* are not making the custody or visitation decision: I am. We want merely advice and counsel" (1995, italics in original).

Some psychologists (Melton, Petrila, Poythress, & Slobogin, 1997; Schutz, Dixon, Lindenberger, & Ruther, 1989; Weithorn & Grisso, 1987) have concluded that it is inappropriate for custody evaluators to give testimony on the ultimate question. Instead, the focus should be on the quality of the relationship between parents and the child.

Mario Dennis (1998), a psychologist, has written:

> I think there are ways of addressing the ultimate issue without giving a final opinion on it. I generally list the advantages and disadvantages of placing the children with each parent, and relate those to the test data,

parenting experience, relationships between the parents and children, environment, etc. I also factor in the potential consequences of disrupting the status quo, whatever that may be.

Regardless, the psychologist as expert witness should resist the temptation to express an opinion that goes beyond his or her information or competence, whatever the pressures from the judge or the lawyers to do so.

Ethical Considerations

The ethical responsibilities of any psychologist testifying as an expert witness apply here. The psychologist should be informed on a variety of topics: the best interests of the child, other applicable legal standards, the effects of divorce on children, and child psychopathology (Ackerman, 1994).

THE APPLIED RESEARCHER ROLE

Forensic psychologists who are on the "firing line" need to be aware of research findings on relevant issues. Psychologists in the applied researcher role have provided useful findings on two topics: the effects of divorce on children and the effects of types of custody arrangements.

The Effects of Divorce on Children

The decision to divorce is a complicated one, and many considerations compete for attention. Some divorcing couples partially justify the decision to divorce by assuming that any detrimental effects on their children will gradually dissipate. This self-serving assumption that "children are resilient; they will eventually get over it" is challenged by a 15-year longitudinal study of 131 children and adolescents from 60 divorced families by Wallerstein and Blakeslee (1989). Only about a tenth of the children in this study felt

relieved when the quarrelling parents separated, and these tended to be the older children who had been observers or recipients of physical abuse from one or both parents.

Judith Wallerstein, one of the authors of the study, has stated: "Almost half of children of divorces enter adulthood as worried, underachieving, self-deprecating, and sometimes angry young men and women" (quoted by Toufexis, 1989, p. 61). Wallerstein and Blakeslee described a "sleeper effect" on females; many of them seemed to have adjusted to their parents' divorce well into adulthood, at which point they suffered "an intolerable level of anxiety about betrayal." They then might drop out of university, become promiscuous, or trap themselves in unsatisfactory relationships—all, according to the authors, to protect themselves from rejection, abandonment, and betrayal. The researchers reported that this reaction occurred in two-thirds of the women between the ages of 19 and 23. Of children whose mothers remarried, half said they did not feel welcome in the new family. Ten years after the divorce, more than a third reported having poor relationships with both parents.

These results are disturbing, but whether they apply to a more representative sample of divorced families may be questioned. The participants were recruited through the offer of counselling, leading some reviewers (cf., Melton, Petrila, Poythress, & Slobogin, 1997, p. 492) to expect them to differ from a broader set of families who were coping with marital separation.

Another major study presents more optimistic conclusions about the effects of divorce on children. The longitudinal study by Hetherington and her colleagues (Hetherington, 1979, 1989, 1993; Hetherington, Stanley-Hagan, & Anderson, 1989) was a quasi-experimental study of 72 white, middle-class four- and five-year-old children and their divorced parents. (In all these families, mothers received custody of the children.) Focus was on the changes in the relationships; for example, the first year after the divorce is conflict-ridden, as everyone deals not only with anger and loss but also with practical problems of separate households. Results often differ from family to family; general trends are summarized by Thompson (1983) and by Melton et al. (1997).

The Effects of Type of Custody

The most consistent innovation by the courts regarding divorce in the last three decades is **joint custody**. Statutes in an increasing number of jurisdictions have come to favour it as an alternative (Rohman, Sales, & Lou, 1990), and in some recent statutes, such custody must be ordered by the judge unless the evidence exists that such an arrangement would be harmful to the child (Scott & Derdeyn, 1984). In some locations, joint custody has become the judicial determination in as many as 80 percent of the cases (Byczynski, 1987). However, definitions of joint custody differ widely from location to location. In some instances, the amount of time the child is in the physical custody of each parent is split relatively equally; in other instances, the child lives mainly with one parent, but both parents retain legal decision making with respect to the child's education, health, and welfare (Felner & Terre, 1987). Simply put, joint legal custody does not necessarily mean shared physical custody (Maccoby & Mnookin, 1992).

During the period of peak interest in the procedure, joint custody was seen as a panacea to the problem of custody, because children could maintain their relationship with both parents, divorced fathers could maintain influence over the lives of their children, and mothers could avoid the burden of being the sole disciplinarian (Press, 1983). Two other reasons for the enthusiasm for joint custody have been offered: (1) fathers who continued to share custody of their children were more likely to make child-support payments and (2) co-parenting would reduce the conflict between divorced parents (Weitzman, 1985).

But then second thoughts surfaced. For example, it has been claimed that joint custody strains the ideal of "psychological parenting" after divorce. The concept of psychological parenting was advanced by Goldstein, Freud, and Solnit (1979), who defined such a parent as "one who, on a continuing, day-to-day basis, through interplay, and mutuality, fulfills the child's psychological needs for a parent, as well as the child's physical needs" (p. 98). Also, the early expectations about the unqualified beneficial effects of joint custody upon the children have been tempered by research findings that are mixed. Box 13.4 reviews these findings.

As noted earlier, the anticipated benefits of joint custody extend beyond the satisfaction level of children and also included possible increased compliance with child-support mandates and a reduction in conflict between the two parents. The detailed review by Sales, Manber, and Rohman (1992), on which we have relied heavily in this chapter, concludes that results are also mixed for each of these. For example, some studies conclude that fathers who are participating in joint-custody arrangements are less often late or delinquent in paying child support (Luepnitz, 1982, 1986; Waddell, 1985), but another study reports no difference between joint-custody and maternal-custody arrangements (Lowery, 1986).

Likewise, it is not clear that joint custody reduces the level of antagonism between divorced parents (Sales, Manber, & Rohman, 1992, p. 32). Hauser (1985), in an extreme view, has concluded that "simply having the designation of joint custody does little, if anything, to ameliorate conflict; nor does it promote, support, or make possible appropriate communication, adequate to children's needs in a population of chronic litigators" (p. 581). It is the case that other studies report no difference in conflict levels from different custody arrangements (Albiston, Maccoby, & Mnookin, 1990), but many studies report the opposite, including greater cooperation between parents and a lower rate of further lawsuits (Shiller, 1986a; Luepnitz, 1986; Ilfeld, Ilfeld, & Alexander, 1982).

BOX 13.4

How Beneficial Is Joint Custody: A Task for Evaluation Research

A review of findings about the effects of joint custody upon children (Felner & Terre, 1987, pp. 126–134) provides mixed conclusions.

On the positive side are the following findings:

1. Luepnitz (1982) compared joint-custody arrangements with single-custody homes. All of the children in the joint-custody arrangements reported that they preferred that system; about half of the children in the single-custody homes wished for more contact with the other parent. In a follow-up of 43 of her 50 families, Luepnitz (1986) concluded that joint custody, at its best, is superior to single custody at its best, but by no means was one always better than the other.
2. Shiller (1986b) concluded that children in joint custody retain more appropriate and realistic feelings about each parent.
3. In another study, Shiller (1986a) found that boys have fewer behavioural difficulties in joint-custody arrangements.

But less optimistic were the findings of a study by Steinman (1981), who interviewed 24 families, all of whom had agreed to a joint-custody arrangement. Although many of the parents and children thrived under this system, about a quarter of the 32 children reported having a difficult time shifting back and forth between the two homes. Another third of these children seemed "overburdened" and were having noticeable adjustment problems. In fact, the child's need for environmental stability is considered by some as the major obstacle to greater use by judges of the joint-custody arrangement (Clingempeel & Reppucci, 1982).

Given that sometimes joint custody is helpful to children and sometimes it is harmful, can we identify factors that increase the likelihood of a beneficial result? Yes. If the parents have an amicable relationship, joint custody seems to have no adverse effect on the emotional health of the children (Kline, Tschann, Johnston, & Wallerstein, 1989). But a continuing conflict-riddled relationship between parents can be detrimental to the children in a joint-custody arrangement. Sales, Manber,

and Rohman (1992) summarized the research findings as follows:

Factors that have been identified as important for joint custody to work beneficially for the children include the parents' willingness to share custody and cooperate; their motivation to provide continued access to the other parent; and their ability to separate their own feelings and issues about the other parent from the child's needs and feelings, to empathize with the child, to respect the other parent's bond with the child, to trust in the other parent's parenting skills, and to maintain objectivity through the divorce process (Keilin & Bloom, 1986; Steinman, Zemmelman, & Knoblauch, 1985; Shiller, 1986a; Volgy & Everett, 1985). The importance of the quality of the interparental relationship for the success of the joint-custody arrangement fits with Koch and Lowery's (1984) findings regarding non-custodial fathers; continued involvement of fathers with their children after divorce is predicted by the relationship between the divorced parents rather than by the parent–child relationship. (p. 33)

As this review implies in its last statement, the specific custody arrangements may be less influential on children's adjustment than the parents' emotional stability and the amount of continuing conflict between them (Grych & Fincham, 1992). In summary, as the review by Felner and Terre (1987) concluded:

Perhaps the clearest statement that can be made is that no particular custody arrangement is "best." Arguments in favor of a resumption of one form over another are ill-suited to the realities of family life and development. The contention of Goldstein et al. (1973) that the child's relationship with the custodial or "psychological parent" may be damaged by the continued coequal involvement of the non-custodial parent does not appear to be necessarily true in all cases. However, neither is the contention by joint custody advocates that joint custody is the best alternative for all children. (p. 140)

SUMMARY

As a part of the decision making when a couple divorces and contests the custody of their children, forensic psychologists can play several roles, including that of marriage counsellor, mediator, child therapist, court–appointed evaluator, expert witness, and applied researcher. In such activities, the forensic psychologist needs to avoid the possibility of dual relationships, such as serving as a therapist for the child and later serving as a consultant to the court on the best disposition for the child.

When the forensic psychologist carries out an evaluation at the request of the court, several procedures are typically included. Each parent and each child are separately interviewed, and each child is often observed interacting with each parent. Usually, the parents are asked to complete a questionnaire or even a battery of psychological assessment techniques. The most frequently used instrument is the MMPI-2, although several instruments have been devised specifically for child custody evaluations.

Upon completion of the evaluation, the forensic psychologist prepares a report for the court. In Canada, the report is made available to the parents' lawyers and to the parents. The psychologist may then testify at a hearing. Judges differ in their desire to hear ultimate-opinion testimony from the psychologist.

A separate role exists for the forensic psychologist in evaluating general claims and assumptions about the nature of custody, as well as the long-term effects of the parents' divorce on their children.

KEY TERMS

applied researcher, p. 279
best interests of the child standard, p. 278
court-appointed evaluator, p. 278
custody evaluation, p. 279
dual relationship, p. 276
expert witness, p. 279
fact witness, p. 278
joint custody, p. 293
mediator, p. 276
tender-years doctrine, p. 282
ultimate-opinion testimony, p. 291

SUGGESTED READINGS

Ackerman, M. J. (1994). *Clinician's guide to child custody evaluations*. New York: John Wiley.

Ackerman presents a detailed description of the comprehensive ASPECT procedure.

Gould, J. W. (1998). *Conducting scientifically crafted custody evaluations*. Thousand Oaks, CA: Sage.

This text offers state-of-the-art application of forensic techniques to child custody evaluations as well as reviews of applicable literature from child development.

Greenberg, S. A., & Shuman, D. W. (1997). Irreconcilable conflict between therapeutic and forensic roles. *Professional Psychology: Research and Practice, 28,* 505–557.

This article analyzes ten critical differences between the role of the psychotherapist and that of the forensic evaluator.

Liss, M. B., & McKinley-Pace, M. J. (1999). Best interests of the child: New twists on an old theme. In R. Roesch, S. D. Hart, & J. R. P. Ogloff (Eds.), *Psychology and law: The state of the discipline* (pp. 339–372). New York: Kluwer Academic/Plenum Publishers.

This recent chapter-length article reviews applications of the best interests of the child standard not only to custody after divorce, but also to adoption cases.

Melton, G. B., Petrila, J., Poythress, N. G., & Slobogin, C. (1997). *Psychological evaluations for the courts* (2nd ed.). New York: Guilford.

Chapter 16, "Child Custody in Divorce," is a sobering but thoughtful treatment of the psychologist's varied roles.

Schutz, B. M., Dixon, E. B., Lindenberger, J. C., & Ruther, N. J. (1989). *Solomon's sword: A practical guide to conducting child custody evaluations*. San Francisco: Jossey-Bass.

This brief guide for the forensic psychologist includes useful examples of interview questions for parents and for children and behavioural observations. It also contains a section on how the psychologist as expert witness should respond when "Ziskinized," or aggressively questioned during cross-examination.

14

Discrimination

Racism and in particular anti-black racism, is a part of our community's psyche. A significant segment of our community holds overtly racist views. A much larger segment subconsciously operates on the basis of negative racial stereotypes. Furthermore, our institutions, including the criminal justice system, reflect and perpetuate those negative stereotypes.
—JUSTICE DOHERTY (*R. v. Parks*, 1993)

WHAT IS DISCRIMINATION?

Although Canada is a country that outwardly values diversity and enjoys an international reputation as an advocate of human rights, the manner in which some members of our society have been treated by the legal system sometimes suggests otherwise. Ours is one of the most ethnically diverse countries in the world. According to a Statistics Canada 2002 report, 23 percent of Canada's adult population (5.3 million people) were born outside of Canada. Of this population, nearly half (46 percent), or about 10.3 million, reported only British, French and/or Canadian ethnic or cultural origins. People of non-European descent accounted for 13 percent of the adult population, or 2.9 million. The most common origins in this group were Chinese and East Indian. Another 22 percent of the adult population, or 4.9 million, reported other mixed ethnic backgrounds, or were not aware of their ethnicity (Statistics Canada, 2003). Further, in 2001, nearly a million people in Canada identified themselves as being Aboriginal.

We are fortunate to be living in such an interesting and diverse cultural landscape. But how often are Canadians discriminated against based on their ethnic background? Section 15 of the Charter of Rights and Freedoms (1982) states that "Every individual is equal before and under the law and has the right to the equal protection and equal benefit of the law without discrimination and, in particular, without discrimination based on race, national or ethnic origin, colour, religion, sex, age or mental or physical disability." However, there is much evidence that large numbers of people in Canada are discriminated against. The Ethnic Diversity Study by Statistics Canada involved surveying 42 500 adults in the ten provinces in 2002. Of these respondents, 7 percent, or about 1.6 million adult Canadians, reported that they had experienced discrimination or unfair treatment in the past five years "sometimes" or "often" because of their ethnocultural characteristics. However, this proportion rises to 20 percent when we consider the respondents who were of a visible minority and who

perceived such discrimination. Of the groups among the visible-minority population, blacks were the most likely (32 percent; an estimated 135 000 people) to report that they had been treated unfairly sometimes or often because of their ethnicity. This compares with 21 percent of South Asians and 18 percent of Chinese people. It is important to note that this survey focused on "visible minorities" defined by the Employment Equity Act, as "persons other than the Aboriginal peoples, who are non-Caucasian in ethnicity and non-white in colour." As such, the level of mistreatment reported above does not include the enormous degree of discrimination suffered by the Aboriginal people in Canada for hundreds of years and to the present day.

The government-controlled, church-run residential school system is perhaps the most obvious and best-known historical example of systematic racism against Aboriginal people. However, there is evidence for continuing racism and bias against this group within the legal system. For example, as documented by the National Anti-Racism Council of Canada (2002), in Saskatoon there have been many instances in which police officers picked up Aboriginal males reported to be intoxicated and drove them to remote areas, where they abandoned them in bitterly cold weather. This practice led to tragic consequences in the winter of 2000 when the frozen bodies of two Aboriginal men—Rodney Naistus and Lawrence Wegner—were found near the Queen Elizabeth Power Plant south of Saskatoon. When Wegner's body was found on February 3, he was wearing only a T-shirt and jeans, with no shoes. In 2001, two Saskatoon police officers admitted to picking up an Aboriginal man named Darrel Night on a downtown street and driving him to the outskirts of the city. Night reported that they took his coat and left him to walk home in the cold. The two officers were suspended and received sentences of eight months each. As a result of this case, city officials set up a 16-officer task force to investigate the practices of the Saskatoon police. The task force found no grounds for charges in the deaths of Wegner and Naistus (National Anti-Racism Council of Canada, 2002).

Would Wegner and Naistus still be alive had they been Caucasian? How do we prove that an act reflects discrimination against an individual based on some personal characteristic? What is the reason that although Aboriginal people constitute approximately 12 percent of the population of Manitoba, they account for over half of the 1600 people incarcerated in Manitoba's correctional institutions (Trevethan, Moore, & Rastin, 2002)? These are difficult questions to answer, but important ones, and ones that are worthy of study by psychologists who wish to apply the knowledge of their profession to the problems facing the legal system.

Prejudice and Discrimination

First, we need to be explicit about the meaning of some terms, especially because words such as *prejudice* and *discrimination* are used frequently and broadly by the public and the media. Social psychologists customarily distinguish between prejudice and discrimination by defining **prejudice** as an attitude and **discrimination** as a behaviour. That is, prejudice is something internal, and is defined as an unjustified evaluative reaction to a member of a group that results from the recipient's membership in that group. The definition implies that the prejudiced person holds the same evaluative attitude toward the group as a whole. A prejudice is considered to be unjustified because it involves prejudgment, because it is illogical (derived from hearsay or from biased sources), or because it leads the person to over-categorize and treat individuals on the basis of the group with which they are identified. A prejudiced attitude can be favourable or unfavourable, positive or negative, but most of society's concern focuses, understandably, on negative prejudices.

In contrast, discrimination is defined as a behaviour—an overt observable action—that accepts one person or rejects another on the basis of his or her membership in a particular group. Negative actions can be ones of aggression and hostility or actions reflecting avoidance and with-

drawal. Often, discrimination is a direct reflection of prejudice. On the one hand, a person may have prejudiced attitudes but not be discriminatory in his or her behaviour; a university student who is homophobic, for example, may not seek a transfer upon learning that his or her new dormitory roommate is gay. On the other hand, a person may be unprejudiced in his or her attitudes and yet reflect discriminatory behaviour; for example, Domino's Pizza employees in several large cities—some of whom were black—refused to deliver to certain minority neighbourhoods because the owner of the company told them not to stop in high-crime areas.

As the deaths of Wegner and Naistus became widely publicized, many claimed the act reflected **racism**. Is racism a type of prejudice or a type of discrimination? The critics of the police referred to such an act as racist, but social scientists would refer to such behaviours as racially discriminatory actions and would ordinarily define racism as a subset of attitudes within the domain of prejudice.

Modern Racism

Strong pressures exist in our society against the endorsement of blatantly racist remarks, and researchers agree that the expression of prejudice is more often subtle now than in the past. When respondents are asked to select the traits that are most typical of specific racial and ethnic groups, those who are willing to attribute negative characteristics to blacks have consistently declined (that is, have left that section of the questionnaire blank) over the last 70 years, as the compilation done by Dovidio and Gaertner (1996), reprinted in Table 14.1, illustrates. In fact, although many Caucasians may regard themselves as unprejudiced, they still may reflect bias and harbour negative feelings and beliefs about certain groups. Hence, social psychologists have developed concepts to refer to a prejudice that fulfills the original definition, but is more nuanced than blatant. When applying it to racial attitudes, it has often been called **modern racism** (McConahay, 1983, 1986), although other terms, such as

Table 14.1	Percent of Subjects Selecting a Trait to Describe Black Americans (Formerly "Negroes") in 1933, 1951, 1967, 1982, 1988, 1990, 1993, and 1996							
	1933	**1951**	**1967**	**1982**	**1988**	**1990**	**1993**	**1996**
Superstitious	84	41	13	6	2	3	1	1
Lazy	75	31	26	13	6	4	5	2
Happy-go-lucky	38	17	27	15	4	1	2	1
Ignorant	38	24	11	10	6	5	5	2
Musical	26	33	47	29	13	27	12	18
Ostentatious	26	11	25	5	0	1	1	0
Very religious	24	17	8	23	20	19	17	23
Stupid	22	10	4	1	1	3	0	0
Physically dirty	17	—	3	0	1	0	1	0
Naive	14	—	4	4	2	3	1	0
Slovenly	13	—	5	2	1	1	0	0
Unreliable	12	—	6	2	1	4	1	0
Pleasure loving	—	19	26	20	14	14	14	12
Sensitive	—	—	17	13	15	9	4	5
Gregarious	—	—	17	4	6	2	4	6
Talkative	—	—	14	5	5	8	13	9
Imitative	—	—	13	9	4	3	0	1
Aggressive	—	—	—	19	16	17	24	21
Materialistic	—	—	—	16	10	3	13	6
Loyal to family	—	—	—	39	49	41	39	39
Arrogant	—	—	—	14	7	7	5	3
Ambitious	—	—	—	13	23	16	24	18
Tradition loving	—	—	—	13	22	16	16	18
Individualistic	—	—	—	—	24	17	19	16
Passionate	—	—	—	—	14	17	19	14
Nationalistic	—	—	—	—	13	13	19	6
Straightforward	—	—	—	—	12	15	24	19
Intelligent	—	—	—	—	—	14	5	21
Sportsmanlike	—	—	—	—	—	13	8	17
Quick-tempered	—	—	—	—	—	12	13	13
Artistic	—	—	—	—	—	12	6	9
Argumentative	—	—	—	—	—	—	14	11
Loud	—	—	—	—	—	—	11	24
Progressive	—	—	—	—	—	—	11	14
Radical	—	—	—	—	—	—	10	8
Revengeful	—	—	—	—	—	—	11	5
Suspicious	—	—	—	—	—	—	10	6
Talkative	—	—	—	—	—	—	13	9
Faithful	—	—	—	—	—	—	—	15

(From "Affirmative Action, Unintentional Racial Biases, and Intergroup Relations," by J. F. Dovidio and S. L. Gaertner, 1996, *Journal of Social Issues, 52(4),* p. 52. Reprinted by permission of Blackwell Publishing.)

Note: This table compares responses in eight different studies done at different times. Respondents were asked to select traits that were most typical of a number of different racial and ethnic groups. All the surveys were conducted using similar procedures.

subtle racism, *symbolic racism* (Sears, 1988), *subtle prejudice* (Pettigrew & Meertens, 1995), *aversive racism* (Dovidio & Gaertner, 1996; Gaertner & Dovidio, 1986), and *racial ambivalence* (Katz & Hass, 1988; Katz, Wackenhut, & Hass, 1986) have also been used. These are described in Box 14.1. Scales measuring these attitudes are evaluated in a useful chapter by Biernat and Crandall (1999).

What might be some of the manifestations of modern racism in Canadian society? According to the National Anti-Racism Council of Canada (2002), the Canadian media frequently misrepresent and stereotype ethnic minorities, including Aboriginal peoples. Such groups are frequently portrayed as outsiders or violent criminals posing a threat to the Canadian way of life. According to this report, some examples of negative stereotypes in the media included:

■ Black people are associated with drugs and guns, and are scapegoats for crime in Canadian society.
■ Immigrants are associated with crime such as drug smuggling and trafficking, or depicted as troublemakers who steal jobs from Canadians.
■ Muslim people are depicted as potential terrorists and fundamentalists, especially since the attacks of September 11, 2001.

■ Tamil Canadians are linked with gangs or terrorism.

Who Is Discriminated Against?

Members of any group can be discriminated against, sometimes for the most trivial of reasons. Certain groups receive protection from the courts, and they have received the most attention from psychological researchers; the qualities that loosely define these groups are:

■ ethnicity, colour, religion, or national origin
■ gender
■ age (particularly older age)
■ disability (both physical and psychological)

In some jurisdictions, persons with a homosexual sexual orientation are provided legal protection against discrimination, but in some jurisdictions they are not.

Overview of the Chapter

Society has raised a number of legitimate issues regarding discrimination that, while not easy to resolve, are better understood by considering the psychological perspectives. These questions include:

BOX 14.1
Contemporary Views of Racism

Social psychologists have offered several conceptions relevant to the distinction between what McConahay (1986) called "old-fashioned racism" and the more nuanced type:

■ McConahay and Hough (1976). *Modern racism*: "the expression in terms of abstract ideological symbols and symbolic behaviors of the feeling that blacks [or other minority groups] are violating cherished values and making illegitimate demands for changes in the racial status quo" (p. 38). For example, the statement "Blacks are getting too demanding in their push for equal rights" reflects modern racism.

■ Dovidio and Gaertner (1986). *Aversive racism*: the possession of racist attitudes and the wish to express them despite the desire to conform to current social norms, which condemn racism.

■ Katz and Hass (1988). *Ambivalent racism*: a white person's possessing, for example, pro-black and anti-black attitudes jointly, resulting in ambivalence.

■ Jackman (1978). *Functional theory of modern racism*: a Marxist position, proposing that Caucasians wish to maintain their advantaged position in society no matter what the cost to other groups of people.

1. Is the use of IQ tests valid for assigning persons of different ethnic backgrounds to special education classes?
2. Do affirmative action programs achieve their goals?
3. How extensive is gender discrimination in the workplace?
4. Is legislation that applies special penalties to hate crimes a deterrent to them?

This chapter examines four topics, reflecting discrimination, that have been studied by psychologists. They are the use of testing to assign students to special education classes; the impact of affirmative action policies; employment discrimination by ethnicity and gender; and hate crimes. These are, of course, only a few of the issues that reflect discrimination and have drawn the interest of social scientists. Racial discrimination in prisons, in jury verdicts, and by judges has been studied (Foley, Adams, & Goodson, 1996; Ruby & Brigham, 1996). Additionally, social scientists have sought to determine what influences businesses' compliance with legislation pertaining to people with disabilities has had on the employment of persons with mental disabilities (Scheid, 1999). The empirical study of age discrimination by employers, especially the impact of expert witnesses on jury awards, has generated useful findings (Greene, Downey, & Goodman-Delahunty, 1999).

WHAT CAN PSYCHOLOGY CONTRIBUTE?

Throughout this book, frequent examples are provided of discrimination based on gender and ethnic background. In the quest to understand and ameliorate these various manifestations of discrimination, the greatest contribution of psychology is its approach to understanding the phenomenon. More specifically, it can contribute in two ways, through a conceptual analysis and through the use of its methodologies. Each is described below.

Conceptual Analysis

We have already noted that psychologists have specified distinctions between prejudice and discrimination and recently focused on their more subtle manifestations. The systematic analysis of racial discrimination began in the 1930s. In contrast, the topic of gender discrimination has been studied only for the last four decades, despite its similarly long history in Canada and around the globe.

Modern Sexism

Just as racism often has become more subtle in its expression, so too the type of **sexism** most typically expressed has been changed by laws that give men and women the same rights and privileges in society. It has been proposed that three differing manifestations of sexism can be distinguished (Benokraitis & Feagin, 1986):

■ Behaviours reflecting blatant or overt sexism: "Those discriminatory actions directed against women that are quite obvious and visible" (Benokraitis & Feagin, 1986, p. 46). Examples of this type are the inequity in pay for women and men in the same jobs, the greater difficulty women experience in obtaining credit and loans, and the frequency of sexual harassment in the workplace.

■ Actions reflecting subtle sexism: "The unequal and harmful treatment of women that is visible but often not noticed because we have internalized sexist behavior as normal" (p. 30). It may take many forms, from effusive chivalry by men to discouragement and exclusion of women.

■ Behaviours related to covert sexism: "The unequal and harmful treatment of women that is hidden, clandestine, maliciously motivated, and very difficult to document" (p. 31).

Consider the case described in Chapter 1, in which Ann Hopkins brought a lawsuit against her employer, Price Waterhouse, claiming sex stereotyping caused her to be denied a partnership (*Price Waterhouse v. Hopkins*, 1989). The partners who made promotion decisions considered Hopkins to be too hard-driving, profane, and aggressive in her behaviour. Is this blatant or subtle sexism? Recall that Susan Fiske, a psychologist, testified about the possible influences of sexual stereotyping on judgments, such as promotion decisions, in organizations. Some observers have concluded that her testimony "was very valuable in providing the courts with a scientific basis for holding that sex stereotyping had a subtle, discriminatory impact on the views that Price Waterhouse's partners had toward Ms. Hopkins' candidacy for partnership" (Tomkins & Pfeifer, 1992, p. 399). However, after Price Waterhouse appealed the court's decision that Hopkins had been unfairly treated, a U.S. Supreme Court judge commented that the Court didn't need a psychologist to point out that sex discrimination had occurred. Although he seemed to be interpreting Price Waterhouse's action as blatant sexism, even members of the U.S. Supreme Court differed. Justice O'Connor wrote that "direct evidence of discrimination is hard to come by" and that U.S. law protects against "discrimination, subtle or otherwise" (*Price Waterhouse v. Hopkins*, 1989, pp. 1804–1805).

Regardless of these labelling distinctions, Fiske's testimony stands as an example of a conceptual analysis of the characteristics of gender stereotyping and their effects on employment and promotion decisions, as Chapter 1 illustrated. In what other ways can psychology contribute?

Methodology

Psychologists and other social scientists have established sophisticated methodological approaches in their research. Because lawyers and judges often are not trained in the use of statistics, psychologists can make a valuable contribution by the application of their methodologies to claims of employment discrimination, and to the evaluation of laws that seek to provide reforms regarding, for example, hate crimes or school segregation. Two types of contributions are described in this section: the use of statistical evidence and the application of experimental designs to assess subtle racism.

The Use of Statistical Analysis

Statistical analysis can be useful in the courtroom. In particular, statistical evidence has been employed in employment discrimination cases (Baldus & Cole, 1980; Dawson, 1980; Kaye, 1982a, 1982b; Kaye & Aicklin, 1986), and some judges have strongly advocated its use. (See an illustration in Box 14.2.) For example, Justice Potter Stewart wrote that U.S. Supreme Court opinions "make it clear that statistical analyses have served and will continue to serve an important role in cases in which the existence of discrimination is a disputed issue" (*International Brotherhood of Teamsters v. United States*, 1977, p. 339).

The courts, in discrimination suits, make a distinction between claims of disparate treatment and disparate impact. **Disparate treatment** is judged to have occurred when an employer treats an employee or some employees less favourably than the other employees because of ethnicity, colour, religion, gender, or national origin. **Disparate impact** (also called **adverse impact**) occurs if the employer's practices appear to be neutral in the treatment of different groups but nevertheless "fall more harshly on one group than on another and cannot be justified by business necessity" (Fienberg, 1989, p. 22). Disparate treatment is more susceptible to illustration by the use of statistical analyses than disparate impact.

Tomkins and Pfeifer (1992) have concluded that judges are especially uncomfortable with the use of statistical evidence, in part because it is hard for them to evaluate. They suggested that social framework evidence, as illustrated in Dr. Fiske's testimony, is more effective than statistical evidence. They wrote:

> The social science evidence that was introduced by Hopkins differed from the kind of social science evidence presented in *McCleskey*. Instead of presenting social science evidence that statistically quantified the influence of discriminatory factors on Price

BOX 14.2

A Judge Who Did His Statistics Homework

Whereas some judges shy away from statistical evidence and base their conclusions on personal experiences rather than empirical data, American Judge Patrick E. Higginbotham, in the case of *Vuyanich v. Republic National Bank* (1984), sought to understand the workings of another approach.

Joan Vuyanich was a black woman who worked as a clerk for the Republic National Bank for three months in 1969. Shortly after she was let go, she filed a charge with the U.S. Equal Employment Opportunity Commission (EEOC), claiming that she had been fired because of her ethnicity and gender. After much delay, the case went to trial in 1979, and Judge Higginbotham took almost a year to announce his opinion. He faced a formidable task; five statistical expert witnesses testified for the plaintiff, and the defence countered with four statistical experts who presented alternative analyses and rebutted the testimony of the plaintiff's experts. Most of the data used by each side were derived from the bank's records, but the two sides chose different variables to evaluate, including different regression analyses.

During the trial, Judge Higginbotham listened to the direct examination and cross-examination of each witness, and then he questioned them himself, usually asking questions about the substantive nature of the evidence. Saks and Van Duizend (1983) observed:

The judge employed flexible procedures in managing the trial. On several occasions he allowed experts to conduct what in essence was an in-court seminar through which they were invited to explain in more detail their underlying conceptualizations or mathematical procedures. Although the attorneys objected to this departure from the traditional procedures for eliciting testimony, they were overruled. (p. 35)

The detail in the decision was worth the wait; it was 127 pages in length; almost 80 pages were devoted to a review of "the mathematics of regression analysis." Judge Higginbotham subsequently observed that he and his law clerks took an entire month off from their other duties in order to understand the statistical evidence presented by the teams of expert witnesses. The judge's eventual opinion—which found for the plaintiff—contains several statistical conclusions that not all experts would agree with, but "on balance it remains a remarkable description of some basic statistical issues in a legal context, something that even the most diligent and able judges can rarely take the time to do" (Fienberg, 1989, p. 21).

Waterhouse's partners' decision and that was designed to make law (i.e., social authority evidence: see Monahan & Walker, 1986, 1990), Hopkins had her expert describe social science evidence in a descriptive, overview manner. The expert provided a scientific context, a framework (Walker & Monahan, 1987), for the consideration of the specific factual information related to Hopkins' term of employment at Price Waterhouse. (Tomkins & Pfeifer, 1992, pp. 398–399)

Warren McCleskey was a black man who participated in the armed robbery of an Atlanta furniture store in the late 1970s; he was convicted of killing a white police officer who responded to the alarm that a robbery was in progress. McCleskey was sentenced to death, but he challenged the constitutionality of this sentence on the grounds that the state of Georgia administered its death-sentencing laws in a racially discriminatory manner, using statistical analysis to demonstrate racial bias. But in 1987 the U.S. Supreme Court rejected his claim, and McCleskey was later executed (*McCleskey v. Kemp,* 1987).

Tomkins and Pfeifer (1992) later contrasted Dr. Fiske's approach with the statistical analysis used by Professor David Baldus in Warren McCleskey's appeal:

In contrast to Dr. Fiske's spending her time instructing the court in Hopkins about the substance of sex stereotyping, Professor Baldus spent a considerable amount of his time teaching the court in *McCleskey* about multiple regression and appropriate techniques for data coding, data reduction, and the like. What if Professor Baldus had been allowed to inform the court about subtle racism and the insidious effect it likely had on decision making in Georgia's criminal justice system? What if Professor Baldus had read from some of the court employees' process notes instead of coding them and regressing them on a bivariate, outcome variable? Certainly, to prove a constitutional violation is a lot more difficult than proving a statutory violation; nonetheless, there might be a greater likelihood of convincing the trial court that discrimination persists if the social science expert offers contextual (and perhaps even concrete, anecdotal evidence: see generally Borgida & Nisbett, 1977; Kahneman & Tversky, 1973; Nisbett, Borgida, Crandall, & Reed, 1982; Tversky & Kahneman, 1973) evidence to complement abstract statistical evidence or if the expert simply provides the background, the social science context, which the fact-finder then can use to consider the other witnesses' evidence. (Tomkins & Pfeifer, 1992, p. 402)

Perhaps so. As Tomkins and Pfeifer acknowledged, the court's rejection of what psychologists consider persuasive statistical differences in the death penalty for blacks and whites can be attributed to a number of causes; for example, constitutional issues extract different considerations. It can be argued that the court would not have been persuaded by *any* type of social-science evidence in McCleskey's appeal, because it would have created tremendous problems for many states' penal systems if McCleskey's death sentence had been overturned on the basis of racial disparities. Such a decision would have unleashed numerous appeals and changes in sentences throughout the United States.

Using Research to Detect Racism and Sexism

■ Two men answer the same advertisement for an entry-level professional position in an engineering firm; they are of the same age and their credentials are quite similar. The white man gets the job; the Aboriginal man does not.

■ Two couples respond to the "Open House" sign displayed in front of a nice house in a prestigious suburban neighbourhood. When the white couple follows up by contacting the real estate agent, they are greeted with enthusiasm; when the black couple does the same, the agent tells them that a buyer has already made a bid on the house.

■ A psychology department chairperson reviews the résumés of two applicants for an assistant professor position; both applicants have recently completed their Ph.D.s at distinguished universities, and each has several publications. The woman is invited to campus for an interview; the man is not.

Each of these scenarios could well occur in real life—and often do—and each reflects the application of traditional research methodology to a new field, the identification of expressions of discrimination. An effort is made by the researchers, just as in any experiment, to keep other factors equivalent—the credentials, the age and apparent affluence of the house-seeking couple, the job experience—while varying the ethnicity or gender. Any difference in response can then plausibly be attributed to this independent variable. Such procedures have been used by investigators working for government agencies charged with identifying and prosecuting examples of racial or gender discrimination in employment or housing (Crosby, 1994). Even the biases of white physicians have been studied by using such procedures; actors posing as cardiac patients solicited evaluation and treatment; only the sex and ethnicity of the patients was varied. Women and blacks—especially black women—were far less likely to be referred for cardiac catheterization, an important diagnostic procedure, than were white men with the same symptoms (Williams, 1999).

The application of this type of methodology has produced findings that illustrate the salience of subtle racism. For example, a program of research by Gaertner and Dovidio (1977; Dovidio & Gaertner, 1996; Frey & Gaertner, 1986) found that in a situation that was clearly an emergency, whites who believed they were the only bystanders came to the aid of a black person as quickly as they did for another white person. But in an ambiguous situation in which it was unclear whether an injury had taken place, whites responded less quickly to a black person than to a white person. Furthermore, if the respondent was led to believe that other bystanders were present, the black victim was helped only half as often as the white victim.

The use of such real-life situations often exposes subtle racism. For example, a person at home receives a phone call. It is clearly a wrong number, but the caller still describes his plight; he's stranded on the freeway and has run out of coins for the pay phone; he needs someone to call the garage for him (Gaertner & Bickman, 1971). Willingness to help was often a function of the perceived ethnicity of the caller, even for recipients who denied any overt racial prejudice.

Results of extensive work on this general topic lead to a conclusion that racism is, indeed, subtly manifested in contemporary life. Returning to the above employment examples, it has been found that, characteristically, if information about job candidates is consistent—that is, each candidate has uniformly positive credentials—applicants of each ethnicity are treated similarly. In some studies, the black candidate with strong credentials is even rated more favourably—reflecting an attitude that has been called reverse racism. But when the information about each candidate is more ambiguous, subtle racism may favour the white individual (Dovidio, 1995). For example, subtle racism may be reflected in attitudes that blacks have received favourable treatment by government organizations or that their family structure prevents them from being reliable employees.

Similar methodologies have been used to detect sexism. More than 35 years ago, Goldberg (1968) asked respondents to evaluate the significance and writing style of articles written either by "John McKay" or "Joan McKay." The articles were, of course, the same, but the respondents rated them more favourably when they thought they were authored by a man. This procedure has been adapted to assess the reactions to women in the workplace, with similar results (Wallston & O'Leary, 1981). Like the results when comparing ethnic backgrounds, these findings often reflect subtle biases. Especially when the criteria for evaluation are vague, subjective, and ill-defined, gender bias is expected to occur (Goddard, 1986).

COURT DECISIONS REGARDING ASSIGNMENT TO SPECIAL EDUCATION CLASSES

Following the decision of the Supreme Court of Canada in the 1997 case *Eaton v. Brant County Board of Education*, Canadian schools now have clear guidance about the factors that must be considered before placing a student in a special education class. In that case, the Supreme Court considered whether such a placement violated the child's equality rights under the Charter of Rights and Freedoms. Twelve-year-old Emily Eaton had cerebral palsy, could not speak or use sign language, and had some visual impairment. After she spent three years in an integrated classroom with the aid of a full-time assistant, the school board decided that she should be placed in a special education class. It believed that Emily was not benefiting from integration, but, rather, was being harmed by it. Against her parents' wishes, Emily was placed in the special education class. After hearing from many expert witnesses, two appeal bodies in the educational system upheld the decision. Subsequently, the Supreme Court of Canada agreed that Emily's placement in a special education class did not represent illegal discrimination. It held that for an action to exhibit illegal discrimination, it must not only involve differential treatment but also have negative consequences for the person.

One consideration in the *Eaton* case concerned the student's intellectual abilities and whether Emily's abilities were best suited in a mainstream environment or special education setting. As Reschly (1999) has observed, the assessment of the educational abilities of schoolchildren has become a major responsibility of psychologists. Should IQ test results be the basis for assigning schoolchildren to special education classes? Should such tests be used even if it is claimed that they are biased against minority children? And what should be the role of the forensic psychologist when such issues are brought before the courts for resolution?

On the issue of the fairness of using IQ results for placement of children in special education classes, American courts have had more to say than Canadian courts, but the issue is similar in the two countries, especially when considering racial bias in the process. Before we turn to some key American court rulings on this issue, it should be noted that the National Anti-Racism Council of Canada (2002) recently observed that "the practice of streaming—the process of placing learners into varying tracks or levels of education through a process of assessment—continues to be one of the greatest affronts to equity in the educational system in Canada. With such assessment and placement procedures and tools being inherently racially, culturally and linguistically biased, learners from some racialized groups, and Aboriginals in particular, end up in the basic, technical, vocational or 'general' tracks and are vastly under-represented in the advanced or university-oriented streams" (p. 70).

Two American federal judges considered the same evidence about the same legal issues; in fact, in both cases the defendant was the board of education, some of the expert witnesses were the same, and both trials were bench trials (trials in which the case was heard only by the judge, without a jury). Yet the two judges reached drastically different conclusions on the question of racial bias in the procedure.

The first of the cases was *Larry P. et al. v. Riles et al.* (1979), which involved litigation over a 15-year period, beginning in 1971. When the suit was initiated, more than 25 percent of the children in special education classes in California were black, although less than 10 percent of the school population in general was of that ethnicity (Elliott, 1987). Initially, the representatives of Larry P. and four other minority students in California—concerned about "dumping" such students in these classes—sought and received an injunction that prevented the use of intelligence test results in making decisions about placement in EMR (educable mentally retarded) classes in the San Francisco school district. The plaintiffs claimed that the tests were culturally biased against minorities and that the school system was acting in violation of Title VI of the U.S. Civil Rights Act of 1964, which stated that recipients of federal aid may not "utilize criteria or methods of administration which have the effect of subjecting individuals to discrimination because of their ethnicity, color, or national origin, or have the effect of defeating or substantially impairing accomplishment of the objectives of the program as respecting individuals of a particular race, color, or national origin" (*Larry P. et al. v. Riles et al.,* 1979, p. 963). Further, the plaintiffs claimed that the school district moved toward the use of what they called "nonobjective" intelligence tests in the early 1970s, and in so doing, intentionally fostered the over-enrolment of black children in EMR classes. They argued that intelligence tests were not valid measures of intelligence in minority children and had not been specifically validated as EMR placement mechanisms.

After a second injunction in 1974, the case went to trial in 1977 and lasted eight months; the judge, Robert F. Peckham, did not announce his decision until a year later. This decision, based on reviewing more than 10 000 pages of testimony from more than 50 witnesses (mostly experts) and 200 exhibits, was a complex one. Judge Peckham acknowledged that "The court has necessarily been drawn into the emotionally charged debate about the nature of 'intelligence' and its basis in 'genes' or 'environment.' This debate, which finds renowned experts disagreeing sharply, obviously cannot be resolved by judicial decree. Despite these problems, however, court intervention has been necessary" (*Larry P. et al. v. Riles et al.,* 1979, p. 932). He also noted that his decision was based on the consensus of expert witnesses' testimony about what intelligence tests could and could not do but acknowledged that the experts disagreed about the utility of intelligence testing for EMR placement.

Judge Peckham's decision affirmed almost all of the plaintiffs' contentions. He concluded that the available data were consistent with a finding of bias against black children, that those children's subculture, socioeconomic status, or environment hampered their ability to acquire the knowledge needed to answer specific items. His ruling included the following conclusions:

1. San Francisco schools were acting in violation of U.S. federal law including the Civil Rights Act of 1964, Section 504 of the Rehabilitation Act of 1973, and the Education for All Handicapped Children Act of 1975 (Elliot, 1987).
2. The school system used intelligence tests that were racially and culturally biased and had a discriminatory impact on black children.
3. These tests had not been validated for the placement of black children into EMR classes, and the result had been the placement of children from that racial group in disproportionate numbers into these classes, thus denying them their guarantee to a right of equal protection.

His remedy was to enjoin the San Francisco Unified School District from using intelligence test results for placement of children in special education classes. This decision was appealed by the school district but upheld in 1984. And two years later, an injunction was issued in California that prohibited the use, statewide, of intelligence tests with black students for *any* reason (Taylor, 1990). Further, an IQ score of a black student transferring into California would not remain as a part of his or her permanent record, nor could parents of black children put into their child's records any privately obtained IQ scores (Elliott, 1987).

Although its locale was different, the second case was strikingly similar in many ways. Filed in 1975 and tried in 1980, the case of *PASE v. Hannon* (1980) was also a class action suit brought by the representatives of black children; PASE stood for "People in Action on Special Education." In contrast to the earlier case, the trial lasted only three weeks and generated fewer witnesses and about 2000 pages of testimony and argument. Judge John F. Grady, based in Chicago, concluded, in contrast, that the tests generally were not biased and that cultural differences had little effect on the differential performance of children of differing ethnic backgrounds; furthermore, he reached his decision in an entirely different manner from Judge Peckham. In fact, he stated that he was uncomfortable relying on expert testimony:

> None of the witnesses in this case has so impressed me with his or her credibility and expertise that I would feel secure basing a decision simply on his or her opinion. In some instances, I am satisfied that the opinions expressed more the result of doctrinaire commitment to a preconceived idea than they are a result of scientific inquiry. I need something more than the conclusions of the witnesses in order to arrive at my own conclusions. (*PASE v. Hannon*, 1980, p. 836)

Judge Grady based his decision on his analysis of specific test items; he wrote:

> It is obvious to me that I must examine the tests themselves in order to know what the witnesses are talking about.... For me to say that the tests are either biased or unbiased

without analyzing the test items in detail would reveal nothing about the tests but only something about my opinion of the tests. (p. 836)

Almost 90 percent of his judicial opinion was devoted to a detailed armchair analysis of items and answers from the three prominent individually administered intelligence tests of that time, the Wechsler Intelligence Scale for Children (WISC), the Wechsler Intelligence Scale for Children-Revised (WISC-R), and the Stanford Binet. He judged each item as either biased or not. For example, consider this item: "Who discovered America?" Dr. Robert L. Williams, a psychologist testifying for the plaintiffs, stated that this question was insulting to Native children because it implied that their homeland had to be "discovered." Furthermore, he said, the question was confusing because the land didn't need to be "discovered" in the first place. But Judge Grady questioned the relevance of Williams's claims; he wanted to know how such a question discriminated against black children (p. 838). After doing his item-by-item check, Judge Grady evaluated very few test items as being biased against any racial or cultural group. Specifically, he concluded the following:

1. One item from the Stanford Binet and eight items from the WISC and WISC-R were culturally biased against black children. These included "Why is it better to pay bills by check than by cash?" and "What are you supposed to do if you find someone's wallet or pocketbook in a store?" (Elliott, 1987, p. 149). In Judge Grady's opinion, those few items did not cause the tests to be unfair, as they made up a small proportion and many of them were higher-level questions that would not usually be administered to a child who had the possibility of placement in an EMR class.
2. Placement in EMR classes was not decided solely by the intelligence test results; other tests were included in the battery. Furthermore, many of those who adminis-

tered the tests in the Chicago area were themselves black, and they would administer them in a culturally sensitive way.
3. He found no evidence that wrong placements of children into EMR classes occurred.

Not only were Judge Grady's findings and ruling opposite those of Judge Peckham, but he went out of his way to acknowledge the differences in his opinion:

As is by now obvious, the witnesses and the arguments that persuaded Judge Peckham have not persuaded me. Moreover, I believe the issue in the case cannot be properly be analyzed without a detailed examination of the items on the tests. It is clear that this was not undertaken in the *Larry P.* case. (*PASE v. Hannon, 1980*, pp. 882–883)

Judge Grady's procedure was roundly criticized by several psychologists. For example, Donald Bersoff (1981) wrote: "If Judge Peckham's analysis is scanty and faulty, Judge Grady's can best be described as naive; at worst it is unintelligent and completely empty of empirical substance. It represents a single person's subjective and personal opinions cloaked in the authority of judicial robes" (p. 1049). But psychologist Rogers Elliott (1987) noted that Judge Grady had pleaded with both sides to provide him with research articles concerned with item analyses. During the testimony he said, "Hasn't anybody ever, in the Chicago school system, ever bothered to take the scores and take the tests and see how these kids do on these various items? I just can't believe that nobody has done that" (quoted by Elliott, 1987, p. 142). But the lawyers chose to emphasize other aspects of the case.

Should judges be making decisions about the potential cultural bias of individual test items? Are they any good at it? Sattler (1991) sought to answer the latter question with respect to the judges in these two cases. He used 25 items from the WISC or WISC-R, including 11 identified as biased by either Judge Peckham or Judge Grady and administered them to 448 randomly selected students (224 black and 224 white) in Grades 4 through 6 in various Ohio schools. Of the 25 items, 12 were found to be significantly more difficult for black children than white children; of these, the judges had identified only six, or 50 percent. Additionally, five items that were singled out by the judges as being biased were found not to be harder for the black children. Neither outcome reflected a high degree of accuracy by the judges. Sattler concluded:

> [T]he results suggest that an armchair inspection of items cannot provide reliable data about differential difficulty levels.... Court judges, untrained in psychometrics and without resort to data, lack the expertise required to decide which items on tests are or are not biased. Such unsupported decisions fall into the realm of personal opinion. (1991, pp. 127–128)

Perhaps Judge Grady's criticism of Judge Peckham's reliance on expert testimony should be re-examined in light of the empirical findings (Brown, 1996). But judges *are* the decision makers, and some judges, as illustrated by Judge Grady's response, are not impressed with the testimony of psychologists.

AFFIRMATIVE ACTION

Most citizens value the principles of equality and fairness; yet when attempts are made to apply these principles to members of diverse groups, reluctance and resistance are often the results (Skedsvold & Mann, 1996a). **Affirmative action** generally refers to any procedure that permits consideration of ethnicity, gender, disability, or national origin, along with other variables, in order to provide equal opportunity to qualified individuals who have been denied those opportunities because of past discrimination (Lasso, 1998). Social programs designed to eliminate discriminatory practices have become unde-

sirable in the eyes of some; the term *affirmative action* has become an emotional hot button, both for its supporters and its opponents. As our society reconsiders its policies, can psychology contribute anything to the understanding and possible resolution of the controversy?

The Courts and Affirmative Action

Affirmative action practices are widely used in both Canada and the United States. In both countries, the rationale for such initiatives was similar: to counteract the legacy of historical discrimination, often systemic in nature, such as the church-run Aboriginal school system in Canada. Canada's current affirmative action law stems from the Abella Royal Commission on Equality in Employment in 1983. This commission recommended that affirmative action be based on the Charter of Rights and Freedoms, which permits discrimination to ameliorate "conditions of disadvantaged individuals or groups." Following the recommendations of the Abella Commission, there are four designated groups for intervention through such practices: women, visible minorities, disabled persons, and Aboriginal persons. Legislated employment equity applies to all federally regulated areas including banking, transportation, communication, and all federal corporations having 100 or more employees.

Before identifying possible psychological contributions in this area, it is useful to examine how the courts have dealt with the legality of affirmative action programs. In doing so, a theme from earlier chapters—the complex, sometimes conflicting, relationship between the law and psychology—resurfaces. According to the Charter of Rights and Freedoms, all Canadians are equal and cannot be treated in a discriminatory fashion. However, as mentioned, the Charter includes a caveat: This principle does not preclude any program or activity that has as its object the amelioration of conditions of peoples who are disadvantaged because of their ethnicity, religion, gender, age, or mental or physical disability. Thus, while disallowing discrimination in principle, it concurrently allows or even encourages it under some conditions. So, most universities in Canada now explicitly encourage women, Aboriginal people, disabled people, and members of visible minorities to apply for faculty positions. The official policy of Dalhousie University, for example, is to:

> take pro-active steps to eliminate discrimination in its two forms: direct discrimination against individuals, and systemic discrimination in the University's employment systems that is often unintentional. The University is committed to reversing the historic under-representation of women, Aboriginal peoples, racially visible persons, and people with a disability on its faculty and staff.

The RCMP and Canadian military have adopted a similar approach in their hiring practices.

Nacoste (1996) has suggested that the U.S. Supreme Court, in its evaluations of the constitutionality of affirmative action policies, has developed procedural standards that are based on reasoning that has as its goal "avoiding government actions that might have negative social psychological effects" (p. 133). Specifically, he concluded that "members of the U.S. Supreme Court appear to have been influenced by an implicit theory that indicates that the use of group membership as a criterion for making personnel decisions will reinforce common, negative group stereotypes" (p. 134). Two cases are illustrative.

Regents of the University of California v. Bakke

In 1973 Allan Bakke was one of 2664 applicants who sought admission to the medical school at the University of California at Davis. From this overwhelming number only 100 were accepted; 84 of these places were filled through the regular admission procedures and 16 by minority applicants who were "disadvantaged." Not only were the applicants separated into two groups, but they were screened by different committees using different criteria. The year that Bakke applied, the 16 applicants who were selected under the spe-

cial program had undergraduate grade point averages of 2.88, as compared to 3.49 for the 84 students admitted through the standard admission process. The "disadvantaged" students' scores on the MCAT (the medical school aptitude test) were also lower (Schwartz, 1988). Bakke's application was rejected, even though his credentials were stronger than those of the 16 minority students who were admitted. Bakke thus filed a lawsuit claiming that the procedure gave preferential treatment to minorities and hence was a form of racial discrimination, denying him equal protection of the law under the Fourteenth Amendment of the U.S. Constitution. After lower courts essentially agreed with Bakke, the Regents of the University of California appealed the case to the United States Supreme Court.

The view of Justice Lewis Powell reflected Nacoste's assessment; he wrote, "preferential programs may only reinforce common stereotypes holding that certain people are unable to achieve success without special protection based on a factor having no relation to individual worth" (quoted by Nacoste, 1996, p. 134). Further, Justice Powell concluded that the set-aside procedure used by the University of California at Davis led to a disregard of individual rights that were guaranteed by the Fourteenth Amendment. But he did not conclude that all affirmative action procedures were unconstitutional; for example, a policy that gave some weight to group membership, but not necessarily decisive weight, would be constitutional because the program would treat each applicant as an individual in the admission process.

More recently, the U.S. Supreme Court decided not to hear the appeal in the case of *Hopwood v. State of Texas* (1996). The University of Texas School of Law had been using a procedure similar to the one Bakke confronted; it set lower test score standards for black and Hispanic applicants than for white applicants and had provided a separate review board for minority applicants. Thus the law school hoped to achieve a diversified student body with a goal of about 10 percent Hispanics and 5 percent blacks in the entering class. The school had already scrapped the procedure after being sued by four unsuccessful white applicants, including Cheryl Hopwood, but the procedure was rejected by the court anyway.

When it decides not to review an appeal stemming from a decision by a lower court, the justices of the U.S. Supreme Court do not have to give a reason for their action. But the decision by the court above to strike down the procedure was certainly in keeping with Justice Powell's concern that separate admissions committees failed to protect individual rights.

Adarand Constructors Inc. v. Pena

Adarand Constructors Company, a small Colorado firm, submitted a bid on a subcontract to Mountain Gravel and Construction Company, which had been awarded a contract from the U.S. Department of Transportation to build a federal highway in that state. In order to receive monetary compensation from the U.S. government for making affirmative-action–related awards (an extra 10 percent), Mountain Gravel—one of the 300 000 organizations a year awarded U.S. federal contracts—had to consider in its decision whether the subcontracting bids it received came from businesses owned by members of "socially and economically disadvantaged groups." Even though its subcontract bid was the lowest, Adarand—a white-owned company—lost out to another company that was Hispanic-owned; thus Randy Pech, the owner of Adarand, sued, claiming that the process interfered with his rights to due process and equal protection. The majority opinion for the U.S. Supreme Court, written by Justice Sandra Day O'Connor, did not go so far as to declare federal affirmative-action programs unconstitutional. But it ruled that this particular affirmative-action procedure was unconstitutional because it was not narrowly tailored to neutralize a documented level of discrimination. That is, the Court said that federal programs must pass the most stringent of tests, a standard of **strict scrutiny**; they must specifically be tailored to address identifiable past discrimination. Under the standard, a challenged

program survives only if it promotes "compelling" governmental interests (Lacovara, 1995). In a concurrence with the majority opinion, Justice Clarence Thomas wrote:

> Inevitably, such programs engender attitudes of superiority or, alternatively, provoke resentment among those who believe that they have been wronged by the government's use of ethnicity. These programs stamp minorities with a badge of inferiority and may cause them to develop dependencies or to adopt an attitude that they are *entitled* to preferences. (concurring opinion by Justice Thomas, *Adarand v. Pena*, 1995, p. 240, italics in original)

Justice Antonin Scalia also reflected this assumption that racial entitlement leads to the kind of thinking that produces divisiveness and hatred between ethnic groups. Both Justices Thomas and Scalia expressed a desire that the decision go further because of their wish to abolish affirmative action completely (Greenhouse, 1995b).

Psychological Contributions

Four potential types of contributions by psychologists to the understanding of affirmative-action procedures can be identified.

Affirmative Action and the Limits of Fairness

As Opotow (1996) has observed, affirmative-action programs have always been controversial. It has been suggested that the major hindrance to the acceptance of affirmative-action programs is that they violate a "sense of fairness" and thus run counter to North Americans' endorsement of the value of equality (Chang, 1996). Opponents of these programs argue that affirmative action provides an "unfair advantage" to members of targeted groups, and the eventual result will be a form of **reverse discrimination** (Gamson & Modigliani, 1987). The perceived fairness of a procedure has an impact on the evaluation of the

CHAPTER 14   DISCRIMINATION

person associated with the procedure (Nacoste, 1985, 1987; Thibaut & Walker, 1975); thus when an affirmative-action procedure is implemented, employees are identified on the basis of their ethnicity and gender, and any perceived group differences become more salient (Chang, 1996).

To understand the diverse reactions, it is helpful to inquire about the **psychological boundary** between those who deserve fair or special treatment and those who do not. Opotow's (1996) analysis emphasized how this boundary between the deserving and the undeserving can shift as social and economic conditions change. For example, as minorities move into professional and managerial positions, white people whose positions are threatened may include only their white friends in their set of persons who deserve fair treatment. Or when the economy is good and jobs are easy to find, white employees may accept the hiring of a minority group member with less experience more easily than they would under a weak economy when jobs are scarce.

An Analysis of Public Opinion of Affirmative Action

Social scientists conduct public opinion polls, but sometimes polls can result in misleading conclusions because of their limited structure. The conventional wisdom is that the public is currently not supportive of affirmative-action policies (Plous, 1996). When the choices are limited to two diverse positions, such as no affirmative action versus extreme programs such as set asides or separate admissions criteria for minorities, the public's reaction is to reject "affirmative action." But public resistance is diminished when the choices include more moderate procedures, such as guarantees of continued employment for current workers (Plous, 1996). And if individual achievement-related characteristics are given weight, as well as the individual's ethnicity or gender, affirmative-action procedures are more likely to be accepted (Heilman, 1994; Kravitz, 1995; Nacoste, 1994). Specifically, a Gallup poll

found that fewer than 25 percent of the respondents wanted to eliminate affirmative-action laws completely (Benedetto, 1995).

The Development of More Acceptable Programs

If it is the case that much of the resistance to affirmative action stems from the reactions described above, psychologists can assist employers and admissions officers in designing programs that do not threaten participants' self-images. Pratkanis and Turner (1996) have offered 12 principles to serve as a guide for improving the effectiveness of affirmative-action programs and removing the stigma of preferential selection; these are described in Box 14.3.

Evaluation of Effectiveness of Affirmative Action

Psychologists and other researchers have contributed to an understanding of the acceptance and effectiveness of affirmative-action policies in several ways. For example, as noted in the proposals of Pratkanis and Turner (1996) in Box 14.3, equal-status contact should be a goal when implementing affirmative-action programs. A program of research by Cook (1971, 1978; see also Wrightsman, 1972, pp. 324–337) showed that prejudice and resentment toward blacks was ameliorated when the interracial working conditions involved common goals, a state of cooperative interdependence between the workers, equal status, and the endorsement of equality by the supervisors. Similarly, Elliot Aronson and his colleagues (Aronson, 1992; Aronson & Bridgeman, 1992; Aronson, Stephan, Sikes, Blaney, & Snapp, 1978), through the ingenious application of a jigsaw technique, showed that students from diverse backgrounds, when placed in learning groups that emphasized interdependence, improved their school performance, as well as reduced the levels of prejudice expressed by the white students toward the minorities.

Recently, two academic administrators, Bowen and Bok (1998), studied the progress of

BOX 14.3
Principles of Effective Affirmative Action

Pratkanis and Turner (1996) proposed that affirmative action can be seen as a type of help but that it is often resisted because its offer of help does not conform to society's values and implies that the recipient lacks certain abilities. Thus it engenders in the beneficiary a sense of being threatened and results in defensive behaviours. Pratkanis and Turner suggested 12 principles, the implementation of which might reduce such reactions (1996, pp. 125–127):

1. Focus the helping efforts away from the recipient and toward a goal of removing social barriers.
2. Establish unambiguous, explicit, and focused qualifications for use in selection and promotion decisions.
3. Communicate clearly the requisite procedures and criteria.
4. Be certain that selection procedures are perceived as fair by relevant audiences.

5. Emphasize the recipients' contributions to the organization and their specific competencies.
6. Develop socialization strategies that deter respondents from coming to believe that they are dependent on the good graces of the organization for their jobs, status, and future advancement.
7. Reinforce the fact that affirmative action is not preferential selection.
8. Establish the conditions of equal status contact and the sharing of common goals.
9. Emphasize that change is inevitable, that participants must bring their attitudes in line with the new reality.
10. Be aware that affirmative-action programs do not operate in isolation.
11. Recognize that affirmative action is not a panacea.
12. Monitor the affirmative-action program to see what works and what doesn't.

black and white students who entered 28 prominent universities in 1976 and 1989, when affirmative-action programs were in effect. They noted that the black students entered these elite colleges and universities with lower test scores and high-school grades than did the white students and they received lower grades in university and had a lower graduation rate. However, after graduation these same black students achieved notable success; for example, they earned advanced degrees at rates identical to those of their white classmates; they were slightly more likely to obtain professional degrees in law, business, and medicine; and they were more active than their counterparts in civic activities. The black students who graduated from elite universities earned 70 percent to 85 percent more than black graduates generally. *Affirmative action* continues to be a term that triggers strong reactions—favourable or unfavourable—from the public, and legislative bodies and the courts will continue to struggle over a proper balance between conflicting values in our society. Forensic psychology can make a contribution by identifying attitudes of co-workers, specifying conditions that lead to acceptance of minority co-workers, and evaluating innovative programs.

EMPLOYMENT DISCRIMINATION

The National Anti-Racism Council of Canada (2002) report outlines some alarming statistics concerning unemployment among Aboriginal peoples in Canada:

- They face the highest overall unemployment rate of any group, at 25 percent.
- One in 17 Aboriginal persons is in the top quintile of income, compared to one in five non-Aboriginal workers.
- Only 13 percent of Aboriginal people with the same education as whites had earnings in the top quintile.
- Many university-educated Aboriginal people still earn in the bottom quintile, at a rate of 38 percent, compared to 15 percent for nonracialized groups.

■ On some reserves, as many as 95 percent of Aboriginal people are forced to rely on welfare.

While such statistics offer *prima facie* evidence for workplace discrimination in Canada, over the last 40 years, statistical analyses have given convincing objective evidence (although often the figures are so extreme that tools of statistical inference may not be required). Much of the relevant research has occurred in the U.S. For example, consider the case of *Jones v. Tri-County Electric Cooperative* (1975), which concerned the hiring practices of a utility company. The firm had hired only one black person (for a janitorial position) from the time the 1964 U.S. Civil Rights Act became law (July 1, 1965) until the initiation of a lawsuit seven years later. After the initiation of the suit, the company hired several more black people, but the number of the newly hired persons who were minorities was only eight out of 43 hires, or 19 percent—a number significantly less than the 40 percent of the local population who were black. The defendant was, on the basis of this disparate impact (an action that is a hindrance to equal opportunity), found to be in violation of the law.

However, sometimes job qualifications, such as past experience or aptitude test scores, were used to prevent minorities from obtaining jobs. In 1971, in the case of *Griggs v. Duke Power Co.*, the U.S. Supreme Court recognized that the lack of equal opportunity can result not only from intentional discrimination but also from practices that, though not intending to discriminate, have a disparate impact on minorities and women. In this case, black employees challenged Duke Power Company's requirements of a high school diploma and a certain level of performance on a scholastic aptitude test for hiring and promotion, when those qualifications were unrelated to performance on the job. It ruled that when a job qualification had such an impact on minorities or women, the Civil Rights Act of 1964 made such a procedure unlawful unless an employer could show that the action was a business necessity; thus the burden of proof was on the employer. But in 1989 the U.S. Supreme Court modified the *Griggs* decision, placing the burden of proof on employees to prove that a challenged job qualification was not really related to the company's needs (Lewis, 1991).

Thus, employment discrimination was permitted to continue in that a differential in test scores could be used as a justification for making minority members ineligible for certain jobs. But the U.S. Department of Labor initiated a procedure that had the goal of reducing the impact of test results on hiring; it revised the scoring system for its General Aptitude Test Battery (GATB), by using a within-group scoring procedure, usually called **race-norming**. Consider the following example:

> John Smith, a white, scores 327 on a vocational-aptitude test. Fred Jones, black, gets only 283. But if the two applicants are sent to a prospective employer, their test results are said to rank identically at the 70th percentile. A computer error? No. The raw score Jones earned was compared only with the marks earned by fellow blacks. Smith's number went into a blend of scores made by whites and "others." If a Hispanic person takes the same test, his raw score is converted on a third curve reserved for Hispanics only. (Barrett, 1991, p. 57)

A fair procedure, to redress past employment discrimination, or a case of reverse discrimination? Psychologists are divided on the legitimacy of the procedure, as are government officials, lawyers, and even civil rights activists (Gottfredson, 1994; Sackett & Wilk, 1994). For example, should police departments that have separate physical-ability requirements for female and male applicants be required to change them?

HATE CRIMES

Since moving into the new millennium, Canadians have been shocked by the news of recent hate crimes, reminding us that hate directed toward certain groups based on their ethnic background or sexual orientation still occurs in our society. On April 12, 2004, a Jewish elementary school in Montreal was set ablaze with a racist note left at the scene. A week earlier, police in Toronto arrested three teenagers in relation to numerous anti-Semitic hate crimes, including the desecration of a Jewish cemetery. In the U.S., hate crimes have extended to murder. Two white supremacists in Texas, unrepentant even after their conviction for murder, chained James Byrd, Jr., a black man, to a pickup truck and dragged him to his death. Two men in Laramie, Wyoming, learning that Matthew Shepard was gay, enticed him into their truck, drove him to an isolated area, tied him to a fence, pistol-whipped him, and left him to die. In April 1999, one of the perpetrators, Russell Henderson, pleaded guilty to kidnapping and murder in order to avoid the death penalty.

Hate crimes are words or actions intended to harm or intimidate an individual because of his or her membership in a minority group; they may include violent assaults, murder, sexual assault, or property crimes motivated by prejudice, as well as threats of violence or acts of intimidation (Finn & McNeil, 1987, cited by Herek, 1989). Hate crimes differ from other serious crimes in that they are based primarily on the victim's membership in an identifiable group; thus any incident with such a victim has threatening implications for other members of that group (Craig & Waldo, 1996). A swastika burned into a synagogue door or a racial epithet scrawled on a sidewalk are actions that assail the identity of group members.

Such crimes seem to be on the rise throughout North America. In fact, B'nai Brith Canada reported an increase in anti-Semitic incidents across the country in 2003, including almost 600 cases of violence, harassment, and vandalism. This represented a 27.2 percent increase from 2002, which also had an increase of 60 percent over 2001. Thus, the number of reported anti-Semitic incidents more than doubled from 2001

to 2003 (i.e., increased by 104 percent). The FBI estimated that more than 8000 hate crimes were committed in the United States in 1997 (Bai & Smith, 1999). Victims of hate crimes are most often members of groups that are stereotyped in this society. Herek (1989) has concluded that lesbians and gay men are often the principal targets of such crimes. Yet social science research on hate crimes is only at its beginning stages.

Meanwhile, Canadian legislation has moved forward in establishing more severe penalties for such crimes. The Criminal Code now includes laws against advocating genocide (up to five years in prison) and public incitement of hatred against a particular group based on colour, race, religion, or ethnic origin (up to two years in prison). In 2004, Bill C-250 passed to extend these laws to hate based on sexual orientation. Unfortunately, in other jurisdictions, there are still no hate-crime laws. The legislature of Wyoming, where Matthew Shepard was killed, has rejected hate-crime legislation that includes sexual orientation three times in recent years.

Psychologists can contribute to the policy debate on the merits of special hate-crime legislation by carrying out evaluation research on the effects of such legislation on crime rates. Do such laws have a deterrent impact? The perpetrators of the heinous hate crimes that took the lives of James Byrd, Jr., and Matthew Shepard are eligible for the death penalty (in the United States), even without such laws. Further, forensic psychologists can identify attitudes and behaviours that lead to crimes directed at minority groups. They can also conduct research on those individuals convicted of such crimes. What are their psychological characteristics? What is their rate of recidivism? Is it possible to prevent their aberrant behaviours against others from recurring?

SUMMARY

Canadians value the principles of equality and fairness. Yet, some members of our diverse society have experienced discrimination and outright racism in the legal system and workplace. Psychologists distinguish between prejudice and discrimination. Prejudice is internal, an unjustified evaluative attitude toward a member of a group that results from the recipient's membership in that group. In contrast, discrimination refers to an observable behaviour in which another person is accepted or rejected on the basis of his or her membership in a particular group. Expressions of prejudiced attitudes are less blatant than in the past, leading to the development of the concept of modern racism, or subtle racism, to refer especially to the attitudes of people in the majority who may regard themselves as unprejudiced, while still harbouring feelings of resentment toward minority or other ethnic groups.

Forensic psychologists can contribute to the amelioration of discrimination by the application of a conceptual analysis and the use of several research and statistical methodologies, including evaluation research procedures that assess the effectiveness of, for example, affirmative-action programs or laws that provide for more severe punishments for hate crimes.

Psychologists have contributed to judicial decisions regarding the use of IQ test results to place children in special education classes and particularly the potential bias against minority group children by the use of individualized intelligence tests in this determination. Researchers have also evaluated the effectiveness of affirmative-action programs and have made suggestions for ways that such programs can be improved.

KEY TERMS

adverse impact, p. 302
affirmative action, p. 309
discrimination, p. 298
disparate impact, p. 302
disparate treatment, p. 302
hate crimes, p. 315

modern racism, p. 298
prejudice, p. 298
psychological boundary, p. 312
race-norming, p. 314
racism, p. 298
reverse discrimination, p. 311
sexism, p. 301
strict scrutiny, p. 311
subtle racism, p. 300

SUGGESTED READINGS

Clayton, S. D., & Crosby, F. J. (1992). *Justice, gender, and affirmative action.* Ann Arbor: University of Michigan Press.

This application of social psychological theory of relative deprivation to the reactions of victims of prejudice and discrimination includes a chapter identifying aspects of affirmative-action programs that promote success.

Cole, D. (1999). *No equal justice: Race and class in the American criminal justice system.* New York: New Press.

This well-written book by a Georgetown University law professor is first a demonstration of racial bias in the U.S. criminal justice system, with an extensive review of its applications to profiling, right to counsel, jury selection, sentencing, and other aspects. Second, it is a claim that the criminal justice system "affirmatively depends upon inequality."

Elliott, R. (1987). *Litigating intelligence: IQ tests, special education, and social science in the courtroom.* Dover, MA: Auburn House.

Elliott, a psychologist, not only provides a detailed analysis of the *Larry P.* and *PASE* cases regarding the use of IQ tests for placement in special education classes but also gives a wide-ranging description of what happens to social-science evidence in an adversary system.

Goodman-Delahunty, J. (1999). Civil law: Employment and discrimination. In R. Roesch, S. D. Hart, & J. R. P. Ogloff (Eds.), *Psychology and law: The state of the discipline (pp. 277–337).* New York: Kluwer Academic/Plenum.

This article presents a recent survey of psychological applications to the study of employment discrimination and sexual harassment.

Kravitz, D., & Platania, J. (1993). Attitudes and beliefs about affirmative action: Effects of target sex and ethnicity. *Journal of Applied Psychology, 78*, 928–938.

In this article, the authors apply traditional social psychological methodology to determinants of opinions about affirmative action.

Skedsvold, P. R., & Mann, T. L. (Eds.). (1996b). The affirmative action debate: What's fair in policy and programs? *Journal of Social Issues, 52 (4),* 1–160.

This special journal issue contains articles by prominent psychologists on the impact of affirmative-action policies.

Tomkins, A. J., & Pfeifer, J. E. (1992). Modern social-scientific theories and data concerning discrimination: Implications for using social science evidence in the courts. In D. K. Kagehiro & W. S. Laufer (Eds.), *Handbook of psychology and law (pp. 385–407).* New York: Springer-Verlag.

Tomkins and Pfeifer's excellent review of the psychological approach to discrimination includes historical antecedent, the early research on prejudice, modern approaches to conceptualization, and applications to recent court cases.

15

Sexual Harassment

By requiring an employee, male or female, to contend with unwelcome sexual actions or explicit sexual demands, sexual harassment in the workplace attacks the dignity and self-respect of the victim both as an employee and as a human being.

—SUPREME COURT OF CANADA (*Janzen v. Platy Enterprises Ltd.*, 1989)

INCREASED AWARENESS OF SEXUAL HARASSMENT

Canadians are becoming increasingly familiar with the problem of sexual harassment in our society. A 1998 National Angus Reid Group/*Globe and Mail*/CTV poll conducted among a representative sample of 1501 people showed that 90 percent of Canadians were aware of the allegations made against Canada's Armed Forces regarding sexual harassment and assaults on women in the military. Half of Canadians aware of the allegations felt that this was "evidence of a widespread problem in the Canadian Armed Forces" rather than just "isolated incidents"; 70 percent wanted to see the federal government open a special investigation into this matter.

Sexual harassment is any unwelcome, sex-based interaction, including verbal interaction, at work or at school that renders harm to the recipient. But the term is the subject of considerable confusion, and one of the contributions of psychology is the analysis of the meanings held by different people, especially relative to the legal definition of sexual harassment (Frazier, Cochran, & Olson, 1995). Certainly, many people fail to realize that some forms of sexual harassment are *illegal*. When sexual harassment cases end up in the courtroom, there can be enormous emotional and financial costs for both parties (e.g., Perry, Kulik, & Bourhis, 2004).

During the past three decades, the Supreme Court of Canada, the Canadian Human Rights Act, and provincial codes (such as the Newfoundland Human Rights Code) have determined that sexual harassment is a serious human rights violation. The Canada Labour Code establishes an employee's right to employment free of sexual harassment and requires employers to take positive action to prevent sexual harassment in the workplace. Some components or manifestations of sexual harassment, such as sexual assault and criminal harassment (stalking), are crimes in the Criminal Code of Canada.

As the chapter describes, psychology can contribute to the understanding of the conditions under which harassment occurs as well as what determines whether claims of sexual harassment will be upheld.

Origins of the Term

The term **sexual harassment** was apparently first coined in 1974 by a group of women at Cornell University, after several female colleagues had been forced off the job by unwanted advances from their male supervisors (Brownmiller & Alexander, 1992). The first widespread media attention came in an article in the *New York Times* ("Women Begin to Speak Out against Sexual Harassment at Work") by Enid Nemy, on August 19, 1975, reporting on hearings held by the New York City Commission on Human Rights, then chaired by Eleanor Holmes Norton. Three years later Lin Farley's breakthrough book *Sexual Shakedown* was published—after 27 publishers had turned it down. Also in the 1970s the Equal Employment Opportunity Commission in the United States emerged as a major means of redress against sexually harassing actions by employers. By 1977, several American cases had established the harassed victim's right, under the 1964 U.S. Civil Rights Act, to sue the company that employed her or him (it stated that to prove a case of sexual harassment, the employee had to show that he or she was subject to unwelcome conduct based on his or her sex and that this unwelcome conduct caused harm). However, American victims are entitled to collect only back pay, not damages (unlike the situation in Canada); if they choose to file a civil suit, instead, they may be embroiled in lengthy court proceedings, and even if they win, they face the possibility that a judge will reduce the amount awarded them by the jury (Fisk, 1998).

Incidence Rates

It is clear that behaviours constituting sexual harassment are pandemic in many segments of our society. In a 1992 Angus-Reid poll, more than a third of the women who had worked outside the home said that they had been sexually harassed on the job (Angus-Reid Report, 1992). Surveys of Canadian university students have found that about half of female respondents have experienced some kind of sexual harassment on campus (e.g., McDaniel & van Roosmalen, 1991). Perhaps the first large-scale survey of the prevalence of sexual harassment was one that used self-reports and was released in 1981 by a U.S. federal regulatory agency. In a random survey of 20 000 federal employees, it found that 42 percent of the female workers had experienced an incident of sexual harassment on the job in the previous two years (Brownmiller & Alexander, 1992). A subsequent survey of 13 000 U.S. government workers, done in 1994, found that 44 percent of the female workers and 19 percent of the men said they had been the targets of unwanted and uninvited sexual attention (McAllister, 1995). A number of more specialized surveys have provided a variety of examples of the pervasiveness of sexual harassment:

1. One out of every seven female faculty members at colleges and universities has reported having experienced sexual harassment, according to a survey of 30 000 faculty members (Henry, 1994).
2. More than 40 percent of women lawyers in large law firms reported "yes" to queries about receiving deliberate touching, pinching, or cornering in the office (Slade, 1994). Similarly, a survey of 4500 female physicians found that nearly half (47.7 percent) reported having experienced some form of harassment, from being told that medicine was not a fit career for a woman to being called "honey" in front of patients; more than a third (36.9 percent) said they had been sexually harassed (Manning, 1998).
3. In general workplace surveys, 40 percent to 60 percent of women say they have been sexually harassed at some point in their careers (Swisher, 1994).
4. In regard to female graduate students, 60 percent in Schneider's (1987) survey said they had been exposed to some form of

everyday harassment by male faculty, such as sexually suggestive remarks, and 22 percent had been asked for dates by male faculty.

Recall that these are surveys using retrospective self-reports. Further, widely varying definitions of sexual harassment were used in the different surveys. Yet, even the critics of the methodology have acknowledged that sexual harassment is "a very real and important problem in organizations" (Arvey & Cavanaugh, 1995, p. 50).

Highly Publicized Cases

It may be said that the decade of the 1990s contributed mightily to public awareness of sexual harassment. In October 1991, many Americans watched their television sets as Professor Anita Hill recounted her claims that a U.S. Supreme Court justice nominee had sexually harassed her. Activities at the "Tailhook" convention of U.S. naval officers in Las Vegas and the actions of Army drill sergeants at Aberdeen Proving Ground received widespread visibility. U.S. Senator Robert Packwood's advances against several of his staff members became fodder for David Letterman's monologues. Mitsubishi Motor Corporation agreed to pay US$34 million to end a lawsuit that claimed that hundreds of its female assembly-line workers at its Normal, Illinois, plant had been sexually harassed. And in the latter part of the decade the United States faced the suit of Paula Jones against the president of the United States.

But do people agree as to what constitutes sexual harassment? Can a woman sexually harass a man? In Michael Crichton's (1993) novel *Disclosure* (and the subsequent movie), one did. In 1997, 12 percent of sexual harassment charges in the U.S. were filed by men (Goodman-Delahunty, 1999). And when a female employer harasses a male employee, his reaction can be as extreme as that of a female who has been sexually harassed; yet the public does not view the female-to-male harassment as negatively (Pigott, Foley, Covati, & Wasserman, 1998).

The 1990s also revealed that courts were in disagreement about what constituted harassment, and some psychological research also revealed gender differences in ratings of what constituted sexual harassment in some "grey-area" situations (Frazier, Cochran, & Olson, 1995; Gutek & O'Connor, 1995). During that decade the courts sought clarification on a number of questions; for example, if the incident involves two people of the same sex, does it constitute sexual harassment? (See Box 15.1 for an exploration of this issue.)

CONCEPTUALIZATIONS OF SEXUAL HARASSMENT

Confusion in the Public

As the media made the public increasingly aware of the problem, the number of complaints by employees increased dramatically in the late 1990s (Cloud, 1998; Mauro, 1993). A significant number of these were by men against female bosses. Yet these represent only the tip of the iceberg. It is estimated that only 6 percent of grievances generate formal complaints; many employees fear repercussions for complaining (Fitzgerald, Swan, & Fischer, 1995; Kantrowitz, 1992). Others— whether employees or students—do not label the act as harassment at the time, or may blame themselves for the interaction (Kidder, Lafleur, & Wells, 1995; Weiss & Lalonde, 1998).

The public lacks consensus as to exactly what statements or acts constitute sexual harassment (Gruber, 1992). For example, men have difficulty labelling a statement or a question as sexually harassing if it attempts to reflect a compliment or if it is intended to be humorous (Gutek, 1985; Terpstra & Baker, 1987). Thus, one of the tasks in the early 1990s was to develop classifications of sexually harassing statements and actions.

Gruber's Typology of Sexual Harassment

Gruber (1992) divided harassment into three types: verbal requests, verbal comments, and

---

BOX 15.1
Is Same-Sex Harassment Sexual Harassment?

If men can be sexually harassed, the protagonist need not always be a predatory female. Men report potentially harassing behaviours from men at least as often as they do from women (Waldo, Berdahl, & Fitzgerald, 1998). Joseph Oncale's case is an example.

For four months in 1991 Joseph Oncale was an off-shore oil-rig worker. While working as part of an eight-man crew for Sundowner Offshore Services, he claimed that he was sexually pursued and threatened with rape by two of his supervisors—who were also male. Once the two men grabbed his genitals and one of them placed his penis against Oncale's head. On another occasion, he claimed, he was sodomized with a bar of soap. He twice reported these incidents to his employer's representative at the job site, but nothing was done. His supervisors portrayed their actions as a type of locker-room horseplay. So Joseph Oncale quit. Does he have the right to sue for sexual harassment? The Fifth Circuit Court of Appeals based in New Orleans said no, that Title VII of the U.S. Civil Rights Act of 1964 did not apply to same-sex encounters; several other circuits have ruled the same way (Ryan & Butler, 1996). Are such decisions justified? Observers have labelled as a loophole the fact that Title VII prohibited discrimination in the workplace based on race, religion, sex, and national origin, but ignored same-sex discrimination (Landau, 1997).

But Oncale pursued his suit to the U.S. Supreme Court, and in the oral arguments held in December 1997, six of the nine justices were quite critical of the circuit court's ruling, and Chief Justice Rehnquist, at one point, said, "I don't see how we could possibly sustain the ruling" (quoted by Carelli, 1997, p. A-1). In its unanimous decision, the Court ruled in favour of Oncale; it stated: "Nothing in Title VII necessarily bars a claim of discrimination ... merely because the plaintiff and the defendant are of the same sex" (*Oncale v. Sundowner Offshore Services*, 1998, p. 1001).

nonverbal displays. Within each type, he generated several subcategories. His typology is reprinted in Box 15.2. Within each of the three categories, the subcategories ranged from more severe to less severe. For example, **sexual bribery** was defined as a request with either a threat or a promise of a reward, whereas the less severe verbal requests, **subtle pressures/advances** were exemplified by ambiguous or inappropriate questions or double entendres.

Fitzgerald's Typology

Louise Fitzgerald and her associates (see Fitzgerald, Drasgow, Hulin, Gelfand, & Magley, 1997; Fitzgerald & Hesson-McInnis, 1989; Fitzgerald, Shullman, et al, 1988) have generated a classification of types of behaviours between students and professors; these also can be ordered from less serious to more serious. Their classifications are as follows:

1. Gender harassment, or generalized sexual remarks and behaviour.
2. Seductive behaviour, or inappropriate and offensive, but sanction-free, advances.
3. Sexual bribery, or solicitation by promise of rewards.
4. Threat of punishment, or use of coercion.
5. Sexual imposition, or gross sexual advances or assault.

These classifications, developed by psychologists, are helpful, but it was up to the courts to decide where to draw the line between borderline acceptable and unacceptable practices. Several key cases and pieces of legislation tried to clarify such questions in both Canada and the United States.

SEXUAL HARASSMENT LEGISLATION

Canada

In Canada, there are three main pieces of legislation that protect people from sexual harassment—the **Canadian Human Rights Act**, the Criminal Code of Canada, and the Canadian Labour Code.

The Canadian Human Rights Act (1985) describes the overriding principles behind harassment policies and gives the specific contexts in which harassment can occur. It states that *all people* have a right to live and work without being harassed, and if harassment occurs, the victim can expect something to be done about it. It specifically states that sexual harassment is a discriminatory practice in the provision of goods, services, facilities or accommodation customarily available

---

> ### BOX 15.2
> ### Gruber's Typology of Sexual Harassment
>
> A. Verbal requests
>   (More to less severe)
>
>   1. Sexual bribery
>
>   2. Sexual advances
>
>   3. Relational advances
>
>   4. Subtle pressures/advances
>
> B. Verbal comments
>   (More to less severe)
>
>   1. Personal remarks
>
>   2. Subjective objectification
>
>   3. Sexual categorical remarks
>
> C. Nonverbal displays
>   (More to less severe)
>
>   1. Sexual assault
>
>   2. Sexual touching
>
>   3. Sexual posturing
>
>   4. Sexual materials

(Adapted from Gruber, 1992, pp. 451–452.)

to the general public; the provision of commercial premises or residential accommodation; or matters related to employment. In other words, Canadians are protected from acts of sexual harassment in their place of employment or anywhere that provides us with goods, services (e.g., a hospital, school, or university), facilities (e.g., a gym), or accommodation (e.g., an apartment).

Such sexual harassment can include verbal abuse or threats, unwelcome remarks or jokes of a sexual nature, displaying of sexually explicit or other offensive pictures, leering or other gestures, and unnecessary physical contact.

The most serious forms of sexual harassment extend into the realm of **criminal behaviour**. When sexual harassment includes sexual assault or stalking, Canadians are protected by the Criminal Code of Canada. **Sexual assault** includes three types of crime: Simple sexual assault (forcing any form of sexual activity on another person without that person's consent, such as kissing, fondling, grabbing, sexual intercourse, etc.), sexual assault with a weapon, and aggravated sexual assault (if the victim is wounded, maimed, or disfigured while being sexually assaulted). In Canada, the crime of **stalking** (section 264 of the Criminal Code) is referred to as **criminal harassment**, and involves the repeated contact (physical, visual, e-mail, verbal, or physical proximity) with a person who does not consent to such contact. The behaviour of the stalker directly or indirectly threatens the other person's safety and security. As such, stalking is defined by the impact it has on the person being stalked and not the intent of the stalker. The Criminal Code (section 264) defines the stalking as:

(a) repeatedly following from place to place the other person or anyone known to them;

(b) repeatedly communicating with, either directly or indirectly, the other person or anyone known to them;

(c) besetting or watching the dwelling-house, or place where the other person,

or anyone known to them, resides, works, carries on business or happens to be; or

(d) engaging in threatening conduct directed at the other person or any member of their family.

The Canada Labour Code (1985) focuses specifically on harassment against employees in the workplace. Division XV.1 of the Code focuses on sexual harassment, which refers to "any conduct, comment, gesture or contact of a sexual nature that is likely to cause offence or humiliation to any employee or that might, on reasonable grounds, be perceived by that employee as placing a condition of a sexual nature on employment or on any opportunity for training or promotion." The Code states that all employees are entitled to a *workplace free of sexual harassment* and that every employer shall make every reasonable effort to ensure that no employee is subjected to sexual harassment. The 1989 case of *Janzen v. Platy Enterprises Ltd.* (see Box 15.3) established that in Canada employers are liable for their employees' acts of sexual discrimination.

The United States

Within the U.S. courts, there has been much disagreement over the meaning and consequences of sexual harassment. Beginning in the 1980s, some courts made rulings that were inconsistent with those of others, partly because of their interpretations of official guidelines. The specific wording of the guidelines is as follows:

Unwelcome sexual advances, requests for sexual favors, and other verbal or physical conduct of a sexual nature constitute sexual harassment when: (1) submission to such conduct is made either explicitly or implicitly a term or condition of an individual's employment, (2) submission to or a rejection of such conduct by an individual is used as a basis for employment decisions affecting such individual, or (3) such conduct has the purpose or effect of unreasonably interfering with an

BOX 15.3
A Key Canadian Supreme Court Decision

The landmark decision on sexual harassment was handed down by the Supreme Court of Canada in 1989. The case of *Janzen v. Platy Enterprises Ltd.* (1989), on appeal to the Supreme Court from the Court of Appeal for Manitoba, established that, in Canada, sexual harassment forms a specific type of **sexual discrimination** and *that employers are liable for their employees' acts of such sexual discrimination.*

The complainants J. and G. were employed as waitresses at Pharos Restaurant in Winnipeg during the fall of 1982. The restaurant was owned and operated by Platy Enterprises Ltd. and the president of the corporation was the manager. While working, J. was sexually harassed by another employee, who repeatedly touched her body and made unwanted sexual advances. This employee was in charge of the cooking during the evening shift and had no actual authority over the waitresses. However, he gave the impression (supported by the manager) that he had control over firing employees. Despite J.'s objections, this harassment persisted for more than a month and included threatening behaviours. Although the manager was informed of the situation, he did not attempt to stop it and J. decided to quit her job. G. was the victim of a similar pattern of harassment by the same employee. Eventually, the manager fired G. from her job. The women filed a complaint with the Manitoba Human Rights Commission against Pharos Restaurant. The adjudicator found that they had been subjected to persistent sexual harassment and had been the victims of sexual discrimination violating the Human Rights Act. The women were awarded punitive damages and damages for loss of wages, and the employee and the employer were found to be jointly liable. However, the Court of Appeal reversed the judgment, stating that sexual harassment of this type is not discrimination on the basis of sex and that the employer could not be held liable for the

sexual harassment perpetrated by its employee. The final judgment came down to the Supreme Court of Canada who disagreed, stating that "Sexual harassment is a form of sex discrimination…. The crucial fact in this case is that it was only female employees who ran the risk of sexual harassment…. It strains credulity to argue that the sole factor underlying the discriminatory action was appellants' sexual attractiveness—a personal characteristic—and that gender was accordingly irrelevant" and that "the respondent Platy Enterprises Ltd. must be held liable for the actions of its employee" (summary para. 7–10).

In addition, the Supreme Court defined sexual harassment as unwelcome conduct of a sexual nature that detrimentally affects the work environment or leads to adverse job-related consequences for the victims of the harassment. With this broad definition, the Court rejected the more rigid categorization emerging from American cases. (American courts have tended to separate sexual harassment into two categories: the "quid pro quo" type of harassment in which an employment benefit, such as promotion, is made contingent upon participation in sexual activity, and the "hostile" or "poisoned" environment type of harassment in which an employee is required to endure sexual touching, comments, gestures, or taunting as a condition of work. We'll look at these two types of harassment shortly.)

The Supreme Court of Canada concluded that sexual harassment can take various forms. It is not limited to the obvious case in which an employer demands sexual favours, nor do victims of harassment need to show that they were not hired, denied a promotion, or fired because of their refusal to participate in sexual activity. It also includes a situation in which an employee endures sexual groping, propositions, and inappropriate comments, in the absence of job consequences.

individual's work performance or creating an intimidating, hostile, or offensive working environment. (U.S. EEOC, 1980, p. 74677)

Two Types of Sexual Harassment

In the U.S., guidelines have been established for distinguishing between two types of sexual harassment, one more clear-cut than the other.

Quid pro Quo Sexual Harassment In the **quid pro quo** type of sexual harassment, sexual demands are made in exchange for employment benefits. More broadly, it involves an implicit or explicit bargain whereby the harasser promises a reward for complying with sexual demands or threatens punishment for not complying with sexual demands (Hotelling, 1991). An example: "Sleep with me or you'll get fired." In most cases, this type of sexual harassment—often manifested by explicit propositions or physical sexual actions—is relatively easy to recognize (McCandless & Sullivan, 1991). It can also be applied to faculty–student relationships, in which the promise of a higher grade (or the threat of a failing one) is the inducement to comply.

Hostile Workplace Environment Overt sexual behaviour or bribery is not required for sexual harassment to have occurred. If ridicule, insult, and/or intimidation are severe or pervasive enough to create an abusive atmosphere or to alter the working conditions of the employee, the situation meets the second criterion of sexual harassment, the presence of a **hostile work environment**. Under the 1964 U.S. Civil Rights Act, it is illegal for employers to create or tolerate "an intimidating, hostile, or offensive working environment" by use of harassment. If, for example, pornographic pictures and sexually explicit language are frequent in the workplace, the environment may—in and of itself—be considered a harassing one.

Although this dichotomy used in the United States may make *prima facie* good sense, the Canadian Supreme Court has rejected this model of sexual harassment, arguing that it is unnecessary. In *Janzen v. Platy Enterprises Ltd.* (1989), Chief Justice Brian Dickson of the Supreme Court stated:

> Canadian human rights tribunals have also tended to rely on the *quid pro quo/hostile work environment dichotomy*. I do not find this categorization particularly helpful. While the distinction may have been important to illustrate forcefully the range of behaviour that constitutes harassment at a time before sexual harassment was widely viewed as actionable, in my view there is no longer any need to characterize harassment as one of these forms. The main point in allegations of sexual harassment is that unwelcome sexual conduct has invaded the workplace, irrespective of whether the consequences of the harassment included a denial of concrete

employment rewards for refusing to participate in sexual activity.

In addition to the concern expressed by the Canadian courts, assessing the presence of this type of harassment is extremely challenging (McCandless & Sullivan, 1991). Is an act a well-intentioned compliment or an attempt to create a difficult working arrangement? How frequently must a co-worker tell obscene jokes for a work environment to be considered hostile? If the only woman on a work team is given the most dangerous tasks (or the most menial ones), is this a hostile work environment? As far back as 1986, the American Supreme Court recognized that sexual harassment that creates a hostile work environment violates their 1964 Civil Rights Act. (See Box 15.4 for a description of a relevant case.) But in ensuing years, other courts differed in what criteria were used to establish a "hostile workplace environment"; for example, did the victim have to suffer "psychological damage"? And what should the standard be—the perspective of the victim or that of an outside observer? Because of these ambiguities, the U.S. Supreme Court agreed to take on the case of *Harris v. Forklift Systems, Inc.* in 1993.

Harris v. Forklift Systems, Inc.

In 1993 the U.S. Supreme Court offered a more refined definition of sexual harassment. It decided that a demonstration of psychological injury was unnecessary as long as the behaviour was physically threatening or humiliating or if it unreasonably interfered with an employee's work performance. Justice Sandra Day O'Connor used a "reasonable person" standard in her decision. She ruled out as sexual harassment "conduct that is not severe or pervasive enough to create an objectively hostile or abusive work environment—an environment that a reasonable person would find hostile or abusive" (*Harris v. Forklift*, 1993, p. 370). She chose not to use the language of the traditional "reasonable man" standard but was unwilling to go so far as to adopt the "reasonable woman" standard (described next).

BOX 15.4
Meritor Savings Bank v. Vinson

A vice-president of the Meritor Savings Bank and manager of one of its branches, Sidney Taylor, had hired Mechelle Vinson as a teller. Four years later, the bank discharged her because it claimed she had used excessive amounts of sick leave. (By that time she had been promoted to assistant branch manager.) Ms. Vinson filed a suit, claiming she had been sexually harassed by her boss (she claimed he had exposed himself and had fondled her in front of other employees) and that she had agreed to have sexual relations with him out of fear of losing her job. She estimated that they had sex 40 or 50 times. The bank responded by claiming that Ms. Vinson had voluntarily agreed to her boss's advances, and hence no grounds for sexual harassment were present. The district court had found for the bank, based on her "voluntary" acquiescence. After several intervening steps, the case was accepted for review by the U.S. Supreme Court,

which in 1986 ruled unanimously that Title VII of the 1964 Civil Rights Act forbade not only quid pro quo type of sexual harassment but also situations in which harassment created an abusive work environment. The decision was written by Justice Rehnquist, who stated that "the correct inquiry is whether respondent by her conduct indicated that the alleged sexual advances were unwelcome, not whether her actual participation in sexual intercourse was involuntary."

The decision was not, however, a complete victory for those in sympathy with women who were harassed in the workplace. At the trial, the bank had introduced evidence about Vinson's style of dress and personal fantasies in support of its rejoinder that the sexual activity was voluntary. The U.S. Supreme Court ruled that it was within the domain of the trial judge to decide whether such evidence was relevant or prejudicial to the case.

The Reasonable Woman Standard   The **reasonable woman standard** was apparently first used in the U.S. in *Ellison v. Brady* (1991). In this case, the court decided to view allegedly harassing behaviour from the perspective of the victim. It explained that "if it examined only whether a 'reasonable person' would find the conduct harassing, it would run the risk of reinforcing the prevailing level of discrimination" (quoted in McCandless and Sullivan, 1991, p. 18). In changing the focus, this court decision reflected earlier psychological research that men and women may hold differing views on sexual harassment, with men more likely to see as "comparatively harmless amusement" (see Wiener, 1995) a behaviour that women would see as sexual harassment. That is, some empirical studies have concluded that men may be more tolerant of sexual harassment than women are, and that women are more likely than men to label sexually aggressive behaviour at work as harassment. But such gender differences should not be overestimated. A meta-analysis of more than 90 comparisons (Blumethal, 1998) concluded that gender differences in the perception of sexual harassment were relatively small,

although they were consistent across age, culture, and professional status. The focus on victims in the *Ellison v. Brady* decision has drawn attention and criticism. Rosen (1993a) noted that the decision used the terms "victim" and "woman" interchangeably, as in "an understanding of the victim's view requires, among other things, an analysis of the different perspectives of men and women. Conduct that many men consider unobjectionable may offend many women" (quoted by Rosen, 1993a, p. 14).

The U.S. Supreme Court's decision in the *Harris v. Forklift* case did not put to rest the issue of the appropriate definition of sexual harassment. What constitutes a "hostile environment" was not precisely specified (Plevan, 1993). Justice O'Connor's opinion painted only broad limits: a hostile environment is more than isolated jokes and comments—a "mere offensive utterance" is not enough to establish such an environment— but an environment can be considered hostile before the harassing conduct present causes the victim to have a nervous breakdown. To assess whether an environment was hostile, the U.S. Supreme Court relied on its frequent focus on the "totality of the circumstances," meaning that the context in which conduct occurs is important. Critics, such as John Leo (1993), have focused their concern on incidents that stretch the standard, such as the banning of photos of women in modest swimsuits.

Another concern is the possible restriction on free speech (Rosen, 1993a, 1993b). Let us say that an employer uses profane language; he claims that his words are merely expletives and protected as free speech. Should he be punished? What about a man who makes a wolf whistle directed toward a woman on the street? Rosen (1993a) went further, to ask: Will gender-based job titles such as "draftsman" or "foreman" become actionable as "sexually suggestive" material? (See an article by Eugene Volokh, 1992, for a review of the free-speech issue; Volokh, a law professor, has been quoted as saying that the liberal court decisions have had a "chilling effect" on the expression of free speech at work [Cloud, 1998, p. 53].) A third issue is concern about the image of women reflected in the opinion. Does the opinion attempt to shield women and reflect a stereotype of them as needing special protection from words and images?

HOW CAN PSYCHOLOGY HELP?

Though ambiguities and disagreements remain, the last two decade have seen great progress in understanding the nature of sexual harassment. Psychological analyses of cases and psychological research have contributed to this understanding; this section reviews several ways that forensic psychologists can build upon these contributions.

Analyzing the Causes of Sexual Harassment

What causes sexual harassment to occur? And do people differ in their explanations of the causes when a complaint of sexual harassment is filed? In answer to the first question, Pryor, Giedd, and Williams (1995; Pryor, 1987) have employed the classic Lewinian model of social behaviour—that it is a function of the person and the environment. Sexual harassment is a social behaviour that some people do some of the time. Specifically, certain persons may possess proclivities to sexually harass others but also the social norms of the organization may either encourage or discourage the expression of harassment. For example, the incidence of sexual harassment is higher in male-dominated workplaces (Gutek, 1985); these workplaces can be environments that make one's sex more salient (Deaux, 1995).

With regard to situational factors, local social norms influence the incidence rate. In some organizations, managers or local work-group leaders may condone such behaviour, so that potential harassers may perceive that they are free to do so (Gutek, 1985)—among military personnel, for example. Women reported being sexually harassed more often in units in which the commanding officers were perceived to be encouraging sexual harassment (Pryor, LaVite, & Stoller, 1993). And it was not only the women who felt that their commanders were insensitive; independent measures of the local social norms showed that other people perceived the managers to be encouraging sexual harassment.

With regard to the second determinant in Pryor's theory, or within-the-person factors such as cynicism about relationships or hostility toward women, Pryor elaborated on a methodological procedure first used by Malamuth (1981) to study rape proclivities. Men were asked to imagine themselves in a series of scenarios in which they have power over an attractive woman. For example:

> [O]ne scenario depicts an interaction between a male university professor and a female student who is seeking to raise her grade in a class. Male subjects are asked to rate the likelihood of their performing an act of quid pro quo sexual harassment in each scenario, given that they could do so with impunity. In the professor/student scenario, for example, how likely is it that the subject would raise the student's grade in

exchange for sexual favors, given that his behavior would go unpunished? (Pryor, Giedd, & Williams, 1995, p. 74)

The scale developed by Pryor, the Likelihood to Sexually Harass (LSH) scale has high reliability. Based on administration of this instrument and other self-report measures to groups of college men, Pryor has drawn the following conclusions about men who report that they would be likely to engage in sexual harassment:

1. They tend to believe common myths about rape and are more sexually aggressive in general.
2. They describe themselves as stereotypically male; they believe men should be mentally, emotionally, and physically self-reliant; they avoid stereotypically feminine occupations and activities. In summary, they view themselves as hypermasculine.
3. They think of women as sex objects, and they can readily provide justifications for actions that others would call sexual harassment. But they are also aware of the situational constraints (such as standards in that particular workplace or the presence of a boss who is sensitive toward attempts to harass co-workers) on such behaviour (Pryor, Giedd, & Williams, 1995).

In an inventive series of studies, Pryor and his colleagues have demonstrated that men with a high LSH score did harass women "when they found themselves in a situation socially engineered such that harassing behavior was convenient and not conspicuous" (Pryor, Giedd, & Williams, 1995, pp. 80–81). Further, they tended to engage in such behaviours only when local norms encouraged or allowed such behaviour.

When it comes to attributions of the cause of specific acts of harassment, a number of factors have been identified, including how flagrant the act was, how frequently it was done, and how the other person responded (Thomann & Wiener, 1987). As is discussed subsequently, these factors are useful in determining whether a complaint of

sexual harassment will receive recognition and compensation in the courts.

Distinctions between Female and Male Victims

The phenomenon of a supervisor or co-worker provoking a person of the same gender, referred to as **same-sex sexual harassment**, is beginning to be studied by psychologists. Several conclusions have emerged from these investigations:

1. When men report being victims of sexual harassment, the perpetrator is much more likely to be of the same sex, in contrast to complaints by women, who almost always list a person of the other sex as the perpetrator. Self-report surveys have found that 40 percent to 50 percent of complaints by males report that the harassment is by another male, whereas only 2 percent of the complaints by women cite another woman (Pryor & Whalen, 1997; Waldo, Berdahl, & Fitzgerald, 1998).
2. Men and women report experiencing different types of sexual harassment. Almost all men reported crude or offensive behaviours, such as jokes or obscene gestures, as the most frequent type of offence (Bastian, Lancaster, & Reyst, 1996; Magley, Waldo, Drasgow, & Fitzgerald, 1998; cited by Foote & Goodman-Delahunty, 1999). Whereas females were more likely to report conduct fulfilling a quid pro quo claim, men more often reported conduct reflecting a hostile work environment.
3. The emotional impact of the harassment on men depends upon many factors, including the setting and the type of harassment. Previously, the chapter reported that women interpret a wider range of behaviours as sexual harassment. Similarly, Foote and Goodman-Delahunty concluded that "From one perspective, men may actually experience sexual harassment as less offensive than do women" (1999, p. 133). They wrote:

First, the harassment may be considered a more acceptable part of male culture; it is an element of men's experience as early as grade school. Second, most of the harassment experienced by men is verbal in nature, rather than sexual touching or coercive sexual behavior.... This "guy talk" is often derisive of women as well as men … and, although it disparages both genders, it enforces stereotypical male roles and behaviors. (p. 133)

Measuring Beliefs

Equally important in understanding the nature of harassment is the assessment of beliefs about what does and does not constitute sexual harassment. Two measures have been developed: the Tolerance for Sexual Harassment Inventory (Lott, Reilly, & Howard, 1982) and the Beliefs about Sexual Harassment Scale (Perot, Brooks, & Gersh, 1992), but little research has been done using them. As noted above, earlier assumptions that men and women differ in their definition of harassment has been qualified, in the sense that egregious cases lead the vast majority of both women *and* men to label them as harassing; gender differences emerge with respect to evaluating less clear-cut actions. As Gutek and O'Connor (1995) noted, "When the harassment is either severe or the behavior is so benign that it is clearly not harassment, the perceptual gap between the two sexes closes" (p. 156).

What factors in a case might influence whether the employer's behaviour constitutes harassment? Wiener, Winter, Rogers, and Arnot (2004) examined the potential effects of the complainant's previous workplace behaviour on such judgments. The authors exposed participants to a female complainant whose conduct was described as aggressive, submissive, ambiguous, or neutral. Results indicated that an aggressive complainant caused participants (especially women) to rate lower the likelihood that a neutral complainant in a second independent case was the victim of gender discrimination.

Across cases, men found less evidence of harassment than women did. Apparently, both the manner in which a person behaved prior to making a complaint and the gender of the "judge" may make a difference.

Predicting the Outcome of Complaints

To bring a complaint of sexual harassment against a supervisor is not easy. Is there a way to predict whether complainants who do so will be successful? Yes. Terpstra and Baker (1988, 1992), after examining a number of cases in two settings, have identified several relevant factors. First, they examined 81 sexual harassment charges filed over a two-year period, to determine what influenced their outcome. About 30 percent of these cases were settled in favour of the complainant. The researchers identified nine characteristics that *may have influenced* the decisions:

1. The perceived seriousness of the harassment behaviour reported.
2. The frequency of the harassment.
3. The status of the harasser (co-worker, immediate supervisor, or higher-up).
4. The severity of the job-related consequences of the harassment.
5. Whether the complainant had witnesses to support the charges.
6. Whether the complainant had documents to support the charges.
7. The nature of management's reasons for the reported adverse employment-related consequences.
8. Whether the complainant had notified management of the harassment prior to filing charges.
9. Whether the employing organization had taken investigative or remedial action when notified of the problem.

Only three of these characteristics were significantly related to the decisions; the sexual harassment charges were more likely to have been resolved in favour of the complainant when the harassment behaviours were serious, when the complainant had witnesses to support the charges, or when the complainant had given notice to management prior to filing formal charges (Terpstra & Baker, 1988).

This type of analysis was repeated by the same researchers (Terpstra & Baker, 1992) for 133 cases that led to court decisions between 1974 and 1989. A total of 38 percent of these cases were decided in favour of the complainants—a figure higher than the 30 percent of cases settled in favour of the complainant (discussed above)—even though the complainants' cases were not as strong as those in the original study. In these cases, five of the nine aspects distinguished between winning and losing. Complainants were more likely to win their cases if the harassment was severe, witnesses or documents supported their cases, they had given notice to management prior to filing charges, or their organization took no action.

If a complainant had none of these factors in her or his favour, the odds of winning the case were less than 1 percent; if all five, almost 100 percent. Specific odds for each of the five alone: severity of harassment, 40 percent; witnesses, 48 percent; supporting documents, 44 percent; notice given to management, 49 percent; and the organization not taking action, 53 percent.

Restructuring the Workplace

As Pryor's analysis discussed above suggested, sexual harassment does not involve only individual attitudes and beliefs, but also practices in the organization, whether it is a factory, an office, or an academic department (Riger, 1991). For example, until recently, universities—as well as businesses—had no policies condemning or punishing sexual harassment, whereas now most do.

Psychologists have played a role in designing and administering training programs that seek to educate workers as to the meaning of sexual harassment. One goal of such programs is to encourage a greater percentage of actual victims to report the harassment. Barak (1992) has suggested a two-phase workshop, as follows:

Intensive, cognitive-behavioral workshops designed to provide women with skills to combat [sexual harassment] might be divided into two phases. The first phase could develop their awareness of the … phenomenon, including its process, causes, and typical consequences. By means of brief lectures, exercises, case-study simulations, and video modeling, participants could be taught to identify, detect, understand, and analyze the many forms of sexual harassment and the ways in which they typically unfold. The second phase could teach practical coping skills. Again, with the help of a range of teaching techniques, such as live simulations and video demonstrations, participants could be taught, among other things, the multiple response options appropriate to various forms of sexual harassment, as well as how to make use of the applicable laws and grievance procedures. (Barak, 1992, p. 818)

Okay. But why not put our emphasis on restructuring the workplace so that sexual harassment is less likely to occur, rather than dealing with ways to respond to it? A first step would be to educate members of both genders about their discrepancies in what is sexual harassment, as Riger (1991) has suggested. Workshops that, for example, explore how men and women interpret the same comment or gesture differently try to address this problem.

SUMMARY

Awareness of the nature and frequency of sexual harassment increased during the 1990s and the new millennium, in large part because of several highly publicized cases, such as those involving the Canadian military. Nevertheless, the term is not fully understood, and one of the contributions of psychology is the analysis of its meaning for different people, especially as these mesh with or conflict with courts' definitions.

The Supreme Court of Canada has defined sexual harassment as unwelcome conduct of a sexual nature that detrimentally affects the work environment or leads to adverse job-related consequences for the victim. With this broad definition, the Supreme Court rejected the model emerging from American cases (using two types of sexual harassment—quid pro quo and hostile workplace harassment). The Supreme Court has determined that sexual harassment is any unwelcome sexual conduct in the workplace. In the Canadian case *Janzen v. Platy Enterprises Ltd.* (1989), the Supreme Court established that sexual harassment forms a specific type of sexual discrimination and that employers are liable for their employees' acts of such sexual discrimination.

Forensic psychologists can make contributions to a better understanding of the nature of sexual harassment and to a decrease in its occurrence, including assessing and analyzing beliefs about what does and does not constitute sexual harassment, developing models to predict when harassment will occur, and identifying factors that increase the likelihood of a complaint being successful. Psychologists have played a role in designing and administering training programs that seek to educate workers as to the meaning of sexual harassment.

KEY TERMS

Canadian Human Rights Act, p. 322
criminal behaviour, p. 323
criminal harassment, p. 323
hostile work environment, p. 325
quid pro quo, p. 324
reasonable woman standard, p. 326
same-sex sexual harassment, p. 328
sexual assault, p. 323
sexual bribery, p. 322
sexual discrimination, p. 324
sexual harassment, p. 319
stalking, p. 323
subtle pressures/advances, p. 322

SUGGESTED READINGS

Borgida, E., & Fiske, S. T. (Eds.). (1995). Gender stereotyping, sexual harassment, and the law. *Journal of Social Issues, 51*(1), 1–207.

This special issue of the *Journal of Social Issues* includes articles on lay definitions of sexual harassment, models for predicting harassment, and the reasonable woman standard. Highly recommended.

Foote, W. E., & Goodman-Delahunty, J. (1999). Same-sex harassment: Implications of the *Oncale* decision for forensic evaluation of plaintiffs. *Behavioral Sciences and the Law, 17,* 123–139.

This article presents a recent review of research on the frequency and types of same-sex sexual harassment.

Mayer, J., & Abramson, J. (1994). *Strange justice: The selling of Clarence Thomas*. Boston: Houghton-Mifflin.

Of the several books about Justice Clarence Thomas's confirmation hearing and the claims of sexual harassment by Professor Anita Hill, this is probably the most thoroughly researched.

Pryor, J. B., Giedd, J. L., & Williams, K. B. (1995). A social psychological model for predicting sexual harassment. *Journal of Social Issues, 51*(1), 69–84.

This article presents a person-X-situation model of sexual harassment, a model that proposes that the likelihood that a person will act in a harassing manner is determined both by that person's proclivities and by aspects of the workplace that encourage or tolerate sexual exploitation.

Wekesser, C., Swisher, K. L., & Pierce, C. (Eds.). (1992). *Sexual harassment*. San Diego: Greenhaven Press.

This collection includes reprinted articles about the extent of sexual harassment, its causes, and its possible solutions.

16

The Promising Future of Forensic Psychology in Canada

> Science knows no country, because knowledge belongs to humanity, and is the torch which illuminates the world. Science is the highest personification of the nation because that nation will remain the first which carries the furthest the works of thought and intelligence.
> —LOUIS PASTEUR (CITED IN DUBOS, 1960, P. 145)

THE STATUS OF FORENSIC PSYCHOLOGY IN CANADA

Undergraduate and graduate students in forensic psychology courses and programs in Canada are a highly enthusiastic bunch. Although what many of them want most is to become Clarice Starling in *Silence of the Lambs* (which is unlikely to happen), there seems to be a high level of interest in most areas falling under the heading of forensic psychology. We hope that this text has inspired some of you to continue on in the field and perhaps come up with your own new research and insights.

As a student of forensic psychology in Canada, there is much to be excited about in this new millennium. A recent special issue of the *Canadian Journal of Behavioural Science* highlighted the field of forensic psychology, and offered an impressive array of the types of work happening in our field today by Canadians and others (see Porter, 2004). As was introduced in Chapter 1, and has become evident throughout this book, Canada long has been a leader in the field of forensic psychology, contributing some of its most important advances in both research and practice. To keep up with continuing progress in the field, students may wish to periodically check out the Web sites of the **Criminal Justice Section of Canadian Psychological Association** (http://www.cpa.ca/CJS/index.html), the **American Psychology-Law Society** (http://www.ap-ls.org/), and the **European Association of Psychology and Law** (http://www.law.kuleuven.ac.be/eapl/).

One reason that forensic psychology is taking off in Canada is that lawyers, members of the judiciary, and other professionals in the legal system are seeing the value of psychology in their fields. As Ogloff (2004) notes, "The law needs psychology" (p. 84). The basis of this positive recognition in recent years is decades of groundbreaking research, without which the foundations of application in the legal system would be weak. And, ultimately, when research effectively informs practice, psychologists are able to gain invaluable experience that then leads to contribute to the effective training and education of others. This pedagogical mission occurs both with students like you and with staff who work on the "front line" in the legal system.

FORENSIC PSYCHOLOGY IN CANADA: THREE ACTIVITIES

Research

The legal system was created because of unacceptable human behaviour (i.e., crime) and is designed to control behaviour (Ogloff & Finkelman, 1999). As outlined by James Ogloff (2004), this attempted control of human behaviour leads to assumptions of human nature, some of which may not be correct or which have been untested. Consider, for example, a long-standing belief in our correctional system is that all offenders have the potential to live as law-abiding citizens. Although this sounds good in principle, forensic psychologists have shown that certain offenders, such as psychopaths, may not have this capacity (e.g., Ogloff, Wong, & Greenwood, 1990; Rice, Harris, & Cormier, 1992; cf. Skeem, Monahan, & Mulvey, 2002). Recent neuroimaging studies suggest possible functional or structural anomalies in the brains of psychopaths (e.g., Raine, Lencz et al., 2003) that could be related to the persistence of their antisocial and often violent behaviour (see Porter & Porter, 2004). Another example would be the frequent acceptance of "recovered" or "repressed" memory evidence by Canadian courts (e.g., *R. v. R. J. H.*, 2000). As we saw in earlier chapters, psychological research has established that many such reports are based on false memories (e.g., Loftus, 2003). As we can see, assumptions in the legal system must be tested scientifically. Being the science of human behaviour, psychology is in the best position to fill this role. It has much to offer to the legal system by shedding light on people's actions as they relate to the law, from someone committing a crime to a witness testifying in court.

As we have witnessed throughout this book, Canada's track record in forensic research has been superb. While some of this work has been large-scale projects occurring in collaboration with researchers from other countries, much of it has been individual researchers "dogging it out" (often with their graduate students) until they find the answers to important psycho-legal questions. Pioneering research on eyewitness memory, criminal behaviour and risk assessment, victim behaviour, deception detection, and other areas has occurred here. Canadian researchers publish at a high rate in the leading academic journals in the field, such as *Law and Human Behavior*, *Behavioral Sciences and the Law*, and *Criminal Justice and Behavior*.

Many of the luminaries in our field set the stage for this work starting in the 1960s and '70s. For example, three of them, whose names you will recognize, obtained their Ph.D.s in the 1960s from the University of Western Ontario, which, interestingly, had little in the way of forensic training or research at the time. Dr. John Yuille, a professor at the University of British Columbia, has published widely on victim, witness, and suspect memory; trauma and memory; interviewing techniques; credibility assessment; and child sexual abuse. Dr. Robert Hare, a professor emeritus at the University of British Columbia, has written extensively about his research on psychopathy, created the major tool for measuring psychopathy, and wrote the 1993 bestseller *Without Conscience: The Disturbing World of the Psychopaths among Us*. And Dr. Daniel Yarmey of the University of Guelph has published numerous articles pertaining to eyewitness memory (as well as many other areas). As we saw earlier, he also wrote one of the first important texts on the psychology of eyewitnesses, *The Psychology of Eyewitness Testimony*, in 1979. Along with Donald Dutton, one of the leading experts on domestic violence, Yuille and Hare established the first formal forensic psychology program in Canada (at the University of British Columbia).

There are many other examples of people in our field who were trained in the 1960s and early 1970s who helped to set the stage for the excellent research currently happening in Canada (and inspired a passion for research in forensic psychology in generations of undergraduate and graduate students). Just to name a few:

- Don Read, current (at the time of writing) director of the Psychology and Law program at Simon Fraser University, obtained his Ph.D. in 1969 and went on to publish important articles on memory in forensic contexts, the recovered memory debate, eyewitness testimony, and other aspects of autobiographical memory. He also testified as an expert witness in some fascinating cases, including one in which the heavy-metal band Judas Priest was accused of planting subliminal messages about suicide in their songs.
- Phil Firestone at the University of Ottawa has conducted research on sexual offenders, diagnostic/intervention issues, and offender recidivism.
- Paul Gendreau at the University of New Brunswick specializes in research and policy in the justice system.
- Vernon Quinsey at Queen's University has conducted research on prediction, modification, and management of violent behaviour, and sexual offending.
- Chris Webster, professor emeritus at Simon Fraser University, has written about violence risk assessment and management.

As mentioned by Ogloff (2004) in Chapter 1, prominent programs of forensic research occurring at the University of Victoria, the University of British Columbia, Simon Fraser University, the University of Saskatchewan, the University of Regina, Queen's University, the University of Toronto, Ryerson University, the University of Guelph, Université de Montréal, Dalhousie University, and the University of New Brunswick are largely because of the seeds planted by people such as those described above.

In fact, many people mentioned above who got the ball rolling for us in Canada are continuing to excel in research. For example, Don Read and his colleague Deborah Connolly recently conducted a very important study of recovered memory evidence in the Canadian courts. Using archival data, they have examined more than 2000 cases of sexual assault from the 1980s and '90s and found that evidence for recovered or delayed memories has emerged in as many as 6 percent of all sexual assault cases. In this innovative work, they continue to look at factors contributing to case outcomes (Connolly & Read, 2003; Connolly & Read, 2004).

Students of forensic psychology need to strive to continue in this tradition of research excellence.

Practice

Our field has a strong empirical basis because of ongoing research programs such as the ones mentioned above. This research foundation has led to the widespread application of psychology in the legal system, as we have seen throughout this text. At virtually every stage of the legal system in Canada, psychologists are being consulted, from the time a crime happens. For example, the RCMP and other police forces are increasingly relying on psychologists and other social scientists during their criminal investigations and interventions. These activities include helping with hostage negotiations, profiling serial offenders, planning interviews and interrogations, and offering counselling to officers who have gone through traumatic experiences (such as shooting a suspect).

If a suspect is apprehended and a trial is planned, psychologists are consulted for many reasons, including giving an opinion about evidence (such as a confession or another expert's report) or conducting assessments of criminal responsibility or fitness to stand trial. For example, at the Provincial Forensic Psychiatry Service in Nova Scotia, psychiatrists and psychologists conduct assessments of defendants prior to trial. In the case of an NCRMD defence, they sometimes are called to give evidence about the accused person's psychological state at the time of the offence. Also, before a trial, psychologists may help to design programs to help especially vulnerable witnesses to prepare for the possible ordeal of giving testimony (as with the London Court Clinic program for child witnesses described in Chapter 12).

Within the trial itself, a psychologist may be asked to give an expert opinion about a psychological issue if he or she meets the *Mohan* criteria, or about the defendant (such as the findings within a psychological assessment). For the purposes of sentencing and other pre-trial hearings (such as a dangerous offender and long-term offender hearings), a psychologist may be asked to conduct a risk assessment, commenting on an offender's likelihood of reoffending or potential for rehabilitation. After a defendant is designated an "offender" (by a guilty verdict) and placed in a correctional facility, psychologists—often full-time staff members in the institution—are heavily involved in the assessment of the person from the time he or she enters prison until that person is conditionally released or finishes the sentence. Sometimes, psychologists will be asked to provide assessment and intervention with an offender who may be suicidal. In fact, the Correctional Service of Canada is one of the largest employers of psychologists in Canada. When a person is found to be NCRMD or not fit to stand trial, he or she often is sent to a psychiatric facility such as the Forensic Psychiatric Institute in British Columbia for ongoing assessment and treatment by psychologists.

Training

As mentioned, there are two main kinds of training that forensic psychologists provide—teaching students like some of you, and training in the form of workshops, lectures, or supervision given to legal staff or psychologists in training. Some of you may have already decided that you would like to pursue a career in forensic psychology. At present, this can involve specific training at the undergraduate level and at the graduate level. If you wish to become a forensic psychologist who teaches and/or practices, you will need at least a masters degree, but in most provinces a Ph.D. will be required in coming years.

As James Ogloff (2004) reviewed, there is some good news for aspiring students. Earlier, he had conducted a survey of universities and law schools in Canada to look at what was then happening in psychology and law (Ogloff, 1990). He discovered that undergraduate courses in forensic psychology were being offered in five universities. However, when he looked at the situation in 2001, the number had increased to 25 (Ogloff, in press)! In terms of graduate courses in the area, the number had risen from four to seven. And, the number of formal programs in the field rose from none to four. This supports our observation that forensic psychology is thriving in Canada. However, Ogloff (2004) expressed some dissatisfaction that there were still few law schools offering courses in psychology and law. He concluded that "ongoing efforts must be made to provide systematic training to psychology graduate students in relevant areas of law and to ensure that some exposure of legal psychology is provided to students of law" (p. 85). In addition, because of a large number of faculty retirements, some formalized forensic psychology programs, such as the one at the University of British Columbia, are at risk of being phased out. In fact, Queen's University recently ended its renowned doctoral program in correctional/forensic psychology for such reasons. There are many unique challenges in conducting research on and working with forensic populations that cannot be met with standard training in clinical or experimental psychology. Further, there is still a huge demand for training in forensic psychology for students entering graduate school but still too few formal programs in the area (Porter, 2004). Thus, Canadian universities must start to recognize and act upon the need for more formalized programs in this field.

Academic Training

As of 2004, a large number of Canadian universities offer at least one course in forensic psy-
chology, psychology and the law, or another similar class at the undergraduate level. These institutions include the University of British Columbia, Simon Fraser University, the University of Alberta, the University of Saskatchewan, the University of Winnipeg, Carleton University, Queen's University, the University of Toronto, Concordia University, the University of Waterloo, York University, the University of New Brunswick, Acadia University, Dalhousie University, St. Francis Xavier University, and Saint Mary's University, although this list is by no means complete.

To our knowledge, at the present time, there is only one university in Canada that has a formalized **undergraduate program in forensic psychology**: Dalhousie University in Halifax. Starting in 2002, the certificate program in forensic psychology may be taken in conjunction with a four-year Bachelor of Science or Bachelor of Arts honours degree. The program allows students to specialize in forensic psychology at the undergraduate level while obtaining hands-on experience working within the criminal justice system. As part of this program, students are required to complete two four-week placements within the criminal justice system, either working at Springhill Institution (a medium-security institution in Nova Scotia), at a local parole office, or at the East Coast Forensic Hospital. In addition, students are required to take two classes in forensic psychology, complete their honours research project on a forensic topic, and take several classes in sociology (such as criminology). One other university—Carleton—offers specialized training in several areas of psychology at the undergraduate level, including forensic psychology. The University of New Brunswick at Saint John also offers a criminal justice minor for undergraduate psychology students.

If you are nearing completion of your undergraduate degree in psychology, you may be wondering where to go from here. Currently, there are several Canadian universities that offer graduate-level training in forensic psychology, either in a formal program in the area or by allowing students to focus their training in that area while completing other programs. The graduate program at the University of British Columbia offers specialized training in both clinical-forensic and forensic research. Students must complete a practicum within a forensic context, complete a portion of their internship at a forensic site, complete three of their option credits in forensic courses, and complete a Ph.D. thesis on a forensic topic. Graduate-level forensic courses available include "Offenders and Their Victims," "Psychology and the Criminal Justice System," "Ethics," and others.

Simon Fraser University offers two graduate-level programs in law and forensic psychology (see Ogloff, 1999). In the experimental forensic program, students are required to take several courses in law and psychology, conduct a research project in law and psychology, and to complete a practicum in the area. In addition, students may use other law and psychology courses to fulfill the requirements for their degree. Students in the clinical-forensic program are required to take several courses in law and psychology in addition to the regular requirements for nonforensic students. They also must complete their research project in forensic psychology, complete a practicum in forensic psychology, and are encouraged to complete their thesis in the area of law and psychology. At the University of Saskatchewan, forensic psychology is considered a specialization within each of the clinical doctoral program and the applied social psychology program. At Carleton University there is not a specific graduate program in forensic psychology but students who are admitted to the graduate program can complete a concentration in basic and applied social psychology (e.g., crime and delinquency, family violence). Carleton offers several courses in the forensic area including "Forensic Assessment," "Adult Offenders," "Witnesses, Victims, and Juries," "Youthful Offenders," and the "Psychology of Family Violence." Similar to Carleton, at Dalhousie University, students can obtain specialized forensic training but there is no formalized forensic program per se. Dalhousie offers two programs in psychology, a doctoral program in clinical psychology and a masters/doctoral program in experimental psychology, with the option of specializing in forensic psychology in either.

Practical Training

In recent years, psychologists have become increasingly active in offering training to Canadian legal staff. There are many examples that we have mentioned in this book. As mentioned in Chapter 1, in one of the most exciting developments in this area, the **National Judicial Institute (NJI)** based in Ottawa has invited psychologists to offer lectures and training to judges across the country. In light of the many well-known cases in which someone was falsely convicted, researchers in forensic psychology have been invited to educate the judiciary in areas such as eyewitness identification and credibility assessment. As Director George Thomson has recently stated, such training is intended to educate judges on "the risk of over-reliance on certain factors, such as demeanour in findings of credibility" (Dotto, 2004, p. 49). He also noted that the NJI is considering having psychologists train judges in other areas.

Another type of training in credibility assessment has been used with Canadian parole officers. Porter, Woodworth, and Birt (2000) combined training and research during a credibility assessment workshop with Correctional Service of Canada parole officers. The ability of officers to detect lying was looked at over two days of deception-detection training. On the first day, 32 officers judged whether 12 (six telling the truth, six lying) videotaped speakers were telling the truth, half of which were judged before and half judged after training. Five weeks later, 20 of the original participants judged the honesty of another 12 speakers (again, six pre- and six post-training). In addition, three groups of undergraduate participants made judgments on the same 24 videotapes: (1) a feedback group, which received feedback on accuracy following each judgment they made; (2) a feedback plus cue information group, which was given feedback and information on empirically based cues to lying; and (3) a control group, which received no feedback or cue information. It was found that at baseline all groups performed at or below chance levels. However, overall, all groups including the parole officers became significantly better at detecting deception than the control group. By the final set of judgments, the parole officers were significantly more accurate (with an average of 76.7 percent) than their baseline performance (average of 40.4 percent). These results indicated that detecting lies is very difficult, but that training could help.

There are many other examples of practical training in Canada. Psychologists such as John Yuille have trained many groups of police officers, lawyers, and social workers in appropriate interviewing techniques with children. For decades, Don Dutton has trained police officers in domestic violence intervention (as well as providing treatment to the abusers). Robert Hare and colleagues such as Adelle Forth (at Carleton University) train staff in the use of the Psychopathy Checklist-Revised (Hare, 1991, 2003). Other psychologists offer training in a variety of well-validated risk-assessment tools developed in Canada. For example, the **Mental Health, Law, and Policy Institute** in British Columbia (director Dr. Ronald Roesch) is associated with the Simon Fraser psychology and law and criminology programs, and offers research and training in areas related to mental health law and policy (see http://www2.sfu.ca/mhlpi/). They offer specialized training to legal staff in the HCR-20 (Webster, Douglas, Eaves, & Hart, 1997) for evaluating risk for violence, the SVR-20 (Boer, Hart, Kropp, & Webster, 1997) for evaluating sexual violence risk, and the FIT (Roesch, Zapf, Eaves, & Webster, 1998) for evaluating fitness to stand trial. Similarly, the mandate of the **Centre for Criminal Justice Studies** (director Dr. Paul Gendreau) at the University of New Brunswick in Saint John is threefold: (1) to disseminate bodies of knowledge in the criminal justice area that meet the policy and practical needs of public and community-based organizations that address antisocial behaviour, (2) to provide consultation and training to legal professionals and community groups (e.g., parole, probation, prisons, policing, victim services, legislative and legal reform, etc.), and (3) to conduct research in areas with practical significance (see http://www.unbsj.ca/arts/psychology/ccjs.html).

SUMMARY

Canada has a tradition of excellence in forensic psychology. Beginning in the 1960s, academic researchers began to set the stage for new generations of researchers and practitioners in our field. While few of them were formally trained in forensic psychology, their research in diverse areas, including forensic aspects of memory, criminal behaviour, and forensic assessment, were pioneering and led to the generation of numerous fertile research programs across the country.

At present, forensic psychologists are having a great impact in Canada, in terms of research, practice, and training. Several Canadian universities offer formalized and less structured training in the field, at both the undergraduate and graduate levels. At the same time, we need to create more such programs in light of the field's basic scientific importance, relevance in the legal system, and the increasing interest from students hoping to pursue a career in forensic psychology.

KEY TERMS

American Psychology-Law Society, p. 333
Behavioral Sciences and the Law, p. 334
Centre for Criminal Justice Studies, p. 338
Criminal Justice and Behavior, p. 334

SUGGESTED READINGS

Canadian Journal of Behavioural Science (April, 2004, Volume 36). Special Issue on Forensic Psychology.

This issue reports seven new empirical studies (six of them Canadian) in forensic psychology. This will give students an idea of the kind of interesting work happening in the field.

The following three papers by James Ogloff give an evolving historical and contemporary overview of graduate education in psychology and law, with attention to the Canadian context:

Ogloff, J. R. P. (1990). Law and psychology in Canada: The need for training and research. *Canadian Psychology, 31*, 61–73.

Ogloff, J. R. P. (1999). Graduate training in law and psychology at Simon Fraser University. *Professional Psychology: Research and Practice, 30*, 99–103.

Ogloff, J. R. P. (2000). Two steps forward and one step backward: The law and psychology movement(s) in the 20th century. *Law and Human Behavior, 24*, 457–483.

References

A. B. v. T. S. (2000) BCSC 976.

Abidin, R. (1990). *Parenting Stress Index* (3rd ed.). Odessa, FL: Psychological Assessment Resources.

Abidin, R. R. (1998, August). *Parenting Stress Index: Its empirical validation.* Paper presented at the meetings of the American Psychological Association, San Francisco.

Acker, J. R. (1990). Social science in Supreme Court criminal cases and briefs: The actual and potential contribution of social scientists as *amicus curiae. Law and Human Behavior, 14,* 25–42.

Acker, J. R., & Toch, H. (1985). Battered women, straw men, and expert testimony: A comment on *State v. Kelly. Criminal Law Bulletin, 21,* 125–155.

Ackerman, M. J. (1994). *Clinician's guide to child custody evaluations.* New York: John Wiley.

Ackerman, M. J., & Ackerman, M. (1997). Custody evaluation practices: A survey of experienced professionals (revisited). *Professional Psychology: Research and Practice, 28,* 137–145.

Ackerman, M. J., & Schoendorf, K. (1992). *Ackerman-Schoendorf Scales for Parent Evaluation of Custody (ASPECT): Manual.* Los Angeles: Western Psychological Services.

Adarand Constructors, Inc. v. Pena, 115 S.Ct. 2097 (1995).

Adler, S. J. (1994). *The jury: Trial and error in the American courtroom.* New York: Times Books.

Adler, T. (1993, September). APA files amicus brief in grant application case. *APA Monitor*, p. 26.

Ainsworth, P. B. (1995). *Psychology and policing in a changing world.* Chichester, UK: Wiley.

Albiston, C. R., Maccoby, E. E., & Mnookin, R. H. (1990). Does joint legal custody matter? *Stanford Law and Policy Review, 2,* 167–179.

Allan, A. & Louw, D. A. (1997). The ultimate opinion rule and psychologists: A comparison of the expectations and experiences of South African lawyers. *Behavioral Sciences and the Law, 15,* 307–320.

Allen, S. W., Cutler, B. L., & Berman, G. L. (1993, August). *Analyses comparing various hostage negotiation techniques.* Paper presented at the meetings of the American Psychological Association, Toronto.

Allison, J. A., & Wrightsman, L. S. (1993). *Rape: The misunderstood crime.* Thousand Oaks, CA: Sage.

American Law Institute. (1962). *Model penal code.* Washington, DC: American Law Institute.

American Psychiatric Association. (1987). *Diagnostic and statistical manual of mental disorders—Revised* (3rd ed.). Washington: American Psychiatric Association.

American Psychiatric Association. (1994). *Diagnostic and statistical manual of mental disorders* (4th ed.). Washington, DC: American Psychiatric Association.

American Psychological Association. (1995). *Lesbian and gay parenting: A resource for psychologists.* Washington, DC: American Psychological Association.

Angus-Reid (1992). Sexual harassment in the workplace. *The Reid Report, 32*(7), 1.

Annin, P. (1970, December 10). Unfriendly persuasion. *Newsweek,* p. 73.

Anson, R. S. (1998, July). The devil and Jeffrey MacDonald. *Vanity Fair,* pp. 46–68.

Arditti, J. A. (1995). Review of the Ackerman-Schoendorf Scales for Parental Evaluation of Custody. In J. C. Conoley & J. C. Impara (Eds.), *Twelfth mental measurements yearbook* (pp. 20–22). Lincoln: University of Nebraska Press.

Arnett, P. A., Hammeke, T. A., & Schwartz, L. (1993, August). *Quantitative and qualitative performance on Rey's 15–item test.* Paper presented at the meetings of the American Psychological Association, Toronto.

Aron, C. J. (1993, July 19). Women battered by life and law lose twice. *National Law Journal,* pp. 13–14.

Aronson, E. (1990, November). *Subtle coercion during police interrogation: The Bradley Page murder trial.* Invited address, Williams College, Williamstown, MA.

Aronson, E. (1992). *The social animal* (6th ed.). New York: W. H. Freeman.

Aronson, E., & Bridgeman, D. (1992). Jigsaw groups and the desegregated classroom: In pursuit of common goals. In E. Aronson (Ed.), *Readings on the social animal* (pp. 430–440). New York: W. H. Freeman.

Aronson, E., Stephan, C., Sikes, J., Blaney, N., & Snapp, N. (1978). *The jigsaw classroom.* Thousand Oaks, CA: Sage.

Arvey, R. D., & Cavanaugh, M. A. (1995). Using surveys to assess the prevalence of sexual harassment: Some methodological problems. *Journal of Social Issues, 51*(1), 39–52.

Asch, S. E. (1956). Studies of independence and conformity: A minority of one against a unanimous majority. *Psychological Monographs, 70* (9, Whole No. 416).

Associated Press. (1986, May 12). A crime that doesn't pay. *Kansas City Star,* p. A5.

Associated Press. (1992, February 23). FBI says 25 serial killers are still at large. *Lawrence Journal-World,* p. 13C.

Associated Press. (1993, November 4). Tape of therapy allowed in trial of two brothers. *New York Times,* p. A7.

Associated Press. (1994a, October 19). Man kills his wife for infidelity, and gets an 18-month sentence. *New York Times,* p. C19.

Associated Press. (1997, March 17). Psychologist report offers insight to O. J. guardianship. *Lawrence Journal-World,* p. 5A.

Aubry, A., & Caputo, R. (1965). *Criminal interrogation.* Springfield, IL: Charles C Thomas.

Aubry, A., & Caputo, R. (1980). *Criminal interrogation* (3rd ed.). Springfield, IL: Charles C Thomas.

B. v. B., 242 S.E. 2d 248 (W. Va. 1978).

Bagby, R. M., Nicholson, R. A., Rogers, R., & Nussbaum, D. (1992). Domains of competency to stand trial: A factor analytic study. *Law and Human Behavior, 16,* 491–508.

Bai, M., & Smith, V. E. (1999, March 8). Evil to the end. *Newsweek,* pp. 22–24.

Bailey, I. (1999, August 11). *Diving rod led searcher to dead girl.* Retrieved on August 23, 2004, from: http://www.100megsfree4.com/farshores/divining.htm.

Baker, M. (1985). *Cops: Their lives in their own words.* New York: Pocket Books.

Bala, N., Lee, K., Lindsay, R., Talwar, V. (2001). A legal and psychological critique of the present approach to the assessment of the competence of the child witness. *Osgoode Hall Law Journal, 38,* 409–451.

Baldus, D. C., & Cole, J. W. (1980). *Statistical proof of discrimination.* New York: McGraw-Hill.

Barak, A. (1992). Combatting sexual harassment. *American Psychologist, 47,* 818–819.

Barbaree, H., Seto, M., Serin, R., Amos, N., & Preston, D. (1994). Comparisons between sexual and non-sexual rapist subtypes. *Criminal Justice & Behavior, 21,* 95–114.

Barber, T. X., & Wilson, S. C. (1978–1979). The Barber Suggestibility Scale and the Creative Imagination Scale: Experimental and clinical applications. *American Journal of Clinical Hypnosis, 21,* 84–96.

Bard, M., & Sangrey, D. (1979). *The crime victim's book.* New York: Basic Books.

Barefoot v. Estelle, 463 U.S. 880 (1983).

Barland, G. H. (1981). *A validity and reliability study of counter-intelligence screening test.* Security Support Battalion, 902nd Military Intelligence Group, Fort Meade, MD.

Barland, G. H., & Raskin, D. C. (1975). An evaluation of field techniques in detection and deception. *Psychophysiology, 12,* 321–330.

Barnett, O. W., & LaViolette, A. D. (1993). *It could happen to anyone: Why battered women stay.* Thousand Oaks, CA: Sage.

Barr, J. (1979). *Within a dark wood.* Garden City, NY: Doubleday.

Barrett, G. V., & Morris, S. B. (1993). The American Psychological Association's amicus curiae brief in *Price Waterhouse v. Hopkins:* The values of science versus the values of the law. *Law and Human Behavior, 17,* 201–215.

Barrett, L. I. (1991, June 3). Cheating on the tests. *Time,* p. 57.

Bartlett, F. (1932). *Remembering: A study in experimental and social psychology.* Cambridge: Cambridge University.

Bartol, C. R. (1991). Predictive validation of the MMPI for small-town police officers who fail. *Professional Psychology: Research and Practice, 22,* 127–132.

Bartol, C. R., & Bartol, A. M. (1999). History of forensic psychology. In A. K. Hess & I. B. Weiner (Eds.), *Handbook of forensic psychology* (2nd ed., pp. 3–23). New York: John Wiley.

Basow, S. (1986). *Gender stereotypes.* Pacific Grove, CA: Brooks/Cole.

Bassuk, E. (1980). The crisis theory perspective on rape. In S. L. McCombie (Ed.), *The rape crisis intervention handbook* (pp. 121–129). New York: Plenum.

Bastian, L. D., Lancaster, A. R., & Reyst, H. E. (1996). *Department of Defense 1995 Sexual Harassment Survey* (DMDC Report 96–014). Washington, DC: Defense Manpower Data Center.

Bazelon, D. (1982). Veils, values, and social responsibility. *American Psychologist, 37,* 115–121.

Beaber, R., Marston, A., Michelli, J., & Mills, M. (1985). A brief test for measuring malingering in schizophrenic individuals. *American Journal of Psychiatry, 144,* 1478–1481.

Becker, J. V., & Murphy, W. D. (1998). What we know and do not know about assessing and treating sex offenders. *Psychology, Public Policy, and Law, 4,* 116–137.

Becker, J. V., Skinner, L. J., Abel, G. G., Axelrod, R., & Treacy, E. C. (1984). Depressive symptoms associated with sexual assault. *Journal of Sex and Marital Therapy, 10,* 185–192.

Bedau, H. A., & Radelet, M. L. (1987). Miscarriages of justice in potentially capital cases. *Stanford Law Review, 40,* 21–179.

Bekerian, D. A., & Jackson, J. L. (1997). Critical issues in offender profiling. In J. L. Jackson & D. A. Bekerian (Eds.), *Offender profiling: Theory, research and practice* (pp. 209–220). New York: John Wiley.

Benedetto, R. (1995, July 25). 3 of 4: Retain programs that combat bias. *USA Today,* p. 3A.

Bennett, C., & Hirshhorn, R. (1993). *Bennett's guide to jury selection and trial dynamics in civil and criminal litigation.* St. Paul, MN: West.

Benokraitis, N.V., & Feagin, J. R. (1986). *Modern sexism: Blatant, subtle, and covert discrimination.* Englewood Cliffs, NJ: Prentice-Hall.

Berlin, F. S. (1994). Jeffrey Dahmer: Was he ill? Was he impaired? Insanity revisited. *American Journal of Forensic Psychiatry, 15,* 5–29.

Berliner, L. (1998). The use of expert testimony in child sexual abuse cases. In S. J. Ceci & H. Hembrooke (Eds.), *Expert witnesses in child abuse cases* (pp. 11–27). Washington, DC: American Psychological Association.

Bermant, G. (1986). Two conjectures about the issue of expert testimony. *Law and Human Behavior, 10,* 97–100.

Bernard, L. C., & Fowler, W. (1990). Assessing the validity of memory complaints: Performance of brain-damaged and normal individuals on Rey's test to detect malingering. *Journal of Clinical Psychology, 46,* 432–436.

Bersoff, D. N. (1987). Social science data and the Supreme Court: Lockhart as a case in point. American Psychologist, 42, 52–58.

Bersoff, D. N. (1981). Testing and the law. *American Psychologist, 36,* 1047–1056.

Bersoff, D. N. (1993, August). *Daubert v. Merrell Dow: Issues and outcome.* Paper presented at the meetings of the American Psychological Association, Toronto.

Beutler, L. E., Nussbaum, P. D., & Meredith, K. E. (1988). Changing personality patterns of police officers. *Professional Psychology: Research and Practice, 19,* 503–507.

Biernat, M., & Crandall, C. S. (1999). Racial attitudes. In J. P. Robinson, P. R. Shaver, & L. S. Wrightsman (Eds.), *Measures of political attitudes* (pp. 297–411). San Diego: Academic Press.

Bischoff, L. G. (1995). Review of Parent Awareness Skills Survey. In J. C. Conoley & J. C. Impara (Eds.), *Twelfth mental measurements yearbook* (pp. 735–736). Lincoln: University of Nebraska Press.

Blackman, J. (1986). Potential used for expert testimony: Ideas toward the representation of battered women who kill. *Women's Rights Law Reporter, 9* (3 & 4), 227–238.

Blackman, J., & Brickman, E. (1984). The impact of expert testimony on trials of battered women who kill their husbands. *Behavioral Sciences and the Law, 2,* 413–422.

Blackshaw, S., Chandarana, P., Garneau, Y., Merskey, H., & Moscarello, R. (1996). *Adult Recovered Memories of Childhood Sexual Abuse.* Retrieved July 16, 2004, from the Canadian Psychiatric Association Web site: http://www.cpa-apc.org/French_Site/Publications/Position_Papers/Adult.asp.

Blagrove, M. (1996). Effects of length of sleep deprivation on interrogative suggestibility. *Journal of Experimental Psychology: Applied, 2,* 48–59.

Blau, T. H. (1994). *Psychological services for law enforcement.* New York: John Wiley.

Blinkhorn, S. (1988). Lie detection as a psychometric procedure. In A. Gale (Ed.), *The polygraph test: Lies, truth and science* (pp. 29–38). London: Sage.

Block, A. P. (1990). Rape trauma syndrome as scientific expert testimony. *Archives of Sexual Behavior, 19,* 309–323.

Blumenthal, J. A. (1998). The reasonable woman standard: A meta-analytic review of gender differences in perceptions of sexual harassment. *Law and Human Behavior, 22,* 33–57.

Boat, B. W., & Everson, M. D. (1988). Use of anatomical dolls among professionals in sexual abuse evaluation. *Child Abuse and Neglect, 12,* 171–174.

Bochnak, E. (Ed.). (1981). *Women's self defense cases: Theory and practice.* Charlottesville, VA: Michie Press.

Boehm, V. R. (1968). Mr. Prejudice, Miss Sympathy, and the authoritarian personality: An application of psychological measuring techniques to the problem of jury bias. *Wisconsin Law Review, 1968,* 734–750.

Boer, D. P., Hart, S. D., Kropp, P. R., & Webster, C. D. (1997). *Sexual Violence Risk-20 (SVR-20): Professional guidelines for assessing violence risk.* Simon Fraser University, BC: Mental Health, Law and Policy Institute.

Boeschen, L. E., Sales, B. D., & Koss, M. P. (1998). Rape trauma experts in the courtroom. *Psychology, Public Policy, and Law, 4,* 414–432.

Boland, P. L., & Quirk, S. A. (1994). At issue: Should child abuse be prosecuted decades after an alleged incident occurred? *American Bar Association Journal, 80,* 42.

Bolton, B. (1985). Review of Inwald Personality Inventory. In J. V. Mitchell (Ed.), *Ninth mental measurements yearbook* (pp. 711–713). Lincoln: Buros Institute of Mental Measurements, University of Nebraska.

Bond, S. B., & Mosher, D. L. (1986). Guided imagery of rape: Fantasy, reality, and the willing victim myth. *Journal of Sex Research, 22,* 162–183.

Bonnie, R., & Slobogin, C. (1980). The role of mental health professionals in the criminal process: The case for informed speculation. *Virginia Law Review, 66,* 427–522.

Borchard, E. M. (1932). *Convicting the innocent: Sixty-five actual errors of criminal justice.* Garden City, NY: Doubleday.

Borgida, E., & Fiske, S. T. (Eds.). (1995). Gender stereotyping, sexual harassment, and the law. *Journal of Social Issues, 51*(1), 1–207.

Borgida, E., & Nisbett, R. (1977). The differential impact of abstract vs. concrete information on decisions. *Journal of Applied Social Psychology, 7,* 258–271.

Borum, R. (1988). A comparative study of negotiator effectiveness with "mentally disturbed hostage-taker" scenarios. *Journal of Police and Criminal Psychology, 4,* 17–20.

Borum, R. (1998). Forensic assessment instruments. In G. P. Koocher, J. C. Norcross, & S. S. Hill, III (Eds.), *Psychologists' desk reference* (pp. 487–491). New York: Oxford University Press.

Borum, R., & Fulero, S. M. (1999). Empirical research on the insanity defense and attempted reforms: Evidence toward informed policy. *Law and Human Behavior, 23,* 117–135.

Bothwell, R. K., Deffenbacher, K. A., & Brigham, J. C. (1987). Correlation of eyewitness accuracy and confidence: Optimality hypothesis revisited. *Journal of Applied Psychology, 72,* 691–695.

Bottoms, B. L., & Davis, S. (1993, September). Scientific evidence no longer subject to "Frye test." *APA Monitor,* p. 14.

Boudreau v. The King (1949). 94 C.C.C. 1 (S.C.C.).

Bovard, J. (1994, November). Drug-courier profiles. *Playboy,* pp. 46–48.

Bowen, W. G., & Bok, D. (1998). *The shape of the river: Long-term consequences of considering race in college and university admissions.* Princeton, NJ: Princeton University Press.

Bragg, R. (1995, July 18). Sheriff says prayer and a lie led Susan Smith to confess. *New York Times,* pp. A1, A8.

Brandt, J. R., Kennedy, W. A., Patrick, C. J., & Curtain, J. J. (1997). Assessment of psychopathy in a population of incarcerated adolescent offenders. *Psychological Assessment, 9,* 429–435.

Braswell, A. L. (1987). Resurrection of the ultimate issue rule: Federal Rule of Evidence 704(b) and the insanity defense. *Cornell Law Review, 72,* 620–640.

Brekke, N., & Borgida, E. (1988). Expert scientific testimony in rape trials: A social-cognitive analysis. *Journal of Personality and Social Psychology, 55,* 372–386.

Brenner, M. (1997, February). American nightmare: The ballad of Richard Jewell. *Vanity Fair,* pp. 100–107, 150–165.

Breslau, N., Davis, G. C. D., Andreski, P., & Peterson, E. (1991). Traumatic events and posttraumatic stress disorder in an urban population of young adults. *Archives of General Psychiatry, 48,* 255–264.

Bricklin, B. (1994). *The Bricklin Perceptual Scales: Child-perception-of-parents series.* Furlong, PA: Village.

Bricklin, B. (1995). *The custody evaluation handbook: Research-based solutions and applications.* New York: Brunner-Mazel.

Brigham, J. C. (1971). Ethnic stereotypes. *Psychological Bulletin, 76,* 15–38.

Brigham, J. C. (1992). A personal account of the research expert in court. *Contemporary Psychology, 37,* 529–531.

Brigham, J. C. (1999). What is forensic psychology, anyway? *Law and Human Behavior, 23,* 273–298.

Brigham, J. C., & Bothwell, R. K. (1983). The ability of prospective jurors to estimate the accuracy of eyewitness identifications. *Law and Human Behavior, 7,* 19–30.

Brigham, J. C., Maass, A., Snyder, L. D., & Spaulding, K. (1982). Accuracy of eyewitness identifications in a field setting. *Journal of Personality and Social Psychology, 42,* 673–681.

Brigham, J. C., & Wolfskeil, M. P. (1983). Opinions of attorneys and law enforcement personnel on the accuracy of eyewitness identifications. *Law and Human Behavior, 7,* 337–349.

Bristow, A. R. (1984). *State v. Marks:* An analysis of expert testimony on rape trauma syndrome. *Victimology: An International Journal, 9,* 273–281.

British Columbia Ministry of Women's Equality (2001). *Women's economic security and pay equity: Discussion paper.* Victoria, BC: Ministry of Women's Equality.

British Psychological Society. (1986). Report of the working group on the use of the polygraph in criminal investigations and personnel screening. *Bulletin of the British Psychological Society, 39,* 81–94.

Brodsky, S. L. (1991). *Testifying in court: Guidelines and maxims for the expert witness.* Washington, DC: American Psychological Association.

Brott, A. A. (1994, August 8–14). The facts take a battering. *Washington Post National Weekly Edition,* pp. 24–25.

Brown v. Board of Education of Topeka, 347 U.S. 483 (1954).

Brown v. Mississippi, 297 U.S. 278 (1936).

Brown, D., Scheflin, A. W., & Hammond, D. C. (1998). *Memory, trauma, treatment, and the law.* New York: Norton.

Brown, E., Deffenbacher, K., & Sturgill, W. (1977). Memory for faces and the circumstances of encounters. *Journal of Applied Psychology, 62,* 311–318.

Brown, L., & Willis, A. (1985). Authoritarianism in British recruits: Importation, socialization, or myth? *Journal of Occupational Psychology, 58,* 97–108.

Brown, N. (1996). *Can judges decide?* Unpublished manuscript, Department of Psychology, University of Kansas, Lawrence, KS.

Browne, A. (1984, August). *Assault and homicide at home: When battered women kill.* Paper presented at the Second National Conference for Family Violence Researchers, Durham, NH.

Browne, A. (1987). *When battered women kill.* New York: Free Press.

Browne, A., & Williams, K. (1989). Resource availability for women at risk and partner homicide. *Law and Society Review, 23,* 75.

Brownmiller, S. (1975). *Against our will: Men, women, and rape.* New York: Simon & Schuster.

Brownmiller, S., & Alexander, D. (1992, January/February). From Carmita Wood to Anita Hill. *Ms. Magazine,* pp. 70–71.

Bruck, M. (1998). The trials and tribulations of a novice expert witness. In S. J. Ceci & H. Hembrooke (Eds.), *Expert witnesses in child abuse cases* (pp. 85–104). Washington, DC: American Psychological Association.

Bruck, M., & Ceci, S. J. (1993). *Amicus brief for the case of State of New Jersey v. Michaels presented by Committee of Concerned Social Scientists.* Supreme Court of New Jersey, Docket #36,333. (Reprinted in *Psychology, Public Policy, and Law,* 1995, *1,* 272–322.)

Bruck, M., & Ceci, S. J. (1999). The suggestibility of children's memory. *Annual Review of Psychology, 50,* 419–439.

Bruck, M, Ceci, S. J., & Francouer, E. (2000). Children's use of anatomically detailed dolls to report on genital touching in a medical examination: Developmental and gender comparisons. *Journal of Experimental Psychology: Applied, 6,* 74–83.

Bruck, M., Ceci, S. J., Francouer, E., & Renick, A. (1995). Anatomically detailed dolls do not facilitate preschoolers' reports of pediatric examination involving genital touching. *Journal of Experimental Psychology: Applied, 1,* 95–109.

Bruck, M., Ceci, S. J., & Hembrooke, H. (1998). Reliability and credibility of young children's reports: From research to policy and practice. *American Psychologist, 53,* 136–151.

Brussel, J. A. (1968). *Casebook of a crime psychiatrist.* New York: Bernard Geis.

Buckhout, R. (1974). Eyewitness testimony. *Scientific American, 231,* 23–31.

Buckhout, R. (1983). Psychologist v. the judge: Expert testimony on identification. *Social Action and the Law, 9*(3), 67–76.

Buckhout, R., & Friere, V. (1975). *Suggestibility in lineups and photospreads: A casebook for lawyers* (Center for Responsive Psychology Monograph No. CR-5). New York: Brooklyn College.

Bulkley, J. A., & Horwitz, M. J. (1994). Adults sexually abused as children: Legal actions and issues. *Behavioral Sciences and the Law, 12,* 65–87.

Bull, R. H. (1988). What is the lie-detector test? In A. Gale (Ed.), *The polygraph test: Lies, truth and science* (pp. 10–18). London: Sage.

Burge, S. K. (1988). Post-traumatic stress disorder in victims of rape. *Journal of Traumatic Stress, 1*(2), 193–209.

Burgess, A. W., & Holmstrom, L. L. (1974). Rape trauma syndrome. *American Journal of Psychiatry, 131,* 981–999.

Burgess, A. W., & Holmstrom, L. L. (1985). Rape trauma syndrome and post-traumatic stress response. In A. W. Burgess (Ed.), *Research handbook on rape and sexual assault* (pp. 46– 61). New York: Garland.

Burtt, H. (1931). *Legal psychology.* Englewood Cliffs, NJ: Prentice-Hall.

Butcher, J. N., Dahlstrom, W. G., Graham, J. R., Tellegen, A., & Kaemmer, B. (1989). *The Minnesota Multiphasic Personality Inventory-2 (MMPI-2): Manual for administration and scoring.* Minneapolis: University of Minnesota Press.

Buxton, A. (1999). The best interest of children of gay and lesbian parents. In R. Galatzer-Levy, L. Krauss, & B. Leventhal (Eds.), *The scientific basis for custody decisions in divorce* (pp. 319–356). New York: John Wiley.

Byczynski, L. (1987, December 29). Is joint custody better? *Kansas City Times,* pp. A1, A4.

Campagna, V. (1998, July 29). Personal communication via e-mail.

Campbell, M. A., Porter, S., & Santor, D. (2004). Psychopathic traits in adolescent offenders: An evaluation of criminal history, clinical, and psychosocial correlates. *Behavioral Sciences and the Law, 22,* 23–47.

CBC News Online (2004, January 19). *Halifax police chief apologizes in discrimination case.* Retrieved on May 14, 2004, from the Canadian Broadcasting Corporation Web site: http://www.cbc.ca/stories/2004/01/19/johnson040119.

CBC News Online (2004, January 20). *Documents detail Toronto drug squad corruption.* Retrieved on May 14, 2004, from the Canadian Broadcasting Corporation Web site: http://www.cbc.ca/stories/2004/01/20/toronto-probe040120.

CBC News Online (2004, July 23). *Peel chief under fire for comments.* Retrieved on August 12, 2004, from the Canadian Broadcasting Corporation Web site: http://toronto.cbc.ca/regional/servlet/View?filename=to_peelzhang20040723.

Canada Labor Code (R.S. 1985, c. L-2). Retrieved on July 7, 2004, from the Department of Justice Canada Web site: http://laws.justice.gc.ca/en/L-2/.

Canadian Centre for Justice Statistics (2000). Statistics Canada Catalogue no. 85-225-XIE.

Canadian Centre for Justice Statistics (2004). *Family violence in Canada: A statistical profile 2004.* Statistics Canada Catalogue no. 85-224-XIE.

Canadian Charter of Rights and Freedoms (1982). Retrieved on May 14, 2004, from the Department of Justice Canada Web site: http://laws.justice.gc.ca/en/charter/.

Canadian Human Rights Act (R.S. 1985, c. H-6). Retrieved on July 7, 2004, from the Department of Justice Canada Web site: http://laws.justice.gc.ca/en/H-6/.

Canadian Professional Police Association (n.d.). *The History of the Memorial Service.* Retrieved on July 5, 2004, from the Canadian Professional Police Association Web site: http://www.cpa-acp.ca/memorial/history.htm.

Canadian Professional Police Association (n.d.). *Canadian Professional Police Association: The Memorial.* Retrieved on October 3, 2004, from the Canadian Professional Police Association Web site: http://www.cppa-acpp.ca/index-english.htm.

Cannon, L. (1998). *Official negligence: How Rodney King and the riots changed Los Angeles and the LAPD.* New York: Times Books.

Caplan, L. (1984). *The insanity defense and the trial of John W. Hinckley, Jr.* New York: David R. Godine.

Carelli, R. (1997, December 7). High court to rule in harassment case. *Kansas City Star,* pp. A1, A22.

Carlson, H. M., & Sutton, M. S. (1975). The effects of different police roles on attitudes and values. *Journal of Psychology, 91,* 57–64.

Carlson, R. A. (1995). Review of the Perception-of-Relationship Test. In J. C. Conoley & J. C. Impara (Eds.), *Twelfth mental measurements yearbook* (p. 746). Lincoln: University of Nebraska Press.

Carr, C. (1994). *The alienist.* New York: Random House.

Carr, C. (1997). *The angel of darkness.* New York: Ballantine.

Carroll, D. (1988). How accurate is polygraph lie detection? In A. Gale (Ed.), *The polygraph test: Lies, truth and science* (pp. 19–28). London: Sage.

Carroll, J. S. (1980). An appetizing look at law and psychology. *Contemporary Psychology, 25,* 362–363.

Carson, D. (1988). Risk: A four letter word for lawyers. In P. J. Hessing & G. Van den Heuvel (Eds.), *Lawyers on psychology and psychologists on law* (pp. 57–63). Amsterdam: Swets & Zeitlinger.

Casey, S. (1994). Homosexual parents and Canadian child custody law. *Family & Conciliation Courts Review, 32,* 379–396.

Cassell, P. G. (1996a). All benefits, no costs: The grand illusion of *Miranda's* defenders. *Northwestern University Law Review, 90,* 1084–1124.

Cassell, P. G. (1996b). *Miranda's* social costs: An empirical reassessment. *Northwestern University Law Review, 90,* 387–499.

Cassell, P. G. (1998). Protecting the innocent from false confessions and lost confessions—and from *Miranda. Journal of Criminal Law and Criminology, 78,* 497–556.

Cassell, P. G., & Hayman, B. S. (1996). Police interrogation in the 1990s: An empirical study of the effects of *Miranda. UCLA Law Review, 43,* 839–931.

Cattell, J. McK. (Ed.). (1894). *Proceedings of the American Psychological Association.* New York: Macmillan.

Ceci, S. J., & Bruck, M. (1993). Suggestibility of the child witness: A historical review and synthesis. *Psychological Bulletin, 113,* 403–439.

Ceci, S. J., & Bruck, M. (1995). *Jeopardy in the courtroom: A scientific analysis of children's testimony.* Washington, DC: American Psychological Association.

Ceci, S. J., & Hembrooke, H. (Eds.). (1998a). *Expert witnesses in child abuse cases.* Washington, DC: American Psychological Association.

Ceci, S. J., & Hembrooke, H. (1998b). Introduction. In S. J. Ceci & H. Hembrooke (Eds.), *Expert witnesses in child abuse cases* (pp. 1–8). Washington, DC: American Psychological Association.

Ceci, S. J., Ross, D. F., & Toglia, M. P. (1987). Suggestibility of children's memory: Psycholegal implications. *Journal of Experimental Psychology: General, 116,* 38–49.

Ceci, S. J., Toglia, M. P., & Ross, D. F. (Eds.). (1987). *Children's eyewitness memory.* New York: Springer-Verlag.

Chamallas, M. (1990). Listening to Dr. Fiske: The easy case of *Price Waterhouse v. Hopkins. Vermont Law Review, 15,* 89–124.

Chandler, J. (1990). *Modern police psychology.* Springfield, IL: Charles C Thomas.

Chang, W. C. (1996). Toward equal opportunities: Fairness, values, and affirmative action programs. *Journal of Social Issues, 52*(4), 93–97.

Chopra, S. R., & Ogloff, J. R. P. (2000). Evaluating jury secrecy: Implications for academic research and juror stress. *Criminal Law Quarterly, 44,* 190–222.

Christianson, S. A., & Hubinette, B. (1993). Hands up! A study of witnesses' emotional reactions and memories associated with bank robberies. *Applied Cognitive Psychology, 7,* 365–379.

Clark, K. B., & Clark, M. P. (1952). Racial identification and preference in Negro children. In G. E. Swanson, T. M. Newcomb, & E. L. Hartley (Eds.), *Readings in social psychology* (Rev. ed., pp. 551–560). New York: Holt.

Clark, M. (1997). *Without a doubt.* New York: Viking Penguin.

Clark, M., & Grier, P. E. (1993, August). *Using the Multiphasic Sex Inventory with child molesters.* Paper presented at the meetings of the American Psychological Association, Toronto.

Clayton, S. D., & Crosby, F. J. (1992). *Justice, gender, and affirmative action.* Ann Arbor: University of Michigan Press.

Clifford, B. R., & Scott, J. (1978). Individual and situational factors in eyewitness testimony. *Journal of Applied Psychology, 63,* 352–359.

Clingempeel, W. G., & Reppucci, N. D. (1982). Joint custody after divorce: Major issues and goals for research. *Psychological Bulletin, 91,* 102–127.

Cloud, J. (1998, March 23). Sex and the law. *Time,* pp. 48–54.

Cockburn, A., & Cockburn, P. (1999). *Out of the ashes: The resurrection of Saddam Hussein.* New York: HarperCollins.

Cohn, D. S. (1991). Anatomical doll play of preschoolers referred for sexual abuse and those not referred. *Child Abuse and Neglect, 15,* 567–573.

Cole, D. (1999). *No equal justice: Race and class in the American criminal justice system.* New York: New Press.

Commission on Accreditation for Law Enforcement Agencies. (2004). Retrieved on October 3, 2004, from the Commission for Law Enforcement Agencies Web site: http://www.calea.org.

Conger, J. (1995). Review of Perception-of-Relationships Test. In J. C. Conoley & J. C. Impara (Eds.), *Twelfth mental measurements yearbook* (pp. 747–748). Lincoln: University of Nebraska Press.

Connolly, D. A., & Read, J. D. (2003). Remembering historical child sexual abuse. *The Criminal Law Quarterly, 47,* 438–480.

Connolly, D. A., & Read, J. D. (2004, in press). *Delayed prosecutions of historic child sexual abuse: Analyses of 2064 Canadian criminal complaints.*

Conte, J. R., Sorenson, E., Fogarty, L., & Rosa, J. (1991). Evaluating children's reports of sexual abuse: Results from a survey of professionals. *American Journal of Orthopsychiatry, 61,* 428–437.

Cook, S. W. (1971). *The effect of unintended interracial contact upon racial interaction and attitude change.* Final report, U.S. Department of Health, Education, and Welfare, Office of Education, Project No. 5–1320.

Cook, S. W. (1978). Interpersonal and attitudinal outcomes in cooperating interracial groups. *Journal of Research and Development in Education, 12,* 97–113.

Cook, S. W. (1979). Social science and school desegregation: Did we mislead the Supreme Court? *Personality and Social Psychology Bulletin, 5,* 420–434.

Cook, S. W. (1984). The 1959 social science statement and school segregation: A reply to Gerard. *American Psychologist, 39,* 819–832.

Cooper, D. K., & Grisso, T. (1997). Five year research update (1991–1995): Evaluations for competence to stand trial. *Behavioral Sciences and the Law, 15,* 347–364.

Cornwell, P. D. (1991). *Body of evidence.* New York: Charles Scribner's.

Correctional Service of Canada (1995). Federal offender family violence: Estimates from a national file review study. *Forum, 7.*

Court TV. (1992). *The insanity trial of Jeffrey Dahmer* (video). New York: Court TV.

Cowan, C. L., Thompson, W. C., & Ellsworth, P. C. (1984). The effects of death qualification on jurors' predispositions to convict and on the quality of deliberation. *Law and Human Behavior, 8,* 53–79.

Cox, G. D. (1991, October 28). Assumption of risks. *National Law Journal,* pp. 1, 24–25.

Cox, G. D. (1992, August 3). Tort tales lash back. *National Law Journal,* pp. 1, 36–37.

Craig, K. M., & Waldo, C. R. (1996). "So, what's a hate crime anyway?" Young adults' perceptions of hate crimes, victims, and perpetrators. *Law and Human Behavior, 20,* 113–129.

Cramer, D. (1986). Gay parents and their children: A review of research and practical implications. *Journal of Counseling and Development, 64,* 504–507.

Crenshaw, M. (1986). The psychology of political terrorism. In M. G. Hermann (Ed.), *Political psychology* (pp. 379–413). San Francisco: Jossey-Bass.

Crichton, M. (1993). *Disclosure.* New York: Knopf.

Criminal Code (R.S. 1985, c. C-46). Retrieved on August 23, 2004, from the Department of Justice Web site: http://laws.justice.gc.ca/en/C-46/.

Crocker, P. L. (1985). The meaning of equality for battered women who kill men in self-defense. *Harvard Women's Law Review, 8,* 121–153.

Crosby, F. (1994, September 8). *Affirmative action: Illusions and realities.* Ferne Forman Fisher Lecture, University of Kansas, Lawrence, KS.

Cutler, B. L., Berman, G. L., Penrod, S. D., & Fisher, R. P. (1994). Conceptual, practical, and empirical issues associated with eyewitness identification test media. In D. F. Ross, J. D. Read, & M. P. Toglia (Eds.), *Adult eyewitness testimony: Current trends and developments* (pp. 163–181). New York: Cambridge University Press.

Cutler, B. L., Moran, G., & Narby, D. J. (1992). Jury selection in insanity defense cases. *Journal of Research in Personality, 26,* 165–182.

Cutler, B. L., & Penrod, S. D. (1988). Context reinstatement and eyewitness identification. In G. M. Davies & D. M. Thomson (Eds.), *Memory in context: Context in memory* (pp. 231–244). New York: John Wiley.

Cutler, B. L., & Penrod, S. D. (1989). Forensically relevant moderators of the relation between eyewitness identification accuracy and confidence. *Journal of Applied Psychology, 74,* 650–652.

Cutler, B. L., & Penrod, S. D. (1995). *Mistaken identification: The eyewitness, psychology, and the law.* New York: Cambridge University Press.

Cutler, B. L., Penrod, S. D., & Martens, T. K. (1987). The reliability of eyewitness identification: The role of system and estimator variables. *Law and Human Behavior, 11,* 233–258.

Dahlstrom, W. G., Welsh, G. S., & Dahlstrom, L. E. (1972). *An MMPI handbook: Vol. 1 Clinical interpretation.* Minneapolis: University of Minnesota Press.

Daily Journal Court Rules Service. (1994, October 21). *The O. J. Simpson juror questionnaire.* Los Angeles, CA: Daily Journal Corporation.

Dallaire, R. (2003). *Shake hands with the devil: The failure of humanity in Rwanda.* Toronto: Random House Canada.

Dane, F. C. (1985). In search of reasonable doubt: A systematic examination of selected quantification approaches. *Law and Human Behavior, 9,* 141–158.

Daubert v. Merrell Dow Pharmaceuticals, Inc., 113 S.Ct. 2786 (1993).

Davis, J. H. (1989). Psychology and the law: The last 15 years. *Journal of Applied Social Psychology, 19,* 199–230.

Davis, J., & Gonzalez, R. (1996, February). *Relative and absolute judgments of eyewitness identification.* Paper presented at the meetings of the American Psychology-Law Society, Hilton Head, SC.

Dawes, R. M. (1988). *Rational choice in an uncertain world.* San Diego: Harcourt Brace Jovanovich.

Dawes, R. M. (1994). *House of cards: Psychology and psychotherapy built on myth.* New York: Free Press.

Dawes, R. M., Faust, D., & Meehl, P.E. (1989). Clinical versus actuarial judgment. *Science, 243,* 1668–1674.

Dawson, J. (1980). Are statistics being fair to employment discrimination plaintiffs? *Jurimetrics Journal, 21,* 1–20.

Deaux, K. (1995). How basic can you be? The evolution of research on gender stereotypes. *Journal of Social Issues, 51*(1), 11–20.

Decker, S. H., & Wagner, A. E. (1982). Race and citizen complaints against the police: An analysis of their interaction. In J. R. Greene (Ed.), *Managing police work: Issues and analysis* (pp. 107–122). Newbury Park, CA: Sage.

Dedman, B. (1998, August 9). Study of assassins concludes there is no common profile. *Kansas City Star,* p. A15.

Deeley, P. (1971). *Beyond the breaking point.* London: Arthur Baker.

Deffenbacher, K. A., & Loftus, E. F. (1982). Do jurors share a common understanding concerning eyewitness behavior? *Law and Human Behavior, 6,* 15–30.

Delprino, R., & Bahn, C. (1988). National survey of the extent and nature of psychological services in police departments. *Professional Psychology, 19,* 421–425.

Dennis, M. (1998, May 8). Personal communication via e-mail.

Devenport, J. L., Penrod, S. D., & Cutler, B. L. (1997). Eyewitness identification evidence: Evaluating common sense evaluations. *Psychology, Public Policy, and Law, 3,* 338–361.

Diamond, S. S. (1990). Scientific jury selection: What social scientists know and don't know. *Judicature, 73*(4), 178–183.

Dietrich, J. F., & Smith, J. (1986). The nonmedical use of drugs including alcohol among police personnel: A critical literature review. *Journal of Police Science and Administration, 14,* 300–306.

Dietz, P. E. (1996). The quest for excellence in forensic psychiatry. *Bulletin of the American Academy of Psychiatry and the Law, 24*(2), 153–163.

Dillehay, R. C., & Nietzel, M. T. (1980). Constructing a science of jury behavior. In L. Wheeler (Ed.), *Review of personality and social psychology* (pp. 246–264). Newbury Park, CA: Sage.

Dingus, A. (1994, September). Wise blood. *Texas Monthly,* pp. 84–88.

Disclosure (2003, January 28a). *Inside the interrogation room: Technique critique.* Retrieved on August 7, 2004, from the Canadian Broadcasting Corporation Web site: http://www.cbc.ca/disclosure/archives/030128_confess/technique.html.

Disclosure (2003, January 28b). *Inside the interrogation room: The Darrelle Exner murder.* Retrieved on August 7, 2004, from the Canadian Broadcasting Corporation Web site: http://www.cbc.ca/disclosure/archives/030128_confess/murder_print.html.

DiVasto, P.V. (1985). Measuring the aftermath of rape. *Journal of Psychosocial Nursing and Mental Health Services, 23,* 33–35.

Dix v. Canada (A.G.), (2002) ABQB 580.

Dodge, K.A. (1991).The structure and function of reactive and proactive aggression. In D. J. Pepler & K. H. Rubin (Eds.), *The development and treatment of childhood aggression* (pp. 1–18). Hillsdale, NJ: Erlbaum.

Doe v. Doe, 111 Va. 736, 284 S.E. 2d 799 (1981).

Doren, D. M. (1998). Recidivism base rates, predictions of sex offender recidivism, and the "Sexual Predator" commitment laws. *Behavioral Sciences and the Law, 16,* 97–114.

Dotto, L. (2004). Liar liar. *National Magazine, 13,* 44–49.

Douglas, J. E., Burgess, A. W., Burgess, A. G., & Ressler, R. (1992). *Crime classification manual.* Lexington, MA: Lexington Books.

Douglas, J. E., & Munn, C. (1992, February).Violent crime scene analysis: Modus operandi, signature, and staging. *F.B.I. Law Enforcement Bulletin,* pp. 1–10.

Douglas, J. E., & Olshaker, M. (1995). *Mindhunter: Inside the FBI's elite serial crime unit.* New York: Charles Scribner's.

Douglas, J., & Olshaker, M. (1997). *Journey into darkness.* New York: Pocket Star Books.

Douglas, J., & Olshaker, M. (1998). *Obsession.* New York: Charles Scribner's.

Douglas, J. E., Ressler, R. K., Burgess, A. W., & Hartman, C. R. (1986). Criminal profiling from crime scene analysis. *Behavioral Sciences and the Law, 4,* 401–421.

Douglas, K., Ogloff, J., Nicholls, T., & Grant, I. (1999). Assessing risk for violence among psychiatric patients: The HCR-20, Violence Risk Assessment Scheme, and the Psychopathy Checklist: Screening Version. *Journal of Consulting and Clinical Psychology, 67,* 917–930.

Douglas, K. S., Huss, M. T., Murdoch, L. L., Washington, D. O. N., & Koch, W. J. (1999). Posttraumatic stress disorder stemming from motor vehicle accidents: Legal issues in Canada and the United States. In E. J. Hickling & E. B. Blanchard (Eds*),* *The international handbook of road traffic accidents & psychological trauma: Current understanding, treatment and law* (pp. 271–289). Oxford: Elsevier.

Dovidio, J. F. (1995). *Bias in evaluative judgments and personnel selection: The role of ambiguity.* Unpublished manuscript, Department of Psychology, Colgate University, Hamilton, NY. (Cited by Dovidio & Gaertner, 1996.)

Dovidio, J. F., & Gaertner, S. L. (Eds.). (1986). *Prejudice, discrimination, and racism.* San Diego, CA: Academic Press.

Dovidio, J. F., & Gaertner, S. L. (1996). Affirmative action, unintentional racial biases, and intergroup relations. *Journal of Social Issues, 52*(4), 51–75.

Doyle, A. C. (1891). A case of identity. In *The original illustrated Sherlock Holmes.* Secaucus, NJ: Castle.

Doyle, A. C. (1892).The man with the twisted lips. In *The original illustrated Sherlock Holmes.* Secaucus, NJ: Castle.

Drinan, R. F. (1973).The rights of children in modern American family law. In A. E. Wilkerson (Ed.), *The rights of children: Emergent concepts in law and society* (pp. 37–46). Philadelphia: Temple University Press.

Drozd, L. M. (1998, August). Domestic Violence and Custody. Paper presented at the meetings of the American Psychological Association, San Francisco.

Dunnette, M. D., & Motowidlo, S. J. (1976, November). *Police selection and career assessment.* Washington, DC: Law Enforcement Assistance Association, United States Department of Justice.

Dubos, R. (1960). *Louis Pasteur: Free Lance of Science.* New York, NY: Da Capo Press.

Durham v. United States, 214 F.2d 862 (D.C. Cir. 1954).

Duthie, B., & McIvor, D. L. (1990). A new system for cluster-coding child molester MMPI profile types. *Criminal Justice and Behavior, 17,* 199–214.

Dutton, D. G. (1981). *The criminal justice system response to wife assault.* Ottawa: Solicitor General of Canada, Research Division.

Dutton, D. G. (1988). *The domestic assault of women: Psychological and criminal justice perspectives.* Boston: Allyn & Bacon.

Dutton, D. G. (1995a). *The batterer: A psychological profile.* New York: Basic Books.

Dutton, D. G. (1995b). *The domestic assault of women: Psychological and criminal justice perspectives* (Rev. ed.). Vancouver: UBC Press.

Dutton, D. G (1998). *The abusive personality: Violence and control in intimate relationships.* New York: Guilford.

Dutton, D. G., & Levens, B. R. (1977). Domestic crisis intervention: Attitude survey of trained and untrained police officers. *Canadian Police College Journal, 1*(2), 75–92.

Dutton, D. G., & McGregor, B. M. S. (1992). Psychological and legal dimensions of family violence. In D. K. Kagehiro & W. S. Laufer (Eds.), *Handbook of psychology and law* (pp. 318–340). New York: Springer-Verlag.

Dutton, M. A. (1992). *Empowering and healing the battered woman: A model for assessment and intervention.* New York: Springer.

Dutton, M. A. (1993). Understanding women's responses to domestic violence: A redefinition of battered woman syndrome. *Hofstra Law Review, 21,* 1191–1242.

Dutton-Douglas, M. A., Perrin, S., & Chrestman, K. (1990, August). *MMPI differences among battered women.* Paper presented at the meetings of the American Psychological Association, Boston.

Dywan, J., Kaplan, R. D., & Pirozzolo, F. J. (1991). Introduction. In J. Dywan, R. D. Kaplan, & F. J. Pirozzolo (Eds.), *Neuropsychology and the law* (pp. xi–xv). New York: Springer-Verlag.

Eaton v. Brant County Board of Education [1997] 1 S.C.R.

Ebbinghaus, H. E. (1885). *Memory: A contribution to experimental psychology.* New York: Dover.

Edens, J. F., Poythress, N. G., & Lilienfeld, S. O. (1999). Identifying inmates at risk for disciplinary infractions: A comparison of two measures of psychopathy. *Behavioral Sciences and the Law, 17,* 435–443.

Egeth, H. E. (1993). What do we *not* know about eyewitness identification? *American Psychologist, 48,* 577–580.

Ekman, P. (1985). *Telling lies: Clues to deceit in the marketplace, politics, and marriage.* New York: Norton.

Ekman, P., & O'Sullivan. M. (1991). Who can catch a liar? *American Psychologist, 46,* 913–920.

Elliott, R. (1987). *Litigating intelligence: IQ tests, special education, and social science in the courtroom.* Dover, MA: Auburn House.

Elliott, R. (1991). Social science data and the APA: The *Lockhart* brief as a case in point. *Law and Human Behavior, 15,* 59–76.

Elliott, R. (1993). Expert testimony about eyewitness identification: A critique. *Law and Human Behavior, 17,* 423–437.

Ellis, H. D., Shepherd, J. W., & Davies, G. M. (1980). The deterioration of verbal descriptions of faces over different delay intervals. *Journal of Police Science and Administration, 8,* 101–106.

Ellison v. Brady, 924 F.2d 871 (9th Cir. 1991).

Ellison, K. W. (1985). Community involvement in police selection. *Social Action and the Law, 11*(3), 77–78.

Ellison, K. W., & Buckhout, R. (1981). *Psychology and criminal justice.* New York: Harper & Row.

Ellsworth, P. C. (1991). To tell what we know or wait for Godot? *Law and Human Behavior, 15,* 77–90.

Emery, R. (1994). *Renegotiating family relationships: Divorce, child custody, and mediation.* New York: Guilford.

Emery, R., & Wyer, M. (1987). Divorce mediation. *American Psychologist, 42,* 472–480.

Engelbrecht, S. B., & Wrightsman, L. S. (1994). Unpublished research, University of Kansas, Lawrence, KS.

Erickson, W. D., Luxenburg, M. G., Walbek, N. H., & Seely, R. K. (1987). Frequency of MMPI two-point code types among sex offenders. *Journal of Consulting and Clinical Psychology, 55,* 566–570.

Ernsdorff, G. N., & Loftus, E. F. (1993). Let sleeping memories lie? Words of caution about tolling the statute of limitations in cases of memory repression. *Journal of Criminal Law and Criminology, 84,* 129–174.

Erven v. The Queen. (1979). 1 S.C.R. 926.

Everson, M. D., & Boat, B. W. (1994). Putting the anatomical doll controversy in perspective: An examination of the major uses and criticisms of the dolls in child sexual abuse evaluations. *Child Abuse and Neglect, 11,* 113–129.

Ewing, C. P. (1987). *Battered women who kill: Psychological self-defense as legal justification.* Lexington, MA: Lexington Books, D. C. Heath.

Ewing, C. P. (1990). Psychological self-defense: A proposed justification for battered women who kill. *Law and Human Behavior, 14,* 579–594.

Ewing, C. P., & Aubrey, M. R. (1987). Battered women and public opinion: Some realities about the myths. *Journal of Family Violence, 4*(2), 143–159.

Ewing, C. P., Aubrey, M., & Jamieson, L. (1986, August). *The battered woman syndrome: Expert testimony and public atti-*

tudes. Paper presented at the meetings of the American Psychological Association, Washington, DC.

Faigman, D. (1986). The battered woman syndrome and self-defense: A legal and empirical dissent. *Virginia Law Review, 72,* 619–647.

Faigman, D. L., Kaye, D. H., Saks, M. J., & Sanders, J. (1997). *Modern scientific evidence: The law and science of expert testimony.* St. Paul, MN: West.

Faigman, D. L., & Wright, A. J. (1997). The battered woman syndrome in the age of science. *Arizona Law Review, 39,* 67–115.

Farley, L. (1978). *Sexual shakedown: The sexual harassment of women on the job.* New York: McGraw-Hill.

Fargo, M. (1994, April). Using juror questionnaires to supplement voir dire. *Court Call,* pp. 1–3.

Faust, D., & Ziskin, J. (1988). The expert witness in psychology and psychiatry. *Science, 241,* 31–35.

Fedorowycz, O. (1999, October). Homicide in Canada—1998. *Juristat 19(10).* Ottawa: Canadian Centre for Justice Statistics, Statistics Canada.

Feigenson, N., Park, J., & Salovey, P. (1997). Effect of blameworthiness and outcome severity on attributions of responsibility and damage awards in comparative negligence cases. *Law and Human Behavior, 21,* 597–617.

Felchlia, M. (1992). Construct validity of the Competency Screening Test. *Dissertation Abstracts International, 53*(1–B), 604.

Feldman-Summers, S., Gordon, P. E., & Meagher, J. R. (1979). The impact of rape on sexual satisfaction. *Journal of Abnormal Psychology, 88,* 101–105.

Felner, R. D., Rowlison, R. T., Farber, S. S., & Primavera, J. (1987). Child custody resolution: A study of social science involvement and input. *Professional Psychology: Research and Practice, 18,* 468–474.

Felner, R. D., & Terre, L. (1987). Child custody dispositions and children's adaptation following divorce. In L. A. Weithorn (Ed.), *Psychology and child custody determinations: Knowledge, roles, and expertise* (pp. 106–153). Lincoln: University of Nebraska Press.

Fernandez, E. (1993, November 15). Dead letters. *People,* pp. 111–112.

Fields, G. (1993, December 16). Indictment: D.C. cops bragged about crimes, *USA Today,* p. 3A.

Fienberg. S. E. (Ed.). (1989). *The evolving role of statistical assessments as evidence in the courts.* New York: Springer-Verlag.

Finkel, N. J., Meister, K. H., & Lightfoot, D. M. (1991). The self-defense defense and community sentiment. *Law and Human Behavior, 15,* 585–602.

Finkelhor, D., Hotaling, G., Lewis, I. A., & Smith, C. (1990). Sexual abuse in a national survey of adult men and women: Prevalence, characteristics, and risk factors. *Child Abuse and Neglect, 14,* 19–28.

Finn, P., & McNeil, T. (1987, October 7). *The response of the criminal justice system to bias crime: An exploratory review.* Contract Report submitted to the National Institute of Justice.

Fisher, R. P. (1995). Interviewing victims and witnesses of crime. *Psychology, Public Policy, and Law, 1,* 732–764.

Fisher, R. P., & Geiselman, R. E. (1992). *Memory-enhancing techniques for investigative interviewing: The cognitive interview.* Springfield, IL: Charles C Thomas.

Fisher, R. P., Geiselman, R. E., & Amador, M. (1989). Field test of the cognitive interview: Enhancing the recollection of actual victims and witnesses of crime. *Journal of Applied Psychology, 74,* 722–727.

Fisher, R. P., Geiselman, R. E., & Raymond, D. S. (1987). Critical analysis of police interview techniques. *Journal of Police Science and Administration, 15,* 177–185.

Fisk, M. C. (1998, April 20). Judges slash worker awards. *National Law Journal,* pp. A1, A20.

Fiske, S. T., Bersoff, D. N., Borgida, E., Deaux, K., & Heilman, M. E. (1991). Social science research on trial: Use of sex stereotyping research in *Price Waterhouse v. Hopkins. American Psychologist, 46,* 1049–1060.

Fiske, S. T., Bersoff, D. N., Borgida, E., Deaux, K., & Heilman, M. E. (1993). What constitutes a scientific review? A majority retort to Barrett and Morris. *Law and Human Behavior, 17,* 217–233.

Fitzgerald, L. F., Drasgow, F., Hulin, C. L., Gelfand, M. J., & Magley, V. J. (1997). Antecedents and consequences of sexual harassment in organizations: A test of an integrated model. *Journal of Applied Psychology, 82,* 578–589.

Fitzgerald, L. F., & Hesson-McInnis, M. (1989). The dimensions of sexual harassment: A structural analysis. *Journal of Vocational Behavior, 35,* 309–326.

Fitzgerald, L. F., Shullman, S. L., Bailey, N., Richards, M., Swecker, J., Gold, Y., Ormerod, A. J., & Weitzman, L. (1988). The incidence and dimensions of sexual harassment in academia and the workplace. *Journal of Vocational Behavior, 32,* 152–175.

Fitzgerald, L. F., Swan, S., & Fischer, K. (1995). Why didn't she just report him? The psychological and legal implications of women's responses to sexual harassment. *Journal of Social Issues, 51*(1), 117–138.

Foa, E. B., Olasov, B., & Steketee, G. (1987). *Treatment of rape victims.* Paper presented at the conference, State-of-the-Art in Sexual Assault, Charleston, SC.

Foa, E. B., & Rothbaum, B. O. (1998). *Treating the trauma of rape: Cognitive behavioral therapy for PTSD.* New York: Guilford Press.

Foley, L. A. (1993). *A psychological view of the legal system.* Madison, WI: Brown & Benchmark.

Foley, L. A., Adams, A. M., & Goodson, J. L. (1996). The effect of race on decisions by judges and other officers of the court. *Journal of Applied Social Psychology, 26,* 1190–1212.

Follingstad, D. R. (1994a, March). *Rape trauma syndrome in the courtroom.* Workshop presented for the American Academy of Forensic Psychology, Santa Fe, NM.

Follingstad, D. R. (1994b, March 10). *The use of battered woman syndrome in court.* Workshop presented for the American Academy of Forensic Psychology, Santa Fe, NM.

Follingstad, D. R., Polek, D. S., Hause, E. S., Deaton, L. H., Bulger, M. W., & Conway, Z. D. (1989). Factors predicting verdicts in cases where battered women kill their husbands. *Law and Human Behavior, 13,* 253–270.

Foote, W. E., & Goodman-Delahunty, J. (1999). Same-sex harassment: Implications of the *Oncale* decision for forensic evaluation of plaintiffs. *Behavioral Sciences and the Law, 17,* 123–139.

Forman, B. (1980). Psychotherapy with rape victims. *Psychotherapy: Theory, Research and Practice, 17,* 304–311.

Forth, A. E., & Mailloux, D. L. (2000). Psychopathy in youth: What do we know? In C. B. Gacono (Ed.), *The clinical and forensic assessment of psychopathy: A practitioner's guide* (pp. 25–54). Mahwah, NJ: Erlbaum.

Foster, H. H. (1969). Confessions and the station house syndrome. *DePaul Law Review, 18,* 683–701.

Fowler, R. D. (1986, May). Howard Hughes: A psychological autopsy. *Psychology Today,* pp. 22–33.

Fowler, R., De Vivo, P. P., & Fowler, D. J. (1985). Analyzing police hostage negotiations: The verbal interaction analysis technique. *Journal of Crisis Intervention, 2,* 16–28.

Fox, R. E. (1991). Proceedings of the American Psychological Association, Incorporated, for the year 1990. *American Psychologist, 46,* 689–726.

Frank, E., & Stewart, B. D. (1984). Depressive symptoms in rape victims: A revisit. *Journal of Affective Disorders, 7,* 77–85.

Frank, G. (1966). *The Boston Strangler.* New York: Signet.

Franklin, B. (1994, August 22). Gender myths still play a role in jury selection. *National Law Journal,* pp. A1, A25.

Franklin, C. (1970). *The third degree.* London: Robert Hale.

Frazier, P. A. (1990). Victim attributions and postrape trauma. *Journal of Personality and Social Psychology, 59,* 298–304.

Frazier, P. A., & Borgida, E. (1988). Juror common understanding and the admissibility of rape trauma syndrome evidence in court. *Law and Human Behavior, 12,* 101–122.

Frazier, P. A., & Borgida, E. (1992). Rape trauma syndrome: A review of case law and psychological research. *Law and Human Behavior, 16,* 293–311.

Frazier, P. A., Cochran, C. C., & Olson, A. M. (1995). Social science research on lay definitions of sexual harassment. *Journal of Social Issues, 51*(1), 21–37.

Fredman, S. G. (1995, August). *Child custody evaluations from the bench: A judge's perspective.* Paper presented at the meetings of the American Psychological Association, New York.

Frey, B. (1994). *Development of a structured preference scale and a deductive preference scale.* Unpublished Ph.D. dissertation, Department of Educational Psychology and Research, University of Kansas, Lawrence, KS.

Frey, D. L., & Gaertner, S. L. (1986). Helping and the avoidance of inappropriate interracial behavior: A strategy that perpetuates a nonprejudicial self-image. *Journal of Personality and Social Psychology, 50,* 1083–1090.

Frick, P. J. (1998). *Conduct disorders and severe antisocial behavior.* New York: Plenum.

Frick, P. J., Bodin, S. D., & Barry, C. T. (2000). Psychopathic traits and conduct problems in community and clinic-referred samples of children: Further development of the Psychopathy Screening Device. *Psychological Assessment, 12,* 382–393.

Frick, P. J., & Ellis, M. (1999). Callous-unemotional traits and subtypes of conduct disorder. *Clinical Child and Family Psychology Review, 2,* 149–168.

Frick, P. J., O'Brien, B. S., Wooton, J. M., & McBurnett, K. (1994). Psychopathy and conduct problems in children. *Journal of Abnormal Psychology, 103,* 700–707.

Friedland, N., & Merari, A. (1985). The psychological impact of terrorism: A double-edged sword. *Political Psychology, 6,* 591–604.

Friedman, G. (1993). *A guide to divorce mediation.* New York: Workman.

Frye v. United States, 293 F. 1013, 34 A.L.R. 145 (D. C. Cir. 1923).

Fulero, S. M. (1988, August). *Eyewitness expert testimony: An overview and annotated bibliography, 1931–1988.* Paper presented at the meetings of the American Psychological Association, Atlanta.

Fulero, S. M. (1997). Babies, bathwater, and being "hoisted by own petard." *National Psychologist, 6*(3), 10–11.

Fulero, S. (1998, May 14). Personal communication via e-mail.

Fulero, S. M., & Finkel, N. J. (1991). Barring ultimate issue testimony: An "insane" rule? *Law and Human Behavior, 15,* 495–507.

Fulero, S. M., & Penrod, S. (1990). The myths and realities of attorney jury selection folklore and scientific jury selection: What works? *Ohio Northern University Law Review, 17,* 229–253.

Furby, L., Weinrott, M., & Blackshaw, L. (1989). Sex offender recidivism: A review. *Psychological Bulletin, 105,* 3–30.

Fuselier, G. D. (1988). Hostage negotiation consultant: Emerging role for the clinical psychologist. *Professional Psychology: Research and Practice, 19,* 175–179.

Gaertner, S. L., & Bickman, L. (1971). Effects of race on the elicitation of helping behavior: The wrong number technique. *Journal of Personality and Social Psychology, 20,* 218–222.

Gaertner, S. L., & Dovidio, J. F. (1977). The subtlety of white racism, arousal, and helping behavior. *Journal of Personality and Social Psychology, 35,* 691–702.

Gaertner, S. L., & Dovidio, J. F. (1986). The aversive form of racism. In J. F. Dovidio and S. L. Gaertner (Eds.), *Prejudice, discrimination, and racism* (pp. 61–89). San Diego, CA: Academic Press.

Galatzer-Levy, R. M. (1997, December 22). Personal communication via e-mail.

Gale, A. (1988). Introduction: The polygraph test, more than scientific investigation. In A. Gale (Ed.), *The polygraph test: Lies, truth and science* (pp.1–9). London: Sage.

Galligan, P. T. (1996, March 15). Report to the Attorney General of Ontario on certain matters relating to Karla Homolka. *Government of Ontario.*

Gamson, W. A., & Modigliani, A. (1987). The changing culture of affirmative action. In R. D. Braungart (Ed.) *Research in political sociology* (vol. 3). Greenwich, CT: JAI Press.

Garb, H. N. (1998). *Studying the clinician: Judgment research and psychological assessment.* Washington, DC: American Psychological Association.

Garrison, E. G. (1991). Children's competence to participate in divorce custody decision making. *Journal of Clinical Child Psychology, 20,* 78–87.

Garven, S., Wood, J. M., Malpass, R. S., & Shaw, J. S., III. (1998). More than suggestion: The effect of interviewing techniques from the McMartin Preschool case. *Journal of Applied Psychology, 83,* 347–359.

Geberth, V. J. (1981, September). Psychological profiling. *Law and Order,* pp. 46–49.

Geberth, V. J. (1990). *Practical homicide investigation: Tactics, procedures, and forensic techniques* (2nd ed.). New York: Elsevier.

Geiselman, R. E., Fisher, R. P., MacKinnon, D. P., & Holland, H. L. (1985). Eyewitness memory enhancement in the police interview: Cognitive retrieval mnemonics versus hypnosis. *Journal of Applied Psychology, 70,* 401–412.

Geiselman, R. E., Fisher, R. P., MacKinnon, D. P., & Holland, H. L. (1986). Enhancement of eyewitness memory with the cognitive interview. *American Journal of Psychology, 99,* 385–401.

Geiselman, R. E., & Machlovitz, H. (1987). Hypnosis in memory recall: Implications for forensic use. *American Journal of Forensic Psychology, 1,* 37–47.

Geiselman, R. E., & Padilla, J. (1988). Interviewing child witnesses with the cognitive interview. *Journal of Police Science and Administration, 16,* 236–242.

Geller, W. A. (1993). *Videotaping interrogations and confessions.* Washington, DC: U.S. Department of Justice.

Genz, J. L., & Lester, D. (1976). Authoritarianism in policemen as a function of experience. *Journal of Police Science and Administration, 4,* 9–13.

George, R., & Clifford, B. R. (1992). Making the most of witnesses. *Policing, 8,* 185–198.

Gerard, A. B. (1994). *The Parent-Child Relationship Inventory: Reflections on form and function.* Paper presented at the meetings of the American Psychological Association, New York.

Gerard, H. (1983). School desegregation: The social science role. *American Psychologist, 38,* 869–872.

Germann, A. C. (1969). Community policing: An assessment. *Journal of Criminal Law, Criminology, and Police Science, 60,* 84–96.

Gilbert, G. (1754/1769). *The Law of Evidence 121-47.* London, His Majesty's Law Printers.

Gillespie, C. (1989). *Justifiable homicide.* Columbus: Ohio State University Press.

Glancy, G. D., Regehr, C., Bryant, A. G., & Schneider, R. (1999). Another nail in the coffin of confidentiality. *Canadian Journal of Psychiatry, 44,* 440.

Goddard, R. W. (1986). Post-employment: The changing current in discrimination charges. *Personnel Journal, 65,* 34–40.

Gold, V. (1987). Covert advocacy: Reflections on the use of psychological persuasion techniques in the courtroom. *North Carolina Law Review, 65,* 481–508.

Goldberg, P. (1968). Are women prejudiced against women? *Transaction, 5,* 28–30.

Golding, S. L. (1990). Mental health professionals in the courts: The ethics of expertise. *International Journal of Law and Psychiatry, 13,* 281–307.

Golding, S. L., & Roesch, R. (1987). The assessment of criminal responsibility: A historical approach to a current controversy. In I. B. Weiner & A. K. Hess (Eds.), *Handbook of forensic psychology* (pp. 395–436). New York: John Wiley.

Golding, S. L., Roesch, R., & Schreiber, J. (1984). Assessment and conceptualization of competency to stand trial: Preliminary data on the Interdisciplinary Fitness Interview. *Law and Human Behavior, 8,* 321–334.

Goldstein, G., & Incagnoli, T. M. (Eds.). (1997). *Contemporary approaches to neuropsychological assessment.* New York: Plenum.

Goldstein, J., Freud, A., & Solnit, A. (1973). *Beyond the best interests of the child.* New York: Free Press.

Goldstein, J., Freud, A., & Solnit, A. J. (1979). *Before the best interests of the child.* New York: Free Press.

Goldstein, R. L. (1989). The psychiatrist's guide to right and wrong: Part IV: The insanity defense and the ultimate issue rule. *Bulletin of the American Academy of Psychiatry and the Law, 17,* 269–281.

Gonzalez, R., Ellsworth, P. C., & Pembroke, M. (1993). Response biases in lineups and showups. *Journal of Personality and Social Behavior, 6,* 1–13.

Goodman, G. S. (1984). Children's testimony in historical perspective. *Journal of Social Issues, 40*(2), 9–31.

Goodman, G. S., Quas, J. A., Batterman-Faunce, J. M., Riddlesberger, M. M., & Kuhn, J. (1997). Children's reaction to and memory for a stressful experience: Influences of age, knowledge, anatomical dolls, and parental attachment *Applied Developmental Science, 1,* 54–75.

Goodman, G. S., Redlich, A. D., Qin, J., Ghetti, S., Tyda, K. S., Schaaf, J. M., & Hahn, A. (1999). Evaluating eyewitness testimony in adults and children. In A. K. Hess & I. B. Weiner (Eds.), *Handbook of forensic psychology* (2nd ed., pp. 218–272). New York: John Wiley.

Goodman-Delahunty, J. (1999). Civil law: Employment and discrimination. In R. Roesch, S. D. Hart, & J. R. P. Ogloff (Eds.), *Psychology and law: The state of the discipline* (pp. 277–337). New York: Kluwer Academic/Plenum.

Gordon, W. L., III. (1997). Reflections of a criminal defense lawyer on the Simpson trial. *Journal of Social Issues, 53,* 417–424.

Gottfredson, L. S. (1994). The science and politics of race-norming. *American Psychologist, 49,* 955–963.

Gough, H. G. (1975). *Manual for the California Psychological Inventory.* Palo Alto, CA: Consulting Psychologists Press.

Gould, J. (1998). *Conducting scientifically crafted child custody evaluations.* Thousand Oaks, CA: Sage.

Gould, K. (1995). A therapeutic analysis of competency evaluation requests: The defense attorney's dilemma. *International Journal of Law and Psychiatry, 18,* 83–100.

Graham, J. R. (1987). *The MMPI: A practical guide* (2nd ed.). New York: Oxford University Press.

Greenberg, L. (1998, November 17). Personal communication via e-mail.

Greenberg, S. A., & Shuman, D. W. (1997). Irreconcilable conflict between therapeutic and forensic roles. *Professional Psychology: Research and Practice, 28,* 505–557.

Greene, E., Downey, C., & Goodman-Delahunty, J. (1999). Juror decisions about damages in employment discrimination cases. *Behavioral Sciences and the Law, 17,* 107–121.

Greene, E., Raitz, A., & Lindblad, H. (1989). Juror's knowledge of battered women. *Journal of Family Violence, 4*(2), 105–126.

Greenhouse, L. (1992, October 14). High court to decide admissibility of scientific evidence in U.S. courts. *New York Times,* p. A9.

Greenhouse, L. (1995, June 14). Split court in step with nation. *Kansas City Star,* p. A6.

Greenstone, J. L. (1995a). Hostage negotiations team training for small police departments. In M. I. Kurke & E. M. Scrivner (Eds.), *Police psychology into the 21st century* (pp. 279–296). Hillsdale, NJ: Lawrence Erlbaum.

Greenstone, J. L. (1995b). Tactics and negotiating techniques (TNT): The way of the past and the way of the future. In M. I. Kurke & E. M. Scrivner (Eds.), *Police psychology into the 21st century* (pp. 357–371). Hillsdale, NJ: Lawrence Erlbaum.

Greenwald, J. P., Tomkins, A. J., Kenning, M., & Zavodny, D. (1990). Psychological self-defense jury instructions: Influence on verdicts for battered women defendants. *Behavioral Sciences and the Law, 8,* 171–180.

Greenwood, P. W., & Petersilia, J. (1976). *The criminal investigation process.* Washington, DC: Law Enforcement Assistance Association.

Greif, G. L., & Hegar, R. L. (1993). *When parents kidnap.* New York: Free Press.

Gretton, H. M., McBride, H. L., Hare, R. D., O'Shaughnessy, R., & Kumka, G. (2001). Psychopathy and recidivism in adolescent sex offenders. *Criminal Justice and Behavior, 28,* 427–449.

Griggs v. Duke Power Co., 401 U.S. 424 (1971).

Grisham, J. (1996). *The runaway jury.* New York, NY: Dell Publishing Company.

Grisso, T. (1984, June). *Forensic assessment in juvenile and family cases: The state of the art.* Keynote address, Summer Institute on Mental Health Law, University of Nebraska, Lincoln.

Grisso, T. (1986). *Evaluating competencies: Forensic assessments and instruments.* New York: Plenum.

Grisso, T., & Saks, M. J. (1991). Psychology's influence on constitutional interpretation: A comment on how to succeed. *Law and Human Behavior, 15,* 205–211.

Grove, W. M., & Meehl, P. E. (1996). Comparative efficiency of informal (subjective, impressionistic) and formal (mechanical, algorithmic) prediction procedures: The clinical statistical controversy. *Psychology, Public Policy, and Law, 2,* 297–323.

Gruber, J. E. (1992). A typology of personal and environmental sexual harassment: Research and policy implications for the 1990s. *Sex Roles, 26,* 447–464.

Grych, J. H., & Fincham, F. D. (1992). Interventions for children of divorce: Toward greater integration of research and action. *Psychological Bulletin, 111,* 434–454.

Gudjonsson, G. H. (1984). A new scale of interrogative suggestibility. *Personality and Individual Differences, 5,* 303–314.

Gudjonsson, G. H. (1988). How to defeat the polygraph tests. In A. Gale (Ed.), *The polygraph test: Lies, truth and science* (pp. 126–136). London: Sage.

Gudjonsson, G. H. (1989). Compliance in an interrogation situation: A new scale. *Personality and Individual Differences, 10,* 535–540.

Gudjonsson, G. H. (1991). Suggestibility and compliance among alleged false confessors and resisters in criminal trials. *Medicine, Science, and the Law, 31,* 147–151.

Gudjonsson, G. (1992). *The psychology of interrogations, confessions, and testimony.* Chichester, UK: Wiley.

Gudjonsson, G. H. (1997). *The Gudjonsson Suggestibility Scales Manual.* East Sussex, UK: Psychology Press.

Gudjonsson, G. H. (2003). *The Psychology of interrogations and confessions: A handbook.* London: Wiley.

Gudjonsson, G. H., & Copson, G. (1997). The role of the expert in criminal investigation. In J. L. Jackson & D. A. Bekerian (Eds.), *Offender profiling: Theory, research and practice* (pp. 62–76). New York: John Wiley.

Gudjonsson, G. H., & Lebegue, B. (1989). Psychological and psychiatric aspects of a coerced-internalized false confession. *Journal of the Forensic Science Society, 29*(4), 261–269.

Gudjonsson, G. H., & Sartory, G. (1983) Blood-injury phobia: A "reasonable excuse" for failing to give a specimen in a case of suspected drunken driving. *Journal of the Forensic Science Society, 23,* 197–201.

Guidubaldi, J., & Cleminshaw, H. (1998, August). *The Parenting Satisfaction Scale: Development, validity, and applications.* Paper presented at the meetings of the American Psychological Association, San Francisco.

Gutek, B. A. (1985). *Sex and the workplace: The impact of sexual behavior and harassment on women, men, and organizations.* San Francisco: Jossey-Bass.

Gutek, B. A., & O'Connor, M. (1995). The empirical basis for the reasonable woman standard. *Journal of Social Issues, 51*(1), 151–166.

Hafemeister, T. L., & Melton, G. B. (1987). The impact of social science research on the judiciary. In G. B. Melton (Ed.), *Reforming the law: Impact of child development research* (pp. 29–59). New York: Guilford.

Hageman, M. J. (1979). Who joins the force for what reason: An argument for "the new breed." *Journal of Police Science and Administration, 15,* 110–117.

Hagen, M. A. (1997). *Whores of the court: The fraud of psychiatric testimony and the rape of American justice.* New York: HarperCollins.

Hagin, R. A. (1992). Review of the Bricklin Perceptual Scales. In J. J. Kramer & J. C. Conoley (Eds.), *Eleventh mental measurements yearbook* (pp. 117–118). Lincoln: University of Nebraska Press.

Hale, M., Jr. (1980). *Human science and social order: Hugo Münsterberg and the origins of applied psychology.* Philadelphia: Temple University Press.

Hall, G. C. N. (1989). WAIS-R and MMPI profiles of men who have assaulted children: Evidence of limited utility. *Journal of Personality Assessment, 53,* 404–412.

Hall, G. C. N. (1995). Sexual offender recidivism revisited: A meta-analysis of recent treatment studies. *Journal of Consulting and Clinical Psychology, 63,* 802–809.

Hall, G. C. N., Maiuro, R. D., Vitaliano, P. P., & Proctor, W. D. (1986). The utility of the MMPI with men who have sexually assaulted children. *Journal of Clinical and Consulting Psychology, 54,* 493–496.

Hall, N. (December, 2000). *Growing the problem: The second annual report of the Mental Health Advocate of British Columbia.* BC: Author.

Hammond, D. L. (1980). *The responding of normals, alcoholics, and psychopaths in a laboratory lie-detection experiment.* Unpublished doctoral dissertation, California School of Professional Psychology, Los Angeles.

Hammond, D. C., Garver, R. B., Mutter, C. B., Crasilneck, H. B., Frischholz, E., Gravitz, M. A., Hibler, N. S., Olson, J., Scheflin, A. W., Spiegel, H., & Webster, W. (1995). *Clinical hypnosis and memory: Guidelines for clinicians and for forensic hypnosis.* Des Plaines, IL: American Society of Clinical Hypnosis Press.

Haney, C. (1980). Psychology and legal change: On the limits of a factual jurisprudence. *Law and Human Behavior, 4,* 147–199.

Hans, V. (1989). Expert witnessing. *Science, 245,* 312–313.

Hans, V. P. (1990). Attitudes toward corporate responsibility: A psychological perspective. *Nebraska Law Review, 69,* 158–189.

Hans, V. P., & Lofquist, W. (1992). Jurors' judgments of business liability in tort cases: Implications for the litigation explosion debate. *Law and Society Review, 26,* 85–115.

Hanson, R. K., & Bussière, M. T. (1998). Predicting relapse: A meta-analysis of sexual offender recidivism studies. *Journal of Consulting and Clinical Psychology, 66,* 348–362.

Hare, R. (1991). *The Hare Psychopathy Checklist—Revised Manual.* Tonawanda, NY: Multi-Health Systems.

Hare, R. D. (1993). *Without conscience: The disturbing world of the psychopaths among us.* New York, NY: Pocket Books.

Hare, R. D. (1996). Psychopathy: A clinical construct whose time has come. *Criminal Justice and Behavior, 23,* 25–54.

Hare, R. D. (1998). The Hare PCL-R: Some issues concerning it's use and misuse. *Legal and Criminological Psychology, 3,* 101–122.

Hare, R. (2003). *The Hare Psychopathy Checklist-Revised Manual* (2nd ed.). Toronto: Multi-Health Systems.

Hare, R. D., & Jutai, J. (1983). Criminal history of the male psychopath: Some preliminary data. In K. T. Van Dusen & S. A. Mednick (Eds.), *Prospective studies of crime and delinquency* (pp. 225–236). Boston: Kluwer-Nijhoff.

Hargrave, G. E., & Hiatt, D. (1987). Law enforcement selection with the interview, MMPI, and CPI: A study of reliability and validity. *Journal of Police Science and Administration, 15,* 110–117.

Hargrave, G. E., & Hiatt, D. (1989). Use of the California Psychological Inventory in law enforcement officer selection. *Journal of Personality Assessment, 53,* 267–277.

Hargrave, G. E., Hiatt, D., Ogard, E., & Karr, C. (1993). *Comparison of the MMPI and the MMPI-2 for a sample of peace officers.* Unpublished manuscript cited by Blau, 1994.

Harris v. Forklift Systems, Inc., 114 S.Ct. 367 (1993).

Harris, G., Rice, M., & Quinsey, V. (1993). Violent recidivism of mentally disordered offenders: The development of a statistical prediction instrument. *Criminal Justice and Behavior, 20,* 315–335.

Harris, T. (1981). *The red dragon.* New York: Putnam.

Harris, T. (1988). *The silence of the lambs.* New York: St. Martin's Press.

Harris, T. (1999). *Hannibal.* New York: Delacorte Press.

Hart, S., & Hare, R. (1992). Predicting fitness for trial: The relative power of demographic, criminal, and clinical variables. *Forensic Reports, 5,* 53–54.

Hassel, C. (1975). The hostage situation: Exploring motivation and cause. *The Police Chief, 42*(9), 55–58.

Hastie, R. (1991). Is attorney-conducted *voir dire* an effective procedure for the selection of impartial jurors? *American University Law Review, 40,* 703–726.

Hathaway, S. R., & McKinley, J. C. (1983). *The Minnesota Multiphasic Personality Inventory: Manual.* New York: Psychological Corporation.

Hauser, B. B. (1985). Custody in dispute: Legal and psychological profiles of contesting families. *Journal of American Academy of Child Psychiatry, 24,* 531–537.

Haynes, J. (1981). *Divorce mediation: A practical guide for therapists and counselors.* New York: Gardner.

Hays, G. (1992). *Policewoman One: My twenty years on the LAPD.* New York: Berkeley Books.

Hazelwood, R. R., & Burgess, A. W. (1995). *Practical aspects of rape investigation: A multidisciplinary approach* (2nd ed.). Boca Raton, Fla.: C.R.C. Press.

Hazelwood, R. R., & Douglas, J. E. (1980). The lust murderer. *FBI Law Enforcement Bulletin, 50*(7), 10–15.

Hedrick, M. (1998, November 15). *Comprehensive child custody evaluations.* Workshop sponsored by American Academy of Forensic Psychology, St. Louis, MO.

Heilbroner, D. (1993, August). Serial murder and sexual repression. *Playboy,* pp. 78, 147–150.

Heilbrun, K. (1998, Spring). Forensic psychology as a specialization: What role for AP-LS? *American Psychology-Law Society News,* pp. 36–41.

Heilbrun, K., & Heilbrun, A. B., Jr. (1995). Risk assessment with the MMPI-2 in forensic evaluations. In Y. S. Ben-Porath, J. R. Graham, G. C. N. Hall, R. D. Hirschman, & M. S. Zaragoza (Eds.), *Forensic applications of the MMPI-2* (pp. 160–178). Thousand Oaks, CA: Sage.

Heilman, M. (1994). Affirmative action: Some unintended consequences for working women. In B. M. Staw &

L. L. Cummings (Eds.), *Research in organizational behavior* (pp. 125–169). Greenwich, CT: JAI Press.

Heinze, M. C., & Grisso, T. (1996). Review of instruments assessing parenting competencies used in child custody evaluations. *Behavioral Sciences and the Law, 14,* 293–313.

Hemphill, J. F., Hare, R. D., & Wong, S. (1998). Psychopathy and recidivism: A review. *Legal and Criminological Psychology, 3,* 139–170.

Hemphill, J., Templeman, R., Wong, S., & Hare, R. D. (1998). Psychopathy and crime: Recidivism and criminal careers. In D. Cooke, A. Forth, & R. D. Hare (Eds.). *Psychopathy: Theory, research and implications for society* (pp. 374–399). Dordrecht, Netherlands: Kluwer.

Henkel, J., Sheehan, E. P., & Reichel, P. (1997). Relation of police misconduct to authoritarianism. *Journal of Social Behavior and Personality, 12,* 551–555.

Henry, T. (1994, April 8). Harassment: It's academic. *USA Today,* p. 1A.

Herbsleb, J. D., Sales, B. D., & Berman, J. J. (1979). When psychologists aid in the voir dire: Legal and ethical considerations. In L. E. Abt & I. R. Stuart (Eds.), *Social psychology and discretionary law* (pp. 197–217). New York: Van Nostrand Reinhold.

Herek, G. M. (1989). Hate crimes against lesbians and gay men. *American Psychologist, 44,* 948–955.

Herman, L. (1992). The unexplored relationship between the privilege against compulsory self-incrimination and the involuntary confession rule (Part I). *Ohio State Law Journal, 53,* 101–209.

Herman, J. L. (1992). Complex PTSD: A syndrome in survivors of prolonged and repeated trauma. *Journal of Traumatic Stress, 5,* 377–392.

Hervé, H. M., Mitchell, D., Cooper, B. S., Spidel, A., & Hare, R. D. (2004). Psychopathy and unlawful confinement: An examination of perpetrator and event characteristics. *Canadian Journal of Behavioural Science, 36,* 137–145.

Hess, A. K., & Weiner, I. B. (Eds.). (1999). *Handbook of forensic psychology* (2nd ed.). New York: John Wiley.

Hetherington, E. M. (1979). Divorce: A child's perspective. *American Psychologist, 39,* 851–858.

Hetherington, E. M. (1989). Coping with family transitions: Winners, losers, and survivors. *Child Development, 60,* 1–14.

Hetherington, E. M. (1993). An overview of the Virginia longitudinal study of divorce and remarriage with a focus on early adolescence. *Journal of Family Psychology, 7,* 39–56.

Hetherington, E. M., Stanley-Hagan, M., & Anderson, E. R. (1989). Marital transitions: A child's perspective. *American Psychologist, 44,* 303–312.

Hibler, N. S. (1995). Hypnosis for investigative purposes. In M. I. Kurke and E. M. Scrivner (Eds.), *Psychology into the 21st century* (pp. 319–336). Hillsdale, NJ: Lawrence Erlbaum Associates.

Hibler, N. S., & Kurke, M. I. (1995). Ensuring personal reliability through selection and training. In M. I. Kurke and

E. M. Scrivner (Eds.), *Police psychology into the 21st century* (pp. 57–91). Hillsdale, NJ: Lawrence Erlbaum Associates.

Hilgard, E. R., & Hilgard, J. R. (1975). *Hypnosis in the relief of pain*. Los Altos, CA: Kaufmann.

Hiltonsmith, R. W. (1995). Review of the Parent Perception of Child Profile. In J. C. Conoley & J. C. Impara (Eds.), *Twelfth mental measurements yearbook* (p. 738). Lincoln: University of Nebraska Press.

Hoffman, L. E, Lavigne, B., Dickie, I, & Women Offender Sector, Correctional Service of Canada. (1998). *Women Convicted of Homicide Serving a Federal Sentence: An Exploratory Study*. Retrieved May 19, 2004, from the Correctional Service of Canada Web site: http://www.csc-scc.gc.ca/text/prgrm/fsw/homicide/toc_e.shtml.

Hogan, R. (1971). Personality characteristics of highly rated policemen. *Personnel Psychology, 24,* 679–686.

Hoge, S., Bonnie, R., Poythress, N., & Monahan, J. (1992). Attorney-client decision making in criminal cases: Client competence and participation as perceived by their attorneys. *Behavioral Sciences and the Law, 10,* 385–394.

Hoge, S., Poythress, N., Bonnie, R., Monahan, J., Eisenberg, M., & Feucht-Haviar, T. (1997). The MacArthur Adjudication Competence Study: Diagnosis, psychopathology, and adjudicative competence-related abilities. *Behavioral Sciences and the Law, 15,* 329–345.

Holbrook, S. H. (1957). *Dreamers of the American dream*. Garden City, NY: Doubleday.

Holmes, R. M., & Holmes, S. T. (1996). *Profiling violent crimes* (2nd ed.). Thousand Oaks, CA: Sage.

Holmes, R. M., & Holmes, S. T. (1998). *Serial murder* (2nd ed.). Thousand Oaks, CA: Sage.

Holt, S. E., Meloy, J. R., & Stack, S. (1999). Sadism and psychopathy in violent and sexually violent offenders. *Journal of the American Academy of Psychiatry and Law, 27,* 23–32.

Honts, C. R. (1994). Assessing children's credibility: Scientific and legal issues in 1994. *North Dakota Law Review, 70,* 879–903.

Honts, C. R., & Hodes, R. L. (1982a). The effect of simple physical countermeasures on the detection of deception. *Psychophysiology, 19,* 564.

Honts, C. R., & Hodes, R. L. (1982b). The effects of multiple physical countermeasures on the detection of deception. *Psychophysiology, 19,* 564–565.

Honts, C. R., Raskin, D. C., & Kircher, J. C. (1983). Detection of deception: Effectiveness of physical countermeasures under high motivation conditions. *Psychophysiology, 20,* 446–447.

Honts, C. R., Raskin, D. C., & Kircher, J. C. (1984). Effects of spontaneous countermeasures on the detection of deception. *Psychophysiology, 21,* 583.

Hopwood v. State of Texas, 78 F.3d 932 (5th Cir. 1996).

Horowitz, I. A. (1980). Juror selection: A comparison of two methods in several criminal cases. *Journal of Applied Social Psychology, 10,* 86–99.

Horowitz, I. A., & Willging, T. E. (1984). *The psychology of law: Integrations and applications*. Boston: Little, Brown.

Horowitz, M. J., Wilner, N., & Alvarez, W. (1979). Impact of event scale: A measure of subjective stress. *Psychosomatic Medicine, 41,* 209–218.

Horvath, F. S. (1977). The effect of selected variables on interpretation of polygraph records. *Journal of Applied Psychology, 62,* 127–136.

Horvath v. The Queen. (1979). 2 S.C.R. 376.

Hotelling, K. (1991). Sexual harassment: A problem shielded by silence. *Journal of Counseling and Development, 69,* 497–501.

Houseman (Guardian of) v. Sewell (1997). Supreme Court of British Columbia. Docket: Docket: 13452.

Howlett, D. (1993, September 9). Lesbian ruling stirs fury, praise. *USA Today*, p. 3A.

Howlett, D. (1995, November 13). He has eluded FBI and police for 17 years. *USA Today*, pp. 1A–2A.

Huber, P. (1988). *Liability: The legal revolution and its consequences*. New York: Basic Books.

Huber, P. W. (1991). *Galileo's revenge: Junk science in the courtroom*. New York: Basic Books.

Hudson, J. R. (1970). Police encounters that lead to citizen complaints. *Social Problems, 18,* 179–193.

Huff, C. R., Rattner, A., & Sagarin, E. (1996). *Convicted but innocent: Wrongful conviction and public policy*. Thousand Oaks, CA: Sage.

Humm, D. G., & Humm, K. A. (1950). Humm-Wadsworth Temperament Scale appraisals compared with criteria of job success in the Los Angeles Police Department. *Journal of Psychology, 30,* 63–75.

Hutchins, R. M., & Slesinger, D. (1928a). Some observations on the law of evidence—spontaneous exclamations. *Columbia Law Review, 28,* 432–440.

Hutchins, R. M., & Slesinger, D. (1928b). Some observations on the law of evidence—memory. *Harvard Law Review, 41,* 860–873.

Hutchins, R. M., & Slesinger, D. (1928c). Some observations on the law of evidence—the competency of witnesses. *Yale Law Journal, 37,* 1017–1028.

Hyman, I. E., Husband, T. H., & Billings, F. J. (1995). False memories of childhood experiences. *Applied Cognitive Psychology, 9,* 181–197.

Iacono, W. G., & Patrick, C. J. (1987). What psychologists should know about lie detection. In I. B. Weiner & A. K. Hess (Eds.), *Handbook of forensic psychology* (pp. 460–489). New York: John Wiley.

Iacono, W. G., & Patrick, C. J. (1999). Polygraph ("lie detector") testing: The state of the art. In A. K. Hess & I. B. Weiner (Eds.), *The handbook of forensic psychology* (2nd ed., pp. 440–473). New York: John Wiley.

Ibn-Tamas v. United States, 407 A.2d 626 (1979).

Ilfeld, F. W., Ilfeld, H. Z., & Alexander, J. R. (1982). Does joint custody work? A first look at outcome data of relitigation. *American Journal of Psychiatry, 139,* 62–66.

Inbau, F. E., & Reid, J. E. (1962). *Criminal interrogation and confessions*. Baltimore: Williams and Wilkins.

Inbau, F. E., Reid, J. E., & Buckley, J. P. (1986). *Criminal interrogation and confessions* (3rd ed.). Baltimore: Williams and Wilkins.

International Brotherhood of Teamsters v. United States, 431 U.S. 324 (1977)

Inwald, R. (1990). *Fitness-for-duty evaluation guidelines: A survey for police/public safety administrators and mental health professionals*. Paper presented at the meetings of the American Psychological Association, Boston.

Inwald, R. E. (1992). *Inwald Personality Inventory Technical Manual (Rev. ed.)*. Kew Gardens, NY: Hilson Research.

Inwald, R., Knatz, H., & Shusman, E. (1983). *Inwald Personality Inventory Manual*. Kew Gardens, NY: Hilson Research.

Inwald, R., & Shusman, E. (1984). The IPI and MMPI as predictors of academy performance for police recruits. *Journal of Police Science and Administration, 12*, 1–11.

Irving, B. L., & Hilgendorf, E. L. (1980). *Police interrogation: The psychological approach* (Research Study No. 2). London: Royal Commission on Criminal Procedure.

Isikoff, M. (1994, March 21–27). The Foster case: Grist for the Whitewater rumor mill. *Washington Post National Weekly Edition*, p. 8.

Iverson, G. L., Franzen, M. D., & Hammond, J. A. (1993, August). *Examination of inmates' ability to malinger on the MMPI-2*. Paper presented at the meetings of the American Psychological Association, Toronto.

Jackman, M. R. (1978). General and applied tolerance: Does education increase commitment to racial integration? *American Journal of Political Science, 22*, 302–324.

Jackson, J. L., & Bekerian, D. A. (1997a). Does offender profiling have a role to play? In J. L. Jackson & D. A. Bekerian (Eds.), *Offender profiling: Theory, research and practice* (pp. 1–7). New York: John Wiley.

Jackson, J. L., & Bekerian, D. A. (Eds.). (1997b). *Offender profiling: Theory, research and practice*. New York: John Wiley.

Jackson, J. L., van den Eshof, P., & de Kleuver, E. E. (1997). A research approach to offender profiling. In J. L. Jackson & D. A. Bekerian (Eds.), *Offender profiling: Theory, research and practice* (pp. 107–132). New York: John Wiley.

Jaffe, P. G., Hastings, E., Reitzel, D., & Austin, G. W. (1993). The impact of police laying charges. In N. Z. Hilton (Ed.), *Legal responses to wife assault* (pp. 62–95). Newbury Park, CA: Sage.

Janik, J. (1993, August). *Pre-employment interviews of law enforcement officer candidates*. Paper presented at the meetings of the American Psychological Association, Toronto.

Janoff-Bulman, R. (1979). Characterological versus behavioral self-blame: Inquiries into depression and rape. *Journal of Personality and Social Psychology, 37*, 1798–1809.

Janofsky, J. S., Spears, S., & Neubauer, D. N. (1988). Psychiatrists' accuracy in predicting violent behavior on an inpatient unit. *Hospital and Community Psychiatry, 39*, 1090–1094.

Janzen v. Platy Enterprises Ltd., [1989] 1 S.C.R.1252.

Jenkins, P., & Davidson, B. (1990). Battered women in the criminal justice system: An analysis of gender stereotypes. *Behavioral Sciences and the Law, 8*, 161–170.

Jobb, D. (28 April 1999). *Mental Disorder Defence "Creates a Legal Limbo."* Retrieved May 19, 2004, from The Chronicle Herald Web site: http://www.herald.ns.ca/cgi-bin/home/package?NSHomicidesIII.

Jobes, D. A., Berman, A. L., & Josselson, A. R. (1986). The impact of psychological autopsies on medical examiners' determination of manner of death. *Journal of Forensic Sciences, 31*, 177–189.

Johnson, H. (1996). Violent crime in Canada. *Juristat, 16*, 6. Canadian Centre for Justice Statistics, Statistics Canada.

Johnson, J. (1994, May 16). Witness for the prosecution. *New Yorker*, pp. 42–51.

Johnson, K. (1998, April 16). New breed of bad cop sells badge, public trust. *USA Today*, p. 8A.

Johnson, W. G., & Mullett, N. (1987). Georgia Court Competency Test-R. In M. Hersen & A. S. Bellack (Eds.), *Dictionary of behavioral assessment techniques*. New York: Pergamon.

Jones v. Tri-County Electric Cooperative, 512 F.2d 13 (5th Cir. 1975).

Jones, A. (1981). *Women who kill*. New York: Holt Rinehart.

Jones, A. (1994a, March 10). Crimes against women. *USA Today*, p. 9A.

Jones, A. (1994b). *Next time, she'll be dead: Battering and how to stop it*. Boston: Beacon Press.

Jones, E. E. (1990). *Interpersonal perception*. San Francisco: Freeman.

Jones, E. E., & Davis, K. E. (1965). A theory of correspondent inferences: From acts to dispositions. In L. Berkowitz (Ed.), *Advances in experimental social psychology* (Vol. 2, pp. 219–266). San Diego: Academic Press.

Jones, E. E., & Harris, V. A. (1967). The attribution of attitudes. *Journal of Experimental Social Psychology, 3*, 1–24.

Jones, J. W. (1995). Counseling issues and police diversity. In M. I. Kurke & E. M. Scrivner (Eds.), *Police psychology into the 21st century* (pp. 207–254). Hillsdale, NJ: Lawrence Erlbaum.

Juni, S. (1992). Review of Inwald Personality Inventory. In J. J. Kramer & J. C. Conoley (Eds.), *Eleventh mental measurements yearbook* (pp. 415–418). Lincoln: Buros Institute of Mental Measurements, University of Nebraska.

Jurgensen, K. (1994, October 20). Again, a "passion killer" gets away with murder. *USA Today*, p. 12A.

Jurow, G. L. (1971). New data on the effect of a "death qualified" jury on the guilt determination process. *Harvard Law Review, 84*, 567–611.

Kagehiro, D. K., & Stanton, W. C. (1985). Legal vs. quantified definitions of standards of proof. *Law and Human Behavior, 9*, 159–178.

Kahneman, D., Slovic, P., & Tversky, A. (Eds.). (1982). *Judgments under uncertainty: Heuristics and biases*. Cambridge, England: Cambridge University Press.

Kahneman, D., & Tversky, A. (1973). On the psychology of prediction. *Psychological Review, 80*, 237–251.

Kahneman, D., & Tversky, A. (1982). On the study of statistical intuitions. *Cognition, 11*, 123–141.

Kalven, H., & Zeisel, H. (1966). *The American jury*. Boston: Little, Brown.

Kaminker, L. (1992, November 16). An angry cry for mute voices. *Newsweek*, p. 16.

Kantrowitz, B. (1992). Sexual harassment in America: An overview. In C. Wekesser, K. L. Swisher, & C. Pierce (Eds.), *Sexual harassment* (pp. 16–23). San Diego: Greenhaven Press.

Kargon, R. (1986). Expert testimony in historical perspective. *Law and Human Behavior, 10,* 15–27.

Kassin, S. M. (1997). The psychology of confession evidence. *American Psychologist, 52,* 221–233.

Kassin, S. M. (1998a). Clinical psychology in court: House of junk science? *Contemporary Psychology, 43,* 321–324.

Kassin, S. M. (1998b). Eyewitness identification procedures: The fifth rule. *Law and Human Behavior, 22,* 649–653.

Kassin, S. M., & Barndollar, K. A. (1992). The psychology of eyewitness testimony: A comparison of experts and prospective jurors. *Journal of Applied Social Psychology, 22,* 1241–1249.

Kassin, S. M., Ellsworth, P. C., & Smith, V. L. (1989). The "general acceptance" of psychological research on eyewitness testimony: A survey of the experts. *American Psychologist, 44,* 1089–1098.

Kassin, S. M., Ellsworth, P. C., & Smith, V. L. (1994). Deja vu all over again: Elliott's critique of eyewitness experts. *Law and Human Behavior, 18,* 203–210.

Kassin, S. M., & Kiechel, K. L. (1996). The social psychology of false confessions: Compliance, internalization, and confabulation. *Psychological Science, 7,* 125–128.

Kassin, S. M., & McNall, K. (1991). Police interrogation and confessions: Communicating promises and threats by pragmatic implication. *Law and Human Behavior, 15,* 233–251.

Kassin, S. M., & Neumann, K. (1997). On the power of confession evidence: An experimental test of the "fundamental difference" hypothesis. *Law and Human Behavior, 21,* 469–484.

Kassin, S. M., & Sukel, H. (1997). Coerced confessions and the jury: An experimental test of the "harmless error" rule. *Law and Human Behavior, 21,* 27–46.

Kassin, S. M., & Wrightsman, L. S. (1980). Prior confessions and mock juror verdicts. *Journal of Applied Social Psychology, 10,* 133–146.

Kassin, S. M., & Wrightsman, L. S. (1981). Coerced confessions, judicial instruction, and mock juror verdicts. *Journal of Applied Social Psychology, 11,* 489–506.

Kassin, S. M., & Wrightsman, L. S. (1983). The construction and validation of a Juror Bias Scale. *Journal of Research in Personality, 17,* 423–442.

Kassin, S. M., & Wrightsman, L. S. (1985). Confession evidence. In S. M. Kassin & L. S. Wrightsman (Eds.), *The psychology of evidence and trial procedure* (pp. 67–94). Thousand Oaks, CA: Sage.

Katsh, M. E. (Ed.). (1998). *Taking sides: Clashing views on controversial legal issues* (8th ed.). Guilford, CT: Dushkin/McGraw-Hill.

Katz, I., & Hass, R. G. (1988). Racial ambivalence and American value conflict: Correlational and priming studies of dual cognitive structures. *Journal of Personality and Social Psychology, 55,* 893–905.

Katz, I., Wackenhut, J., & Hass, R. G. (1986). Racial ambivalence, value duality, and behavior. In J. Dovidio & S. L. Gaertner (Eds.), *Prejudice, discrimination, and racism* (pp. 35–59). San Diego: Academic Press.

Kaye, D. H. (1982a). The numbers game: Statistical inference in discrimination cases. *Michigan Law Review, 80,* 833–856.

Kaye, D. H. (1982b). Statistical evidence of discrimination. *Journal of American Statistical Association, 77,* 773–783.

Kaye, D. H., & Aicklin, M. (Eds.). (1986). *Statistical methods in discrimination litigation.* New York: Marcel Dekker.

Kebbell, M. R., & Wagstaff, G. F. (1997). Why do the police interview eyewitnesses? Interview objectives and the evaluation of eyewitness performance. *Journal of Psychology, 131,* 595–601.

Kebbell, M. R., Wagstaff, G. F., & Covey, J. A. (1996). The influence of item difficulty on the relationship between eyewitness confidence and accuracy. *British Journal of Psychology, 87,* 653–662.

Keilin, W. G., & Bloom, L. J. (1986). Child custody evaluation practices: A survey of experienced professionals. *Professional Psychology: Research and Practice, 17,* 338–346.

Kelliher (village of) v. Smith, [1931] S.C.R. 672.

Kelly, J. F., & Wearne, P. K. (1998). *Tainting evidence: Inside the scandals at the FBI crime lab.* New York: Free Press.

Kendall-Tackett, K. A., Williams, L. M., & Finkelhor, D. (1993). Impact of sexual abuse on children: A review and synthesis of recent empirical studies. *Psychological Bulletin, 113,* 164–180.

Kennedy, M.A., & Yuille, J.C. (1999, November). *Recent complaint: The fallacy of raising a "hue and a cry" after a sexual assault.* 48th Annual Conference of the Canadian Society of Forensic Science, Edmonton, AB.

Kessler, R. (1994, March 8). Spies, lies, averted eyes. *New York Times,* p. A19.

Kidder, L. H., Lafleur, R. A., & Wells, C. V. (1995). Recalling harassment, reconstructing experience. *Journal of Social Issues, 51*(1), 53–67.

Kilpatrick, D. G. (1983, Summer). Rape victims: Detection, assessment and treatment. *Clinical Psychologist,* pp. 92–95.

Kilpatrick, D. G., & Amick, A. E. (1985). Rape trauma. In M. Hersen & C. G. Last (Eds.), *Behavior therapy casebook* (pp. 86–103). New York: Springer.

Kilpatrick, D. G., Best, C. L., Veronen, L. J., Amick, A. E., Villeponteaux, L. A., & Ruff, G. A. (1985). Mental health correlates of criminal victimization: A random community survey. *Journal of Consulting and Clinical Psychology, 53,* 866–873.

Kilpatrick, D. G., Resick, P., & Veronen, L. (1981). Effects of a rape experience: A longitudinal study. *Journal of Social Issues, 37*(4), 105–112.

Kilpatrick, D. G., & Veronen, L. J. (1984). *Treatment of fear and anxiety in victims of rape* (Final report, NIMH Grant No. HMH29602). Rockville, MD: National Institute of Mental Health.

Kilpatrick, D. G., Veronen, L. J., & Best, C. L. (1985). Factors predicting psychological distress among rape victims. In C. R. Figley (Ed.), *Trauma and its wake* (pp. 113–141). New York: Brunner/Mazel.

Kissel, S., & Freeling, N. W. (1990). *Evaluating children for courts using psychological tests*. Springfield, IL: Charles C Thomas.

Kitzmann, K. M., & Emery, R. E. (1993). Procedural justice and parents' satisfaction in a field study of child custody dispute resolution. *Law and Human Behavior, 17,* 553–568.

Klein, R. & Bromberg, A. (2003). *Audit of Antisemitic Incidents 2003*. Retrieved on May 20, 2004, from the B'Nai Brith Canada Web site: http://www.bnaibrith.ca/publications/audit2003/audit2003.pdf.

Kleinmuntz, B., & Szucko, J. (1984). A field study of the fallibility of polygraph lie detection. *Nature, 308,* 449–450.

Kline, M., Tschann, J. M., Johnston, J. R., & Wallerstein, J. S. (1989). Children's adjustment in joint and sole physical custody families. *Developmental Psychology, 25,* 430–438.

Kluger, R. (1976). *Simple justice*. New York: Alfred A. Knopf.

Knapp, S. J., & Vandecreek, L. (1985). Psychotherapy and privileged communications in child custody cases. *Professional Psychology: Research and Practice, 16,* 398–407.

Knight, R. A., & Prentky, R. A. 1993. Exploring characteristics for classifying juvenile sex offenders. In H. E. Barbaree, W. L. Marshall, & S. M. Hudson (eds.) *The Juvenile Sex Offender* (pp. 45–83). New York, NY: Guilford.

Koch, M. A., & Lowery, C. R. (1984). Visitation and the noncustodial father. *Journal of Divorce, 8,* 47–65.

Kolasa, B. J. (1972). Psychology and law. *American Psychologist, 27,* 499–503.

Kolb, B., & Whishaw, I. A. (1990). *Fundamentals of human neuropsychology* (3rd ed.). New York: W. H. Freeman.

Konecni, V., & Ebbesen, E. (1981). A critique of the theory and method in social psychological approaches to legal issues. In B. D. Sales (Ed.), *The trial process* (pp. 481–498). New York: Plenum.

Konecni, V. J., & Ebbesen, E. B. (1986). Courtroom testimony by psychologists on eyewitness identification issues: Critical notes and reflections. *Law and Human Behavior, 10,* 117–126.

Koocher, G. P., Goodman, G. S., White, C. S., Friedrich, W. N., Sivan, A. B., & Reynolds, C. R. (1995). Psychological science and the use of anatomically detailed dolls in child sexual-abuse assessments. *Psychological Bulletin, 118,* 199–222.

Koss, M. P. (1988). Hidden rape: Incidence, prevalence, and descriptive characteristics of sexual aggression and victimization in a national sample of college students. In A. W. Burgess (Ed.), *Sexual assault* (Vol. II, pp. 3–25). New York: Garland.

Koss, M. P. (1993). Detecting the scope of rape: A review of prevalence research methods. *Journal of Interpersonal Violence, 8,* 198–222.

Koss, M. P., & Harvey, M. R. (1991). *The rape victim: Clinical and community interventions* (2nd ed.). Thousand Oaks, CA: Sage.

Kosson, D. S., Kelly, J. C., & White, J. W. (1997). Psychopathy-related traits predict self-reported sexual aggression among college men. *Journal of Interpersonal Violence, 12,* 241–254.

Kotlowitz, A. (1999, February 8). The unprotected. *New Yorker,* pp. 42–53.

Kovera, M. B., & Borgida, E. (1998). Expert scientific testimony on child witnesses in the age of Daubert. In S. J. Ceci & H. Hembrooke (Eds.), *Expert witnesses in child abuse cases* (pp. 185–215). Washington, DC: American Psychological Association.

Kramer, M. (1997, December 15). How cops go bad. *Time,* pp. 78–83.

Kraske, S. (1986, November 25). Victim of abduction, rapes recounts ordeal of terror. *Kansas City Star,* pp. 1A, 8A.

Krauss, E., & Bonora, B. (1983). *Jurywork: Systematic techniques* (2nd ed.). St. Paul, MN: West.

Kravitz, D. A. (1995). Attitudes toward affirmative action plans directed at blacks: Effects of plan and individual differences. *Journal of Applied Social Psychology, 25,* 2192–2220.

Kravitz, D. A., Cutler, B. L., & Brock, P. (1993). Reliability and validity of the original and revised Legal Attitudes Questionnaire. *Law and Human Behavior, 17,* 661–677.

Kravitz, D., & Platania, J. (1993). Attitudes and beliefs about affirmative action: Effects of target sex and ethnicity. *Journal of Applied Psychology, 78,* 928–938.

Kretschmer, E. (1925). *Physique and character.* New York: Harcourt.

Kroes, W., Margolis, B., & Hurrell, J. (1974). Job stress in policemen. *Journal of Police Science and Administration, 2*(2), 145–155.

Kropp, P. R., & Hart, S. D. (1997). Assessing risk of violence in wife assaulters: The Spousal Assault Risk Assessment Guide. In C. D. Webster & M. A. Jackson (Eds.), *Impulsivity: Theory, assessment, and treatment.* New York: Guilford.

Kropp, P. R. & Hart, S. D. (2000). The Spousal Assault Risk Assessment (SARA) guide: Reliability and validity in adult male offenders. *Law and Human Behavior, 24,* 101–118.

Kropp, P. R., Hart, S. D., Webster, C. D., & Eaves, D (1994). *Spousal Assault Risk Assessment Guide.* North Tonawanda, NY: Multi-Health Systems.

Kropp, P. R., Hart, S. D., Webster, C. D., & Eaves, D (1995). *Spousal assault risk assessment guide (SARA): Users Manual* (version 2). Vancouver: British Columbia Institute Against Family Violence.

Kropp, P. R., Hart, S. D., Webster, C. D., & Eaves, D. (1998). *Manual for the Spousal Assault Risk Assessment Guide* (3rd ed.). Toronto: Multi-Health Systems.

Kuehnle, K. (1996). *Assessing allegations of child sexual abuse.* Sarasota, FL: Professional Resource Press.

Kurke, M. I., & Scrivner, E. M. (Eds.). (1995). *Police psychology into the 21st century.* Hillsdale, NJ: Lawrence Erlbaum.

Kwong, M. J., Bartholomew, K. & Dutton D. G. (1999) A gender comparison of domestic violence in Alberta. *Canadian Journal of Behavioural Science, 31*(3), 150–160.

Labaton, S. (1993a, July 12). Pursuers grappling with smoke on bomber's long trail of fear. *New York Times,* pp. A1, A8.

Labaton, S. (1993b, October 7). Clue and $1 million reward in case of serial bomber. *New York Times,* p. A10.

Laboratory of Community Psychiatry. (1974). *Competency to stand trial and mental illness.* Northvale, NJ: Jason Aronson.

Lacayo, R. (1991, April 8). Confessions that were taboo are now just a technicality. *Time,* pp. 26–27.

Lacovara, P. A. (1995, July 17). The Supreme Court ruling that curtailed race-based federal affirmative-action programs has left the private sector wondering if its programs may be next. *National Law Journal,* pp. B5–B6.

LaFortune, K. A., & Carpenter, B. N. (1998). Custody evaluations: A survey of mental health professionals. *Behavioral Sciences and the Law, 16,* 207–224.

Landau, J. (1997, May 5). Out of order. *New Republic,* pp. 9–10.

Landers, S. (1988, June). Use of "detailed dolls" questioned. *APA Monitor,* pp. 24–25.

Landsman, S. (1995). Of witches, madmen, and products liability: A historical survey of the use of expert testimony. *Behavioral Sciences and the Law, 13,* 131–157.

Langer, W. C. (1972). *The mind of Adolf Hitler.* New York: Basic Books.

Langevin, R., Paitich, D., Freeman, R., Mann, K., & Handy, L. (1978). Personality characteristics and sexual anomalies in males. *Canadian Journal of Behavioural Science, 10,* 222–238.

Larry P. et al. v. Riles et al., 343 F.Supp. 306, 1972; 495 F.Supp. 929 (1979).

Lassiter, G. D., & Irvine, A. A. (1986). Videotaped confession: The impact of camera point of view on judgments of coercion. *Journal of Applied Social Psychology, 16,* 268–276.

Lasso, R. (1998, September 11). *Affirmative action: One step in the struggle for civil rights.* Invited address, University of Kansas, Lawrence, KS.

Laufer, W. S., & Walt, S. D. (1992). The law and psychology of precedent. In D. K. Kagehiro & W. S. Laufer (Eds.), *Handbook of psychology and law* (pp. 39–55). New York: Springer-Verlag.

Laurentide Motels v. Beauport (City). (1989). 1 S.C.R. 705.

Lavin, M., & Sales, B. D. (1998). Moral justifications for limits on expert testimony. In S. J. Ceci & H. Hembrooke (Eds.), *Expert witnesses in child abuse cases* (pp. 59–81). Washington, DC: American Psychological Association.

Lawlor, R. J. (1998). The expert witness in child sexual abuse cases: A clinician's view. In S. J. Ceci & H. Hembrooke (Eds.), *Expert witnesses in child abuse cases* (pp. 105–122). Washington, DC: American Psychological Association.

Lawrence, R. (1984). Checking the allure of increased conviction rates: The admissibility of expert testimony on rape trauma syndrome in criminal proceedings. *University of Virginia Law Review, 79,* 1657–1704.

Lecci, L., & Myers, B. (1996, August). *Validating the factor structure of the Juror Bias Scale.* Paper presented at the meetings of the American Psychological Association, Toronto.

Lee, G. P., Loring, D. W., & Martin, R. C. (1992). Rey's 15–item visual memory test for the detection of malingering: Normative observations on patients with neurological disorders. *Psychological Assessment, 1,* 43–46.

Leichtman, M. D. & Ceci, S. J. (1995). The effects of stereotypes and suggestions on preschooler's reports. *Developmental Psychology, 31,* 568–578.

Leippe, M. R. (1995). The case for expert testimony about eyewitness memory. *Psychology, Public Policy, and Law, 1,* 909–959.

Leippe, M. R., Wells, G. L., & Ostrom, T. M. (1978). Crime seriousness as a determinant of accuracy in eyewitness identification. *Journal of Applied Psychology, 63,* 345–351.

Lemmon, J. A. (1985). *Family mediation practice.* New York: Collier.

Leo, R. A. (1992). From coercion to deception: The changing nature of police interrogation in America. *Crime, Law, and Social Change, 18,* 35–39.

Leo, R. A. (1996a). The impact of Miranda revisited. *Journal of Criminal Law and Criminology, 86,* 621–692.

Leo, R. A. (1996b). Inside the interrogation room. *Journal of Criminal Law and Criminology, 86,* 266–303.

Leo, R. A. (1996c). Miranda's revenge: Police interrogation as a confidence game. *Law and Society Review, 30,* 259–288.

Leo, J. (1993, November 29). An empty ruling on harassment. *U.S. News and World Report,* p. 20.

Levens, B. R., & Dutton, D. G. (1980). *The social service role of the police: Domestic crisis intervention.* Ottawa: Solicitor General of Canada.

Levy, C. J. (1994, December 12). F.B.I. says fatal mail blast is work of serial bomber. *New York Times,* pp. A1, A12.

Lewin, T. (1994, October 21). Outrage over 18 months for man who killed his wife in "heat of passion." *New York Times,* p. A9.

Lewis, A. (1991, August 5). Defining the issue. *New York Times,* p. A13.

Lewis, A. (1993, April 23). After the buck stops. *New York Times,* p. A19.

Lezak, M. D. (1995). *Neuropsychological assessment* (3rd ed.). New York: Oxford University Press.

Lind, E. A., & Tyler, T. R. (1988). *The social psychology of procedural justice.* New York: Plenum.

Lindsay, D. S., & Read, J. D. (1994). Psychotherapy and memories of childhood sexual abuse: A cognitive perspective. *Applied Cognitive Psychology, 8,* 281–338.

Lindsay, R. C. L. (1994). Biased lineups: Where do they come from? In D. Ross, J. Read, & M. Toglia (Eds.), *Adult eyewitness testimony: Current trends and developments* (pp. 182–200). New York: Cambridge University Press.

Lindsay, R. C. L., Pozzulo, J. D., Craig, W., Lee, K., & Corber, S. (1997). Simultaneous lineups, sequential lineups, and showups: Eyewitness identification decisions of adults and children. *Law and Human Behavior, 21,* 391–404.

Lindsay, R. C. L., Wallbridge, H., & Drennan, D. (1987). Do the clothes make the man? An exploration of the effect of lineup attire on eyewitness identification accuracy. *Canadian Journal of Behavioural Science, 19,* 463–478.

Lindsay, R. C. L., & Wells, G. L. (1980). What price justice? Exploring the relationship of lineup fairness to identification accuracy. *Law and Human Behavior, 4,* 303–314.

Lindsay, R. C. L., Wells, G. L., & Rumpel, C. (1981). Can people detect eyewitness identification accuracy within and across situations? *Journal of Applied Psychology, 66,* 79–89.

Linedecker, C., & Burt, W. (1990). *Nurses who kill.* New York: Windsor.

Lipsitt, P. D., Lelos, D., & McGarry, A. L. (1971). Competency for trial: A screening instrument. *American Journal of Psychiatry, 128,* 105–109.

Lipton, J. P. (1977). On the psychology of eyewitness testimony. *Journal of Applied Psychology, 62,* 90–93.

Liss, M. B., & McKinley-Pace, M. J. (1999). Best interests of the child: New twists on an old theme. In R. Roesch, S. D. Hart, & J. R. P. Ogloff (Eds.), *Psychology and law: The state of the discipline* (pp. 339–372). New York: Kluwer Academic/Plenum.

Livingston, J. D., Wilson, D., Tien, G., & Bond, L. (2003). A follow-up study of persons found not criminally on account of metal disorder in British Columbia. *Canadian Journal of Psychiatry, 48,* 408–415.

Lloyd-Bostock, S. (1989). *Law in practice.* Chicago: Lyceum.

Locke, D. and Code, R. (2001) "Canada's shelters for abused women, 1999–2000." *Juristat, 21.* Ottawa: Canadian Centre for Justice Statistics, Statistics Canada.

Loftus, E. F. (1975). Leading questions and the eyewitness report. *Cognitive Psychology, 7,* 560–572.

Loftus, E. F. (1979). *Eyewitness testimony.* Cambridge: Harvard University Press.

Loftus, E. F. (1983). Silence is not golden. *American Psychologist, 65,* 9–15.

Loftus, E. F. (1993a). Psychologists in the eyewitness world. *American Psychologist, 48,* 550–552.

Loftus, E. F. (1993b). The reality of repressed memories. *American Psychologist, 48,* 518–537.

Loftus, E. F. (2003). Memory in Canadian courts of law. *Canadian Psychology, 44,* 207–212.

Loftus, E. (2003). Our changeable memories: Legal and practical implications. *Nature Reviews: Neuroscience, 4,* 231–234.

Loftus, E. F., & Hoffman, H. G. (1989). Misinformation and memory: The creation of new memories. *Journal of Experimental Psychology: General, 118,* 100–104.

Loftus, E. F., & Ketcham, K. (1991). *Witness for the defense: The accused, the eyewitness, and the expert who puts memory on trial.* New York: St. Martin's Press.

Loftus, E. F., & Ketcham, K. (1994). *The myth of repressed memory: False memories and allegations of sexual abuse.* New York: St. Martin's/Griffin.

Loftus, E. F., Miller, D. G., & Burns, H. J. (1978). Semantic integration of verbal information into a visual memory.

Journal of Experimental Psychology: Human Learning and Memory, 4, 19–31.

Loftus, E. F., & Pickrell, J. (1995). Formation of false memories. *Psychiatric Annals, 25,* 720–25.

Loftus, E. F., & Rosenwald, L. A. (1995). Recovered memories: Unearthing the past in court. *Journal of Psychiatry and Law, 23,* 349–361.

Loh, W. D. (1981). Perspectives on psychology and law. *Journal of Applied Social Psychology, 11,* 314–355.

London Family Court Clinic (2002, May). *Child Witnesses in Canada: Where we've been, Where we're going.* Retrieved on August 17, 2004, from the Centre for Children & Families in the Justice System of the London Family Court Clinic Web site: http://www.lfcc.on.ca/Cwp_2002.pdf.

Loo, R. (1986). Suicide among police in a federal force. *Suicide and Life-Threatening Behavior, 16,* 379–88.

Lopez, S. (1998, May 11). Hide and seek. *Time,* pp. 56–60.

Los Angeles Times. (1993, April 23). President defends Reno, calls for investigation. *Kansas City Star,* p. A1.

Lott, B., Reilly, M. E., & Howard, D. (1982). Sexual assault and harassment: A campus community case study. *Signs, 8,* 296–319.

Louisell, D. W. (1955). The psychologist in today's legal world. *Minnesota Law Review, 39,* 235–260.

Louisell, D. W. (1957). The psychologist in today's legal world: Part II. *Minnesota Law Review, 41,* 731–750.

Low, P. W., Jeffries, J. C., & Bonnie, R. J. (1986). *The trial of John W. Hinckley, Jr.: A case study in the insanity defense.* Mineola, NY: Foundation Press.

Lowery, C. R. (1981). Child custody in divorce proceedings: A survey of judges. *Professional Psychology, 12,* 492–498.

Lowery, C. R. (1984). The Wisdom of Solomon: Criteria for child custody from the legal and clinical points of view. *Law and Human Behavior, 8,* 371–380.

Lowery, C. R. (1986). Maternal and joint custody: Differences in the decision process. *Law and Human Behavior, 10,* 303–315.

Luepnitz, D. A. (1982). *Child custody: A study of families after divorce.* Lexington, MA: D. C. Heath.

Luepnitz, D. A. (1986). A comparison of maternal, paternal, and joint custody: Understanding the varieties of post-divorce family life. *Journal of Divorce, 9,* 1–12.

Lukacs, J. (1997). *The Hitler of history.* New York: Alfred A. Knopf.

Lukas, J. A. (1997). *Big trouble.* New York: Simon & Schuster.

Lunde, D. T., & Morgan, J. (1980). *The die song: A journey into the mind of a mass murderer.* New York: W. W. Norton.

Lupfer, M., Cohen, R., Bernard, J. L., Smalley, D., & Schippmann, J. (1985). An attributional analysis of jurors' judgments in civil cases. *Journal of Social Psychology, 125,* 743–751.

Luus, C. A. E. (1991). *Eyewitness confidence: Social influence and belief perseverance.* Unpublished doctoral dissertation, Iowa State University, Ames.

Luus, C. A. E., & Wells, G. L. (1994). The malleability of eyewitness confidence: Co-witness and perseverance effects. *Journal of Applied Psychology, 79,* 714–723.

Lykken, D. T. (1981, June). The lie detector and the law. *Criminal Defense, 8*(3), 19–27.

Lykken, D. T. (1985). The probity of the polygraph. In S. M. Kassin & L. S. Wrightsman (Eds.), *The psychology of evidence and trial procedure* (pp. 95–123). Newbury Park, CA: Sage.

Lykken, D. T. (1988). The case against polygraph testing. In A. Gale (Ed.), *The polygraph test: Lies, truth and science* (pp. 111–125). London: Sage.

Lykken, D. T. (1998). *A tremor in the blood: Uses and abuse of the lie detector.* New York: Plenum.

Lynam, D. R. (2002). Fledgling psychopathy: A view from personality theory. *Law and Human Behavior, 26,* 255–259.

Lynn, S. J., & Nash, M. R. (1994). Truth in memory: Ramifications for psychotherapy and hypnotherapy. *American Journal of Clinical Hypnosis, 36,* 194–208.

Lyons, A., & Truzzi, M. (1991). *The blue sense: Psychic detectives and crime.* New York: Mysterious Press.

M. (K.) v. M. (H.) [1992] 3 S.C.R.

Maccoby, E. E., & Mnookin, R. H. (1992). *Dividing the child: Social and legal dilemmas of custody.* Cambridge: Harvard University Press.

Macdonald, J. M., & Michaud, D. L. (1987). *The confession: Interrogation and criminal profiles for police officers.* Denver: Apache.

MacKinnon, C. A. (1987). *Feminism unmodified: Discourses on life and law.* Cambridge: Harvard University Press.

Magley, V. J., Waldo, C. R., Drasgow, F., & Fitzgerald, L. F. (1998). *The impact of sexual harassment on military personnel: Is it the same for men and women?* Unpublished manuscript, University of Illinois at Urbana-Champaign. (Cited by Foote & Goodman-Delahunty, 1999.)

Maher G. (1977). *Hostage: A police approach to a contemporary crisis.* Springfield, IL: Charles C. Thomas.

Malamuth, N. (1981). Rape proclivity among males. *Journal of Social Issues, 37*(4), 138–154.

Malcolm, J. (1995, October 16). Easy time. *New Yorker,* pp. 98–107.

Malcolm, P. B., Andrews, D. A., & Quinsey, V. L. (1993). Discriminant and predictive validity of phallometric measured sexual age and gender preference. *Journal of Interpersonal Violence, 8,* 486–501.

Malpass, R. S., & Devine, P. G. (1980). Realism and eyewitness identification research. *Law and Human Behavior, 4,* 347–358.

Malpass, R. S., & Devine, P. G. (1981). Eyewitness identification: Lineup instructions and the absence of the offender. *Journal of Applied Psychology, 66,* 482–489.

Malpass, R. S., & Devine, P. G. (1983). Measuring the fairness of eyewitness identification lineups. In S. M. A. Lloyd-Bostock & B. R. Clifford (Eds.), *Evaluating witness evidence* (pp. 81–102). New York: John Wiley.

Mandelbaum, R. (1989, November). Jury consultants: What can they do, and is it worth it? *Inside Litigation, 3*(11), 1, 13–19.

Manning, A. (1998, February 23). Operating with sexism. *USA Today,* pp. 1D–2D.

Manson v. Braithwaite, 432 U.S. 98 (1977).

Marafiote, R. A. (1985). *The custody of children: A behavioral assessment model.* New York: Plenum.

Marcil-Gratton, N. & Le Bourdais, C. (1999). *Custody, access and child support: Findings from the National Longitudinal Survey of Children and Youth.* Ottawa, Department of Justice Canada.

Marxsen, D., Yuille, J. C., & Nisbet, M. (1995). The complexities of eliciting and assessing children's statements. *Psychology, Public Policy, and Law, 1,* 450–460.

Mason, M. A. (1991). The McMartin case revisited: The conflict between social work and criminal justice. *Social Work, 36,* 391–395.

Mason, M. A. (1998). Expert testimony regarding the characteristics of sexually abused children: A controversy on both sides of the bench. In S. J. Ceci & H. Hembrooke (Eds.), *Expert witnesses in child abuse cases* (pp. 217–234). Washington, DC: American Psychological Association.

Mauro, T. (1993, November 10). Court clears air on sexual harassment. *USA Today,* pp. 1A–2A.

Mayer, J., & Abramson, J. (1994). *Strange justice: The selling of Clarence Thomas.* Boston: Houghton Mifflin.

McAlary, M. (1987). *Buddy boys: When good cops turn bad.* New York: G. P. Putnam's.

McAllister, B. (1995, November 20–26). The problem that won't go away. *Washington Post National Weekly Edition,* p. 33.

McAuliff, B. D., & Kovera, M. B. (1998, August). *Are laypersons' beliefs about suggestibility consistent with expert opinion?* Paper presented at the meetings of the American Psychological Association, San Francisco.

McCandless, S. R., & Sullivan, L. P. (1991, May 6). Two courts adopt new standard to determine sexual harassment. *National Law Journal,* pp. 18–20.

McCann, J. T. (1998). A conceptual framework for identifying various types of confessions. *Behavioral Sciences and the Law, 16,* 441–453.

McCleskey v. Kemp, 481 U.S. 279 (1987).

McCloskey, M., & Egeth, H. E. (1983). Eyewitness identification: What can a psychologist tell a jury? *American Psychologist, 38,* 550–563.

McCloskey, M., Egeth, H., & McKenna, J. (1986). The experimental psychologist in court: The ethics of expert testimony. *Law and Human Behavior, 10,* 1–13.

McConahay, J. B. (1983). Modern racism and modern discrimination: The effects of race, racial attitudes, and context on simulated hiring decisions. *Personality and Social Psychology Bulletin, 9,* 551–558.

McConahay, J. B. (1986). Modern racism, ambivalence, and the Modern Racism Scale. In J. F. Dovidio & S. L. Gaertner (Eds.), *Prejudice, discrimination, and racism* (pp. 91–125). San Diego: Academic Press.

McConahay, J. B., & Hough, J. C. (1976). Symbolic racism. *Journal of Social Issues, 32*, 23–45.

McCord, D. (1985). The admissibility of expert testimony regarding rape trauma syndrome in rape prosecutions. *Boston College Law Review, 26*, 1143–1213.

McDaniel, S. A., & van Rossmalen, E. (1991). Sexual harassment in Canadian academe: Explorations in power and privilege. *Atlantis: A Women's Studies Journal, 17*, 3–13.

McIver, W., Wakefield, H., & Underwager, R. (1989). Behavior of abused and non-abused children in interviews with anatomically correct dolls. *Issues in Child Abuse Accusations, 1*, 39–48.

McMains, M. (1988). Psychologists' roles in hostage negotiations. In J. Reese & J. Horn (Eds.), *Police psychology: Operational assistance* (pp. 281–317). Washington, DC: U.S. Government Printing Office.

McNally, R. J. (2003). *Remembering trauma*. Cambridge, MA: Belknap/Harvard University.

McNamara, J. (1967). Uncertainties in police work: The relevance of police recruits' backgrounds and training. In D. Bordua (Ed.), *The police: Six sociological essays* (pp. 163–252). New York: John Wiley.

McPoyle, T. J. (1981). The investigative technique of criminal profiling. *Your Virginia State Trooper, 3*(1), 87.

McQuiston, J. T. (1994, May 6). Rifkin depicted as delusional. *New York Times*, p. B16.

Meadows, R. J. (1987). Beliefs of law enforcement administrators and criminal justice educators toward the needed skill competencies in entry-level police training curriculum. *Journal of Police Science and Administration, 15*, 1–9.

Meddis, S. V. (1993, October 7). $1 million for clues to "Unabomber." *USA Today*, p. 3A.

Meehl, P. E. (1954). *Clinical versus statistical prediction: A theoretical analysis and a review of the evidence*. Minneapolis: University of Minnesota Press.

Meloy, J. R. (Ed.). (1998). *The psychology of stalking: Clinical and forensic perspectives*. San Diego: Academic Press.

Melton, G. B. (1995). Review of the Ackerman-Schoendorf Scales for Parental Evaluation of Custody. In J. C. Conoley & J. C. Impara (Eds.), *Twelfth mental measurements yearbook* (p. 22). Lincoln: University of Nebraska Press.

Melton, G. B., Goodman, G. S., Kalichman, S. C., Levine, M., Saywitz, K. J., & Koocher, G. P. (1995). Empirical research on child maltreatment and the law. *Journal of Clinical Child Psychology, 24*, 47–77.

Melton, G. B., Huss, M. T., & Tomkins, A. J. (1999). Training in forensic psychology and the law. In A. K. Hess and I. B. Weiner (Eds.), *Handbook of forensic psychology* (2nd ed., pp. 700–720). New York: John Wiley.

Melton, G. B., & Limber, S. (1989). Psychologists' involvement in cases of child maltreatment: Limits of role and expertise. *American Psychologist, 44*, 1225–1233.

Melton, G. B., Petrila, J., Poythress, N. G., & Slobogin, C. (1987). *Psychological evaluations for the courts*. New York: Guilford Press.

Melton, G. B., Petrila, J., Poythress, N. G., & Slobogin, C. (1997). *Psychological evaluations for the courts* (2nd ed.). New York: Guilford Press.

Melton, G. B., & Saks, M. J. (1990). AP-LS's pro bono amicus brief project. *American Psychology-Law Society News, 10*, 5.

Melton, G. B., Weithorn, L. A., & Slobogin, C. (1985). *Community mental health centers and the courts: An evaluation of community-based forensic services*. Lincoln: University of Nebraska Press.

Meritor Savings Bank v. Vinson, 106 S.Ct. 2399 (1986).

Meyer, C., & Taylor, S. (1986). Adjustment to rape. *Journal of Personality and Social Psychology, 50*, 1226–1234.

Mezzo v. The Queen (1996) 1 S.C.R. 802.

Michaud, S. G. (with Hazelwood, R.). (1998). *The evil that men do: FBI profiler Roy Hazelwood's journey into the minds of sexual predators*. New York: St. Martin's Press.

Micheels, P. A. (1991). *Heat: The fire investigators and their war on arson and murder*. New York: St. Martin's Press.

Milano, C. (1989, August). Re-evaluating recruitment to better target top minority talent. *Management Review*, pp. 29–32.

Milgram, S. (1974). *Obedience to authority*. New York: Harper & Row.

Mills, R. B., McDevitt, R. J., & Tonkin, S. (1966). Situational tests in metropolitan police recruit selection. *Journal of Criminal Law, Criminology, and Police Science, 57*, 99–104.

Miner v. Miner, 11 Ill. 43 (1849).

Miranda v. Arizona, 384 U.S. 436 (1966).

Miron, M. S., & Douglas, J. E. (1979, September). Threat analysis: The psycholinguistic approach. *FBI Law Enforcement Bulletin*, pp. 1–8.

Monahan, J. (1992). Mental disorder and violent behavior: Perceptions and evidence. *American Psychologist, 47*, 511–521.

Monahan, J., & Steadman, H. (1994). Toward the rejuvenation of risk research. In J. Monahan & H. Steadman (Eds.), *Violence and mental disorder: Developments in risk assessment* (pp. 1–17). Chicago: University of Chicago Press.

Monahan, J., & Walker, L. (1986). Social authority: Obtaining, evaluating, and establishing social science in law. *University of Pennsylvania Law Review, 134*, 477–517.

Monahan, J., & Walker, L. (1988). Social science research in law: A new paradigm. *American Psychologist, 43*, 465–472.

Monahan, J., & Walker, L. (1990). *Social Science in Law: Cases and Materials*. (2nd ed.) Westbury, NY: Foundation.

Monahan, J., & Walker, L. (1991). Judicial use of social science research. *Law and Human Behavior, 15*, 571–584.

Monahan, J. (1997). Foreword. In C. D. Webster & M. A. Jackson (Eds.), *Impulsivity: Theory, assessment, and treatment* (pp. ix–xi). New York: Guilford.

Moran, G., & Comfort, J. C. (1982). Scientific jury selection: Sex as a moderator of demographic and personality predictors of impaneled felony juror behavior. *Journal of Personality and Social Psychology, 43*, 1052–1063.

Moran, G., & Cutler, B. L. (1989, August). *Dispositional predictors of criminal case verdicts*. Symposium paper presented at the meetings of the American Psychological Association, New Orleans.

Moran, G., Cutler, B. L., & DeLisa, A. (1994). Attitudes toward tort reform, scientific jury selection, and juror bias: Verdict inclination in criminal and civil trials. *Law and Psychology Review, 18,* 309–328.

Morison, S., & Greene, E. (1992). Juror and expert knowledge of child sexual abuse. *Child Abuse and Neglect, 16,* 595–613.

Morris, R. J. (1995, August). *Ethical issues in the conduct of child custody evaluations*. Paper presented at the meetings of the American Psychological Association, New York.

Morris, W. (1998). *The ghosts of Medgar Evers: A tale of race, murder, Mississippi and Hollywood*. New York: Random House.

Morse, S. J. (1978). Law and mental health professionals: The limits of expertise. *Professional Psychology, 9,* 389–399.

Morse, S. J. (1990). The misbegotten marriage of soft psychology and bad law: Psychological self-defense as a justification for homicide. *Law and Human Behavior, 14,* 595–618.

Mossman, D. (1994). Assessing predictions of violence: Being accurate about accuracy. *Journal of Consulting and Clinical Psychology, 62,* 783–792.

Mossman, K. (1973, May). Jury selection: An expert's view. *Psychology Today,* pp. 78–79.

Motiuk, L.L. & Belcourt, R. I. (1995). *A statistical profile of homicide, robbery, sex and drug offenders in federal corrections.* Ottawa: Solicitor General Canada Brief B-11.

Motiuk, L. L., & Belcourt, R. I., (1997). *Homicide, sex, robbery, and drug offenders in federal convictions: An end of 1996 review.* Ottawa: Research Branch, Correctional Service of Canada.

Mullin, C. (1986). *Error of judgement.* London: Chatto & Windus.

Münsterberg, H. (1908). *On the witness stand.* Garden City, NY: Doubleday.

Murdock Hicks, M., Rogers, R., & Cashel, M. L. (2000). Predictions of violent and total infractions among institutionalized male juvenile offenders. *Journal of the American Academy of Psychiatry and the Law, 28,* 183–190.

Murphy, W. D., & Peters, J. M. (1992). Profiling child sexual abusers: Psychological considerations. *Criminal Justice and Behavior, 19*(1), 24–37.

Murray, D. M., & Wells, G. L. (1982). Does knowledge that a crime was staged affect eyewitness performance? *Journal of Applied Social Psychology, 12,* 42–53.

Myers, B., & Lecci, L. (1998). Revising the factor structure of the Juror Bias Scale: A method for the empirical validation of theoretical constructs. *Law and Human Behavior, 22,* 239–256.

Myers, J. E. B. (1992). *Legal issues in child abuse and neglect.* Thousand Oaks, CA: Sage.

Myers, J. E. B., Bays, J., Becker, J., Berliner, L., Corwin, D. L., & Saywitz, K. J. (1989). Expert testimony in child sexual abuse litigation. *Nebraska Law Review, 68,* 1–145.

Nacoste, R. W. (1985). Selection procedure and responses to affirmative action: The case of favorable treatment. *Law and Human Behavior, 9,* 225–242.

Nacoste, R. W. (1987). Social psychology and affirmative action: The importance of process in policy analysis. *Journal of Social Issues, 43*(1), 127–132.

Nacoste, R. W. (1994). If empowerment is the goal …: Affirmative action and social interaction. *Basic and Applied Social Psychology, 15,* 87–112.

Nacoste, R. W. (1996). How affirmative action can pass constitutional and social psychological muster. *Journal of Social Issues, 52*(4), 133–144.

Nagel, T. W. (1983, October). *Tensions between law and psychology: Fact, myth, or ideology?* Paper presented at the meetings of the American Psychology-Law Society, Chicago.

Nathan, D. (1987). The making of a modern witch trial. *Village Voice, 33,* 19–32.

Narby, D. J., Cutler, B. L., & Moran, G. (1993). A meta-analysis of the association between authoritarianism and jurors' perceptions of defendant culpability. *Journal of Applied Psychology, 78,* 34–42.

National Advisory Commission on Criminal Justice Standards and Goals. (1973). *Report on police.* Washington, DC: U.S. Government Printing Office.

National Anti-Racism Council of Canada (2002). *Racial discrimination in Canada: The status of compliance by the Canadian government with the International Convention on the Elimination of All Forms of Racial Discrimination.* Toronto: CultureLink. Retrieved on May 20, 2004, from: http://www.narc.freeservers.com/whats_new.html.

National Missing Children Services, National Police Services & Royal Canadian Mounted Police (2001). *Canada's missing children: Annual report 2001.* Ottawa: National Missing Children's Services.

Niederhoffer, A. (1967). *Behind the shield: The police in urban society.* Garden City, NY: Doubleday.

Neiderland, W. G. (1982). The survivor syndrome: Further observations and dimensions. *Journal of American Psychoanalytic Association, 30,* 413–425.

Neil v. Biggers, 409 U.S. 188 (1972).

Nemy, E. (1975). Women begin to speak out against sexual harassment at work. *New York Times.*

Nichols, H. R., & Molinder, I. (1984). *Muliphasic Sex Inventory Manual.* Tacoma, WA: Nichols & Molinder.

Nicholson, R. (1999). Forensic assessment. In R. Roesch, S. D. Hart, & J. R. P. Ogloff (Eds.), *Psychology and law: The state of the discipline* (pp. 121–173). New York: Kluwer Academic/Plenum.

Nicholson, R. A., Briggs, S. R., & Robertson, H. C. (1988). Instruments for assessing competency to stand trial: How do they work? *Professional Psychology: Research and Practice, 19,* 383–394.

Nicholson, R. A., & Johnson, W. G. (1991). Prediction of competency to stand trial: Contribution of demographics, type of offense, clinical characteristics, and psychological ability. *International Journal of Law and Psychiatry, 14,* 287–297.

Niederhoffer, A. (1967). *Behind the Shield: The police in urban society.* Garden City, NY: Doubleday.

Nietzel, M. T., & Dillehay, R. C. (1986). *Psychological consultation in the courtroom.* New York: Pergamon Press.

Nims, J. (1998, August). *NIMS Observation Checklist.* Paper presented at the meetings of the American Psychological Association, San Francisco.

Nisbett, R., Borgida, E., Crandall, C., & Reed, H. (1982). Popular induction: Information is not necessarily informative. In D. Kahneman, P. Slovic, & A. Tversky (Eds.), *Judgment under uncertainty: Heuristics and biases* (pp. 101–116). New York: Cambridge University Press.

Noguchi, T. T. (with DiMona, J.). (1985). *Coroner at large.* New York: Simon & Schuster.

Norris, J. (1992). *Jeffrey Dahmer.* New York: Pinnacle Books.

Note. (1953). Voluntary false confessions: A neglected area in criminal investigation. *Indiana Law Journal, 28,* 374–392.

O'Brien, D. (1985). *Two of a kind: The hillside stranglers.* New York: New American Library.

Office of Technology Assessment. (1983). *Scientific validity of polygraph testing: A research review and evaluation.* Washington, DC: U.S. Congress.

Ofshe, R. (1992). Inadvertent hypnosis during interrogation: False confessions due to dissociative state, misidentified multiple personality, and the satanic cult hypothesis. *International Journal of Clinical and Experimental Hypnosis, 40,* 125–156.

Ofshe, R. J., & Leo, R. A. (1997). The social psychology of police interrogation: The theory and classification of true and false confessions. *Studies in Law, Politics, and Society, 16,* 189–215.

Ofshe, R., & Watters, E. (1994). *Making monsters: False memories, psychotherapy, and sexual hysteria.* New York: Charles Scribner's.

Ogloff, J. R. P. (1990). Law and psychology in Canada: The need for training and research. *Canadian Psychology, 31,* 61–73.

Ogloff, J. R. P. (1999). Graduate training in law and psychology at Simon Fraser University. *Professional Psychology: Research and Practice, 30,* 99–103.

Ogloff, J. R. P. (2000). Two steps forward and one step backward: The law and psychology movement(s) in the 20th century. *Law and Human Behavior, 24,* 457–483.

Ogloff, J. (2001). Supreme Court refused to hear from CPA. *Psynopsis, 2,* 2–4.

Ogloff, J. R. P. (2004). Invited introductory remarks to the special issue. *Canadian Journal of Behavioural Science, 36,* 84–86.

Ogloff, J. R. P. (in press). Into the public forum: Experiences from legal psychology in Canada. *Canadian Psychology.*

Ogloff, J. R. P., & Finkelman, D. (1999). Law and psychology: An overview. In R. Roesch, S. D. Hart, & J. R. P. Ogloff (Eds.), *Psychology and law: The state of the discipline* (pp. 1–20). New York, NY: Kluwer Academic/Plenum.

Ogloff, J. R. P., & Otto, R. K. (1993). Psychological autopsy: Clinical and legal perspectives. *Saint Louis University Law Journal, 37,* 607–646.

Ogloff, J. R. P., Roberts, C. F., & Roesch, R. (1993). The insanity defense: Legal standards and clinical assessment. *Applied and Preventive Psychology, 2,* 163–178.

Ogloff, J. R. P., & Vidmar, N. (1994). The impact of pretrial publicity on jurors: A study to compare the relative effects of television and print media in a child sex abuse case. *Law and Human Behavior, 18,* 507–525.

Ogloff, J., Wong, S., & Greenwood, A. (1990). Treating criminal psychopaths in a therapeutic community program. *Behavioral Sciences & the Law, 8,* 81–90.

O'Hara, C. E., & O'Hara, G. L. (1956). *Fundamentals of criminal investigation.* Springfield, IL: Charles C Thomas.

O'Hara, C. E., & O'Hara, G. L. (1980). *Fundamentals of criminal investigation* (5th ed.). Springfield, IL: Charles C Thomas.

Okpaku, S. R. (1976). Psychology: Impediment or aid in child custody cases? *Rutgers Law Review, 29,* 1117–1153.

Oldfield, D. (1997). What help do the police need with their enquiries? In J. L. Jackson & D. A. Bekerian (Eds.), *Offender profiling: Theory, research and practice* (pp. 93–106). New York: John Wiley.

Olson, W. K. (1991). *The litigation explosion: What happened when America unleashed the lawsuit.* New York: Dutton.

Oncale v. Sundowner Offshore Services, 118 S.Ct. 998 (1998).

Ontario Human Rights Commission (2003). *Paying the price: The human cost of racial profiling.* Retrieved on July 2, 2004, from the Ontario Human Rights Commission Web site: http://www.ohrc.on.ca/english/consultations/racial-profiling-report.shtml.

Opotow, S. (1996). Affirmative action, fairness, and the scope of justice. *Journal of Social Issues, 52*(4), 19–24.

Orlando, J. A., & Koss, M. P. (1983). The effect of sexual victimization on sexual satisfaction: A study of the negative association hypothesis. *Journal of Abnormal Psychology, 92,* 104–106.

Orne, M. T. (1979). The use and misuse of hypnosis in court. *International Journal of Clinical and Experimental Hypnosis, 27,* 311–341.

Orne, M. T., Soskis, D. A., Dinges, D. F., & Orne, E. C. (1984). Hypnotically induced testimony. In G. L. Wells & E. F. Loftus (Eds.), *Eyewitness testimony: Psychological perspectives* (pp. 171–213). New York: Cambridge University Press.

Orth, M. (1999). *Vulgar favors: Andrew Cunanan, Gianni Versace, and the largest failed manhunt in U.S. history.* New York: Delacorte.

Ostrov, E. (1985, August). *Validation of police officer recruit candidates' self-reported drug use on the Inwald Personality Inventory.* Paper presented at the meetings of the American Psychological Association, Los Angeles.

Ostrov, E. (1986). Police/law enforcement and psychology. *Behavioral Sciences and the Law, 4,* 353–370.

Otto, R. (1996, August). *Outline on custody evaluations.* Tampa: Florida Mental Health Institute.

Otto, R. K., & Collins, R. P. (1995). Use of MMPI-2/MMPI-A in child custody evaluations. In Y. S. Ben-Porath, J. R. Graham, G. C. N. Hall, R. D. Hirschman, & M. S. Zaragoza (Eds.), *Forensic applications of the MMPI-2* (pp. 222–252). Thousand Oaks, CA: Sage.

Otto, R. K., Edens, J. F., Poythress, N. G., & Nicholson, R. A. (1998, March). *Psychometric properties of the MacArthur Competence Assessment Tool-Criminal Adjudication (MacCAT-CA).* Paper presented at the meetings of the American Psychology-Law Society, Redondo Beach, CA.

P. (D.) v. S. (C.). (1993). 4 S.C.R. 141.

Palmer, S. (1960). *A study of murder.* New York: Thomas Crowell.

Palmore v. Sidoti, 466 U.S. 429 (1984).

Paris, M. L. (1996). Trust, lies, and interrogation. *Virginia Journal of Social Policy and Law, 3,* 15–44.

Park, L. & Renner, K. (1998). The failure to acknowledge differences in developmental capabilities leads to unjust outcomes for child witnesses in sexual abuse cases. *Canadian Journal of Mental Health, 17,* 5–19.

Parker, L. (1998, April 24–26). The "great pretender." *USA Today,* pp. 1A–2A.

PASE v. Hannon, 506 F.Supp. 831 (1980).

Paterson, E. J. (1979). How the legal system responds to battered women. In D. M. Moore (Ed.), *Battered women* (pp. 79–99). Newbury Park, CA: Sage.

Patterson, C. J. (1992). Children of lesbian and gay parents. *Child Development, 63,* 1025–1042.

Payne, D. G., Neuschatz, J. S., Lampinen, J. M., & Lynn, S. J. (1997). Compelling memory illusions: The phenomenological qualities of false memories. *Current Directions in Psychological Science, 6,* 56–60.

Peace, K. A. P., & Porter, S. (2004). A longitudinal investigation of the reliability of memories for trauma and other emotional experiences. *Applied Cognitive Psychology, 18,* 1143–1159.

Peak, K. J., & Glensor, R. W. (1996). *Community policing and problem solving: Strategies and practices.* Upper Saddle River, NJ: Prentice-Hall.

Pekkanen, J. (1976). *Victims: An account of rape.* New York: Popular Library.

Pence, E., & Paymor, M. (1985). *Power and control: Tactics of men who batter: An educational curriculum.* Duluth, MN: Minnesota Program Development.

Pennebaker, J. W. (1993). Putting stress into words: Health, linguistic, and therapeutic implications. *Behavior Research and Therapy, 31,* 539–548.

Pennebaker, J. W. & Beall, S. K. (1986). Confronting a traumatic event: Toward an understanding of inhibition and disease. *Journal of Abnormal Psychology, 95,* 274–281.

Pennington, N., & Hastie, R. (1981). Juror decision making models: The generalization gap. *Psychological Bulletin, 89,* 246–287.

Penrod, S. D., & Cutler, B. L. (1987). Assessing the competence of juries. In I. B. Weiner & A. K. Hess (Eds.), *Handbook of forensic psychology.* New York: John Wiley.

Penrod, S., & Cutler, B. (1995). Witness confidence and witness accuracy: Assessing their forensic relation. *Psychology, Public Policy, and Law, 1,* 817–845.

Penrod, S. D., Fulero, S. M., & Cutler, B. L. (1995). Expert psychological testimony on eyewitness reliability before and after Daubert: The state of the law and the science. *Behavioral Sciences and the Law, 13,* 229–259.

People v. Raymond Buckey et al., Los Angeles Sup. Ct. No. A750900 (1990).

People v. Torres, 128 Misc.2d 129, 488 N.Y.2d 358 (Sup. Ct. 1985).

Perez-Pena, R. (1994, December 12). Investigators describe a meticulous maker of bombs. *New York Times,* p. A12.

Perkins, D. D. (1988). The use of social science in public interest litigation: A role for community psychologists. *American Journal of Community Psychology, 16,* 465–485.

Perot, A. R., Brooks, L., & Gersh, T. L. (1992, August). *Development of the Beliefs about Sexual Harassment Scale.* Paper presented at the meetings of the American Psychological Association, Washington, DC.

Perry, E. L., Kulik, C. T., & Bourhis, A. C. (2004). The reasonable woman standard: Effects of sexual harassment court decisions. *Law and Human Behavior, 28,* 9–27.

Perry, N. W., & Wrightsman, L. S. (1991). *The child witness: Legal issues and dilemmas.* Thousand Oaks, CA: Sage.

Peterson, C., Moores, L., & White, G. (2001). Recounting the same events again and again: Children's consistency across multiple interviews. *Applied Cognitive Psychology, 15,* 353–371.

Pettigrew, T. F., & Meertens, R. W. (1995). Subtle and blatant prejudice in Western Europe. *European Journal of Social Psychology, 25,* 57–75.

Pezdek, K., & Banks, W. P. (Eds.). (1996). *The recovered memory/false memory debate.* San Diego: Academic Press.

Pezdek, K., Finger, K., & Hodge, D. (1997). Planting false childhood memories: The role of event plausibility. *Psychological Science, 8,* 437–441.

Pezdek, K., & Taylor, J. (2000). Discriminating between accounts of true and false events. In D. F. Bjorklund (Ed.), *Research and theory in false-memory creation in children and adults* (pp. 69–92). Mahwah, NJ: Lawrence Erlbaum and Associates.

Pigott, M. A., Foley, L. A., Covati, C. J., & Wasserman, A. (1998, March). Mock jurors' *perceptions of a male plaintiff in sexual harassment litigation.* Paper presented at the meetings of the American Psychology-Law Society, Redondo Beach, CA.

Pinkney v. Canada (Attorney General) (1998), 145 F.T.R. 311.

Pinizzotto, A. J. (1984). Forensic psychology: Criminal personality profiling. *Journal of Police Science and Administration, 12,* 32–40.

Pinizzotto, A. J., & Finkel, N. J. (1990). Criminal personality profiling: An outcome and process study. *Law and Human Behavior, 14,* 215–233.

Pirozzolo, F. J., Funk, J., & Dywan, J. (1991). Neuropsychology and its applications to the legal forum. In J. Dywan, R. D. Kaplan, & F. J. Pirozzolo (Eds.), *Neuropsychology and the law* (pp. 1–23). New York: Springer-Verlag.

Plass, P. S., Finkelhor, D., & Hotaling, G. T. (1997). Risk factors for family abduction: Demographic and family interaction characteristics. *Journal of Family Violence, 12,* 313–332.

Plevan, B. P. (1993, December 6). Harris won't end harassment questions. *National Law Journal,* pp. 19–20.

Plous, S. (1996). Ten myths about affirmative action. *Journal of Social Issues, 52*(4), 25–31.

Podlesny, J. A., & Raskin, D. C. (1977). Physiological measures and the detection of deception. *Psychological Bulletin, 84,* 782–799.

Pogrebin, M. R., Poole, E. D., & Regoli, R. M. (1986). Stealing money: An assessment of bank embezzlers. *Behavioral Sciences and the Law, 4,* 481–490.

Pokorny, A. D. (1983). Prediction of suicide in psychiatric patients: Report of a prospective study. *Archives of General Psychiatry, 40,* 249–257.

Poole, D. A., & White, L. T. (1991). Effect of question repetition on the eyewitness testimony of children and adults. *Developmental Psychology, 27,* 975–986.

Porter, S. (2004). Forensic psychology. *Canadian Journal of Behavioural Science, 36,* 81.

Porter, S. (1996). Without conscience or without active conscience? The etiology of psychopathy revisited. *Aggression and Violent Behavior, 1,* 179–189.

Porter, S., Birt A. R., & Boer, D. P. (2001). Investigation of the criminal and conditional release histories of Canadian federal offenders as a function of psychopathy and age. *Law and Human Behavior, 25,* 647–661.

Porter, S., Birt, A. R., Yuille, J. C., & Hervé, H. (2001). Memory for murder: A psychological perspective on dissociative amnesia in forensic contexts. *International Journal of Law and Psychiatry, 24,* 23–42.

Porter, S., Campbell, M. A., Birt, A. R., & Woodworth, M. T. (2003). "He said, She Said": A psychological perspective on historical memory evidence in the courtroom. *Canadian Psychology, 44,* 190–206.

Porter, S., Campbell, M. A., Birt, A. R., & Woodworth, M. T. (2003). "We said, she said": A response to Loftus (2003). *Canadian Psychology, 44,* 213–215.

Porter, S., Campbell, M. A., Woodworth, M., & Birt, A. R. (2001). A new psychological conceptualization of the sexual psychopath. In F. Columbus (Ed.) *Advances in Psychological Research (Volume 7).* Huntington, NY: Nova Science Publishers, Inc.

Porter, S., Drugge, J., Fairweather, D., Herve, H., Birt, A. R., & Boer, D. (2000). Profiles of psychopathy in incarcerated sex offenders. *Criminal Justice and Behavior, 27,* 196–215.

Porter, S., & Porter, S. (2004, in press). Psychopathy and violent crime. In H. Hervé & J. C. Yuille (Eds.), *Psychopathy in the third millennium: Research and practice.* New York: Academic Press.

Porter, S., & Yuille, J.C. (1996). The language of deceit: An investigation of the verbal clues to deception in the interrogation context. *Law and Human Behavior, 20,* 443–458.

Porter, S., Yuille, J. C., & Lehman, D. R. (1999). The nature of real, implanted and fabricated memories for emotional childhood events: Implications for the recovered memory debate. *Law and Human Behavior, 23,* 517–537.

Porter, S., & Woodworth, M. (2004, in press). Patterns of violent behavior in the criminal psychopath. In C. Patrick (Ed.). *Handbook of psychopathy.* New York: Guilford.

Porter, S., Woodworth, M., & Birt, A. R. (2000). Truth, lies, and videotape: An investigation of the ability of federal parole officers to detect deception. *Law and Human Behavior, 24,* 643–658.

Porter, S., Woodworth, M., Earle, J., Drugge, J., & Boer, D. P. (2003). Characteristics of violent behavior exhibited during sexual homicides by psychopathic and non-psychopathic murderers. *Law and Human Behavior, 27,* 459–470.

Post, J. M. (1991). Saddam Hussein of Iraq: A political psychology profile. *Political Psychology, 12,* 279–289.

Potter, J. A., & Bost, F. (1995). *Fatal justice: Reinvestigating the MacDonald murders.* New York: Norton.

Powitsky, R. J. (1979). The use and misuse of psychologists in a hostage situation. *The Police Chief, 46*(6), 30–33.

Poythress, N. G. (1980). Assessment and prediction in the hostage situation: Optimizing the use of psychological data. *The Police Chief, 47*(8), 34–38.

Poythress, N., Bonnie, R., Hoge, S., Monahan, J., & Oberlander, L. (1994). Client abilities to assist counsel and make decisions in criminal cases: Findings from three studies. *Law and Human Behavior, 18,* 437–452.

Pratkanis, A. R., & Turner, M. E. (1996). The proactive removal of discriminatory barriers: Affirmative action as effective help. *Journal of Social Issues, 52*(4), 111–132.

Prentky, R. A., Lee, A. F. S., Knight, R. A., & Cerce, D. (1997). Recidivism rates among child molesters and rapists: A methodological analysis. *Law and Human Behavior, 21,* 635–659.

Press, A. (1983, January 10). Divorce American style. *Newsweek,* pp. 42–48.

Price Waterhouse v. Hopkins, 109 S.Ct. 1775 (1989).

Proulx, J., Pellerin, B., Paradis, Y., McKibben, A., Aubut, J., & Ouimet, M. (1997). Static and dynamic predictors of recidivism in sexual aggressors. *Sexual Abuse: A Journal of Research and Treatment, 9,* 7–27.

Pryor, J. B. (1987). Sexual harassment proclivities in men. *Sex Roles, 17,* 269–290.

Pryor, J. B., Giedd, J. L., & Williams, K. B. (1995). A social psychological model for predicting sexual harassment. *Journal of Social Issues, 51*(1), 69–84.

Pryor, J. B., LaVite, C., & Stoller, L. (1993). A social psychological analysis of sexual harassment: The person/situation interaction. *Journal of Vocational Behavior, 42,* 68–83.

Pryor, J. B., & Whalen, N. J. (1997). A typology of sexual harassment: Characteristics of harassers and the social circumstances under which harassment occurs. In W. O'Donohue (Ed.), *Sexual harassment: Theory, research, and treatment* (pp. 129–151). Boston: Allyn & Bacon.

Pulaski, C. (1980). Criminal trials: "A search for truth" or something else? *Criminal Law Bulletin, 16,* 41, 44–45.

Quen, J. M. (1981). Anglo-American concepts of criminal responsibility: A brief history. In S. J. Hucker, C. D. Webster & M. H. Ben-Aron (Eds.), *Mental disorder and criminal responsibility.* Toronto: Butterworths.

Quinsey, V. L., Arnold, L. S., & Pruesse, M. G. (1980). MMPI profiles of men referred for a pretrial psychiatric assessment as a function of offense type. *Journal of Clinical Psychology, 36,* 410–417.

Quinsey, V. L., Harris, G. T., Rice, M. E., & Cormier, C. A. (1998). *Violent offenders: Appraising and managing risk.* Washington, DC: American Psychological Association.

Quinsey, V. L., & Lalumiere, M. L. (2001). *Assessment of sexual offenders against children* (2nd ed.). Thousand Oaks, CA: Sage Publications, Inc.

Quinsey, V. L., Rice, M. E., & Harris, G. T. (1995). Actuarial prediction of sexual recidivism. *Journal of Interpersonal Violence, 10,* 85–105.

R. v. Armstrong (1959) 125 C.C.C. 56.

R. v. Béland (1987), 2 S.C.R. 398, File No. 18856.

R. v. Bain (1992) 1 S.C.R.

R. v. Brown (2003). 64 O.R. (3d).

R. v. Burns [1994] 1 S.C.R. 656.

R. v. Calderon (2004) Court of Appeal for Ontario, Docket C38499; C38500.

R. v. Chaulk [1990] 3 S.C.R. 1303.

R. v. Clark (1984). 17 Queens Bench of Alberta.

R. v. D. D. (2000) 148 C.C.C. (3d) 41.

R. v. Darrach [2000] 2 S.C.R. 443, 2000 SCC 46.

R. v. Fagundes (1997) Court of Appeal for Ontario, Docket c16059.

R. v. François [1994] 2 S.C.R. 827.

R. v. Gruenke (1991) 3 S.C.R. 263.

R. v. Hodgson (1998). 2 S.C.R. 449.

R. v. Jabarianha, [2001] 3 S.C.R. 430.

R. v. Jabarianha (1997), cited in *R. v. Jabarianha* (1999) 140 C.C.C. (3d) 242.

R. v. Malott [1998] 1 S.C.R. 123.

R. v. Marquard [1993] 4 S.C. R. 223.

R. v. McCraw (1991) 3 S.C.R. 72.

R. v. McLean (2003). Provincial Court of Newfoundland and Labrador. Docket: 130A-0001.

R. v. McIntosh and McCarthy (1997). 117 C.C.C. (3d) 385.

R. v. Mills, (1999) BCCA 159.

R. v. Mohan, [1994] 2 S.C.R. 9.

R. v. Lavallee, [1990] 1 S.C.R. 852.

R. v. Lomax (2002). NSPC 31.

R. v. Normore (2002). Provincial Court of Newfoundland. Docket 1301A-00470.

R. v. O'Connor, [1995] 4 S.C.R. 411.

R v. Oickle (2000). S.C.C. 38, File no. 26535.

R. v. Pan; R. v. Sawyer (2001). 2 S.C.R. 344, 2001 SCC 42.

R. v. Parks (1993) 84 C.C.C. (3d) 353.

R. v. Parks (1992) 75 C.C.C. (3d) 287.

R. v. R. J. H. (2000) 145 C.C.C. (3d) 202.

R. v. Ranger (2003) Court of Appeal for Ontario. Docket C31117.

R. v. Redbreast (2004) ABQB 504.

R. v. Regan (1999) Nova Scotia Court of Appeal, Docket C.A.C. 147242.

R. v. Regan, [2002] 1 S.C.R. 297, 2002 SCC 12.

R v. Samra (1998). Court of Appeal for Ontario. Docket: C18884.

R. v. Savoy (1997). Supreme Court of BC. Docket: CC940826.

R. v. Smierciak (1946), 87 C.C.C. 175.

R v Sterling (1995) S. J. No. 612 (C.A.).

R v. Stone (1999). 2 SCR 290.

R. v. Swain, [1991] 1 S.C.R. 933.

R. v. Taillefer and Duguay (1995), 100 C.C.C. (3d) 1.

R. v. W. (R.), [1992] 2 S.C.R. 122.

R. v. Whynot (1983), 9 C.C.C. 449 (N.S.C.A).

Rabinowitz, D. (1990, May). From the mouths of babes to a jail cell: Child abuse and the abuse of justice. *Harper's Magazine,* pp. 52–63.

Rachlin, H. (1991). *The making of a cop.* New York: Simon & Schuster.

Rachlin, H. (1995). *The making of a detective.* New York: W. W. Norton.

Rafter, N. H., & Stanko, E. A. (1982). *Judge, lawyer, victim, thief: Women, gender role, and criminal justice.* Boston: Northeastern University Press.

Raine, A., Lencz, T., Taylor, K., Hellige, J. B., Bihrle, S., Lacasse, L., Lee, M., Ishikawa, S., & Colletti, P. (2003). Corpus callosum abnormalities in psychopathic antisocial individuals. *Archives of General Psychiatry, 60,* 1134–1142.

Rappeport, M. (1993, October 11). Statistics fine-tune simple courtroom evidence. *National Law Journal,* pp. 15–16.

Raskin, D. C. (1981, June). Science, competence, and polygraph techniques. *Criminal Defense, 8*(3), 11–18.

Raskin, D. C. (1989). Polygraph techniques for the detection of deception. In D. C. Raskin (Ed.), *Psychological methods in criminal investigation and evidence* (pp. 247–296). New York: Springer.

Raskin, D. C., & Esplin, P. W. (1991). Statement validity assessment: Interview procedures and content analysis of children's statements of sexual abuse. *Behavioral Assessment, 13,* 265–291.

Raskin, D. C., & Hare, R. (1978). Psychopathy and detection of deception in a prison population. *Psychophysiology, 15,* 126–136.

Rattner, A. (1988). Convicted but innocent: Wrongful conviction and the criminal justice system. *Law and Human Behavior, 12,* 283–293.

Re Moore and the Queen (1984), 10 C.C.C. (3d) 306.

Read, D., & Lindsay, S. D. (Eds.) (1997). *Recollections of trauma: Scientific evidence and clinical practice.* New York, NY: Plenum.

Reese, J., Horn, J., & Dunning, C. (Eds.). (1991). *Critical incidents in policing.* Washington, DC: U.S. Government Printing Office.

Regents of the University of California v. Bakke, 438 U.S. 265 (1978).

Regehr, C., & Glancy, G. (1995). Battered woman syndrome defense in the Canadian courts. *Canadian Journal of Psychiatry, 40*, 130–135.

Reich, J., & Tookey, L. (1986). Disagreements between court and psychiatrist on competency to stand trial. *Journal of Clinical Psychiatry, 47*, 616–623.

Reid, J. E. (1945). Stimulated blood pressure responses in lie detection tests and a method for their detection. *Journal of Criminal Law, Criminology and Police Science, 36*, 201–204.

Reiser, M. (1972). *The police department psychologist.* Springfield, IL: Charles C Thomas.

Reiser, M. (1974). Some organizational stressors on policemen. *Journal of Police Science and Administration, 2*, 156–159.

Reiser, M. (1980). *Handbook of investigative hypnosis.* Los Angeles: LEHI.

Reiser, M. (1982a). Crime specific psychological consultation. *The Police Chief, 49*(3), 53–56.

Reiser, M. (1982b). *Police psychology: Collected papers.* Los Angeles: LEHI.

Reiser, M. (1982c). Selection and promotion of policemen. In M. Reiser (Ed.), *Police psychology: Collected papers* (pp. 84–92). Los Angeles: LEHI.

Reiser, M. (1985). Investigative hypnosis: Scientism, memory tricks, and power plays. In J. K. Zeig (Ed.), *Ericksonian psychotherapy: Vol. I. Structures.* New York: Brunner/Mazel. (Cited by Steblay and Bothwell, 1994.)

Reiser, M. (1989). Investigative hypnosis. In D. C. Raskin (Ed.), *Psychological methods in criminal investigation and evidence* (pp. 151–190). New York: Springer.

Reschly, D. J. (1999). Assessing educational disabilities. In A. K. Hess & I. B. Weiner (Eds.), *The handbook of forensic psychology* (2nd ed., pp. 127–150). New York: John Wiley.

Ressler, R., Burgess, A., & Douglas, J. (1988). *Sexual homicide.* Lexington, MA: Lexington Books.

Ressler, R. K., Burgess, A. W., Douglas, J. E., Hartman, C. R., & D'Agostino, R. B. (1986). Sexual killers and their victims: Identifying patterns through crime scene analysis. *Journal of Interpersonal Violence, 1*, 288–308.

Ressler, R. K., Burgess, A. W., Hartman, C. R., Douglas, J. E., & McCormack, A. (1986). Murderers who rape and mutilate. *Journal of Interpersonal Violence, 1*, 273–287.

Ressler, R. K., & Shachtman, T. (1992). *Whoever fights monsters.* New York: St. Martin's Press.

Reynolds, M. (1994, November). The scariest criminal in America. *Playboy*, pp. 120–122, 128, 146–154.

Rice, M., & Harris, G. (1995). Violent recidivism: Assessing predictive validity. *Journal of Consulting and Clinical Psychology, 63*, 737–748.

Rice, M. E., & Harris, G. T. (1997). Cross-validation and extension of the Violence Risk Appraisal Guide for child molesters and rapists. *Law and Human Behavior, 21*, 231–241.

Rice, M., Harris, G., & Cormier, C. (1992). An evaluation of maximum-security therapeutic community for psychopaths and other mentally disordered offenders. *Law and Human Behavior, 16*, 399–412.

Rider, A. O. (1980, June-August). The firesetter: A psychological profile. *F.B.I. Law Enforcement Bulletin*, pp. 2–23.

Riger, S. (1991). Gender dilemmas in sexual harassment policies and procedures. *American Psychologist, 46*, 497–505.

Riley, J. A. (1998, March). *The Revision of the Competency Assessment Instrument.* Paper presented at the meetings of the American Psychology-Law Society, Redondo Beach, CA.

Ring, K. (1971). *Let's get started: An appeal to what's left in psychology.* Unpublished manuscript, Department of Psychology, University of Connecticut, Storrs, CT.

Robinette, P. R. (1999). *Differential treatment of corporate defendants as a form of actor identity and evaluator expectations.* Unpublished doctoral dissertation, Department of Communication Studies, University of Kansas, Lawrence, KS.

Robinson, E. (1935). *Law and the lawyers.* New York: Macmillan.

Rodriguez, J. H., LeWinn, L. M., & Perlin, M. L. (1983). The insanity defense under siege: Legislative assaults and legal rejoinders. *Rutgers Law Journal, 14*, 397–430.

Roediger, H. L., III, & McDermott, K. B. (1995). Creating false memories: Remembering words not presented in word lists. *Journal of Experimental Psychology: Learning, Memory and Cognition, 21*, 803–814.

Roesch, R., & Golding, S. L. (1980). *Competency to stand trial.* Urbana: University of Illinois Press.

Roesch, R., & Golding, S. L. (1987). Defining and assessing competence to stand trial. In I. Weiner & A. Hess (Eds.), *Handbook of forensic psychology* (pp. 378–394). New York: John Wiley.

Roesch, R., Golding, S. L., Hans, V. P., & Reppucci, N. D. (1991). Social science and the courts: The role of amicus curiae briefs. *Law and Human Behavior, 15*, 1–11.

Roesch, R., Webster, C., & Eaves, D. (1984). *The Fitness Interview Test: A method for examining fitness to stand trial.* Toronto: Centre of Criminology, University of Toronto.

Roesch, R., Webster, C., & Eaves, D. (1994). *The Fitness Interview Test—Revised: A method for examining fitness to stand trial.* Burnaby, BC: Department of Psychology, Simon Fraser University.

Roesch, R., Zapf, P. A., Eaves, D., & Webster, C. D. (1998). *The Fitness Interview Test—Revised.* Burnaby, BC: Mental Health, Law, and Policy Institute, Simon Fraser University.

Rogers, R. (1984). *Rogers Criminal Responsibility Assessment Scales (R-CRAS) and test manual.* Odessa, FL: Psychological Assessment Resources.

Rogers, R. (1986). *Conducting insanity evaluations.* New York: Van Nostrand Reinhold.

Rogers, R. (1987). APA's position on the insanity defense: Empiricism versus emotionalism. *American Psychologist, 42*, 840–848.

Rogers, R. (1988). Structured interviews and dissimulation. In R. Rogers (Ed.), *Clinical assessment of malingering and deception* (pp. 250–268). New York: Guilford Press.

Rogers, R. (1990). Models of feigned mental illness. *Professional Psychology: Research and Practice, 21,* 182–188.

Rogers, R., & Cavanaugh, J. L. (1981). The Rogers Criminal Responsibility Assessment scales. *Illinois Medical Journal, 160,* 164–169.

Rogers, R., Cavanaugh, J. L., Seman, W., & Harris, M. (1984). Legal outcome and clinical findings: A study of insanity evaluations. *Bulletin of the American Academy of Psychiatry and the Law, 12,* 75–83.

Rogers, R., Dolmetsch, R., Wasyliw, O. E., & Cavanaugh, J. L. (1982). Scientific inquiry in forensic psychology. *International Journal of Law and Psychiatry, 5,* 187–203.

Rogers, R., & Ewing, C. P. (1989). Ultimate opinion pro-scriptions: A cosmetic fix and plea for empiricism. *Law and Human Behavior, 13,* 357–374.

Rogers, R., & Ewing, C. P. (1992). The measurement of insanity: Debating the merits of the R-CRAS and its alternatives. *International Journal of Law and Psychiatry, 15,* 113–123.

Rogers, R., Gillis, J. R., Bagby, R. M., & Monteiro, E. (1991). Detection of malingering on the Structured Interview of Reported Symptoms (SIRS): A study of coached and uncoached simulators. *Psychological Assessment: A Journal of Consulting and Clinical Psychology, 3,* 673–677.

Rogers, R., Johansen, J., Chang, J.J., & Salekin, R. (1997). Predictors of adolescent psychopathy: Oppositional and conduct-disorders symptoms. *Journal of the American Academy of Psychiatry and Law, 25,* 261–270.

Rogers, R., Sewell, K. W., & Goldstein, A. M. (1994). Explanatory models of malingering: A prototypical analysis. *Law and Human Behavior, 18,* 543–552.

Rogers, R., Wasyliw, O. E., & Cavanaugh, J. L. (1984). Evaluating insanity: A study of construct validity. *Law and Human Behavior, 8,* 293–303.

Rohman, L. W., Sales, B. D., & Lou, M. (1990). The best interests standard in child custody decisions. In D. Weisstub (Ed.), *Law and mental health: International perspectives* (Vol. 5, pp. 40–90). Elmsford, NJ: Pergamon.

Rooke, A. Justice. (1996 March 20). Assessing credibility in arbitrations and in court: A difficult task for judge, jury or arbitrator. Presentation to the Canadian Bar Association. Edmonton, AB.

Rose, V.G., & Ogloff, J.R.P. (2001). Evaluating the comprehensibility of jury instructions: A method and an example. *Law and Human Behavior, 25,* 409–431.

Rosen, J. (1993a, November 1). Reasonable women. *New Republic,* pp. 12–13.

Rosen, J. (1993b, November 16). Fast-food justice. *New York Times,* p. A15.

Rosen, P. (1972). *The Supreme Court and social science.* Urbana: University of Illinois Press.

Rosenbaum, R. (1993, April). The F.B.I.'s agent provocateur. *Vanity Fair,* pp. 122–136.

Rosenbaum, R. (1998). *Explaining Hitler.* New York: Random House.

Rosenberg, C. E. (1968). *The trial of the assassin Guiteau: Psychiatry and the law in the Gilded Age.* Chicago: University of Chicago Press.

Rosenhan, D. L. (1973). On being sane in insane places. *Science, 179,* 250–258.

Rosenthal, R. (1995). *State of New Jersey v. Margaret Kelly Michaels:* An overview. *Psychology, Public Policy, and Law, 1,* 246–271.

Rossi, D. (1982). Crime scene behavioral analysis: Another tool for the law enforcement investigator. *The Police Chief, 49*(1), 152–155.

Rossmo, D. K. (1996). Targeting victims: Serial killers and the urban environment. In O'Reilly-Fleming (ed.), *Serial and Mass Murder: Theory, Research and Policy* (pp. 133–153). Toronto, ON: Canadian Scholars Press.

Rossmo, D. K. (1997). Geographic profiling. In J. L. Jackson & D. A. Bekerian (Eds.), *Offender profiling: Theory, research and practice* (pp. 159–175). New York: John Wiley.

Roth, S., & Lebowitz, L. (1988). The experience of sexual trauma. *Journal of Traumatic Stress, 1*(1), 79–107.

Rowland, C. K. (1994, February 28). Personal communication.

Royal Canadian Mounted Police (2004). *Truth verification.* Retrieved on August 20, 2004, from the Royal Canadian Mounted Police Web site: http://www.rcmp.ca/techops/truth_ver_e.htm.

Royal, R. F., & Schutt, S. R. (1976). *The gentle art of interviewing and interrogation: A professional manual and guide.* Englewood Cliffs, NJ: Prentice-Hall.

Ruby, C. (2000, October 17). Supreme justice. *The Globe and Mail.* Accessed on August 7, 2004, from the Fathers Are Capable Too Web site: http://www.fact.on.ca/news/news0010/gm00101c.htm.

Ruby, C. L., & Brigham, J. C. (1996). A criminal schema: The role of chronicity, race, and socioeconomic status in law enforcement officials' perception of others. *Journal of Applied Social Psychology, 26,* 95–112.

Ruby, C. L., & Brigham, J. C. (1997). The usefulness of the criteria-based content analysis technique in distinguishing between truthful and fabricated allegations: A critical review. *Psychology, Public Policy, and Law, 3,* 705–737.

Ruch, L. O., Gartrell, J. W., Amedeo, S. R., & Coyne, B. J. (1991). The Sexual Assault Symptom Scale: Measuring self-reported sexual assault trauma in the emergency room. *Psychological Assessment, 3,* 3–8.

Ruch, L. O., Gartrell, J. W., Ramelli, A., & Coyne, B. J. (1991). The Clinical Trauma Assessment: Evaluating sexual assault victims in the emergency room. *Psychological Assessment, 3,* 405–411.

Ruddy, C. (1997). *The strange death of Vincent Foster.* New York: Free Press.

Ryan, J., & Butler, J. M. (1996, December 23). Without Supreme Court precedent, federal courts struggle with the issue of whether Title VII lawsuits may be brought for same-sex sexual harassment. *National Law Journal,* p. B8.

Sackett, P. R., & Wilk, S. L. (1994). Within-group norming and other forms of score adjustment in preemployment testing. *American Psychologist, 49,* 929–954.

Saks, M. J. (1976). The limits of scientific jury selection. *Jurimetrics Journal, 17,* 3–22.

Saks, M. J. (1987). Social scientists can't rig juries. In L. S. Wrightsman, S. M. Kassin, & C. E. Willis (Eds.), *In the jury box: Controversies in the courtroom* (pp. 48–61). Thousand Oaks, CA: Sage.

Saks, M. J. (1992). Normative and empirical issues about the role of expert witnesses. In D. K. Kagehiro & W. S. Laufer (Eds.), *Handbook of psychology and law* (pp. 185–203). New York: Springer-Verlag.

Saks, M. J. (1993). Improving APA science translation amicus briefs. *Law and Human Behavior, 17,* 235–247.

Saks, M. J., & Van Duizend, R. (1983). *The use of scientific evidence in litigation.* Williamsburg, VA: National Center for State Courts.

Salekin, R. T., Rogers, R., & Sewell, K. W. (1996). A review and meta-analysis of the Psychopathy Checklist-Revised: Predictive validity of dangerousness. *Clinical Psychology Science and Practice, 3,* 203–215.

Sales, B., Manber, R., & Rohman, L. (1992). Social science research and child-custody decision making. *Applied and Preventive Psychology, 1,* 23–40.

Sales, B. D. (Ed.). (1995, June). [Special issue]. *Psychology, Public Policy, and Law, 1* (2).

Sales, B. D., & Shuman (Eds.). (1996). *Law, mental health, and mental disorder.* Pacific Grove, CA: Brooks/Cole.

Samra, J., & Connolly, D. A. (2004). Legal compensability of symptoms associated with Posttraumatic stress disorder: A Canadian perspective. *International Journal of Forensic Mental Health, 3,* 55–66.

Samra, J., & Yuille, J. C. (1996). Anatomically-neutral dolls: their effects on the memory and suggestibility of 4- to 6-year-old eyewitnesses, *Child Abuse & Neglect 20,* 1261–1272.

Sanders, L. (1981). *The third deadly sin.* New York: Berkeley Books.

Sattler, J. M. (1991). How good are federal judges in detecting differences in item difficulty on intelligence tests for ethnic groups? *Psychological Assessment, 3,* 125–129.

Saunders, D. (1992). A typology of men who batter women: Three types derived from cluster analysis. *American Journal of Orthopsychiatry, 62,* 264–275.

Saywitz, K. J., & Dorado, J. S. (1998). Interviewing children when sexual abuse is suspected. In G. P. Koocher, J. C. Norcross, & S. S. Hill, III. (Eds.), *Psychologists' desk reference* (pp. 503–509). New York: Oxford University Press.

Saywitz, K., Geiselman, R. E., & Bornstein, G. (1992). Effects of cognitive interviewing and practice on children's recall performance. *Journal of Applied Psychology, 77,* 744–756.

Saywitz, K. J., Goodman, G. S., Nicholas, E., & Moan, S. F. (1991). Children's memories of a physical examination involving genital touch: Implications for reports of child sexual abuse. *Journal of Consulting and Clinical Psychology, 59,* 682–691.

Saywitz, K., & Snyder, L. (1996). Narrative elaboration: Test of a new procedure for interviewing children. *Journal of Consulting and Clinical Psychology, 64,* 1347–1357.

Schaer, J. (1999). *Suicide prevention in law enforcement.* Employee and Family Assistance Program: Toronto Police Service.

Schall v. Martin, 467 U.S. 253 (1984).

Scheflin, A. W., & Shapiro, J. L. (1989). *Trance on trial.* New York: Guilford Press.

Scheflin, A. W., Spiegel, H., & Spiegel, D. (1999). Forensic uses of hypnosis. In A. K. Hess & I. B. Weiner (Eds.), *The handbook of forensic psychology* (2nd ed., pp. 474–498). New York: John Wiley.

Scheid, T. L. (1999). Employment of individuals with mental disabilities: Business response to the ADA's challenge. *Behavioral Sciences and the Law, 17,* 73–91.

Schmalleger, F. (1995). *Criminal justice today* (3rd ed.). Englewood, Cliffs, NJ: Prentice Hall.

Schneider, B. E. (1987). Graduate women, sexual harassment, and university policy. *Journal of Higher Education, 58*(1), 46–65.

Schneider, E. M. (1986). Describing and changing: Women's self-defense work and the problem of expert testimony on battering. *Women's Rights Law Reporter, 9* (3–4), 195–222.

Schretlen, D. (1986). *Malingering: Use of a psychological test battery to detect two kinds of simulation.* Ann Arbor, MI: University Microfilms International.

Schuller, R. A. (1992). The impact of battered woman syndrome evidence on jury decision processes. *Law and Human Behavior, 16,* 597–620.

Schuller, R. A. (1994). Applications of battered woman syndrome evidence in the courtroom. In M. Costanzo & S. Oskamp (Eds.), *Violence and the law* (pp. 113–134). Thousand Oaks, CA: Sage.

Schuller, R. A. & Hastings, P. A. (2002). Complainant sexual history evidence: It impact on mock jurors' decisions. *Psychology of Women Quarterly, 26,* 252–261.

Schuller, R. A. & Rzepa, S. (2002). Expert testimony pertaining to battered woman syndrome: Its impact on jurors' decisions. *Law and Human Behavior, 6,* 655–673.

Schuller, R. A., Smith, V. L., & Olson, J. M. (1994). Jurors' decisions in trials of battered women who kill: The role of prior beliefs and expert testimony. *Journal of Applied Social Psychology, 24,* 316–337.

Schuller, R. A., & Vidmar, N. (1992). Battered woman syndrome evidence in the courtroom: A review of the literature. *Law and Human Behavior, 16,* 273–291.

Schuller, R. A., Wells, E., Rzepa, S., & Klippenstine, M. A. (2004). Rethinking Battered Woman Syndrome evidence: The impact of alternative forms of expert testimony on mock juror's decisions. *Canadian Journal of Behavioural Science, 36,* 127–136.

Schulman, J., Shaver, P., Colman, R., Emrich, B., & Christie, R. (1973, May). Recipe for a jury. *Psychology Today,* pp. 37–44, 77–84.

Schulman, M. (1979). *A survey of spousal violence against women in Kentucky.* Washington, DC: Law Enforcement.

Schutz, B. M., Dixon, E. B., Lindenberger, J. C., & Ruther, N. J. (1989). *Solomon's sword: A practical guide to conducting child custody evaluations.* San Francisco: Jossey-Bass.

Schwartz, B. (1988). *Behind Bakke: Affirmative action and the Supreme Court.* New York: New York University Press.

Scogin, F., Schumacher, J., Howland, K., & McGee, J. (1989, August). *The predictive validity of psychological testing and peer evaluations in law enforcement settings.* Paper presented at the meetings of the American Psychological Association, New Orleans.

Scott, E., & Derdeyn, A. P. (1984). Rethinking joint custody. *Ohio State Law Journal, 45,* 455–498.

Sears v. Rutishauser, 466 NE.2d 210, Ill. (1984).

Sears, D. O. (1988). Symbolic racism. In P. A. Katz & D. A. Taylor (Eds.), *Eliminating racism: Profiles in controversy* (pp. 53–84). New York: Plenum.

Seelau, S. M., & Wells, G. L. (1995). Applied eyewitness research: The other mission. *Law and Human Behavior, 19,* 319–324.

Seligman, M. E. P. (1975). *Helplessness: On depression, development, and death.* San Francisco: W. H. Freeman.

Seligman, M. E. P., & Maier, S. F. (1967). Failure to escape traumatic shock. *Journal of Experimental Psychology, 74,* 1–9.

Selkin, J. (1987). *The psychological autopsy in the courtroom: Contributions of the social sciences to resolving issues surrounding equivocal deaths.* Denver: Self-published.

Selkin, J., & Loya, J. (1979, February). Issues in the psychological autopsy of a controversial public figure. *Professional Psychology,* pp. 87–93.

Serin, R. C., & Amos, N. L. (1995). The role of psychopathy in the assessment of dangerousness. *International Journal of Law and Psychiatry, 18,* 231–238.

Serin, R. C. , Malcolm, P.B., Khanna, A., & Barbaree, H. E. (1994). Psychopathy and deviant sexual arousal in incarcerated sexual offenders. *Journal of Interpersonal Violence, 9,* 3–11.

Serrill, M. S. (1984, September 17). Breaking the spell of hypnosis. *Time,* p. 62.

Seto, M.C., & Barbaree, H. E. (1997). Sexual aggression as antisocial behavior: A developmental model. In M. Stoff, & J.D. Maser (Eds.). *Handbook of antisocial behavior* (pp. 524–533). New York, NY: John Wiley & Sons.

Shaffer, M. B. (1992). Review of the Bricklin Perceptual Scales. In J. J. Kramer & J. C. Conoley (Eds.), *Eleventh mental measurements yearbook* (pp. 118–119). Lincoln: University of Nebraska Press.

Sharn, L. (1993, November 4). Typical arsonist is young, unfulfilled. *USA Today,* p. 3A.

Shaw, J. S., III. (1996). Increases in eyewitness confidence resulting from postevent questioning. *Journal of Experimental Psychology: Applied, 2,* 126–146.

Shaw, J. S., Garven, S., & Wood, J. M. (1997). Co-witness information can alter witnesses' immediate memory reports. *Law and Human Behavior, 21,* 503–523.

Shaw, J. S., III, & McClure, K. A. (1996). Repeated postevent questioning can lead to elevated levels of eyewitness confidence. *Law and Human Behavior, 20,* 629–653.

Sherman, L. W., & Berk, R. A. (1984). The specific deterrent effects of arrest for domestic assault. *American Sociological Review, 49,* 261–272.

Shiller, V. M. (1986a). Joint versus maternal custody for families with latency age boys: Parent characteristics and child adjustment. *American Journal of Orthopsychiatry, 56,* 486–489.

Shiller, V. M. (1986b). Loyalty conflicts and family relationships in latency age boys: A comparison of joint and maternal custody. *Journal of Divorce, 9,* 17–38.

Shneidman, E. S. (1981). The psychological autopsy. *Suicide and Life-Threatening Behavior, 11,* 325–340.

Shusman, E. J., & Inwald, R. E. (1991a). A longitudinal validation study of correctional officer job performance as predicted by the IPI and the MMPI. *Journal of Criminal Justice, 19*(4), 173–180.

Shusman, E. J., & Inwald, R. E. (1991b). Predictive validity of the Inwald Personality Inventory. *Criminal Justice and Behavior, 18,* 419–426.

Shusman, E. J., Inwald, R. E., & Knatz, H. F. (1987). A cross-validation study of police recruit performance as predicted by the IPI and MMPI. *Journal of Police Science and Administration, 15,* 162–169.

Shusman, E., Inwald, R., & Landa, B. (1984). A validation study of correction officer job performance as predicted by the IPI and MMPI. *Criminal Justice and Behavior, 11,* 309–329.

Shuy, R. W. (1998). *The language of confession, interrogation, and deception.* Thousand Oaks, CA: Sage.

Siegal, M., Waters, L. J., & Dinwiddy, L. S. (1988). Misleading children: Causal attributions for inconsistency under repeated questioning. *Journal of Experimental Child Psychology, 45,* 438–456.

Silverstein, J. M. (1985). The psychologist as panel member. *Social Action and the Law, 11*(3), 72–74.

Silverton, L., & Gruber, C. (1998). *Malingering Probability Scale (MPS) Manual.* Los Angeles, CA: Western Psychological Services.

Silverton, L., Gruber, C. P., & Bindman, S. (1993, August). *The Malingering Probability Scale for Mental Disorders (MPS-MD): A scale to detect malingering.* Paper presented at the meetings of the American Psychological Association, Toronto.

Simon, D. (1991). *Homicide: A year on the killing streets.* New York: Ivy Books.

Simpson, B., Jensen, E., & Owen, J. (1988, October). Police employee assistance program. *Police Chief,* pp. 83–85.

Singleton, G. W., & Teahan, J. (1978). Effects of job related stress on the physical and psychological adjustment of police officers. *Journal of Police Science and Administration, 6,* 355–361.

Skafte, D. (1985). *Child custody evaluations: A practical guide.* Thousand Oaks, CA: Sage.

Skedsvold, P. R., & Mann, T. L. (1996a). Affirmative action: Linking research, policy, and implementation. *Journal of Social Issues, 52*(4), 3–18.

Skedsvold, P. R., & Mann, T. L. (Eds.). (1996b). The affirmative action debate: What's fair in policy and programs? *Journal of Social Issues, 52* (4), 1–160.

Skeem, J. L., Golding, S. L., Cohn, N. B., & Berge, G. (1998). Logic and reliability of evaluations of competence to stand trial. *Law and Human Behavior, 22,* 519–547.

Skeem, J. L., Monahan, J. & Mulvey, E. P. (2002). Psychopathy, treatment involvement, and subsequent violence among civil psychiatric patients. *Law and Human Behavior, 26,* 577–603.

Skeem, J. L. & Mulvey, E. P. (2001). Psychopathy and community violence among civil psychiatric patients: Results from the MacArthur violence risk assessment study. *Journal of Consulting and Clinical Psychology, 69,* 358–374.

Skinner, L. J., & Berry, K. K. (1993). Anatomically detailed dolls and the evaluation of child sexual abuse allegations. *Law and Human Behavior, 17,* 399–421.

Skolnick, J. H. (1966). *Justice without trial: Law enforcement in a democratic society.* New York: John Wiley.

Skolnick, J. H., & Bayley, D. H. (1986). *The new blue line: Police innovation in six American cities.* New York: Free Press.

Skolnick, J. H., & Leo, R. A. (1992). The ethics of deceptive interrogation. In J. W. Bizzack (Ed.), *Issues in policing: New perspectives* (pp. 75–95). Lexington, KY: Auburn House.

Slade, M. (1994, February 25). Law firms begin reining in sex-harassing partners. *New York Times,* p. B12.

Slobogin, C. (1996). Dangerousness as a criterion in the criminal process. In B. D. Sales & D. W. Shuman (Eds.), *Law, mental health, and mental disorder* (pp. 360–383). Pacific Grove, CA: Brooks/Cole.

Slobogin, C. (1997). Deceit, pretext, and trickery: Investigative laws by the police. *Oregon Law Review, 76,* 775–816.

Slobogin, C., Melton, G. B., & Showalter, C. R. (1984). The feasibility of a brief evaluation of mental state at the time of the offense. *Law and Human Behavior, 8,* 305–321.

Slovic, P., & Fischhoff, B. (1977). On the psychology of experimental surprises. *Journal of Experimental Psychology: Human Perception and Performance, 3,* 545–551.

Smith v. Jones, [1999] 1 S.C.R. 455.

Smith, D. H., & Stotland, E. (1973). A new look at police officer selection. In J. R. Snibbe & H. M. Snibbe (Eds.), *The urban policeman in transition* (pp. 5–24). Springfield, IL: Charles C. Thomas.

Smith, G. P., & Burger, G. (1993, August). *Detection of malingering: A validation test of the SLAM Test.* Paper presented at the meetings of the American Psychological Association, Toronto.

Smith, M. C. (1983). Hypnotic memory enhancement of witnesses: Does it work? *Psychological Bulletin, 94,* 387–407.

Sophonow Inquiry Report (2001). Retrieved on August 20, 2004, from the Government of Manitoba Web site: http://www.gov.mb.ca/justice/sophonow/.

Soskis, D. A. (1983). Behavioral sciences and law enforcement personnel: Working together on the problem of terrorism. *Behavioral Sciences and the Law, 1,* 47–58.

Spanos, N. (1996). *Multiple identities & false memories: A sociocognitive perspective.* Washington, DC: American Psychological Association.

Spanos, N. P., Menary, E., Gabora, N. J., DuBreuil, C., and Dewhirst, B. 1991. Secondary Identity Enactments During Hypnotic Past-life Regression: A Sociocognitive Perspective. *Journal of Personality and Social Psychology 61:* 308–320.

Spanos, N.P., Weekes, J.R., & Bertrand, L.D. (1985). Multiple personality: A social psychological perspective. *Journal of Abnormal Psychology, 94,* 362–376.

Sparrow, M. K., Moore, M. H., & Kennedy, D. M. (1990). *Beyond 911: A new era of policing.* New York: Basic Books.

Spencer, J. R. (1998). The role of experts in the common law and the civil law: A comparison. In S. J. Ceci & H. Hembrooke (Eds.), *Expert witnesses in child abuse cases* (pp. 29–58). Washington, DC: American Psychological Association.

Spiegel, D., & Spiegel, H. (1987). Forensic uses of hypnosis. In I. B. Weiner and A. K. Hess (Eds.), *Handbook of forensic psychology* (pp. 490–507). New York: John Wiley.

Spiegel, H., & Spiegel, D. (1978). *Trance and treatment: Clinical uses of hypnosis.* New York: Basic Books.

Spielberger, C. D. (Ed.). (1979). *Police selection and evaluation: Issues and problems.* Washington, DC: Hemisphere.

Sporer, S.L. (1981). *Toward a comprehensive history of legal psychology.* Unpublished manuscript, University of Erlagen-Nürnberg.

Sporer, S. L. (1993). Eyewitness identification accuracy, confidence, and decision times in simultaneous and sequential lineups. *Journal of Applied Psychology, 78,* 22–33.

Stahl, P. M. (1994). *Conducting child custody evaluations: A comprehensive guide.* Thousand Oaks, CA: Sage.

State v. Cressey, 628 A.2d 696 (N.H. 1993).

State v. Marks, 231 Kan. 647 P.2d 1292 (1982).

State v. Michaels, 625 A.2d 489 (N.J. Sup. Ct. App. Div. 1993).

Statistics Canada (1998). *Family violence in Canada: A statistical profile.* Retrieved August 14, 2004, from the Statistics Canada Web site: http://www.statcan.ca/english/freepub/85-224-XIE/0009885-224-XIE.pdf.

Statistics Canada (1999). *Family violence in Canada: A statistical profile.* Retrieved August 14, 2004, from the Statistics Canada Web site: http://www.statcan.ca/english/freepub/85-224-XIE/0009985-224-XIE.pdf.

Statistics Canada (2001, 19 July). Crime statistics 2000. *The Daily.* Retrieved August 25, 2004, from the Statistics Canada Web site: http://www.statcan.ca/Daily/English/010719/d010719b.htm.

Statistics Canada (2001a). Canada's shelters for abused women, 1999–2000. *Juristat, 21(1),* catalogue number: 85-002-XIE2001001.

Statistics Canada (2001b). Spousal violence after marital separation. *Juristat, 21(7),* catalogue number: 85-002-XIE.

Statistics Canada (2002, 25 September). Homicides 2001. *The Daily.* Retrieved May 19, 2004, from the Statistics Canada Web site: http://www.statcan.ca/Daily/English/020925/d020925b.htm.

Statistics Canada (2003). *Ethnic diversity study: Portrait of a multicultural society* (2002). Retrieved on August 25, 2004, from the Statistics Canada Web site: http://www.statcan.ca/english/freepub/89-593-XIE/free.htm.

Steadman, H. J., Robbins, P. C., Monahan, J., Appelbaum, P., Grisso, T., Mulvey, E. P., & Roth, L. (1996). The MacArthur Violence Risk Assessment Study. *American Psychology-Law Society News, 16*(3), 1–4.

Steblay, N. M. (1997). Social influence in eyewitness recall: A meta-analytic review of lineup instruction effects. *Law and Human Behavior, 21,* 283–297.

Steblay, N. M., & Bothwell, R. K. (1994). Evidence for hypnotically refreshed testimony: The view from the laboratory. *Law and Human Behavior, 18,* 635–651.

Steinman, S. (1981). The experience of children in a joint-custody arrangement: A report of a study. *American Journal of Orthopsychiatry, 51,* 403–414.

Steinman, S. B., Zemmelman, S. E., & Knoblauch, T. M. (1985). A study of parents who sought joint custody following divorce: Who reaches agreement and sustains joint custody and who returns to court. *Journal of the American Academy of Child Psychiatry, 24,* 554–562.

Steketee, G., & Foa, E. B. (1987). Rape victims: Post-traumatic stress responses and their treatment. *Journal of Anxiety Disorders, 1,* 69–86.

Steller, M., & Koehnken, G. (1989). Criteria-based statement analysis. In D. C. Raskin (Ed.), *Psychological methods in criminal investigation and evidence* (pp. 217–245). New York: Springer.

Stets, J.E., & Straus, M.A. (1990). Gender differences in reporting marital violence and its medical and psychological consequences. In M.A. Straus & R.J. Gelles (Eds.), *Physical violence in American families: Risk factors and adaptations to Violence in 8,145 Families* (pp. 227–244). New Brunswick, NJ: Transaction Publishing.

Stern, L. W. (1903). *Beiträge zur Psychologie der Aussage.* (Contributions to the Psychology of Testimony). Leipzig: Verlag Barth.

Stevens, J. A. (1997). Standard investigatory tools and offender profiling. In J. L. Jackson & D. A. Bekerian (Eds.), *Offender profiling: Theory, research and practice* (pp. 76–91). New York: John Wiley.

Stewart, S. H., Mitchell, T. L., Wright, K. D., & Loba, P. (2004). The relations of PTSD symptoms to alcohol use and coping drinking in volunteers who responded to Swissair Flight 111 airline disaster. *Journal of Anxiety Disorders, 18, 51–68.*

Stovall v. Denno, 388 U.S. 293 (1967).

Stratton, J. (1978). The police department psychologist: Is there any value? *The Police Chief, 45*(5), 70–74.

Stratton, J. A. (1980). Psychological services for police. *Journal of Police Science and Administration, 8,* 31–39.

Straus, M. A. (1979). Measuring family conflict and violence: The conflict tactics scale. *Journal of Marriage and the Family, 41,* 75–88.

Straus, M. A., & Gelles, R. J. (1986). Societal change in family violence from 1975 to 1985 as revealed by two national surveys. *Journal of Marriage and the Family, 48,* 465–479.

Straus, M. A., & Gelles, R. J. (1988). How violent are American families? Estimates from the National Family Violence Resurvey and other studies. In G. T. Hotaling, D. Finkelhor, J. T. Kirkpatrick, & M. A. Straus (Eds.), *Family abuse and its consequences* (pp. 14–36). Newbury Park, CA: Sage.

Strawbridge, P., & Strawbridge, D. (1990). *A networking guide to recruitment, selection, and probationary training of police officers in major police departments in the United States of America.* New York: John Jay College of Criminal Justice.

Strier, F. (1998, March). *The future of trial consulting: Issues and projections.* Paper presented at the meetings of the American Psychology-Law Society, Redondo Beach, CA.

Strier, F. (1999). Whither trial consulting: Issues and projections. *Law and Human Behavior, 23,* 93–115.

Stuntz, W. J. (1989). Waiving rights in criminal procedure. *Virginia Law Review, 75,* 761–824.

Sugg, R. (1992). Primary care physician's response to domestic violence: Opening Pandora's box. *Journal of American Medical Association, 267,* 3157–3160.

Sullivan, K., & Sevilla, G. (1993, August 30–September 5). A look inside a rapist's mind. *Washington Post National Weekly Edition,* p. 32.

Summit, R. (1992). Abuse of the child sexual abuse accommodation syndrome. *Journal of Child Sexual Abuse, 1*(4), 153–161.

Swartz, J. D. (1985). Review of Inwald Personality Inventory. In J.V. Mitchell (Ed.), *Ninth mental measurements yearbook* (pp. 713–714). Lincoln: Buros Institute of Mental Measurements, University of Nebraska.

Swartz, M. (1997, November 17). Family secret. *New Yorker,* pp. 90–107.

Swenson, W. M., & Grimes, P. B. (1969). Characteristics of sex offenders admitted to a Minnesota state hospital for pre-sentence psychiatric investigation. *Psychiatric Quarterly Supplement, 34,* 110–123.

Swisher, K. (1994, February 14–20). Corporations are seeing the light on harassment. *Washington Post National Weekly Edition,* p. 21.

Tanford, J. A. (1990). The limits of a scientific jurisprudence: The Supreme Court and psychology. *Indiana Law Journal, 66,* 137–173.

Tanford, J. A., & Tanford, S. (1988). Better trials through science: A defense of psychologist-lawyer collaboration. *North Carolina Law Review, 66,* 741–780.

Tapp, J. L. (1976). Psychology and the law: An overture. *Annual Review of Psychology, 27,* 359–404.

Tapp, J. L. (1977). Psychology and the law: A look at the interface. In B. D. Sales (Eds.), *Psychology in the legal process* (pp. 1–15). New York: Spectrum.

Tasker, F., & Golombok, S. (1995). Adults raised as children in lesbian families. *American Journal of Orthopsychiatry, 65,* 203–215.

Taylor, R. (1990). The Larry P. decision a decade later: Problems and future directions. *Mental Retardation, 28*(1), 3–6.

Terman, L. M. (1917). A trial of mental and pedagogical tests in a civil service examination for policemen and firemen. *Journal of Applied Psychology, 1,* 17–29.

Terpstra, D. E., & Baker, D. D. (1987). A hierarchy of sexual harassment. *Journal of Psychology, 121,* 599–605.

Terpstra, D. E., & Baker, D. D. (1988). Outcomes of sexual harassment charges. *Academy of Management Journal, 31,* 185–194.

Terpstra, D. E., & Baker, D. D. (1992). Outcomes of federal court decisions on sexual harassment. *Academy of Management Journal, 35,* 181–190.

Terr, L. C. (1979). Children of Chowchilla. *Psychoanalytic Study of the Child, 34,* 547–623.

Terr, L. C. (1983). Chowchilla revisited: The effects of psychic trauma four years after a school-bus kidnapping. *American Journal of Psychiatry, 140,* 1543–1550.

Thibaut, J., & Walker, L. (1975). *Procedural justice: A psychological analysis.* Hillsdale, NJ: Lawrence Erlbaum.

Thomann, D. A., & Wiener, R. L. (1987). Physical and psychological causality as determinants of culpability in sexual harassment cases. *Sex Roles, 17,* 573–591.

Thompson, R. A. (1983). The father's case in child custody disputes: The contributions of psychological research. In M. E. Lamb & A. Sagi (Eds.), *Fatherhood and family policy.* Hillsdale, NJ: Lawrence Erlbaum.

Tomkins, A. J., & Oursland, K. (1991). Social and social science perspectives in judicial interpretations of the Constitution: A historical view and an overview. *Law and Human Behavior, 15,* 101–120.

Tomkins, A. J., & Pfeifer, J. E. (1992). Modern social scientific theories and data concerning discrimination: Implications for using social science evidence in the courts. In D. K. Kagehiro & W. S. Laufer (Eds.), *Handbook of psychology and law* (pp. 385–407). New York: Springer-Verlag.

Toobin, J. (1994, October 31). Juries on trial. *New Yorker,* pp. 42–47.

Toobin, J. (1996a, September 9). The Marcia Clark verdict. *New Yorker,* pp. 58–71.

Toobin, J. (1996b). *The run of his life.* New York: Simon & Schuster.

Toufexis, A. (1989, February 6). The lasting worlds of divorce. *Time,* p. 61.

Toufexis, A. (1991, May 6). Mind games with monsters. *Time,* pp. 68–69.

Tremper, C. (1987). Organized psychology's efforts to influence judicial policy-making. *American Psychologist, 42,* 496–501.

Trevethan, S., Moore, J. P., & Rastin, C. J. (2002). A profile of aboriginal offenders in federal facilities and serving time in the community [Electronic version]. *Forum on Corrections Research, 14.* Retrieved August 17, 2004, from http://www.csc-scc.gc.ca/text/pblct/forum/e143/143f_e.pdf.

Trocmé, N., MacLaurin, B., Fallon, B., Daciuk, J., Billingsley, D., Tourigny, M., Mayer, M., Wright, J., Barter, K., Burford, G., Hornick, J., Sullivan, R., & McKenzie, B. (2001). *Canadian incidence study of reported child abuse and neglect (CIS): Final Report.* Ottawa, ON: Minister of Public Works and Government Services Canada.

Turvey, B. (1999). *Criminal profiling: An introduction to behavioral evidence analysis.* London: Academic Press.

Tversky, A., & Kahneman, D. (1973). Availability: A heuristic for judging frequency and probability. *Cognitive Psychology, 5,* 207–232.

Tversky, A., & Kahneman, D. (1974). Judgment under uncertainty: Heuristics and biases. *Science, 185,* 1124–1131.

Tversky, A., & Kahneman, D. (1983). Extensional versus intuitive reasoning: The conjuction fallacy in probability judgment. *Psychological Bulletin, 90,* 293–315.

Tyler, T. R., & Folger, R. (1980). Distributional and procedural aspects of satisfaction with citizen-police encounters. *Basic and Applied Social Psychology, 1,* 281–292.

Ulrich, D., & Trumbo, D. (1965). The selection interview since 1949. *Psychological Bulletin, 63,* 100–116.

Undeutsch, U. (1982). Statement reality analysis. In A. Trankell (Ed.), *Reconstructing the past: The role of psychologists in criminal trials* (pp. 27–56). Stockholm, Sweden: Norstedt & Somers.

Undeutsch, U. (1984). Courtroom evaluations of eyewitness testimony. *International Review of Applied Psychology, 33,* 51–67.

Undeutsch, U. (1989). The development of statement reality analysis. In J. C. Yuille (Ed.), *Credibility assessment* (pp. 101–120). Dordrecht, The Netherlands: Kluwer.

United States v. Brawner, 471 F.2d 969 (D.C. Cir. 1972).

United States v. Hall, 93 F.3d 1337 (7th Cir. 1996).

United States Equal Employment Opportunity Commission. (1980, November 10). Final amendment to guidelines on discrimination because of sex under Title VII of the Civil Rights Act of 1964, as amended. 29 CAR Part 1604. *Federal Register, 45,* 74675–74677.

Ustad, K. L., Rogers, R., Sewell, K. W., & Guarnaccia, C. A. (1996). Restoration of competency to stand trial: Assessment with the Georgia Court Competency Test and the Competency Screening Test. *Law and Human Behavior, 20,* 131–146.

Vallee, B. (1986). *Life with Billy.* Toronto, ON: Seal Books.

Van den Haag, E. (1960). Social science testimony in the desegregation cases: A reply to Professor Kenneth Clark. *Villanova Law Review, 6,* 69–79.

Verhovek, S. H. (1993, May 5). Investigators puzzle over last minutes of Koresh. *New York Times,* p. A10.

Vermunt, R., Blaauw, E., & Lind, E. A. (1998). Fairness evaluations of encounters with police officers and correctional officers. *Journal of Applied Social Psychology, 28,* 1107–1124.

Veronen, L. J., Kilpatrick, D. G., & Resick, P. A. (1979). Treatment of fear and anxiety in rape victims: Implications for the criminal justice system. In W. H. Parsonage (Ed.), *Perspectives on victimology* (pp. 148–159). Thousand Oaks, CA: Sage.

Vidmar, N. (1995). *Medical malpractice and the American jury.* Ann Arbor: University of Michigan Press.

Visher, G. (1987). Juror decision making: The importance of evidence. *Law and Human Behavior, 11*, 1–14.

Volgy, S. S., & Everett, C. A. (1985). Joint custody reconsidered: Systemic criteria for mediation. *Journal of Divorce, 8*, 131–150.

Vollers, M. (1991, July). The haunting of the New South. *Esquire*, pp. 58–63, 120.

Volokh, E. (1992). Freedom of speech and workplace harassment. *U.C.L.A. Law Review, 39*, 1791–1872.

Vorpagel, R. E. (1982). Painting psychological profiles: Charlatanism, charisma, or a new science? *The Police Chief, 49*(1), 156–159.

Vrij, A. (2001). Implicit lie detection. *The Psychologist, 14*, 58–60.

Vrij, A. (2000). *Detecting lies and deceit: The psychology of lying and the implications for professional practice.* Chichester, England: Wiley.

Vrij, A., Akehurst, L., Soukara, S., & Bull, R. (2002). Will the truth come out? The effect of deception, age, status, coaching, and social skills on CBCA scores. *Law and Human Behavior, 26*, 261–283.

Vuyanich v. Republic National Bank, 723 F.2d 1195 (1984).

W. M.Y. v. Duncan Scott, B.C. Soccer Assoc. et al, (2000) BCSC 1294.

Waddell, F. E. (1985). Borrowing child support payments. *Mediation Quarterly, 9*, 63–83.

Wagenaar, W. A. (1988). *Identifying Ivan*. Cambridge: Harvard University Press.

Wagenaar, W. A., & Groenewed, J. (1990). The memory of concentration camp survivors. *Applied Cognitive Psychology, 4*, 77–87.

Waid, W. M., Orne, E. C., Cook, M. R., & Orne, M. T. (1981). Meprobamate reduces accuracy of physiological detection of deception. *Science, 212*, 71–73.

Waid, W. M., Orne, E. C., & Orne, M. T. (1981). Selective memory for social information, alertness, and physiological arousal in the detection of deception. *Journal of Applied Psychology, 66*, 224–232.

Wakefield, H., & Underwager, R. (1998). Coerced or non-voluntary confessions. *Behavior Sciences and the Law, 16*, 423–440.

Wald, M., Ayres, R., Hess, D. W., Schantz, M., & Whitebread, C. H. (1967). Interrogations in New Haven: The impact of Miranda. *Yale Law Journal, 76*, 1519–1648.

Waldo, C. R., Berdahl, J. L., & Fitzgerald, L. F. (1998). Are men sexually harassed? If so, by whom? *Law and Human Behavior, 22*, 59–79.

Walker, L., & Monahan, J. (1987). Social frameworks: A new use of social science in law. *Virginia Law Review, 73*, 559–612.

Walker, L. E. (1998, August). *Forensic psychology: Psychologists, Solomon, and child custody decisions.* Symposium introduction presented at the meetings of the American Psychological Association, San Francisco.

Walker, L. E. A. (1979). *The battered woman.* New York: Harper & Row.

Walker, L. E. A. (1984). *The battered woman syndrome.* New York: Springer.

Walker, L. E. A. (1992). Battered woman syndrome and self-defense. *Notre Dame Journal of Law, Ethics, and Public Policy, 6*, 321–334.

Walker L. E. A. (1993). Battered women as defendants. In N. Z. Hilton (Ed.), *Legal responses to wife assault: Current trends and evaluation* (pp. 233–257). Thousand Oaks, CA: Sage.

Walker, L. E. A., Thyfault, R. K., & Browne, A. (1982). Beyond the juror's ken: Battered women. *Vermont Law Review, 7*, 1–14.

Walker, N. E., Brooks, C. M., & Wrightsman, L. S. (1998). *Children's rights in the United States: In search of a national policy.* Thousand Oaks, CA: Sage.

Walkley, J. (1987). *Police interrogation: Handbook for investigators.* London: Police Review Publications.

Waller, N. G. (1992). Review of Inwald Personality Inventory. In J. J. Kramer & J. C. Conoley (Eds.), *Eleventh mental measurements yearbook* (pp. 418–419). Lincoln: Buros Institute of Mental Measurements, University of Nebraska.

Wallerstein, J. S., & Blakeslee, S. (1989). *Second chances: Men, women, and children a decade after divorce.* New York: Ticknor and Fields.

Wallerstein, J., & Kelly, J. B. (1980). *Surviving the breakup: How children and parents cope with divorce.* New York: Basic Books.

Wallston, B. S., & O'Leary, V. E. (1981). Sex and gender make a difference: The differential perceptions of men and women. In L. Wheeler (Ed.), *Review of personality and social psychology* (Vol. 2, pp. 9–41). Thousand Oaks, CA: Sage.

Ward v. The Queen, [1979] 2 S.C.R. 30.

Warshaw, R. (1988). *I never called it rape.* New York: Harper & Row.

Waschbusch, D., Porter, S., Carrey, N., Kazmi, O., Roach, K., & D'Amico, D. (2004). A comparison of conduct problems in elementary age children. *Canadian Journal of Behavioural Science, 36*, 97–112.

Watkins, J. G. (1989). Hypnotic hypernesia and forensic hypnosis: A cross-examination. *American Journal of Clinical Hypnosis, 32*(2), 71–83.

Webster, C. D., Douglas, K. S., Eaves, D., & Hart, S. (1997). HCR-20 (version 2): Historical, clinical, risk-20. Simon Fraser University, BC: Mental Health, Law and Policy Institute.

Webster, M. (2004). Do crisis negotiators practice what they preach? *The Canadian Review of Policing Research, 1.* Retrieved on August 17, 2004, from http://crpr.icaap.org/issues/issue1/mwebster.html.

Wecht, C. (1994). *Cause of death.* New York: Penguin.

Weiner, T. (1994, March 8). Spy suspect replied deceptively on lie test in 1991, F.B.I. says. *New York Times*, pp. A1, A12.

Weisman, J. (1980). *Evidence.* New York: Viking.

Weiss, D. S., & Lalonde, R. N. (1998, August). *Responses of female undergraduates to sexual harassment by male instructors.*

Paper presented at the meetings of the American Psychological Association, San Francisco.

Weithorn, L. A. (Ed.). (1987). *Psychology and child custody determinations: Knowledge, roles, and expertise*. Lincoln: University of Nebraska Press.

Weithorn, L. A., & Grisso, T. (1987). Psychological evaluations in divorce custody: Problems, principles, and procedures. In L. A. Weithorn (Ed.), *Psychology and child custody determinations: Knowledge, roles, and expertise* (pp. 157–180). Lincoln: University of Nebraska Press.

Weitzenhoffer, A. M., & Hilgard, E. R. (1959). *Stanford Hypnotic Susceptibility Scale: Forms A and B*. Palo Alto, CA: Consulting Psychologists Press.

Weitzman, L. J. (1985). *The divorce revolution: The unexpected social and economic consequences for women and children in America*. New York: Free Press.

Wekesser, C., Swisher, K. L., & Pierce, C. (Eds.). (1992). *Sexual harassment*. San Diego: Greenhaven Press.

Wells, G. L. (1978). Applied eyewitness testimony research: System variables and estimator variables. *Journal of Personality and Social Psychology, 36,* 1546–1557.

Wells, G. L. (1984a). How adequate is human intuition for judging eyewitness testimony? In G. L. Wells & E. F. Loftus (Eds.), *Eyewitness testimony: Psychological perspectives* (pp. 256–272). New York: Cambridge University Press.

Wells, G. L. (1984b). The psychology of lineup identifications. *Journal of Applied Social Psychology, 14,* 89–103.

Wells, G. L. (1986). Expert psychological testimony: Empirical and conceptual analysis of effects. *Law and Human Behavior, 10,* 83–95.

Wells, G. L. (1993). What do we know about eyewitness identification? *American Psychologist, 48,* 553–571.

Wells, G. L. (1995). Scientific study of witness memory: Implications for public and legal policy. *Psychology, Public Policy, and Law, 1,* 726–731.

Wells, G. L., & Bradfield, A. L. (1998). "Good, you identified the suspect": Feedback to eyewitnesses distorts their reports of the witnessing experience. *Journal of Applied Psychology, 83,* 360–376.

Wells, G. L., & Leippe, M. R. (1981). How do triers of fact infer the accuracy of eyewitness identification? Using memory for peripheral detail can be misleading. *Journal of Applied Psychology, 66,* 682–687.

Wells, G. L., Leippe, M. R., & Ostrom, T. M. (1979). Guidelines for empirically assessing the fairness of a lineup. *Law and Human Behavior, 3,* 285–293.

Wells, G. L., Lindsay, R. C. L., & Ferguson, T. (1979). Accuracy, confidence, and juror perceptions in eyewitness identification. *Journal of Applied Psychology, 64,* 440–448.

Wells, G. L., & Loftus, E. F. (1984). Eyewitness research: Then and now. In G. L. Wells & E. F. Loftus (Eds.), *Eyewitness testimony: Psychological perspectives* (pp. 1–11). Cambridge: Cambridge University Press.

Wells, G. L., Malpass, R. S., Lindsay, R. C. L., Fisher, R. P., Turtle, J. W., & Fulero, S. M. (2000). From the lab to the police station: A successful application of eyewitness research. *American Psychologist, 55,* 581–598.

Wells, G. L., & Murray, D. M. (1984). Eyewitness confidence. In G. L. Wells & E. F. Loftus (Eds.), *Eyewitness testimony: Psychological perspectives* (pp. 155–170). Cambridge: Cambridge University Press.

Wells, G. L., Rydell, S. M., & Seelau, E. P. (1993). On the selection of distractors for eyewitness lineups. *Journal of Applied Psychology, 78,* 835–844.

Wells, G. L., & Seelau, E. (1995). Eyewitness identification: Psychological research and legal policy on lineups. *Psychology, Public Policy, and Law, 1,* 765–791.

Wells, G. L., Seelau, E., Rydell, S., & Luus, C. A. E. (1994). Recommendations for properly conducted lineup identification tasks. In D. F. Ross, J. D. Read, & M. P. Toglia (Eds.), *Adult eyewitness testimony: Current trends and developments* (pp. 223–244). New York: Cambridge University Press.

Wells, G. L., Small, M., Penrod, S., Malpass, R. S., Fulero, S. M., & Brimacombe, C. A. E. (1998). Eyewitness identification procedures: Recommendations for lineups and photospreads. *Law and Human Behavior, 22,* 603–647.

Whipple, G. M. (1909). The observer as reporter: A survey of the "psychology of testimony." *Psychological Bulletin, 6,* 153–170.

Whipple, G. M. (1910). Recent literature on the psychology of testimony. *Psychological Bulletin, 7,* 365–368.

Whipple, G. M. (1911). The psychology of testimony. *Psychological Bulletin, 8,* 307–309.

Whipple, G. M. (1912). The psychology of testimony and report. *Psychological Bulletin, 9,* 264–269.

White, E. K., & Honig, A. L. (1995). The role of the police psychologist in training. In M. I. Kurke & E. M. Scrivner (Eds.), *Police psychology into the 21st century* (pp. 257–277). Hillsdale, NJ: Lawrence Erlbaum.

White, S. (1988). Should investigatory use of anatomical dolls be defined by the courts? *Journal of Interpersonal Violence, 3,* 471–475.

White, S., & Santilli, G. (1988). A review of clinical practices and research data on anatomical dolls. *Journal of Interpersonal Violence, 3,* 430–442.

White, S., Strom, G., Santilli, G., & Halpin, B. (1986). Interviewing young sexual abuse victims with anatomically correct dolls. *Child Abuse and Neglect, 10,* 519–529.

Wiener, R. L. (1995). Social analytic jurisprudence in sexual harassment litigation: The role of social framework and social fact. *Journal of Social Issues, 51*(1), 167–180.

Wiener, R. L., Winter, R., Rogers, M., & Arnot, L. (2004). The effects of prior workplace behavior on subsequent sexual harassment judgments. *Law and Human Behavior, 28,* 47–67.

Wiggins, E. C., & Brandt, J. (1988). The detection of simulated amnesia. *Law and Human Behavior, 12,* 57–78.

Wigmore, J. H. (1909). Professor Münsterberg and the psychology of testimony: Being a report of the case of Cokestone v. Münsterberg. *Illinois Law Review, 3,* 399–455.

Wildman, R. W., II, Batchelor, E. S., Thompson, L., Nelson, F. R., Moore, J. T., Patterson, M. E., & DeLaosa, M. (1978). *The Georgia Court Competency Test: An attempt to develop a rapid, quantitative measure of fitness for trial.* Unpublished manuscript, Forensic Services Division, Central State Hospital, Milledgeville, GA.

Williams, A. L. (1999, March 26). Did doctors' biases speed mother's death? *USA Today,* p. 15A.

Williams, W., & Miller, K. (1981). The processing and disposition of incompetent mentally ill offenders. *Law and Human Behavior, 5,* 245–261.

Wilson, J. P., & Keane, T. M. (Eds.). (1997). *Assessing psychological trauma and PTSD.* New York: Guilford Press.

Wilson, P., Lincoln, R., & Kocsis, R. (1997) Validity, utility and ethics of profiling for serial violent and sexual offenders. *Psychiatry, Psychology and Law, 4,* 1–11.

Wolfgang, M. E., & Ferracuti, F. (1967). *The subculture of violence.* London: Tavistock.

Wood, J. M., Schreiber, N., Martinez, Y., McLaurin, K., Strok, R., Velarde, L., Garven, S., & Malpass, R. S. (1997). *Interviewing techniques in the McMartin Preschool and Kelly Michaels cases: A quantitative analysis.* Unpublished paper, University of Texas at El Paso.

Woodworth, M. & Porter, S. (1999). Historical foundations and current applications of criminal profiling in violent crime investigations. *Expert Evidence, 7,* 241–264.

Woodworth, M., & Porter, S. (2002). In cold blood: Characteristics of criminal homicide as a function of psychopathy. *Journal of Abnormal Psychology, 111,* 435–445.

Woychuk, D. (1996). *Attorney for the damned: A lawyer's life with the criminally insane.* New York: Free Press.

Wright, L. (1994). *Remembering Satan.* New York: Alfred A. Knopf.

Wrightsman, L. S. (1972). *Social psychology in the seventies.* Pacific Grove, CA: Brooks/Cole.

Wrightsman, L. S., & Heili, A. (1992, September). *Working paper—Measuring bias in civil trials.* Unpublished paper, Department of Psychology, University of Kansas, Lawrence, KS.

Wrightsman, L. S., & Kassin, S. M. (1993). *Confessions in the courtroom.* Thousand Oaks, CA: Sage.

Wrightsman, L. S., Nietzel, M. T., & Fortune, W. H. (1998). *Psychology and the legal system* (4th ed.). Pacific Grove, CA: Brooks/Cole.

Wyer, M. M., Gaylord, S. J., & Grove, E. T. (1987). The legal context of child custody evaluations. In L. A. Weithorn (Ed.), *Psychology and child custody evaluations* (pp. 3–22). Lincoln: University of Nebraska Press.

Y.(S.) v. C. (F.G.) (1997), 26 B.C.L.R. (3d) 155 (C.A.).

Yakir, D. (1991, February 24). I had to realize how angry I was. *Parade Magazine,* pp. 4–5.

Yarmey, A. D. (1979). *The psychology of eyewitness testimony.* New York: Free Press.

Yarmey, A. D. (1984). Age as a factor in eyewitness memory. In G. L. Wells & E. F. Loftus (Eds.), *Eyewitness testimony: Psychological perspectives* (pp. 142–154). Cambridge: Cambridge University Press.

Yarmey, A. D. (1986). Ethical responsibilities governing the statements experimental psychologists make in expert testimony. *Law and Human Behavior, 12,* 101–116.

Yarmey, A. D. (2001). Expert testimony: Does eyewitness memory research have probative value for the courts? *Canadian Psychology, 42,* 92–100.

Yarmey, A. D. (2003). Eyewitness identification: Guidelines and recommendations for identification procedures in the United States and Canada. *Canadian Psychology, 44,* 181–189.

Yarmey, A. D., & Jones, H. P. T. (1983). Is the psychology of eyewitness identification a matter of common sense? In S. M. A. Lloyd-Bostock & B. R. Clifford (Eds.), *Evaluating witness evidence: Recent psychological research and new perspectives* (pp. 13–40). Chichester, UK: Wiley.

Yarmey, A. D., Yarmey, M. J., & Yarmey, A. L. (1996). Accuracy of eyewitness identifications in showups and lineups. *Law and Human Behavior, 20,* 459–477.

Yonah, A., & Gleason, J. M. (Eds.). (1981). *Behavioral and quantitative perspectives on terrorism.* New York: Pergamon.

Young, D. (1996). Unnecessary evil: Police lying in interrogations. *Connecticut Law Review, 28,* 425–477.

Young v. Young [1993] 4 S.C.R.

Youngstrom, N. (1991, October). Spotting serial killer difficult, experts note. *APA Monitor,* p. 32.

Yuille, J. C. (1980). A critical examination of the psychological and practical implications of eyewitness research. *Law and Human Behavior, 4,* 335–345.

Yuille, J. C. (1988). The systematic assessment of children's testimony. *Canadian Psychology, 29,* 247–262.

Yuille, J. C. (1989). Expert evidence by psychologists: Sometimes problematic and often premature. *Behavioural sciences and the law, 7,* 181–196.

Yuille, J. C. (1993). We must study forensic eyewitnesses to know about them. *American Psychologist, 48,* 572–573.

Yuille, J. C., & Cutshall, J. (1986). A case study of the eyewitness memory of a crime. *Journal of Applied Psychology, 71,* 291–301.

Yuille, J.C., Davies, G., Gibling, F., Marxsen, D. & Porter, S. (1994). Eyewitness memory of police trainees for realistic role plays. *Journal of Applied Psychology, 79(6),* 931–936.

Yuille, J. C., Daylen, J., Porter, S., & Marxsen, D. (1996). Challenging the eyewitness expert. In J. Ziskin (Ed.) *Coping with psychiatric and psychological testimony,* (5th ed., pp. 1266–1298). Los Angeles, CA: Law and Psychology Press.

Yuille, J.C., Hunter, R., & Harvey, W. (1990). A coordinated approach to interviewing in child sexual abuse investigations. *Canada's Mental Health,* 38(2/3), 14–17.

Yuille, J. C., Hunter, R., Joffe, R., & Zaparniuk, J. (1993). Interviewing children in sexual abuse cases. In G. Goodman & B. Bottoms (Eds.), *Understanding and improving children's testimony: Clinical, developmental and legal implications.* Guilford Press.

Yuille, J. C., Marxsen, D., & Cooper, B. (1999). Training investigative interviewers: Adherence to the spirit, as well as the letter. *International Journal of Law and Psychiatry, 22,* 323–336.

Yuille, J.C., Tymofievich, M. & Marxsen, D. (1995). The nature of allegations of child sexual abuse. In T. Ney

(Ed.), *True and false allegations of child sexual abuse* (pp. 21–46). New York: Bruner Mazel.

Zaccardelli, G. (2003). *Directional statement 2004/2005.* Retrieved on May 14, 2004, from the Royal Canadian Mounted Police Web site: www.rcmp-grc.gc.ca/dpr/dir_stat_2004_05_e.htm.

Zapf, P. (1998, March). *An examination of the construct of competence in a civil and criminal context: A comparison of the MacCAT-T, the MacCAT-CA, and the FIT-R.* Paper presented at the meetings of the American Psychology-Law Society, Redondo Beach, CA.

Zapf, P., & Roesch. R. (1997). Assessing fitness to stand trial: A comparison of institution-based evaluations and a brief screening interview. *Canadian Journal of Community Mental Health, 16,* 53–66.

Zapf, P., Roesch, R., & Viljoen, J. L. (2001). Assessing fitness to stand trial: The utility of the Fitness Interview Test (Revised Edition). *Canadian Journal of Psychiatry, 46,* 423–432.

Zimbardo, P. G. (1967). The psychology of police confessions. *Psychology Today, 1,* 17–27.

Ziskin, J. (1995). *Coping with psychiatric and psychological testimony* (Vol. 1–3, 5th ed.). Los Angeles: Law and Psychology Press.

Ziskin, J., & Faust, D. (1988). *Coping with psychiatric and psychological testimony* (4th ed., Vols. 1–3). Los Angeles: Law and Psychology Press.

Zizzo, F. (1985). Psychological intervention and specialized law enforcement groups. *Emotional First Aid: A Journal of Crisis Intervention,* 2(1), 25–27

Name Index

Subject Index

Labadie, Joel, 144
La Forest, Gérard V., 113
Lamer, Antonio, 113, 114
Larry P. et al. v. Riles et al., 306–8
Laurentide Motels v. Beauport, 99
Lavallee, Angelique Lyn, 226–27
Law
    criticisms of psychology, 14–15, 19–20
    dichotomies of psychology and, 17
    intuition *vs.* empiricism, 7–11, 17–18
    mental health and, 20
    proof in, 19
    social science and, 21
    truth in, 17–19
    and values, 6–7
Law and Human Behavior, 334
Law Enforcement Hypnosis Institute (LEHI), 99
Leading questions, 127, 261
    and false memories, 128–29
Learned helplessness, 222
Le Dain, Gerald Eric, 113
Legal Attitudes Questionnaire (LAQ), 173–74
Legal defence
    battered woman defence, 215, 226–230
    self-defence, 228
    See also NCRMD (not criminally responsible by reason
        of a mental disorder)
L'Heureux-Dubé, Claire, 99, 149
Likelihood to Sexually Harass (LSH) scale, 328
Lindsay, Stephen, 7
Lineups, 122, 130, 131, 132–34
List, John, 86
Litigation explosion, 179
Lombroso, Césare, 11
London Family Court Clinic, 260
Long, Allan, 26
Long-term reactions phase, of rape trauma syndrome, 241,
    243–45
L Scale, 54, 210
Lulow, Jeffrey, 275

M. [K.] v. M. [H.], 249
MacArthur Competence Assessment Tool-Criminal
    Adjudication (MacCAT-CA), 206–7
MacDonald, Jeffrey, 70–71
"Mad Bomber" case, 82–85
Malcolm, Andrew, 27
Malingering, 209–11
Malingering Probability Scale, 210
Malingering Scale (MS), 210–11
Malleus Malificarum, 75
Malott, Margaret Ann, 228
Malott, Paul, 228
Malvar, Marie, 92
Manson v. Braithwaite, 138
Marriage counsellor, 276
Marshall, Thurgood, 39

Martensville case, allegation of sexual abuse, 256–57
Mass arson, 73
Mass murder, 86
Maximization, 155
McCleskey, Warren, 303
McCleskey v. Kemp, 41, 302–3
McConnell, James, 74
McGillis, Kelly, 241
McLachlin, Beverley, 282
McLellan, Anne, 7, 9
McMartin, Virginia, 257
McMartin case, allegation of sexual abuse, 257, 261–62, 268
McNaughton Rules, 192–93
Mediator, 276–77
Memory
    associative, 129
    of children, 12, 263
    cognitive interview and, 106
    demand characteristics and, 127–28
    estimator variables and, 121
    hypnosis and, 99–106
    repeated questioning and, 127–28
    study of, 12–13
    traumatic experiences and, 126
    unconscious transference, 127
    for violence, 121
    See also Eyewitness identification; False memory;
        Recovered memory
Memory Assessment Procedure (MAP), 264
Memory testimony, 120
Menendez, Erik, 43
Menendez, Lyle, 43
Mens rea, 192
Mental Health, Law, and Policy Institute, 338
Mental Screening Evaluation (MSE), 197
Meritor Savings Bank, 326
Meta-analysis, 103
Metesky, George, 84–85
Mezzo v. the Queen, 123
Michaels, Margaret Kelly, 269–70, 271
Milgram, Stanley, 151
Military, sexual harassment in, 320
Milosevic, Slobodan, 77
Miner v. Miner, 282
Minimization, 154
Minnesota Multiphasic Personality Inventory
    (MMPI/MMPI-2), 25, 52–54, 55, 79–80, 210, 248,
    287–88
Minorities, and affirmative action, 309, 310
Miranda v. Arizona, 154
Miranda warning, 151
Miron, Murray S., 78
Mitsubishi Motor Corporation, 320
Mock jury approach, 168
Mode of death, 93
Modern racism, 298
Modlin, H., 239
Modus operandi (MO), 80, 81